W9-AUX-749

THE
ULTIMATE
BOOK OF
BIZARRE
LISTS

FASCINATING FACTS AND SHOCKING TRIVIA ON MUSIC, CRIME, CELEBRITIES, HISTORY AND MORE FROM LISTVERSE.COM

JAMIE FRATER

MJF BOOKS
New York

Published by MJF Books
Fine Communications
322 Eighth Avenue
New York, NY 10001

The Ultimate Book of Bizarre Lists
LC Control Number: 2013936347
ISBN-13: 978-1-60671-193-4
ISBN-10: 1-60671-193-8

Copyright © 2010 by Jamie Frater
Design copyright © 2010 by Ulysses Press and its licensors.

This book was originally published as *Listverse.com's Ultimate Book of Bizarre Lists*

This edition is published by MJF Books in arrangement with Ulysses Press.

Acquisitions Editor: Keith Riegert
Managing Editor: Claire Chun
Editor: Lauren Harrison
Proofreaders: Elyce Petker, Lily Chou
Production: Judith Metzener, Abigail Reser
Design: what!design @ whatweb.com
Cover photos: all from shutterstock.com: coffin @ SOMATUSCAN; bottles
© Fribus Ekaterina; ant © Evgeniy Ayupov; carved head © Mikhail Levit; mannequin
© david harding; man as baby © Dmitry Shironosov; skull © CreativeHQ

Interior photos: see page 701

All rights reserved. No part of this publication may be reproduced or transmitted in any form or by any means, electronic or mechanical, including photocopy, recording, or any information storage and retrieval system, without the prior written permission of the publisher.

Printed in the United States of America.

MJF Books and the MJF colophon are trademarks of Fine Creative Media, Inc.

BG   10   9   8   7   6   5   4   3   2   1

I dedicate this book to my brothers, Stewart and Andrew Frater, and to my sisters, Catriona Anderson and Sarah Jones.
With all my love.

Table of Contents

THE
ULTIMATE
BOOK OF
BIZARRE
LISTS

Life and Death

10 STORIES OF BIZARRE BIRTHS

10 TWINS WITH DIFFERENT FATHERS

Mia Washington had twin boys, but her husband is the biological father of only one. Washington had an usual case of birthing fraternal twins with two separate fathers. This story has become more common because of occasional in-vitro-treatment tales of lab error in which a few eggs were contaminated with the wrong sperm; however, Washington's story unfolds much more naturally. She first became pregnant when having a little fun with either her husband or her lover. Very soon afterward, she met up with the other man and a second egg was released and fertilized. This is a medical rarity known as heteropaternal superfecundation, and only a handful of cases have ever been documented. When the two babies were born and one looked nothing like the father, the truth was discovered. Mr. Washington adopted Mia's other son and took the fatherly role for both children.

9 DIFFERENT COLORED TWINS

The chances of a mixed-race couple having twins who look as if they are of different races are a million to one, but there are occasional stories that pop up about them, like Kian and Remee Hodgson and Ryan and Leo Gerth. A British couple has become even more of an exception by having two sets of twins who

look remarkably different. Miya and Leah Durrant were born in December 2008, and their older sisters, Hayleigh and Lauren, were born seven years earlier. Miya has the black hair and dark complexion of her father Dean Durrant and older sister Hayleigh, while Leah has blue eyes and paler skin just like mom Alison Spooner and older sister Lauren.

8 OLDEST MOTHER

In 2008 and at the age of 70, Rajo Devi became the oldest woman to give birth. She and her husband had unsuccessfully tried to conceive all throughout their 50 years of marriage and thought it was impossible after she went through menopause in her late 50s. However, after entering a fertility program at an in-vitro clinic, Devi was successfully impregnated by a donor egg that was fertilized with the sperm of her 72-year-old husband. On December 6, she gave birth to a baby girl, and both mother and daughter are healthy. Latest reports claim that the happy septuagenarians are attempting in-vitro fertilization again in hopes of having a baby boy.

7 YOUNGEST MOTHER

Lina Medina of Peru holds the record as the world's youngest mother. When she gave birth to her son on May 14, 1939, Lina was only five years old. Her son, Gerardo, spent his childhood believing his grandmother was his mother and his true mother was his older sister. He died at the age of 40 from bone marrow disease, but there was no indication that his unusual birth had anything to do with his problem. Although studies about the pair are hard to find, what is known is that both mother and son were both healthy and suffered no visible affects of such a bizarre birth. Lina married in 1972 and gave birth to her second child that same year—33 years after Gerardo was born. To this day, Gerardo's biological father is unknown and Lina refuses to disclose that information.

6 TINIEST BABIES

James Elgin Gil was born May 20, 1987, in Ottawa, Canada, and is the world's youngest surviving premature baby. He was born 21 weeks and 5 days into gestation (more than 18 weeks too early). To understand the gravity of the situation, one should know that the survival rates for premature babies born at 22 weeks is less than 10 percent. Many hospitals will refuse to give medical attention to babies born before the 22-week mark. This baby lucked out by weighing a "hefty" 1.1 pounds (482 grams) at birth, which increased his chances of survival. The title for tiniest single baby goes to Amillia Sonja Taylor of Florida. She was born at 21 weeks and 6 days but weighed only 10 ounces (283 grams). Remarkably, the hospitals where both of them were born decided to bring the babies to the intensive care units, and they are now both healthy and doing fine.

5 BIGGEST BABIES

The record for birthing the world's heaviest (surviving) newborn belongs to Sig. Carmelina Fedele of Aversa, Italy. In September 1955, she gave birth to a baby boy who weighed 22 pounds 8 ounces (10.2 kilograms), but not much else is known about the boy. Second place belongs to a boy born in September 2009 weighing 19 pounds 3 ounces (8.7 kilograms). The name of the child wasn't released, but what is known is that he was born to an Indonesian woman with a history of diabetes. Due to insulin problems, diabetic women tend to have larger-than-average babies. Her three previous children were also heavier-than-average kids, but this little boy was significantly bigger!

4 TOILET BABY

There's an alarming number of stories to be found of babies born near or even in the toilet, but Bhuri Kalbi's daughter has the distinction of being born while mom was on a toilet of an Indian train. Kalbi was only seven months pregnant when she rode this particular train, so she hadn't anticipated the outcome of her trip to the bathroom. She felt like she needed to use the toilet, but what actually happened was a precipitous birth, or a quick birth commonly associated with pregnancy complications. Toilets on Indian trains are chutes that empty directly onto the tracks, so after the precipitous birth, Kalbi's baby fell through the hole and onto the tracks as the train was in motion. After receiving the alert, staff at a nearby station found the baby girl still alive on the tracks.

3 BORN IN A TREE

Carolina Chirindza gave birth to her baby, Rositha, in a tree. In 2000, Chirindza's home in Mozambique was overcome by rapidly moving high floodwaters, so she climbed up a tree to avoid the crocodile-infested waters. For four days without food or water, she waited for rescue. Baby Rositha was born on the fourth day, and fortunately, a South African military helicopter rescued them shortly thereafter. There is also a tree-birth story from Papua New Guinea. The pregnant Nolan Yekum and her husband were hung from a tree after being accused of witchcraft. She gave birth mere moments before she and her husband freed themselves from their nooses and went into hiding. Both tree babies and moms were eventually admitted to hospitals and given good bills of health.

2 A COUNTRY'S QUINTS

Their names are Annette, Cecile, Emilie, Marie, and Yvonne, but they are better known as the Dionne Quints. They are the only recorded set of identical quintuplets and one of the very few sets of naturally conceived high multiples to survive infancy. On May 28, 1934, the Dionne Quints were born to the impoverished Elzire and Oliva Dionne of Canada. When the quints were nine months old, they were taken from their parents and became wards of the state to live in an estate that became known as Quintland. There, they lived a rigid schedule consisting of either medical testing or structured playtime outdoors in the observatory field where tourists could watch them without interacting with the children. In fact, they had very little contact with people, aside from the nurses and house staff. When they were nine years old, their parents won back custody of the children, but they continued the girls' "fish-bowl" existence with various engagements, photo-ops, and tourist attractions to turn a profit from the publicity. The sisters claimed they never saw any of the purported millions of dollars made by the government and their parents from this bizarre upbringing. With their privacy severely abused and their childhoods traumatized, the Dionne Quints severed ties with the rest of their family, and the three surviving sisters currently share a modest house and an intensely private life in Montreal.

1 THE GREAT STORK DERBY

Charles Vance Miller had an ordinary birth and never had children of his own, but he certainly deserves a spot on a list of bizarre birth stories. By the time of his death in 1926, the Canadian lawyer amassed a large fortune but had no one to leave it to. He was a strange fellow whose puckish attitude was reflected in his will. Among his many oddball bequests was that his Jamaican vacation home be given to three lawyers who absolutely hated each other. When the last lawyer died, the house would be sold and the money given to Toronto's poor. The will also stated that any extra money was to be given to the mother who gives birth to the highest number of legitimate children within the ten years after his death. The event became known as the Great Stork Derby, and by the end of the ten-year period, six moms split the fortune: $125,000 each to four women who gave birth to nine children apiece, and $12,500 to two women, one of whom had two stillbirths and the other who had children with someone who was not her husband. The prizes may not seem like much now, but each was a fortune given the Great Depression of the early '30s. Happily, all of the families used their money wisely, and the children's educations were the top priority.

10 BIZARRE BIRTH DEFECTS

10 SIAMESE TWINS

We are all familiar with the tales of Siamese twins (named for the country of birth of the first known conjoined twins). It is, of course, a rare disorder in which twins are born joined together at one or more parts of their bodies. In the most rare cases, children can be born joined at the top of their head. Sometimes Siamese twins can be separated, allowing both to live full lives, but more frequently, this is not possible.

9 AMBRAS SYNDROME

Ambras Syndrome is a disorder that causes someone to be born with excessive hair over the face and body. This is fortunately a very rare disease; in fact, there are only 40 humans in the world with it at present. The disease is extremely debilitating for children, as they are often rejected by their peers.

8 FUSED LIMBS

Fused limbs are two limbs which are joined together. This can happen in some cases with toes or fingers, but in a recent case in Peru, a young girl was born with her legs completely fused, giving her the appearance of a mermaid. One in every 70,000 babies has this disorder.

7 CYCLOPIA

Cyclopia is named for the famous mythical creature the Cyclops. Children born with cyclopia have one eye in the middle of their head. It is believed that the cause may be related to certain cancer treatment drugs taken by pregnant women.

6 CRANIOPAGUS PARASITICUS

Craniopagus parasiticus is a condition in which a child is born with a parasitic extra head from their unborn twin. There have only been ten cases of it in documented history, with only three surviving birth. In one bizarre case, the second head was able to smile, blink, cry, and suckle.

5 FETUS IN FETU

Fetus in fetu is when a child is born with his twin inside him, giving the appearance of pregnancy. Both twins are usually formed from one egg, but during the pregnancy, one is absorbed by the other and it begins to live off it like a parasite. Surgery can usually remove the undeveloped twin from the stronger one with no ill effects.

4 FIBRODYSPLASIA OSSIFICANS PROGRESSIVA

Children who are born with this disease grow bone in areas that are hurt. Where a child is injured and would normally scar or have their skin grow back, the child suffering from fibrodysplasia ossificans progressiva develops bone in sufficiently large quantities that it can become debilitating, with the excess bone fusing joints. The bone cannot be removed in surgery because it would cause more bone to grow in the surgery wounds.

3 PROGERIA

Progeria occurs in one in eight million births. It causes a child to look aged well beyond their years. Children with progeria lose their hair, develop wrinkles, and take on the facial characteristics of the very old. Severe arterial damage caused by the disease means that most sufferers die by the time they hit adolescence.

2 VESTIGIAL TAIL

Vestigial tail is when a child is born with a semi-functional tail, complete with muscles, nerves, skin, and blood vessels. It is believed to be caused by a mutation of the genes that exist in infants to cause the cellular death of body parts that are not needed.

1 ANENCEPHALY

Anencephaly is the absence of a brain and spinal cord. There is no cure and most anencephalic babies die during childbirth. According to the National

Institute of Neurological Disorders and Stroke, "a baby born with anencephaly is usually blind, deaf, unconscious, and unable to feel pain. Although some individuals with anencephaly may be born with a main brain stem, the lack of a functioning cerebrum permanently rules out the possibility of ever gaining consciousness. Reflex actions such as breathing and responses to sound or touch occur."

10 PAINFUL RITES OF PASSAGE

10 SEPIK SCARIFICATION

The tribes living along the Sepik River in Papua New Guinea have used the tradition of scarification to mature their boys into men for decades. The ceremony requires the youth to be cut along his back, chest, and buttocks in elaborate patterns to mimic the coarse skin of a crocodile. It is thought that this reptilian divinity consumes his youth during the bloody process, leaving behind a man in his place.

Before he can be treated as a man, though, the boy is subjected to humiliation in a ritual that can take weeks. In fact, the boys are referred to as women and regarded that way in order to psychologically toughen them. The scarification, parallel to the taunts, strengthens them physically because it requires a vast amount of discipline to go through the ritual, withstanding hundreds of cuts. The raw wounds are cleaned after the scarification is complete but the pain endured continues for days as their bodies heal.

9 NAGHOL—LAND DIVING

In the South Pacific Ocean on Pentecost Island, tribe members construct a tower 60 to 90 feet (20 to 30 meters) high made from the trees surrounding a clearing. Rocks and wood are removed from the ground and the soil is tilled before the tower is built. The rickety structure is then used as a foundation for the world's most extreme form of bungee jumping, with only two vines and faith supporting a diver.

The ritual is done to ensure the yam harvest that year will be successful; the higher they dive, the better the harvest will be. It's also thought to strengthen participants spiritually as they take the leap of faith. While diving is not required, those that do are revered in the community and seen as true warriors. After all, to dive means to sacrifice your life for the tribe. They embrace the possibility of death during the initiation; it would be like taking one for the team. Boys around seven and eight (once they are circumcised) can participate, and they're considered men after they survive the fall.

The risks are obvious. Divers are prone to concussions and broken hips and necks, and that's if the vines don't snap (and if they don't impale themselves). If the vine is measured correctly, the only pain a diver will experience is the sudden harsh pull at his ankles once he drops, a painful feeling which will stay with him for days. It's common to see tribe members' heads hit the ground after a jump, but for the most part, they survive unscathed.

8 MARDUDJARA ABORIGINAL SUBINCISION

In Australia, a Mardudjara Aboriginal youth must go through a lengthy process to become a real man. Between six and eight years of age, he's considered dead, prohibited from speaking. He travels with the men of his tribe to neighboring communities where he's given a special ceremony around a bonfire. Elders dance and chant for him to ensure a successful initiation. He lies down on the backs of his brethren who form a human table so that the surgeon may sit on his chest. The boy is offered an object to bite down on as the foreskin of his penis is sliced off. To complete this stage of the rite of passage, he must then swallow the severed foreskin, without chewing, so that it may strengthen him from within.

Several weeks later, the final phase is ready to be undertaken. Lying down, he's given yet another object to bite while his penis is held erect. Another surgeon cuts along the underside of the penis. To ensure that the incision is done properly, a thin wooden stick is inserted into the urethra to guide the blade. Cut lengths vary, some only an inch while others go as low as to the scrotum. Once the operation is complete, the boy is guided to the fire so that the flames may heal his fresh wound. He is now a man.

7 ROMAN INFIBULATIONS

Speaking of penis, the ancient Romans also had their own initiation method. Infibulation is the process of suturing the foreskin. Using string or a metal clasp, the foreskin was closed and the penis was drawn to the side. Most infibulations were self-inflicted.

This was done for several reasons. For singers, infibulations helped keep their voice through the years. It also was thought to capture and retain gladiators' might and vitality. In some cases, an exposed penis was thought to be vulgar, especially the head of the penis, so infibulations were done to show modesty and restraint. Youths were exposed to the process to keep them from masturbating and to help them abstain from sexual intercourse. It was a show of maturity to suture your own foreskin.

6 MENTAWAI TEETH CHISELING

Female Mentawaians of Sumatra experience an agonizing practice known as teeth chiseling. A local shaman sharpens a crude blade as best he can to make the chiseling as least painful as possible. The young girl is given nothing to numb the feeling in her mouth before he takes a rock and begins to hack away. Using careful strikes, the blade carves the corners of the teeth, leaving behind pointed ends similar to shark teeth. To finish the process, her teeth are filed to achieve the desired shape.

This is done to young girls because it is believed to make them more attractive. It's also said that sharpened teeth please the spirits the tribes believe in and bring balance to a female's life. It's an old tradition the Mentawaians have been following for years, but the practice isn't as common anymore. Today, it's up to the girl to decide if she wants her teeth chiseled to become beautiful.

5 XHOSA MALE CIRCUMCISIONS

It's a celebration when a boy has the opportunity to become a man for the Xhosa people of South Africa. The *abakwetha* (male initiate) is shaved, and he's given a feast before he's taken to the mountains, where a hut is built for him by his family. The hut will be his home for the next several weeks, so it's fortified to keep insects and animals away (primarily to protect from disease).

Without any preparation, the surgeon appears and conducts the circumcision. The foreskin is removed, often with a dull blade, and the boy is left alone. He takes refuge in his hut, where he cannot eat or drink water until he's healed. The risk of infection is high. The blade alone, which is used on multiple boys transitioning into men, can often carry STDs. One of the big fears of the boys going into the procedure is news of previous *abakwetha* that have been hospitalized because of the circumcision.

4 FULANI WHIP MATCH

The Fulani people from Benin live nomadically in West Africa. For their boys to be considered men, they must endure a tormenting, bloody whip match that will test their strength, self-control, and bravery. The initiate picks a long stick and sharpens it in a way that will guarantee the most painful blow with every whip. Once he has his weapon, clans from all over gather for the ceremony, in which two youths are pitted against each other.

His goal is to hit his opponent the hardest and to wince the least when he's struck. Three blows are given by each boy. The crowd decides who has shown the most courage through the ordeal and is the winner of the match.

3 SABINY FEMALE CIRCUMCISIONS

Girls of the Sabiny tribe in Uganda go through genital mutilation to achieve womanhood. The pain that comes with the tradition is part of the experience that can't be matched. If a girl can survive the ordeal, she proves herself strong enough to endure any and all obstacles that she may face in the rest of her life. Female circumcisions are complete when the clitoris is partially cut or completely removed. The Sabiny believe this will make a woman faithful to her husband and keep her from sexual promiscuity. Infection and likeliness of death is high. This, among other health complications, is just part of the tradition that a woman must withstand to prove herself.

2 MATAUSA BLOOD INITIATION

Papua New Guinea isn't known just for the crocodile scarification ritual, as seen earlier in the list. Deep in the highlands, an equally gruesome rite of passage exists. The Matausa believe that if a boy doesn't complete the blood initiation, he may suffer the consequences his entire life. He will never be seen as a real man and he won't experience the vigor and strength that the others have. That's why boys are eager to go through the initiation, regardless of pain, to become warriors.

In order to do this, they must cleanse themselves of any remaining female influences left in them from their mothers. First, they must slide two thin wooden canes down their throats to induce vomiting several times to empty their stomachs. Afterward, a collection of reeds are inserted into the initiate's nose to further expel bad influence. Finally, they must endure repeated stabbings to the tongue. This bloody ritual thus purifies them and they are truly men afterward.

1 SATERE-MAWE BULLET ANT GLOVE

The Brazilian Satere-Mawe tradition that makes young boys into warriors has become notorious in recent years. Explorers, adventurers, and documentarians flock to the Amazon to catch a glimpse of what is considered to be one of the most painful rites of passage on earth. What makes the initiation so torturous? The culprit is the bullet ant.

According to the Schmidt Sting Pain Index, the bullet ant has the worst known insect sting. A single sting is comparable to being shot with a bullet (hence the name). The intense pain lasts a full 24 hours and can lead to vomiting, nausea, and cardiac dysrhythmia. And that's all from one sting. The Satere-Mawe don't use just one ant.

More than 30 bullet ants are submerged in a liquid natural sedative drug until they are unconscious. A glove weaved from leaves is fashioned and then completed by placing the ants in the tight openings, stingers pointed inward. Once the ants are conscious, they struggle to free themselves from the weaving,

 growing more anxious and desperate with each passing second. The boy being initiated has his hands coated in a thin layer of charcoal before slipping on two bullet-ant gloves. He must endure

their stings for ten minutes. The goal is to keep from screaming or showing signs of weakness. He and the tribe members present chant and dance to take his mind off the pain. Once the ritual is complete, he will suffer from the stings for days, but he's one step closer to being a warrior; this process must be repeated an additional 20 times in the following months for it be officially complete.

10 TRULY BIZARRE DEATHS

10 THE DONATISTS

Donatism was an early Christian heretical movement that was named after Donatus Magnus, Bishop of Carthage, in AD 313. The Donatists believed that the church should be a church of saints and not sinners. This view led huge numbers of followers to seek out martyrdom, either by suicide or by asking strangers to kill them (often in large groups). This was such a widespread belief that it is surprising to know that they survived—albeit as a very small sect—until the 7th or 8th century.

9 AL-MUSTA'SIM

In 1258, Hulagu Khan, the grandson of Genghis Khan, invaded the Abbasid region, comprising modern Iraq and Syria. Al-Musta'sim, the Caliph, raised no repelling army and consequently fell into the hands of Kahn who, being a relatively decent man, needed to execute him but didn't want to spill royal blood. Khan came up with a brilliant idea. He had Al-Musta'sim rolled up in a rug and ordered his men to trample him to death with their horses. Such compassion was not shown for Al-Musta'sim's sons, most of whom were summarily executed.

8 CLEMENT VALLANDIGHAM

Vallandigham was a member of the U.S. House of Representatives and he suffered not just a bizarre death, but an ironic one. While working as a lawyer, Vallandigham needed to prove that his client, who was on trial for murder, had accidentally shot the victim when taking his gun out of his pocket. To prove that it was possible, Vallandigham put the gun in his pocket and drew it. The gun fired as he had predicted but unfortunately it killed him. His client was acquitted.

7 ALEXANDER I OF GREECE

While walking in his royal gardens, King Alexander I of Greece was bitten by two monkeys. He contracted sepsis and died three weeks later. His death had a serious impact on Greece because it restored his pro-German father, the deposed Constantine I, to the throne.

6 J. G. PARRY-THOMAS

John Godfrey Parry-Thomas was a famed engineer and racecar driver from Wales. In his attempt to break his own world land-speed record, a chain in the car's engine snapped, hitting him in the head and killing him. At the time he was traveling at 170 miles per hour.

5 TENNESSEE WILLIAMS

Tennessee Williams, the author of some of the greatest plays in U.S. history, died by choking on the lid of an eye drop bottle. He took the eye drops regularly and would open the bottle with his teeth. While holding the lid in his mouth as he tilted his head back to administer the drops, he accidentally swallowed the lid and died.

4 GARRY HOY

Garry Hoy was a lawyer who worked on the 24th floor of the Toronto-Dominion Centre. Hoy insisted that the glass windows of the office were unbreakable; to prove it, he threw himself at one full force. Alas, the windows were not unbreakable, and he hurtled to his death 24 floors below. For his efforts, he was awarded a Darwin award in 1996.

3 ALLAN PINKERTON

Allan Pinkerton was a spy and a detective who is best known for creating the Pinkerton National Detective Agency, the first of its kind in the United States. In 1884, he slipped on the pavement and bit his tongue. The tongue became infected, and within two weeks it caused him to die of gangrene as he refused to get treatment for it.

2 FRANK HAYES

Frank Hayes is most well-known for the honor of being the only man to win a horse race while he was dead! In the middle of the race, he suffered a fatal heart attack. Despite carrying dead weight, his horse, Sweet Kiss, ran on to win the race.

1 MITHRIDATES

Mithridates was a Persian soldier who accidentally killed Cyrus the Younger, son of Darius II of Persia. For such a blunder, he was put to death by scaphism. Here is an ancient account of his grueling 17-day death:

> [The king] decreed that Mithridates should be put to death in boats; which execution is made in the following manner: Taking two boats framed exactly to fit and answer each other, they lay down in one of them the malefactor that suffers, upon his back; then, covering it with

the other, and so setting them together that the head, hands, and feet of him are left outside, and the rest of his body lies shut up within, they offer him food, and if he refuse to eat it, they force him to do it by pricking his eyes; then, after he has eaten, they drench him with a mixture of milk and honey, pouring it not only into his mouth, but all over his face. They then keep his face continually turned towards the sun; and it becomes completely covered up and hidden by the multitude of flies that settle on it. And as within the boats he does what those that eat and drink must needs do, creeping things and vermin spring out of the corruption and rottenness of the excrement, and these entering into the bowels of him, his body is consumed. When the man is manifestly dead, the uppermost boat being taken off, they find his flesh devoured, and swarms of such noisome creatures preying upon and, as it were, growing to his inwards. In this way Mithridates, after suffering for seventeen days, at last expired.—Plutarch

10 BIZARRE DEATH-RELATED FACTS

10 GREGORY BIGGS

The film *Struck* is loosely based on the death of Gregory Biggs, a homeless man from Texas. He was struck by a car driven by a woman who was high on drugs. He became lodged in her windshield, and she drove home with him stuck there. She left him in the garage and visited him throughout the night, apologizing for hitting him. Several hours later, he died of his injuries. The driver was eventually given a 50-year prison sentence.

9 DISENFRANCHISED GRIEF

Disenfranchised grief is the name given to the types of grief that society generally does not acknowledge as serious, such as the death of a pet, a miscarried pregnancy, the loss of a parent, or giving a child up for adoption. Some people even suffer disenfranchised grief at the loss of celebrities. This can create serious problems for the sufferer as there are seldom any support systems in place to help the grieving process.

8 SAFETY COFFINS

Safety coffins are surprisingly common throughout modern history, with the first being recorded in 1792. A safety coffin is a normal coffin that is fitted with special attachments for use in the event that a person be buried alive in it. These devices usually consist of breathing tubes and some system for the victim to alert the living of their plight.

7 DEATH ERECTION

A death erection (also called terminal erection) is a postmortem erection that is observed in the bodies of executed men. It is particularly common in cases of hangings. The cause of the erection is the swift movement of blood to the lower regions of the body.

6 WALKING GHOST

The ominously named "walking ghost" is a phase of radiation poisoning in which the victim still appears to have good health. It can last for days, but in all cases it is followed by death. The reason for the syndrome is that it takes time for radiation poisoning to take effect in the body.

5 LAZARUS SYNDROME

Lazarus syndrome is when a dead person returns to life unexpectedly after an unusually long period of time. In one case, a man arose 17 minutes after resuscitation efforts were ended and he was declared dead. This obviously has implications for medical ethics with regards to knowing whether a person is truly dead in order to harvest their organs for transplant.

4 REPUBLICAN MARRIAGE

The republican marriage is a sometimes disputed practice in which a man and a woman are tied naked together and then drowned. It was originally described in the 18th century in relation to the French revolution (hence the name). Some reports also state that the couple is run through with a sword prior to drowning.

3 LONDON NECROPOLIS RAILWAY STATION

Unbeknownst to most Londoners, beneath their feet runs the London Necropolis Railway Station, a specially constructed station designed to service the Brookwood cemetery. The line opened in 1854 and ran until it was hit by a bomb during World War I. The entrance can still be seen on Westminster Bridge Road.

2 LAL BIHARI

Lal Bihari, born in 1961, is a farmer who was officially declared dead after his uncle bribed an official to do so in order for him to gain ownership of his nephew's land. Bihari launched a campaign to have himself declared alive again, and in the course of his efforts found at least 100 others who had suffered the same fate. By 2004, four members (including Bihari) of the Association of the Dead had had their status as living restored.

1 MASCHALISMOS

Maschalismos is a practice dating back to ancient Greece in which corpses are mutilated to prevent them from inflicting their anger on the living. In some parts of Europe, people who committed suicide had a stake driven through their hearts before burial, and in some parts of Australia, dead bodies are beaten to break their bones. This unusual practice is found all over the world.

10 HORRIFYING PREMATURE BURIALS

10 VIRGINIA MACDONALD, 1851

Virginia Macdonald lived with her father in New York City and became ill, died, and was buried in Greenwood Cemetery, Brooklyn. After the burial, her mother declared and persistently asserted her belief that her daughter was not dead when she was buried. The family tried in vain to assure the mother of the death of her daughter. Finally, the mother insisted so strenuously that her daughter was buried alive that the family consented to have the body dug up. To their horror, they discovered the body lying on its side, the hands badly bitten, and every indication of a premature burial.

Interesting Fact: When the Les Innocents cemetery in Paris, France, was moved from the center of the city to the suburbs, the number of skeletons found face down convinced many people and several doctors that premature burial was very common.

9 MADAM BLUNDEN, 1896

When Madam Blunden was thought to be dead, she was buried in the Blunden family vault at Holy Ghost Chapel in Basingstoke, England. The vault was situated beneath a boys' school. The day after the funeral, when the schoolboys were playing, they heard a noise from the vault below. After one of the boys ran and told his teacher about the noises, and the sexton was summoned. The vault and the coffin were opened just in time to witness Madam Blunden's final breath. All possible means were used to resuscitate her, but they were unsuccessful. In her agony, she had torn frantically at her face and had bitten the nails off her fingers.

Interesting Fact: A large number of designs for safety coffins were patented during the 18th and 19th centuries. Safety coffins were fitted with a mechanism to allow the occupant to signal that he or she has been buried alive.

8 *NEW YORK TIMES* ARTICLE, 1886

"WOODSTOCK, Ontario, Jan. 18—Recently a girl named Collins died here, as it was supposed, very suddenly. A day or two ago the body was exhumed, prior to its removal to another burial place, when the discovery was made that the girl had been buried alive. Her shroud was torn into shreds, her knees were drawn up to her chin, one of her arms was twisted under her head, and her features bore evidence of dreadful torture."

Interesting Fact: In the 19th century, Dr. Timothy Clark Smith of Vermont was so concerned about the possibility of being buried alive that he arranged to be buried in a special crypt that included a breathing tube and a glass window in his grave marker that would permit him to peer out to the living world six feet above.

7 *DAILY TELEGRAPH* ARTICLE, 1889

"GRENOBLE, Jan. 18—A gendarme was buried alive the other day in a village near Grenoble. The man had become intoxicated on potato brandy, and fell into a profound sleep. After twenty hours passed in slumber, his friends considered him to be dead, particularly as his body assumed the usual rigidity of a corpse. When the sexton, however, was lowering the remains of the ill-fated gendarme into the grave, he heard moans and knocks proceeding from the interior of the 'four-boards.' He immediately bored holes in the sides of the coffin, to let in air, and then knocked off the lid. The gendarme had, however, ceased to live, having horribly mutilated his head in his frantic but futile efforts to burst his coffin open."

Interesting Fact: The fear of being buried alive is called "taphephobia." The word comes from the Greek *taphos*, meaning "grave," and "phobia" is from the Greek *phobos*, meaning "fear"; literally, it is the fear of the grave, or fear of being put in the grave while still alive.

6 *THE SUNDAY TIMES* ARTICLE, 1838

"TONNEINS, Dec. 30—A frightful case of premature interment occurred not long since, at Tonneins, in the Lower Garonne. The victim, a man in the

prime of life, had only a few shovelfuls of earth thrown into his grave when an indistinct noise was heard to proceed from his coffin. The grave-digger, terrified beyond description, instantly fled to seek assistance, and some time elapsed before his return, when the crowd, which had by this time collected in considerable numbers round the grave, insisted on the coffin being opened. As soon as the first boards had been removed, it was ascertained beyond a doubt, that the occupant had been interred alive. His countenance was frightfully contracted with the agony he had undergone, and, in his struggles, the unhappy man had forced his arms completely out of the winding sheet, in which they had been securely enveloped. A physician, who was on the spot, opened a vein, but no blood flowed. The sufferer was beyond the reach of art."

Interesting Fact: In *The Complete Worst-Case Scenario Survival Handbook,* one of the scenarios listed is how to survive if you are buried alive in a coffin. If anyone finds themselves in the same predicament as the people on this list, you can read some life-saving information there.

5 BRITISH MEDICAL JOURNAL, 1877

"December 8—It appeared from the evidence that some time ago a woman was interred with all the usual formalities, it being believed that she was dead, while she was only in a trance. Some days afterwards, the grave in which she had been placed being opened for the reception of another body, it was found that the clothes which covered the unfortunate woman were torn to pieces, and that she had even broken her limbs in attempting to extricate herself from the living tomb. The Court, after hearing the case, sentenced the doctor who had signed the certificate of decease, and the mayor who had authorized the interment, each to three months' imprisonment for involuntary manslaughter."

Interesting Fact: Today, when a definition of death is required, doctors usually turn to "brain death" to define a person as being clinically dead. People are considered dead when the electrical activity in their brain ceases.

4 NEW YORK TIMES ARTICLE, 1884

"DAYTON, Feb. 8.—A sensation has been created here by the discovery of the fact that Miss Hockwalt, a young lady of high social connections, who was supposed to have died suddenly on Jan. 10, was buried alive. The terrible truth was discovered a few days ago, and since then it has been the talk of the city. The circumstance of Miss Hockwalt's death was peculiar. It occurred on the morning of the marriage of her brother to Miss Emma Schwind at Emannel's Church. Shortly before 6 o'clock the young lady was dressing for the nuptials and had gone into the kitchen. A few moments afterward she was found sitting on a chair with her head leaning against a wall and apparently lifeless. Medical aid was summoned in, Dr. Jewett who, after examination, pronounced her dead. Mass was being read at the time in Emannel's Church and it was thought best to continue, and the marriage was performed in gloom. The examination showed that Anna was of excitable temperament, nervous, and affected with sympathetic palpitation of the heart. Dr. Jewett thought this was the cause of her supposed death. On the following day, the lady was interred in the Woodland. The friends of Miss Hockwalt were unable to forget the terrible impression and several ladies observe that her eyes bore a remarkably natural color and could not dispel an idea that she was not dead. They conveyed their opinion to Annie's parents and the thought preyed upon them so that the body was taken from the grave. It was stated that when the coffin was opened it was discovered that the supposed inanimate body had turned upon its right side. The hair had been torn out in handfuls and the flesh had been bitten from the fingers. The body was reinterred and efforts made to suppress the facts, but there are those who state they saw the body and know the facts to be as narrated."

Interesting Fact: In 1822, Dr. Adolf Gutsmuth was buried alive several times to demonstrate a safety coffin he had designed. Once he stayed underground for several hours and ate a meal of soup, sausages, and beer delivered to him through the coffin's feeding tube.

3 MARY NORAH BEST, 1871

Seventeen-year-old Mary Norah Best was the adopted daughter of Mrs. Moore Chew. Mary was pronounced dead from cholera and entombed in the Chew's vault in an old French cemetery in Calcutta. The surgeon who pronounced her dead was a man who would have benefited from her death and had tried to kill her adopted mother. Before Mary "died," her adoptive mother fled to England after the second attempt on her life and left Mary behind. Mary was put into a pine coffin, and it was nailed shut. Ten years later, in 1881, the vault was unsealed to admit the body of Mrs. Moore's brother. On entering the vault, the undertaker's assistant found the lid off of Mary's coffin on the floor. The position of her skeleton was half in and half out of the coffin. Apparently after being entombed, Mary awoke from the trance and struggled violently until she was able to force the lid off of her coffin. It is surmised that after bursting open her casket, she fainted from the strain and while falling forward over the edge of her coffin she struck her head against the masonry shelf and was killed. It is believed the surgeon poisoned the girl and then certified her death.

Interesting Fact: Some believe Thomas A. Kempis, a German Augustinian monk who wrote *The Imitation of Christ* in the 1400s, was denied canonization because splinters were found embedded under his nails after his death. Canonization authorities determined that anyone aspiring to be a saint would not fight death if he found himself buried alive.

2 *NEW YORK TIMES* ARTICLE, 1885

"ASHEVILLE, N.C., Feb. 20.–A gentleman from Flat Creek Township in this (Buncombe) County, furnishes the information that about the 20th of last month a young man by the name of Jenkins, who had been sick with fever for several weeks, was thought to have died. He became speechless, his flesh was cold and clammy, and he could not be aroused, and there appeared to be no action of the pulse and heart. He was thought to be dead and was prepared for burial, and was noticed at the time that there was no stiffness in any of the limbs. He was buried after his supposed death, and when put in the coffin it was remarked that he was as limber as a live man. There was much talk in the neighborhood about the case and the opinion was frequently expressed that Jenkins had been buried alive. Nothing was done about the matter until the 10th inst., when the coffin was taken up for the purpose of removal and internment in the family burying ground in Henderson County. The coffin being wood, it was suggested that it be opened in order to see if the body was in such condition that it could be hauled 20 miles without being put in a metallic casket. The coffin was opened, and to the great astonishment and horror of his relatives the body was lying face downward, and the hair had been pulled from the head in great quantities, and there was scratches of the finger nails on the inside of the lid and sides of the coffin. These facts caused great excitement and all acquainted personally with the facts believe Jenkins was in a trance, or that animation was apparently suspended, and that he was not really dead when buried and that he returned to consciousness only to find himself buried and beyond help. The body was then taken to Henderson County and reinterred. The relatives are distressed beyond measure at what they term criminal carelessness in not being absolutely sure Jenkins was dead before he was buried."

Interesting Fact: Because of the concern of premature burials, a group was formed called Society for the Prevention of People Being Buried Alive. They encouraged the slow process of burials.

1 MADAME BOBIN, 1901

In 1901, a pregnant Madame Bobin arrived on board a steamer from Western Africa and appeared to be suffering from yellow fever. She was then transferred to a hospital for those affected with contagious diseases. There she became worse and apparently died and was buried. A nurse later said she noticed that the body was not cold and that there was tremulousness of the muscles of the abdomen; the nurse expressed the opinion that she could have been prematurely buried. After this was reported to Madame Bobin's father, he had the body exhumed. They were horrified to find that a baby had been born and died with Madame Bobin in the coffin. An autopsy showed that Madame Bobin had not contracted yellow fever and had died from asphyxiation in the coffin. A suit against the health officials resulted in £8,000 ($13,000) damages against them.

Interesting Fact: Historical records indicate that during the 17th century when plague victims often collapsed and seemed to be dead, there were 149 actual cases of people being buried alive.

10 BIZARRE APOCALYPSE SCENARIOS

10 IMPENDING DISASTER OF PLANET X

This one started life as an archaeological find. Years ago, a mysterious clay tablet made by the Sumerians, the earliest inhabitants of the Middle East, was found in the Middle East. Upon this tablet was a depiction of something that looked like our solar system; all the planets were there, and all of them were rotating around the sun. But there were 11 celestial bodies. Now, we know there are only nine planets. Maybe one of them was our moon or the recently discovered mini-planet Sedna? But where did the 11th come from? At the same time that the tablet was found, astronomers were perplexed by a strange force in the outer solar system. It seemed as though the outer planets were being pulled out of their orbit. Something massive must be out there. These combined findings led to the theory of the mysterious Planet X.

Planet X is predicted to be hundreds of times larger than Earth and to have a massive orbit of about 3600 years. When it comes through the inner solar system, it could cause cataclysmic disaster upon our planet. It is so massive that it could turn the poles upside down, and slow the earth's rotation or even stop it. If Planet X gets close enough, it could even peel the Earth's crust off or push us into the sun. All bad scenarios.

9 RUNAWAY GREENHOUSE EFFECT

Here is one we're heading straight for right now. In a few decades, our climate may just go completely insane. Temperatures might rise rapidly,

melting the ice caps, turning our planet's climate into something comparable to that of Venus. We all know about global warming; for the past ten years you haven't been able to open a newspaper without reading something about it. But the Runaway Greenhouse Effect is basically what will happen if we reach that point of no return.

As temperatures rise, water evaporates, which makes the atmosphere thicker, which in turn traps in more heat, which causes more water to evaporate. In this chain reaction, Earth's atmosphere will really become similar to Venus' because that is exactly what is happening there. The atmosphere there is so thick that solar heat never escapes, so it just keeps getting hotter. And there is nothing to stop it. Just like there will be nothing stop it here on Earth.

The threshold could happen as soon as 2015. The polar ice caps hold trillions of tons of carbon dioxide trapped in tiny bubbles of ancient air. If this is released, it could literally break the atmosphere. It could cause the initial rapid temperature rise and start the water-vapor reaction. We could possibly be heading for a world where tin and lead would melt instantly in our atmosphere. When all the water is trapped as an evaporate, the atmosphere will be too hot to support 99 percent of all life, and we humans will be able to do nothing to stop it.

8 FINE-TUNING OF THE UNIVERSE

Is the world we live in and perceive real? Like the movie *The Matrix*, are we just a simulation? Perhaps we're being played out by a superior alien race that is watching us on a TV or controlling us with a computer. One of the best pieces of evidence for this theory is the Universal Fine-Tuning Factor. The fact that the universe is so precisely tuned to support life is a huge astronomical coincidence. I don't just mean animal or plant life; I mean all life—stars, black holes, galaxies, and even atoms and particles. The entire universe seems to be fine-tuned.

A British cosmologist, Fred Hoyle, was the first to realize the implications of this "coincidence." You see, there is a very peculiar thing about the fundamental constants (like atomic masses or the speed of light) in that if they were slightly different, nothing would exist. Take the strong force inside atomic nuclei: if the force were just slightly stronger, it would boost the burning of stars so much that they would explode only seconds after they were formed. We wouldn't have a sun—or even a planet. If, on the other hand, the force were a tad weaker, it would be too weak to hold together elements, like the heavy hydrogen isotope deuterium. Stars wouldn't light up, and humans wouldn't be here, either. And the same goes for everything else. Slightly more or less of any constant, and the universe won't work. So the question is, why are all the fundamental constants tuned to support the universe?

7 THE INFERTILITY PROBLEM

As you probably know, there are lots of men and women out there who cannot conceive children. But did you know that the amount of people who cannot conceive is rising? And rising very fast, might I add. So fast, in fact, that scientists predict it to be a very serious problem for the future of our species. There are a few theories about why infertility is on the rise. One is that pollution, or the chemicals in pollution, have over the years caused damage to our cells and in turn our reproductive systems. Another theory is that evolution has determined who can have kids and who can't. You know, survival of the fittest? But in truth, rising infertility is most likely caused by a combination of lots of things, including these two, as well as diseases.

This causes a slow extinction. At first, the streets will be a little less crowded, there will be no more traffic jams, it will be easier to get a house, and there will be more jobs. There will also be a lot more fertility clinics that are crowded. People will know that there is a problem, but think the fertility treatment will help them. Cut to a few generations later. The roads will empty, most of the buildings (including the fertility clinics) will be abandoned. A few people will still be alive, but there will be no one running things like power plants or treatment plants; society will be thrown back to the Middle Ages. People will be living in small communes, and children will be very rare. And someday, the last child will be born.

6 THE SOLAR COLLISION

A comet is going to hit the Earth. Pah! I'm much more concerned about Gliese-710. Haven't heard of it? I'm not surprised, with a name like that. It is a red dwarf star, and you probably can't see it with the naked eye. Yet! As time passes, it will become more noticeable. Then one day it will hit us. Not directly you understand, but it will be close enough to destroy the solar system, either by ripping it apart by gravity or by hitting the Oort cloud. The Oort cloud is a huge collection of solar dust, ice, and planet-sized rocks—millions of them—that surrounds our solar system. If Gliese-710 hits this cloud it would send these planet-sized asteroids hurtling in our direction. Not just a few of them but enough that we would have to defend our planet for thousands of years.

This star is far away, so don't start panicking just yet. It would take over a million years to make it to our solar system. But Gliese-710 isn't the only star heading toward us. There are about eight to come before this one. The nearest is called Barnard's Star and will hit us in 10,000 years. After that, there is a twin system called Alpha Cen A/B. This one could pull us in and burn us up, or it could slingshot us out into open space and we'd freeze (or both). One thing's for sure, though. It is very difficult to predict the path of a star, so hopefully they will miss by enough not to do any permanent damage. But don't hold your breath. They would have to miss us by billions of miles.

5 QUANTUM VACUUM COLLAPSE INEVITABILITY

This one's simple enough: scientists will destroy the universe. I'm sure you've all heard of the Large Hadron Collider (LHC). It was in the news in 2009 and was deemed a doomsday device because theorists said that it could destroy the planet. Well they're wrong; it could, in theory, destroy the entire universe. Quantum physics predicts that the universe is filled with something called vacuum energy. Now, think of this energy as gunpowder. It's ready to explode, and all you need is a fuse. So scientists built the Large Hadron Collider.

They have recently fixed the LHC. One day during a collision experiment, the use of specific elements could trigger the quantum vacuum collapse. Less than a second later, the Earth will be wiped out, gone without a trace. A wave of destruction will spread through the universe at the speed of light, destroying everything in its path. Nothing will stop it until the universe is completely gone. Scientists argue that elements smash into each other in nature all the time and that the universe is still here, so there is no risk of this catastrophe. But what they fail to realize is that the particles they use in the collider, such as gold, are rare. Or they play around with elements that are so unstable they don't exist in "nature"; who knows what will happen with those ones.

4 INCREASE OF THE CONSTANTS

Do you remember what I said about how the universe is fine-tuned and that if the constants weren't exactly right then the universe just wouldn't happen? Well, unfortunately, in 2001, physicists discovered something bizarre. One of these constants, the "fine-structure constant" seems to be very, very slowly getting bigger. Surely this can't be true? Constants are by definition *constant* and should be impossible to change. This sparked a massive physics debate, which still goes on today. In the meantime, more evidence has been gathered that more constants are on the move, like the mass of the proton and the speed of light, are all going a bit iffy.

What this means to us is that one day the universe may just collapse. All the stars will burn up within seconds, light will bend around corners, and then everything will eventually go dark. Some truly weird things could also occur; you could witness buildings turn into liquid rock and metal; you could see people just start vanishing into thin air (given that the air is still there—the atmosphere will disappear pretty much instantly). All this sounds too far-fetched to believe, but if we take what the scientists have seen to be true, then we are heading to this kind of universe quite soon. Well...like, a few million years.

3 VANISHING ACT

This one is just about as serious as this list will get (apart from number 9). This one comes straight from the mouths of high-ranking UN officials, government agencies, and scientists and is locked away among thousands of reports that hardly anyone reads. Basically, it says that in three generations, there will be half the population on Earth as there is now, and that number will keep declining. No, it's not a virus; there is no prophecy saying that a comet will hit the Earth, killing three billion people. The truth is as simple as not having enough children.

Decades ago, people had to have lots of children. The main reason was the more children you had, the more hands you had to help farm lands, work in shops, and look after you when you were older. Modern technology combined with social programs has replaced our need for many children. We only really have children now because we want them, and the problem now is that fewer and fewer people want children. There are many possible reasons for this change, such as poor finances or the inability to find a suitable home. It could have to do with the fact that more women work now than ever before, so they have children later and bear fewer. Fifty years ago women had, on average, five children. Today that number is 2.7. On average, a couple needs to have 2.1 children (compensating for children who die young) to ensure the continuation of the species. The decline is rapidly reaching that crunch point of 2.0. When that happens, the population of the planet will go down, and it will happen faster than you think. Three generations from now, the planet's population will be three billion and falling. Think of it: we could all die out because we just don't do enough conceiving. Breed, people!

2 GRAIN SITUATION

This one is seriously stupid, but it is taken very seriously among biologists. Someday our planet could be completely covered in grain. And I mean absolutely everywhere: on the beaches, in the swamps, through cracks in the pavement. Sure, there will be enough food, but the only food will be bread. Grain will overrun all other crops, pushing back all other agriculture, until the entire biosphere is swamped with grain. Forests will turn into roaming fields of grain, the food chain will break down, and all the land on earth will be one endless grain desert. Grain dust will cause fires that may burn an entire continent (or two), or all the water could be sucked up by the grain, causing irreversible damage to our water supplies. We may even experience an ice age because of the extra carbon dioxide in the atmosphere from all the fires.

I know, stupid right? I mean, taken down by grain. Well, biologists seem to believe that one day the human race is going to create the mother of all genetically modified crops. With genetic modification, you can take out a certain gene, or add another here and there, so that the crop is resistant to certain diseases or insects. What is predicted, however, is a Super Grain capable of withstanding anything: diseases, insects, extreme temperatures. They will be able to grow in practically any soil, maybe even rocks, and would probably be immune to anything mankind can throw at them.

And it doesn't have to be grain—that was for argument's sake. In Canada, for instance, genetically modified canola leaked from a test field and into the countryside. Now Super Caonla is shooting up all over Canada. But it could be anything. Not just stuff that will make bread or vegetable oil. What if it turns out to be cotton? We're totally screwed.

1 GRAY GOO HYPOTHESIS

This is my favorite scenario because it's utterly terrifying. As technology progresses, it gets smaller and smaller. Pretty soon we are going to enter the realms of nano technology. For this scenario, we have to go a little bit into the future; not long—say ten years. Nanobots are what I'm talking about. They will be microscopic robots designed to do all sorts of tasks, mostly in the medical field where they can seek out and eradicate bacterial infections, repair tissue damage, and mend blood vessels, lots of things that would be very helpful to everyone. They will be able to rearrange single atoms and, for instance, make water out of sand. They will be able to take carbon atoms and turn them into diamonds. They will pick up raw materials and rearrange them into what they need. Well, obviously these nanobots will be extremely difficult to make, being microscopic and everything. And herein lies the problem. Scientists realize the only way to make them would be to use the nanobots themselves and to make them self-replicating so that each one is a microscopic nanobot factory.

Here's the scary part: what would happen if just one of them were accidentally thrown away? Well, it would pretty much go around changing atoms into robots. Then those robots would make more, and more, and more at an exponential rate until the horror has unfolded. Scientists believe within 72 hours, every single atom on earth will be turned into a nanobot. All buildings, cars, plants, rocks, oceans, animals, and yes, even us humans… will be nanobots. There it is, an endless sea of gray goo. And if ever some extraterrestrial were to land on the planet, then they, too, would be turned into nanobots. What's even scarier is that scientists are really working on creating nanobots and are very close to achieving them.

10 FASCINATING AND BIZARRE DISINTERMENTS

10 LEE HARVEY OSWALD

Conspiracy theorists, like Michael Eddowes, believed that an elaborate plan had taken place prior to Oswald's transfer from one jail to another; Oswald was killed while en route to his new holdings. Eddoes believes that a Soviet spy had taken Oswald's place and that it was this spy who had been fatally shot and not the real Oswald. So, with the consent of Oswald's widow, Eddowes was granted permission to exhume the body in 1981. Unfortunately, a leak in the casket had caused a lot of damage, but investigators were able to positively match the body to Oswald through dental records. Eddowes believed that was not enough, given that there were a number of physical discrepancies between Oswald and the body they had exhumed. Eddowes continued to promote his Soviet Spy Theory despite the positive match.

9 VIRGINIA POE

In 1847, at the age of 24, Virginia Poe, the wife and cousin of renowned poet Edgar Allan Poe, died from tuberculosis. Two years later, Edgar Allen Poe died and was buried in a small, unkempt family lot at the Westminster Cemetery in Maryland. Funds were raised to give Edgar Allan Poe a grander monument, and in 1875 he was reinterred in a more prominent section of the same cemetery, but no one thought to move his wife, who was buried in New York. During the same year as his reburial, the cemetery in which Virginia Poe was buried was destroyed and her gravesite disturbed. William Gill, a Poe enthusiast and biographer, claimed her bones and kept them in a box under his bed for the next ten years. She was later reburied next to her husband.

8 KING ARTHUR

The legendary king of the Britons may or may not be a historical figure, but King Arthur's body (or possibly someone else's, with the thought that it is his) has been dug up a few times over the centuries. The story begins in 1191, when the monks of the Glastonbury Abbey claimed to have found Arthur's remains in their burial grounds. The exhumation was recorded and published in 1193 by Arthurian biographer Geoffrey of Monmouth. He described a hollowed-out oak log containing the bones of two people—one being Guinevere, Arthur's second wife, and the other being Arthur himself—and a lead cross with Arthur's name on it. The bones were again disturbed in 1278 by order of Edward I to have a ceremonial transfer into a marble tomb. In 1539, the monastery, along with the majority of Catholic Church property, was taken by King Henry VIII and the tomb was destroyed, although the site is still marked today.

7 JESSE JAMES

Near the end of James' criminal career as an outlaw of the American Wild West, the James-Younger Gang had diminished to a few players, including Robert Ford, who killed Jesse James to claim the bounty on his head. Despite Ford's very public declarations about killing him and despite the positive identification of the body made by physical anomalies matching that of James, rumors still persisted that he faked his own death. In the late 1940s, a man who went by the name J. Frank Dalton insisted he was the real Jesse James. In 1995, James' body was exhumed, and DNA testing proved it to be the real Jesse James. Despite the test results, those who sided with Dalton still believed that he was the real James, so in 2000, a permit was granted to dig up Dalton's body. The wrong body was exhumed and so the court granted yet another permit to dig up Dalton, making him the third person to be studied as a possible Jesse James.

6 CHRISTOPHER COLUMBUS
Columbus may have arguably traveled more in death than in life! He died in 1506 in Spain and was first buried in Valladolid. His remains were then moved to a monastery in Seville. In 1542, he was moved yet again to Santo Domingo, Hispaniola. When the French took control of Hispaniola, Columbus' remains were moved to Havana, Cuba. When Cuba became independent in 1898, Columbus was moved yet again, and this time went back to Seville. At least, it's assumed what was moved back to Seville were the remains of Christopher Columbus, although there are some who are skeptical. In 1877, the cathedral in Santo Domingo was undergoing repairs and workers had found a tomb inscribed to Christopher Columbus. One theory is that the bones that were constantly moved were those of Columbus' son, Diego, who had the grave site next to his father.

5 SAMMY DAVIS, JR.
Sammy Davis, Jr., died in 1990 due to complications from throat cancer and was buried in a cemetery in Glendale, California. When it was discovered that he was nearly bankrupt, his wife, Altovise, had his body exhumed so she could remove $70,000 worth of jewelry that was buried with him.

4 FARINELLI
There are no conspiracies saying a fake Farinelli was buried in his grave, nor was he disturbed to move to another site. Farinelli was exhumed in the name of science. Farinelli, one of Italy's most famous *castrato*, was one of many 18th-century singers who were castrated before puberty so they could continue to sing the higher ranges. Farinelli was one of the few *castrati* who had a successful singing career later in life. The goal of the exhumation was to study the anatomical effects of prepubescent castration on the body.

3 "STONEWALL" JACKSON

This American Civil War general was not exhumed, but his left arm was. As a result of friendly fire, Jackson had to have his left arm amputated. The arm was buried at the battlefield in Chancellorville, Virginia, and Jackson was taken from battle to a safe place to recuperate. He contracted pneumonia and died eight days after the amputation. Jackson's body was buried in Lexington, Virginia. In 1929, Jackson's left arm was dug up and reburied in the Ellwood Family Cemetery in Spotsylvania, Virginia, nearly 150 miles away from the rest of his body. The Ellwood tombstone reads, "Arm of Stonewall Jackson."

2 JOHANN SEBASTIAN BACH

Bach may very well hold the record for most graves dug up for a single exhumation. In 1750, he was buried at the Johanneskirsche in an unmarked grave. The expansion of the graveyard in 1894 provided a chance to determine the exact location of his grave site. Based on scant clues the authorities could collect—clues like "the grave most likely was located within either the second or third section of the churchyard, but it also could have been in the first section"—they selected the most likely Bach grave sites and dug them all up. Based on the casket type, gender, and age of the skeleton and a few distinctive characteristics of the skull, they found what they believe is a high probability to be the remains of Johann Sebastian Bach. He was reinterred in the newly enlarged Johanneskirsche with a marked grave and was moved yet again to the Thomaskirsche when the first church was destroyed in World War II.

1 JOSEF HAYDN

Shortly after Haydn's burial in 1809, Johan Peters bribed the gravediggers to allow him to steal Haydn's head. He had a strong interest in the pseudoscience phrenology, which determines someone's personality and traits by the shape of their skull. To his delight, Haydn's musical bump was "fully formed," further proving the man's musical genius. However, as hard as it was to obtain the skull in the first place, it proved near impossible to return it to its rightful owner afterward. Peters kept the skull until the end of the Austrian War of 1809, after which he gave the skull to Josef Rosenbaum who had worked for Haydn's patrons. Rosenbaum's wife was extremely pleased with this acquisition and would prominently display the skull in a glass box during musical recitals. It wasn't until 1820 that the skull's story became public. Prince Esterhazy, of the patron family Rosenbaum worked for, decided to move Haydn's remains to the family church, only to discover it was missing a head. When Rosenbaum was found out, he gave the prince a skull close to shape and age of Haydn's and that was buried with the rest of the bones. The skull passed ownership a number of times through the decades not to reunite with the rest of Haydn's bones until 1954, 145 years since they were last together.

10 BIZARRE DISAPPEARANCES

10 JOHN BRISKER

John Brisker was an American basketball player who played in the ABA and NBA in the early 1970s. Brisker averaged over 20 points per game and was considered a solid defensive player, too. But his volatile personality and penchant for fighting caused him to be cut from the Seattle Supersonics at the end of the 1975 season.

According to a teammate, Charlie Williams, Brisker "was an excellent player, but say something wrong to the guy and you had this feeling he would reach into his bag, take out a gun, and shoot you."

In 1978, Brisker traveled to Uganda, telling his family he was entering the import-export business. What happened next is one of the enduring mysteries of the 1970s. The prevailing theory is that Brisker went to Uganda, not to become a business man, but as a guest of Ugandan strongman Idi Amin. When Amin was overthrown in 1979, Brisker was allegedly executed by firing squad. His body has never been recovered.

9 WILLIAM MORGAN

William Morgan was a would-be author who disappeared near Batavia, New York, in 1826. What makes his disappearance noteworthy was the involvement of local Freemasons in a conspiracy to silence him. A failed business man, Morgan attempted but failed to join the fraternal order of Freemasons in Batavia. Angered by his rejection, Morgan declared his intention to reveal the secrets of the group in an upcoming book. This action angered local Freemasons, who took out newspaper ads denouncing Morgan and even attempted to burn his newspaper office down. Morgan was eventually arrested on charges that he owed money and was jailed in Canandaigua, New York.

Later that same night, an unknown man came to the jail claiming to be Morgan's friend. He offered to pay the debt and have Morgan released. Morgan left the jail with the man and was never seen again. Three Masons were eventually convicted of kidnapping Morgan, but his body was never found. The most widely accepted theory is that Morgan was drowned in the Niagara River. Freemasons, of course, deny this is what happened and claim that Morgan was paid $500 to leave the country. In 1827, a badly decomposed body was found on the shores of Lake Ontario. The body was thought to be Morgan's, but no positive identification could be made.

The disappearance of William Morgan created widespread anti-Masonic sentiment. The Anti-Masonic party even fielded a presidential candidate in 1832.

8 BOBBY DUNBAR

On August 23, 1912, Lessie and Percy Dunbar came face to face with every parent's worst nightmare when their four-year-old son, Bobby, disappeared on a fishing trip near Swayze Lake in St. Landry Parish, Louisiana. Eight months later, Bobby was found in the custody of William Cantwell Walters. Walters was convicted of kidnapping, and Dunbar was returned to his family.

But the story doesn't end there. A woman named Julia Anderson claimed this was case of mistaken identity and that "Bobby Dunbar" was actually her

son, Charlie Bruce Anderson. For some reason, Anderson's claim was dismissed, and Bobby Dunbar was returned to his parents. More than 90 years later, one of Bobby Dunbar's grandchildren decided to put an end to the mystery once and for all. A DNA test conducted on Bobby Dunbar, Jr., and the son of Lessie and Percy Dunbar's other child, Alonzo, established there was no blood relation. The child raised as Bobby Dunbar wasn't Bobby Dunbar!

It is now presumed that the real Bobby Dunbar either drowned in the swamp or was killed by an alligator. The true identity of the fake Bobby Dunbar remains a mystery.

7 PERCY FAWCETT

Percy Fawcett was a British archaeologist and the inspiration for Indiana Jones. In 1925, Fawcett, his eldest son, Jack, and Raleigh Rimell set off deep into the Amazon to find a mythical lost city Fawcett named "Z." They never returned. They were last reported crossing the Upper Xingu River, a southeastern tributary of the Amazon. It is assumed the trio was either killed by natives or simply succumbed to the elements. Wilder theories have Fawcett going mad and living out his days as the crazed chieftain of a tribe of cannibals! In 1927, one of Fawcett's name plates was found by locals, and in 1933 a compass, of the type used by Fawcett, was found by Colonel Aniceto Botelho.

Over 100 people have died on numerous expeditions to discover the fate of Fawcett and his companions. A set of bones, thought to be Fawcett's, were discovered in 1951. However, DNA testing proved they were not. The ultimate fate of Fawcett, his son, and Rimell will probably never be known.

6 CHARLES NUNGESSER AND FRANCOIS COLI

Charles Eugène Jules Marie Nungesser and Francois Coli were French World War I pilots and rivals of Charles Lindbergh to make the first nonstop transatlantic flight. On May 8, 1927, Nungesser and Coli set off from Paris in a modified Levasseur PL.8 biplane named the *White Bird*. The plan was to fly a great circle route over the southwestern part of England and Ireland, cross the Atlantic to Newfoundland, and then head south to a water landing in New York.

When the plane didn't arrive, an international search was launched. Nothing was ever found. There are two popular theories as to the fate of the *White Bird* and its crew. One theory holds that a sudden squall caused the plane to crash in the Atlantic. A second theory maintains that Nungesser and Coli made it as far as Newfoundland or even Maine before crashing. This theory is supported by numerous eyewitnesses, including Anson Berry, who claimed to have heard a sputtering aircraft fly over his isolated camp at Round Lake, Maine, late in the afternoon of May 9, 1927.

To date, nothing conclusive has been proven, but small pieces of wreckage found in Maine suggest the plane did reach the coast.

5 WALLACE FARD MUHAMMAD

Wallace Fard Muhammad was the founder of the Nation of Islam. Muhammad's life is shrouded in mystery. He was either born in Afghanistan, Mecca, or New Zealand sometime between 1877 and 1896. Even his true name is disputed. Alternative names on record include Wallace/Wallie Dodd Ford, Wallace Dodd, Wallie Dodd Fard, W. D. Fard, David Ford-el, Wali Farad, and Farrad Mohammed.

What is known is that Muhammad preached in Detroit from 1930 to 1934 before vanishing without a trace on a trip to Chicago. Numerous theories surround his disappearance. Some maintain he was killed by police or possibly his successor, Elijah Muhammad. Other theories have him returning to Mecca or even being called back to the so-called Mother Plane. There is some evidence that Muhammad lived into the 1960s. An alleged former lover claimed he returned to New Zealand. Despite Muhammad's disappearance in 1934, the FBI maintained an open file on him until 1960.

4 HEINRICH MÜLLER

Heinrich Müller was head of the Gestapo and played a leading role in the planning and execution of the Holocaust. He was one of the last Nazi loyalists to remain in the Führerbunker as Soviet forces closed in. He disappeared on May 1, 1945, the day after Hitler committed suicide. Müller was one of the highest-ranking Nazi party members to escape justice, and CIA files reveal an exhaustive search to find him in the months after the war. But there were never any solid leads, and the search was complicated by there being several Heinrich Müllers among the Nazi high command.

During the Cold War, it was believed by some in the CIA that Müller was being hidden by the Soviets. But a thorough examination of Soviet documents following the end of the Cold War found no evidence. While his ultimate fate remains a mystery, it is now widely believed Müller died in Berlin shortly after World War II.

3 MICHAEL ROCKEFELLER

Michael Rockefeller was the youngest son of New York governor Nelson Rockefeller and a fourth-generation member of the legendary Rockefeller family. While working for the Peabody Museum, Rockefeller developed a love for archaeology. In 1961, he took part an expedition to explore New Guinea, one of the last uncharted areas of the world.

On November 17, 1961, Rockefeller was riding in a 40-foot dugout canoe with Dutch anthropologist René Wassing when the boat became swamped and overturned.

Wassing managed to swim to shore, but Rockefeller was not so lucky. Despite an extensive search, no trace was ever found. It is presumed that Rockefeller either drowned or was killed by a shark or crocodile. However, there is circumstantial evidence that Rockefeller may have met with a much stranger and far more gruesome fate.

Even in 1961, New Guinea was home to tribes of headhunters and cannibals, some of whom lived not far from where Rockefeller disappeared. It is entirely possible that he was captured and killed as revenge for several tribesmen who were killed by a Dutch patrol three years earlier. An unsubstantiated claim by author Paul Toohey, holds that Rockefeller's mother hired a private investigator to discover what became of her son. According to Toohey, the investigator brought back three skulls local tribesmen claimed were white men they had killed. One of these skulls was supposedly Michael's. The Rockefeller family has never confirmed the story.

2 RAY GRICAR

Ray Gricar has only been missing since 2005, yet the circumstances surrounding his disappearance are as strange as any other on this list. Gricar was the District Attorney for Centre County, Pennsylvania. On April 15, 2005, Gricar took the day off to travel to Lewisburg, Pennsylvania, and was never seen again. His abandoned car was discovered in a parking lot in Lewisburg. Although Gricar was not a smoker, authorities discovered cigarette ashes in the car and a faint odor of smoke.

The discovery of Gricar's laptop, recovered from the Susquehanna River several months later, yielded even stranger clues. The hard drive had been removed and damaged beyond repair. In April 2009, police reported that Gricar had made Internet searches for information on how to destroy a hard drive. The investigation is ongoing, although authorities believe his death to be a suicide.

1 "SWEET" JIM ROBINSON

"Sweet" Jim Robinson was a boxer, best remembered for being one of Muhammad Ali's first professional opponents. Robinson was not a very good boxer and was often used as an easy win for up-and-comers. He fought Ali in February, 1961, losing in the first round. He retired after seven years, with a dismal 5–23 record.

In 1979, *Sports Illustrated* reporter Michael Brennan interviewed Robinson at his home in the Liberty City district of Miami. This was the last-known interview with the former heavyweight. ESPN reporter Wright Thompson spent six years searching the Miami area for any sign of the missing boxer. Even famed Ali collector Stephen Singer, who has collected autographs from every Ali opponent except Robinson, has come up empty. Although not officially considered a missing person, Robinson's current whereabouts are unknown.

10 COMPOSERS WHO DIED ODD DEATHS

10 CHARLES-HENRI VALENTIN ALKAN, 1813–1888

Charles-Henri Valentin Alkan (born Charles-Henri Morhange) was one of the most prominent piano virtuosos of his time and was of Jewish descent. He was a highly talented child prodigy who was admitted at the age of six to the Paris Conservatoire, where he won numerous awards during his youth and later developed close friendships with noted persons such as Frederic Chopin, Franz Liszt, George Sand, and Victor Hugo. Alkan was considered by his contemporaries to be one of the most masterful pianists, and subsequently, he composed almost exclusively for the piano.

Alkan was also well-known for being rather eccentric and hypersensitive. At the height of his performing career, several episodes, including his failure to secure the position as head of the piano department at the Conservatoire, and the death of Chopin pushed him into reclusion; he no longer performed and interacted little with society. He also spent much of his time studying the Bible and the Talmud. For many years, it was believed that his death occurred while reaching for a copy of the Talmud on a high bookshelf, causing the shelf to topple and crush him under the weight of the books. This tale has recently been disproved upon the discovery of a contemporary letter from his concierge who said that he had found Alkan in his kitchen moaning under a coat rack (possibly from fainting, or suffering a stroke or heart attack) and that he died later that night. He was 74 at the time of his death.

9 JEAN-MARIE LECLAIR, 1697–1764

Another famous virtuoso of his time, Leclair was one of the most celebrated violinists in Europe during the 18th century, having composed one opera, 48 violin sonatas, and an assortment of other chamber works. Leclair had remarried after his first wife prematurely passed away, however, the second marriage didn't last, and the couple separated in 1758. Leclair was forced to purchase a small apartment in an otherwise rough neighborhood of Paris, and in 1764 he was found stabbed to death in his home. His death has always remained a mystery, but it was believed that his estranged wife was somehow responsible because she stood to benefit financially. His nephew, Guillaume-François Vial, was the primary suspect, but according to my research, he was never arrested or put to trial.

8 JEAN-BAPTISTE LULLY, 1632–1687

Sticking with the Baroque era, Lully (born in Florence as Lulli) was Louis XIV's favorite and main court composer. Lully was famous as a dancer, violinist, and composer and composed numerous ballets, operas, and even incidental music for Molière's comedies. He was the founder of French opera and responsible for determining the elements that would develop overtime to create Romantic French grand opera (for which Giaochino Rossini is considered the founder with his opera Guillaume Tell) such as the inclusion of ballet music, faster plot development, an expanded orchestration than previously employed, and a revolutionary method of combining recitatives (the sung dialogue of opera in which most of the action takes place) and arias (the main set pieces which served to showcase the singer and the character portrayed).

Lully was also well-known for his many sexual escapades with both men and women, and there has been rumor for centuries of an illicit affair with the Sun King himself. In January 1687, Lully had been conducting a performance of his Te Deum in honor of Louis XIV's recovery from illness when he inadvertently struck his foot with the pointed staff he had been using to keep time (this is long before batons were used to conduct). The wound became gangrenous and he died on March 22 of that year.

7 ALESSANDRO STRADELLA, 1644–1682

His life and death the subject of a great opera by Friedrich von Flotow, Alessandro Stradella was one of the great Italian composers of the early Baroque period. A predecessor to the likes of Arcangelo Corelli and Antonio Vivaldi, he was a highly respected and famous composer of mostly operas, oratorios, and cantatas as well as church chamber music during a time when the Vatican had outlawed secular musical dramas, namely opera. As a result, Stradella pioneered much in the oratorio and cantata genres, as setting Biblical subjects to music was not considered heretical or sinful.

For all of his musical success, Stradella's life had a darker side. In 1677, he was employed by a powerful Venetian nobleman to tutor his mistress. The two had a torrid affair, and Stradella fled after it was exposed. The nobleman had hired several hit men to kill the great composer, but he managed to escape unharmed. He settled in Genoa, where he continued to compose great works for the church and stage until yet another affair caught up to him. He was chased through the streets of Genoa by a hired assassin who did manage to catch him and brutally stabbed and murdered him.

6 BEDR ICH SMETANA, 1824–1884

While Beethoven's hearing loss happened gradually overtime, Smetana lost his in a matter of a few weeks after suffering awful tinnitus for years (he was subjected to an extremely high, unending pitch through most of his life). A highly talented and nationalistic Czech composer, Smetana is mostly famous for several operas, his enormous orchestral symphonic suite, *Má Vlast (My Country)*, and an array of chamber music, namely his first String Quartet "From My Life," in which each movement depicts a pivotal event from his life, including the onset of his deafness. His musical style was the first to really steep itself in Czech folk music, dance rhythms, myths, and fairy tales.

Smetana, like several other prominent Czech composers, had a very difficult time developing his reputation and fame, and he struggled against many intrigues from his opponents in Bohemian musical circles. Ultimately, his professional hardships and his deafness preyed on his mind, and he began to suffer severe neurological illness. Family life was not easy, either, as three of his four children from his first marriage, as well as his first wife, had died by the time he was 35 years old. He did remarry and had two more children with his second wife. Smetana suffered a stroke-seizure in 1882 and was forbidden to compose any further. He ignored this and attempted to finish his last opera, but the strain on his mind drove him to a breakdown and he spent his last months in the Prague Insane Asylum where he died of a progressive paralysis, possibly caused by complications from syphilis.

5 HUGO WOLF, 1860–1903

A German eccentric known for his prolific song-writing skills, Hugo Wolf led a very sad and disturbed life. He was a child prodigy, having studied piano, violin, and composition, but his rebellious nature, severe mood swings, and bouts of depression impeded his completion of his studies; he was constantly dismissed from the various musical institutions where he enrolled. He managed to survive through the financial backing of noted patrons who were swept away by his musical talents. He was most strongly influenced by the music and compositional language of Richard Wagner, but Wolf was not inclined to compose large-scale works and focused mainly on songs for voice and piano. He had a great passion for poetry and was determined to set to music many poems neglected by other composers. When he did use text previously set to music, it was because he felt that the other composer did not do the words justice. With his outspoken criticisms of other composer's works he considered inferior, Wolf made numerous enemies, such as Anton Rubenstein and Johannes Brahms; however, paradoxically, during the time he served as a critic, he composed very little.

It was from 1888 to 1892 that Wolf was most productive as a composer, with an output of his most famous song cycles (the *Mörike-Lieder*, *Eichendorff-Lieder*, *Goethe-Lieder*, and the Spanish and Italian songbooks) and he began to receive

high recognition for his talents. In early 1897, Wolf began to show signs of mental derangement, brought on mainly by syphilis, and eventually he had to stop composing altogether. He attempted to drown himself before requesting admission to an insane asylum where he eventually died completely and utterly mindless.

It's also interesting to note that Wolf had an affair with the wife, Melanie, of his good friend and patron Heinrich Köchert. The affair was exposed after a time, but Heinrich remained Hugo's friend. Melanie had visited him frequently during those last years, but she was so struck with grief over Wolf's death and guilt for cheating on her husband that she committed suicide in 1906.

4 ERNEST CHAUSSON, 1855–1899

The composer of the famous and beloved *Poème for Violin and Orchestra* as well as many songs and orchestral works, met his end in a freak accident. Chausson came from a very wealthy family and originally pursued a career in law, but he was unhappy and eventually turned to music when he was 25 years old. He began his studies with the great Jules Massenet at the Paris Conservatoire, and eventually his music evolved into very dramatic, poetic, and psychologically emotional pieces, drawing much inspiration from Richard Wagner, Johannes Brahms, and César Franck. He is credited for being the first composer to use the celeste, a keyboard instrument, in an orchestral setting (the celeste was made most famous by Tchaikovsky's "Dance of the Sugarplum Fairy" in *The Nutcracker* ballet). Chausson was not the most prolific of composers, but his music is still regularly performed today. He held the position as secretary of the Société Nationale de Musique and became friends with the majority of the Paris musical and artistic elite. He also had an affinity for Russian literature and French Impressionistic artwork. At the age of 44, Chausson was on for a bicycle ride outside his property in Limay when he lost control of the bike on a downhill slope and crashed into a brick wall. He died instantly.

3 PYOTR ILYICH TCHAIKOVSKY, 1840–1893

The most famous and recognizable composer on this list, Tchaikovsky was a Russian composer whose music still pervades our lives today. Constantly faced with exposure of his homosexuality, he tried to force himself into very unhappy relationships with women and even married, but the couple separated without divorce after a short time. In 1877, he came into contact with a devoted fan, Nadezhda von Meck, a very wealthy widow who would become his patron and, in a way, soul mate; however, she insisted that the two never meet face to face. They embarked on a remarkable journey together, exchanging over 1000 letters that have provided great insight into the personality and the emotional tribulations of this great man, until Meck finally severed their correspondence, claiming bankruptcy in 1890. This was devastating to Tchaikovsky, as Meck provided emotional and financial stability for him.

After several years of traveling around Europe and composing, Tchaikovsky mysteriously died a mere nine days after the premiere of his sixth symphony, the *Pathétique*, which is a highly personal and autobiographic work. The circumstances of Tchaikovsky's death remain a mystery. It was believed for many years that he died of cholera, and there were more than eight completely different "eyewitness" reports of him taking that "fateful sip of unboiled water." It is believed that Tchaikovsky may have had an illicit relationship with a young nobleman or royal he was tutoring at the time, and several alumni from the School of Jurisprudence held a Court of Honor to discuss the punishment options, of which two were proposed: exile from Russia (something Tchaikovsky could not bear) or suicide with a cover-up. It's more widely accepted that to protect both his and the school's reputations, Tchaikovsky was forced to commit suicide. Unfortunately, the exact circumstances around his death will never be truly known.

2 ENRIQUE GRANADOS, 1867–1916

Most famous for his piano suite *Goyescas* and his opera of the same name, Enrique Granados was a Spanish nationalistic composer who sought to captivate the flavor and culture of Spain in his music, and he was also heavily influenced by the paintings of Francisco Goya (whom he also modeled his painting style after). He led a rather successful life that ended tragically. His opera's premiere was canceled in Europe due to the outbreak of World War I and subsequently received its premiere at the Metropolitan Opera in New York City, where it had a huge success. He was invited to give a piano recital at the White House by President Woodrow Wilson, but in doing so, he and his wife missed the boat back to Spain. Instead, they took a boat to England, where they boarded the French ferry *Sussex* to take them to France.

On March 24, 1916, while crossing the English Channel, the *Sussex* was victim to a German U-boat torpedo. Granados, despite a life-long fear of water, drowned after he jumped out of his lifeboat in a futile attempt to save his wife, Amparo, who also drowned. Ironically, the area of the boat where his cabin was located did not sink, and the passengers in that part of the boat survived the attack.

1 ANTON VON WEBERN, 1883–1945

This very influential and important Austrian serial composer lost his life in a very unfortunate manner. Webern studied with Arnold Shoenberg at Vienna University, where he also met Alban Berg. These three composers were responsible for creating a mathematically based musical compositional language and style known as serialism, or the 12-tone technique. There are 12 tones in the Western musical scale, and the basic foundation of this compositional style was to use all 12 tones of the chromatic scale in various permutations to create subversive atonal atmospheres. Of the three composers, Webern took serialism the furthest into what is known as total serialism, and his music is still not well-received by many today.

At first he was privately outspoken against the Nazi party, who had called his music "degenerate," but after the advent of World War II Webern became a supporter of Adolph Hitler. He continued to struggle to earn his living as a composer, as his music was considered far too radical to be enjoyed. He had moved to Salzburg toward the end of the war to ensure his safety. In an effort to not wake his sleeping grandchildren, Webern left his house to enjoy a cigar, oblivious that a curfew had been established by the Allied occupying forces, when he was shot dead by an American soldier who saw him light the cigar. Webern was 61 when he was killed on September 15, 1945. The soldier who shot him was so distraught after the event that he turned to the bottle and died of alcoholism ten years later.

5 PROMINENT PEOPLE PUT ON TRIAL AFTER THEIR DEATH

5 JOHN WYCLIFFE

Wycliffe was a Catholic in the 14th century who opposed papal power in the secular world. During his lifetime, he made a translation of the Latin Bible into English. Even though he was a very controversial figure, he was never excommunicated. After his death in 1385, the Council of Constance declared him a heretic, and ordered all his books to be burned. Twelve years later, at the behest of Pope Martin V, his bones were dug up and rendered to ashes, which were thrown into the River Swift.

4 MARTIN BORMANN

Bormann was a high-up Nazi official who had the dubious honor of hiding out with Hitler in the last days of World War II. After the end of the war, there were various reports as to his whereabouts; all were contradictory. The Military Tribunal at Nuremberg tried Bormann in absentia and sentenced him to death. DNA was later used to prove that Bormann was in fact dead at the time of the trial.

3 SAINT JOAN OF ARC

Twenty-four years after Joan of Arc was tried and executed by renegade bishops, Pope Callixtus III re-opened her case. The trial found overwhelmingly that a miscarriage of justice had been done and the saintly soldier was vindicated. The bishops who condemned her were implicated with heresy and condemning an innocent woman. It would take another 500 years before the Patron of France was declared a saint by Pope Benedict XV.

2 SAINT THOMAS BECKET

Thomas Becket was a 12th-century Archbishop of Canterbury who fought vehemently against the proposed chuch reforms of King Henry II. The king ordered Becket killed. He was murdered in the cathedral. Some 300 years later, King Henry VIII, who created the Anglican religion because he could not otherwise divorce his wife, ordered the bones of Becket to be put on trial. He was found guilty, and his bones were publicly burned. In an ironic twist, Saint Thomas Becket is now venerated by the Anglican church.

1 POPE FORMOSUS

Pope Formosus was a 9th-century pope who tried to resign the papal throne amid great scandal but eventually returned to it. When he died, Pope Stephen VI had the corpse of Formosus dug up and put on trial. He was accused of breaching church law, pretending to be a bishop, and lying. Stephen had Formosus' papal clothing removed and two fingers from his right hand cleaved off. The body was then tossed into the Tiber River. Eventually, public support turned against Pope Stephen and he was strangled to death.

12 PEOPLE WHO DIED PERFORMING

12 JOHNNY ACE

Johnny Ace was a rhythm-and-blues musician active from 1949 to 1954. Born in Tennessee in 1929 as John Marshall Alexander, Jr., he served his country in the Navy during the Korean War before becoming a musician. On Christmas Day 1954, Ace was performing in Houston, Texas, when, during a break in the set, he began playing with a .22-caliber revolver as band members often did for fun. It is widely reported that Ace was either playing Russian roulette during the break or bragging about how the gun wasn't loaded when in fact it was. It's reported he had been drinking and was warned to "Be careful" as he waved his pistol around, before stating, "It's okay, gun isn't loaded, see?" while putting it to his head and pulling the trigger.

11 EDITH WEBSTER

Edith Webster was an actress who performed on stage in theaters. She was performing in Baltimore, Maryland, and while singing her swan song, "Please Don't Talk About Me when I'm Gone," collapsed and died both in the play and in real life. She had suffered a heart attack at the exact moment her character was meant to collapse and die. Obviously, the audience thought it was part of the act and applauded unknowingly at both her death and the stagehand's call for help, thinking it was part of the play.

10 J. I. RODALE

Jerome Irving Rodale was a playwright, editor, author, and publisher born in 1898. During his life, he published various organic farming magazines. While not technically a performer, he died while appearing as a guest on *The Dick Cavett Show* in 1971. Rodale finished his interview but was still on stage, and Cavett brought out his second guest, Pete Hamill, a columnist for the *New York Post*. It was during this interview that Rodale let out a "snoring sound," which got laughs from the audience, before the camera zoomed in on his face and Hamill said jokingly, "This looks bad." Still, the audience laughed, although Cavett didn't—he says he "knew" Rodale was dead. Two interns rushed onto the stage to try and revive him but couldn't. Ironically, during his interview, Rodale said, "I'm in such good health that I fell down a long flight of stairs yesterday and I laughed all the way," "I've decided to live to be a hundred," as well as "I never felt better in my life!" He had also previously bragged that "I'm going to live to be 100, unless I'm run down by some sugar-crazed taxi driver."

9 PAUL MANTZ

Stunt pilots live on the edge of life and death all the time, but Paul Mantz avoided this inevitability throughout his long career as a stunt pilot and racing-pilot champion. It was during the filming of *The Flight of the Phoenix* in 1965 that Mantz died while attempting a very low flight over a desert site in Arizona. According to reports, Mantz's plane struck a small hillock and he lost control. After Mantz tried to save the aircraft, it split in two and nosed into the ground, killing him instantly. Officials have blamed alcohol consumption before the stunt as the reason his judgment and efficiency were not as they should have been. The final credit in *The Flight of the Phoenix* says, "It should be remembered... that Paul Mantz, a fine man and a brilliant flier, gave his life in the making of this film..."

8 KARL WALLENDER

Karl Wallender was a German daredevil born in 1905. He was the founder of The Flying Wallendas—an international daredevil circus act. He was most famed for his wire walks, which he would perform between two very high structures without a safety net, particularly in his later years. In 1978, at age 73, he died while attempting to cross between two towers of a ten-story hotel in Puerto Rico. While crossing the gap, winds of around 30 miles per hour were enough to cause Wallender to lose his balance and fall 121 feet to his death. He was quoted as saying, "Life is being on the wire; everything else is just waiting."

7 LESLIE "LES" HARVEY

Leslie Harvey, born in 1945, was a Scottish guitarist for many bands during the 1960s and 1970s, most notably Stone the Crows. Before the band's formation in 1969, however, Harvey played with the band Cartoone as they toured the United States opening for Led Zeppelin. On May 3, 1972, while performing with Stone the Crows at the Swansea Top Rank Ballroom in Wales, he touched an ungrounded microphone with wet hands and was electrocuted. The shock killed him.

6 ERIC MORECAMBE

John Eric Bartholomew OBE was an English comedian who together with Ernie Wise formed the award-winning comedy duo "Morecambe and Wise." He took his stage name from the seaside town of Morecombe in which he grew up. He became a famed presenter and comedian throughout the years, co-hosting the hugely popular *The Morecambe and Wise Show*, which hit a record 28 million viewers on one of their Christmas specials. Throughout his career, Morecambe suffered two heart attacks before succumbing to the third on May 28, 1984. He was appearing at a comedy show at the Roses Theater in Tewkesbury, England, and due to his huge popularity, he returned to the stage six times after the end of his show. After his sixth return he announced, "That's your lot!" before leaving the stage. After walking off-stage, he joked, "Thank goodness that's over," before collapsing. He was pronounced dead at 4 a.m. the next morning. He was 58.

5 JON-ERIC HEXUM

Jon-Eric Hexum was an actor and model born in the '50s in New Jersey. He played various roles in American television programs before landing his big lead role in the series *Cover Up* in 1984, in which he played a model turned weapons expert and CIA agent. As with most shows that include guns, the prop .44-Magnum was loaded with blanks; however, it is reported that Hexum was unaware that this prop gun would still shoot out paper wadding, which was used to seal gun powder in the shell. During the shooting of a scene where he was to empty the gun of real bullets and load it with blanks, a technical problem meant the scene was delayed, and Hexum fell asleep. Upon waking he realized the scene still wasn't done and began playing with the gun. It is reported that he was playing Russian roulette with the gun, which was loaded with three empty cartridges and two blanks. He put it to his head and said, "Let's see if I've got one for me" before pulling the trigger. While the paper wadding didn't penetrate his skull, it hit with enough force to dislodge a quarter-sized piece of skull and propel it into his brain. The accident happened on October 12, 1984, and despite five hours of surgery, Hexum died six days later; he was declared brain-dead due to the massive bleeding in his brain. His mother flew his body to San Francisco to be harvested for organ transplants before he was buried.

4 BRANDON LEE

Brandon Bruce Lee was the son of martial arts legend Bruce Lee and was born in 1965. During his relatively short career, he walked in his father's footsteps and starred in many kung fu and action films throughout the '80s and '90s. In 1992, he landed the starring role in *The Crow*, a film based on an underground comic book about an undead musician. On March 31, 1993, the crew was filming a scene in which Lee's character, Eric Draven, finds his girlfriend being beaten and raped by thugs. As Lee walked onto set, an actor playing one of the thugs was supposed to shoot at him with a gun loaded with blanks. Because of various tampering with the gun and the blanks being used (the extent of which is still not fully understood), the gun was left with enough primer to push the bullet cartridge out of the gun. Although at a speed much slower than a true bullet, from close range it could still prove dangerous. The malfunction went unnoticed, and Lee was hit in the abdomen as the bullet traveled through his body and got lodged in his spine. The scene was immediately cut and an ambulance called, though it is believed his heart stopped beating on the way to the hospital. Despite a six-hour operation and 60 pints of blood transfusions, Brandon Lee died at 1:04 p.m. He was just 28 years old. He was later buried next to his father in Washington.

3 DIMEBAG DARRELL

Dimebag Darrell (real name Darrell Lance Abbott) was an American guitarist famous for being a founding member of the metal bands Pantera and Damageplan. Born in 1966, throughout his music career he was praised and widely regarded as "one of the most influential stylists in modern metal." He was killed on stage while performing with Damageplan on December 8, 2004, by an ex-Marine named Nathan Gale. Gale shot Abbott

five times, including once in the head, before turning on others and shooting another ten shots. He killed three more people, including an employee of the arena and Damageplan's head of security, both of whom tried to wrestle the handgun from his hands, and also an audience member who tried to perform CPR on Abbott. Gale also wounded seven others. He was killed by a policeman who approached him from behind as he had a hostage in a headlock, and he was shot in the head with a 12-gauge shotgun. A nurse tried to revive Darrell, but he was dead by the time paramedics arrived.

The reasons for Gale's attack have been debated. An initial motive that was theorized was that Gale was angry at the breakup of Pantera and blamed Abbott for this, or that apparently Pantera had stolen a song written by Gale. Another theory suggested Gale was a paranoid schizophrenic and was convinced Damageplan members were reading his mind and stealing his thoughts. Darrell Abbott was buried in a KISS casket, with Eddie Van Halen's Charvel Hybrid VH2 guitar.

2 OWEN HART

Owen James Hart was a Canadian wrestler born in 1965 who won multiple titles during his career, most notably during his time at the WCW and the WWF. He started his wrestling life in Japan, wrestling for the NJPW (New Japan Pro-Wrestling) circuit and gained popularity throughout his time in America, most memorably for his relationship with his brother Bret and his feud with Jerry Lawler, as well as his winning his tag-team title with Yokozuna. Hart died on May 23, 1999, during his arrival to the ring for an Intercontinental Championship match with The Godfather, during the Over-the-Edge pay-per-view event. He was supposed to be lowered into the ring on a harness, where he would be dropped a meter or so from the surface for comedic effect. Tragically, his harness malfunctioned and released Hart too early. He fell 78 feet into the ring and landed chest first on the top rope before being propelled into the middle of the ring. He was able to sit up for a short while after the accident before losing consciousness. He was rushed to hospital but pronounced dead on arrival. Hart had died from internal bleeding, due to a severed aorta.

1 TOMMY COOPER

Tommy Cooper was a Welsh-born British prop comedian and magician famous for his red fez he always wore and the persona he crafted of a magician whose tricks always go wrong. Cooper died on April 15, 1984, as he performed live on television for a variety show entitled *Live from Her Majesty's*. During a sketch in which he was to pull numerous objects from a gown, just after his assistant helped him put the gown on, Cooper collapsed and sat against the curtain while the audience and his assistant laughed, thinking it was an impromptu part of his act. He then fell backward onto his back, creating more laughs, however, as the minutes passed it was apparent that something had actually gone wrong and it wasn't part of his act. Another curtain was closed to hide where he had fallen and other acts continued on the front of the stage. People backstage tried to resuscitate Cooper but couldn't. He was pronounced dead on arrival at Westminster hospital, from a heart attack. He was 63 years old. Controversy later arose from the fact that the video of him collapsing was posted on YouTube. It can be found by searching "Tommy Cooper death."

10 MOST TERRIFYING NATURAL DISASTERS

10 TYPHOON TIP

Pacific typhoons are generally more powerful than Atlantic hurricanes because the former have much more water over which they can gather strength.

On October 12, 1979, Typhoon Tip made history with the lowest air pressure ever recorded at sea level on earth: 870 mbars. Standard sea-level air pressure is 1013.25 mbars. Hurricane Andrew only made it to 922 mbars.

Tip had one-minute sustained winds of 190 mph. It killed 99 people, a low number compared to some of the others on this list, but this must be placed in the perspective of a long warning before the typhoon strikes.

Of the fatalities, 44 were fishermen in the open Pacific. Tip sank or grounded eight ships. One of these was a giant freighter that the storm broke in half. Not only was it the strongest cyclone ever recorded, it was also the largest at half the size of the continental United States.

9 THE LAKE NYOS LIMNIC ERUPTION

Limnic eruptions are some of the most bizarre natural disasters known. The criteria required for one to occur make them very rare. Lake Nyos is in a very remote area of the Cameroonian jungle. It is not very large, only 1.2 miles by 0.75 miles, but it is quite deep, at 682 feet. Under the lake bed, a magma chamber is leaking carbon dioxide into the water. This changes the water into carbonic acid. Carbon dioxide is 1.5 times denser than air, which is why it will not rise from the bottom of a lake, unless shoved up by another force. There are only three such lakes known on earth.

On August 21, 1986, the carbon dioxide at the bottom of the lake suddenly erupted all at once, 1.6 million tons of it, and released a cloud of carbon dioxide from the water. This cloud, being heavier than air, hugged the ground contours and blew out of the lake at 60 mph; it then went downhill throughout the area at up to 30 mph and displaced all the oxygen in several small villages, suffocating between 1700 and 1800 people, not counting all their livestock.

The force of the gas expulsion also blew out the lake water itself, in an 80-foot-high tsunami that stripped the trees, shrubs, and soil off one side of the shore.

8 THE 1960 CHILE EARTHQUAKE

The most powerful earthquake ever recorded struck near Valdivia, Chile, on May 22, 1960, at 2:11 p.m. local time. As many as 6000 people were killed. Many more would have been, had it not been for Chile's preparedness for earthquakes and the remote location of the epicenter.

Eyewitnesses reported that it appeared as if God has seized the entire world from one end like a rope and swung it as hard as he could. Forty percent of the houses in Valdivia were razed to the ground. Cordon Caulle, a nearby active volcano, was ripped open and forced to erupt.

The quake measured 9.5 in magnitude, and 35-foot-high waves were recorded 6000 miles away. Of all the seismic energy of the 20th century plus the 2004 Indian Ocean quake, 25 percent was concentrated in the 1960 Chile quake.

It caused 82-foot-high waves to travel down the Chilean coast. Hilo, Hawaii, was destroyed. The quake possessed twice the surface-energy yield as the 2004 Indian Ocean quake, and equaled 178 billion tons of dynamite. This would have powered the entire United States, at 2005 energy consumption levels, for 740 years.

7 THE 2003 EUROPEAN HEAT WAVE

Europe is not accustomed to hot summers. Give them a break—hot summers almost never happen there. But in 2003, they got hit with one that would make the southeastern United States or the Australian outback sit back and marvel.

In Europe, most of the homes built within the last 50 years before 2003 did not have air conditioners because none had ever been needed. Now, well over half of them have equipped themselves for the future.

There were at least 14,802 deaths from the heat in France alone, most of them old people in nursing homes or in single-family homes without the ability to cool off. The heat dried up most of Europe, and severe forest fires broke out in Portugal. Some 2000 people died there from the heat.

About 300 died in Germany, where the weather is usually very cold to delightfully mild; 141 died in Spain, where the temperature actually gets into the 90s once in a great while; 1500 died in the Netherlands. Multiple temperature records, having lasted since the 1700s, were broken, then broken again a week later: 106.7°F in Brono, Switzerland, which melted a lot of Alpine glaciers into flash floods; 104.7 in Bavaria, Germany; 103 in Paris. The new record in Edinburgh, Scotland, is now 91.2°F, which is unheard of there.

6 THE STORM OF THE CENTURY

From March 12 to 13, 1993, a cyclonic storm formed off the East Coast of the United States so vast in size that it caused a unique hodgepodge of severe weather.

Rarely does a single storm system cause blizzards from the Canada–U.S. border all the way down to Birmingham, Alabama, but this one did, and Birmingham received 12 to 16 inches of snowfall in one day and night. This was accompanied everywhere with hurricane-force wind gusts. The Florida panhandle

received up to four inches of snow, and the strange thing is that five people were killed by tornadoes in the middle of this blizzard.

The Appalachians of North Carolina, Virginia, and West Virginia received as much as 3.5 feet of snow, with drifts up to 35 feet. Throughout the eastern half of the country, 300 people froze to death when the electrical power was knocked out by falling trees. Wind gusts of 100 mph reached all the way to Havana, Cuba.

5 THE GREAT FLOOD OF 1931

The deadliest natural disaster ever recorded occurred through the winter, spring, and summer of 1931 in central China. There are three major rivers draining this area: the Yangtze, the Yellow, and the Huai. All three flooded catastrophically because the winter snowstorms were particularly heavy in the mountains around the river basins, and when spring began, all this snow melted and flowed into the rivers.

Then the spring brought particularly heavy rains. Then the cyclone season, which usually brings only two storms per year, brought ten, seven of them in July. All this water swelled the three major rivers, especially the Yellow River, and because they drain a very large, very flat area of China, somewhere between 3.7 and 4 million people were drowned or starved.

Nanjing City, China's capital at the time, became an island surrounded by over 100,000 square kilometers of water, more area than the state of Indiana, or all of Portugal.

4 THE TUNGUSKA EXPLOSION

On June 30, 1908, at about 7:14 a.m. local time, an asteroid or comet plummeted over the lower Tunguska River in Krasnoyarsk, Russia, a remote area of Siberia, and detonated at an altitude of three to six miles.

It exploded with the energy of the largest thermonuclear bomb the United States has ever tested, the Castle Bravo bomb, at 10 to 15 megatons. This is one-third the power of the largest thermonuclear weapon ever detonated, the Tsar Bomba. The airburst toppled about 80 million trees over 772 square miles of Siberian taiga, and would have registered at 5.0 on the Richter scale.

Thankfully, no one was killed, because the nearest eyewitnesses were about 40 miles away from ground zero. They reported seeing a bright blue column of light streak across the sky, almost as bright as the sun, then a flash, and a report like artillery fire right beside them.

For 100 miles around the epicenter, people were blown off their feet by the shockwave; their clothes were scorched off, windows were shattered, and trees were seared to death and blown over. Iron locks were snapped off barn doors. This detonation was more than sufficient to incinerate the entire population of Japan, the São Paolo metropolitan area, the Buenos Aires metropolitan area, or the entire United States' New England megalopolis from Boston to Washington, D.C.

3 THE 1999 BRIDGE CREEK F5 TORNADO

On May 3, 1999, a tornado outbreak lasting for three days began with a bang when an F5 tornado formed at about 7:12 p.m. local time. This tornado was the most powerful windstorm ever recorded on earth, at 318 mph. It killed 36 people and traveled northeast from Amber, Oklahoma, through Bridge Creek and Moore. Moore is a southern suburb of Oklahoma City, and had the tornado veered north into the city, it would have probably caused more deaths than any other tornado in history and become the costliest.

The tornado obliterated 8000 houses. It shredded large vehicles with debris and then wrapped them around telephone poles, threw them completely through warehouses, whipped two-by-fours through wheel hubs, and shot pine straw all the way through eight-inch-thick pine trees.

This was the first time that the local weather stations reported over radio that if residents were not securely underground, they would be killed. Hiding under mattresses in bathtubs, in ditches, or under highway overpasses was insufficient.

2 THE 1815 TAMBORA ERUPTION

Mt. Tambora is on Sumbawa Island, in south Indonesia. It erupted from April 6 to 11, 1815, but the worst of this was at the end, from April 10 to 11. The power is rated as seven on the Volcanic Explosivity Index, making this eruption the most powerful in recorded history, four times more powerful than the 1883 Krakatoa eruption.

This means that the Tambora eruption was 52,000 times more powerful than the Hiroshima bomb. All the vegetation on Sumbawa was incinerated or uprooted, mixed with ash, and washed out to sea. The trees formed rafts three miles across. Pumice ash does not mix well with water, and one of these rafts of ash and wood drifted all the way to Calcutta, India.

In the largest loss of life caused by a volcanic eruption in recorded history, 92,000 people were killed, most by starvation.

The finer ash remained in the atmosphere for three years and covered the entire planet, causing brilliant sunsets and the famous "Year without a Summer" in both North America and Europe. The ash disrupted the weather and caused global temperatures to decrease as much as 1.3°F on average, an enormous drop.

1816 was the coldest year of the 1810s, and that was the coldest decade of the century because of the eruption. From June 6 to 10, 1816, 12 inches of snow fell in Quebec City. Crops in the entire Northern Hemisphere were severely damaged.

1 THE 1958 LITUYA BAY MEGATSUNAMI

Megatsunamis were only theoretical until July 9, 1958, when, in Lituya Bay, a very narrow fjord of the Alaskan panhandle, a 7.7-magnitude earthquake shook 90 million tons of rock and glacial ice off the mountainside at the head of the bay. It dropped off all at once, almost vertically, and landed as a monolith into the bay's deep headwaters.

This generated the highest wave ever recorded on earth at 1720 feet. That's 470 feet taller than the tip of the Empire State Building's antenna. It is, in fact, taller than all but the five tallest skyscrapers on earth today, and most scientists agree that it had sufficient power to rip these buildings from their foundations.

The wave traveled from the head of the bay out toward the open ocean, and because the bay is so narrow, the wave was funneled up the mountainsides. It snapped all the trees off at three to six feet above the ground everywhere up to 1720 feet high around the bay. Most of these were six-foot-thick spruce trees.

There were a total of three fishing boats in the bay, near the mouth, and the wave sank one, killing the two on board. The other two were lucky to ride this wave up the mountainsides and then slosh with it back into the bay.

One of the boats was anchored, and the three-foot-thick iron anchor chain was snapped like thread when the wave lifted the boat. One of the survivors estimated the length of time between the wave's overtopping of the island in the bay to its arrival at his boat as two seconds. If this is true, the wave was traveling at 600 mph.

The megatsunami stripped away all the trees, grass, and soil down to the bedrock, and then dissipated in the open ocean.

10 TRULY AWFUL WAYS TO BE KILLED BY AN ANIMAL

10 ELECTROCUTION—ELECTRIC EELS

Electric eels are elongated, freshwater fish, native to the Amazon and Orinoco rivers in South America. They are not really eels, but a kind of knifefish (and related to catfish). They are among the deadliest denizens of the South American rivers. The electric eel has not one, but three specialized organs to produce electric currents strong enough (600 volts, sometimes more) to stun or kill an adult human. It is believed that many "unexplained" disappearances of people swimming in the Amazon and Orinoco rivers could be due to their being stunned by an electric eel and drowning, or dying because of the eel's shock itself. Many of these deaths are often blamed on attacks by predatory animals such as piranha or caiman.

The electric eel doesn't eat human beings; it feeds on smaller fish, crabs, and small mammals. It only attacks in self-defense, and handling an electric eel or even entering the water wherever these fish are common should be avoided at all costs.

9 CONSTRICTION—PYTHONS AND ANACONDAS

Pythons and anacondas, a kind of boa constrictor, are not venomous. They have very sharp teeth to hold on to their prey, but they rely on constriction for the actual kill. This means once they have secured their prey with their teeth, they coil around the victim and squeeze so that the unfortunate animal doesn't have any space to breathe. Every time the victim tries to inhale, the snake squeezes harder. This deadly "hug"  is so powerful that even blood can't flow. As a matter of fact, death comes usually because of cardiac arrest or stroke, and not asphyxia, as was once believed.

Although some smaller snakes, such as king snakes and gopher snakes, use constriction to kill prey, pythons and anacondas are the best-known constrictors, and the scariest, too, since these cold-blooded predators have been known to kill and eat humans once in a while.

8 DROWNING AND DISMEMBERMENT—CROCODILE

Among large predatory animals, crocodiles are the ones that kill the greatest number of people every year. They are often said to be among the few animals that still see humans as perfectly suitable prey. To deal with large prey, crocodiles use the "death roll." Called by some "the most powerful killing mechanism" of any animal, the death roll consists of the crocodile holding its prey with its jaws (usually by the neck or a limb), dragging it to the water and spinning its entire body; this is usually enough to dismember the unfortunate victim. They can do this on dry land as well.

The scariest part is that the crocodile really doesn't care if the prey is alive or dead when it starts feeding; by doing a death roll, it is really trying to tear the prey into smaller, easier-to-swallow pieces. Many humans lucky enough to escape a crocodile attack have lost entire limbs to this devastating feeding method. But most victims die of blood loss, shock, or simply drown before they have a chance to escape.

7 BITTEN THROUGH THE BRAIN—JAGUAR

Most big cats kill prey by strangulation. From the house cat to the tiger and lion, they all go for the neck or throat in most cases, biting so hard and holding so tight that the victim either chokes or has a stroke. In some cases, the bite is deep enough to pierce the windpipe, the jugular vein, or even to snap the neck vertebrae. It often takes a few minutes for a big cat to strangle a large prey to death.

But the jaguar is a completely different story. This formidable cat, found in Mexico and Central and South America, has been known to strangle prey once in a while, but it usually goes for a faster, deadlier method: it simply bites through the skull and pierces the brain, causing instant death. It has particularly long and thick fangs, and incredibly powerful jaws to do this (actually, its bite is much stronger than a lion's or a tiger's, relative to the jaguar's size). The skull bite allows the jaguar to kill armored prey, such as caimans, as well as the now-extinct glyptodonts (giant relatives of armadillos), and they have also been known to use this killing method successfully against feral bulls weighing almost half a ton.

You may ask, if the jaguar kills its victims so quickly and efficiently, why is it in this list? Shouldn't the other cats be worse, since it takes minutes for them to strangle prey? Maybe, but it seems that for some not-so-big or not-so-armored prey, the jaguar doesn't bite through the top of the skull, but rather sinks its fangs into the victim's ears! Can you imagine the fangs of a giant cat stabbing through your ears and going into your brain? That's the stuff of nightmares.

6 GUTTED BY A GIANT BIRD—CASSOWARY

The cassowary is the only bird that made it into this list. Sure, protective parent owls clawing your eyes out and causing you to fall down a tree to your death (it has happened) are scary, but these birds are usually harmless, unless you do something really stupid. While the vegetarian cassowary (found in the rainforests of Australia and New Guinea) is usually a shy animal and will try to avoid confrontations, males can be extremely aggressive at times, and zookeepers agree that cassowaries are among the most dangerous creatures to keep in a zoo.

Listed by the *Guinness Book of World Records* as the world's most dangerous bird, the cassowary has an enormous, daggerlike claw on the second toe of each foot. When confronted, the bird will leap into the air and kick its enemy, kung fu–style, using the deadly claws to cause serious injury. It can, literally, claw your guts out. And even if it doesn't, the kick is mighty enough to rupture your internal organs and cause massive internal bleeding and death. Needless to say, you should never approach one of these birds, particularly if they are captive or protecting their chicks.

5 HAVING YOUR FACE RIPPED OFF—SLOTH BEAR

Sloth bears are among the least known bear species. They are found mostly in India and Sri Lanka, where natives fear them even more than they do tigers or snakes. And with good reason: it has been said that these bears maul at least one person per week in India, and they often seem to attack without provocation. They feed mostly on ants and termites, and only very rarely eat meat, but they seem to dislike humans (which shouldn't be surprising, since these bears have been subjected to centuries of hunting and cruelty). They are also nearsighted and easily taken by surprise. If confronted, a sloth bear is as likely to attack as it is to run away.

Being mauled by any kind of bear is a horrible way to go, but the sloth bear is particularly nasty due to its trademark killing method: it uses its teeth and its incredibly long, sharp claws to literally rip the victim's face off. Those who are lucky enough to escape death after a sloth bear attack are usually badly scarred for life and often left without an eye, a lip, or a nose.

4 CHOKING ON ANTS—SIAFU ANT

Also known as the driver ant, this African species is the only insect known to actually attack and devour humans, although you have to be very unlucky to die in a siafu attack. These ants are very slow and blind; unless you are unable to stay out of their way, you really don't have to be afraid of them. Usually these ants feed on smaller animals, but attacks on sleeping people, babies left unattended, and at least one drunken man who broke a leg and couldn't run away from the ant army, have all been reported.

Domestic animals such as cows and goats that were left tied to a pole for the night, and thus rendered unable to escape, have also been known to be devoured by siafu ants. What makes these insects so scary is that they can bite and sting, but that's not the way they kill you. During the attack, they will attempt to go into any opening they can find, including your mouth and nose, and victims are said to die of asphyxia after the ants crawl into their lungs! If that's not scary...

3 DEADLY INFECTION AFTER RAPE—CANDIRU

Candiru are rather sinister creatures to start with. These small, slender, almost transparent catfish relatives are among the few hematophagous vertebrates, feeding on the blood of other fish. They do this by going into their prey's gills and anchoring themselves there with a series of hooked spines they have in their bodies. A severe candiru infestation can weaken and eventually kill the unfortunate victim. They also feed on dead fish, eating them from the inside out. Although candiru used to be little-known denizens of the South American rivers, they have lately gained some fame as the most feared fish in the Amazon. That's right, more so than piranhas and electric eels.

This is because candiru will sometimes swim into the urethra or anus of men and women, and become stuck in there via the hooked spines. This is very painful and potentially deadly, because when the human victim leaves the water, the fish dies and its body starts to rot. The resulting infection has caused many deaths in remote parts of South America where there aren't any hospitals, since a delicate surgical procedure is needed to remove the fish from your private parts. Ouch.

2 EATEN ALIVE—WOLVES AND HYENAS

Big cats will usually make sure you're dead before they start feeding on your flesh. They are perfectly equipped to kill their victims quickly and with no mess. However, some of their distant carnivorous relatives are a completely different story. Although they kill smaller prey by violently shaking them and breaking their spines, wolves and hyenas lack any efficient killing weapons to deal with larger prey, so they usually don't waste time and start eating as soon as the victim is brought down.

Indeed, it is not uncommon for a large animal to still be alive when the wolf pack or hyena clan is already munching on its intestines. Of course, death follows soon after, due to shock or blood loss, but still, the idea of being alive while a snarling group of voracious predators feeds on your entrails is particularly disturbing to most people, hence the wolf's and hyena's place as number 2 in this list.

1 STARVATION—TAPEWORM

Tapeworms are gigantic (up to 12 meters long or more, depending on the species) but very slender parasites, whose eggs or larvae can be ingested via eating raw or badly cooked meat. Once ingested, the creature will anchor itself to the walls of the host's intestine and absorb all the nutrients from the host's food; in other words, you eat, your intestine absorbs the nutrients, and the tapeworm steals the nutrients for itself. The result? You can eat incredible amounts of food and you will still be malnourished.

If left untreated, a tapeworm infection can eventually lead to death by starvation, no matter how much you eat. And just in case you thought it couldn't be worse, sometimes the tapeworm larvae can find their way into your brain, causing seizures, and all sorts of neurological problems. So, having seizures due to a worm infestation in your brain before you starve to death due to the big, adult worm in your gut: the tapeworm just had to be number 1.

40 FAMOUS
LAST WORDS

40 PARDON ME, SIR. I DID NOT DO IT ON PURPOSE.
Said by: Queen Marie Antoinette after she accidentally stepped on the foot of her executioner as she went to the guillotine.

39 I CAN'T SLEEP.
Said by: J. M. Barrie, author of *Peter Pan*.

38 I SHOULD NEVER HAVE SWITCHED FROM SCOTCH TO MARTINIS.
Said by: Humphrey Bogart.

37 I AM ABOUT TO—OR I AM GOING TO—DIE; EITHER EXPRESSION IS CORRECT.
Said by: Dominique Bouhours, famous French grammarian.

36 I LIVE!
Said by: Roman emperor, as he was being murdered by his own soldiers.

35 DAMN IT...DON'T YOU DARE ASK GOD TO HELP ME.
Said by: Joan Crawford, to her housekeeper who began to pray aloud.

34 I AM PERPLEXED. SATAN GET OUT.
Said by: Aleister Crowley, famous occultist.

33 NOW, WHY DID I DO THAT?
Said by: General William Erskine, after he jumped from a window in Lisbon, Portugal, in 1813.

32 HEY, FELLAS! HOW ABOUT THIS FOR A HEADLINE FOR TOMORROW'S PAPER: "FRENCH FRIES!"

Said by: James French, a convicted murderer, who was sentenced to death by the electric chair. He shouted these words to members of the press who were to witness his execution.

31 BUGGER BOGNOR.

Said by: King George V, whose physician had suggested that he relax at his seaside palace in Bognor Regis, England.

30 IT'S STOPPED.

Said by: Joseph Henry Green, upon checking his own pulse.

29 LSD, 100 MICROGRAMS I.M.

Said by: Aldous Huxley, author, to his wife. She obliged and he was injected twice before his death.

28 YOU HAVE WON, O GALILEAN.

Said by: Emperor Julian, having attempted to reverse the official endorsement of Christianity by the Roman Empire.

27 NO, YOU CERTAINLY CAN'T.

Said by: John F. Kennedy, in reply to Nellie Connally, wife of Governor John Connelly, who commented, "You certainly can't say that the people of Dallas haven't given you a nice welcome, Mr. President."

26 I FEEL ILL. CALL THE DOCTORS.

Said by: Mao Zedong, Chairman of China.

25 TOMORROW, I SHALL NO LONGER BE HERE.

Said by: Nostradamus.

24 HURRY UP, YOU HOOSIER BASTARD, I COULD KILL TEN MEN WHILE YOU'RE FOOLING AROUND!

Said by: Carl Panzram, serial killer, shortly before he was executed by hanging.

23 PUT OUT THE BLOODY CIGARETTE!
Said by: Saki, a British writer, to a fellow officer while in a trench during World War I, for fear the smoke would give away their position. He was then shot by a German sniper who had heard the remark.

22 PLEASE DON'T LET ME FALL.
Said by: Mary Surratt, before being hanged for her part in the conspiracy to assassinate Abraham Lincoln. She was the first woman executed by the United States federal government.

21 NOW, NOW, MY GOOD MAN, THIS IS NO TIME FOR MAKING ENEMIES.
Said by: Voltaire, when asked by a priest to renounce Satan.

20 LONG LIVE FREEDOM!
Said by: Hans Scholl, German resistance leader, spoken from the guillotine before his execution in 1943.

19 GO ON, GET OUT! LAST WORDS ARE FOR FOOLS WHO HAVEN'T SAID ENOUGH!
Said by: Karl Marx, when asked by his housekeeper if he had any last words.

18 I HAVE NOT TOLD HALF OF WHAT I SAW.
Said by: Marco Polo, Venetian traveler and writer.

17 A KING SHOULD DIE STANDING.
Said by: Louis XVIII, king of France, who suffered from gout, which left him wheelchair-bound most of his adult life.

16 BROTHERS! BROTHERS, PLEASE! THIS IS A HOUSE OF PEACE!
Said by: Malcom X, breaking up a fight moments before he was shot.

15 DIE, MY DEAR? WHY, THAT'S THE LAST THING I'LL DO!
Said by: Groucho Marx.

14 HELLO. WE'RE LOOKING IN ... WE'RE OVERLOOKING THE FINANCIAL CENTER. THREE OF US. TWO BROKEN WINDOWS — OH, GOD! OH, G—

Said by: Kevin Cosgrove, an office worker who called for help during the 9/11 attacks and was cut off as the building collapsed around him.

13 IN KEEPING WITH CHANNEL 40'S POLICY OF BRINGING YOU THE LATEST IN BLOOD AND GUTS, AND IN LIVING COLOR, YOU ARE GOING TO SEE ANOTHER FIRST—ATTEMPTED SUICIDE.

Said by: Christine Chubbuck, anchorwoman, who shot herself live on the air.

12 NOW I CAN CROSS THE SHIFTING SANDS.

Said by: L. Frank Baum, author of *The Wizard of Oz*. The Shifting Sands are the impassable deserts surrounding the Land of Oz.

11 FRANCE, ARMY, JOSÉPHINE...

Said by: Napoleon Bonaparte, emperor of France, on his deathbed.

10 RELAX—THIS WON'T HURT.

Said by: Hunter S. Thompson, author, in the final sentence of his suicide note.

9 THE PLAY IS OVER, APPLAUD!

Said by: Attributed to Caesar Augustus, ruler of the Roman Empire. The phrase was commonly used to signal the end of a show in Roman theaters.

8 I KNOW YOU ARE HERE TO KILL ME. SHOOT, COWARD, YOU ARE ONLY GOING TO KILL A MAN.

Said by: Ernesto "Che" Guevara, right before his execution in Bolivia.

7 MY WALLPAPER AND I ARE FIGHTING A DUEL TO THE DEATH. ONE OR THE OTHER OF US HAS TO GO.

Said by: Oscar Wilde.

6 THIS IS A HELL OF A WAY TO DIE.

Said by: George S. Patton, who died from a car accident, while out hunting.

5 WE GOT A BAD FIRE! LET'S GET OUT—WE'RE BURNING UP...
Said by: An *Apollo 1* astronaut, probably Roger Chaffee. All three crew members died in a launch-pad fire in 1967.

4 HOME TO THE PALACE TO DIE...
Said by: Czar Alexander II of Russia, after an anarchist assassination attempt. He died of his wounds mere hours later.

3 DON'T DISTURB MY CIRCLES!
Said by: Archimedes, a Greek mathematician who was killed by the Romans, while proving geometric theorems in the sand before him.

2 DON'T LET ME DIE LIKE THIS; SAY I SAID SOMETHING.
Said by: Emiliano Zapata, Mexican revolutionary.

1 WELL, GENTLEMEN, YOU ARE ABOUT TO SEE A BAKED APPEL.
Said by: George Appel, a convicted murderer, who was sentenced to death by the electric chair. He shouted these words to members of the press who were to witness his execution.

CHAPTER TWO
Work and Play

10 UNUSUAL MAIL DELIVERIES AND EVENTS

10 THE PONY EXPRESS

In 1860, William H. Russell was sure that his Central Overland California and Pike's Peak Express Company could beat the time of stagecoach wagons, which made the trip from Missouri to California in 24 days. The company built way stations every 10 to 15 miles and published the following advertisement:

> Wanted: Young, skinny, wiry fellows not over 18.
> Must be expert riders, willing to risk death daily.
> Orphans preferred.
> Wages, $25.00 per week.

Johnny Fry and Sam Hamilton were first to sign up, pledging an oath under which they swore not to cuss, fight, abuse animals, or lie. The Pony Express was born to great expectations: "No danger or difficulty must check his speed or change his route, for the world is waiting for the news he shall fetch and carry... God speed to the pony and the boy!" (*Western Journal of Commerce*, Kansas City.) Russell's prediction proved accurate: the first run was completed in ten days—less than half the stagecoach's time. Riders covered 75 to 100 miles each day, stopping at the way stations only long enough to change horses.

Sending a letter on the Pony Express was not cheap: $5.00 for one-half ounce, compared to standard U.S. postage, which was 10 cents. But if you were in a hurry, there was no better choice. In 1861, President Lincoln's inaugural address made the fastest transcontinental trip up until that time: St. Joseph, Missouri, to Sacramento, California, in seven days, 17 hours. But that same year, the transcontinental telegraph was completed, and on October 26, 1861, the Pony Express came to an end after just 18 months of operation.

9 MISSILE MAIL

Mail has been delivered by horses, boats, sleds, snowshoes, skis, trucks, motorcycles, automobiles, mules, pole boats, airplanes, hovercraft, dog sleds, parachutes, and snowmobiles. But none is stranger than missile mail. In 1936, two rockets transported mail about 2000 feet across a frozen lake toward Hewitt, New Jersey, from Greenwood Lake, New York. The rockets crash-landed and slid across the ice. The Hewitt postmaster walked onto the ice and dragged the mail bags the rest of the way.

Postmaster General Arthur Summerfield later attempted again to shoot the mail. On June 8, 1959, Summerfield declared, "Before man reaches the moon, mail will be delivered within hours from New York to California, to England, to India, or to Australia by guided missiles."

The submarine USS *Barbero* fired a guided missile with 3000 letters toward the naval air station in Mayport, Florida. The missile, at 600 mph, covered the 100 miles in 22 minutes. The cost, however, was too great to justify missiles as a standard method of mail delivery.

8 MULE TRAIN

In Supai, Arizona, a sign in the local café reads, "No fries til mail." The town of Supai eats more mail than it reads. At the bottom of the south rim of the Grand Canyon, and home to 525 Havasupai Native Americans, Supai is the last place in the United States to get its mail by mule-train delivery. Helicopters and air drops are impractical here, so the three- to five-hour trip is made by mule five days a week, with each mule carrying up to 200 pounds of mailed supplies.

7 MILLION DOLLAR DELIVERY

When New York jeweler Harry Winston decided to donate the fabled Hope Diamond to the Smithsonian Institution, he chose to send it first-class mail. "It's the safest way to mail gems," Winston is quoted as saying. The delivery from New York City to Washington, D.C., cost Winston $2.44 in postage, and an additional $142.85 for a million dollars' worth of insurance.

Letter carrier James Todd picked up the diamond at City Post Office in Washington and drove to the Natural History building, where he delivered it to the museum curator. Afterward, Todd told the Washington Post that he felt "a little shaky," not because of the enormous value of the 45.52-carat diamond, but because he was not used to getting so much attention at his job.

6 PET POST

In December 1954, the postmaster in Orlando, Florida, received the following letter:

Dear Sir:

I am sending my chameleon because I live in Fostoria, Ohio, and it is too cold for him here. Will you please let him loose.

Sincerely yours,

David _____

P.S. Could you let me know if he arrives there OK? Thank you very much. I am so worried about him.

On December 7, 1954, David received the following response:

Dear David,

I received your chameleon yesterday and he was immediately released on the post office grounds. Best wishes for a merry Christmas!

Sincerely,

L.A. Bryant, Jr.
Postmaster

5 CHILD POST

In 1914, a four-year-old named May Pierstorff, who lived with her parents in Grangevillle, Idaho, was going to visit her grandmother in Lewiston. Her parents calculated that sending her there via parcel post was cheaper than full fare by traditional transportation. At 48.5 pounds, the child came in under the parcel post weight requirement of less than 50 pounds. It was then legal, and still is today, to mail chickens, so her parents were charged postage at the chicken rate. The Pierstorffs pinned the 53 cents in postage to her coat and put May in the baggage car, under the care of the postal clerk. Though it was customary to leave packages in the post office overnight, when May arrived in Lewiston, the postmaster took her to her grandmother. By 1920, it was illegal to mail human beings, although not before an angry mother mailed a baby to the husband who had left her.

4 PNEUMATIC TUBES

Pneumatic-tube systems represented a new kind of tunnel vision. Under New York City, workers still occasionally encounter remnants of what was once a flourishing underground mail-delivery system. Powered by positive rotary blowers and reciprocating air compressors, pneumatic mail tubes could fly under the city at a rate of 100 mph, regardless of snow or traffic snarls overhead. At one time, there were 136 pneumatic tube operators, called racketeers, in New York City. They could send one tube every 12 seconds. By the 1950s, 55 percent of New York City's mail was sent by tubes.

There were problems, however. Each container could hold only five pounds, and could not carry more than one kind of mail. The process was expensive, partly because each container needed to be sorted twice. The time saved by shooting the mail through the tubes was lost in sorting and resorting. The system was suspended from 1919 to 1922, briefly resurrected in New York and Boston, and finally discontinued in 1953.

3 RURAL FREE DELIVERY

Rural Free Delivery (RFD) was born when Postmaster General John Wanamaker thought it made more sense for one person to deliver mail to country homes than for 50 people to go to town for their mail. Until that time, postmasters would often hire a boy to deliver mail, and schoolteachers sent the mail home with their students. The post office also stayed open for one hour after church on Sundays, but none of these systems seemed satisfactory.

The problem with delivery to country homes was, of course, mailboxes. Soon the roadsides were "littered" with orange crates, lard cans, feed boxes, and many other contrivances to hold mail. By 1901, Congress went into action, deciding after prolonged debate that country mailboxes needed to be of a standard size, have a signal flag to show when mail was inside, and be of a height and proximity to the road to be convenient for the mail carrier. The standard basic mailbox cost 50 cents, but there were some locked boxes that cost several dollars. As a result of this expense, some customers refused to buy a mailbox, and the post office refused to deliver their mail, resulting in some contentious exchanges.

When Sears, Roebuck and Montgomery Ward began sending out large catalogs each year, they hit upon a retailing gold mine. But the mailboxes needed to be resized, and in the 1920s, Congress approved the larger mailboxes still in use today.

2 FIRST AIR MAIL

History's first air-mail flight happened in 1859, aboard the hot air balloon *Jupiter*. The historic flight took place on August 17, with

the temperature in the 90s. John Wise, the aeronaut, was given 123 letters in Lafayette, Indiana, to deliver to New York City. The balloon had to ascend to 14,000 feet to pick up any wind, but that wind, unfortunately, carried it south. After covering only 30 miles in five hours, Wise descended in Crawfordsville, Indiana, where his trip was labeled a "trans-county-nental" flight. Wise gave the mail to a postal agent, who put it on a train for New York.

1 POSTED TO FREEDOM

Henry "Box" Brown, a slave who had seen his wife and children sold away from him, mailed himself to freedom on March 29, 1849. With the help of a storekeeper in Louisa County, Virginia, Brown had himself packed into a crate that was 3 x 2 x 2.6 feet and labeled "This Side Up With Care," to be sent to the home of Philadelphia abolitionist James Miller McKim.

At five feet eight inches and weighing 200 pounds, Brown curled himself into the box with only a small container of water and traveled in that position for 27 hours. The crate was loaded onto a wagon, then to the baggage car of a train, then another wagon, then a steamboat, then another wagon, then a second baggage car, then a ferry, then a third railroad car, and finally a wagon that delivered him to McKim's house. When no sound was heard from the box delivered to his house, McKim asked, "Is all right within?" and Brown answered, "All right." When the box was opened, Brown stood up and passed out.

Public outrage at his story led to the passage of the Fugitive Slave Act of 1850, which made it illegal to help escaping slaves. When the law was passed, Brown moved to England, where he remained until 1875.

10 CURIOUS EVERYDAY INVENTIONS

10 GARDEN GNOMES

Philip Griebel has the honor of being known as the inventor of garden gnomes. Originally he created other small creatures out of terra cotta, but he was struck by the idea of using characters from local mythology. Griebel lived in Thuringia, Germany, in the mid-1800s, so gnomes were his character of choice. His gnomes became popular and spread from Germany to France and then to the rest of Europe and the world. Griebel's descendants still make garden gnomes. Sadly, only one of the original batch still survives; he is named Lampy and is valued at a whopping 1.5 million dollars.

9 FRICTION MATCHES

Matches have been around so long it is hard to imagine that they were not always with us. While the first matches existed in China in the 6th century and Europe in the 16th, the friction match as we know it today was not invented until the early 1800s. The very first friction match was invented by John Walker, an English chemist, in 1826. Nearly 40 years later, the famous match company Bryant and May began mass production.

8 CONTACT LENSES

The first contact lenses were successfully invented and worn in 1888. Their inventor, Adolf Eugen Fick, tested his invention first on rabbits, then on himself and friends. The lenses were made of blown glass and were very thick in comparison to modern lenses, so much so that they could only be worn for a few hours at a time. Contact lenses as we know them today arrived in 1949.

7 WASHING MACHINE

The first washing machine was invented in (believe it or not) 1692! It was, however, non-electric. The electric washing machine came about in the late 1800s when Ford Motor Company employee Louis Goldenberg invented it for the company.

6 SODA CAN

The first soda cans had no pull tabs, and a metal punch was required to open it. By 1936, patents were flying as various inventors tried to come up with ways to provide easy can opening tools. In 1962, the old-style pull tab (which was removed entirely and discarded) was invented, and in 1975, it was replaced by the modern tabs, which remain on the can.

5 CONDOMS

In 1855, the first rubber condom was invented. They were made by wrapping strips of raw rubber around penis-shaped moulds. They were, revoltingly, reusable, and had a shelf life of a few months. The modern latex condom was invented in 1912.

4 TIN FOIL

Modern aluminum foil was predated by tin foil—foil made from thinly beaten sheets of tin. In fact, in many countries, aluminum foil is still called tin foil. Modern aluminum foil was invented in the 20th century, and it was even used for audio recordings in some of the earliest phonograph machines.

3 BALLPOINT PEN

The first ballpoint pen was invented in 1888 by leather tanner John Loud. He needed a writing implement that would be able to mark the leather he tanned, since fountain pens were not suitable for the task. It was virtually identical to the modern ballpoint pen and had been in use for 50 years when László Bíró patented an improved pen with freer movement of the ball in the tip. He is remembered as the slang name for the ballpoint: the biro.

2 SHAMPOO

Modern shampoo arrived in the 1930s under the brand name Drene. It was a synthetic shampoo, meaning it included no soap. But the earliest shampoo appeared in 1814, when an English entrepreneur opened a beauty salon that washed hair with soap shavings dissolved in water.

1 CHOCOLATE BARS

The very first molded chocolate bar (as we know it today) was invented by Fry's Chocolates in 1847 in Bristol, England. The company still exists today but has merged with the Cadbury company. The Fry's Cream (a chocolate bar with a flavorful filling) is arguably their best chocolate bar, and that was invented in 1866. It is still available today.

10 UTTERLY USELESS MILITARY COMMANDERS

10 REDVERS BULLER

Known as "Reverse" Buller by his troops during the Second Boer War, the Englishman was first defeated at the Battle of Colenso and subsequently lost his position as overall commander. He continued on to suffer defeats at Spion Kop and Vaal Krantz, almost letting the war slip away from the British.

9 RODOLFO GRAZIANI

After achieving moderate success in Libya and Ethiopia, the "Butcher of Ethiopia" became Commander-in-Chief of the Italian Royal Army's General Staff and of Italian North Africa at the start of World War II. In 1940, after facing increasing pressure from dictator Benito Mussolini and possible demotion, Graziani followed orders and invaded Egypt with his Tenth Army. In 1941, Graziani resigned his commission after the British counterattacked and the Tenth Army was completely defeated during Operation Compass.

8 GEORGE B. MCCLELLAN

With high hopes set upon his shoulders at the beginning of the American Civil War and quickly becoming General-in-Chief of the Union Army, McClellan would earn the distinction as a general of little action. McClellan truly disappointed President Lincoln at the Battle of Antietam where the North and South would fight the bloodiest battle of the war. Despite the Union fighters outnumbering the Confederates, McClellan was unable to crush Robert E. Lee after failing to pursue him into Virginia. McClellan was removed from command immediately after.

7 WILLIAM WESTMORELAND

Under Westmoreland's leadership as Deputy Commander of Military Assistance Command, the Vietnam War began smoothly as the U.S. "won every battle." But in 1968, when Westmoreland was promoted to Army Chief of Staff, Communist forces baited him into committing nearly 40 percent of his strength to the military outpost at Khe Sanh, then attacked cities and towns throughout South Vietnam. This would be known as the Tet Offensive and would become a major turning point in the war. Westmoreland's strategy throughout the war was to win through attrition warfare (pounding the enemy with greater numbers and resources), which military strategists caution against using. This strategy inevitably failed, as the North Vietnamese and Viet Cong maintained control over how the war was fought, which was through guerilla warfare. Westmoreland's general mistake: severely underestimating the Communists.

6 MAURICE GAMELIN

Gamelin was commander of the French forces in World War II and was largely responsible for the fall of France to German control during the Battle of France. Gamelin made the mistake of viewing the forested, mountainous Ardennes area as impenetrable and chose to defend it with ten of his weakest, least well-equipped and least well-trained divisions. Gamelin also chose not to disperse France's vast number of superior tanks. Despite reports of the buildup of German forces and even knowing the date of the Germans' attack, Gamelin did nothing, stating that he would "await events." After the Germans attacked, Gamelin was eventually removed from his post, but by then it was too late.

5 ARTHUR PERCIVAL

In World War II, Percival commanded British Malaya. After only ten weeks into the Pacific War, he became responsible for the largest surrender of British-led forces in history. Percival surrendered Malaya to Japanese forces in early 1942, defying Winston Churchill's instructions for prolonged resistance. A common view holds that 138,708 allied personnel surrendered or were killed by fewer than 30,000 Japanese. Some historians are a little more sympathetic toward Percival's legacy, arguing that he had been dealt an unusually bad hand.

4 PAVEL GRACHEV

Grachev played a key role in initiating and leading the First Chechen War. He was responsible for coming up with the idea of using force to "restore constitutional order" in Chechnya. Grachev publicly promised to swiftly crush the Chechen separatist forces "in a couple of hours with a single airborne regiment." He led the disastrous storming of Grozny while drunk after celebrating his birthday on January 1. The initial assault resulted in very high casualties for the Russians and an almost complete breakdown of morale in the Russian forces.

Grachev once said that only an "incompetent commander would order tanks into the streets of central Grozny, where they would be vulnerable." Yet near the end of the war, he did exactly that. The war soon ended in a Russian defeat, with hundreds of thousands of military and civilian casualties. Grachev has also been linked to corruption among the higher ranks of the military, specifically the assassination of journalist Dmitry Kholodov.

3 ANTONIO LOPEZ DE SANTA ANNA

The self-proclaimed "Napoleon of the West" didn't quite leave the same legacy as his idol. After early success in the Mexican War of Independence, the rest of his career didn't pan out the way he would have liked. Santa Anna, a lifetime gambler, was known for his risk-taking in battle, but also for his brutality. Soon after Santa Anna declared himself dictator of Mexico, rebels who opposed the Mexican dictatorship created three new republics, one of them being the Republic of Texas. In the famous Battle of the Alamo, Santa Anna struggled to defeat about 250 Texans with 2400 Mexicans and subsequently lost nearly 600 men. Santa Anna later stunningly lost Texas at the Battle of San Jacinto, at which the Mexicans again outnumbered the Texans. The Texans only suffered two casualties, while the Mexicans lost hundreds of men. Santa Anna was found wearing a private's uniform, hiding in a marsh.

2 DARIUS III OF PERSIA

The last king of the Achaemenid Empire of Persia, Darius was not quite as qualified to rule a mighty empire as his predecessors were. In 334 BC, Alexander the Great invaded the Persian Empire. Darius never showed up for the first battle and defeat (the Battle of Granicus) because he didn't see Alexander as much of a threat to his empire. Darius did not take the field against Alexander until a year and a half after Granicus, at the Battle of Issus. His forces outnumbered Alexander's men by at least a two-to-one ratio, but Darius was still outflanked, defeated, and forced to flee. Later, although many factors were in his favor, Darius lost the Battle of Gaugamela and his family was captured. He again was the first to flee the battle, abandoning all of his soldiers and his property to be taken by Alexander. Darius quickly lost everything and became nothing but a fugitive. He was eventually betrayed and killed by a friend. Thus it was under Darius' rule that the Persian Empire fell and was conquered.

1 PUBLIUS QUINCTILIUS VARUS

After occupying Jerusalem and crucifying 2000 Jewish rebels in Judaea, Varus went off to govern Germania and tame barbarian tribes. Varus was stationed with three of his legions, the 17th, 18th, and 19th when news arrived of a revolt growing in the Rhine area. The man who appealed for Varus' help was Arminius, a Romanized Germanic prince. Varus' trust in Arminius was an obvious and terrible misjudgment. Varus placed his legions in a position in which their fighting strengths would be minimized and that of the Germanic Cherusci tribesman maximized. The Romans marched right into the ambush that Arminius laid, thus leading to the Battle of the Teutoburg Forest. The heavily forested, swampy terrain made the Varus' legions' maneuvers impossible. The Germanic fighters demolished the three Roman legions. Some captured Romans were placed in wicker cages and burned alive, while others were enslaved or ransomed. Germanic tribes sacrificed Roman officers on altars to their gods. Varus himself, seeing all hope was lost, committed suicide. Arminius cut off his head and sent it to another Germanic leader as a present. The legion numbers 17, 18, and 19 never again appeared in the Roman Army's order of battle due to the shame and bad luck they carried. The Battle of the Teutoburg Forest darkened Emperor Augustus' remaining years, and he was heard, upon occasion, to moan, "Quinctilius Varus, give me back my legions!"

10 ANCIENT JOBS THAT SUCKED BIG TIME

10 NOMENCLATOR

The nomenclator held a vitally important job. He was, effectively, a living human-calendar-cum-address-book. These days we have our iPhones, our Blackberrys, and all manner of digital devices to remember the people we are introduced to at meetings or (more embarrassingly) those we meet when we drink a little too much at a work party. We have all, no doubt, had that experience in which we meet a person, take down their name and number, promise to contact them soon, and, in the sober light of day, wonder who the hell they are. The ancients had a much better way of dealing with this.

They dragged a slave—a nomenclator—to their parties and forced him to remember the names and numbers. Now, the most important difference between the iPhone and the nomenclator is that the nomenclator could tell you who the guy was, what you talked about, and whether he was worth contacting. He could also clarify whether that gorgeous lady you met was made gorgeous by beer goggles or not. Frankly, if it weren't for an exorbitantly high minimum wage, we would all be better off tossing the iPhone and taking on a modern nomenclator. But alas, who would want the job? Who would want to be paid two bucks an hour to remain sober while everyone else was partying on down? Not me, that's for sure!

9 SLAVER

Okay, be prepared for a sensitive topic. A slaver was a gentleman (used in the most liberal sense of the word possible) who sold slaves—for work or pleasure. He would travel behind armies who were off fighting in battle so he could capture the losers and sell them to rich Greeks as slaves; or he would buy "unwanted" boys (but only the handsome ones) from parents so he could castrate them and sell them as lovers to wealthy Greek men who had a taste for young flesh. This provided, in a rather repulsive way, an alternative to adoption for those parents who didn't want their children. The downside to this somewhat repellent career choice, was that despite the demand for handsome young boys, the slavers were often murdered by those who didn't approve of their trade.

8 ORNATRIX

An ornatrix is a hairdresser, a job that is so often looked down upon these days, and it was no more prestigious in ancient times. But a modern hairdresser really ought to appreciate her job because she has it so much better now than ever in the past. Picture this: the imperial queen is balding and blonde, but the fashion this week is dark lustrous locks. Today, a hairdresser would either shove a wig on the lady or glue in some extensions. This was, sadly, not an option for the work-weary ornatrix of days gone by.

In order to provide her mistress with a coal-colored mane, a hairdresser had to work with a mixture of bile, rotten leeches (which made for an especially rich black color), and squid ink. But it gets worse. Occasionally, fashion would demand blonde hair, and the mistress was a natural brunette. There was no peroxide in those days. To give her a lovely golden hue, the hairdresser had to mix pigeon poop and ashes together in the hopes that the chemical combination would strip out the healthy color of the hair. Oh, and to set the color, the hairdresser had to pee on the hair. Worse still was being a slave with beautiful hair, which was often cut from the slave's head and fashioned into a wig for a rich woman.

7 VESTAL VIRGIN

Let's start with the job description: "Teen female virgin wanted for 30-year service. Must be Roman, have all limbs, and not be the child of a slave." This

was the job description of the vestal virgin. These attractive and fully limbed girls were to spend 30 years giving service to Vesta, goddess of the family. They had to keep the vestal flame burning and were in positions of great honor as the only female priests in ancient Rome. Now, if one of these pretty young girls absent-mindedly forgot to keep the fire going, she would be flogged till she bled. If, the heavens forbid, she slipped up in the area of virginity, she was buried alive. Oh, and to make matters worse, the lazy vestal virgin who slept in and let the fire go out was not just likely to get a flogging: letting the fire die was a sign of loss of virginity. In other words, she got flogged, then buried alive—just for sleeping in!

6 DENTIST

Imagine the mouths of the Romans, who didn't brush their teeth, ate craploads of rotten fish sauce, and spent a huge amount of time feasting and vomiting. Now imagine one with an abscess or a toothache and being the dentist who had to deal with that. Wine was commonly used as an anesthetic, but when things got really bad, the poor dentist had to take drastic measures. This (sadly) involved taking a red-hot poker to the patient's gums after the tooth was ripped out and stuffing rotten fish into the resulting charred hole. One can't help but wonder who had it worse—the dentist or the patient!

5 WINE MAKER

Speaking of my favorite subject, wine, what job could be better than that of the wine maker? Harvesting the grapes in the early hours while the dew still drips from the vines; pressing the fat grapes with one's feet while singing bawdy epic songs; and finally, after fermentation, drinking the delicious nepenthe on the terrace. Hmm…perhaps drinking wine that wasn't laced with lead!

That's right, unfortunately, the Romans didn't understand the dangers of lead, and they regularly sweetened their wine with sugar of lead (much in the same way as we fill our drinks with a variety of cancer-causing sugar replacements these days). To make matters worse, they often served their "lead wine" in lead cups! The average Roman who enjoyed a quaff or two consumed up to one gram of lead per day!

4 PRAEGUSTATOR

Praegustator: in other words, a taster. Who wouldn't want to be paid a handsome sum every day for doing nothing but chowing down on the emperor's dinner? Daily tastes of peacock, swamp hen, wild boar—the list is virtually endless. But, as is to be expected on this list, there is a caveat. Most of the emperors were jerks, and a lot of people wanted them dead. And in those days, the easiest way to kill someone was to poison them. So, the emperors were certain to be dished up a plate of some rancid poisonous delicacies at least once or twice in their career. Herein steps the praegustator. This poor schmuck was the guy who had to have a mouthful of everything the emperor planned to eat. Needless to say, history has shown us that more pre-tasters died than emperors.

3 ROWER

Most of us are aware of the experience of going to the gym to lose a few pounds. The burning ache in the shoulders and arms when our personal trainer forces us onto the satanic rowing machine with no desire other than to make us feel bad because we dragged them out of bed at 6 a.m. Fortunately for us, we're paying the bills, so we can tell the trainer to shove off and stop after three minutes. And that brings us to the poor, unfortunate souls who had to row the Greek war boats during the good old ancient days.

First of all, most rowers were slaves and were paid nothing more than a daily meal. Second, when that nasty burn set in, they couldn't just stop and demand a latte break. They would get flogged if they stopped. Imagine your innocuous personal trainer pulling out a cat-o'-nine-tails when your arms started to ache. Imagine being flayed because the chubby guy on the machine next to you is going half a mile faster than you. That was the life of the rower.

2 ARMPIT PLUCKER

I was tempted to say nothing about this item, as the title is disgusting enough! But, alas, it would feel like cheating were I to stop there. Some years ago, I was a student of pugilism. We were a small class of teenage boys being taught by an ex-Soviet nuclear submarine commander who had emigrated to New Zealand, and he worked us hard. Now, I was a teen who was very concerned about personal hygiene. Sadly, the same was not true for the majority of my class. The gym smelled like someone had sprayed body odor especially to "man" us up. This is not a new thing.

The ancients were incredibly fond of their sports. Because these athletes were working out all day in the hot sun and were aware of hair's natural ability to retain unpleasant odors, the men, both young and old, went through a daily routine of having their underarm hairs plucked out by the armpit plucker; after all, they were most likely to spend the evening in very close company with others at the public baths. The armpit plucker was not the same as a modern beautician who plucks eyebrows; these were professionals who were dealing with incredibly hairy armpits full of smells that one doesn't want to think about at all. No amount of grappa could prepare you for this job.

1 DELATOR

Latin is an amazing language—it manages to make everything sound lovely. For example, *pedacabo* (pronounced "ped-a-cah-bo") just rolls right off the tongue. Unfortunately, it means "one who is anally penetrated." *Delator* is similar. In modern English, the delator might be called a snitch, a rat, a fink, an informant, a stoolie, and a huge variety of other unpleasant names for a person who is, basically, a nark. These were men whose sole job in life was to tell on their neighbors for every little misdemeanor. They make the Nazi Youth look good! These bastards even reported people for failure to pay their taxes! Unfortunately, power often goes to their heads, and these sneaky scumbags started making stuff up because they were paid regardless of the truth behind their accusations. If there were ever social pariahs, these guys were them. The most famous delator, although he wasn't Roman, was, of course, Judas.

10 TRULY WEIRD JOBS FROM HISTORY

10 SILVER MINER

This isn't so much strange as it is downright dangerous and dirty. Not having tools strong enough to do the job without labor, the ancients had to mine everything by hand, and those hands were usually those of children. Life expectancy in the silver mines was three months, but that didn't bother the Romans because it was slaves who did the work. Young boys would be pushed down very small holes that were extraordinarily deep, considering they were dug manually. The holes were hot and stuffy and prone to collapse. Outside the mines the silver ore was melted down, producing poisonous gasses. Needless to say, this added to the danger of the job.

9 STERCORARIUS

Rome was famous for its extensive sewer system, but despite having such an advanced method of dealing with poop, most Romans didn't have access to it (either because they lived in the hills or were too poor for plumbing). And sometimes even those who could afford it didn't want it due to the smells that leaked into people's homes and the rats and other vermin that lived in the sewers. This meant that most houses needed to deal with their poop in some other way. This is where the stercorarius comes in. He would travel door to door collecting all the human waste and cart it off to the edge of town, and farmers would buy the dung for their crops. Effectively, the Romans had a better way of dealing with their waste than we do in modern times.

8 URINATORES

The urinatores were salvage divers from Ostia, a harbor city in ancient Rome. The name, with its similarity to "urine" is probably a reference to the fact that the deep diving caused so much pressure on their abdomens that they urinated a lot. The divers had but one tool—a kettle-shaped diving bell filled with air for breathing and weighed down with lead weights—to help the divers reach up to 30 meters below the surface. Their job was primarily to salvage, but they also moved construction equipment around. The dangers in this job are obvious, but the pay was good, and many of divers became very affluent members of Roman society.

7 LITTER CARRIER

The litter carrier was a slave whose job it was to cart women (and later men) around in little carriages. It was a hard job and a tedious one and could be dangerous (picture carrying a carriage up a flight of stairs!). The litter carriers were usually dressed in fine garments, and the litters became more and more extravagant over the years. In fact, in later years, many wealthy Romans had windows of glass in their litters instead of the traditional curtains. Documents from the Roman times tell us that it was very uncomfortable to travel by litter, as it could make one sea sick. To a certain extent, this job still exists in that there is a group of men trained to carry the papal sedia gestatoria, a throne carried on men's shoulders. The sedia was last used in the 1980s, but may make a comeback due to security complications surrounding Pope Benedict XVI.

6 GYMNASIARCH

The gymnasiarch had a busy job in ancient Greece due to the popularity of athletics. Despite being a dirty job—the gymnasiarch had to oil and scrape the athletes, as well as tidy up after wrestling matches and maintain the gymnasium in general—the position was highly sought after by the rich, as it was considered the epitome of philanthropic occupations. To qualify as gymnasiarch you had to be between 30 and 60 and have a large net worth. One benefit of the job was that you got to carry a stick with which to beat sullen youths who misbehaved in the gym.

5 CURSE TABLET MAKER

Curse tablets were thin sheets of soft lead that had curses written on them. The curses were then affixed by nails to the altars or walls of temples. The poor curse tablet writer had sit day in and day out hearing the complaints and woes of his customers who needed curses written. Fortunately, many of these curse tablets have survived to modern times so we can get a glimpse of the Romans' life and way of thinking. Here is one example: "bind every limb and sinew of Victorius, the charioteer for the Blue team… the horses he is about to race… blind their eyes so they cannot see and twist their soul and heart so they cannot breathe."

4 ORGY PLANNER

The orgy planner had a very unusual but very exciting job—he got to plan festivities for the rich members of society and, in some cases, got many perks (which I am sure you can imagine without me spelling them out). The orgy planner had to organize food, women, music, and accommodations. The downside to the job was that the orgy planner wasn't liked by all members of society (particularly those who were never invited to orgies) and the trade was even banned for a short time. The most famous orgy planner was Gaius Petronius, who is most famous for writing the satirical book about Roman debauchery called *Satyricon*.

3 FUNERAL CLOWN

The funeral clown was paid to dress up as the dead person, wear a mask of his face, and dance around, acting like him. The Romans believed that this would placate the spirits of the dead and bring joy to the living. As the funeral progressed, the funeral clown would run alongside the corpse with other clowns making jokes and mimicking the dead. Some clowns were very highly regarded and even got to mock the emperor at his funeral. They were well paid, and it must have been an oddly happy diversion from the clowns' regular jobs as the heads of mime troupes.

2 SLINGER

A slinger was a man trained to use the sling. The sling was an essential part of Roman military strategy because it was more effective (both in distance and damage) than an arrow. As children, slingers-in-training were required to kill their dinner—no kill, no food. It was an extremely good way to get youths trained fast. The slinger could throw stones up to one pound in weight, and they could be used accurately up to 200 meters.

1 WATER ORGANIST

The hydraulis was a type of pipe organ blown by air, where the power source pushing the air was derived by water from a natural source (like a waterfall) or by a manual pump. Consequently, the water organ lacked a bellows, blower, or compressor. The instrument was extremely popular in ancient Rome, and there were regular competitions for it. At one competition, a player named Antipatros won a prize for playing the instrument for two days straight. A water organist was guaranteed a long career, as the instrument was used at all holidays and social events. Even Emperor Nero played the hydraulis. Another benefit to the job was that you got the best seat in the house at the gladiator events because the organ was used to accompany the fights.

10 WORST URBAN JOBS IN AMERICA

10 POLICE OFFICER

Unless they're patrolling Mayberry, police officers risk their lives every day as they start their shifts. Most cities have budget constraints that prevent an adequate number of police on the street in the first place. They are often undertrained and out-gunned in the most dangerous situations. Every traffic stop, domestic-dispute report, or drug bust could be their last. Although the benefits are great, the pay is only adequate, and many officers moonlight as private security officers or bodyguards. Moving through the ranks and reaching a non-street-level position, like a detective, is usually the best option for a long career.

9 FIREFIGHTER

Arson for profit. Old abandoned buildings full of homeless people. These are a couple of reasons that big city firefighters have to risk their lives every day. They have to go in, save lives, and put out a fire before it spreads to surrounding buildings. In times of riots (like in Detroit and Watts in the 1960s

and LA after the Rodney King verdict) they are actually the victims of attack from angry mobs. It's a demanding job that's not for those weak in mind or body.

8 EXTERMINATOR

If a roach- or rat-infested house is your idea of fun, then this job is for you. For the rest of us, the prospect of going into a stranger's house that is overrun by disease-spreading vermin is a nightmare job. This is such an awful occupation that it even inspired a Stephen King short story!

7 CONVENIENCE STORE WORKER

This is a job where your life could be lost over a few dollars in the cash register. Some stores are family-run mom-and-pop businesses. Others are large 24-hour conglomerates that offer a chance for people to work hours suitable to their lifestyle. Despite closed-circuit security cameras and even an occasional gun hidden under the counter, many employees are shot even before a demand of money is made.

6 PROSTITUTE

The world's oldest profession is alive and well on city streets all across the planet. Besides the risk of being raped, assaulted, or even killed, there is always the real chance of catching an STD or AIDS. Since prostitution is illegal in most of the U.S., prostitutes also run the risk of being arrested and jailed.

5 FACTORY WORKER

The five dollars a day that Henry Ford offered people to work in his Detroit factories almost 100 years ago was life changing for some families. Many laborers and skilled tradesman jumped at the chance to double their income. Although conditions are safer nowadays and the pay is much more thanks to unions and collective bargaining agreements, the typical factory job is still dirty, hard, and tedious.

4 OFFICE WORKER

A long commute to spend an even longer day in a cube. As motivational speaker Les Brown put it, "You work just hard enough to keep from getting fired and get paid just enough to keep from quitting." Most people spend a lot of time at the office surfing the web, exchanging humorous e-mails, or updating their resumes. It's a wonder any business gets done at all!

3 CAB DRIVER

Most drivers have to put in long hours behind the wheel to make a living. You have to deal with traffic jams and passengers that don't tip. Sometimes passengers are actually out to rob you of the few dollars you have made and will kill you in a heartbeat. This is why some cabbies will not pick up certain fares, which of course leads to more controversy.

2 DRUG DEALER

Crack, weed, meth—they're available on any street corner for a few dollars a hit. In neighborhoods where drug use is rampant and jobs are scarce, many people choose this fast-money option to make some cash to pay the bills. Whether it is the low-level, street-corner dealer or someone in a "middle management" capacity, the risks are high and the pay is surprisingly low.

1 TELEMARKETER

They call at dinner time, in the middle of your favorite movie, or right when you finally get the baby to sleep. They are pre-scripted, auto-call generated denizens calling to sell us magazines or insurance. The truth is most of those telemarketers are hard-working young people who are paying their way through college or older people in between "real jobs," trying to keep up with their mortgage payments. They are practically tied to the phone by a headset, and breaks and lunches are also tightly monitored.

10 BIZARRE HOBBYIST COLLECTIONS

10 HUBCAPS AND LICENSE PLATES

It seems that hubcaps and license plates go hand in hand and that this collection of rusted and otherwise useless car parts can get way out of control. Imagine towering stacks of meticulously placed hubcaps and entire garage walls emblazoned with license plates from the world over, and you have a car enthusiast's dream workshop. For some reason, be it nostalgia or just another psychological compulsion, some people just love the idea of having more hubcaps than necessary. License plates? OK, maybe. But hubcaps? Why?

9 NEWSPAPERS

In this practice that's often called hoarding, or "newspaper squalor," many people have the compulsive urge to save up unread papers or magazines in the hopes of reading them some day. Yes, I have a *MAD* magazine collection and a stash of comic books, but those are generally kept neatly filed in a box. Oh, and some folks have a nice little stack of *Maxim* or *Playboy* for bathroom perusing, but most of those people don't have towering stacks of magazines along every wall and in every corner  of their home. As it turns out, mass collections of such fire-hazardous reading materials can be particularly deadly and have, in the past, trapped people under collapsing piles and even caused fatal fires.

8 DUCT TAPE

Though still bizarre, collecting duct tape has become more common lately since someone discovered its use in making all sorts of fun crafts. You can, with minimal folding and swearing, create wallets, purses, small bags, belt, hats, and, apparently, entire outfits made from rolls upon rolls of the multicolored adhesive. Now everyone's favorite mispronounced product (just so we're clear, it's not "duck tape") can be worn or collected.

7 FOOD

Daisy Randone (Brittany Murphy's character in *Girl, Interrupted*) ate nothing but rotisserie chicken from her father's restaurant. Granted, she was in a mental institution at the time, during which she amassed quite the collection of mostly eaten bones from said meals under her bed. It was only the smell that alerted the others to her filthy situation. Strangely, this is not just a Hollywood concept. As it turns out, there are people obsessed with a specific taste and smell of a food, who will go to great lengths to guard it, regardless of the fact that it is half-eaten and prone to rotting. The neurological phenomenon is classified as hoarding, or the bizarre desire to want to collect useless things.

6 DEAD ANIMALS

Here is an excerpt from the *San Francisco Chronicle* about a woman who collects animals for a living:

As a kid growing up in Oakland, Nancy Valente had one reaction to the idea of a dead animal: "Eeeuuuw!" Now friends call her up and say, "I saw something dead on the road and thought of you." "Did you pick it up?" is Valente's comeback. "It's a standard joke," says Valente, known as "Roadkill Nancy" among local park rangers who are used to the Mill Valley zooarchaeologist's unconventional ways of adding to her impressive collection of animal bones. "I'm the bone lady," says Valente, 67. "I don't know why I like them so much. I have a lot of them around the house, like the elk skull with a whole rack of antlers. I'd love to show it to people, but I can't even put it in my car.

For years, Valente's cheery mix of nature and the macabre thrilled kids and grossed out parents at the Marin Headlands Visitors Center with "Bones, Bones, Bones," her monthly presentation of bones and skins of local animals. Valente has now moved her program to Muir Woods National Monument, and is also venturing into the East Bay.

5 SPIT

Yes, there is a whole club of people who collect spit and enjoy doing it. There is really nothing else that can be said about this. The sooner we move to item 4, the better.

4 SKULLS

In Mexico, many religious celebrations relating to the dead involve the extensive use of skulls. These are normally very old skulls that are often kept in crypts full of old bones. However, the collecting of skulls is also occasionally found outside of religious circles. The *Chicago Sun Times* reported this in May 2007:

It certainly seemed suspicious—a skull boiling in a pot of water on the stove. That was the ghoulish report Chicago Police received Tuesday night when they were summoned to a Bucktown apartment in the 2100 block of North Damen. Sure enough, police found four human skulls, as the witness reported. But by Wednesday detectives had determined this was a legal case of bone collecting. "There's a market—a legal market—for bones, and I import and sell bones for medical research on the auction Web site eBay," said 26-year-old Brian Sloan.

3 BOOGERS

Strangely, some people do collect these. One Baron VonKlyf posted this on Dave Berry's website blog in 2006. To some, booger collecting is revolting, but to a few, it's just another hobby. After successfully rooting through their noses, many people will randomly wipe their found treasures wherever they can find a conveniently discreet spot. But then there are those folks who have a designated location for their nose discoveries.

2 SKIN

Let's kick this one off with an excerpt from *The Harvard Crimson* (Harvard University's newspaper) on November 13, 2005:

> *Langdell's curator of rare books and manuscripts, David Ferris, says of his library's man-bound holding: "We are reluctant to have it become an object of fascination." But the Spanish law book, which dates back to 1605, may become just that.*
>
> *Accessible in the library's Elihu Reading Room, the book, entitled "Practicarum quaestionum circa leges regias…," looks old but otherwise ordinary. Delicate, stiff, and with wrinkled edges, the skin's coloring is a subdued yellow, with sporadic brown and black splotches like an old banana. The skin is not covered in hair or marked by tattoos—except for a "Harvard Law Library" branding on its spine. Nothing about it shouts "human flesh" to the untrained eye.*

However, collecting skin is not just for the discriminating book binder anymore. Many people collect bits of their own flesh for pleasure. There's something just a bit wrong with that.

1 EYEBALLS

The collection that stares back at you. I guess to some that would be appealing enough to make them want to amass a big bunch of eyeballs. Objects resembling eyeballs have appeared in many gift shops, vending machines, and even on websites devoted to the sole purchasing of ocular memorabilia.

You can find pillows, serving bowls, Christmas tree lights, gum balls, and pajamas all with images of eyeballs on them, but there are people known to collect real human eyeballs. Lest they deflate or become dried out and unappealing, the eyeballs must be kept in a jar of formaldehyde. Now that is dedication.

10 MOST ANNOYING WASTES OF TIME

10 BLOW-IN CARDS

How much time does the average person waste picking up off the floor and throwing away the magazine subscription cards that fall out when you open a magazine? These annoyances are meant to fall out into your lap, but this assumes the reader is sitting down when they open the magazine, and also assumes it won't land on the floor or be blown away by the wind or a fan. Invariably, these little cards end up everywhere you don't want them—under the couch, in between the seat cushions, on the kitchen floor, or blowing down the driveway as you get the mail. These cards are typically three by five inches in size and are called "blow-in" cards, because in the magazine-manufacturing process, the cards are typically blown into the magazine, between the pages, one at a time. Of course, sometimes the machines accidentally blow in more than one card, so your issue of *Sports Illustrated* barfs nine of these cards onto the floor when you open it.

How effective are these blow-in cards for magazines? One magazine estimates that 12 percent of their subscriptions come in as a result of blow-in cards (compared to only 10 percent through Internet subscription services). And cost is another reason blow-in cards are not going away anytime soon. It costs the magazine, on average, about $10 to acquire a new subscriber using blow-in cards, compared to $25 or more using direct mailing.

There are also subscription cards called "bind-in" cards, and these aren't as annoying—they're bound into the magazine and don't fall out. Typically they have perforated edges and can be torn out by the reader.

9 EXTENSION CORDS AND WATER HOSES

It may be possible to go through life and never have to use an extension cord or a water hose, but for the average homeowner, these are essential tools of the trade, and both can be incredibly frustrating to use and waste many hours of one's life. No matter how carefully one unwinds and rewinds extension cords and water hoses, no matter what anti-snag device one uses, inevitably, they become twisted, ensnared, tangled, pinched, and stuck. Untangling an especially complicated knot in an extension cord or water hose can take minutes. Sometimes, the extent of the tangle is so maddening that one throws the cord or hose down in disgust and simply walks away in defeat. All manner of hose-reeling devices and extension-cord-wrapping gadgets are available—all of which promise to prevent tangles, kinks, and snares and all of which inevitably fail.

8 TAMPER-RESISTANT PACKAGING

Tamper-resistant devices or features are common on modern packaged products. There are also tamper-evident packaging methods, which make it noticeable that a product has been tampered with or opened. Whether they are seals, caps, wrappings, twist-off devices, hooks, anchors, twist-ties, or the dreaded hard-plastic clamshell packaging used on such items as children's toys, all manner of tamper-resistant and tamper-evident packaging wastes hours in an average lifetime as you pry, cut, twist, shear, punch, and otherwise manipulate the packaging to get at what you want.

Tamper-resistant packaging as we now know it is a relatively new invention that dates back to the Chicago Tylenol murders in the autumn of 1982. Seven people died after taking pain-relief capsules that had been poisoned. The Tylenol poisonings took place when Extra-Strength Tylenol capsules were maliciously laced with potassium cyanide. The crime led to reforms in the packaging of over-the-counter substances and to federal anti-tampering laws. The case remains unsolved, and no suspects have been charged. However, the incident did inspire the pharmaceutical, food, and consumer-product industries to develop tamper-resistant packaging. Moreover, product tampering was made a federal crime.

The benefits of tamper-resistant packaging are therefore substantial; they have prevented untold loss of life and bodily injury since the new packaging measures were implemented. However, there is no denying that modern packaging wastes many hours of the average American's lifetime as they struggle to open or get through these devices.

7 RED LIGHTS

They have been around almost as long as the automobile, yet red traffic lights are a huge time waster. Why? Because there are other options to control traffic flow at many intersections, like the traffic circle, or roundabout. A roundabout is a type of circular junction in which road traffic must travel in one direction around a central island. Signs usually direct traffic entering the circle to slow down and give the right of way to drivers already in the circle. These junctions are sometimes called modern roundabouts in order to emphasize

 the distinction from older circular-junction types, which had different design characteristics and rules of operation. Older designs, called traffic circles or rotaries, were typically larger, operated at higher speeds, and often gave priority to entering traffic.

In countries where people drive on the right side of the road, the traffic flow around the central island of a roundabout is counterclockwise. In countries where people drive on the left, the traffic flow is clockwise. Statistically, modern roundabouts are safer for drivers and pedestrians than both older traffic circles and traditional intersections. Because low speeds are required for traffic entering roundabouts, they are not designed for high-speed motorways.

Under many traffic conditions, an unsignalized roundabout can operate with less delay to users than traffic-signal control or all-way-stop control (intersections with red lights). Unlike an all-way-stop intersection, a roundabout does not require a complete stop by all entering vehicles, which reduces both individual delay and delays resulting from vehicle lines. A roundabout can also operate much more efficiently than a signalized junction because drivers are able to proceed when traffic is clear without the delay incurred while waiting for the traffic signal to change. Roundabouts can, however, increase delays in locations where traffic would otherwise not be required to stop, and do have some disadvantages such as motorcycle safety concerns. But, over an average lifetime, modern roundabouts would save the typical driver many hours otherwise spent sitting at red lights at intersections.

The first modern roundabout in the United States was constructed in Summerlin, Nevada, in 1990, and roundabouts have since become increasingly common in North America.

6 MICROSOFT PRODUCTS

"Do you want to send this error message?" "Sorry but Windows needs to shut down." How many times were you moving along through your PC and suddenly one of these annoying messages popped up on the screen and you were cut off, stopped dead in your tracks and had to wait for your computer to reboot? If you are like most PC users, it is a lot of wasted time. And most hated of all is the dreaded "blue screen of death," which appears with no warning or error message at all, just a blank blue screen staring back at you. And, of course, how much time have you wasted redoing the content that was lost when Microsoft products decided to just shut down or lock up on you?

This is not meant to be a specific criticism of Microsoft; all computer programs, operating systems, and hardware have problems and can lock up or shut down or lose data for unexpected reasons. However, because Microsoft has the lion's share of the PC and software market, they account for the vast majority of the time we waste because of computer software and hardware malfunctions. And, of course, they were responsible for the travesty that was Windows 98, which single-handedly wasted millions of hours of human time until Windows XP was released.

5 TELEMARKETERS

One bright spot on this depressing list is the advent of "do not call lists," which have drastically cut down on the number of telemarketing phone calls the average person receives. But the time wasted by answering the phone at 5 p.m., in the middle of dinner, as some telemarketer peddled their product can never be recovered. These calls are, perhaps, not one of the biggest time wasters (measured in sheer volume of minutes wasted) because you could always just hang up or screen incoming telemarketing calls with an answering machine, but they are certainly one of the most annoying.

The sheer intensity and volume of the annoyance led people to finally say, "Enough is enough" and demand legislation, which led to the creation of the National Do Not Call Registry in 2003. How effective has this legislation been? In 2007, it was estimated that over 70 percent of Americans had registered their telephone number with the registry, and 77 percent felt the registry had drastically reduced the number of telemarketing calls they received (down from an average of thirty calls per month to only six).

Note: The same system was introduced in Canada in 2008 and has had far less success. With over 300,000 complaints received, and over $73,000 in fines levied against telemarketing companies, only $250 has been collected, as of March 1, 2010. Sadly, Canadians are still having their time wasted by this modern day menace!

4 TELEPHONE DIRECTORIES

If you like this list, press one now. If you dislike this list, press two. If you hate telephone directories, press three, or stay on the line and an operator will assist you. We all have these annoying menu options branded into our brains. Seldom can you call a company, or an individual, and not be confronted with a menu of options or recorded messages you must wait through, or push through, to reach the person you want to speak with. Anyone old enough to remember the days when there were no answering machines and you called a person and either they picked up or they didn't, or you called a company and an actual human being picked up the phone and talked to you, knows just how far we have devolved over the last 30-plus years and how much time we waste. Telephone directories may help companies route incoming calls and improve their operating efficiency, but they are certain to annoy callers and waste their time.

3 MALWARE

An especially virulent form of modern time wasting is caused by various forms of computer malware that infect and slow down your computer, or slow down your interface with the computer (or both). Of course, if we simply didn't use computers, this extreme time waster wouldn't be an issue. However, in our modern high-tech lives, not using a computer is becoming more and more difficult. It is estimated that at least 60 percent of all home PCs are infected with some form of malware. Many PCs are so infected as to render the machines almost unusable. Unknowing and not especially tech-literate home PC users waste untold hours on slow, unresponsive malware-infested computers and don't even know it. It's debatable which is worse: living with things that waste your time, unbeknownst to you, or living with things that waste your time, and of which you are painfully aware. Regardless, computer malware (not to mention the time spent installing anti-malware programs and time spent running and maintaining them) is a huge waste of time.

2 CUSTOMER SUPPORT

Very closely related to telephone directories is the modern annoyance of poor (or nonexistent) customer support. You have a problem or a question, or perhaps a complaint about a product or service? You pick up the phone and call the company (or you can e-mail them, but the result is typically the same). You weave your way through the labyrinth of confusing telephone-directory menu options until you finally arrive at (possibly) a human being to talk to. You think you've wasted too many minutes of your life so far? The time wasting has only begun. If you're lucky, you will have called a company that has good or even excellent customer support, and you will reach a knowledgeable, helpful, trained, and friendly customer-support employee. But sadly, more often than not, you reach a person who is just the opposite. In fact, many companies today deliberately use customer-support people who are anything but supportive. The customer-support person you reach is often overworked, burned out, and doesn't care. Whatever the reason, you're about to enter the Twilight Zone of time-wasting frustration.

You all know the routine: the customer-support person can't help you or delays helping you because "their computers are down." Or they can't help you so they transfer you to someone else who can, and you wait on hold for untold scores of minutes. This other support person never answers, or takes a very long time to answer, and it ends up that they can't help you either, in which case they transfer you to a third person, or refer you back to the person you first spoke to. In the phone-call-transfer process, often you get disconnected and the line goes dead and you need to call back and start through the labyrinth all over again. All of this wastes hours, days, weeks, or possibly months of your life.

1 TOO MANY CHOICES

Have you ever gone into a grocery store to buy, say, a box of Wheat Thins and been confronted with an entire wall of different varieties of Wheat Thins? You just want regular, old-fashioned Wheat Thins. But to find them, you must search your way through a dozen or more different types of Wheat Thins in the grocery store display. Big Wheat Thins (an oxymoron George Carlin would have loved), Artisan Cheese Wheat Thins, Ranch Wheat Thins…the list goes on and on. This takes time and becomes very frustrating. In fact, research has shown that when confronted with too many different choices, grocery store shoppers tend to not buy the product at all out of sheer overload and frustration. Now, take the Wheat Thin choice overload model and apply it to most every other product you want to buy in a grocery store. You end up spending half a day shopping for groceries when before it took an hour, simply because you can't find what you are looking for or have to ponder too many choices.

The "tyranny of choice" is not just about grocery shopping. It's in almost every consumer decision we have to make. For example, there used to be GM,

Ford, and American Motors (and a few European and Japanese car models). Now there are dozens of car manufacturers and hundreds of available models to choose from. It used to be that you worked a job and received healthcare benefits and a retirement program. Now there are many different "benefit menus" and "plan options" to review and choose from. All of this takes time and can be very frustrating.

Do we really need such an overabundance of choice in almost every aspect of our modern lives? Multiple options to choose from may or may not be a modern benefit to life, but there is one thing too many choices always are: time wasters.

10 ARTISTS WHO WORK WITH BIZARRE MEDIA

10 POST-IT NOTES

Alumni of Eisenhower Junior High School in Taylorsville, Utah, must be proud of their alma mater, for the school claims to "have set more world records than any other school"! They currently hold nine world records, and their record-breaking attempts have appeared in Guinness World Records and Ripley's Believe It or Not! One of the records the school broke is the World's Largest Post-it Mosaic. On November 6, 2009, 151 pupils participated in constructing a 60- by 40-foot mosaic using 38,400 colorful Post-it Notes. The resulting mosaic illustrated the theme "Go Green." The Post-it Notes were later recycled.

9 PLAYING CARDS

David Alvarez, a 20-year-old art student from Leavenworth, Washington, proved that you don't need to be good at drawing to be an artist when he unveiled his 25-foot-high portrait of Jimi Hendrix made from more than 8500 Bicycle playing cards (or 168 decks). Using a computer program, he divided a picture of Jimi Hendrix into parts and mapped out where the colored playing cards should go. Then, in a single day, Alvarez worked for 21 hours straight, painstakingly placing each card in its right position on a Styrofoam-core board with double-sided tape, only resting for an hour and half before working again.

8 JUNK MAIL

Americans get swamped every year by millions of tons of junk mail. Sandy Schimmel, an Arizona artist, decided to put them to good use. She creates beautiful, vivid mosaic pictures out of her junk mail in a process known as "upcycling." Inspired by a mosaic that she saw while in Venice, Italy, Schimmel's works are mostly portraits, including a piece featuring Madonna called *All American Blonde* and a re-creation of the famous painting *The Birth of Venus*.

7 GUMBALLS

Franz Spohn, illustrator, sculptor, and professor of art at Edinboro University in Pennsylvania, specializes in creating large mosaic murals depicting famous people like Barack Obama, Rosa Parks, and Robert Ripley from hundreds of gumballs. Spohn fills plastic tubes with gumballs, stacked according to color, and lines the tubes up to create his masterpieces.

6 POSTAGE STAMPS

Pete Mason from Staffordshire, England, claims to be the "Post Pop Art" man. Combining pop art and graphic design, he creates portraits of famous icons like Martin Luther King, Jr., and Princess Diana out of recycled postage stamps. To make a portrait, Mason first draws a picture of his subject on a canvas. Then he divides the picture in stamp-sized squares. Then the stamps, which are sorted out by color, design, and postmark pattern, are applied to the surface. Typically, Mason's larger works use around 20,000 stamps.

5 COMPUTER PARTS

In an art exhibition in Beijing, China, in 2006, a group of computer engineers displayed a re-creation of da Vinci's *Mona Lisa* made out of computer parts. Constructed with various circuits and chip sockets, the work, entitled *Technology Smiling*, fascinated audiences.

4 APPLES

Since 1988, Emma Karp and her father, Helge Lundstrom, have been creating huge apple mosaics for the annual Kivik Apple Festival. The Swedish town has long been an important fruit supplier in Sweden, and the festival celebrates the end of the harvest there, which is around late September. The centerpiece of the festival is the apple mosaic, which can contain up to 75,000 apples of different varieties, or about 8820 pounds.

3 FRUIT AND VEGGIE STICKER LABELS

Barry Snyder of Erie, Colorado, creates amazing mosaic artworks out of those annoying stickers that come on store-brought fruit and vegetables. His four-square-foot creations are typically made out of around 4000 stickers and take him about six months to create. Many of the stickers he uses are sent to him by people from around the globe. His original works are so popular that they can sell for up to $10,000.

2 BAR CODES

Scott Blake specializes in creating portraits of famous icons out of bar codes. His bar-code art was inspired by the Y2K computer bug, when he used Photoshop to create his first bar-code mosaic of Jesus Christ. Since then, he has created around 30 portraits of famous icons such as Andy Warhol and Arnold Schwarzenegger. Scott also created several interactive pieces, where scanning the bar codes on the mosaic flashes up images of the person pictured in the mosaic on a screen. This was done in Scott's portraits of Bruce Lee and Elvis Presley.

1 BURNT TOAST

Maurice Bennett of New Zealand tops the list for his mosaic portraits of famous people made from thousands of pieces of toasted bread, burned in varying degrees to create different shades. His works have depicted such greats as New Zealand Prime Minister John Key and director Peter Jackson. His works are typically displayed on billboards, where they are best viewed.

10 MOST BIZARRE MODERN JOBS

10 ARMPIT SNIFFER

When we go to the supermarket to buy deodorant, we are drawn in by all the colorful packaging and the nice scents. But before those bottles hit the shelves, someone needs to make sure they actually do what they are meant to do: mask body odor. This job is left to the armpit sniffers, who get to sniff smelly armpits all day long to ensure that the deodorant is effective.

9 CHICKEN SEXER

The job of the chicken sexer is to determine the sex of baby chickens when they hatch so that they can be sent off to the appropriate location for their future life as an egg-laying hen or dinner for four. This job requires a gentle hand (so as

to not damage the wee chicks) a good eye (to recognize whether they have a penis or not), and the ability to drift off and forget that your whole working life is going to be spent looking at chickens' sex organs.

8 FURNITURE TESTER

Next time you buy a new bed or sofa, think of the many men and women whose job it is to sit or lie on those things for hours to test their comfort level. Furniture design is not just a matter of science or ergonomics—someone needs to actually make sure they function and are comfortable.

7 SNAKE MILKER

Snake venom is used for all manner of things, but the most important is undoubtedly for its use in medical research. A lot of venom is needed every year for this research, and some poor guy has to spend all day pushing snake fangs into a plastic container in order to milk them. At least he can have the satisfaction of knowing that his dangerous task may one day save a person's life.

6 AIRPLANE REPO MAN

I bet you have never thought about what happens when someone forgets to make payments on their private jet. Well, the finance company sends in the airplane repo man! He has to have an excellent flying record, because when he finds your plane, he has to fly it to its destination, undoubtedly an auction house for repossessed planes. This can be a dangerous job (imagine repossessing a plane from the mob), so sometimes plane repo men need to bring backup with them.

5 SPORTS MASCOT

Sports mascots are not just fans running around in furry costumes. They are actually paid staff of the sports team they support. To be a mascot, you need to be athletic and fit, and you definitely should not apply if you are shy. Some mascots are so popular they are more famous than the team's players!

4 BODY PART MODEL

Modeling is not just for the beautiful—if you have good hands or attractive feet, there may be a job in modeling for you. In fact, depending on the product needing a model, sometimes you need to have ugly hands or other parts of your body (don't forget that someone needs to be photographed for the "before" photos). Body models can make a lot of money, so don't discount it as an employment option if you lose your job.

3 BALL DIVING

Have you ever wondered what happens to all the golf balls that go into the water on golf courses? Now you know: golf ball divers go in occasionally to retrieve them. It's a highly paid position and it can be extremely dangerous (at least two people have died on the job). The best part is that when the ball divers are done, then can put on their plus fours and play a round of golf.

2 BARNYARD MASTURBATOR

The job of the barnyard masturbator is to stimulate farm animals for artificial insemination. They usually have two options. The first is to use a rectal electrifier, which sends small shots of electricity up the bottom of the animal to stimulate it from behind. The other option is to do it the old-fashioned way—with their hands. Either way, I think the less said about this job the better.

1 VOMIT COLLECTOR

As we all know from experience, roller coasters and other carnival rides can make us a little queasy. More often than not, at least one person on the more exciting rides will have a little spew. Unfortunately, this produces quite a lot of vomit every day, and some very unlucky people get the job of cleaning it up. Next time you hate your job, think of the poor vomit collector working at your local amusement park.

CHAPTER THREE
Between the Sheets

10 BIZARRE AND ICKY RELATIONSHIPS

10 DAUVEED
Relationship: Man and mannequin

This is item 10 on the list because I can't for the life of me work out whether it is for real. In June 2009, Dauveed (whose surname is so complex I can't work out what it is) had a faux wedding ceremony in which he married Clara, a mannequin. From my research, I have found comments by people who claim to have seen Dauveed with his mannequin walking around Hollywood, which would imply that he took the marriage seriously. Regardless of whether Dauveed really is in love with Clara or not, it is kind of nice to know that society has offbeat people in it to add color to our lives.

9 LOT'S DAUGHTERS
Relationship: Daughters rape father

First, the appropriate Bible quote:

> *And the elder said to the younger Our father is old, and there is no man left on the earth, to come in unto us after the manner of the whole earth. Come, let us make him drunk with wine, and let us lie with him, that we may preserve seed of our father. And they made their father drink wine that night: and the elder went in and lay with her father: but he perceived not neither when his daughter lay down, nor when she rose up. And the next day the elder said to the younger: Behold I lay last night with my father, let us make him drink wine also to night, and thou shalt lie with him, that we may save seed of our father. They made their father drink wine that night also, and the younger daughter went in, and lay with him: and neither then did he perceive when she lay down, nor when she rose up. So the two daughters of Lot were with child by their father. (Genesis 19:31–36)*

It doesn't really get much more blatant than that. The two daughters had sex with their father, Lot, in order to preserve his family line. Incidentally, this all happened shortly after they had fled from Sodom and Gomorrah, which were destroyed by God for their immorality—ironic? Lot had no memory of the events described above (maybe it was the liquor), and nine months later the daughters gave birth to two sons, Moab (father of the Moabites), and Ammon (father of the Ammonites).

8 MUNDA DHANDA VILLAGER
Relationship: Girl and dog

In a bizarre ceremony, villagers from the East Indian Jharkhand region marry young girls to dogs in order to ward off evil spirits. They believe that the ceremony will protect the girl and her family from curses. Once the girl comes of age, she is free to marry a human without needing to get a divorce from her canine husband.

7 NEJDET BOYANAY
Relationship: Man and alien

Turkish man Nejdet Boyanay claims to have been experiencing sexual relations with an alien visitor since he was ten years old. This bizarre relationship lasted until Boyanay was 21. After speaking to reporters about the incident, he claimed that the alien returned and tried to kill him in the shower because he had made their love affair public. You couldn't make this stuff up if you tried!

6 CALIGULA
Relationship: Man and horse

It's a well-known fact that Caligula loved his horse Incitatus. But there is no evidence that their strange relationship ever became sexual. Nevertheless,  Caligula provided Incitatus with a stable built with marble and filled with ivory and purple cloth, the imperial color. The horse was looked after by a team of 18 servants and was fed oats mixed with gold. Incitatus even held special dinner parties for the local dignitaries.

5 JOHN DEAVES
Relationship: Father and daughter

If you are currently eating your breakfast, might I advise you to put it aside for just a moment. On March 20, 2008, John Deaves and his daughter, Jenny, were sentenced to a three-year good-behavior bond after pleading guilty to two counts of performing an act of incest, which led to the birth of their daughter, Celeste.

The "couple" met 30 years after John had left his daughter's mother. Jenny was 31, and just two weeks after meeting, the father and daughter had sex. Jenny Deaves said soon after reuniting with her father, she began to see him as a man first and her father second. "I was looking at him, sort of going, 'Oh, he's not too bad,'" she said. Mr. Deaves admits that he "initially" thought having sex with his daughter was wrong.

4 POPE PIUS IX
Relationship: Pope and kidnapped son

Pope Pius IX raised a young boy as if he were his son in an extraordinarily unusual act for a Pope. The boy had been removed from his Jewish parents because their servant girl baptized him thinking he was dying. Because Christians were not legally allowed to be raised by Jews, he became a ward of the state. Interestingly, after the death of the Pope, the boy spoke strongly in his favor at the first steps in his canonization process.

3 KENNETH PINYAN
Relationship: Man and horse

Kenneth Pinyan, also known as Mr. Hands, loved horses so much that he took to having sexual relations with them at night. His friend videotaped him, and the footage was released onto the Internet. On the fateful night of July 2, 2005, while in the act of performing for the camera, the horse got overexcited and perforated Pinyan's colon during anal sex. Pinyan died of his injuries.

2 EIJA-RIITTA BERLINER-MAUER
Relationship: Woman and wall

Eija-Riitta Berliner-Mauer (which means Berlin Wall) married the famous wall in 1979 after being diagnosed with a condition called object-sexuality. She claimed to have fallen in love with the structure in her childhood and began collecting images of it. After five visits—during which she wooed the wall—she married it in front of a handful of guests. She insisted that she had a full and loving relationship with the wall. While the rest of mankind rejoiced when the Berlin Wall, erected by the Soviets in 1961 to halt an exodus from East to West Berlin, was largely torn down in 1989, its "wife" was horrified. Having gotten over the "death" of her husband, the wall, Eija-Riitta has finally found love again and is now dating her garden fence.

1 CARL TANZLER
Relationship: Man and corpse

Carl Tanzler, a doctor from Florida, was so in love with his young tuberculosis patient Elena Milagro that when she died, he dug her body up from the graveyard and used bizarre techniques to embalm her. He used coat hangers to keep her joints together, gave her glass eyes, and as her skin decomposed, he replaced it with silk soaked in wax and plaster of Paris. He dressed her corpse in fine clothes and jewelry and kept her body in his bed. After rumors got out that Tanzler was sleeping with Milagro's corpse, he was confronted at his home and the body was found. He was arrested and charged. He was given a preliminary hearing for the trial, but the case was dropped because it had been over ten years since he had stolen her body.

10 BIZARRE PLACES TO GET MARRIED

10 BUNGEE JUMP

Some people are just too literal. This couple decided to take the plunge into marriage from 164 feet in the air, and even had the ceremony on a platform with 22 relatives and friends suspended along with them.

The guests were securely strapped to their chairs with tuxedos, dresses, and all. The platform was slowly raised as the ceremony went on, until the entire assembly reached 164 feet in the air, where Sandra Eens and Jeroen Kippers exchanged rings and took a leap of faith together.

9 HAPPY MEAL OR BEAN BURRITO

We have two contenders for this one, and you can decide which is more romantic:

The first comes to us from Fairborn, Ohio, where McDonald's coworkers Tyree Henderson and Trisha Lynn Esteppe married at the restaurant where they met three years prior. The restaurant didn't skip a beat—the wedding took place while customers came and went, placing orders and eating their Big Macs. The lucky bride stated that she could "not imagine a more romantic setting for their wedding." Not sure which is worse: the fact that she thought that was romantic or that they have worked there for three years.

Our second couple decided to tie the knot at their favorite fine dining establishment, Taco Bell. The bride and groom, Paul and Caragh Brooks, wedded while sitting in a booth while customers looked on. Instead of personalized mints, they had hot sauce packets labeled "Will you marry me?" The saucy bride wore a $15 hot pink dress while a friend, who got ordained online, read the vows wearing a nice T-shirt. The Brooks met online and were a step ahead, as they already had the same last name. I guess that's a good enough reason as any to get married at Taco Bell.

Stay classy guys!

8 CLOWNING AROUND

This one is kind of creepy, but once you get past the makeup it's not so bad, assuming you aren't terrified of clowns, of course.

Roadkill Raccoon and Reddish Raddish married at the Alberta Street Clown House (their nonclown names are Carol Banner and Morgan Nilsen.) Naturally, the bride and groom love everything clown and decided to share that with their friends and family. Guests dressed up as clowns and had all kinds of activities that other weddings should have, such as mud wrestling, minibike tricks, and, of course, jousting. The couple ended the ceremony with a bike parade to the reception. It's a little strange but seems like lots of fun (again, unless you're afraid of clowns).

7 MIDAIR WEDDING

Sometimes love makes you feel sky high. Apparently that wasn't enough for this couple who got married in midair on top of several biplanes!

The activity known as "wing walking" was taken to another level when the British couple, Darren McWalters and Katie Hodgson, were married while the minister stood backwards on another plane and administered the ceremony. In total, three biplanes were used, one for each person as they flew close together. All three of the participants were securely strapped to the planes and wore traditional wedding attire, complete with a tux and a wedding dress. Everything was transmitted wirelessly and broadcast to the guests on the ground via a speaker system.

6 WEDDING ON WHEELS

In a hurry to get married? You might want to hit the road and try the hot-rod wedding from Reverend Darrell Best.

The reverend turned a 1942-edition American La France fire engine into a mini chapel on wheels. Located in Shelbyville, Illinois, the holy matrimony ride is complete with stained-glass windows, a pipe organ, and even an altar for the special occasion. The fire engine fits everyone you need for the wedding: bride, groom, best man, and maid of honor. Reverend Best charges a $200 fee plus $2 per mile for the ride and ceremony.

5 MARRIAGE IN HELL

Who says weddings have to be pretty and fancy—how about dark and morbid? This couple took their love of the macabre and their relationship to the next level when they got married at the haunted house where they both worked.

Tina Milhoane, 22, and Robert Seifer, 24, married at 7 Floors of Hell in the haunted house's cemetery. Everyone dressed the part, with the groom making his entrance in a hearse and coming out of a coffin to his beloved bride. The bride, meanwhile, was dressed in white, with a splash of red added to mimic the character Carrie. The minister was outfitted as the Grim Reaper and even read the Lord's Prayer to the guests.

4 UNDERWATER WEDDING

Sometimes marriage can be sink or swim, and for some, it's sink, swim, and scuba. But forget just getting married while you scuba dive. How about staying in an underwater hotel?

You can make it all happen at the Jules Undersea Lodge, where you can make your underwater adventure come true 21 feet below in Key Largo, Florida. For a mere $1750 plus tax, you can have the lodge all to yourself and even stay there for the honeymoon. Guests scuba dive to the underwater lodge and have plenty of room to relax in two bedrooms, a dining area, a kitchen, and a living area.

3 NUDIST WEDDING

Looking to let your vows hang loose? Then a nudist wedding may be for you. Just think, you don't have to worry about a tux or wedding dress, and your pictures will be very popular.

Many people do this every year, from Dallas, Texas, to Australia, but one of the most well-known places to have a nude wedding is at the Hedonism III Resort in Runaway Bay, St. Ann's Bay, Jamaica. On Valentine's Day in 2003, 29 couples exchanged vows in the buff there, making it one of the largest nude weddings ever. The resort provides everything free of charge with a minimum four-night stay. No word yet if Viagra is available as party favors.

2 GARBAGE DUMP

Think marriage stinks? It certainly did for Rockie Graham and Dave Hart, who got married at the Bethel Transfer Station where they first met. Rockie Graham was there recycling when she caught a dirty look from Dave, and three years later, they were married in this garbage dump with 250 of their closest friends. The bride wore a $7000 white dress with the dump as the picture-perfect background.

The idea came from Dave, who wanted to exchange vows where they originally met. Rockie stated she was "reluctant" at first but eventually gave in to Dave's idea. Now that is compromise, but I suppose if you are going to start a lifelong relationship in a dump, you can only go up from there.

1 ON TOP OF MOUNT EVEREST

Finally, we have a wedding that was a first-ever.

A Nepalese couple actually got married on the peak of Mount Everest, the first-ever wedding in history there. Pem Dorjee and Moni Mulepati made it to the top as part of the Rotary Centennial Everest Expedition and kept their plan a secret until the last minute, since they didn't know if they would make it all the way. The couple spent a mere 10 minutes at the peak and briefly took off their oxygen masks to exchange vows while friends took pictures. There have been couples in the past who have tried to make the same trip, but none were able to make it all the way up.

10 INCREDIBLY BIZARRE SEXUAL PRACTICES

10 AGALMATOPHILIA

Agalmatophilia is a paraphilia concerned with the sexual attraction to a statue, doll, mannequin, or other similar figurative object. The attraction may include the desire for actual sexual contact with the object; a fantasy of having sexual (or nonsexual) encounters with the animate or inanimate object; the act of watching encounters between more than one of the objects; or sexual pleasure gained from thoughts of being transformed or transforming another person into the object. Agalmatophilia may also encompass pygmalionism, which describes a state of love for an object of one's own creation.

9 NYOTAIMORI

Nyotaimori, often referred to as "body sushi," is the practice of eating sashimi or sushi from the body of a woman, typically while she is naked. Nantaimori refers to the same practice using a male model. This sexual fetish is a subdivision of food play. As a result of being served on a human body, the

 temperature of the sushi or sashimi comes closer to body temperature. Before becoming a living sushi platter, the person is trained to lie down for hours without moving. She or he must also be able to withstand the prolonged exposure to the cold

food. Body hair, including pubic hair, is shaved, as a display of pubic hair may be seen as a sexual act. Before service, the individual takes a bath using a special fragrance-free soap and then finishes off with a splash of cold water to cool the body down somewhat for the sushi.

8 PONYPLAY

Ponyplay is a form of bondage that involves a "pony" and a rider. The pony is often outfitted with straps, a leather saddle, blinders, reins, and a bit in the mouth. The rider, sometimes using a riding crop or whip, either gets pulled in a cart or rides the pony directly. The principal theme of animal roleplay is usually the voluntary or involuntary reduction (or transformation) of a human being to animal status and focuses on the altered mind-space created. The most common examples are probably canines (puppy, dog, wolf), felines (cat, kitten, lion), and equines (pony, horse).

7 CANNIBAL FANTASIES

Cannibal fantasies are obviously pretty self-explanatory. On the Deviant Desires website (based on the book of the same name), Katharine Gates explains that some people actually bring these fantasies to life in consensual roleplaying! One of her friends "painted the woman's nude body with dotted lines to represent cuts of meat." One very tasteful website, Muki's Kitchen, features photographs of female models trussed up in pans filled with vegetables, and stuffed with apples and carrots in every possible orifice. Thus, erotic feeding, messy fun, bondage, gags, and vaginal or anal penetration may be incorporated into this practice.

6 PSEUDONECROPHILIA

Unlike real necrophilia, pseudonecrophilia is actually legal (not that that's a good thing)! It's quite simple, actually: one partner remains quiet and still, while the other has sex with him or her. For added realism, the "pseudodead" partner can lay in cold water for a while before the act! This particular practice met some notoriety, thanks to its appearance in the show *Law & Order: Special Victims Unit*.

5 SALIROPHILIA

Salirophilia is a sexual fetish or paraphilia that involves deriving erotic pleasure from soiling or disheveling the object of one's desire, usually an attractive person. It may involve tearing or damaging their clothing, covering them in mud or filth, or messing their hair or makeup. The fetish does not involve harming or injuring the subject, only their appearance. The fetish sometimes manifests itself in the defacing of statues or pictures of attractive people, especially celebrities. The fetishist finds this sexually exciting, not just mere vandalism. They sometimes form collections of defaced art for future enjoyment.

4 MUMMIFICATION

Mummification as a bondage practice involves restraining a living person's body in a nondamaging way by wrapping it head to toe, or neck to toe, in materials like plastic wrap, cloth, bandages, rubber strips, duct tape, plaster bandages, body bags, or straitjackets. The end result is a person completely immobilized and looking like an Egyptian mummy. They may then either be left bound in a state of sensory deprivation for a period of time, or sensually stimulated in their state of bondage before being released from the wrappings.

3 AUTOPEDERASTY

Autopederasty is the near-impossible act of sticking one's own fully erect penis in one's own rectum. Yes. Only a small percentage of people can do it, but it's possible! There's a porn movie called *Go Fuck Yourself* that is devoted to the act, even going so far as to instruct people on how to do it. There are two other more familiar variants of this: autofellatio (when a man gives himself oral sex) and autocunnilingus (when a woman gives herself oral sex).

2 EMETOPHILIA

This is also known as erotic vomiting—talk about blowing chunks! Obviously, the words "erotic" and "vomiting" are not often used together. However, they do have similarities: both trigger the release of hormones that make you feel better; both are caused by stimulus; and, for men at least, both involve having fluids forced through a tube and out of an orifice.

The primary dissimilarity is that most people do not associate throwing up with a pleasurable experience. Dr. Robert J. Stoller, a renowned sexologist and psychiatrist, begs to differ. He studied the cases of three women: The first woman doesn't do the Technicolor-yawn herself; instead, she says "…I can reach a sure orgasm by imagining someone vomiting in a hard, humiliating fashion…"; The second woman actually experiences an orgasm every time she throws up; The third and final woman describes it like this: "…Vomiting for me is like…an orgasm in that I'm tensed, I feel the…intense flood of good feelings almost continually throughout the vomiting and experience relief and quiet warmth in my body when I'm finished. It is not identical to an orgasm. I do not feel it intensely in my genitals alone, but I do feel it there as well as the rest of my body and…in my mouth…."

There is also a practice known as a "Roman shower," which is to become aroused by being vomited upon.

1 TERATOPHILIA

Teratophilia is the sexual attraction to deformed or monstrous people. One version of teratophilia is acrotomophilia, or sexual attraction to amputees. Considerable commercial and amateur erotica is published apparently targeting people with such a fetish.

❧❧❧❧❧❧❧

10 MOST FAMOUS PENISES

10 JUAN BAPTISTA DOS SANTOS

Juan Baptista dos Santos was born in Faro, Portugal, around 1843. He was in all ways normal except for his third leg and second penis. Both of his penises were fully functional, and he claimed that he could use both during intercourse—after using one, he would start on the other. He apparently had an extremely high sexual appetite. Juan was famous for having a relationship with a French courtesan who had three legs and two vaginas.

9 BANNED ½ MM PENIS

It is rare that a German book generates any interest in the United States, and German children's books are usually completely off the radar. So it came as quite a surprise to many when the huge scandal arose over the German children's book by Rotraut Susanne Berner. A request was made for an American publishing house to print English translations of the book for distribution in the U.S. "It was really a sensation at first," said Berner. "As it turned out, there were a couple of changes that had to be made before the books could be unleashed on the American public. First off, smokers had to be removed from the illustrations. But that wasn't all. One image shows a scene from an art gallery — and for realism's sake, there is a cartoonish nude hanging on the wall along with a tiny, seven-millimeter-tall statue of a naked man on a pedestal." The publisher said, "American kiddies, obviously, could never be expected to handle such a depiction of the human body." The series is popular all around the world, and the United States is the only country to kick up a stink and the books are still unpublished here because of a tiny penis on a cartoon of a statue.

8 DIRK DIGGLER
Boogie Nights is a 1997 film that follows the life of nightclub dishwasher Dirk Diggler. Due to his enormous penis, he becomes a famous porn star and engages in drug abuse. While this is essentially a film about Dirk's penis, it does everything possible to conceal it from the viewers until a brief glimpse in the last scene.

7 BART SIMPSON
In *The Simpsons Movie* viewers of all ages (due to its PG-13 rating) were surprised to see a full-frontal image of a naked, skateboarding Bart. The scene involves Bart eagerly accepting Homer's dare to skateboard at high speed to Krusty Burger, stark naked. After a series of fortuitous cover-ups, there is a fleeting glimpse of the ten-year-old's modest, but distinctly yellow, penis. Fortunately, audiences around the world took it for what it was: a humorous drawing.

6 LILI ELBE
What is this? A woman on a list of penises? Well, Lili Elbe happens to be the first documented case of a transexual. Einar Wegener (born in Denmark) was a famous artist in Paris in the Roaring Twenties. After Einar's wife asked him to pose as a woman for a portrait she was painting, he realized that he wanted to be a woman. He was subjected to a series of experimental operations that involved removing his penis and having ovaries and a uterus implanted (the surgeries were unsuccessful). Despite the conservatism of the times, Einar became Lili, and the government annulled his marriage and granted him a new birth certificate listing him as male.

5 JESUS
The Catholic Feast of the Circumcision is considered so important that on January 1 every year, all Catholics in the world are obliged to attend Mass under pain of mortal sin. The feast remembers the Biblical tale in which Jesus was taken to the temple to be circumcised. It is considered by many to be the first moment that Jesus bled, which is significant for those who consider that his blood gave man redemption. The actual account of the circumcision can be read in Luke 2:21.

4 RASPUTIN

Rasputin is famed as the bizarre mystic who cast a spell over the ladies of the court in Imperial Russia. In 1916, he was murdered by a group of noblemen who believed that he was convincing their wives to sleep with him and influencing the affairs of the state. After many attempts to kill him, they finally succeeded and also mutilated his sexual organs, severing his penis. The penis ended up in a museum for all to see.

3 JOHN WAYNE BOBBITT

John Wayne Bobbitt's name will forever be remembered in history after his wife cut off his penis on the night of June 23, 1993. John fortunately managed to find his penis (which his wife tossed into a field) and it was reattached. Bizarrely, he went on to star in a number of very tacky porn movies.

2 JOHN HOLMES

John Curtis Holmes was one of the most popular male adult film stars in the 1970s. His popularity was mostly due to his enormous penis, which was 13-and-a-half inches long. His co-stars likened having sex with him to "doing it with a big, soft kind of loofah." His notable size was the cause of much mirth. A popular joke in the industry said that Holmes was incapable of achieving an erection because the blood flow from his head to his penis would cause him to pass out.

1 DAVID

Undoubtedly the most looked at penis in the world, Michelangelo's "David" is a masterpiece of Renaissance sculpture. The statue is 17 feet tall, and although he was a Jew, David does not appear circumcised. This is in keeping with the rules of style governing that period of art. During the Victorian era when the Victorians destroyed the genitalia of many statues in a fit of repressed sexual energy, David survived unscathed. However, for the benefit of royal visits by Queen Victoria, a detachable ivy leaf was fashioned to gird his loins.

10 BIZARRE DATING WEBSITES

10 ASHLEY MADISON AGENCY

This site, dedicated to married and single folks seeking out "arrangements" with other married people, sadly has (to date) 4,255,000 members. This site took off in America and spread like a rash over popular radio-station commercial breaks with the tagline "Life is short. Have an affair!" The site *guarantees* an affair if you sign up, although they do mention in their disclaimer that they are not to be held liable for personal injury or death that may happen to you if you use their services.

9 SCIENTIFIC MATCH

At a measly $2000 for a lifetime membership, this site boasts that it will find you a match based on physical chemistry. To find you that perfect someone, their "CLIA/ASH-accredited lab" analyzes your supplied DNA sample and then destroys it after they're done. What are the benefits of DNA comparison?

- Chances are increased that you'll love the natural body fragrance of your match.
- You have a greater chance of a more satisfying sex life.
- Women tend to enjoy a higher rate of orgasms with their partners.
- Women have a much lower chance of cheating in their exclusive relationships.
- Couples tend to have higher rates of fertility.
- All other things being equal, couples have a greater chance of having healthier children with more robust immune systems.

8 WOMEN BEHIND BARS

You have a better-than-average shot at hooking up with this website, for obvious reasons. Unfortunately, the site doesn't list what offenses landed these women in prison, so you're taking your chances. Surprisingly, if you get the opportunity to read the "What People Are Saying About Us" page on the site, the percentage is high for satisfied customers. It costs you a mere three dollars to obtain one inmate's address through which you can converse via snail mail. The site even has an "Add to Cart" and "Checkout" button after you're done shopping for your badass beauties! A huge plus is you can pretty much rely on the fact that they're not going to cheat on you with your best friend (or anyone else, for that matter).

7 TALL FRIENDS

If you happen to suffer from tinyophobia (the fear of little people), you might want to check this website out. It specifically caters to like-minded singles who are of a specific height, meaning *tall*. Verbatim, their introduction is, "Welcome to the best, largest, and most effective tall-dating site in the world. This is the best place for looking for tall dating relationship or marriage. We bring together tall-dating minded singles from USA, UK, Canada, Australia, Europe, and more. Here you could mingle with tall singles, tall beautiful women, and tall handsome men."

Other than the height criterion, the site is standard fare, with chat, forums, and the like. As an alternative, they also have a dating site for short people.

6 NO LONGER LONELY

Are you schizophrenic? Do you suffer from paranoia? Do you play with your own waste with great delight? Well, thankfully, a site has been created to match up people with histories of mental illness. Costing nothing to join with full access to all of its features, No Longer Lonely boasts that it's the only dating site of its kind. Now what could possibly go wrong here? And as an alternative, there's also a site for people suffering with an STD. Now if only they would combine these two.

5 TREK PASSIONS

Here you can find that special someone who can debate whether Jean-Luc or James T. was the better captain, and then go snuggle under your Ewok/Death Star matching sheets. From the home page: "A 100% free online community and SciFi personals site for science-fiction lovers, including but not limited to lovers of *Star Trek* and *Star Wars*." Its tagline is, "Love long and prosper!" Just remember to have your partner checked for Tribble infestation before becoming, ahem, intimate.

4 DARWIN DATING

Yes, online dating has been reduced to the shallowest end of the mud puddle with this matchmaking service. The criteria to join are strict, as they allow "beautiful people only." (And that doesn't include inner beauty.) They even have what they affectionately call the "Chimp Calculator" to test your unattractiveness level! Their tagline? "Online dating minus ugly people." One can only imagine how much Photoshopping has been done to these profiles!

3 420 DATING

For those of you who have been living on the moon as of late, the term "420 friendly" is slang for "I smoke weed." Finally, stoners have an online community where they can find someone to share the munchies with. Strangely enough, the site's terms of service state, "The following is a partial list of the kind of Content that is illegal or prohibited on the Website. It includes Content that promotes information that you know is false, misleading or promotes illegal activities." It also states at the bottom of the home page: "420dating.com does not advocate the use of any illegal substances." And yet, on the front page are photos of the latest "Featured Smokers" enjoying a nice, healthy dose of hydroponics. Uhhhh, what?

2 CRAZY BLIND DATE

This site is for intrepid souls only! In a nutshell, you are not allowed to see any photos of your potential dates beforehand, and the service will match you up according to where you live. At the time of this review, the website only boasted services for eight major U.S. cities, but there is an option to select your own location to see if they have any listings. There are three options to choose from: a solo date, a double date, or either. The novelty steps in when you next have the option of going out on a date that very same night! Next, you select the area in your chosen city you wish to go to, then sit back and wait for an e-mail confirmation that the date is scheduled. Not for the faint of heart!

1 DAILY DIAPERS

No, this isn't a site for the aged and infirm wearing Depends. It's the Internet's premiere free community for Adult Babies, Diaper Lovers, Big Kids, and fetishists galore who relish returning to a more peaceful time in their life: childhood. Apparently, these adult children grew up wearing plastic pants and "sissy clothes," as well. According to the site, "Adult Babies like to wear diapers, but also enjoy other babyish things. They may wear baby or sissy clothes such as Onesie-like snap-crotch T-shirts, rompers, or play suits. They tend to like more colorful diaper covers and even frilly ruffled panty-style covers. Adult Babies may also enjoy drinking formula from baby bottles, or eating baby food. Generally they like to be treated totally like a baby during this play time, being changed, bathed, and even spanked by their partner who serves as their Mommy or Daddy." There's someone out there for everyone, huh?

10 FASCINATING FACTS ABOUT SEX

10 WEIGHT LOSS
Fascinating Fact: Sexual acts lead to weight loss.

The average human loses 26 calories when kissing for a minute. Furthermore, vigorous sex for half an hour burns 150 calories (you can lose three pounds in a year if you have sex seven to eight times a month). Kissing is also very good for your teeth: the extra saliva released during the act helps to keep the mouth clean, reducing the risk of tooth decay.

9 PUBIC WIGS
Fascinating Fact: In Victorian times, whores wore pubic wigs.

The pubic wig (a merkin) has been around since the 1400s, when it was originally worn by women who had shaved their pubic hair off to prevent lice. In the Victorian times, it was frequently worn by prostitutes who wanted to conceal the fact that they had diseases like syphilis (honest—we aren't "merkin" this up). Pubic wigs are also used in the film industry to conceal actor's genitals in nude scenes.

8 CONDOMS

Fascinating Fact: Condoms were originally made of animal intestines or linen.

In Asia before the 15th century, some use of glans condoms (devices covering only the head of the penis) is recorded. In China, glans condoms may have been made of oiled silk paper or of lamb intestines. In Japan, they were made of tortoise shell or animal horn (ouch). In the 16th century, condoms were often made with linen sheaths soaked in a chemical solution and allowed to dry before use. The cloths were sized to cover the glans of the penis and were held on with a ribbon.

7 NOT TONIGHT, JOSEPHINE

Fascinating Fact: Sex cures headaches.

Next time your significant other refuses your advances by claiming to have a headache, remember this fact: the sex act can help to cure a headache. Sex causes the body to release endorphins that naturally reduce the pain of a headache.

6 SKIN CARE

Fascinating Fact: Sperm is good for the skin.

The proteins in sperm have a tightening effect on the skin. When sperm is left to dry, the evaporation of the water in it leaves behind protein, which can help to reduce wrinkles. While this may be an excellent anti-aging treatment, the obvious downside is that you have to walk around with sperm on your face.

5 PUBIC HAIR

Fascinating Fact: Pubic hair is designed to grow a certain amount.

All hair on the body is controlled by a "growth program," which determines the growth duration, and consequently the length, of hair. Pubic hair has a shorter growth duration (just a few months, on average) compared to hair on the head. This is what stops pubic hair growing to unmanageable lengths.

4 BLOWSY GAL

Fascinating Fact: The term "blow job" comes from Victorian times.

In the Victorian era, a slang term for a prostitute was "blowsy." At the same time, "blow" was slang for ejaculation. Consequently, by the 1930s, the act of fellatio came to be known as a blow job. It was also used to describe jet planes in World War II. In ancient Greece, the common slang for a blow job was "playing the flute."

3 MALE PORN
Fascinating Fact: Men looking at male porn produce more sperm.
Studies have shown that men who looked at porn of two men and one woman produced more sperm than those who looked at just women. Scientists speculate that seeing competition makes men step up their baby-making capacity.

2 SEX FOR FUN
Fascinating Fact: Humans aren't the only creatures that have sex for fun.
Dolphins and bonobo chimps have also been observed engaging in sexual activity when they are not in their natural reproductive cycles. With the exception of a single pair of cohan gorillas who were seen having sex, bonobos are the only nonhuman animals to have been observed engaging in all of the following sexual activities: face-to-face intercourse, tongue kissing, and oral sex. When bonobos come upon a new food source or feeding ground, the increased excitement will usually lead to communal sexual activity, presumably decreasing tension and allowing for peaceful feeding. Interestingly, bonobo chimps also play and experience joy like humans.

1 ANIMAL PROSTITUTION
Fascinating Fact: Some female penguins engage in prostitution.
Believe it or not, in the wild, certain female penguins (even when in a committed relationship) will exchange sexual favors with strange males for the pebbles they need to build their nests. According to zoologist Dr. Fiona Hunter, "It tends to be females targeting single males, otherwise the partner female would beat the intruder up." On some occasions, the prostitute penguins trick the males. They carry out the elaborate courtship ritual, which usually leads to mating. Having bagged their catch, they then run off.

10 MURDERERS YOU SECRETLY LOVE

10 PATRICK BATEMAN, *AMERICAN PSYCHO*

Bateman is a unique psychopathic serial killer. He's unbelievably handsome, fit, rich, and narcissistic, and he listens to Phil Collins. The shallow, ornamental, material-based society Bateman inhabits is starting to drive him insane. The creepy, self-narrated scenes in which Bateman describes his mind unraveling while he's doing 2000-plus sit-ups, lying on a tanning bed, or putting on kiwi facial masks more expensive than most people's cars, are beyond disturbing.

The reason Bateman is on this list, beyond being a yuppie serial killer, which admittedly is kind of cool, is that somehow, at some point in the movie, we begin to feel sorry for this shallow, egotistical monster who has everything we could ever dream of.

Because as the audience we are given access to the lives of these rich-boy yuppies, we see that their internal lives are empty. Everything's an ornament: business cards and attractive blonde fiancées are just won to compare with the business cards and attractive blonde fiancées of other yuppies. We see that spending and social climbing lead only to more spending and social climbing. Bateman's character only evokes pity. While he does have a certain unique sense of cool, ultimately we just feel sorry for the poor demented bastard.

During one of the final scenes of the movie, in which Bateman sobbingly confesses to his lawyer on the phone—"I guess I've killed 20 people....maybe 40...I ate some of their brains, and I tried to cook a little"—we feel how scared he really is for his sanity, his freedom, and for being revealed for who he really is. This is how Dostoevsky portrays a person who has just committed murder in *Crime and Punishment*—scared, guilty, ashamed, alone—and I imagine this is how it really feels.

From the final monologue of the movie: "There is no catharsis. My punishment continues to elude me. And I gain no deeper knowledge of myself. No new knowledge can be extracted from my telling. This confession has meant nothing."

Note: I know some of you will say that the murders in this movie never even occurred—that it was all in Bateman's head. But you're wrong. You're dead wrong.

9 BUTCH COOLIDGE, JULES WINNFIELD, AND MARSELLUS WALLACEM, *PULP FICTION*

One of Quentin Tarantino's greatest strengths is his ability to combine the ultraviolent with the everyday, which is why *Pulp Fiction* was so original and accessible to almost everyone who watched it. There's murder, violence, and obscenity, but there are also *Seinfeld*-like discussions about the most mundane topics. That these hit men might talk about the same things we talk about with our friends is surreal, and just really freaking cool. Not to mention that all the characters above are all three-dimensional and accessible. They're bad people, but they're not just bad. They can be charming and worrisome and kind, as well. Tarantino makes them human.

All three of these guys are ultimate badasses. They take crap from absolutely no one. Ving Rhames and Bruce Willis' characters, Marsellus Wallace and Butch Coolidge, get the nod for their scene in that awful pawnshop, where they were about to murder each other and instead bond with a shared decency and the disgust they both have for sexual deviants. As much as they might dislike each other, they respect each other. They might be killers, but they're not perverted sickos.

Samuel L. Jackson's character, Jules Winnfield, gets the nod for the redemption he finds. He feels like God intervened in his life, and, not willing to ignore it or pass it off as coincidence, he decides to change his murdering ways. "I'm trying real hard here, Ringo," he says. And, though we never see what happens to him, we do witness what happens to his partner, John Travolta's character, who passes intervention off as a coincidence. Jackson's character is the only one on this list who changed his ways. Because of that, he deserves our respect, and is possibly even more badass because of it.

8 JOHN DOE, *SE7EN*

The movie *Se7en* is disturbing, frightening, dark, and melancholy. And the scope of what John Doe does is jaw-dropping. A lot of serial killers brag about numbers or trophies or the pain they've caused. A lot of serial killers kill for no reason except to cause pain, but they have no vision beyond the murders, which are ends in themselves. But all of John Doe's murders, even his own, are means to an end.

His immense scope and patience would be respectable if, say, he were doing research on cancer or studying ancient cultures, but he's a killer. Not just a killer—a monster. The most sadistic, depraved, frightening, intelligent monster ever shot on screen. What Hannibal Lecter did was peanuts compared to John Doe. While he only commits six murders, and never once on screen, and appears in the film for only 15 or 20 minutes, he still remains one of the grittiest, most visceral sadists every conceived.

7 VIC VEGA (MR. BLONDE), *RESERVOIR DOGS*

Vic Vega is the smoothest, most reserved psychopath ever shot on camera. Before he ever comes on screen, Mr. White and Mr. Pink create a myth of his actions in the foiled bank robbery. They imply that he's an unhinged psycho deviant without any self-control. But when he finally arrives at the warehouse sipping soda out of a straw, he's the epitome of cool and calm. He stands up to the most badass actor of all time: Harvey Keitel, who plays Mr. White. "Are you gonna bark all day, little doggy," he asks, "or are you gonna bite?"

He's in bewilderment that Mr. White and Mr. Pink are giving him a hard time for assassinating a few expendable hostages. His calm presence makes Mr. White and Mr. Pink look like two little schoolgirls at their first dance. On reflection, Mr. Blonde makes every other person in this entire movie look like whiny little babies (besides maybe Joe, the ringleader of the whole thing, and his son).

We feel bad for the cop getting his ear cut off—for his family—for staring into the face of a real-life psychopath, who couldn't care less if he knows anything—just wants to torture him because he enjoys it, but dammit, it's still one of the coolest scenes in all of cinema. Thank you, Mr. Blonde.

6 DANIEL PLAINVIEW, *THERE WILL BE BLOOD*

As the title of the movie suggests, there is blood, and it's Daniel Plainview who spills it. He's a self-proclaimed oil man, with a menacing mustache, dark beady eyes, and a stubborn limp—he drags around his leg as if it were an albatross he's been cursed to carry. He's stubborn and impatient; he's an alcoholic, a self-made millionaire, and a father to his creepy little son. And he murders exactly two people in this movie. The first is a vagabond who makes the mistake of impersonating his brother, and the second is the whiny, creepy preacher, Eli Sunday, who is the only character in the movie as unhappy and misguided as Plainview.

Plainview works his whole life to build an empire, and then when he's sitting on it he has no idea what to do next. He uses everything at his disposal to advance himself, but what he's really doing is taking steps backward toward depravity.

He's on this list because he's empathetic. A lot of people really do only care about themselves. A lot of people in the world really are not good people. Plainview hates other people, but he genuinely wants one person to whom he can relate. His son is this person until he goes deaf in a drilling accident and becomes unreachable to someone as impatient as Plainview. He then meets someone he believes to be his long-lost brother, and he opens up and lets himself be vulnerable until he finds out that it's not his brother at all, but just some drifter who wants to cash in on Plainview's fortune. Plainview murders the vagabond and tries to reconnect with his son, but it's too late.

He's lost. He becomes exceptionally lonely and drowns himself in decadence and alcohol in his mansion. Then he murders Eli Sunday because he's a slimy little weasel and he has nothing to live for, but, fundamentally, because Plainview sees himself in Sunday. And he hates himself more than anything else in the entire world.

5 TOMMY DEVITO, *GOODFELLAS*

Even though he's only about five-feet-four-inches tall, Joe Pesci plays the ultimate badass in this Martin Scorsese film. Whether he's stabbing someone in the chest with a pen or shooting an innocent waiter to death for a mild insult, nobody ever willingly crosses Tommy DeVito. He's ruthless, dangerous, prone to violent outbursts, has severe anger issues, and can kill people who cross him with any object that happens to be lying around. Basically, he's a psychotic, murderous Mafioso.

But he still functions. He has beautiful girlfriends and cool friends, and he's rich. Not to mention he's entertaining as hell to watch. He's somebody who would be cool to hang out with, if there weren't a substantial chance he would stab you to death in the face. He kills because he enjoys it. But at least he's honest.

More than any other person on this list, Tommy DeVito possesses undeniable charisma. After murdering a guy by stabbing him in the chest with a pen, and then later with a knife in his trunk, he goes and eats pasta at his sweet mother's house with his friends, laughing and drinking like nothing happened. The scariest thing about Tommy is that he might not even be insane. He just doesn't care. He'll shoot you, or stab your sister, for error in tact. But he's still a funny guy. ("What do you mean I'm funny? What, like a clown? What, I'm a clown?")

Even though he got what was coming to him in the end, and was extremely unstable, we all still kind of wished that Tommy was getting made in his last scene instead of getting whacked.

4 KARL CHILDERS, *SLING BLADE*

Another unforgettable movie. While most of the characters on this list are cold-blooded murderers without any morals or empathy, Karl Childers is not one of them (even though he does eat his dinner of french fried "petaters" on a table not three meters from where he just clobbered someone over the head with a lawn-mower blade).

In Billy Bob Thornton's directorial debut, in which he also plays the murderous Childers, Karl Childers is a semiretarded inmate being let go from a mental hospital in the South, decades after killing his mother with a sling blade (which some people call a Kaiser blade). Days later, he befriends a slow, fatherless young boy who quickly convinces his loving, but submissive mother to let Karl live in their garage. This sounds like a simple movie, and inherently it is, but it remains one of the sweetest, most uplifting, most genuine movies ever made. Thorton's character has been the butt of countless jokes, impersonations, and even a mock movie, but he rode it all the way to the upper echelons of Hollywood.

There is no doubt in my mind that Karl Childers is the most harmless character to ever murder two people using long, sharp objects. He's sweet and has the mental capacity of his slow 12-year-old friend and so cannot be anything but honest about what he sees, does, or witnesses. Before murdering the abusive stepfather character, Doyle (portrayed exceptionally well by country singer Dwight Yoakam), Childers asks him what numbers to dial for the police. Then when Doyle asks him why he wants to know he says, "I reckon I'm gonna kill you with this here lawn-mower blade."

That last scene pretty much sums up the entire mood of the movie. When Childers, a simpleton who was abused by his parents, sees the same thing happening to the boy he loves more than the world itself, he will not allow it. This movie would be funny, if it weren't so heart-wrenching: the story of a simple, kind man let out into a world that's too big for him to comprehend.

Note: Dwight Yoakam's character, Doyle, would also definitely earn a spot on a list of the top ten people that you want to see get brutally murdered in a movie.

3 MICKEY AND MALLORY KNOX, *NATURAL BORN KILLERS*

They're cool, casual, confident, and hot. They're funny, obnoxious, and unhinged. They're the sexiest serial killers in the world. Say hello to Mickey and Mallory Knox.

Oliver Stone got a lot of heat for making this movie. And more than one psychotic couple has cited the film as the inspiration for their own shooting sprees. John Grisham tried to sue Oliver Stone for inciting violence. Quentin Tarantino wrote the story and then removed his name from the film entirely, which I don't understand, because I'm not sure that Tarantino could have made this movie any better himself.

A lot of people think this movie promotes senseless violence, but I disagree wholeheartedly. This movie is a social commentary on the United States: the media and the phoniness stuffed down our throats at every turn. Are Mickey and Mallory psychotic? Yes. Are they evil? Maybe. But they weren't born psychotic and evil. Stone tries to make it very clear that they are products of their environment.

Neither of them were killers when they met. But there is something about their love that sparks their endless killing spree. The first time Mickey kills, it is to protect Mallory, who symbolizes natural love. Then something is unleashed. They go on a rampage, killing people because at least murder is something real. And while they kill randomly, without remorse or empathy, all the other main characters in the film are worse.

The cop chasing them is just as psychotic as they are, the warden is a masochistic sociopath, and the journalist, played by Robert Downey, Jr., is a phony who represents everything wrong with America. He's the worst because, even though he doesn't have blood on his hands (at least before the ending), he represents something more damaging and irreparable. He perpetuates the tenets of mindless passivity—to just put filler out for the lost generation out in TV land to sit back and watch.

In contrast to Robert Downey, Jr.'s phony character is the Native American shaman who tries to help Mickey and Mallory and who is not a part of the society that created and shunned them. Because of his polar separation from American culture, he represents the only purity in the movie. It's important to note that he is the only victim Mickey and Mallory regret killing and that his murder is unintentional.

They eventually slay Robert Downey, Jr.'s character at the end of the movie, even though he helps them escape and has an "epiphany," which is just as fake as everything else he represents. And maybe, just maybe, the audience could perceive Mickey and Mallory as agents of rightful retribution, wiping out all the fakeness they see around them because there's no other solution. Or maybe they're just insane.

2 ANTON CHIGURH, *NO COUNTRY FOR OLD MEN*

No Country for Old Men is a masterpiece. And while the two other male leads in this movie played their roles so well that I found myself gripping (literally gripping) the theater seat in anticipation of the ending, what truly makes this movie stand out as one of the best of all time is Javiar Bardem's character, Anton Chigurh.

He's a vicious, cold-blooded psychopath with a bad haircut who murders everything in his path. On the surface it might appear that he's after money or that he enjoys killing, but he's really just an avenger, seeking justice for every mistake ever made on earth. He doesn't care whether his victims are specifically responsible. He's not a cause, but a byproduct of the new evilness hinted at by the sheriff and the title of the film. He's the embodiment of retribution and death, killing the majority of people who have the misfortune to cross his path.

He kills out of some purpose we aren't ever shown and has morals that we can sense but can't really imagine. But while his otherworldliness should create a distance between himself and the audience, it is contrasted by his regular human actions, like eating a bag of peanuts while he's deciding whether to kill an innocent (or is he only innocent by how we see things?) gas-station owner, or drinking a bottle of milk inside Llewelyn's trailer, which he has just broken into and where he murdered everyone inside. He is human, which we can forget. He can be hurt. He gets shot and he bleeds and cringes and limps just like anyone else would. He's not from another planet.

And he's comedic in some way only Joel and Ethan Cohen could have conveyed: this dry, matter-of-fact, awkwardly candid, honest humor that's so bewildering and hypnotizing that we're not even sure if it's funny, or even whether it was meant to be. It's this contrast that makes him so accessible. Not to mention he's super badass, self-sufficient, intelligent, and cool, and he uses probably the most kickass weapon in any movie, ever: a captive bolt pistol (aka stun gun).

1 DR. HANNIBAL LECTER, THE HANNIBAL TRILOGY

Of course Dr. Lecter had to be number 1 on this list. Throughout three movies, he dazzled us with his charm and wit. In *Silence of the Lambs*, we heard about his vile crimes before we ever met the man. And, at first, we might have believed that Hannibal was just a kindly old man, trapped in a brick cell for crimes that sound a little too exaggerated. But very soon we see that isn't the case at all. His creepiness and power are cerebral. Within minutes of meeting her, he puts dainty Clarice Starling on her psychological ass. His murders are some of the most violent, and yet he remains sophisticated and respectable, no matter how deranged his actions. Not only does he have a svelte, hypnotic voice that manipulates victims and other serial killers alike, he is also the most intelligent and classy serial killer we've ever met.

While Mickey and Mallory Knox might dine on some greasy breakfast food at a truck stop, our dear Hannibal requires nothing less than the finest caviar and Chianti to be found anywhere in the world. Whether cutting off guard's faces, feeding an out-of-tune violinist to a table of aristocrats, getting one of his patients to cut off his own face and feed it to his dogs, or biting off a nurse's tongue while his heartbeat remains under 85 beats per minute, Dr. Lecter remains a true gentleman to the end, not killing good people unless he has to and cutting off his own hand instead of Clarice's—his muse—when push comes to shove.

And just as we can see the progression of affection our dear Clarice feels for this man (although she would never admit it), we, too, become paralyzed by his charm, even knowing all that we know. Detective Will Graham calls him insane, and he probably is—must be—but a part of all Hannibal Lecter's fans realize how thin the line between genius and insanity really is.

CHAPTER FOUR
Food and Drink

10 BIZARRE FOOD FESTIVALS

10 NOCHE DE RÁBANOS (NIGHT OF THE RADISHES)
Where: Oaxaca, Mexico
When: December 23–24

This is a food festival where eating is discouraged! This festival originated in the 16th century when Spanish monks brought the radish to the new colonies. To gain attention in the food markets, sellers would carve the edible roots into eye-catching sculptures. This tradition continued throughout the centuries and became an official festival in 1987. Radishes as big as two feet long and weighing upward of ten pounds are carved into intricate religious or cultural scenes. The artisans can compete in three different categories for cash prizes.

9 ANNUAL TESTICLE FESTIVAL
Where: Clinton, Montana
When: Early August

There are several imitators, but this is the original ballfest. Usually known by its classier name, the Rocky Mountain Oyster Festival, this whole event is dedicated to serving deep-fried bull testicles. You can have your choice of plain, deep-fried, beer-battered, or marinated, as well as some newly concocted delectables. For the indecisive, five dollars can provide a sampler plate of testicles. Those on a low-testicle diet can have fun as well! One of the highlights of the festival is Bullshit Bingo, with a grand prize of $100 for the lucky person who can correctly predict where a cow will do its doodie. The motto of this dignified event? "I had a ball at the Testicle Festival."

8 WORLD PEA-SHOOTING CHAMPIONSHIP
Where: Witcham, Cambridgeshire, UK
When: July

This is loosely called a food festival since the food isn't celebrated; rather, it's like a block party that grew out of a simple target-shooting competition. In 1971, local headmaster Mr. Tyson held the first pea-shooting competition as a way to fundraise for the upkeep of the village hall. The entrance fee is only one pound for adults and 50 pence for children, but be warned! The competitors take this extreme sport seriously, and you'll need hi-tech gear (like the laser-guided pea shooter) to stand a chance on the field with these seasoned pea-shooting veterans.

7 ROADKILL COOK-OFF AT THE AUTUMN HARVEST FESTIVAL
Where: Marlington, West Virginia
When: Late September

Nobody panic! None of the entries in this harvest festival competition has any tire marks since they aren't actually unfortunate outcomes of "Why did the chicken cross the road?" jokes. This competition utilizes wild game such as raccoon, opossum, and deer...basically any of Bambi's friends that could be potential roadkill. Does that make it better? No? Oh, well... notables among the past wild-game entries are Spicy Venison, Buffalo, and Sausage Stew, Pulled BamBiTo under Saboogo, and Biscuits and Squirrel Gravy.

6 GILROY GARLIC FESTIVAL
Where: Gilroy, California
When: Late July

Gilroy is the unofficial "Garlic Capital of the World" and proudly shows it off in this festival that attracts over 100,000 visitors annually who consume an

 estimated two-and-a-half tons of garlic at the event. The official Gilroy Garlic Festival website claims to have used 72 tons of garlic in the 29 years this festival has existed. Cooking demonstrations and lectures discuss traditional uses and health benefits, but the innovative can always express their love for this pungent food in the Great Garlic Cook-off, which has had entries like garlic ice cream, garlic soft drinks, and last year's winner, "Walnut-Garlic Tart with Garlic-Infused Cream and Chili Syrup." Anyone need a Tic Tac?

5 WAIKIKI SPAM JAM
Where: Waikiki, Hawaii
When: Late April

An area with a scarce meat supply during World War II, this archipelago embraced the blue-canned pink meat and has now become SPAM's most loyal market. During this street festival, hula dancers perform while judges crown a Mr. and Miss Spam, and Hawaii's top chefs create new recipes celebrating the gelatinous meat product. Pedestrians get to sample everything from SPAM burgers to SPAM *musubi* (kind of like sushi but with SPAM instead of fish). This festival benefits the Hawaii Food Bank, the largest nonprofit in Hawaii that feeds the needy.

4 IVREA ORANGE FESTIVAL
Where: Ivrea, Italy
When: Last date: Mid to Late February

The Ivrea Orange Festival originated in the 12th century, when during parades and city celebrations, girls would throw oranges from their balconies to gain the attention of the boy they liked. The boys began to reciprocate—there's no mention anywhere if the secret admiration was returned, but the oranges certainly were!—and this evolved into a messy rivalry between the balcony girls and the street boys. It wasn't until World War II that the intricate citrus battle rules were finally laid out. It's free for anyone to participate by joining one of the nine teams on foot or becoming a member of the carriage crew.

3 CANDY-THROWING FIGHT, CARNIVAL AT VILANOVA I LA GELTRÚ
Where: Vilanova i La Geltrú, Spain
When: Fat Tuesday

Originally a protest of the Franco regime's Carnivale prohibition, this annual festival is by far the sweetest food fight in the world! Celebrations begin on Fat Tuesday with the Meringue Wars, where bakeries open their stores and pass out free pie ammunition to children. The adults dress in the colors of their respective Carnival societies and attend parties and masquerades before joining the children in the streets in what becomes a sweet tooth free-for-all! Over 200,000 pounds of food, ranging from pies to candy to cereal, have been donated to the food fight—it's a dentist's nightmare! The festival officially ends with the ceremonial burial of a sardine to mark the beginning of Lent and the fast.

2 OLNEY PANCAKE RACE
Where: Olney, England, UK
When: Pancake Day (Fat Tuesday)

At 11:55 a.m. on Shrove Tuesday (aka Pancake Day, aka Fat Tuesday), the local ladies assemble, dressed in traditional housewife attire (including skirts, aprons, and scarves), and run 415 yards through the streets of Olney carrying pancakes in frying pans. The pancakes are tossed at the start of the race and the winner must toss her pancake again at the finish. The race has been an Olney tradition since 1445, and in 1950, the competition expanded to include a friendly flapjack rivalry with the housewives and young women of Liberal, Kansas. The ladies of Liberal won this past year's race with a new record of 57.5 seconds.

1 ANNUAL YUMA LETTUCE DAYS
Where: Yuma, Arizona
When: Late January

Yuma is known as "The Winter Lettuce Capital of the World." Sounds silly, yes, but considering Yuma produces $1.5 billion of Arizona's agriculture revenue and provides 90 percent of North America's winter vegetables, it's appropriate to respect the lettuce. Among the highlights of this veggie fair are the lettuce sculptures, cabbage bowling, Homegrown Cooking Contest, and the "World's Largest Salad."

10 BIZARRE EATING DISORDERS

10 ORTHOREXIA
Characterized by the obsession with eating healthy foods, this disease can be confused with and/or diagnosed as anorexia; the main difference is the reasoning behind the eating habits. Anorexics are obsessed with losing weight, while orthorexics feel a need for healthy or "pure" foods. Orthorexia is not recognized by the Diagnostic and Statistical Manual of Mental Disorders (DSM-IV) and, in general, will not be diagnosed, but it is seeing a greater stronghold across the U.S.

9 PRADER-WILLI SYNDROME
Prader-Willi Syndrome (PWS) is caused by a chromosomal defect that brings on an insatiable appetite. It is nonhereditary and affects both sexes and

all races. PWS can bring with it a number of symptoms, including motor-skill deficiency, incomplete growth, and mental retardation. Left unchecked, sufferers can literally eat themselves to death. Treatment includes taking growth hormones and eating a low-cal diet that absolutely must be maintained. A fictionalized account of Prader-Willi was seen on the show *CSI* in 2005.

8 PICA

Pica is both an eating disorder and a psychiatric problem. People with pica feel a compulsion to eat non-nutritional and non-food items. These can include anything from cigarette butts to paint. It is quite easy to get sick or even die from pica, as the sufferer can eat dangerous chemicals or sharp objects that can puncture their vital organs.

7 BIGOREXIA

Often called the opposite of anorexia, bigorexia is the only disorder on this list with more male sufferers than women. Bigorexics compulsively workout, take supplements, and severely restrict their diets. No matter how muscular and sculpted their bodies are, those with the disease are shy or even humiliated to show off their figures because in their minds they just aren't big enough. Statistics vary widely, since in addition to the embarrassment from the illness, eating disorders have long been seen as women's or girls' diseases, and many bigorexic men will not come forward.

6 BINGE EATING DISORDER

Binge eating is a separate condition from bulimia. It is thought to be the most common eating disorder, yet is specified in the DSM-IV as a part of a broad category of EDNOS, or Eating Disorder Not Otherwise Specified. Binge eating sufferers do not have the love of food that most compulsive food hoarders do. Like anorexics and bulimics, binge eaters are ashamed of their bodies and generally are embarrassed about their eating habits.

5 ANOREXIA ATHLETICA

While not technically an eating-related illness in and of itself, this condition is almost never diagnosed without the presence of another eating disorder. As the name suggests, a person with anorexia athletica goes beyond the normal feeling most of us have after a nice long run or a good session in the gym.

The feeling is not optional for those with the disease, and they will often push themselves to overexertion or even serious injury to achieve the perfect body.

4 NIGHT EATING SYNDROME

NES is a new disorder, yet, like orthorexia, it is gaining in diagnosis. Night eating sufferers, who are usually obese or morbidly obese, eat almost nothing in the morning and during the day and eat over half of their daily calories at night. They often experience insomnia or wake up during the night to indulge. Like others with eating disorders, people with NES are often secretive about their habits and are loathe to admit there is a problem.

3 BODY DYSMORPHIC DISORDER

While BDD can be diagnosed without the presence of an eating disorder, it is nearly almost diagnosed along with the "big two" (bulimia and anorexia nervosa) and often lingers long after other symptoms have lessened. People with BDD are convinced they have any number of defects, including but not limited to being fat and ugly and having bad hair and teeth, and an unpleasant odor. This goes beyond the normal teenage insecurities about how someone looks. When a BDD sufferer looks in the mirror, they see something completely different than those around them do.

2 BULIMIA NERVOSA

Bulimia is characterized by binge-purge cycles. When most people think of bulimics, they think of self-induced vomiting. While this is one of the most common ways to purge, bulimics will also use diuretics and enemas. Additionally, bulimics will use ipecac syrup or may overexercise to induce vomiting. Bulimics are very aware that their behavior is both abnormal and frowned upon and will go to great lengths to hide it. Interestingly, bulimics with a balanced binge-purge cycle are generally a normal weight. It is only those who purge more than they binge who exhibit the external signs of an eating disorder.

1 ANOREXIA NERVOSA

Newest studies estimate that 1 out of 100 teenage girls suffers from anorexia. Girls as young as eight have been hospitalized with the condition. Brain mapping anorexics shows their addiction to not eating is just as great as those with heavy drug or alcohol addiction. Anorexics are at great risk for relapse because anorexia and other eating disorders, like most addictions, never go away. Those who have been through treatment and no longer show symptoms or signs of their condition are considered in remission and must keep their impulses and urges in check. Even years down the line, one event can retrigger the illness. However, those who do manage to keep the disease in line can recover fully and live and eat normally.

10 WEIRDEST FOODS TO GET YOU IN THE MOOD

10 SOUP #5

"Strong like a bull" is a phrase that attracts some lovers to this four-legged mammal with a notorious temper. In areas of Southeast Asia, a soup (known as Soup #5) composed of onions, carrots, broth, and bull's penis and testicles, is a popular dish noted for its aphrodisiac properties. The parts in question are given a good scrubbing and are scalded in boiling water for good measure before they wind up in an aromatic soup loaded with vegetables. Unlike some truly wild aphrodisiacs that are potentially harmful, bull's soup is pretty tame by any stretch of the imagination. And while ostrich testicles are said to be tasty, they fall short in the bedroom when compared to the hardy bull variety.

9 FUGU

The sea offers a bounty of strangely arousing aphrodisiacs. One of the weirdest is also one of the deadliest. The blowfish is heralded "fugu" by Japanese chefs who must be specially licensed to prepare and serve this potentially deadly delicacy. Studies show that the toxin in these creatures is far more lethal than cyanide. Eating this specially prepared dish causes the mouth to feel numb. As the numb feeling wears off, people remark on a lingering tingling on their lips and inside their cheeks. This tingling is said to greatly promote sexual arousal.

8 COBRA

Clearly, many of the world's weirdest aphrodisiac dishes come from dangerous animals. Shark fin soup is a notorious aphrodisiac whose popularity is causing the shark population to drop alarmingly in some waters, particularly in Asia. While hunting shark is no walk in the park, catching cobras for their sweet meat is no sport for shrinking violets either. Snakes have sexual connotations that go back centuries, but eating cobras to enhance sex is a thoroughly contemporary practice in many parts of Asia. In some concoctions, cobra blood is mixed with a beverage containing alcohol. Cobra meat is also eaten for its aphrodisiac qualities. Of course, before eating this preparation, it would be wise to know the cook's credentials first.

7 BIRD'S NEST SOUP

Bird's nest soup is an Asian delicacy that lovers must pay top dollar to procure. Bird's nest soup is, indeed, the edible nests made from the saliva of cave-dwelling swiftlet birds. The nests are formed along cave walls and are extremely difficult to obtain, even by experienced cave-wall climbers. Nevertheless, they have been served to royalty and other highly respected people for centuries and are renowned for their ability to stimulate the libido. The soup is one of the most expensive animal-based dishes in the world; save it for a special occasion!

6 CATERPILLAR FUNGUS

Cordyceps, historically known as caterpillar fungus, or *dong chong xia cao* in China, has been revered in the East as an aphrodisiac extraordinaire. This most incredible fungus is a parasite of sorts; it invades the brains of caterpillar larvae and grows there, eventually replacing native tissue with its own. One can wonder how its aphrodisiac properties were
discovered, but this mushroom has been a popular libido-booster for centuries. Today it is actually cultivated so that it can be purchased quite inexpensively, unlike many other weird culinary aphrodisiacs. A plate of cordyceps and a glass of champagne could be the making of the Valentine's night of your life!

5 SPANISH FLY

Some people will do anything for love—even ingest a potentially lethal substance that makes the privates swell up, itch, and secrete a bloody discharge. Ingesting Spanish fly is a famously historic way to stimulate the libido. The Spanish fly, actually a beetle, would be crushed and eaten for a substance it produces called cantharidin. Humans dispel this substance through urine, which is how it comes to irritate the genitals. Of course, Spanish fly enthusiasts are lucky if all they get is an itch. A moderate dose can lead to death by causing fever, convulsions, and seizures. Many love shops try to sell Spanish fly potions, but these are, fortunately, mostly imitations that offer a placebo effect. The use of Spanish fly as an aphrodisiac goes all the way back to the ancient Roman world.

4 BALUT

Balut is another popular Asian dish served with love in mind. Balut is a duck egg that contains a fetus. The egg is boiled and served. This dish is said to have Viagra-like properties, so it is of particular interest to men. Once the fetus or embryo is consumed, the stimulation is thought to begin. Often served nestled within its broken outer shell, this dish is a weird aphrodisiac that is a real bargain compared with bird's nest soup. And because ducks are not on the endangered species list, this dish is quite legal to order, unlike the next item on this list…

3 HORN AND PENIS

Rhino horn and tiger's penis are definitely outlawed, but that does not stop poachers and a thriving black market from continuing to offer them. For centuries, people have eaten parts of these wild animals to stimulate or enhance their sexual ability. Men suffering from impotence are the usual market for these aphrodisiacs in some parts of the world. Although weird and illegal, these continue to be revered sexual stimulants.

2 AMBERGRIS

Ambergris should be a familiar term to all you English students who read *Moby Dick* in high school. The sweet, expensive stuff was the sperm whale's elixir, which went into perfumes during the height of the whaling industry. This heady stuff was prized during the 18th and 19th centuries when whale oil powered the world. Melville didn't mention its aphrodisiac properties, but some Arabian texts recommend its use in the bedroom. Today, many believe that ambergris can boost sexual excitement and vigor. Ambergris is rare and not easy to procure; it is another of the sea's sexually charming elements that doubles as a weird aphrodisiac.

1 ASS'S MILK

Some weird aphrodisiacs are merely topical in nature. For example, ass's milk was a renowned aphrodisiac for ancient Arabs and Romans. Women who rubbed the milk on their genitals felt stimulated by its effects, and men were thought to increase their virility by likewise using it topically. Legend has it that the wife of Nero bathed in the milk for its sexually stimulating effects.

9 UNUSUAL FOOD COMBINATIONS

9 CARROTS AND SUGAR

While it may seem strange to add sugar to vegetables, it is a very common method of preparing carrots in France. The proper name for this dish is Vichy Carrots, in which you combine carrots, salt, pepper, sugar, and Vichy water (a sparkling water from the Vichy region) and cook them down until the carrots are glazed. The sugar heightens the flavor of the carrots, and the end result is a stunning dish of brilliant-orange vegetables.

8 COFFEE AND SALT

Add a touch of salt to coffee to heighten the flavor, just like salt is used in virtually all dishes, including sweets. Just a pinch is enough to make a fantastic espresso.

7 TOMATOES AND SUGAR

Use sugar, not salt. Tomatoes are already acidic, and the addition of salt just increases that acidic flavor. Sugar sweetens and increases the tomato flavor. Tomatoes are fruits, after all.

6 MEAT AND ANISEED

When stewing meat, throw in a star anise; you won't taste the aniseed, but the flavor adds a deep richness to the meat. This is a trick used in all meat dishes created by Heston Blumenthal, the owner of the Fat Duck, voted the world's best restaurant for three years in a row and the bearer of three Michelin stars.

5 TOMATOES AND FOLIAGE

When you cook tomatoes, throw in a tomato branch. The branch contains all the flavor that we love in tomatoes; pick a leaf and smell it and you'll see what I mean. Simply throw in a small stick from the tomato plant to give your cooked tomatoes a much stronger tomato flavor.

4 POTATOES AND NUTMEG

Add nutmeg—just a little—to add a depth to the potatoes that people won't recognize, but they'll definitely like. This works for virtually every potato dish.

3 CHILI AND CHOCOLATE

Add chocolate to a pot of chili. It deepens the meaty flavor of the chili while giving a strong base note to the chile peppers in the dish. This is a trick well-known in the Southwest, where chili cook-offs are common.

2 APPLES AND VANILLA

Apples are very acidic and normally require some sugar in their cooking. Most people add nutmeg or cinnamon to their apple dishes, but vanilla extract adds a surprisingly deep layer of flavor.

1 STRAWBERRIES AND PEPPER

Fresh strawberries are often served with a sprinkling of confectioners' sugar, but the addition of very finely ground pepper (from fresh peppercorns) heightens the flavor.

10 MOST BIZARRE SOUPS

10 MENUDO

This is a personal favorite of mine, but some may find cow stomach soup to be a little odd. Menudo is a traditional Mexican soup that is very popular and often made for special occasions. It is also widely known as a cure all for hangovers. Menudo consists of tripe or cow stomach, onions, cilantro, oregano, chiles, and hominy. It takes anywhere from seven to ten hours to make, as the meat needs to cook for an extended time to make it tender. Some people wonder how stomach lining can be delicious, but when you add all of the other ingredients and let it simmer for hours, what you get is an insanely good soup. The tripe is so tender it almost melts in your mouth. Add some corn tortillas for dipping and you've got yourself a meal. Who knew cow stomach could be so good? The origin of menudo varies; found throughout Mexico, the soup most likely came from a need to use every part of the cow, in this case stomach lining. You can find the soup in most Mexican restaurants.

9 KIBURU SOUP

Perhaps the simplest soup on the list comes to us from the Chagga tribe that lives at the base of Mount Kilimanjaro. The tribe depends on agriculture, mostly bananas and coffee, for their livelihood. A no-frills lifestyle gets you a no-frills soup made of sweet bananas, beans, and dirt, or "earth," as they call it. Essentially, the ingredients are all mixed together to form the soup. The dirt, including bits of twigs, supposedly gives the soup a saltiness and an earthy flavor.

8 SUPU SOUP

This soup reminds me a little of menudo, with many parts of the animal being used to create a flavorful soup or stew. "*Supu*" simply means "soup," but the breakfast version of this Tanzanian soup is the most extravagant, made from goat lungs, heart, liver, and head, as well as cow stomach, intestines, and tongue. If you're lucky, you might even get a cow hoof and tail thrown in. The hooves are sometimes boiled, and then the soup is called *supu ya makongoro*. The version of the soup that's eaten for breakfast is a traditional dish in Tanzania and is widely known to cure hangovers.

7 CHICKEN TESTICLE SOUP

This is very similar to our traditional chicken noodle soup, except that it has chicken testicles instead of other chicken meat. The soup, simply made from testicles and vegetables, is cooked in broth until tender. The testicles are creamy on the inside and very soft, like tofu but with tight skin like a sausage. Some have compared it to an undercooked egg with a custard consistency. Again, the testicles are said to have good side effects; in this case, good skin for the women and stamina for the men. The soup can be made from both black and white chicken testicles.

6 BIRD'S NEST SOUP

One of the most expensive soups on the list, bird's nest soup is made from the nests of swiftlet birds. The Chinese dish is a delicacy and sells for as much as $30 to $100 per bowl; a kilogram (2.2 pounds) of the nest can cost up to $2000. The bird's nests have been in Chinese cooking. Male swiftlet birds take more than 35 days to make their nests in caves. The cup-shaped nests are interwoven strands of salivary cement, so soup made from the nests is almost entirely from the birds' sticky saliva. The nests

dissolve and become gelatinous in water. Some common health benefits that are associated with the soup are better focus, improved breathing, increased libido, and a strengthened immune system.

5 DEER PLACENTA SOUP

In Shanghai, China, you can have deer placenta soup that will help your sex drive, kidneys, skin, and vitality (I'm starting to see a trend here). The soup is made from mushrooms, flowers, black chicken (which must be where the black testicles come from), and deer tendon in a broth. While the soup actually sounds good, the placenta is elastic, which makes it chewy. If you don't know exactly what a placenta is, here is the definition to make it even more appetizing: it's the sac-shaped organ that attaches the embryo or fetus to the uterus during pregnancy in most mammals. Blood flows between mother and fetus through the placenta, supplying oxygen and nutrients to the fetus and carrying away fetal waste products. The placenta is expelled after birth.

4 SHIRAKO SOUP, OR COD'S SPERM SOUP

Known as cod's milk soup in the U.S. and *shirako* in Japan, this soup is essentially the sperm sac of male codfish. The sperm sac cooks until it melts down into a chowderlike broth and becomes creamy, almost like custard. "*Shirako*" appropriately means "white children" and is available in the winter. As with many animal parts that have special qualities in Asian cuisine, cod's sperm supposedly gives you stamina in bed. There is a restaurant in New York that serves the dish as a specialty.

3 FRUIT BAT SOUP

This next soup wouldn't be so bad if they would at least take the fuzzy fur off the bat. In the islands of Palau, this soup is again a delicacy (although I'm starting to think many of these "delicacies" came from unknowing tourists willing to try anything). The island has two types of bats: insect-eating bats and large fruit bats. The latter are cooked in coconut milk, ginger, and spices and are boiled for several hours. At some restaurants, the customer is able to choose his or her bat before cooking it alive in boiling water. Many people who have tried the soup say it's delicious, although having a furry rodentlike head staring at you can be unsettling.

2 TIGER PENIS SOUP

There are many penis soups out there, but this is by far one of the most rare and expensive. Tiger penis soup has been around for centuries in Asian cultures, known for its almost mythical properties akin to Viagra. The dried tiger penis is soaked in water for a week and then simmered for up to 24 hours with other spices and medicines, at times with tiger bone. A single bowl of soup can cost you up to $400.

Tigers are a protected endangered species, yet many Asian markets still carry tiger parts in their shops. A recent survey of New York's Chinatown revealed that 60 percent of the shops claimed to carry tiger parts, although it is illegal. Some shop owners claiming to sell tiger penis often substitute ox or deer tendons for the real thing.

1 *TIET CAHN*, OR VIETNAMESE BLOOD SOUP

Finally, we have a soup so bizarre it can hardly be called a soup at all. It's a traditional soup in Vietnamese cuisine made from simple ingredients: raw blood (usually duck), cooked gizzards, and topped with peanuts and herbs. The soup is refrigerated so the blood coagulates and can then be eaten chilled before the blood loses its Jell-O–like consistency. Supposedly, the soup gives both the person making and eating it strength. Its popularity has declined since the bird flu spread through Asia. Although many still eat it, there is concern for the public's health in consuming raw blood from ducks. Did I really have to tell you that, though?

10 CRAZIEST DIETS EVER

10 MACROBIOTIC DIET

The macrobiotic diet is actually quite ancient. It involves eating grains as a staple food, supplementing with foods such as vegetables and beans, and avoiding the use of highly processed or refined foods. This is probably the least bizarre diet on the list, but it does have one noticeable quirk: some leaders in the field of macrobiotics advocate smoking for good health, claiming that nonmacrobiotic foods—not smoking—cause cancer. Michio Kushi, who introduced macrobiotics to the U.S., had surgery on his colon in 2004. After speaking with the doctor, Michio's son said, "In spite of years of his smoking, a fact well-known to many, recent x-rays of Michio's lungs were surprisingly clean, like that of a 20 year old."

9 CABBAGE SOUP DIET

The cabbage soup diet is a radical weight-loss plan designed around heavy consumption of a low-calorie cabbage soup over a period of seven days. The diet is actually surprisingly popular and has spawned a whole slew of similar fads. The origins of the diet are unknown, but it gained popularity by word of "faxlore" in the 1980s because it spread virally through people sharing it via fax machines. The diet is almost universally condemned by doctors because it lacks any substantial nutrition and the weight loss it causes is mostly water-loss, not fat-loss, and is, therefore, not permanent. The diet is usually touted as being used in hospitals to dramatically reduce weight in patients needing heart surgery; this is not true. Most people trying this diet lose energy and experience light-headedness. The most common side effect is flatulence—a lot of it.

8 PALEOLITHIC DIET

This diet harkens back to cavemen and their eating habits. It's based on the presumed ancient diet of wild plants and animals that various human species habitually consumed during the Paleolithic period—a span of about 2.5 million years that ended around 10,000 years ago with the development of agriculture. Proponents of the diet say that Paleolithic men were free of diseases known in modern times and, therefore, following their diet should keep us from getting sick. Centered around commonly available modern foods, the "contemporary" Paleolithic diet consists mainly of lean meat, fish, vegetables, fruit, roots, and nuts. It excludes grains, legumes, dairy products, salt, refined sugar, and processed oils.

Now we move from a diet based on evolution to one based on creationism:

7 FRUITARIANISM

Fruitarianism is a diet of nothing but fruit, though some people consider themselves fruitarian if their diet is 75 percent or more fruit. Some fruitarians

believe fruitarianism was the original diet of mankind in the form of Adam and Eve based on Genesis 1:29: "And God said: Behold I have given you every herb bearing seed upon the earth, and all trees that have in themselves seed of their own kind, to be your meat." Fruitarians believe that a return to an Eden-like paradise will require simple living and a holistic approach to health and diet. A fruitarian diet can cause deficiencies in calcium, protein, iron, zinc, vitamin D, most B vitamins (especially B-12), and essential fatty acids. Additionally, the Health Promotion Program at Columbia University reports that food restrictions in general may lead to hunger, cravings, food obsessions, social disruptions, and social isolation. Gandhi followed a fruit-only diet from time to time, but eventually gave it up due because it was unsustainable.

Now, if you didn't think that was weird enough, how about the Bible Diet?

6 BIBLE DIET

The Bible diet (or Maker's diet) is based on the idea that certain foods are either forbidden ("unclean") or acceptable ("clean") to God. The main promoter of the Bible diet is Jordan S. Rubin, who claims that the diet was responsible for his recovery from Crohn's disease at the age of 19. In 2004, the United States Food and Drug Administration ordered Rubin's company, Garden of Life, Inc., to stop making unsubstantiated claims about eight of its products and supplements. The diet begins and ends each day with prayers of thanksgiving, healing, and petition. The individual should perform exercises of "life purpose" for two to five minutes before the day gets too stressful. To achieve the utmost spiritual benefits from the partial fast days, it is suggested that dieters pray each time hunger is experienced.

5 SHANGRI-LA DIET

For people who love to eat, the Shangri-La diet is a godsend. Basically, you can eat what you like. The principle behind this diet is that the body has a set point (the weight that it wants to sustain) and appetite is moderated by the body to ensure that you stay there. The inventor of the diet, Seth Roberts, says that you can lower your set point using his method, thereby lowering appetite and eventually weight. The method? Every day you must drink 100 to 400 calories of extra-light olive oil or sugar water in a two-hour window in which you must experience no flavors (including cigarette smoke). It is the consumption of extra flavorless calories that supposedly lowers the set point. While there are some critics of the method (which earned Roberts a spot on the *New York Times* bestseller list), most doctors believe the diet, while lacking scientific evidence, is benign.

4 FLETCHERIZING

"Nature will castigate those who don't masticate." These were the words used by Horace Fletcher at the turn of the 20th century to market his new diet: Fletcherizing. On this diet, a person must chew each mouthful of food 32 times while keeping their head tilted forward. After the chewing is complete, the dieter tilts their head back, allowing the contents of their mouth to slide down their throat. Any food that does not naturally slip down must be spat out. In addition, Fletcher advocated chewing liquids and said that one must not eat when angry or sad. Fletcher died a millionaire at age 69, with the majority of his money having come from promoting his diet, which was wildly popular.

3 BREATHARIANISM

Breatharianism consists of eating nothing. That's right—it's called breatharianism because you survive on nothing but your breath. There are some elements of esotericism in this diet, and some practitioners believe that they're sustained by energy from the sun or a "vital life force" called prana. The Breatharian Institute of America promotes the diet and offers a workshop to help you get started for the low price of just $10,000, which, according to their website "is not a misprint." These courses are run by Wiley Brooks, who previously charged up to $25 million for his courses. Occasionally Wiley eats a cheeseburger and a diet coke, claiming that when he's surrounded by junk culture and junk food, consuming them adds balance. At least three people have died while on this "diet."

2 SLEEPING BEAUTY DIET

As its name implies, this diet involves sleep—a lot of it. The principle behind this diet is "if you aren't awake, you aren't eating." Consequently, advocates take heavy sedatives and sleep for days at a time in order to lose weight. Obviously the diet works, but it's such an unhealthy approach to weight loss that it's insane to try it. The diet was originally formulated in the 1970s and was reportedly popular with Elvis Presley, who was beginning to have difficulty bending down to tie up his blue suede shoes.

1 TAPEWORM DIET

This is as disgusting as it sounds. On this diet, you eat a tapeworm and let it grow in your body until it's fully mature. You then worm yourself and poop out the worm. Advocates of this insane diet assure people that they can lose one to two pounds per week using the method. Because it is illegal to import tapeworms into the U.S., some organizations run tapeworm farms in Africa and Mexico, which tourists can visit to get infected "safely." On these farms, cows are intentionally infected with tapeworm for harvesting for human consumption. This diet is alleged to work because once ingested, the worm attaches in the intestinal tract and absorbs nutrients from the food you eat.

10 FAILED MCDONALD'S PRODUCTS

10 MCGRATIN CROQUETTE

This special McDonald's burger designed for the Japanese market was a dismal failure. Why did it fail? Perhaps it was the fact that it contained deep-fried macaroni, shrimp, and mashed potatoes. Perhaps it was the fact that it was served on a bed of cabbage. Or maybe it was the name, which really is unlike anything ever seen at McDonald's. Despite all of its faults, it does still show up as a seasonal offering in parts of Japan. This one wins the fail award not for losing money, but for being plain awful.

9 HULABURGER

The Hulaburger was the most famous flop of Ray Krok, the man who bought the small-time McDonald's company and turned it into the megafranchise we know today. The burger, which was created in 1963, was aimed at Roman Catholics who were forbidden to eat meat on Fridays. It was basically a cheeseburger but with a slice of pineapple instead of meat. The burger was a disaster, unlike the Filet-O-Fish, which was being marketed at the same time by a Cincinnati franchise.

8 MCDLT

The McDonald's Lettuce and Tomato was given to consumers in a special split package that held the two parts of the burger. The consumer would then combine the two parts and eat them together. The packaging was unwieldy and the entire thing went against the general principle of fast food in that you had to prepare it yourself. Needless to say, despite extensive advertising, the product flopped. McDonald's relaunched the McDLT already assembled for you under the new name "Big N' Tasty."

7 ARCH DELUXE

The Arch Deluxe was meant to be a burger marketed at adults, with more expensive ingredients and a marketing campaign that cost over $100 million. Despite the advertising, which involved scenes of Ronald McDonald enjoying adult activities, the product was a failure and heads of management fell.

6 MCLOBSTER

Why did it fail? The price! Who wants to spend $5.99 on a fast food burger that you know won't satisfy your hunger? And let's face it—it looked like someone threw up in a bun! This product is actually still available in some Canadian franchises and occasionally in Maine. Frankly, if you want lobster, you aren't going to McDonald's to get it. Perhaps next they'll introduce the McFoieGras or the McCaviar.

5 MCHOTDOG

McDonald's was originally prohibited from selling hotdogs because the founder considered them unhygienic, but some stores began selling them in the 1990s. For unknown reasons, the product has never taken off, despite repeated attempts to reintroduce it to the market.

4 MCPIZZA

The McPizza just never took off because people generally preferred to buy their pizzas from trusted pizza parlors. Despite a huge marketing campaign, the McPizza was eventually abandoned and has not been seen since.

3 MCPASTA

McDonald's has tried on more than one occasion to market pasta, with the likes of lasagna, fettuccine, and spaghetti and meatballs being added to the menu. The most likely cause of the McPasta's demise is that, unlike fries and burgers, people want their pasta to be flavorsome, not bland. The company tried pasta meals for kids in New Zealand and Australia, but both countries are considering removing them from their menus due to low demand.

2 MCAFRICA

What is the worst thing you could possibly do when widespread famine in Africa is all over the news? Release and market a McAfrica burger—something to chow down on while watching poor, starving children on TV. The problem with this product was not in the bad flavor, it was in the terrible timing of the advertising campaign. This wasn't the first time McDonald's made this mistake—in Norway in 2002, they released the McAfrica, which contained beef and vegetables in pita bread. The backlash was severe, so McDonald's put donation boxes for famine relief in all stores selling the product. With such brilliant marketing, perhaps we can look forward to a McHolocaust in the future.

1 MCLEAN DELUXE
The first problem with this burger was that men were turned off it (much like they were Diet Coke, which lead to Coke Zero). The next problem was its taste. In the ads, McDonald's sold it as "low fat but tastes great"—but it didn't. The fat that was removed was replaced with water, but to make the water stay in the meat, it was mixed with carrageenan—that's seaweed to you and me. The burger tasted awful, had a limited market, and failed dismally, which is really no surprise.

10 UNUSUAL USES FOR COCA-COLA

10 RUST BUSTER
Coca-Cola is an excellent rust buster. If you have a bunch of small objects that need de-rusting, soak them in Coke overnight and give them a good scrub in the morning. The properties of Coke help to break down the rust particles, making cleaning much easier. You can also apply Coke to a chrome finish that has rust spots—pour some on a rough-textured cloth and rub it in a circular motion on the rust. Be sure to throw out the used Coke when you are done with it, or you might be taking a trip to the doctor.

9 CLEAN A WINDOW
Like in number 10, the citric acid in Coke makes for an excellent window cleaner. This is especially useful for car windows, which can get tough buildups

of gunk. Pour the can of Coke over the window and rub, then wipe it off with a damp cloth to ensure the removal of any sticky residue from the sugars in the drink. Think of this as a cheap alternative to the many citrus-based cleaners that are sold on TV.

8 EAT IT

Coke can be used for a variety of cooking techniques. You can mix it half and half with BBQ sauce for an excellent marinade, and you can even cook an entire chicken in it. The sugars give the chicken a deep, glossy coating and caramelized flavor, while the citric acid gives a nice tang. Coke also makes a great glaze for baked ham.

7 DE-SKUNK

For those of you who live in areas where skunk smells can be an issue from time to time, one can of Coke added to a bucket of water with detergent really helps to break the odor down. If you've been sprayed, stand in the shower and cover yourself from head to toe with Coke; wait for a few minutes, then rinse off. The added bonus is that Coke is an excellent hair treatment, so this list item is two for the price of one!

6 PAIN KILLER

The chemicals in Coca-Cola can be very effective to help neutralize the pain of jellyfish stings. The best thing about this is that while most people at the beach are unlikely to be carrying anti-sting lotions, there's a good chance they have a bottle of Coke. Just pour the Coke over the area in which you have been stung, then feel the relief. If you don't happen to have any Coke, the alternative treatment is to pee on the stung part of your body—or to have someone else pee on it for you.

5 DE-BLACKEN POTS

Pots can sometimes get a black film on the bottom that is almost impossible to remove; this is caused by overcooking or just natural discoloration due to contact with highly acidic foods. To remove the black and restore your pot to new, pour in a can of Coke (or as much as you need to cover the blackened area by an inch) and put it on the stove on a low heat. After an hour or so, wash the pot as normal.

4 CLEAN CLOTHES

Grease stains are infamously difficult to remove from clothing, and stain removers can be very expensive. Here is a cheap solution: empty a can of Coke into your wash along with the usual detergent, and run it through a normal cycle. This is also quite effective for removing blood spots, and it helps to deodorize smelly clothes.

3 KILL BUGS

Pour some Coke into a shallow dish, and place it in the garden near the problem area. Slugs, snails, and other bugs will go in for a drink and never come out again! This is a very good first line of attack in your garden, and it can obviously save you an enormous amount of money by reducing the need for pesticides. You can pour the leftover Coke (minus the bugs) onto plants that like acidic soil, like azaleas and gardenias.

2 HEAL YOURSELF

Coca-Cola is useful for relieving a variety of ailments. The most common use is for soothing upset stomachs. Just slowly sip a glass of flat coke, and it should help to alleviate nausea. It's also good for people suffering from diarrhea or a sore throat. I would say that it can also cure hiccups, but frankly, a glass of water should do the same thing, as the chemicals in Coke don't offer any special "anti-hiccup" magic.

1 MAKE AN EXPLOSION

Most people who have been around on the Internet for at least a few years will be familiar with the Diet Coke–Mentos volcano. The idea is that you drop a Mentos into a bottle of Coke and the chemical reaction will cause the Coke to spurt for miles (not literally, of course).

10 WORST
HALLOWEEN TREATS

10 GOOD & PLENTY

OK, there are some people who like black licorice, but for many others, and for many kids who haven't grown into the taste yet, it's nasty. Not to mention that Good & Plenty are a tease—colorful pink and white candy shells outside, anise-flavored hell underneath. Licorice Allsorts also fall into this category. And I won't even mention how easy it would be to slip a few quaaludes into the mix!

9 HOMEMADE CANDY OR BAKED GOODS

They looked scrumptious and were usually given to you by the sweet little old lady who lived down the street. But, if you were born after 1970, you weren't allowed to eat them, and your folks just threw them out for fear that those gooey Rice Krispie squares, homemade fudge, or caramel apples were filled with razor blades and poison.

8 MR. GOODBAR

This is the bastard stepchild of the Hershey Miniatures pack. Whether or not you like nuts and chocolate together, these yellow goofballs just never quite worked. They always tasted like two separate taste treats thrown together, unlike better chocolate-peanut combinations, like Reese's Peanut Butter Cups, Butterfingers, Baby Ruths, and Snickers. I always came away wishing I had gotten the Krackle, the regular Hershey Chocolate bar, or even the Hershey Dark.

7 APPLES

Apples are not treats! As a kid, I probably ate an apple every day in my lunch. It's Halloween—gimme some candy!

6 MONEY

OK, at first money seems pretty cool, even if you figured you could pool it with your friends and spend it on candy from the store. But you never got more than a couple of stray nickels, or even pennies from the really cheap people! It never came to enough cash to do real candy damage; usually just enough to get a few watermelon Jolly Ranchers. And on that note...

5 JOLLY RANCHERS
They stuck your teeth together until you thought you would have to go to the dentist to pry them apart! Much too much work for way too little candy thrill. And the grape ones just tasted strange. Not quite cough medicine, not quite candy—just weird.

4 NECCO WAFERS AND SMARTIES
I don't even know where to start. These were like eating pastel-colored dust formed into little round discs. Flavorless and not nearly sweet enough, these cheap, powder pellets were weak at best, tasteless at worst, and just cluttered the bottom of the treat bag.

3 ANY GENERIC OR SUPERCHEAP LOLLIPOP
A Tootsie Pop or equivalent could be a somewhat plausible treat—at least you're working toward getting either a Tootsie Roll or bubble gum on the inside after all your efforts. But these crappy little teeny lollipops were just the worst. They tasted like old shoes.

2 WRONG-HOLIDAY CANDY
It was just off-putting to get jellybeans (Easter), peppermints (Christmas), or other strange candies that just didn't fit with Halloween. And of course you wondered, "How long have they been saving these to hand out?"

1 MARY JANES
What exactly were these? Toffee? Peanut chews? Sawdust? To the best of my recollection, they were some kind of molasses concoction, but for anyone born after the days of *Little House on the Prairie* (when the big treat was taking hot molasses out and throwing it down in the snow to cool it in order to make candy) these were a huge disappointment.

10 UTTERLY DISGUSTING FOODS

10 KOPI LUWAK

There is no beating around the bush on this one: Kopi luwak are coffee beans that come from civet (a cat-sized mammal) poo. The animals gorge on only the finest ripe berries and excrete the partially digested beans, which are then harvested for sale. Kopi luwak is the most expensive coffee in the world, selling for between $120 and $600 per pound, and is sold mainly in Japan and the United States, but it is becoming increasingly available elsewhere. The beans are washed and given only a light roast so as to not destroy the complex flavors that develop through the digestive process.

9 OX PENIS

In Western countries, ox penis is usually dried and sold as dog treats, but in many Asian nations, they are commonly eaten by humans. The penis is generally cooked by steaming or deep-frying, but it can also be eaten raw. Some Westerners compare the taste of ox penis with overcooked squid.

8 CENTURY EGG

Century egg is a Chinese ingredient made by preserving duck, chicken, or quail eggs in a mixture of clay, ash, salt, lime, and rice straw for several weeks to several months, depending on the processing method. After the process is completed, the yolk becomes a dark green, creamlike substance with a strong odor of sulphur and ammonia (aka farts or rotten eggs), while the white becomes a dark brown, transparent jelly with little flavor or taste. Century eggs can be eaten as is or chopped and used as an ingredient in another recipe. But whichever way you look at it, you're still eating rotten egg.

7 CATERPILLAR FUNGUS

Caterpillar fungus is a species of parasitic fungus that grows on insect larvae. The fungus invades the body of the thitarodes caterpillar, eventually killing and mummifying it. The dark brown to black fruiting body (or mushroom) emerges from the ground in spring or early summer, always growing out of the caterpillar's forehead. The fungus is commonly found in Chinese or Tibetan medicine, where it's used as an aphrodisiac and as a treatment for a variety of ailments, from fatigue to cancer. It's also served in soup.

6 RATS

Rats are a surprisingly common food in some parts of the world. In North Korea, they're eaten because there's often little else to eat in the villages. They're generally field rats rather than the city rats that most of us are familiar with.

They're described as being tough and stringy, with a chickenlike taste (surprise!). Reuters had this to say: "Live rats are being trucked from central China, suffering a plague of a reported 2 billion rodents displaced by a flooded lake, to the south to end up in restaurant dishes, Chinese media reported."

5 MONKEY BRAINS

This is disgusting primarily because of the very high risk of contracting fatal transmissible spongiform encephalopathies, such as Variant Creutzfeldt-Jakob disease and other similar brain diseases. In parts of China, monkey brains are eaten raw. While it's most likely an urban legend, some people claim that monkey brains are, or were, eaten from the head of a live monkey.

4 SPIDERS

These spiders from Skuon in Cambodia are similar to North American tarantulas. They're bred in holes in the ground specially for eating and are deep-fried. The texture is described as crispy-chewy, and some say it tastes similar to crab. Like tarantulas, these spiders can bite. They were a regular survival food of the Khmer Rouge.

3 BEE LARVAE

Bee larvae is eaten in China and Japan (where it is called *hachinoko*). *Hachinoko* became popular years ago when country people, deprived of fish and meats, turned to other wildlife in search of protein. The larvae are cooked in soy sauce and sugar and taste mildly sweet with a crumbly texture. These days, it is mainly a nostalgia item at parties. It makes a grand entrance in the festivities, and the older folks grin with expectation. The actual task of eating *hachinoko*, however, is not nearly so exciting.

2 BALUT (DUCK FETUS)

Balut is a fertilized duck egg with a nearly developed embryo inside that is boiled and eaten in the shell. Balut are considered delicacies in Asia, especially the Philippines, Cambodia, and Vietnam. Popularly believed to be an aphrodisiac and considered a high-protein, hearty snack, balut are mostly sold by street vendors at night in the regions where they are available. They are often served with beer. Michael from WeirdMeat describes the experience thus:

> After you choose what kind you want, the vendor grabs them piping hot from the basket and passes you a little stool, salt, and a vinegar-onion sauce. You hold the hot egg and flick carefully but forcefully at the top of it with your middle finger. It cracks a bit and you gently remove a small hole from the top, so you can sip the savory broth before removing the whole shell. I agree that the 18-day one is better than the younger ones. You might come across some small chunkies but it's usually just eaten all the way through, in about 3 mouthful bites. You can see feathers, head, wings, and skeleton forming, but it's basically an extra-chewy Easter egg.

Fertilized duck eggs are kept warm in the sun and stored in baskets to retain warmth. After nine days, the eggs are held to a light to reveal the embryo inside. Approximately eight days later, the balut are ready to be cooked, sold, and eaten.

1 SNAKE BLOOD AND BILE

This is less a food than a medicine, but it's so disgusting that it warrants a place on the list. In central Jakarta, a man who calls himself the Cobra Man specializes in preparing blood and bile for medicinal uses. Typically, he cuts off the snake's head and drains the blood into a glass of arrack (a type of alcohol). He adds the bile and serves the drink as a treatment for respiratory ailments, skin problems, aches, or indigestion. It's also said to improve a man's stamina and sex life. Drinking the blood straight from a snake can also be done as an act of bravery or manliness. In defense of the blood eaters, I should remind everyone that pig blood is very commonly eaten in most European nations in the form of black pudding or blood sausage.

10 FASCINATING AND STRANGE FOOD FACTS

10 BUTTER TEA

Fascinating Fact: In Tibet, a common drink is butter tea made from yak butter, salt, and tea.

The average Tibetan can drink 50 to 60 cups of this tea in any one day! It is made by drying Chinese tea in the road for several days to let it acquire a strong flavor. The tea is then boiled for up to half a day and churned in bamboo churns to which salt, a pinch of soda, and rancid butter have been added. When drinking the tea, you blow the scum from the butter away from the edge of the cup and sip. Some Tibetans add flour and *tsu*, a mixture of hardened cheese, butter, and sugar, to their tea in much the same way as Westerners add milk and sugar. When you sip the tea, your host will refill your cup, as it should always remain full.

9 HOT CHOCOLATE

Fascinating Fact: The ancient Mayans made truly hot chocolate—they added chilies and corn to it!

The first records of chocolate being used for drinking come from residue found in ancient Mayan pots—it dates back to the 5th century AD. The drink was made by pounding chocolate beans in to a paste, which was then mixed with water, chile peppers, cornmeal, and assorted spices. The drink was then poured back and forth between a cup and a pot, which gave it a foamy head. This was drunk cold, and people of all classes drank it regularly. The drink tasted spicy and bitter, unlike today's hot chocolate. When chocolate finally reached the West, it was very expensive, costing between $50 to $70 per pound in equivalent modern U.S. dollars. If you ever get to Paris, be sure to visit a café called Angelina for the best hot chocolate in the world—try the Chocolat l'Africain. In case you can't visit Paris, here's the recipe:

Combine ¾ cup whole milk, ¼ cup heavy cream, and 1 teaspoon confectioners' sugar and heat over medium-high until bubbles appear around the edges. Remove from the heat and add 4 ounces, chopped, of the best bittersweet chocolate (72% cacao). Stir until melted (you may need to return it to low heat). Serve with whipped cream.

8 MYSTERIOUS HISTORY OF DOUGHNUTS

Fascinating Fact: No one really knows when doughnuts were invented or who invented them.

Doughnuts (or donuts), were originally made as long twists of dough, not as the rings that are most common these days. It has long been common in England for doughnuts to be made in ball shapes and injected with jam after they were cooked. Both methods of cooking involve no human intervention, as the ball and twist will turn themselves over when the underside is cooked. The ring doughnut common to America just seemed to appear, but one  Hansen Gregory, an American, claimed to have invented it in 1847 when he was traveling on a steamboat; he wasn't satisfied with the texture of the center of the doughnut, so he pressed a hole through it with the ship's pepper box.

7 APPLE, POTATO, OR ONION?

Fascinating Fact: Apples, potatoes, and onions all taste the same when eaten with your nose plugged.

As a child, I had a science class in which we were blindfolded, had our noses plugged, and were given an apple or onion to eat, but we weren't told which of the two we would be given. Not one person was able to state which was which. This shows the incredibly important role that the nose plays in the sense of taste. The fact that the three items have a similar consistency makes them virtually impossible to tell apart without the sense of smell. If you try this, I should warn you: once you unblock your nose, you *can* tell what you have just eaten.

6 FLOATING EGGS

Fascinating Fact: When an egg floats in water, it is "off" and should not be eaten.

As eggs age, gases build up inside the shells, making them more buoyant. This is the best way to test whether an egg has gone rotten without having to break open the shell, risking the foul odor escaping. When an egg is extremely fresh it will lie on its side at the bottom of a glass of water. As it ages, the egg will begin to point upward; it finally floats completely when it has gone bad. Fresh eggs have a very firm white, while old eggs have a very watery white. This is why it is best to use the freshest eggs possible for poaching and frying. Older eggs are perfectly good for omelets or scrambling.

5 VANILLA JUNKIE

Fascinating Fact: The consumption of natural vanilla causes the body to release catecholamines, including adrenalin; for this reason it's considered to be mildly addictive.

When vanilla plants were first exported from Mexico to other tropical climates, they flowered but wouldn't produce vanilla pods. It was discovered that a bee native to Mexico was the only creature that could pollinate vanilla flowers (vanilla comes from a special species of orchid). Attempts to move the bee to other countries failed, and it was not until a slave boy discovered a method of artificial pollination that Mexico lost its monopoly on vanilla. As well as being mildly addictive, vanilla has also been found to block bacterial infections.

4 BANANA TREES

Fascinating Fact: Banana trees are not actually trees—they're giant herbs.

The large stem that's mistaken for a trunk on a banana tree is actually a "pseudostem," meaning "fake stem." Each pseudostem provides a single bunch of yellow, green, or red bananas. This first pseudostem then dies and is replaced by second one. Smaller bunches of bananas (such as the ones we buy in stores) are actually called "hands," not "bunches," which can weigh up to 110 pounds (50 kilograms). The bananas that we eat are specially cultivated to exclude seeds; therefore, you can't plant a banana tree from a commercially grown banana. Wild bananas have many large hard seeds.

3 BRAIN FREEZE

Fascinating Fact: The term "brain freeze" was invented by 7-Eleven to explain the pain one feels when drinking a Slurpee too fast.

Believe it or not, there is a real scientific name for "brain freeze": sphenopalatine ganglioneuralgia (try saying that five times fast!). When something very cold touches the top palate of the mouth, it causes the blood vessels to constrict. This makes the nerves send a signal to the brain to reopen them. The rapid reopening of the vessels causes a buildup of fluid in the tissues, causing a slight swelling in the forehead and, therefore, pain. It normally takes 30 to 60 seconds for the fluid to drain, relieving the pain.

2 ANCIENT SAUCE

Fascinating Fact: Ketchup was originally an Asian fish sauce.

Two words from the Fujian region of China were used to describe a fish brine sauce and a tomato sauce; both words bear a striking resemblance in sound to the word "ketchup": *ke-tsap* and *kio-chiap*. Early Western ketchups were made with fish and spices, or with mushrooms. In fact, mushroom ketchup is still available in the United Kingdom, and it is prized by some modern chefs for its natural inclusion of monosodium glutamate, the only substance known to stimulate the fifth human taste sense, *umami* (savory).

1 FEEL GOOD WITH 7UP

Fascinating Fact: When it was invented in 1920, 7UP contained lithium, the drug commonly prescribed now to sufferers of bipolar disorder.

The drink was originally marketed as a hangover cure due to the inclusion of lithium citrate. It was released just a few years before the Wall Street crash of 1929, and it was marketed under the name "Bib-Label Lithiated Lemon-Lime Soda"—quite a mouthful! The name was changed to 7UP shortly after its release, but lithium remained one of the ingredients until 1950. Some popular myths surround the name of the drink, but the name is most likely due to the fact that the original recipe contained seven ingredients (with the "up" portion relating to the lithium), or the fact that lithium has an atomic mass of seven.

10 FOODS WE LOVE THAT CAN KILL US

10 CASSAVA

Cassava is a South American shrub famed as a great source of carbohydrates. It is so popular that it is used for liquor, candies, cakes, and savory foods. Unfortunately, there have been reports from Southeast Asia that consuming large quantities from various parts of the plant and its relatives can cause death. Unless it's properly prepared, cassava can cause severe cyanide poisoning and a paralyzing disorder known as Konzo.

9 NUTMEG

Nutmeg (and its outer husk, called mace) is a spice native to Indonesia. It has been prized for its flavor since the 18th century. In small doses it is perfectly safe, but in large doses it causes hallucinations followed by convulsions, nausea, and death. It is particularly dangerous to pregnant women when taken in large quantities.

8 BITTER ALMONDS

Almonds are one of the most useful and wonderful of seeds (an almond is not a nut, as many people would have you believe). Its unique taste and excellent suitability for use in cooking have made it one of the most popular ingredients in pastry kitchens for centuries. The most flavorsome almonds are bitter almonds (as opposed to "sweet" almonds). They have the strongest scent and are the most popular in many countries. But there is one problem: they are full of cyanide. Before consumption, bitter almonds must be processed to remove the poison. Despite this requirement, some countries make the sale of bitter almonds illegal. In fact, you may not know that it is now illegal in the U.S. to sell raw almonds—all almonds sold are now heat-treated to remove traces of poison and bacteria.

7 CHERRY PITS

Cherries are a very popular fruit; they are used in cooking, liqueur production, or eaten raw. They are from the same family as plums, apricots, and peaches. All of the previously mentioned fruits on this list contain highly poisonous compounds in their leaves and seeds. (Almonds are also a member of this family, but they are the only fruit that is harvested especially for its seeds.) When the seeds of cherries are crushed, chewed, or even slightly injured, they produce prussic acid (hydrogen cyanide). Next time you are eating cherries, remember not to suck on or chew the pit.

6 APPLE SEEDS

Like the previous two items, apple seeds also contain cyanide, but obviously in much smaller doses. Apple seeds are very often eaten accidentally, but you would need to chew and consume a fairly high number to get sick. There are not enough seeds in one apple to kill, but it is absolutely possible to eat enough to die. (I recommend avoiding apple-eating competitions!) Incidentally, if you eat an apple and end up finding a worm in it, you can drop the apple in a bowl of salt water to kill the worm.

5 RHUBARB

Rhubarb is a very underrated plant—it produces some of the best-tasting desserts and is incredibly easy to grow at home. Rhubarb is something of a wonder plant; in addition to an unknown poison in its leaves, it also contains a corrosive acid. If you mix the leaves with water and soda, it becomes even more potent. The stems are edible (and incredibly tasty) and the roots have been used for over 5000 years as a laxative and stool softener.

4 TOMATOES

First off, a little interesting trivia: in the U.S., thanks to a Supreme Court decision in 1893, tomatoes are vegetables. In the rest of the world, they are considered to be fruit (or more accurately, berries). The reason for this decision was a tax that applied to vegetables but not fruit. You may also be interested to know that, technically, a tomato is an ovary. But they are on this list because the leaves and stems of the tomato plant contain a chemical called glycoalkaloid, which causes extreme nervousness and stomach upset. Despite this, they can be used in cooking to enhance flavor, but they must be removed before eating. Cooking in this way does not allow enough poison to seep out but can make a huge difference in taste. Finally, to enhance the flavor of tomatoes, sprinkle a little sugar on them. Now we just need to work out whether they are "toe-mah-toes" or "toe-may-toes."

3 MUSHROOMS

We have all heard of toadstools and know that they are poisonous, but what many people don't know is that a toadstool is actually a mushroom, not a separate type of plant. Toadstool is slang for "poisonous mushroom." While there are some useful signs that a mushroom is poisonous, they are not consistent, and all mushrooms of unknown origin should be considered dangerous to eat. Some of the things you can look for to try to determine whether a mushroom is poisonous are: it should have a flat cap with no bumps; it should have pink or black gills (poisonous mushrooms often have white gills); and the gills should stay attached to the cap (not the stalk) if you pull it off. But remember, while this is generally true of many types of mushrooms, it is not always the case.

2 CASTOR OIL

Castor oil, the bane of many of our childhoods, is regularly added to candies, chocolate, and other foods. Furthermore, many people still consume a small amount daily or force it on their unwilling children. Fortunately, the castor oil we buy is carefully prepared, because the castor bean is so deadly that it takes just one bean to kill a human and four to kill a horse. The poison is called ricin, which is so toxic that workers who collect the seeds have strict safety guidelines to prevent accidental death. Despite this, many people working in the fields gathering the seeds suffer terrible side-effects.

1 FUGU (PUFFER FISH)

The fugu is so poisonous that in Japan, fugu chefs are trained specially for the job and are tested before being a given certificate of practice. The training takes two or three years. In order to pass, the chef must answer a written test then give a demonstration of his cutting abilities. The final part of the test involves the chef eating the pieces of fugu that he has cut. Only 30 percent of apprentices pass the test, which is not to say that the rest die by eating their fugu—they can fail in earlier parts of the test. Only the flesh of the fugu is consumed, as it is the least likely part to have high amounts of poison, which causes a slight tingling sensation in the mouth. Fugu is the only food officially illegal for the emperor of Japan to eat—for his safety.

10 ANIMALS YOU WOULDN'T BELIEVE PEOPLE EAT

10 ELEPHANTS

The most endangered type of elephant, the forest elephant, is not just hunted for its ivory—it is also hunted for its meat. One animal can provide over 1000 pounds of flesh, resulting in the poacher making a fortune from one kill. This, combined with the popularity of eating its meat, makes it a difficult animal to protect.

9 GORILLAS
Gorillas are endangered, but the native populations of the various African nations in which they are eaten don't care. The eating of gorillas (and chimpanzees) is a very old tradition in Africa, one that continues to this day.

8 SILK WORMS
Silk worms make up the main ingredient in a very popular Korean dish. It was originally made with rotten baby worms but evolved to use freshly dead male worms. The worms are battered, breaded, and fried in oil.

7 ANTS
Ants are a popular addition to candy in some nations, and in other countries where the ants are huge, they are eaten fried or baked. Frankly, the idea seems repellent to me, but to each his own. If you want to enjoy ants in France, you can buy them as an ingredient in chocolate bars.

6 FUGU (PUFFER FISH)
This has already appeared on a list here but honestly, who can imagine eating a deadly poisonous fish? It means that someone once actually tasted each part of the animal to determine what was poisonous or not.

5 RAT
This is possibly not such a surprise, as rat is well-known as a staple food in countries with scare supplies of protein. In some places, rat is commonly eaten as a result of starvation (as is the case in North Korea). The ancient Romans used to eat dormice—and some European countries still do—and it was considered a delicacy.

4 HORSE
Horse meat is not just for dogs. And you may be surprised to know that it is very, very popular in many Western countries. France, for example, has special butchers who sell nothing but horse meat. A horse-meat butcher is called a *boucherie chevaline*. In the top eight horse-eating nations in the world, over four million horses are eaten each year.

3 DOGS

It's not popular for us in the West to imagine people eating dog, but it's actually extremely common in Asia and in the South Pacific. Dogs are a good source of nourishment, and they are far larger than rats and thus feed more people. We all feel awful about the thought of people eating dog, but the animals are killed in the kindest possible manner, and it really is no worse than someone eating beef (cow).

2 TURTLES

Turtle was a popular delicacy in the Victorian era, but due to a dwindling population and the increase in environmental protesting, they have become protected around most of the world. Some species of freshwater turtle are plentiful in the U.S., and they are not protected, so eating them is allowed; but in parts of Asia, the endangered sea turtle is routinely caught illegally and eaten. Given the slow growth rate of sea turtles, this is a tragedy in the making.

1 SPIDERS

This had to be the number 1 entry on the list. The thought of eating spiders ought to make most of us queasy, to say the least. But in various parts of the world, spiders are a delicacy. You can buy them at roadside stalls in Cambodia, where people developed a taste for them when they were being starved to death by Pol Pot.

CHAPTER FIVE
Days Gone By

10 BIZARRE MUSEUMS THAT WILL SCARE YOUR SOCKS OFF

10 THE HOUSE ON THE ROCK

Originally designed to house a collection of basically anything, the House on the Rock in Deer Shelter Rock, Wisconsin, first opened in 1959. The house contains fascinating exhibits, such as a re-creation of an early 20th-century American town and a 200-foot-long model of a sea monster. Now, this doesn't sound too scary, but that's only because I forgot to mention that the entire collection is basically left to rot in dark, dusty rooms. Now imagine such a room—filled with the stench of rot—in which you can just make out a scattering of decayed mannequins sawing at old broken musical instruments, playing what sounds like a symphony written in hell! Having seen it, I can assure you that the real thing is far worse than the description.

9 GLORE PSYCHIATRIC MUSEUM

Who wouldn't want to check out a museum dedicated to the history of such wonderful things as electroshock treatment and lobotomies? Well, most people probably. But if you have a taste for the downright shocking, the Glore Psychiatric Museum is for you. And if you find the horrifying parts of the museum too much to cope with, you can relax in the "Awful Things People Have Swallowed" exhibition. Don't forget to check out the ancient treatments area, where you can see instruments for bleeding patients and fascinating dioramas that take you step by step through a psychosurgical operation.

8 NEW HAVEN VENTRILOQUIST MUSEUM

In New Haven, Connecticut, there is a museum that contains nothing but a theatre filled with row upon row of old ventriloquist's dummies. Every seat in the theater has a dummy in it; in fact, when you visit, you have to stand on the stage because there is no room anywhere else. Most people don't suffer from autonomatonophobia (the fear of artificial humanoid figures), but even the staunchest of the staunch will be horrified by this awful display. Just think *Chuckie* times 1000.

7 CAPUCHIN CATACOMBS OF PALERMO

Not intending to be a museum, that is exactly what the Catacombs of Palermo have become: a museum of death. Deep in the bowels of the Capuchin monastery in Palermo, Italy, you can view hundreds of corpses of both monks and local community members. The bodies are lined up along the walls in the clothes in which they were buried. Bodies were put in the catacombs from the end of the 16th century to the last interment, little Rosalia Lombardo in the 1920s. The cool air and dry environment mean that the bodies are extremely well preserved—so well, in fact, that some look like they are just sleeping. But most look like hideous corpses ready to wake up at any moment to attack the visitors. A must-see vacation spot.

6 LONDON DUNGEON

The London dungeon is really famous, so you may wonder why it isn't in the top five of this list. It's mainly because it's scary in a different way from the rest of the items here. It's scary in the sense that no one wants a random stranger dressed as the grim reaper to jump at them and scream. That aside, the dungeon does present a great selection of macabre torture devices from the Middle Ages. (Mind you, your local army base probably has an equally terrifying array of torture devices from the last decade!) If you go to the dungeon, take your heart medication with you—those actors can certainly give you a fright. Oh, and be prepared to wait for a long time to get in—it's a popular attraction.

5 LOMBROSO'S MUSEUM OF CRIMINAL ANTHROPOLOGY

Cesare Lombroso founded the Italian school of criminology. It's no wonder then that this museum, filled with objects from his work, is a terrifying place indeed. Combined with the macabre collectibles are images of crimes, weapons used to slaughter humans, and even Lombroso's own head perfectly preserved in a bottle of formaldehyde. If you're interested in crime or just want to spend a day gazing at skulls, human remains, and other horrifying objects, this is the place to go.

4 MADAME TUSSAUDS

This is probably the most famous entry on this list. Madame Tussauds in London is best known for its enormous collection of wax figures, mostly of famous people. But the museum had a more grisly start. Madame Tussaud herself started the collection during the French Revolution. She would run up to the guillotine after people had been executed and make wax imprints of their severed heads. The most famous is probably that of the last king of France. These heads are all on display at the museum, along with a horrifying collection of monstrous historical displays in the chamber of horrors. When you see the life-sized reproduction of one of Jack the Ripper's victims, you will never be quite the same again. Oh, and to make matters worse, the chamber of horrors now employs actors to jump out and terrify visitors. Take along a change of underwear.

3 MUSEUM OF ANATOMY

Honoré Fragonard was a professor of anatomy, or at least he was until he got canned for showing the symptoms of insanity! Twenty years later he began the work that would be his life's crowning achievement. In 1794 he started gathering dead bodies for what would become his museum of anatomy. The Paris museum was designed to house a gigantic collection of corpses that he personally stripped of their skin and embalmed with a secret recipe, a recipe that remains a mystery to this day. The collection contains the preserved flayed bodies of animals, children, and executed criminals, as well as a collection of skulls from asylums for the mentally disturbed. The museum is so horrifying that entry is available by appointment only.

2 THE MUTTER MUSEUM

The Mutter Museum is best known for its large collection of skulls and anatomical specimens, including a wax model of a woman with a human horn growing out of her forehead; the tallest skeleton on display in North America; a five-foot-long human colon that contained over 40 pounds of poop; and the petrified body of the mysterious Soap Lady, whose entire corpse was turned into soap after she died. The museum also houses a malignant tumor removed from President Grover Cleveland's hard palate; the conjoined liver from the famous Siamese twins Chang and Eng Bunker; and a growth removed from President Abraham Lincoln's assassin, John Wilkes Booth. It may not terrify you, but I guarantee that it will haunt your dreams.

1 THE PURGATORY MUSEUM

According to Catholic doctrine, a person who dies with only slight sins on their soul goes to purgatory to be cleansed by fire before floating off to heaven. At the Church of the Sacred Heart in the Prati district of Rome, there is a small museum tucked away behind a side altar called the Purgatory Museum. This truly scary place has exhibits that document cases of souls in purgatory coming back to earth to haunt the living. Some of the items on display are a table with scorch marks and lines carved out of it by an otherworldly hand, as well as fingerprints burned on clothing and bed linens. But perhaps the scariest item of all is a book with an entire human handprint scorched deeply into the pages—the handprint of a long-dead monk suffering in the fires for some unknown sin.

10 GRUESOME MEDIEVAL TORTURE DEVICES

10 HEAD CRUSHER

The head crusher was a terrible instrument of torture that resembled a modern vice grip turned on its side. The person to be tortured placed his chin on a bar while a metal cap attached to a bolt was screwed onto the top of his head. The bolt was turned slowly, causing the victim's head to be crushed. A lack of confession could result in death, beginning with the eyeballs popping out of their sockets, the teeth shattering, and finally the skull being fractured—releasing the brain.

9 CAT'S PAW

It sounds innocuous, but it was far from it. The cat's paw (also called the Spanish tickler) looked like a garden rake with the ends sharpened and curved. It was often attached to a handle for ease of use. The person performing the torture would rake the victim's body with the claw, which was so sharp it would strip skin and flesh from bones.

8 KNEE SPLITTER

The name of this is enough to send shivers down anyone's spine. As its name implies, this device built of spiked wooden blocks would be placed on either side of a person's knee and screwed together until their knees split. The device's design made it possible to use on other joints, such as elbows and wrists.

7 SCAVENGER'S DAUGHTER

This torture tool was designed at the behest of the foul King Henry VIII by William Skevington, Lieutenant of the Tower of London. It was an A-shaped frame that would completely encircle a kneeling man, who would then be squashed until he bled from nose and ears. This is, effectively, the opposite of the rack.

6 JUDAS CHAIR

This is the only torture device on the list that is still in use today (in some Latin American countries). The Judas chair is effectively a tall stool, but in place of the seat there is a very sharp-tipped pyramid. The poor "Judas" would be lowered anus- or vagina-first onto the tip of the pyramid. The torturer could apply as much of the victim's body weight onto the sharp point as was needed to elicit a confession.

5 THE SPANISH DONKEY

If you have recovered from the images evoked by the previous item, hold onto your seat (or perhaps you might want to stand for this one). The Spanish donkey was similar to the Judas chair, but instead of lowering the victim onto a spike, they were lowered (with a leg on either side) onto a long board shaved to have a razorlike edge; heavy weights would be tied to the victim's legs. Unsurprisingly, there are accounts of victims being cut entirely in two.

4 CHOKE PEAR

The choke pear resembled forceps used in child birth. They were inserted into the mouth or anus of the victim (or the vagina, in the case of women) and expanded by the use of a screw. The tips of each segment of the device were spiked, causing two-fold damage: ripping and cutting. The device was used on different parts of the body, depending on the crime. Homosexuals were punished by having the device inserted into their anus; women guilty of sexual relations with the devil had it inserted into their vagina; and heretics and unorthodox preachers had it inserted into their mouth. One can only hope that it was washed between uses!

3 LEAD SPRINKLER

The lead sprinkler was used, as its name suggests, to sprinkle molten lead or boiling oil on the victim, who was strapped to a table. The device was essentially a ladle with a lid with a hole in it over the bowl. The bowl was filled with liquid and the lid was closed over it. The man inflicting the torture would exercise extreme caution so as to not get splashed himself.

2 BREAST RIPPER

The breast ripper looked like a pair of forceps but with two very large claws at the end of each handle. The ripper could be heated until it was red-hot and used to brand the breasts of unmarried mothers. For those condemned for worse sins, the ripper was used to tear the entire breast off. A rather hideous variation of this was the spider, which was a series of spikes sticking out of a wall. The condemned woman would be dragged along the spikes until her breasts were torn away.

1 CROCODILE SHEARS

These horrible shears were reserved for men who attempted to kill a king. They were shaped like pincers, but instead of having jaws or blades, they formed a pipe lined with jagged teeth when closed. The shears would be heated until they were red-hot and clamped over the victim's penis, which was then ripped from his body. You can be sure that a man who suffered the crocodile shears would not be shedding crocodile tears.

10 CREEPY ASPECTS OF VICTORIAN LIFE

10 VIGNETTES

The Victorian upper class had no televisions to entertain them, so they entertained themselves. One of the popular forms of entertainment was for friends and family to dress up in outrageous costumes and pose for each other. This sounds innocent, but just think: can you imagine your grandmother dressing up as a Greek wood nymph posing on a table in the living room while everyone applauds? No. You can't. The idea is, in fact, creepy. But for the Victorians, this was perfectly normal and fun.

9 POORHOUSES

Poorhouses were government-run facilities where the poor, infirm, or mentally ill could live. They were usually filthy and full to the brim of society's unwanted people. At the time, poverty was seen as dishonorable, as it came from a lack of the moral virtue of industriousness. Many of the people who lived in the poorhouses were required to work to contribute to the cost of their board, and it was not uncommon for whole families to live together with other families in the communal environment. In the Victorian era, life didn't get much worse than that of a poorhouse resident.

8 PEA-SOUPERS

London during the Victorian era was famed for its pea-soupers—fogs so thick you could barely see through them. Pea-soupers were caused by a combination of fog from the River Thames and smoke from the coal fires that were an essential part of Victorian life. Interestingly, London had suffered from these pea-soupers for  centuries. In 1306, King Edward I banned coal fires because of the smog. This creepy environment made the acts of criminals like Jack the Ripper possible. In 1952, 12,000 Londoners died due to the smog, which caused the government to pass the Clean Air Act, creating smog-free zones. In literature and modern film, the Victorian atmosphere is greatly enhanced by the use of thick smog.

7 FOOD

English food can be creepy at the best of times, but it was especially so during the Victorian era. The Victorians loved offal and ate virtually every part of an animal. This is not entirely creepy if you are a food fanatic (like me), but for the average person, the idea of supping on a bowl of brains and heart is not appealing. Another famous dish from the Victorian era was turtle soup. The turtle was prized for its green Jell-O–like fat, which was used to flavor the soup made from the animal's long-boiled stringy flesh. Due to dwindling numbers, turtles are seldom eaten nowadays, though it is possible to purchase them in some states in the U.S. where they are plentiful.

6 SURGERY

In a time when one in four patients died after surgery, you were very lucky in Victorian times to have a good doctor with a clean operating room. There was no anesthesia, no painkillers for after the operation, and no electric equipment to reduce the duration of an operation. Victorian surgery wasn't just creepy, it was outright horrific. Here is a description of one surgery:

> The assembled crowd of anxious medical students dutifully check their pocket watches, as two of Liston's surgical assistants—'dressers' as they are called—take firm hold of the struggling patient's shoulders.
>
> The fully conscious man, already racked with pain from the badly broken leg he suffered by falling between a train and the platform at nearby King's Cross, looks in total horror at the collection of knives, saws, and needles that lie alongside him.
>
> Liston clamps his left hand across the patient's thigh, picks up his favourite knife, and in one rapid movement makes his incision. A dresser immediately tightens a tourniquet to stem the blood. As the patient screams with pain, Liston puts the knife away and grabs the saw.
>
> With an assistant exposing the bone, Liston begins to cut. Suddenly, the nervous student who has been volunteered to steady the injured leg realises he is supporting its full weight. With a shudder he drops the severed limb into a waiting box of sawdust.

At this time, castration was also still widely practiced, along with other revolting surgeries like lobotomies, which were first performed in the Victorian era.

5 GOTHIC NOVEL

How could the gothic novel (a genre of literature that combines elements of both horror and romance) not be included on a list like this? It was the Victorian period that gave us such great works of terror as *Dracula* and *The Strange Case of Dr. Jekyll and Mr. Hyde*. Even Americans got in on the act, with Edgar Allen Poe producing some of the greatest gothic literature of the time. The Victorians knew how to frighten people, and they knew how to do it in grand style. These works still form the basis of much modern horror, and their power to thrill has not dwindled in the least.

4 JACK THE RIPPER

In the late Victorian era, London was terrorized by the monster known as Jack the Ripper. Using the pea-soupers (number 8 on this list) as a cover, the Ripper ultimately slaughtered five or more prostitutes working in the East End. Newspapers, whose circulation had been growing during this period, bestowed widespread and enduring notoriety on the killer because of the savagery of the attacks and the failure of the police to capture the murderer. Because the killer's identity has never been confirmed, the legends surrounding the murders have become a combination of genuine historical research, folklore, and pseudohistory. Many authors, historians, and amateur detectives have proposed theories about the identity of the killer and his victims.

3 FREAK SHOWS

A freak show is an exhibition of rarities, "freaks of nature"—such as unusually tall or short humans, or people with both male and female secondary sexual characteristics or other extraordinary diseases and conditions—and performances that are expected to be shocking to the viewers. Probably the most famous member of a freak show is the Elephant Man. Joseph Carey Merrick (August 5, 1862–April 11, 1890) was an Englishman who became known as the "Elephant Man" because of his physical appearance, which was caused by a congenital disorder. His left side was overgrown and distorted, causing him to wear a mask for most of his life. There can be no doubt that Victorian freak shows were some of the creepiest aspects of society at the time.

2 MEMENTO MORI

Memento mori is a Latin phrase meaning "remember you shall die." In the Victorian era, photography was a new and extremely costly technology. When a loved one died, their relatives would sometimes have a photograph taken of the corpse in a pose, oftentimes with other members of the family. For the vast majority of Victorians, this was the only time they would be photographed. In these postmortem photographs, the effect of life was sometimes enhanced by either propping the subject's eyes open or painting pupils onto the photographic print, and many early images have a rosy tint added to the cheeks of the corpse. Adults were often posed in chairs, or even braced on specially designed frames. Flowers were also a common prop in postmortem photography of all types.

1 QUEEN VICTORIA

Queen Victoria has to have position number 1 on this list because the era is named for her, and, frankly, she was really creepy. When her husband, Albert, died in 1861, she went into mourning, donning black frocks until her own death many years later, and she expected her nation to do the same. She avoided public appearances and rarely set foot in London in the following years. Her seclusion earned her the name "Widow of Windsor." Her somber reign cast a dark pall across Britain, and her influence was so great that the entire period was fraught with creepiness. Ironically, since Queen Victoria disliked black funerals so much, London was festooned in purple and white when she died.

20 FASCINATING HISTORICAL ODDITIES AND FACTS

20 ASBESTOS-LACED CLOTHES

The Romans used to use asbestos in their cloths for daily use, such as dish towels, napkins, and tablecloths. Pliny the Elder, a Roman naturalist, said that they could be cleaned whiter than normal cloth by simply throwing them in the fire because the asbestos made them flame-retardant. He also noted that the slaves who wove the mineral for cloth often suffered from lung disorders.

19 BRAIN: STUFFING FOR THE HEAD

In ancient Egypt, the heart was considered to be the seat of intelligence, not the brain. Egyptians thought the brain was just stuffing for the head. For this reason, they scraped it out of the head during embalming and discarded it, while treating the heart with special care.

18 HAZMAT SUITS OF THE MIDDLE AGES

During the plague in the Middle Ages, some doctors wore a primitive form of biohazard suits called "plague suits." The mask included red glass eyepieces, which were thought to make the wearer impervious to evil. The beak of the mask was often filled with strong aromatic herbs and spices to overpower the miasma, or bad air, which was also thought to carry the plague.

17 WAR AND PEACE

During the last 3500 years, it is estimated that the world has had a grand total of 230 years in which no wars took place. That's enough to make one wonder whether there's any benefit at all to the "peace movement."

16 THE BEARD TAX

In urban circles of Western Europe and the Americas, beards were out of fashion after the early 17th century. The trend went to such an extent that, in 1698, Peter the Great of Russia ordered men to shave off their beards, and in 1705 he levied a tax on beards in order to bring Russian society more in line with contemporary Western Europe.

15 POPE PENS EROTIC NOVEL

The best-selling book of the 15th century was an erotic novel called *The Tale of the Two Lovers*; it is even still read today. The author of this book was none other than Aeneas Sylvius Piccolomini, otherwise known as Pope Pius II, who reigned from 1458 to 1464.

14 SACRED CATS OF EGYPT

In ancient Egypt, cats were considered sacred. When a family pet cat died, the entire family would shave off their eyebrows and remain in mourning until they had grown back.

13 UNCLE SAM POSTER

The model for Uncle Sam on the famous 1917 poster "I Want You" is the face of the painter, James Montgomery Flagg. Flagg used his own picture in order to avoid the need to find a model. For effect, he aged his portrait and added the goatee beard.

12 MEDAL OF HONOR

There is no such thing as the Congressional Medal of Honor. In 1862, President Lincoln signed into law a resolution creating a "Medal of

Honor," which is the official and only title for what most people think is the "Congressional Medal."

11 SLAVES IN SPARTA
In 200 BC, when the Greek city of Sparta was at the height of its power, there were 20 slaves for every citizen. Imagine how tidy their houses must have been!

10 THE COUNTRY THAT PEACE FORGOT
Andorra declared war on imperial Germany during World War I but did not actually take part in the fighting. It remained in an official state of belligerency until 1957, as it was not included in the Treaty of Versailles.

9 DECLARATION OF INDEPENDENCE
Only two people signed the Declaration Independence on July 4, 1776: John Hancock and Charles Thomson. The majority of the other members of Congress signed on August 2, although the final signature wasn't added for another five years.

8 DRINK AND DUNG
As a restorative medicine in ancient Rome, people would drink a mixture of wine and the dung of wild boars.

7 THREE POPES ON THE THRONE
During the Western Schism (1378 to 1417), three men simultaneously claimed to be the legitimate pope. When the cardinals didn't like the pope they originally elected, they invalidly elected a second. This caused great troubles in the church, which lead to the election of a third pope by the council of Pisa (also invalidly). Thus there were three claimants to the throne: Pope Gregory XII, Antipope Benedict XIII, and Antipope John XXIII. This finally ended when the original election was considered the only valid one.

6 BANK PIRACY
Sir William Paterson, founder of the Bank of England, is suspected to have been a pirate in his years before founding the bank.

5 INVENTION OF TEA BAGS

In 1904, tea bags were invented accidentally. The inventor, Thomas Sullivan, a tea merchant, decided that it was cheaper to send small samples to prospective customers in silk bags rather than in boxes. The recipients mistakenly believed they were meant to be dunked, and soon Sullivan was inundated with orders for his "tea bags."

4 PARACHUTE DESIGN

The oldest parachute design appears in an anonymous manuscript from 1470s Renaissance Italy (over 400 years before the airplane appeared), showing a free-hanging man clutching a cross bar frame attached to a conical canopy. As a safety measure, four straps run from the ends of the rods to a waist belt.

3 BLOWING SMOKE UP YOUR...

In the late 1700s, a tobacco enema was used to infuse tobacco smoke into a patient's rectum for various medical purposes, primarily the resuscitation of drowning victims. A tube inserted into the anus was connected to a fumigator and bellows that forced the smoke toward the rectum.

2 NO INCOME TAX

Income tax, along with many other taxes imposed during the Civil War, was repealed after 1865 because the government simply had no need for the extra revenue. The majority of federal income came from taxes on tobacco and alcohol, which were hot commodities at the war's end.

1 HAIRLESS ARMPITS

In Rome, there were people who specialized in armpit plucking. Somewhere around AD 1, Roman aristocrats interested in fashion removed all of their body hair and employed someone to pluck it. Requirements for the profession were tweezers, a strong arm, and the ability to deal with the customer's pain.

10 HISTORICAL MONSTERS

10 ONI (JAPANESE)
The *oni* are gigantic creatures in Japanese mythology. They're usually shown with horns, and while most often they appear in humanoid form, they're sometimes given extra eyes, fingers, or toes and are red or blue and carry an iron club. There is a striking similarity between the *oni* and traditional depictions of Satan.

9 OGRE (FRENCH)
Ogres are popular characters in Western folk tales. They are usually seen as having large heads with beards and wild hair. In fairy tales they are often human-eaters and are almost always extremely strong and ferocious.

8 VAMPIRE (SLAVIC)
Vampires are well-known characters that are generally described as needing blood—mostly human but sometimes animal—in order to sustain themselves. They were especially popular in the 18th century, and the original vampires lacked fangs and were usually described as being bloated and dark skinned, as opposed to the very slim, pale versions we see today.

7 MUMMY (EGYPTIAN)
A mummy is, of course, the preserved corpse of a dead Egyptian that's preserved through the clever use of spices and resins. The most likely cause of the tales of monster mummies probably comes from the curses associated with the violation of the mummy tombs.

6 WEREWOLF (GERMANIC)
Werewolves usually come in two varieties: men who become half-man and half-wolf, or who turn entirely into wolves. They are often described as being placed under a curse, and the association between werewolves and the full moon arose in the Middle Ages, although some evidence does suggest that the notion may even go back as far as the ancient Greek writer Petronius.

5 GOBLIN (ANGLO-SAXON)

Goblins are small creatures found in folklore that are usually depicted as evil, mischievous, disfigured humanoids. Some tales have short goblins while, more rarely, some describe them as the size of an adult human. There are many similarities between goblins and the Celtic brownie, so there is a likely connection somewhere in the mists of history.

4 GHOUL (MIDDLE EASTERN)

Ghouls are monsters from Arabian folklore that are usually found haunting the places humans tend to avoid, like graveyards and abandoned areas. They were classified as *jinn*, evil spirits, from which the word "genie" comes. Folklore states that a ghoul would lure unwary travelers into the desert to kill and eat them. The creature also preyed on young children, robbed graves, and ate the dead.

3 BANSHEE (CELTIC)

When a banshee appears, watch out. In Celtic folklore, the banshee is a forewarning of a coming death, especially of someone of great position in society. Usually depicted as a type of ghost, the banshee is sometimes described as a fairy. In almost all cases, they are dressed in pale, flowing garments and have long, fair hair.

2 GORGON (GREEK)

The gorgon is a famed ancient Greek monster: a woman with sharp fangs and live writhing snakes for hair. When a human looks upon the face of a gorgon, he is said to turn to stone. By far the most famous gorgon is Medusa, the queen of gorgons. She alone is said to be mortal.

1 ZOMBIE (LATIN AMERICAN)

A zombie is a contradiction in terms: a human who's both living and dead. These undead corpses originate in Afro-Caribbean folklore and have become an extremely popular subject for modern horror films and books.

10 TRULY BIZARRE TRADITIONS

10 IYOMANTE RITUAL

The Ainu people (an indigenous tribe from parts of Japan and Russia) are a once-suppressed ethnic minority whose religious roots are animist. Because of their worship of nature, they developed a tradition in which bears were killed in order to send their soul to heaven to bless mankind. This ritual (*Iyomante*) involves the slaughter of a hibernating mother bear in her cave. Her cubs are raised in captivity for two years and then fatally choked or speared in a sacramental act meant to show religious devotion. The villagers then drink the bear's blood and eat its flesh. The skull is placed on an upturned spear that's wrapped with the bear skin. The Ainu then worship this bizarre type of scarecrow. They people believe bears are gods walking among humans. Unfortunately, due to a law change in Japan that revoked the ban on the ritual, it is now occurring again in some places.

9 LIVING WITH THE DEAD

Because funerals are an incredibly important aspect of life for the Torajan people, an ethnic group in South Sulawesi, Indonesia, it can take many months for a family to raise sufficient funds to pay for the festivities. During this period of months, the dead body is wrapped in clothes and kept under the family home. The Torajans believe that the deceased soul remains with them until the burial. Torajan funerals are grand affairs that frequently involve the sacrifice of buffalo (the more important the deceased, the more buffalo are killed). When the person is finally ready to be buried for good, their coffin is usually put in a cave and their effigy is placed at the cave mouth looking out.

8 MASAI SPITTING

This isn't just regular spitting we are talking about. The Masai tribe, an African group found in Kenya and Tanzania, has an unusual way of greeting friends: they spit on one another. Furthermore, when a new child is born, the Masai men spit on it and say it is bad, believing that if they praise the child, they will curse it to a bad life. When greeting an elder, a Masai warrior will spit in his hand as a sign of respect before offering it to be shaken. Masai tribesmen are well-known through the media because of their practice of elongating their earlobes.

7 FEEDING THE DEAD

Fairly recent discoveries of old Roman burial grounds in the Vatican have uncovered a fascinating tradition that was previously forgotten: the Romans would eat with their dead and even feed them. Many of the graves found contained pipes that led from the outside of the grave to the body within; this was used to pour honey, wine, and other foods into the dead. Similar pipes in Roman graves have also been found in England. Ancient Romans would often picnic at the graves of the dead, as they believed they were feeding the souls of their departed loved ones.

6 YANOMAMÖ ASH EATING

The Yanomamö are a large tribe of people from Venezuela and Brazil. They have been largely untouched by modern life and so retain many of their ancient customs, one of which is the focus of this item. Yanomamö religious tradition forbids the keeping of any part of the body of the dead; for this reason, when a Yanomamö dies, his body is taken to be burned and the bones are crushed and combined with the ashes. These are then divided among the family and eaten. Because absolutely no part of the body must remain, the vessel that contained the ashes is then destroyed. The tribesmen believe that a person dies because a shaman or member of another tribe has sent evil to him. This leads to much conflict and intertribe battles.

5 HANGING COFFINS

The limestone caves surrounding Sagada in the Philippines are home to the region's dead. While many people are buried in the caves, a long-standing tradition in the area also means that the faces of the cliffs are dotted with coffins. Hanging coffins can also be found in other places around the world, particularly China, where the nearly extinct Bo people (an indigenous Chinese minority tribe) practice this tradition regularly. The Toraja people (featured in number 9) also sometimes hang coffins of young children, although wealthy adults are normally placed in caves.

4 MOURNING OF MUHARRAM

To commemorate the death of Husayn ibn Ali (a grandson of Muhammad), some groups of Shia Muslims take to the streets and whip themselves with specially designed chains with razors or knives attached. Other groups slit their heads open with knives. This awful tradition (called *matam*) is also practiced by children or forced on them by parents who do the cutting. *Matam* is mostly found in Bahrain, Pakistan, India, Afghanistan, Lebanon, and Iraq, and while some Muslims frown upon the practice, many major Muslim leaders endorse it.

3 SATERE-MAWE INITIATION RITE

The Satere-Mawe people from the Amazon region of Brazil have an agonizing initiation rite for their boys. In order to become a man, the boy must insert his hand into a glove that is woven with drugged bullet ants, which have one of the most painful stings in nature. The boy must wear the glove for a full ten minutes and he must do this 20 times over the course of several months. Steve Backshall, a television reporter, undertook the ordeal and described it thus:

> I put my hands into the gloves. Actually, it wasn't that bad: pretty unpleasant, but bearable; just like the single sting, but repeated over and over again. I stuck it out for the full 10 minutes....My crew took me out of the line-up and off to get some medical tests done. That's when things started to go wrong. I had suffered several hundred stings, and all of a sudden I went beyond pain. First, I started wailing, then, once that had passed, the floodgates opened—deep, guttural sobbing, uncontrollable shaking, writhing, convulsing. I started to drool, and suddenly I wasn't responding to anything at all. My legs wouldn't hold me up, and our doctor was shouting at me to keep moving and not to give in to the urge to lie down and let it take me. If there'd been a machete to hand, I'd have chopped off my arms to escape the pain.

2 BABY TOSSING

Every year in Solapur, a region in Maharashtra, India, parents get together to throw their babies off the top of a 50-foot tower. The babies are caught in a sheet held by other villagers on the ground. The parents believe that the practice will give their children long and healthy lives. This is practiced mostly by Muslims, but some Hindu families also engage in it. Parents that partake in the ritual are usually those who have become pregnant after praying at the Shrine of Baba

Umer Dargah. Local authorities provide policing for the event, despite the fact that the national government is opposed to it.

1 EATING DEATH

The Aghoris are members of a Hindu sect who worship Shiva, whom they see as the supreme god. Because they believe that Shiva created everything, they consider nothing to be bad. For this reason, they engage in a variety of sexual practices, drink alcohol, take drugs, and eat meat. Nothing is considered taboo. But the thing that makes their ancient traditions bizarre is that they are also practicing cannibals and their temples are cremation grounds. An Aghori lives in the cremation ground and is able to support himself there; his clothing comes from the dead, his firewood comes from the funeral pyres, and his food comes from the river. When a person is cremated, an Aghori will coat himself in the ashes of the body and meditate on the dead. Dead bodies that are found floating in the river are gathered up and meditated on. The limbs are then removed by the Aghori and eaten raw.

10 SCANDALOUS FACTS ABOUT HISTORICAL FIGURES

10 ADOLF HITLER

Fact: Hitler was a tax evader.

Recent research into papers relating to Hitler has uncovered the fact that when he became chancellor of Germany in 1934, he had evaded paying 405,500 million Reichsmarks in tax ($6.3 million in today's currency). Fortunately for Hitler, he was forgiven his tax debts when he was elected. It is believed that he earned 1.2 million Reichsmarks for sales of *Mein Kampf* alone, and avoided paying

600,000 Reichsmarks in tax on it. The official who forgave Hitler's tax debt was "rewarded" with a tax-free allowance of 2000 Reichsmarks per month (a huge amount, considering teachers at the time were paid 4800 per annum).

9 WINSTON CHURCHILL

Fact: Churchill was racist.

Sir Winston Churchill is so highly regarded for his skills as an orator and statesman that he was voted Britain's greatest individual by the BBC in 2002. There is no doubt that his speech writing was a class above virtually every other modern writer of English speeches, and we are all familiar with at least one or two of his famous quotations, but what many people don't know is that he also had a dark side. The best way to illustrate that is to let the man speak for himself:

> *"I do not admit... that a great wrong has been done to the Red Indians of America, or the black people of Australia... by the fact that a stronger race, a higher grade race... has come in and taken its place."*—Churchill to Palestine Royal Commission, 1937

> *"I do not understand the squeamishness about the use of gas. I am strongly in favor of using poisonous gas against uncivilised tribes."*—Churchill writing as president of the Air Council

> *"First there are the Jews who, dwelling in every country throughout the world, identify themselves with that country, enter into its national life, and, while adhering faithfully to their own religion, regard themselves as citizens in the fullest sense of the State which has received them... In violent opposition to all this sphere of Jewish effort rise the schemes of the International Jews. The adherents of this sinister confederacy are mostly men reared up among the unhappy populations of countries where Jews are persecuted on account of their race. Most, if not all, of them have forsaken the faith of their fathers...This worldwide conspiracy for the overthrow of civilisation...has steadily growing"*—Churchill writing on "Zionism versus Bolshevism" in the Illustrated Sunday Herald, February 1920

8 GANDHI

Fact: Gandhi was a dirty old man.

At age 36, Gandhi declared himself celibate in order to become enlightened. Despite this, in his later years he became increasingly fascinated with sex to the point that it was his favorite topic of conversation after nonviolence. In order to prove and perfect his state of celibacy, he would sleep naked with young naked women. In one case, he told the father of a young girl that they were sleeping together so Gandhi could correct her posture. (Sure Gandhi, if you say so.)

7 GEORGE WASHINGTON

Fact: Washington cleverly tricked Congress into paying him obscene amounts of money.

Unfortunately, what schoolbooks miss entirely about Washington's life is the fact that he turned down a salary of what would have amounted to a little over $1000 per month, but said, "Sir, I beg leave to assure the Congress that as no pecuniary consideration could have tempted me to have accepted this arduous employment, I do not wish to make any profit from it. I will keep an exact account of my expenses. Those I doubt not they will discharge, and that is all I desire." So, honest Washington offered to be paid expenses only—a generous and touching move. But then the shopping began.

He spent $831.45 on leather goods, maps, and glasses to use in his military position; $3776 through the army's retreat across the countryside; and from September 1775 to March 1776, Washington spent over $6000 dollars on liquor. In eight years, by turning down a salary and taking an expense account, instead of being paid around $12,000, he was paid $449,261.51 in 1780 dollars (around $4,250,000 in today's money).

Washington, being a clever man, tried the same ploy when he was elected president, but he was turned down and given a set salary of $25,000 per year.

6 MARTIN LUTHER

Fact: Martin Luther was an anti-Semite

Martin Luther, the famous monk who started the Protestant Reformation, is often touted as a hero for standing up against excesses in the Catholic Church at the time, but what most people don't know is that he was violently anti-Jewish and he made no secret of it. In 1543, he wrote "On the Jews and Their Lies," in which he recommends that Jews be deprived of money, civil rights, religious teaching, and education, and that they be forced to labor on the land or else be expelled from Germany and possibly killed (sound like someone familiar from more recent times?). He referred to the Jews as a "base, whoring people, that is, no people of God, and their boast of lineage, circumcision, and law must be accounted as filth." He said that Jews were "full of the devil's feces ... which they wallow in like swine," and the synagogue is an "incorrigible whore and an evil slut ..."

He also put together an eight point plan to get rid of the Jews:

> "First to set fire to their synagogues or schools and to bury and cover with dirt whatever will not burn, so that no man will ever again see a stone or cinder of them. ..."

> "Second, I advise that their houses also be razed and destroyed. ..."

> "Third, I advise that all their prayer books and Talmudic writings, in which such idolatry, lies, cursing and blasphemy are taught, be taken from them. ..."

> "Fourth, I advise that their rabbis be forbidden to teach henceforth on pain of loss of life and limb. ..."

> "Fifth, I advise that safe-conduct on the highways be abolished completely for the Jews. ..."

> "Sixth, I advise that usury be prohibited to them, and that all cash and treasure of silver and gold be taken from them. ... Such money should now be used in ... the following [way]... Whenever a Jew is sincerely converted, he should be handed [a certain amount]..."

> "Seventh, I commend putting a flail, an ax, a hoe, a spade, a distaff, or a spindle into the hands of young, strong Jews and Jewesses and letting them earn their bread in the sweat of their brow... For it is not fitting that they should let us accursed Goyim toil in the sweat of our faces while they, the holy people, idle away their time behind the stove, feasting and farting, and on top of all, boasting blasphemously of their lordship over the Christians by means of our sweat. No, one should toss out these lazy rogues by the seat of their pants."

> "If we wish to wash our hands of the Jews' blasphemy and not share in their guilt, we have to part company with them. They must be driven from our country [and] we must drive them out like mad dogs." [Source: Martin Luther, "On the Jews," 47:268–288, 292.]

5 THOMAS JEFFERSON

Fact: Jefferson preached against whites having children with blacks, while doing that very thing and denying his offspring.

Jefferson said, "The amalgamation of whites with blacks produces a degradation to which no lover of his country, no lover of the excellence in the human character, can innocently consent." While preaching this rubbish, he had several children with his slave Sally Hemings, who happened to be the illegitimate half-sister of his wife. While the rumors were around during their lifetime (which Jefferson strenuously denied), it was not until recent times that DNA testing proved that at least one of Hemings' children was indeed fathered by Jefferson. In a letter to Secretary of the Navy Robert Smith dated July 1, 1805, Jefferson also admitted to having tried to seduce his married neighbor, Betsey Walker.

4 ALBERT EINSTEIN
Fact: Einstein was a philanderer.

Einstein is considered the greatest mind of the 20th century, and he and his most famous formula, $E=MC^2$, are known by virtually everyone. Most people know he had a passion for the violin and that he started out life as a clerk in a patent office, but what most people don't know is that he cheated on both of his wives repeatedly. After splitting up with his first wife (because of his infidelity), he married his cousin Elsa. Shortly after that he had an affair with his secretary, Betty Neumann. In a new volume of letters held by the Hebrew University in Jerusalem, Einstein described about six women with whom he spent time and from whom he received gifts while being married to Elsa.

3 ELVIS PRESLEY
Fact: Elvis was unhealthily obsessed with James Dean.

Elvis Presley was a very obsessive and compulsive man. He was passionate about acting and wanted to be the next James Dean, which led him to an obsession with the young star. Elvis memorized all of Dean's lines in *Rebel without a Cause*, and he even sought out Natalie Wood because of her connection to the film. The obsession finally drove him to intentionally befriend Nick Adams, a close friend of James Dean's. Since Dean's death, rumors have been flying that Adams had a sexual relationship with both Dean and Elvis.

2 ANDREW JOHNSON
Fact: Vice President Andrew Johnson took his oath of office while completely drunk.

Andrew Johnson was the vice president during Lincoln's administration. He had a strong dislike for the aristocracy, whom he thought were there by the labor of the poor, such as his own family. An observer reported that the president was "glassy-eyed and smelling of whiskey, [as] he reminded Congress, the Supreme Court, the Cabinet, and pretty much everyone within hearing distance that they owed their positions to 'plebeians' such as himself, then kissed the Bible and staggered away." In response, the *New York Times* said, "To think that one frail life stands between this insolent, clownish creature and the presidency! May God bless and spare Abraham Lincoln!" History shows us that God didn't spare Lincoln, and Johnson eventually became president. His presidency was such a disaster that Congress tried to impeach him twice— successfully on the second attempt! He avoided being fired by just one vote.

1 POPE PIUS IX

Fact: Pope Pius IX kidnapped a Jewish child and had him raised as a Catholic.

On the evening of June 23, 1858, in Bologna, then part of the papal states, police arrived at the home of a Jewish couple, Salomone ("Momolo") and Marianna Padovani Mortara, to seize one of their eight children, six-year-old Edgardo, and transport him to Rome to be raised as a ward of the state. The police had orders from Holy Office authorities in Rome, authorized by Pope Pius IX. Church officials had been told that a 14-year-old Catholic servant girl of the Mortaras, Anna Morisi, had baptized Edgardo while he was ill because she feared that he would otherwise die and go to hell. According to Catholic Church doctrine, Edgardo's baptism, even if it was illegal under canon law, was valid and made him a Christian. Under the canon law, non-Christians could not raise a Christian child, even their own. Edgardo was taken to a house for Catholic converts in Rome, maintained at state expense. His parents were not allowed to see him for several weeks, and then not alone. Pius IX took a personal interest in the case, and all appeals to the Church were rebuffed. Church authorities told the Mortaras that they could have Edgardo back if they abandoned their faith and converted to Catholicism, but they refused.

Despite international protests (including those from the United States government), Pope Pius IX did not relinquish Edgardo, who eventually went on to become a priest. He was also a vehement supporter of the Vatican taking the first steps toward making Pius IX a saint.

10 MEDIEVAL URBAN LEGENDS

10 INCUBUS AND SUCCUBUS

Incubuses are male demons who were reputed to lie upon sleeping women in order to have sex with them. Their aim in doing this was to father children with the woman. The female version of an incubus is called a succubus. The legends of incubuses and succubusses most likely arose due to the preoccupation of medieval people with sin, sexual sins in particular.

9 THE LOST TRIBES

The ten lost tribes of Israel refer to ten ancient tribes that vanished from the Biblical account after Israel was destroyed by ancient Assyrians. All over the world can be found ethnic groups who lay claim to being members of the tribes. In another bizarre connection, the Book of Mormon (the primary religious text of the Church of Jesus Christ of Latter Day Saints) suggests that Native Americans are from two of the lost tribes.

8 FOUNTAIN OF YOUTH

The fountain of youth—still much yearned for today—was an urban legend in Europe after the discovery of America. Its location (ironically) was said to be Florida. Eternal youth featured heavily in urban mythology of the Middle Ages; in addition to the fountain of youth, we hear of elixirs of life and universal panaceas.

7 THE WANDERING JEW

The wandering Jew is a figure from medieval Christianity who was first spoken of in the 13th century. He is said to be a Jew who mocked Christ on his way to the crucifixion and was, consequently, cursed to walk the earth until the second coming. It's possible that the tale was partly derived from the Biblical punishment of Cain, who was also forced to wander the earth scavenging.

6 POPE JOAN

Pope Joan (also called *la Papessa*) is the name of a legendary female pope who supposedly reigned for less than three years around 850, between the papacies of Leo IV and Benedict III (although there were only two months between the two reigns). She is known primarily from a legend that circulated in the Middle Ages. Pope Joan is regarded by most modern historians and religious scholars as fictitious, possibly originating as an antipapal satire. She is known mainly from the 13th-century chronicler Martin of Opava, who did her writing 500 years after the alleged Popess' life. Most scholars dismiss Pope Joan as a medieval legend. *The Oxford Dictionary of Popes* acknowledges that this legend was widely believed for centuries, even among Catholic circles, but declares that there is "no contemporary evidence for a female pope at any of the dates suggested for her reign," and goes on to say that "the known facts of the respective periods make it impossible to fit [a female pope] in." For those who wonder what would happen if this were true (or were to ever be true): a female is not able to be a priest, and a Pope cannot be crowned unless he is a priest first.

5 ROBIN HOOD

Robin Hood is a character from English folklore whose fame has long survived the Middle Ages. He is such a popular character that even today people constantly search through the history books in the hopes of finding evidence that he was a living man and not just a myth. Perhaps the strangest thing is that he is most often lauded for his acts of stealing, which is otherwise condemned by modern society.

4 THE HOLY GRAIL

The Holy Grail has been the source of many controversial books and movies in modern times. It is supposed to be the plate or cup used by Jesus at the last supper, and it appears in much medieval folklore. Adding to its mysteriousness is its alleged connection to the Knights Templar. The Knights (a medieval organization surrounded by mystery) are said to have been the keepers of the Holy Grail. Like the Robin Hood myth, treasure seekers and the curious continue to try to find it to this day.

3 KING ARTHUR

King Arthur, as in the previous two entries, is believed by many to have been a real man, but a complete lack of evidence in the historical record strongly suggests that he is merely a legendary king invented to describe the ideal monarch. Tales of King Arthur include heroic stories of the Knights of the Round Table, the dashing Sir Lancelot, and the ravishingly beautiful Guinevere.

2 THE CHILDREN'S CRUSADE

A medieval myth that has persisted to this day is that of the children's crusade. The myth says that children were forced by the Catholic Church to launch a crusade that resulted in their slaughter. In fact, it never happened at all. The crusade was most likely a voluntary band of men from the countryside who decided to launch their own battle in the Holy Land. The reason the true nature of the crusade turned into a medieval myth was over a misunderstanding of the Latin word "*pueri*," which means "boy." People mistakenly thought that the members of the crusades were *pueri*, but the term was commonly used as slang for a "country bumpkin." There is no historical evidence that a children's crusade ever took place.

1 PRESTER JOHN

From the 12th century to the 17th, legends of Prester John spread across Europe. He was said to be a great and holy king who ruled over a lost Christian nation somewhere in the midst of the Orient. It was believed that he descended from one of the three magi who appeared at the birth of Christ, and his kingdom was described as being full of great riches. Interestingly, these tales largely contributed to the great voyages of discovery in the Middle Ages.

10 FORGOTTEN FACTS ABOUT MOMENTOUS EVENTS

10 MAN ON THE MOON

While the moon landing may arguably be the single most remembered event in the history of mankind and President John F. Kennedy is remembered as the man who championed and led this accomplishment, often forgotten is Kennedy's true motive for the daunting task. In a conversation with James Webb, the director of NASA at the time, Kennedy was quoted as saying, "Everything we do ought to really be tied into getting on to the moon ahead of the Russians ... otherwise we shouldn't be spending that kind of money, because I'm not interested in space ... The only justification for [the cost] is because we hope to beat [the USSR] to demonstrate that instead of being behind by a couple of years, by God, we passed them." Due to this passion to push the U.S. past the Soviets, Kennedy essentially diverted all of NASA's funds to the moon landing, much to the dismay of Webb, who favored a broader approach of discovery and programs.

9 MASS SUICIDE AT JONESTOWN

Due to the powerful images conjured up while recalling the horrific incident in Jonestown that saw more than 900 men, women, and children die through suicide or murder, the world often only remembers the victims who were actually in the compound itself and forgets those who tried to flee with Congressman Leo Ryan, who was there to determine whether or not U.S. citizens were being held against their will. The day before the mass suicide, Ryan and other U.S. government officials landed in Guyana. During their visit, many of the cult members asked to leave with Ryan's delegations. Arriving at the airport, the delegation was ambushed by the cult with the help of a member who had embedded himself into the group of people who wanted to leave. This cult member drew a gun on the plane and summarily shot the passengers. Additionally, the cult sent a small force to attack the delegation from a tractor with a trailer. Congressman Ryan was one of those murdered, becoming the first and only congressman killed in the line of duty in the history of the U.S.

8 JAPAN'S EMPEROR AFTER HIROSHIMA

When U.S. history recalls Japan in World War II, it often only remembers the mushroom clouds that scarred Japan's physical geography and overlooks the strong psychological moorings that were devastated after the surrender. Following the surrender of Japan, General MacArthur forced Hirohito to issue the Humanity Declaration, or the *Ningen-sengen*. In the declaration, the emperor proclaimed that, in fact, contrary to the Shinto religion, which the culture at the time was largely built upon, he was not a god. Interestingly, however, the confession was given in an archaic, formal form of Japanese that allowed the emperor to be deliberately vague. It's theorized that he substituted the common word *arahitogami* or "living god," with the much less common word *akitsumikami*, meaning "an incarnation of god." Many scholars have noted that one could be a living god without being an incarnation of god.

7 THE TERRORIST ATTACKS OF 9/11

Because of the sensational images of the two 110-story Twin Towers of the World Trade Center falling, many people forget the overall tremendous devastation that the 9/11 terrorist attacks truly resulted in. On September 11, 2001, in addition to the Twin Towers, other World Trade Center buildings—7 World Trade Center (47 stories tall), 6 World Trade Center (8 stories tall), and 3 World Trade Center—and the St. Nicholas Greek Orthodox Church were all completely destroyed, the latter entirely buried by debris of Tower 2. Also, 5 World Trade Center (9 stories tall), 4 World Trade Center (9 stories tall), the Deutsche Bank Building (40 stories tall), and Manhattan Community College's Filterman Hall (15 stories tall) were all damaged beyond repair and have been or are slated for demolition.

6 2004 INDIAN OCEAN TSUNAMI

Immediately following the 2004 tsunami, the world was so rocked with the staggering death toll of nearly 240,000 individuals that it is often forgotten that many of the more rural and traditional citizens were able to survive through an indigenous understanding of the signs of an approaching tsunami. For example, scientists in the area were initially convinced that the aboriginal population of the Andaman Islands would be significantly ravaged by the tsunami; however, all but one of the tribes in the islands (oddly enough, the one that had largely converted to Christianity and thus a change of lifestyle) suffered only minor casualties. When questioned, the tribesmen explained to the scientists that the land and ocean often fought over boundaries, and when the earth shook they knew that the sea would soon enter the land until the two could realign their borders. Because of this, the villagers fled to the hills and suffered few or no casualties. Additionally of note is the story of Tilly Smith, a ten-year-old British student vacationing on Mikakhao Beach in Thailand. Tilly had recently studied tsunamis in school and immediately recognized the frothing bubbles and receding ocean as a harbinger of a tsunami. Along with her parents, they warned the beach and it was entirely evacuated safely.

5 THE BOBBY KENNEDY ASSASSINATION

While nearly everyone can name the place (the Ambassador Hotel in Los Angeles) and perpetrator of the assassination (Sirhan Sirhan), few people recall the man who captured and disarmed the gunman when Bobby Kennedy was assassinated. That man was Rosie Grier, an American football sensation (Super Bowl champion, two-time pro-bowler, member of the Ram's "Fearsome Foursome," and five-time All-Pro defensive tackle). On the night of the assassination, Grier was the bodyguard for Kennedy's pregnant wife. Along with Rafer Johnson, an Olympic gold-medal decathlete, Grier heard the shots and tackled Sirhan. Grier then jammed his finger behind the trigger of the gun and broke Sirhan's arm. Grier fought off those who were literally ready to rip Sirhan apart. Later Grier would explain that he "would not allow more violence." Additionally, Grier would later testify to Judge Lance Ito during the O.J. Simpson trial that he had been present when O.J. confessed to the crimes in prison. Judge Ito, however, ruled that the testimony was inadmissible.

4 THE MOSCOW THEATRE MASSACRE

When the news broke that the Russian military had ended the standoff in which 850 people were held hostage by a Chechen separatist group in Moscow, the focus of the news quickly turned to the dramatic rescue. Because of this, the heroism and sacrifice of Olga Romanova is often overlooked. When Romanova, a 26-year-old perfume-shop clerk, heard of the crisis, she left the safety of her parent's house and walked to the theater alone. Convinced that she could reason with the terrorists and at the very least convince them to free the women and children, Romanova somehow managed to bypass the intense security in the area and enter the theater. She then confronted the rebels and pleaded for the immediate release of the hostages. The terrorists, suspecting that she was FSB (Russian Federal Security Service), marched her into an adjoining room and executed her with a shot to the head.

3 KENT STATE SHOOTINGS

Due to the iconic photo of a student lying dead and another leaning over his body and weeping, the Kent State Massacre has largely been accepted as a single event that took place in Ohio and resulted in four students being killed by the U.S. National Guard. What is often forgotten about the event is the sheer size and scale of the overall national unrest at the time of the shootings. Immediately following the shooting and based on the common belief that "they can't kill us all," 900 college campuses were closed because of violent and nonviolent protests. Also, 100,000 people descended on Washington, D.C., smashing car windows, lighting fires, looting, and barricading streets and freeways. President Nixon was evacuated to Camp David, and the 82nd Airborne was brought in to defend the White House. Additionally, Nixon organized a special commission to focus solely on campus unrest. Ray Price, Nixon's chief speechwriter, was quoted as saying, "That's not student protest, that's civil war." Overall, four million people took part in the protests. It was at the time the only nationwide protest on college campuses.

2 ALTAMONT FREE CONCERT OF 1969

When the Altamont Concert is remembered, it is often solely for the Hell's Angels providing "security" and the ensuing riot that left an 18-year-old man dead. According to sources, the Rolling Stones had hired the Hell's Angels to keep people off the stage and to escort the Stones through the concert site. According to some witnesses, the Angels were hired for $500 worth of beer. As the evening went on, the crowd and the Angels got increasingly agitated with one another. The crowd pressed the stage and the Angels fought them back. In the ensuing melee, Meredith Hunter was killed and the death has ever since been remembered as an example of the Angel's inherent lawlessness and violence. However, what is not often recalled is the actual event that spawned the killing. Meredith Hunter, high on methamphetamines, was captured on camera approaching the stage and brandishing a pistol. In response to the imminent danger, an Angel drew a knife and stabbed him. The act of violence was determined by a judge to be one of justifiable homicide, as the Angel had every reason to believe his life was in jeopardy.

1 THE BOSTON MASSACRE

The Boston Massacre was one of the most critical events that led the American colonies to revolt against King George III. While it is well remembered in this fashion, the fates of the British soldiers who fired on the civilians are often forgotten. In fact, the Captain and eight of the soldiers who were present were arrested and tried. What's interesting is that the defender of the soldiers was none other than John Adams, Founding Father and future president of the United States. No lawyer in Boston would take the case, so the court asked Adams to represent the men. Although he was hesitant, he so believed that everyone deserved a fair trial that he finally relented. Adams successfully convinced the jury that six of the men were afraid for their lives and therefore had the right to defend themselves. Interestingly, two of the men were convicted of murder; however, Adams presented a loophole to the court whereby, according to English law, if the men could read, then they could claim to be clergy and thereby were not bound by secular law. Adams had the men read out loud from the Bible, and the charges were reduced to manslaughter, for which they were punished by a branding on the thumb.

10 REASONS THE DARK AGES WERE NOT DARK

10 UNIVERSITIES BORN

The Classical education—still used today in some schools—was the system used by the universities that were created in the early Middle Ages (the first in history). The universities taught the arts, law, medicine, and theology. The University of Bologna, founded in 1088, was the first ever to grant degrees. In addition to the Classical structure, which was based on ancient Greek education, these medieval universities were heavily influenced by Islamic education, which was thriving at the time. While women were not admitted to universities in the early days, the education of women did exist. The convents of the day educated young women, who often entered at a very young age. One such woman, Hildegard Von Bingen, is one of the most celebrated women of the medieval era, and she had great influence over the men in power at the time.

9 SCIENTIFIC FOUNDATIONS LAID

While progress in science was slow during this period in the West, it was steady and of a very high quality. The foundation was laid for the wonderful blossoming of science that was to occur in the High Middle Ages to come. It can be safely said that without the study of science in the early Middle Ages, we would be considerably behind in our scientific knowledge today. Ronald Numbers, a professor at Cambridge University, has said, "Notions such as: 'the rise of Christianity killed off ancient science,' 'the medieval Christian Church suppressed the growth of the natural sciences,' 'the medieval Christians thought that the world was flat,' and 'the Church prohibited autopsies and dissections during the Middle Ages' [are] examples of widely popular myths that still pass as historical truth, even though they are not supported by historical research."

8 CAROLINGIAN RENAISSANCE

The Carolingian Renaissance was a period of advancements in literature, writing, the arts, architecture, jurisprudence, and liturgical and scriptural studies that occurred in the late 8th and 9th centuries. The Carolingians were Franks, and the most well-known is Charlemagne. The Carolingian Empire was considered a rebirth of the culture of the Roman Empire. At the time, vulgar Latin was beginning to be replaced by various dialects as the main spoken languages in Europe, so the creation of schools was vital to spread knowledge further among the common people. It was also this period that gave us the foundation of Western classical music.

7 BYZANTINE GOLDEN AGE

Under Emperor Justinian, this period gave us the *Corpus Juris Civilis* (Body of Civil Law), an enormous compendium of Roman law. Literacy was high, elementary education was widespread, even in the countryside, middle education was available to many people, and higher education was also widely accessible. In the Byzantine Empire during this period there was a massive outpouring of books: encyclopedias, lexicons, and anthologies. While the people of the Byzantine Empire didn't create a lot of new thinking, they solidified and protected for the future much of what was already known.

6 RELIGIOUS UNITY

This is a sticky topic, but the fact is, during the early Middle Ages, Europe had a united church, an agreed upon canon of the Bible, and a well-developed philosophical tradition. This led (as one would expect) to a great period of peace among the Western nations. While Islam was not in agreement with the doctrines of the West, much mutual sharing of information happened and the Islamic contribution to the West is still felt today. This union of beliefs allowed for intellectual progress unseen since the Roman Empire at its heyday. In a sense, you might consider this period as the calm before the storm, as it was merely a hundred years later that the first Crusade would be called to take Jerusalem back from the Muslims, an event that ended the flow of knowledge between groups.

5 ALGEBRA ARRIVED

Thanks to the learnings of the Islamic people in the East, the world received its first book on algebra. The *Compendious Book on Calculation by Completion and Balancing* was written by Al-Khwārizmī (790–840) and the Arabic title of the book gave us the word "algebra." The word "algorithm"

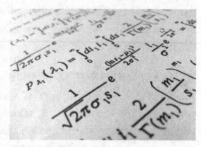

comes from Al-Khwārizmī's name. This book gave us the first systematic solution of linear and quadratic equations. Later translations of his books also gave us the decimal-positional number system we use today. Al-Khwārizmī, along with Diophantas, is considered the father of algebra.

4 ART AND ARCHITECTURE

During the early Middle Ages, architecture was diverse and innovative. It introduced the idea of realistic images in art and it laid the groundwork for the Romanesque period that was to come in the High Middle Ages. The period also included the introduction and absorption of classical forms and concepts in architecture. It can safely be said that this period was the first period of high art, with previous styles being much more functional and less "artistic." In the early Middle Ages, we witness the birth of an astonishing and beautiful history of art and building.

3 FANTASTIC WEATHER

Trivial as it may seem, the weather played a great part in the lives of the average people during the Middle Ages and beyond. When we think of the "Dark Ages," we tend to see images of snow storms, rain, thunder, and darkness, such as we see in films like *The Name of the Rose*. The fact is, in the early Middle Ages, the North Atlantic region was warming up, so much so that at the opening of the High Middle Ages (AD 1100), the area was 100 years into an event now known as the Medieval Warm Period. This period thawed much ice and enabled the Vikings to begin their colonization of Greenland and other northern nations. Ironically, the Protestant Reformation, from the 16th century up until the 19th century, suffered the Little Ice Age, meaning that the period of "enlightenment" was literally darker and colder than the "Dark" Ages. During the Middle Ages, reforms and better knowledge of agriculture provided a boost to food supplies.

2 LAW BECOMES FAIR

The early Middle Ages had a complex system of laws that were often not connected, but they were effective and fair for the most part. For merchants traveling around the world, there was the *Lex Mercatoria* (Law Merchant), which had evolved over time. This law included arbitration and promoted good practice among traders. At the same time, Anglo-Saxon law was formed with a focus on keeping peace in the land. While this eventually led to some very tough laws, living under the legal system in the early Middle Ages was probably the best time to be alive, as it was still flexible and fair for the majority. The third important legal system was the Early Germanic law, which allowed each person to be tried by his own people so as to not be disadvantaged by ignorance or major cultural differences.

1 AGRICULTURAL BOOM

If you wanted to die a martyr by starvation, the early Middle Ages was not the time to do it! As a consequence of the excellent weather and improving agricultural knowledge, the West did extremely well. Iron tools were in wide use in the Byzantine Empire, feudalism in other parts of the world introduced efficient management of land, and massive surpluses were created so that animals were fed on grains and not grass. Public safety was also guaranteed under the feudal system, so peace and prosperity were the lot for most people.

15 QUIRKY FACTS ABOUT MEDIEVAL ENGLAND

15 BATTLE OF HASTINGS

This famous battle did not take place in Hastings! It was actually waged at Senlac Hill, about six miles northwest of Hastings. "The Battle at Senlac Hill" certainly doesn't have the same ring to it as the Battle of Hastings.

14 LONDON BRIDGE IS FALLING DOWN

One of the earliest versions of the London Bridge was destroyed in 1014 when the Saxons rowed up the Thames, tied ropes to the bridge, and pulled it down! This helped regain London for the Anglo-Saxon king from the Danes. It's possible that this event may have been the inspiration for the nursery rhyme "London Bridge is Falling Down."

13 CONTINENTAL QUEEN

Berengaria of Navarre was the Queen of England through her marriage to King Richard I (King Richard the Lionheart). Little is known of her life, but what is known is that she is the only queen of England never to step foot in England! The entire time she was married to Richard, she lived in Continental Europe. In fact, Richard himself only spent about six months in England because he was so busy traveling on Crusade business.

12 SLAVERY

In 1086, 10 percent of the population recorded in the *Domesday Book*, a large census, were slaves. In some areas, that number was as high as 20 percent.

11 BROWN BEARS

England used to be the native home of brown bears, but they became extinct around the 11th century. In later parts of the Middle Ages, the bears were imported into England for sport.

10 GAY KING

There's much evidence to suggest that King Richard I was a homosexual. There's a possibility that he met his wife, Berenegaria, while in a sexual relationship with her brother, the future King Sancho VII of Navarre. It's also reported that he and King Philip II of France were involved. A historian of the time, Roger of Hoveden, said they "ate from the same dish and at night slept in one bed" and had a "passionate love between them."

9 CRIMES COMMITTED BY...ANIMALS?

It was not uncommon in England during the medieval period for animals to be put on trial for crimes. They could be sentenced to death if found guilty. Take that, PETA!

8 PIGGY BANKS

The Middle English term *"pygg"* referred to a type of clay. In the Middle Ages, people often kept coins in jars or pots made of *pygg*; these were called *"pygg* jars," By the 18th century, with the evolution of language, these came to be known as "pig banks" or "piggy banks."

7 PUBLIC BATHS

Contrary to popular belief, medieval English people bathed quite regularly in public baths designed for that purpose. This was due to the belief that "cleanliness is next to Godliness." Public baths were eventually opposed by the Protestants in the 16th century because prostitution was common there.

6 LET THEM EAT RYE BREAD

Most common folk in medieval England had to produce their own food. For this reason, rye and barley bread was common among the poor, who could not afford the large quantities of manure needed to grow wheat for white bread.

5 TRIAL BY ORDEAL

This practice was common in England in the Middle Ages. In the trial, the accused was subjected to a very painful task, such as being burned by a hot iron; if they survived the trial or their wounds healed quickly, they were found not guilty since it was believed that God had performed a miracle to help the accused. The Catholic Church forbade participation in these trials and demanded the use of compurgation instead. Compurgation was the taking of an oath of innocence by the accused, which 12 peers must believe.

4 HOME REMEDIES

One bizarre recipe for a medicine to protect against the plague involved drinking ale that had crushed roasted eggshells, leaves and petals of marigold flowers, and treacle added to it. Needless to say, this was not particularly effective.

3 BARBERS WERE DOCTORS

The barber's pole symbolizes blood and bandages, as most barbers also performed the roles of surgeons and dentists in their towns. Bandages stained with blood would be washed and hung from a pole outside the barber's shop. These would then twist in the wind to form the spiral pattern we're familiar with today. Macabre, but true.

2 NO LAST NAMES

Prior to the introduction of surnames in England in 1066, everyone born had just one name. When surnames were introduced, they would often include a nickname, such as Robert Red (symbolic of his hair color). If Robert went bald over time, his name could change to Robert Ball ("ball" meaning "bald" in Middle English). In time, the system evolved to the point where people would take the same name as their father, giving us the modern surname system.

1 DECORATIVE DRAINS

Contrary to popular belief, gargoyles were not added to churches and buildings to ward off evil spirits—they were drain pipes! True gargoyles project out of a wall (decorative monsters are not gargoyles) and rainwater flows out their mouths away from the building rather than down the side of it, which would cause damage. Gargoyles can be found all over Great Britain and are visible on virtually every church built there during the Middle Ages.

10 ABSOLUTELY AWFUL ROMAN EMPERORS

10 DOMITIAN

The Apocalypse of Saint John, the last book of the Bible, is believed to have been written during Domitian's reign at the end of the 1st century. Domitian was a staunch advocate for the Roman gods and goddesses, the worship of whom had fallen out of practice by the time of his rise to power.

Eusebius of Caesarea, writing 300 years later, recounts that the first large-scale Christian and Jewish persecution began during Domitian's reign. There is no non-Christian history of such activities, but Domitian is known to have been tyrannically opposed to all other religions other than Roman.

Like so many other emperors, Domitian dealt with dissent among his close advisors and friends by means of death. He executed a few too many prominent politicians and wealthy citizens, and the straw that broke the camel's back was his murder of his secretary, Epaproditus.

A man named Stephanus, and several others, conspired to kill Domitian. Stephanus pretended to be wounded for several days so he could conceal a dagger under his bandages. He approached Domitian in his bedroom and stabbed him in the groin, whereupon the emperor was beset by several men, one of whom was a fearsome gladiator, who all stabbed him to death.

9 SEPTIMIUS SEVERUS

There is no doubt that Christians and Jews were persecuted severely during Severus' reign. He believed in a draconian interpretation of Roman law, which did not tolerate any religion but Roman. He did not seek out any particular religious culture, but simply persecuted all foreign ones.

Christians and Jews were the most commonly persecuted, and 1000 to 3000 were executed after being given the option of cursing Jesus or Yahweh, or being beheaded or crucified. Severus had absolutely no respect or care for anyone except his army, since they were the ones who could rise up and depose him. He managed to stabilize the empire through draconian fear, but this stability did not last long once his son, number 4 on this list, took the throne.

8 MAXIMINUS THRAX

Maximinus was, by all accounts, a huge man, well over six feet tall, perhaps seven feet or more. He has been blamed for causing the Crisis of the 3rd Century, largely due to his murders of several dozen of his closest friends, advisors, and benefactors. He did not trust anyone and intended to make the people love him by conquest and expansion.

His first campaign was against the Alamanni people of Germania. They were absolutely no threat to Rome at the time, but Maximinus invaded them and conquered them, albeit at a terrible cost to his army. The people did not love him for this, but hated him. But he went right on invading Sarmatia and Dacia, modern-day Ukraine and Romania, respectively. These people had not instigated anything against Rome.

Meanwhile, a revolt began in North Africa, which set up two men as claimants to the Roman throne, Gordianus Sempronianus and his son. The Roman senate supported them, and in response, Maximinus marched his army on Rome, but his troops had been fighting for so long that they were exhausted and sick. They were unable to enter the closed city gates and many deserted. His

Praetorian Guard had finally had enough and stabbed Maximinus in the back. Then they beheaded his son and advisors and put their heads on poles around the city walls, whereupon they were let in.

7 DIOCLETIAN

Diocletian reigned at the end of the Crisis of the 3rd Century, and although he significantly stabilized and improved the empire's military and economy, he will forever be remembered as the worst persecutor of Christians in history.

He issued several edicts in 303 that removed all rights from Christians until they converted to the Roman religion. Of course, the Christians refused, and from 303 to 311, at least 3000 were martyred. At first, those who refused were simply imprisoned, but it was not long before they were executed by both crucifixion and beheading. Christian churches were sought all over the empire and burned to the ground and looted, and even Christian senators were stripped of their jobs, imprisoned, and executed.

When the persecution didn't seem to be working, since the Christians simply went into hiding and continued to spread their religion, Diocletian advocated their torturous and entertaining executions in the Circus Maximus and Colosseum, and this was the time when most Christians were thrown to the lions, much to the delight of the Roman citizens who worshiped Roman gods.

The murders did not truly stop until Constantine's rise to absolute power in 324.

6 TIBERIUS

Tiberius was emperor after Augustus, from AD 14 to 37, and he didn't care for the job. All he wanted was the luxury, and he left the senate to do all the ruling. The senate despised him for this and they criticized him to the Roman populace until he no longer trusted his safety in Rome and left for the island of Capri. He erected statues of his captain of the guard, Lucius Sejanus, all over the city, and gave all the tasks of ruling to him. Tiberius more or less retired to Capri for the rest of his long life, only returning to Rome a few times.

While he lived on Capri, he had a huge villa built for himself, Villa Jovis, (the Villa of Jupiter), in which he indulged his pedophilia. He swam naked with and raped infants, toddlers, and young boys. He did not otherwise physically harm them in any way, but even in his late 70s, sex with young children was one of his favorite pastimes.

5 NERO

Nero used the office of emperor to suit his desire for an opulent lifestyle and had absolutely no care for the welfare of the people. He never trusted his mother, Agrippina, and tried to kill her by having her ship sunk. This didn't work, and he simply ordered her to be executed. He routinely executed anyone close to him whom he did not trust, always under mysterious circumstances, because he feared the Praetorian Guard.

He managed to reign for 15 years in this way, killing anyone who dissented. He was accused of treason beginning in AD 62, and simply executed the accusers, several dozen of them. He loved to go to bars and whorehouses and didn't even disguise himself.

The Great Fire of Rome, in AD 64, has given rise to the legend that Nero fiddled while Rome burned. This is not true. He was away in Antium (Anzio) and returned to Rome to try to have the fire put out. He even paid for this out of his own pocket.

He did help out the survivors tremendously, letting them stay in the palace until their homes were rebuilt. But the fire largely destroyed the city center, and Nero had a large part of this destruction rebuilt as his Domus Aurea. This was his gift to himself, a gigantic palatial garden complex of 100 to 300 acres, for which he heavily taxed the citizens throughout the empire.

The city wanted a scapegoat, so Nero blamed the fire on the Christians and they were terribly persecuted. He had many people arrested, impaled, and burned to death as torches to light his gardens in the Domus Aurea. He is said to have breathed in the stench and laughed heartily, then turned to his lyre and sung his own songs.

The taxes irritated the populace sufficiently to begin revolts in various provinces, and by AD 68 Nero was no longer loved, but hated by all. His guards deserted him in the palace, and he fled to a nearby villa, where a messenger appeared to tell him that the senate had declared him a public enemy, whom they would beat to death. He had a grave dug, while he repeated, "What an artist dies within me!"

Then he stabbed a dagger into his throat and bled to death. It is believed by most scholars that Nero is the "great beast" whose number is 666, referred to in the last book of the Bible, the Apocalypse.

4 CARACALLA

Caracalla was not insane. He was malicious and sadistic. From 211 to 217 he presided over an awe-inspiring spectacle of fearsome acts. He had his brother and co-emperor, Geta, and Geta's wife assassinated.

The citizens of Alexandria, Egypt, ridiculed this crime with a public play, and when Caracalla got wind of it, he traveled with an army to Alexandria, invited the citizens into their city square, and slaughtered them, looting and burning the whole city; 20,000 died.

This was the sort of emperor he showed himself to be in almost every Roman province, putting down all hints of rebellions, even where they were not imminent. At the slightest whiff of discord, he ordered death. Wherever he went, his army killed, raped, and destroyed.

He was murdered by one of his guardsmen, on April 8, 217, while urinating on the side of the road outside Carrhae. Caracalla had had the guard's brother executed on a false accusation.

3 COMMODUS

Commodus was the son of Marcus Aurelius, one of Rome's greatest rulers, and this only enhanced Commodus' crimes in the public mind.

He adored the gladiatorial games, so much so that he personally entered many of them and fought alongside the gladiators, who were all criminals or slaves. This severely offended the entire empire, especially the senate.

Commodus once ordered all the cripples, hunchbacks, and general undesirables in the city to be rounded up, thrown into the arena, and forced to hack one another to death with meat cleavers.

He especially adored killing animals, and killed 100 lions in one day, to spectators' disgust. He singlehandedly killed three elephants in the arena, beheaded an ostrich and laughed at the senators attending, brandishing the head and motioning that they were next. He speared a giraffe to death, an animal which the spectators did not see as fearsome at all.

The senators conspired to have him killed and poisoned him, but he threw the poison up. They then sent in his favorite wrestler, a gladiator named Narcissus, who strangled him in his bath. His reign lasted 12 years, from 180 to 192.

2 ELAGABALUS

It can be argued that Elagabalus' assassination reign, from 218 to 222, began the Crisis of the 3rd Century, during which Rome was ripped to pieces from the inside out by civil war after civil war, rampant anarchy, uprisings, economic hysteria, and assaults from Germania and elsewhere.

Elagabalus took the throne at the ripe old age of 14 and immediately indulged his most sordid, depraved fantasies and desires. He was a man, yes, but wanted dearly to be a woman, and offered gargantuan sums of money to the physician who could turn him into one for real.

Until then, he enjoyed cross-dressing and whored himself out to common men in whorehouses throughout Rome, wearing female disguises and facial makeup. He even solicited men in the Imperial Palace, standing completely naked in the doorway of his favorite bedroom and purring at every passerby, even his Praetorian Guards.

He confided to the head of the Guard that he would like to castrate himself and asked what the most painful method would be: cutting, crushing, or cooking on open coals. He had hundreds, perhaps thousands, of affairs with men and women while he was married to a Vestal virgin, which was a serious outrage among Romans.

He installed El-Gabal, the Syrian sun god, as the chief god of Rome, surpassing Jupiter, and it is this sun god from which we derive the emperor's nickname. He transferred all Roman sacred relics from their respective temples to a new temple he had built for El-Gabal, the Elagabalium, and named himself the high priest.

After four years of this, Rome erupted into riots as the citizens demanded his death or deposition. Elagabalus responded by walking right into the Praetorian encampment and demanding the arrest and execution of everyone. Instead, everyone descended on him and his mother. He tried to hide in a large clothes chest, but they opened it and stabbed him to death. He and his mother were beheaded and dragged throughout Rome. He was then flung into the Tiber River and spat upon. He was 18 years old.

1 CALIGULA

"Little Boots" took the throne on the death of his second cousin Tiberias, who was something of a great-uncle to him. Some say Caligula ordered the head of the Praetorian Guard to smother him with a pillow.

Upon his ascension, everyone in the empire rejoiced. For the first seven months or so, he was loved by all. He paid handsome bonuses to the military to get them on his side, and recalled many whom Augustus and Tiberias had exiled.

But he became very sick in October of AD 37, and the disease has never been pinned down. Philo blames it on his extravagant lifestyle of too much food, wine, and sex. After the disease passed and Caligula made a full recovery, he had turned into one of the most evil men in human history. Some Jewish, Christian, and Muslim historians for centuries afterward even considered that Caligula might have been possessed by a demon.

He has been accused of the most awesomely disgusting, insane, luridly depraved crimes against humanity and morality, and this lister is sorry to say that the accusations are all absolutely true.

He began ordering the murders of anyone who had ever crossed him or even disagreed with him on mundane matters. He had a very good memory. He exiled his own wife and proclaimed himself a god, dressing up as Apollo, Venus (a goddess), Mercury, and Hercules. He demanded that everyone, from senators to guards to guests and public crowds, refer to him as divine in his presence.

When he was a boy, a seer told him that he would never be emperor until he walked on water. So he built a pontoon bridge across the Bay of Naples, put on the breastplate of Alexander the Great, and paraded night and day across the bay, throwing lavish sex orgies in the light of bonfires.

He attempted to instate his favorite horse, Incitatus ("Galloper"), as a priest and consul, and ordered a beautiful marble stable built for him, complete with chairs and couches on which Incitatus never sat.

Once, at the Circus Maximus, the games ran out of criminals, and the next event was the lions, his favorite. He ordered his guards to drag the first five rows of spectators into the arena, which they did. These hundreds of people were all devoured for his amusement.

A citizen once insulted him to his face in a fit of rage, and Caligula responded by having him tied down and beaten with heavy chains. He made this last for three months, having the man brought out from a dungeon and beaten, until Caligula and the whole crowds that gathered were too offended by the smell of the man's gangrenous brain, whereupon he was beheaded.

Caligula's favorite torture was sawing. The saw blade filleted the spine and spinal cord from crotch to chest, and the victim was unable to pass out due to excess blood to the brain.

He also relished chewing up the testicles of victims without biting them off, while they were restrained upside down before him.

He had one man who insulted him and his entire family publicly executed, one after another, in front of a crowd. The man and wife were first, followed by the oldest child, then the second oldest, and so on. The crowd became outraged and began to disperse, but many stayed, watching in morbid fascination. The last of the family was a 12-year-old girl, who was sobbing hysterically at what she had been forced to watch. A member of the crowd shouted that, as a virgin, she was exempt from execution. Caligula smiled and ordered the executioner to rape her and then strangle her, which he did.

Caligula publicly had sex with his three sisters at banquets and games, sometimes on the table amid the food. He was finally murdered by the Praetorian Guard and some senators as he was leaving the Circus Maximus after the games. His body was left in the street to rot, and dogs finally ate it. He had ruled for four years.

10 UNFORTUNATE FATES OF ENGLISH KINGS

10 A KING'S POWER

A king's power depended on his ability to win battles and gain land and treasure to give his supporters. He was obliged to keep fighting. If he didn't, he would find himself out of a job or deprived of his life; probably both. The power of any kingdom was only as solid as the strength of its king in battle.

To be able to cut down several enemies in quick succession when in a tight spot, and to be a more efficient killer than one's subordinates, was essential for a king living in a society that regarded warfare as the natural way of life. What was gained by the sword needed to be defended by the sword; of the eight kings who ruled Northumbria between 600 and 700, six died in battle.

One successful monarch was Aethelbald of Mercia, a kingdom that was an amalgamation of 30 different tribes. In a style that was typical of the era, he usurped the throne from his father, Aethelwulf, while the old man was visiting Rome. By 731 he controlled all England south of the Humber, and was styled as "King not only of the Mercian's but also of all the provinces which are called South English." However, his supremacy was neither easily won nor stable and he had many enemies. Saint Boniface, Archbishop of Canterbury, for example, constantly reproached him for not taking a wife and instead fornicating with nuns.

Aethelbald did marry eventually. On his way back from Rome, his father had married Judith, the 13-year-old daughter of the Frankish King Charles the Bald, and when his father died, Aethelbald took her for his own wife. Even that didn't satisfy the clergy, who castigated him for marrying his stepmother (she was by then an ancient 15-year-old). The marriage was annulled and the girl returned to France, where her own father sent her to a nunnery because her marriage had been deemed incestuous. In a rare breach of Anglo-Saxon fidelity (but not a unique one) Aethelbald was murdered by his bodyguard at Seckingham near Tamworth.

9 THE BAYEUX TAPESTRY

The image of the last Anglo-Saxon king on the hill above Senlac, staggering back with an arrow in his eye, has come to epitomize the drama at the Battle of Hastings. It's graphically illustrated on the Bayeux Tapestry, a piece of embroidery 70 meters (230 feet) long created by the women of Canterbury in the early 1070s (so it should really be called the Canterbury Tapestry), and then taken to France.

But this tapestry is not the reliable witness that it seems. The stitching we see today is not necessarily the original, and indeed, some of it might be described as a stitch-up. In the years of its existence, two major tracings and a photographic record of the tapestry have been made, so we have three sets of images, dating from 1729, 1819, and 1872—and there are some dramatic variations. Swords and stirrups appear and disappear, a griffin becomes an angel, and, most significantly, the depiction of the king's slaying are altered.

In the 1729 version, the king has his arm raised and appears about to hurl a spear. In 1819, the shaft of the spear has sprouted a flight of feathers and become an arrow pointed toward his forehead. Fifty-three years later, the angle of the arrow has shifted downward to point directly at his right eye. So it would seem that occasional restoration work coincided with trying to improve the story.

The truth may be less complicated. According to Guy, Bishop of Amiens, the crucial moment came when the Normans finally broke the Saxon shield-wall. With Harold and a few of his faithful retainers still holding out, William handpicked a hit squad to go and hack him down. Four knights overpowered Harold, one striking him in the breast, a second cutting off his head, while another disemboweled him. We are then told that the fourth knight cut off one of the Saxon king's legs, but the standard battlefield mutilation was full castration, so the bishop's account was probably being polite.

8 THE BASTARD

During his lifetime, William I was not known as the Conqueror; his nickname was William the Bastard, owing to the scandal of his birth when his father had an affair with a lowly tanner's daughter. But since he was a ruler who thought nothing of having a man's tongue ripped out and nailed to his front door, people didn't call him that to his face.

There was oppression in England after the conquest, but this was a consequence of the new king's need for security as much as anything. William subdued the south and east easily, but the year after the Battle of Hastings, his former ally, Count Eustace of Boulogne (brother-in-law to Edward the Confessor), tried an invasion of his own and was only stopped by the formidable nature of Dover castle.

Harold Godwinson's sons tried a landing in 1068, and there were more attempts the following year. The most dangerous of these saw a Viking army joining up with the northern earls. They seized York and declared independence, while in answer William took his own army north and began killing everyone who lived there.

The ferocious "Harrying of the North" in 1069 was designed to punish and deter, and it devastated the north of England in a broad swath from York to Durham. Villages and crops were burned and livestock slaughtered. Those who escaped a quick death at the hands of the royal army faced a slow one by starvation. During the winter of that year, many people turned to cannibalism. The death toll has been estimated at 150,000, and the destruction left much of the area depopulated for generations.

From 1066 to 1204 most of the great Norman barons, including King William I, had estates on both sides of the Channel, and they frequently had to return to Normandy to put down rebellions. While burning out the inhabitants of Mantes in 1087, the Conqueror's horse shied at the flames and the pommel of his saddle inflicted a fatal rupture to an already sick man of 61 years.

The king had a very corpulent figure when he died, and his corpse swelled even larger during its transit to the abbey of Saint Stephen in Caen for burial. It became so bloated that it wouldn't fit the coffin prepared for it, and heavy-handed attempts to force the issue resulted in bursting its belly. It follows that William the Conqueror's funeral was less than a sweet-smelling affair.

7 DEATH IN THE FOREST

Robert, William the Conqueror's eldest son, was given the dukedom of Normandy. William Rufus, the second son, became King of England. He was a dashing warrior, but he was a cruel, greedy liar (he was also homosexual, which was a definite negative with the church in those days).

Rufus treated the priesthood with contempt and seemed to glory in wickedness. The filling of a bishopric was a lengthy business, and while a position was vacant, a trustee collected the revenues on behalf of the next bishop. Rufus liked this system. The revenues were directed straight into his own treasury, and at the time of his death, Rufus was enjoying the incomes from 12 abbeys that he deliberately kept without an abbot.

In an incident that will always remain a mystery, Rufus died in 1100, killed by an arrow while hunting in the New Forest (strangely, his favorite nephew had been killed by an arrow in the same place three months earlier). Evidently, he was in the sole company of one William Tyrrell. Tyrrell wasn't sure that his claim that he had nothing to do with the king's death would be believed, and he fled abroad, but even when feeling safe, he denied anything to do with murder.

So was it a hunting accident or an assassination? No one really knows. People cared so little they never bothered to inquire too deeply as to what had happened. Disposal was left to a humble charcoal burner, who, on the payment of a couple of coins, dumped the king's body in his cart and took it to Winchester Cathedral. There, because Rufus had been king, he was buried under the floor, but there was no great ceremony. A year later the tower of the cathedral collapsed, destroying his tomb.

6 HENRY I

Henry, William the Conqueror's youngest son, leapt onto the throne, and he quickly went to war with his brother Robert and added Normandy to his cap. Poor Robert spent the next 28 years shut up in Cardiff Castle as a captive. But we know from surviving accounts that considerable amounts of money were spent on his food and clothes, so he can't have been treated too harshly, and he lived to the ripe old age of 80.

Henry I was quite an effective king, and all over England there was peace and law. He had little interest in living large and lavish, and concentrated on advancing the nation's administration. One of the ways he raised money was by selling charters to towns. Charters were a special privilege that allowed town walls to be built and for those living inside them to elect their own local councils.

Also during his reign, the Court of the Exchequer was formed to handle financial matters, taking its name from the checked cloth on which the accounts were calculated. Henry was the last king for 400 years to leave no debts behind him when he died. He passed away in 1135, apparently from eating too many lampreys (a small parasitic eel-like fish that latches onto trout and salmon, considered a delicacy of cuisine at the time), which is a warning to everyone to go easy on the lampreys.

5 THE ANGEVIN MAN

Henry II was one of the greatest kings to sit on the English throne. He was an energetic, intelligent, and determined operator who ruled for 35 years over a huge territory. He brought peace and order to a war-torn England, defeated rebels on all fronts, and set down the principles of English law. His father had developed a habit of wearing a sprig of bright yellow broom in his hat, from which came his nickname of Plantagenet, and Henry made the name his own.

Including his father's estates, Henry II's kingdom not only encompassed England and Normandy, but Brittany and the duchies of Anjou, Touraine, and Maine, in northeastern France, too. Henry's marriage to Eleanor of Aquitaine added to this her lands in southwestern France, and their domain then stretched from the Scottish borders to the Pyrenees, a realm bigger in area than that ruled by the French king. This was embarrassing for the French, because William the Conqueror had been no more than a French duke, so the King of England was still technically a vassal of the French monarchy.

Later, when he was an aging man, Henry began to show favoritism to his youngest son, John (nicknamed John Lackland because he had been promised no great inheritance). The elder sibling, Richard (later called the Lionheart), became fearful for his promised kingdom and allied with his father's greatest rival, King Phillip of France, and invaded Anjou, the Plantagenet heartland. They overran Maine and Tours, and Henry made such a mess of clearing the ground before the citadel at Le Mans, he accidentally burned down the town.

Defeated, weak, ill, and deserted by almost everyone, Henry sent John off to safety in Normandy while he galloped off through the forest toward a stronghold at Chinon. Richard followed his father, blowing a hunting horn as if he were chasing an animal. Henry became too weak to resist, and at Chinon he surrendered to his son. As an agreed part of the terms, he was shown a list of those nobles who favored rebellion against him, and on the top of the list was John, the younger son whose interests he'd been trying to protect.

He gave up the fight against his sickness, saying, "Let things go as they will; I shall struggle no longer." A few hours later, he was dead. Once he had been the greatest king in the West, now he was nothing. His servants at once ran off after first stealing everything they could, including the clothes off his body. A handful of faithful knights arranged for his burial at a convent. They had to dress him in makeshift finery; a crown of gold lace from a woman's dress, and a lead scepter taken from a statue.

4 EDWARD II

Edward II is famous today for being cuckolded by Mel Gibson's character in *Braveheart* and losing the Battle of Bannockburn. He was certainly a feckless playboy who shared a close relationship with one Piers Gaveston. When Edward became king, he made Gaveston the earl of Cornwall. Being lower-class, foreign, and gay, the king's boyfriend was always going to have to work on his popularity at court. But he didn't bother. Instead, the chirpy Gaveston began a scornful, teasing campaign about his success, much to the annoyance of the other noblemen, all of whom had short tempers and long memories.

A king was expected to marry, so the year after his father's death, Edward took as his wife Isabella, the beautiful 13-year-old daughter of the French king. Edward took the opportunity to give large numbers of wedding presents to Piers Gaveston, who proceeded to maliciously flaunt them in front of their donors. This was too much for the barons at the royal court. They later sought out the insolent young man at Scarborough Castle, dragged him off to a hillside, and cut off his head.

Years passed. The times were desperate, rife with famine and war. All looked to Edward II, for it was a king's duty to lead a nation in times of strife. Unfortunately, Edward II had little inclination or expertise for it and simply consoled himself in the company of a new friend named Hugh le Despenser. A despairing population increasingly looked to Edward's estranged wife, Queen Isabella, to develop a movement against her listless husband.

During a trip to France with her 12-year-old son (Edward III), Isabella fell in love with a disenfranchised marcher lord named Roger Mortimer, and together they hatched a plot to place the younger Edward on the throne, with themselves serving as co-regents. In 1326, the queen was able to return to England with her paramour and a band of German mercenaries. The country rose to support them and Edward II fled from London.

After the popular accession of his young son, there was no place for a deposed monarch like Edward II, and he was eventually confined in Berkeley Castle. The chances are he would have given no more trouble, but one day, probably at the instigation of Mortimer, Edward II's jailors murdered him. In the village of Berkeley, tales were told of hideous screams emanating from the castle, but it was many years before the truth was known. Edward had been killed with a hot poker that was inserted into his anus.

3 RICHARD II

This king started out with great promise. In 1381, at the age of 14, he fearlessly rode out to meet thousands of disenchanted peasants who were in rebellion; he then led them out of London and sent them home. However, facing down the rebels was Richard's one and only hour of glory. In adulthood, he proved to be a bad-tempered, dishonest, and vain sovereign, and he was the first king to demand he be addressed as "Your Majesty."

He married Anne of Bohemia, a sister to King Wenceslas the Good, whom he adored, but after her death, during a wave of plague in 1394, Richard became increasingly irrational. Two years later he wed the French king's daughter, Isabella, but the marriage wasn't a hit, possibly because she was only six.

Richard was afraid of John of Gaunt, the last survivor of the days of the Black Prince, whose reign ended in 1376. The immensely wealthy and influential John was the effective center of power and the key figure in the royal family tree in those days. When the old man died in 1399, Richard was bold enough to confiscate his vast estates, which had been promised to John's son, Henry Bolingbroke. In doing this, Richard made one enemy too many. Henry was a tough character with many friends, and none of them felt safe if the great Duchy of Lancaster could be seized at the royal whim.

Since the English were a warlike race, Richard planned to go Ireland, where English settlers had been driven back to a small pale around Dublin. However, when Richard made a visit there to assess things, Henry Bolingbroke turned up with a force of mercenaries, and by the time the king reached Flint Castle in Wales on his return journey, he found himself opposed by 60,000 men.

Lacking enough loyal nobles to fight himself out of trouble, Richard was compelled to surrender. Henry had started out with the intention of just reclaiming his inheritance, but the unpopularity of the king among the nobles of England was such that his arrival developed into a full-blown takeover.

A short time later, Richard abjectly handed over his crown and was imprisoned in Pontefract Castle. He probably knew he didn't have long to live. The official version is that he went on a hunger strike, and Henry put the dead corpse on display to prove Richard hadn't been physically harmed. However, it's likely he was purposely starved to death or poisoned. With the connivance of Parliament, now as strong as it had ever been, Henry Bolingbroke was then installed as King Henry IV. He addressed his Parliament in English, the first king to ever do so.

2 UNEASY KINGSHIP

Henry Bolingbroke, now Henry IV, had been talked into seizing the crown, and he didn't particularly enjoy being king. He came to learn that anyone who seizes the crown is likely to face attempts by others to take it from him. He was constantly troubled by rebellions and was so nervous of assassination that he sometimes slept in his armor when on campaign.

When he was older, he began to suffer from poor health, and his son (later Henry V) took more and more responsibility on himself as his father slowly rotted with leprosy, or possibly syphilis. Either way, the poor man was pretty much falling to pieces.

During his illness, Henry IV was comforted by the prophecy that he would die in Jerusalem, and he swore that when he felt well enough, he would go the Holy Land. One day in 1413, he passed out while praying in Westminster Abbey, and his courtiers carried him to the apartments of the abbot. "Where am I?" Henry asked when he briefly revived. "In the Jerusalem Chamber at Westminster," came the reply.

1 KING OLIVER

Oliver Cromwell—what? Hold on, you might say: Cromwell wasn't a king. Strictly speaking that's true, but his friends did suggest that since he commanded 40,000 war-hardened veterans he could easily take the crown and give birth to a new dynasty. He refused, of course, and took the title Lord Protector, which was OK because it was just like being a king, anyway. Since the Puritan Parliament failed to find a way of governing the country sensibly,

Cromwell dismissed it and ruled as an autocrat, just as the Stuart kings had done.

After much dour pondering, in 1547, Parliament had the Catholic-sounding "mass" taken out of "Christmas" and changed the name to "Christ-tide." It then quickly prohibited the holiday's observance altogether. Parliament also abolished feasts at Easter and Whitsun, and ordered a monthly fast. When Parliament ordered a fast day, soldiers were authorized to enter private houses and confiscate any meat found in the kitchens.

Parliament wouldn't allow dancing, not even around a maypole on a village green, and they closed all the theaters in London. They were very strict about the observance of Sunday, too, and forbade the playing of sports and games on that day. Even sex was deemed sinful if it was enjoyed. Cromwell didn't instigate any of these changes, but the rules were in force when he gained power, and they remained unchanged until the restoration of the monarchy.

In 1658, Oliver Cromwell died of malaria, a disease he probably contracted during his Irish campaign. His body was preserved, and after the Restoration it was ripped from its tomb and hung on public display from the gallows. Later it was dismembered and the body was thrown into a pit dug for the disposal of common criminals. The head was stuck on a stake, and for 30 years it decorated the front of Westminster Hall. Afterward, it was passed around the town to be used as a conversation piece at high-society parties.

10 NOTABLE COINCIDENCES OF THE AMERICAN CIVIL WAR

10 TWO FOR ONE

Coincidence: Two future presidents served in one Union regiment. Of the hundreds and hundreds of regiments raised in the North and sent to war, only one included two future presidents: Rutherford Hayes and William McKinley. Hayes began his Civil War career as an officer in the 23rd regiment in Ohio. He attained the rank of general and spent much of the war in western (soon West) Virginia, where he was wounded four times. William McKinley served under Hayes in the 23rd. Hayes recognized McKinley's courage and leadership abilities, promoting him to supply sergeant for actions while the regiment fought in western Virginia, and to second lieutenant for bravery under fire at Antietam. McKinley greatly admired his fellow Ohioan, and he followed Hayes into the Ohio governor's mansion and then the White House

9 LAST WORDS

Coincidence: General Sedgwick's last words.
During the opening stages of the battle of Spotsylvania, Virginia (May 8–22, 1864), Union commander Major General Sedgwick tried to rally his men, who were ducking from Confederate sniper fire. The general started to say, "They couldn't hit an elephant at this distance," when a rebel nailed him in the head and killed him instantly.

8 FALLING SWORD

Coincidence: Stonewall Jackson's sword falls over.
One morning, as Stonewall Jackson prepared for battle, his sword, which had been left leaning against a tree, fell over on its own. Now, you may think, "So what?" but many people then believed it was an ominous sign, because later that day, Jackson's own men accidentally shot him (see number 2 on this list) and he soon died. Confederate General A. L. Long was among those who recorded the incident in his memoirs and helped foster the legend of the falling sword as an omen, instead of a mere coincidence.

7 IRISH AGAINST IRISH
Coincidence: Irish fight Irish.

Like all civil wars, America's pitted brother against brother, and friend against friend. One of the most poignant episodes occurred during the battle of Fredericksburg, on December 13, 1862. Irish immigrants had flocked to America since the 1840s, some going to Northern ports and some to Southern. At Fredericksburg, Virginia, some of these men met in battle. In the final stages of the battle, the Union's Irish Brigade (which was literally all Irish) fought a Confederate regiment composed mainly of Irish immigrants, with terrible results. (The movie *Gods and Generals* depicts this episode powerfully.)

6 BAD MEDICINE
Coincidence: Bad Civil War medical practices kill President James Garfield.

James Garfield came out of the Civil War with nary a scratch, but after he became president, he succumbed to ghastly Civil War medicine. The medical field had not yet made the now-obvious connection between dirt and infection, and surgeons rarely, if ever, scrubbed their hands before seeing a new patient or changed rags, water, and instruments. When a would-be assassin shot President Garfield in July 1881 in a train station, a doctor soon arrived and took command: Doctor Willard Bliss, a wartime gunshot expert, chief surgeon for the U.S. Army's hospital in Washington, and member of the Washington, D.C., Board of Health. Bliss probed for the bullet with what was most likely a dirty finger. Subsequent probing and surgeries by Bliss and others were also likely done with unwashed hands and nonsterile instruments. Garfield could have recovered from the wounds, but not the massive infections the doctors unwittingly introduced. Following Garfield's death in September 1881, a major push was made in American medicine toward sterilizing hands and instruments.

5 HOLE IN THE HAT
Coincidence: A hole in the hat saves John Brown Gordon.

One of the South's most notable and outspoken postwar figures would have died at Sharpsburg on September 17, 1862, were it not for a hole in his hat. During the Maryland Battle of Antietam, Confederate John Brown Gordon was among the officers who led the defense of the rebel center in a sunken lane. While some of Gordon's account of this battle is, shall we say, embellished, the story of his wounding is not. Shot in the face, Gordon pitched forward and fell face first into his hat. The hat started to fill with blood, but fortunately, there was a bullet hole big enough to let the blood drain. Otherwise, he would have drowned in it. Gordon, one heck of a fighter, recovered from his wounds and rose to the rank of lieutenant general by the war's end. He later served as the Georgia governor and U.S. senator, and, sadly, was an early supporter of the Ku Klux Klan.

4 CLOSE TO HOME
Coincidence: Rebel solider returns home only to die near his house.
In 1861, Todd Carter of Franklin, Tennessee, joined what would eventually become the Army of Tennessee. Four years later, he returned home when that army's commander, John Bell Hood, launched a furious frontal assault on Federals who were holding Franklin on November 30, 1864. Some of the fiercest fighting took place right in front of the Carters' house. The Carters took refuge in their basement while fighting raged above them. Upon sighting his house, Todd cried out, "Follow me boys, I'm almost home," but he was struck down near his house and died two days later. Fascinating note: The Confederates lost five generals at Franklin, including the uniquely named States Rights Gist.

3 BATTLE ROUSER
Coincidence: Everywhere Davis went, a battle was sure to follow.
In one of the most freak coincidences of the war, battle followed in the wake of President Jefferson Davis in his swing around the Confederate circle in November and December 1862. Davis visited several commands, including those stationed at Fredericksburg, Virginia, Murfreesboro, Tennessee, and Vicksburg, Mississippi. The Union and Confederate armies clashed shortly after Davis left each place: December 13 at Fredericksburg, December 31 to January 2 at Murfreesboro, and December 28 at Vicksburg.

2 SAME PLACE SAME MANNER
Coincidence: Jackson and Longstreet were shot one year apart in same place and same manner.
As Stonewall Jackson once said, "Friendly fire isn't." In May 1863, Jackson was riding ahead of his men in the darkness just after his smashing flank attack at Chancellorsville. In the confused darkness in that heavily thicketed terrain, Confederate soldiers accidentally fired on Jackson's party, thinking they were Federal cavalry. A week later, the wounded Jackson died of pneumonia. Almost exactly one year later, during the horrible 1864 Battle of the Wilderness, Confederate Lieutenant General James Longstreet was riding with his staff a

half-mile east on the same road, following his own successful attack that rolled up the Federal left flank. Confederate soldiers accidentally shot Longstreet and his party, thinking they were the enemy. Longstreet took a bullet in the neck. Unlike Jackson, however, Longstreet recovered and rejoined the army that November.

1 LIKE FATHER, LIKE SON

Coincidence: Booth threatened the president.

No, not that Booth and not that president. Junius Booth, father of John Wilkes Booth, sent a death threat to President Andrew Jackson in 1835. Booth wanted Jackson to commute the sentences of two men accused of piracy. Booth never followed through on his threat to cut Jackson's throat, and clerks filed the letter away with other similar notes, undoubtedly figuring Booth was just a crackpot. For 175 years, historians disputed whether Booth actually wrote the message, but in January 2009, the director of the Andrew Jackson Papers Project at the University of Tennessee said they had determined that the elder Booth most certainly did write the letter. The note itself is unremarkable as death threats go, and it would have remained just one of many cantankerous letters to Jackson had it not been for Junius Booth's notorious son. After all, the son actually did what the father only threatened.

10 REALLY ANCIENT INVENTIONS YOU THINK ARE MODERN

10 SOCCER

The ancient Greeks and Romans are known to have played many ball games, some of which involved the use of the feet. These games appear to have resembled rugby. The Roman game *harpastum* is believed to have been adapted from a team game known as *episkyros*. The Roman politician Cicero (106–43 BC) describes the case of a man who was killed while getting a shave when a ball was

kicked into the barber's shop. Also, documented evidence of an activity resembling soccer can be found in the Chinese military manual *Zhan Guo Ce* compiled between the 3rd and 1st century BC. It describes a practice known as *cuju* (literally, "kick ball"), which originally involved kicking a leather ball through a small hole in a piece of silk cloth that was fixed on bamboo canes.

9 TOOTHBRUSHES

A variety of oral hygiene measures have been used since before recorded history. This has been verified by various excavations done all over the world in which chewsticks, tree twigs, bird feathers, animal bones, and porcupine quills were recovered. Many people used different forms of toothbrushes. Indian medicine (Ayurveda) has used the neem tree (also known as the *daatun*) and its products to create toothbrushes and similar products for millennia. A person chews one end of the neem twig until it somewhat resembles the bristles of a toothbrush, and then uses it to brush the teeth. In the Muslim world, the *miswak*, or *siwak*, made from a twig or root with antiseptic properties, has been widely used since the Islamic Golden Age.

8 SUTURES

Physicians have used sutures to close wounds for at least 4000 years, and the fundamental principles of suturing have changed little over time. Archaeological records from ancient Egypt show that Egyptians used linen and animal sinew, as well as things like hair and tree bark. In ancient India, physicians used the pincers of beetles or ants to staple wounds shut. They then cut the insects' bodies off, leaving their jaws in place like staples. Other natural materials used to close wounds include flax, grass, cotton, silk, pig bristles, and animal gut.

7 MAPS

A Babylonian clay tablet that has been generally accepted as the earliest-known map was the artifact unearthed in 1930 at the excavated ruined city of Ga-Sur at Nuzi, 200 miles north of the site of Babylon (present-day Iraq). Small enough to fit in the palm of your hand (3 inches by 2.7 inches), this map-tablet is dated from the dynasty of Sargon of Akkad (2300–2500 BC). The surface of the tablet is inscribed with a map of a district bounded by two ranges of hills and bisected by a water course. This particular tablet is drawn with cuneiform characters and stylized symbols impressed, or scratched, on the clay. Inscriptions identify some features and places. [Source: Turkish Ministry of Culture]

6 SOAP

The earliest recorded evidence of the production of soaplike materials dates back to around 2800 BC in ancient Babylon. A formula for soap consisting of water, alkali, and cassia oil was written on a Babylonian clay tablet around 2200 BC. The Ebers Papyrus, an important Egyptian medical document dating to 1550 BC, indicates that ancient Egyptians bathed regularly and combined animal and vegetable oils with alkaline salts to create a soaplike substance. Egyptian documents mention that a similar substance was used in the preparation of wool for weaving. The Greek physician Galen described making soap using lye, and prescribed using it to wash the body and clothes. This is the first record of soap used as a detergent.

5 SHIPYARDS

The world's earliest dockyards were built in the Harappan port city of Lothal, circa 2400 BC in Gujarat, India. Lothal's dockyards connected to an ancient course of the Sabarmati River on the trade route between Harappan cities in Sindh and the peninsula of Saurashtra when the surrounding Kutch Desert was a part of the Arabian Sea. Lothal engineers gave high priority to the creation of a dockyard and a warehouse to serve the purposes of naval trade. The dock was built on the eastern flank of the town and is regarded by archaeologists as an engineering feat of the highest order. It was located away from the main current of the river to avoid silting, but provided access to ships at high tide as well. The name of the ancient Greek city of Naupactus means "shipyard"; Naupactus' reputation in this field extends to the time of legend, where it is depicted as the place where the Heraclidae built a fleet to invade the Peloponnesus.

4 SPECULUM

A speculum (Latin for "mirror") is a medical tool for investigating body cavities; its form is dependent on the body cavity for which it's designed. Vaginal specula were used by the Romans, and specula artifacts have been found in Pompeii. The original instruments were excavated from the House of the Surgeon at Pompeii, so named because of the materials that were recovered there. The original speculum comprises a priapiscus with two (or sometimes three or four) dovetailing valves which are opened and closed by a handle with a screw mechanism, an arrangement that was also found in the specula of 18th-century Europe. Soranus is the first author who makes mention of the speculum specially made for the vagina. Greco-Roman writers on gynecology and obstetrics frequently recommend its use in the diagnosis and treatment of vaginal and uterine disorders, yet it is one of the rarest surviving medical instruments. [Source: University of Virginia Health Sciences Library]

3 PROCESSED RUBBER

Although vulcanization is a 19th-century invention, the history of rubber cured by other means goes back to prehistoric times. The name Olmec means "rubber people" in the Aztec language. Ancient Mesoamericans, spanning from ancient Olmecs to Aztecs, extracted latex from *Castilla elastica*, a type of rubber tree found in the area. The juice of a local vine, Ipomoea alba, was then mixed with this latex to create an ancient processed rubber as early as 1600 BC. Archaeological evidence indicates that rubber was already in use in Mesoamerica by the Early Formative Period—a dozen balls of it were found in the Olmec El Manati sacrificial bog. By the time of the Spanish Conquest 3000 years later, rubber was being exported from the tropical zones to sites all over Mesoamerica. Iconography suggests that although there were many uses for rubber, rubber balls, both for offerings and for ritual ballgames, were the primary products made.

2 UMBRELLAS

In the sculptures at Nineveh, the parasol appears frequently. Austen Henry Layard gives a picture of a bas-relief representing a king in his chariot, with an attendant holding a parasol over his head. It has a curtain hanging down behind, but is otherwise exactly like those in use today. The parasol was

reserved exclusively for the monarch (who was bald), and was never carried over any other person. In Egypt, the parasol is found in various shapes. In some instances, it is depicted as a fan of palm leaves or colored feathers fixed on a long handle, resembling those now carried behind the Pope in processions. In China, the 2nd-century commentator Fu Qian noted that the collapsible umbrella of Wang Mang's carriage had bendable joints that enabled it to be extended or retracted.

1 TOOTHPASTE

The earliest known reference to toothpaste is in a manuscript from Egypt in the 4th century AD, which prescribes a mixture of iris flowers. Many early toothpaste formulations were based on urine. However, toothpastes or powders did not come into general use until the 19th century. The Greeks, and then the Romans, improved the recipes for toothpaste by adding abrasives such as crushed bones and oyster shells. In the 9th century, the Persian musician and fashion designer Ziryab is known to have invented a type of toothpaste, which he popularized throughout Islamic Spain. The exact ingredients of this toothpaste are currently unknown, but it was reported to have been both "functional and pleasant to taste."

20 ODDITIES YOU DON'T KNOW FROM HISTORY

20 SURVIVAL OF THE INCESTUOUS

Charles Darwin married his first cousin.

19 COINCIDENCE OR CONSPIRACY?

John F. Kennedy, Anthony Burgess, Aldous Huxley, and C. S. Lewis all died on the same day.

18 335-YEAR WAR

Officially, the longest war in history was between the Netherlands and the Isles of Scilly. It lasted from 1651 to 1986, and there were no casualties.

17 GAY MARRIAGE
Gay marriage was legally recognized in Rome, and Nero himself married at least two gay couples.

16 HITLER VS. HITLER
Adolf Hitler's nephew, William Hitler, immigrated to the United States in 1939 and fought against his uncle.

15 AN AMERICAN IN PARIS
Thomas Paine was elected to the first post-Revolution French parliament, despite not speaking a word of the language.

14 FAIL TO THE CHIEF
William Howard Taft is the only U.S. president to come third in his campaign for re-election, losing to eventual winner Woodrow Wilson and fellow Republican Theodore Roosevelt.

13 MARRIAGES OF HENRY VIII
Technically, Henry VIII had only two wives. Four of his marriages were annulled.

12 HANKY PANKY
King Richard II invented the handkerchief.

11 OLDEST PARLIAMENT IN THE WORLD
The Parliament of Iceland is the oldest still-active parliament in the world. It was established in 930.

10 FUTURE FASCISTS
The people who started the art movement of futurism also founded the first Italian Fascist party in 1918.

9 PRESIDENT EINSTEIN
Albert Einstein was offered the role of Israel's second president in 1952 but declined.

8 GIRL POWER
New Zealand was the first country to enfranchise women. It gave them the vote in 1895.

7 THE 27TH AMENDMENT
The 27th amendment to the U.S. Constitution took 202 years to ratify. It was proposed in 1789 and finally ratified in 1992.

6 THE SERFS OF SARK
Until April 2008, the island of Sark remained the last feudal state in Europe.

5 TOXIC TOMATOES
Tomatoes were considered poisonous for many years in Europe, and they were grown for ornamental reasons only. In fact, the leaves and stems of tomatoes are poisonous (but they can be used in moderation for food flavoring).

4 POOR PISA
Soon after construction started in 1173, the foundation of the tower of Pisa settled unevenly. The work was stopped and wasn't continued until 100 years later. Therefore, the leaning tower was never straight.

3 PILLOWS IN ANCIENT EGYPT
Ancient Egyptians used slabs of stone as pillows.

2 SPECTACULAR SPECTACLES
People have been wearing glasses for about 700 years.

1 MAGICAL MUMMY DUST
King Charles II often rubbed dust from the mummies of pharaohs so he could absorb their ancient greatness.

10 BRUTAL HISTORICAL WEAPONS OF WAR

10 KNOBKERRIE

A knobkerrie refers to any blunt-impact implement located at the end of a shaft weapon or staff. Usually a small ball of wood or metal, a knobkerrie was slammed into the nose or groin at close range. This type of weapon has been used in many different incarnations over time, but was originally used in Africa by tribal groups as a means of self-defense. This weapon is still seen today and can be found on the end of most hunting knives in the form of a small ball or point of metal at the end of the handle.

Notable Appearance: The knobkerrie is employed by numerous Zulu warriors in the movie *Zulu*.

9 CALTROP

Most famously used in ninja movies, caltrops are objects with multiple sharp points, designed to be dropped when you're being chased in order to catch your pursuer off guard and cause nasty injury to their feet, or to force approaching enemies to follow a certain path as a trap. The primary idea behind these nasty implements is to render your foes immobile, or at least inflict great pain!

Notable Appearance: Caltrops appear in a number of James Bond movies as a feature of Bond's car; they're dropped from the vehicle to puncture the tires of pursuers.

8 MORNING STAR

The mace's nastier cousin, the morning star, consists of a solid wooden or metal shaft atop which sits (in most designs) a large metal ball adorned with a number of spikes or blades. The morning star was used in medieval times by infantry and horsemen. The primary method of attack was to simply swing the weapon at a foe. The most common target was, logically, the face or head, although the blow could be directed at the legs or knees in order to disable an enemy. The morning star has been seen in different forms since medieval times and is often confused with the mace; the difference between them is that a mace has metal studs, not spikes. Another well-known form of this weapon is the flail, which incorporates a chain between the shaft and spiked ball, allowing the weapon to be swung harder with less exertion.

Notable Appearance: The cave troll appearing in The Lord of the Rings books and movies wields a huge morning star as his weapon of choice.

7 CHAKRAM

Often misidentified as a glaive, which is actually a pole weapon similar to a pike, a chakram is akin to a large throwing star (or *shuriken*). Also known as a war quoit, the chakram is of Indian origin and was usually a large-bladed metal disk. Chakrams were used both for throwing, like Frisbees, or in melee combat, where slashing was the usual method of attack. Another form of the chakram was the chakkar, another bladed throwing weapon in the shape of a hoop rather than a disk. The weapons have a frightening range of up to 100 meters, if they're well manufactured.

Notable Appearance: Xena in *Xena: Warrior Princess* often uses a chakram as a throwing weapon.

6 MAUL

Similar to a modern sledgehammer, the maul is a nasty blunt-force weapon that was initially used by French citizens. Mauls were originally used as tools, but over time they have been employed by various factions for combat purposes. There's no particular method for using a maul, aside from striking almost anywhere on the body for severe damage. Common target areas were (as is common with blunt-force weapons) the head, arms, and legs. A single blow from a maul was sufficient to shatter bones and smash in skulls, even when a helmet was worn. The length of the handle allowed for the maul to be wielded with two hands. A common tactic was to break a victim's legs with a stout blow to the knees or shins, then finish the poor guy off with an overhead smash to the skull.

Notable Appearance: Leatherface in the original *Texas Chainsaw Massacre* movie uses a sledgehammer as a maul to incapacitate one unlucky victim.

5 WAR SCYTHE

Adapted from the common farming tool, the war scythe was altered so that the blade pointed straight from the top of the shaft. War scythes were used as both slashing and stabbing weapons; their weight and aerodynamic shape made them devastating. Capable of cutting through a metal helmet, the weapon is thought to have originated from use by peasants as an improvised weapon that was then adapted for military use. Arguably worse than the military form, the version wielded by peasants in revolts was often blunt from use in farming, meaning the victim was likely to survive numerous slashes before dying.

Notable Appearance: The grim reaper, death himself, is usually depicted wielding a scythe-type weapon.

4 DRAGON BEARD HOOK

This nasty bit of weaponry was employed by Chinese warriors as a means of ensnaring and immobilizing a victim. The weapon consists of a metal head bearing two or more serrated hooks that attach to a length of rope or chain. Used by "casting" out the head, the aim was to pierce or snag a part of the enemy's body with one of the hooks and then reel them in for the kill by pulling on the rope. This often resulted in tearing the victim's body as they struggled to escape. Arterial damage was common, and the victim was often killed by the hook itself before they could be reeled in. The dragon beard hook originates from the Song Dynasty.

Notable Appearance: The *Mortal Kombat* character Scorpion uses a weapon similar to a dragon beard hook to drag distant opponents into close range.

3 NUNCHAKU

Originating as tools for threshing crops, *nunchaku* are Okinawan weapons consisting of two lengths of wood, or sometimes metal, joined by a chain. The weapon is used by holding onto one of the wooden arms and swinging the other extremely quickly at the

victim. The target area was usually the face or arms, with the aim of breaking bones or causing blunt trauma. *Nunchaku* come in various designs, ranging from the basic wooden or metal arms to arms with attached blades or razors for extra damage. *Nunchaku* use is considered an art, and a skilled wielder can operate the weapon at such speed, passing it from hand to hand, that they could potentially strike a victim multiple times per second. A trained *nunchaku* user is also able to "bluff" swings, making the weapon very difficult to defend against, since it's nearly impossible to predict where the blow will come from. *Nunchaku* can also be used in pairs, with one in each hand.

Notable Appearance: Almost any martial arts movie!

2 BARDICHE

This weapon lies somewhere between a polearm and an axe (a family of weapons known as poleaxes), consisting of a long pole with a wide axe head attached along the side and tip of the shaft. The bardiche is of Eastern European and Russian origin. Used as a slashing or cleaving weapon, it was wielded in two hands and swung both horizontally and vertically. The bardiche was often wielded alongside a firearm for use in the event of a close-quarters encounter, although weapons of this style were in use long before the arrival of firearms. The power of the bardiche came from the weight of the blade, which was usually over two feet wide. The method of attack would usually consist of cleaving at the limbs or torso of the enemy.

Notable Appearance: Bardiche variants are often seen in fantasy and *manga* stories, often in the form of a giant axe with a short handle running behind the blade.

1 BLUNDERBUSS

The only firearm to make this list, the blunderbuss was an early form of shotgun, using powder and shot. The weapon was muzzle loaded and identified by the distinctive flared muzzle. The nasty part of the blunderbuss was actually a flaw in the design: the flared muzzle caused the shot to spread quite wide and reduced the muzzle velocity, meaning that shots outside of very close quarters resulted only in shrapnel wounds rather than death. A blunderbuss could, in theory, be loaded with any kind of shrapnel or shot, and small stones or scraps of metal were used as ammunition at times. The gun was used by armies of various nationalities, although it originated in Europe. A smaller, one-handed version of the blunderbuss, called a dragon, was also used. Wounds sustained from a close-range hit from a blunderbuss were brutal, potentially blowing away whole chunks of the body.

Notable Appearance: In the Pirates of the Caribbean movies, Jack Sparrow wields a handgun similar to a dragon, while at least one member of the undead pirate crew seen in the first movie uses a blunderbuss-type firearm.

CHAPTER SIX

Fact and Fiction

10 COMMON MISCONCEPTIONS

10 BRAINPOWER

Common Misconception: Humans use only 10 percent of their brains.
This is utterly false. No one really knows how this myth started, but we do know how it has been perpetuated for so long. When people first began making this false claim, psychics "decided" that it explained why some people had paranormal abilities and others didn't: paranormal powers were unleashed in people who had developed the use of more than 10 percent of the brain. They believed that some region of the brain, if tapped, could provide psychic abilities. This certainly helped their bottom line, as thousands of books have since come out aiming to "teach" people how to develop this power. So, the truth of the matter? Humans use 100 percent of their brain—that is why it's there! Here is a case in point: when a hemispherectomy—the surgical procedure that removes an entire half of the brain—is performed, the patient becomes paralyzed in half of their body.

9 SHAVING

Common Misconception: Shaving makes hair grow back thicker or coarser.
The reason that so many people believe this myth is that uncut hair develops

a taper or split end, both of which feel softer than freshly cut hair. It is for this reason that a man's full beard feels soft, but stubble feels rough. Of course, if this myth were true, every man going bald, and every woman with thinning hair, would simply get a haircut in order to make his hair grow back thicker. It's surprising that so obvious a myth (when you really think about it) is believed by so many!

8 PENIS ENLARGING

Common Misconception: You can extend your penis or widen its girth with special devices or medications.
This is patently untrue and the source of millions of spam e-mails sent around the world every day. Vacuum pumps, pills, stretching techniques: none of them make one iota of difference to the size of your manhood (and consequently the engine-

size of your car). The only way to enlarge your penis is to have enhancement surgery. This is, obviously, extremely expensive, extremely painful, and extremely gruesome—or so I'm told!

7 MSG IS BAD BAD BAD

Common Misconception: Monosodium glutamate (MSG) is evil and must be avoided at all costs.

First off, MSG is a naturally occurring substance found in things like tomatoes, mushrooms, and seaweed. It was first isolated in 1907 and presented in pure powder form in 1909. MSG is a flavor enhancer that excites the fifth taste sense, umami (the others being salty, sweet, sour, and bitter). MSG is to umami as sugar is to sweet. Another term for umami (and a relatively good description of it) is "savory." When you add MSG to a bland soup or stock, it can greatly increase the flavor and add a roundness that cannot be obtained elsewhere. Most fine chefs will use natural MSG when possible—through the inclusion of tomatoes or mushrooms—but many will also use the powder directly.

It is a myth that MSG makes you ill. Thanks to media scares around the world, people have a great horror of MSG, but those same people have no problems scoffing chips and other fast food and pre-packaged foods, almost all of which contain it. Many seasonings and sauces that are available at supermarkets around the world contain MSG, and it is labeled as "flavor enhancer 621" in Australia and New Zealand. An Australian study on "Chinese Restaurant Syndrome" reported that "rigorous and realistic scientific evidence linking the syndrome to MSG could not be found." Enjoy MSG!

6 POPULATION EXPLOSION

Common Misconception: Half, or more than half, of all humans ever born, are alive today.

This is a myth that is probably perpetuated by eugenicists and other people who believe the planet should be saved by population control of the human species. This is not a new myth either: in 1798, Thomas Malthus predicted that population growth would surpass the world food supply by the mid 1800s. The Population Reference Bureau estimates that the earth has held over 106 billion humans throughout history. With a current world population of over 6 billion, that means that roughly 6 percent of people ever born are alive today, a significantly lower number than that given by population explosion alarmists. What is perhaps more frightening is the fact that many nations today are not producing enough children to replenish the population. In other words, many countries are suffering negative birthrates.

5 PLANT MAGIC

Common Misconception: Plants turn carbon dioxide into oxygen.

I suspect this will come as a surprise to most people, but while plants do produce oxygen, they do not do it by converting carbon dioxide. To put it simply, plants convert carbon dioxide into carbohydrate precursors and water (fuel for the plant). This is a light-independent process—the plant doesn't need light to perform this task. So how do plants make oxygen for us to breathe? It uses a light-dependent process: photosynthesis. This is a relatively complex process that takes the light and converts it to potential energy—the byproduct of this process is oxygen.

4 ANTARCTIC-ARCTIC

Common Misconception: The North Pole is north and the South Pole is south.

Actually, in terms of physics, the North Pole (while geographically in the north) is actually a south-magnetic pole, and the South Pole (geographically in the south) is a north-magnetic pole. When your compass is pointing north, it is actually pointing to the south pole of earth's magnetic field. This would not have been the case 780,000 years ago, as the magnetic poles of the earth were reversed (this is called a geomagnetic reversal). Oh, and just to complicate things further, the poles drift around randomly—they are not in a fixed spot. This is most likely due to movements in the molten nickel-iron alloy in the earth's core.

3 MIRROR MIRROR ON THE WALL

Common Misconception: A mirror image reverses left and right.

When we look in a mirror, our left and right sides appear to be reversed—left is right and right is left. In fact, what has really happened is that the mirror has inverted us front and back. The reason that we think it is a left-to-right reversal is that we are used to a person's left and right being reversed when they turn to face us. So what is the mirror doing? Imagine a person with their back to you doing a hand stand to face you rather than turning around; their right and left remain the same but their top and bottom swap. Looking into a mirror has the same effect: nothing reverses in the mirror—not bottom and top, not left and right.

2 MELTING GLASS

Common Misconception: Glass is actually a very slow-flowing liquid.

First of all, this is not true. Second, the reason many people believe it is due to the nature of old panes of glass in which the bottom appears to be thicker than the top, suggesting that the glass is "melting" and pooling at the bottom. The reason for this distortion in the glass is the older method of glass manufacturing. You will notice that you don't see this "melting" behavior in modern glass windows. Glass is actually an amorphous ceramic.

1 FREE AS A BIRD

Common Misconception: Abraham Lincoln's Emancipation Proclamation freed the slaves.

In fact, it freed little or no slaves. Why? Because the Emancipation Proclamation (1862) declared the freedom of all slaves in the Confederate states, that is, the states over which Lincoln and the Union government had no control. Furthermore, it did not free slaves from any of the states that were already under Union control. This would be, in a sense, like Australia trying to declare a binding law on New Zealanders when they are two separate nations. The Emancipation Proclamation was, effectively, worthless. It was not until the Thirteenth Amendment was passed on December 6, 1865, that slavery was officially abolished in full in the U.S.

15 QUITE BIZARRE FACTLETS

15 PAREIDOLIA

Have you ever looked into the sky and seen shapes of animals or people in the clouds? This is pareidolia. It is a psychological phenomenon that is relatively common. This can affect not just sight but hearing, as in the case of people who hear voices when playing music backward. This can also account for many modern so-called miracles in which religious images appear in everyday items like toast.

14 GLEEKING

You may have noticed from time to time that a little saliva is suddenly ejected from under your tongue—this is called gleeking. It is usually accidental—when yawning for example—but some people have developed the knack of making it happen on demand by pushing their tongue forward while moving the lower jaw forward. Why you would want to do this I do not know.

13 HAWAIIAN

The Hawaiian language—yes, it isn't just English—only uses 12 letters from the English alphabet. It also uses an apostrophe to signify the sound of a glottal stop, like in "Hawai'i." In Hawaiian, this symbol is called the 'okina.

12 CRYPTOMNESIA

Plagiarism is not always intentional. Cryptomnesia is the term used to refer to a memory bias in which a person sees something, forgets they saw it, and then re-creates it at a later date thinking it is original. Either that, or it's a darn good excuse when you get caught!

11 CLINICAL LYCANTHROPY

This is a truly bizarre mental disorder in which a person comes to believe they have been transformed into an animal. The sufferer can experience hallucinations and often mimics the behavior of the animal they think they have become. Thankfully, this is an extremely rare disorder.

10 KRAMPUS

Come Christmastime we all love to dream of Santa, presents, good food, and loved ones. But did you know that happy old Santa Claus has a friend who is less than pleasant? His name is Krampus, and for centuries parents in parts of Europe have used him to frighten their children  into behaving. Krampus looks like a cross between a goat and the most hideous demon you can imagine. He has a predilection for beating children with sticks and, in particular, likes beating young girls. Where this aspect of his mythology comes from I know not.

9 ALIEN ASTRONAUTS
In general these days, people believe that man originated in one of two ways: divine creation (in which God created everything) or scientific randomness (in which a quantum fluctuation brought about the physical world as we see it and man evolved from there). But there is a third and infinitely more unusual belief than either of the previous two: alien astronauts. This theory, which is surprisingly popular, posits that aliens came to the earth in prehistory and either gave man's predecessors intelligence or they impregnated man's ancestors, giving rise to modern humans.

8 MARY TOFT
In 1726, the extraordinary case of Mary Toft caused a media storm. Mary claimed to have given birth to rabbits! According to a contemporary report, "[Male midwife John Howard] delivered 'three legs of a Cat of a Tabby Colour, and one leg of a Rabbet: the guts were as a Cat's and in them were three pieces of the Back-Bone of an Eel … The cat's feet supposed were formed in her imagination from a cat she was fond of that slept on the bed at night.'" Needless to say, her deception was eventually uncovered much to the embarrassment of the doctors who treated and believed her.

7 HYPERTHYMESIA
Imagine remembering every single detail of everything you have experienced from the moment of your birth to the present time. Four people (yes, only four) in history have had this ability. It is called hyperthymesia. A hyperthymesiac can describe all of the trivial details of what happened on any given date of their life.

6 INTRUSIVE "R"
Intrusive "r" is the term given to the grammatical oddity in which English speakers who normally don't pronounce a final "r" (such as in British English) insert an "r" into a word to make the language flow better. Sometimes the letter is present (but normally not pronounced) and other times it is added. While normally a British English person would pronounce "far" as "fah," in the

sentence "far away" the "r" is pronounced. Those grammar fanatics seem to have a name for everything!

5 ZEBROIDS
We all know about zebras and donkeys, but do you know about the zebroid? It's a zebra crossed with a horse or donkey. Depending on the combination of parents, you can also get a zorse, zonkey, zebrass, or a zedonk. In the case of a zebroid, the stripes are usually confined to a small portion of the body, as opposed to its zebra parent, which has stripes all over.

4 CRIKEY STEVEIRWINI
There exists, believe it or not, a genus of animal called "crikey." It has one species, which is called "steveirwini." This, of course, is in memory of the late wildlife expert Steve Irwin (also known as the Crocodile Hunter). Crikey steveirwini is a type of land snail. For those who may not be familiar with slang in Australia (the country of Steve Irwin's origin), "crikey" is a common Australian cussword that is most likely derived from "Christ."

3 LAST RESTING PLACE OF JESUS
We all know that Jesus died in Judea. Well, actually, not all of us believe that. In the Shingo village in Japan, the inhabitants believe that Jesus moved there when he was 21 years old to study theology. They also believe that his brother "Isukiri" was crucified in his place. They say that after escaping execution Jesus returned to Japan, became a rice farmer, raised a family, and eventually died and was buried in Shingo.

2 ENORMOUS TREE
The African Baobab tree can grow so huge that if the trunk were hollow, you could stand 20 people side-by-side inside it! Its maximum recorded circumference is 180 feet. That would provide a lot of firewood!

1 ARABIC NUMERALS...OR NOT
Arabic numerals, the numbering system used in English, is a misnomer. Arabic numerals actually originated in India 300 years before the birth of Christ. Fortunately, this is becoming more widely known, and some people now refer to them as the "Hindu-Arabic numerals."

10 FASCINATING FACTS ABOUT THE ROMANS

10 CHURCH AND STATE

The Romans are well-known for having worshipped many gods, but what is not so well-known is the fact that there was also an official state god. This god was called *Sol invictus*, which means "the unconquered sun." *Sol invictus* was the state god from the time of Emperor Aurelian until Constantine I abolished paganism and made Catholicism the state religion. December 25 was named as the feast day of *Sol invictus*.

9 DWELLINGS

Surprisingly, our modern homes are not that unlike the ancient Romans'. They had a variety of styles of homes depending on class, just as we have both slums and McMansions. There were building regulations for safety, just as we have, and most of the apartments had windows. What may be most surprising is that many Roman homes (those of the rich) had central heating by way of hot air circulating beneath the floors. And just like any modern suburb, the Roman suburbs were dotted with fast-food restaurants for those who simply couldn't be bothered with cooking.

8 UNDERWEAR

The subligaculum was the Roman equivalent of modern underwear, but in Roman times it was unisex. It came in the form of either shorts or a loincloth that was wrapped around the nether regions. Roman women sometimes word a band of cloth or leather around their upper body in an ancient form of a bra.

7 EDUCATION

Education was extremely important to the Romans and of a high standard. The rich parents would either homeschool their children or send them to public schools (boys only). The methods of education would be frowned upon today— there were lots of beatings and yelling—but the children learned nevertheless. Even poor children received some education, and most Romans could read and write.

6 HISTORIC IRONY

Saint Peter, the first Bishop of Rome and the Pope, was crucified upside down in the Circus of Nero by the Roman emperor. This was an attempt to squash Christianity. Ironically, 200 years later, the circus was donated to the Church by the Emperor Constantine, and upon that spot was built Saint Peter's Basilica, the home of the Catholic Church and current Pope.

5 AVERAGE DIET

Due to their lifestyle, the Roman diet was very different from our own. Breakfast was usually eaten in bed and consisted of wheat pancakes with dates and honey. Wine was also drunk. At lunchtime (*prandium*) the Romans would have breads and cheese and occasionally meat. This was earlier than our lunchtime and usually occurred around 11 in the morning. The main meal was eaten in the afternoon or early evening and could last as long as four hours. While not big meat-eaters, the Romans would occasionally have dormice for dinner, and there is even a recorded case of a stuffed donkey being dished up!

4 GUARD DOGS

The Romans not only had guard dogs, they, like many of us, had "Beware of Dog!" signs attached to their walls. In Latin. This reads *Cave Canem*—it certainly has a nicer ring to it than our version. These were so common that many *Cave Canem* dog signs exist to this day.

3 SEWERS

The Romans were very clean and loved bathing together. This helped to promote a community spirit and keep the city smelling fresh. In 600 BC, the king of Rome had a sewer system built under the city, and parts of it remain in use today. In fact, it is still the main sewer of the Roman amphitheater. The success of the sewers was so great that the system was duplicated in many other parts of the Roman Empire.

2 PECUNIA NON OLET

Emperors Nero and Vespasian introduced a tax on urine. This may seem strange, but there is actually a good reason for it: urine was collected from the lower classes and paid for by tanners and launderers because it contains ammonia, which was very useful in their trades. When Vespasian's son complained about the disgusting nature of the tax, his father showed him a gold coin and said the famous phrase *pecunia non olet* which means "money doesn't stink." I am not so sure that Vespasian would be pleased to know that his tax ultimately led to his name being used for urinals to this day—in France they are called *vespasiennes*, in Italy *vespasiani*, and in Romania *vespasiene*.

1 CATALLUS XVI

Catallus (ca. 84 BC–ca. 54 BC) is one of the most renowned Roman poets of the 1st century BC. He continues to influence poetry to this day. We are all familiar with the famous Roman poems of heroic endeavor, but most don't know that the Romans loved to get down and dirty from time to time. Here is the shocking translation of Catallus' poem, known as "Catallus XVI":

> I'm gonna fuck you guys up the ass and shove my cock down
> your throats,
>
> yes, you, Aurelius–you fucking cocksucker–and you too, Furius,
> you faggot!
>
> Just because my verses are tender doesn't mean
>
> that I've gone all soft. Sure, a poet should focus
>
> on writing poetry and not on sex; but does that
>
> mean they can't write about sex? If a poem is
>
> in good taste, well-written and erotic,
>
> it can give massive boners to hairy old men,
>
> not just to horny teenagers. You think I'm a sissy
>
> just because I write about thousands of kisses?
>
> I'm gonna fuck you guys up the ass and shove my cock down
> your throats!

It definitely sounds nicer in the Latin original!

10 FASCINATING FACTS ABOUT THE MAYANS

10 CONTINUING CULTURE

Fact: There are numerous Mayans still living in their home regions. At present there are more than seven million Mayans living in their original regions, and many of them have retained large parts of their ancient culture, including their original languages. We owe our thanks to the Mayans for many English words such as "shark" and "cocoa." If you want to say thank you in Yucatec Maya, you say *"Jach Dyos b'o'otik."*

9 MAYAN CHILDHOOD

Fact: The Mayans "enhanced" the beauty of their children.

The Mayans, like modern people who pierce their children's ears, believed in adorning their children with decorations. At very young ages, boards were pressed into babies' foreheads, making a flattened surface. This was mostly found amongst the upper class. Another—and certainly more unusual—practice was dangling objects in front of a newborn baby's eyes until they became permanently crossed.

8 EXCELLENT DOCTORS

Fact: The Mayans had many excellent medical practices.

The Mayans were very concerned about health, and their doctors (shamans) used a combination of magic and nature to bring about healing. These men often had vast medical knowledge. The even used human hair and needles to suture open wounds. They used iron pyrite to fill teeth with cavities and made false teeth from jade and turquoise.

7 BLOOD SACRIFICE

Fact: Some Mayans still practice blood sacrifice.

Most of us are familiar with the blood sacrifices of the early Mayans, but did you know that blood offerings are still often made these days? Instead of human sacrifices, some modern Mayans sacrifice chickens. As part of their festivities, they still burn incense, dance, feast, and have ritual drinking sessions.

6 PAINKILLERS
Fact: The Mayans used painkillers.

In religious rituals, the Mayans often used hallucinogenic drugs, which were also frequently used as painkillers. The most popular painkillers were peyote, morning glory, and even alcohol, which was made from a variety of plants. For faster painkilling, these various herbs and liquids were taken by enema.

5 BALL COURTS
Fact: The Mayans built ball courts so they could play games.

For 3000 years, Mesoamericans played a ball sport that involved the building of courts. One of these games (*ulama*) is still played today. In classic Mayan culture, the game was called *pit* and the act of playing was *pitziil*. The ball was made of rubber and was around the size of a modern volleyball.

4 SAUNAS
Fact: The Mayans used saunas.

The Mayans believed in ritual purification and would often use a sweat bath (*zumpulche*) similar to our modern day saunas. They were used to refresh women after childbirth, to heal the sick, and simply to get clean. They were built like modern saunas, and the steam was produced by pouring water over hot stones.

3 THE LAST MAYAN STATE
Fact: The last Mayan state existed until 1697.

The last independent Mayan state was the island city of Tayasal. It remained independent from Spain until March 13, 1697, when it submitted to a force

led by Martin de Ursua, who was then the governor of Yucatán. The beautiful archeological site Chichén Itzá is located in this area.

2 LIFE GOES ON

Fact: The Mayan calendar does not predict the end of the world in 2012. The Mayans don't have one specific calendar that ends in 2012. They actually used a variety of different interlocking calendars. The long-count calendar is the one that has given rise to this myth about the world ending. But this is due to a misunderstanding. Mayan mythology states that we are in the fourth world, or creation. In 2012, we will move to the fifth world. For the Mayans, this is a cause for celebration, as entering a new age is considered a good thing. The myth about the world ending was originally suggested by José Argüelles in his 1987 book, *The Mayan Factor: Path Beyond Technology.*

1 ANCIENT MYSTERY

Fact: No one really knows what caused the collapse of the Mayan culture. During the 8th and 9th centuries, the Mayan centers in the Southern Lowlands went into decline and were shortly after abandoned. No one knows what the reason is for this, but there is much speculation, including overpopulation, invasion, peasant revolt, environmental disaster, or epidemic disease, and some even postulate that it was the result of a climatic event.

10 FASCINATING FACTS ABOUT THE SCYTHIANS

10 THE DEFEAT OF THE ASSYRIANS

The Assyrians attempted to imitate the grandeur of the Babylonians, but their despotic rule was held together by the might of their army and the terror of their secret agents. The Scythians displaced and drove another steppe tribe, the Cimmerians, toward Assyrian territory. These Cimmerians created havoc for the Assyrian army, who had great difficulty reacting to the raids of these swiftly moving horsemen. The increasing encroachment of the Cimmerians weakened the Assyrians and provided their vassals with opportunity to rebel. Egypt expelled the Assyrians and regained its independence. Ashurbanipal, king of Assyria, panicked at his contracting frontiers and sacked Babylon and destroyed Susa in an attempt to terrorize his remaining peoples into submission. Meanwhile, in the wake of the Cimmerian attacks, the Scythians were provided with increasingly tempting opportunities to raid Assyria. They surged into the Middle East, overwhelming the Assyrian infantry with their speed and firepower. The Babylonians and Medes formed an alliance, and with the mercenary aid of the Scythians they shattered the Assyrian Empire.

9 EQUIPMENT

The full-bearded Scythians wore tall pointed caps, long coats clasped around their waists by belts, and pants tucked into their boots. The wealthier warriors had jackets made of iron scales sewn to leather, while the average Scythian relied on their round, oblong wicker shields draped in leather for protection.

The primary weapon of the Scythians was their short composite bow, which could fire an arrow up to 80 yards. When they hunted birds, the Scythians used fine arrowheads, because they aimed for the eyes. When they shot at other warriors, however, the Scythians used barbed arrowheads designed to tear a wound open on the way out. They also brewed their own poisons for their arrow tips, a mixture of snake venom, putrefied human blood, and, to hasten infection, dung. Their secondary weapons were the *sagaris*, a curved battle-axe, and the *akinakes*, a short, curved sword.

8 BURIAL MOUNDS

The Scythians' culture may have disappeared long ago, but their burial mounds remain. These *kurhans* were built as repositories for the great Scythian chieftains and kings. Atop the strange mounds stood crudely carved stone figures, guarding the bodies and possessions of the deceased interned within. The largest of these *kurhans* are the height of a six-story building and are more than 90 meters across. The mounds were not just piles of dirt or refuse, but were actually layers of sod to provide grazing in the afterlife for the many horses buried along with the deceased.

7 DEATH OF A GREAT MAN

As mentioned in the previous item, the burial of Scythian nobility was quite elaborate. In one *kurhan* uncovered in 1898, archaeologists found 400 horses arrayed in a geometric pattern around the body of the slain warrior. It was not only horses who were slaughtered, but consorts and retainers also had the dubious honor of joining their lord in the afterlife. Herodotus reported that mourners would pierce their left hands with arrows, slash their arms, and cut off portions of their ears in demonstration of their sorrow. A year after the burial, 50 horses and 50 slaves were killed, gutted, stuffed, and impaled on posts around the *kurhan*. The horses stood upright, mounted by the dead slaves, ghastly sentinels guarding the tomb of their slain lord.

6 GOLDEN ARTIFACTS

Before the Scythians can be dismissed as blood-thirsty barbarians, one really needs to see their elaborate golden artwork. Scythian gold came from the Altai district and from frequent raids on Greek and Persian cities. Gold was sewn into their garments in the form of plates, fashioned into belts, broaches, necklaces, torques, scabbards, helmets, earrings, and ornaments, and worked into their weapons. The Scythians had an eye for design, especially depictions of griffins, lions, wolves, stags, leopards, eagles, and—the Scythians' favorite motif—animals in deadly combat. The historian William Montgomery McGovern claimed, "From the mass of evidence now before us, it seems highly probable that this Scytho-Sarmatian animal style spread to all parts of the ancient world and had an important effect not only upon European art but upon the art of ancient China."

5 TATTOOS

Herodotus testified that the Scythians wore tattoos as a sign of their nobility. A Scythian without tattoos showed that he was of low station. The existence of Scythian tattoos was confirmed in 1948, when a Russian archaeologist uncovered the frozen body of a Scythian chieftain. His tattoos included stylized images of a stag and a ram on his right arm, two griffins on his chest, and a fish on his right leg. These findings were seen by some experts as further evidence that fanciful Scythian depictions of wild animals had influenced the art of China, Persia, India, and Eastern Europe.

4 SCALPS AND HEADS

After battle, a Scythian warrior would drink the blood of the first enemy he had killed. With the bloody taste still in his mouth, the warrior would decapitate the corpses of his slain enemies to use as grisly vouchers in the distribution of booty. Only warriors who presented the heads of their slain enemies would receive their share from the chieftain or king. After receiving his share, a warrior would take the scalps from his collection of heads as a lurid inventory of martial prowess. The scalps were affixed to bridles and clothing and even sewn into cloaks. The skulls of the strongest, most respected enemies were cut, gilded with gold, and made into wine goblets. Scythians also used the skin from their victims' limbs as covers for the quivers that hung on the right sides of their belts.

3 MARIJUANA

The Scythians were fond of marijuana and were responsible for bringing it from Central Asia to Egypt and Eastern Europe. In one Scythian grave, archaeologists found a skull with three small holes drilled into it, probably to ease swelling. Beside the skull, the archaeologists found a cache of marijuana, ostensibly to relieve the man's headache in the next life. From Herodotus comes what is, in all likelihood, the most ancient description of hotboxing: "After the burial . . . they set up three poles leaning together to a point and cover them with woolen mats . . . They make a pit in the centre beneath the poles and throw red-hot stones into it . . . they take the seed of the hemp and creeping under the mats they throw it on the red-hot stones, and being thrown, it smolders and sends forth so much steam that no Greek vapour-bath could surpass it. The Scythians howl in their joy at the vapour-bath."

2 AMAZONS

Herodotus relates the tale of a clash between Scythians and Amazons near the Sea of Azov. When the Scythians learned that their fierce opponents were, in fact, women, they sent their most virile warriors to woo, rather than war, these female warriors. Somehow, the Amazons were seduced by the charms of the wily Scythians. They were, however, unwilling to be the brides of their Scythian lovers, turning their noses up at the domestic role that Scythian wives were relegated to. Eventually, according to the tale, the two groups formed a joint tribe.
There is likely little truth to this tale, but archaeologists have recently found the remains of a number of well-armed Scythian women. In all likelihood, this means that Scythian society saw a place for female warriors.

1 **SHOWDOWN WITH DARIUS**
In 513 BC, the Scythians were attacked by Darius the Great, who raised a force of 700,000 men to put an end to their bothersome raids into his territory. Taking advantage of the vast region, the Scythians merely retreated when the Persians advanced and advanced when the Persians retreated. The Scythian scouts milled about, striking from a distance if any of the Persians ever had the misfortune of breaking formation or exposing a flank. Herodotus reports that, at one point, both sides had drawn up battle lines when a loud whooping arose from among the Scythian warriors. The Scythian horsemen suddenly broke their battle line and galloped impulsively after a hare. "These fellows have a hearty contempt for us," Darius is reported to have muttered to an aide. Running low on food and morale, Darius eventually withdrew his army.

15 FASCINATING FACTS ABOUT ANCIENT EGYPT

15 **PHARAOHS HID THEIR HAIR**
Pharaohs of ancient Egypt never let their hair be seen. This is the reason that all of the statues and images of these great rulers are always seen with either a crown or a *neme*, the striped head cloth most well-known for appearing on the mask of Tutankhamen.

14 **HUMAN FLY PAPER**
Pepi II of Egypt hated flies—and there were lots in ancient Egypt—so he came up with a cunning plan: he smeared naked slaves with honey and made them stand near him at all times so the flies were attracted away from him.

13 **MAKEUP USED AS MEDICINE**
Egyptians wore makeup, both men and women. This was originally to protect them from the sun as an early form of sunscreen. Over time they came to believe that the makeup had healing powers, but considering that some of it was made from lead, it was probably more of a health hazard than a healer.

12 MOLDY BREAD TREATED INFECTIONS
Modern science discovered that the mold on bread was penicillin and it revolutionized the health industry. But the ancient Egyptians (while not knowing the reason or its nature) often treated infections with moldy bread, thereby healing themselves with antibiotics.

11 CHILDREN WENT NAKED
Until they became teenagers, Egyptian children were completely naked. The heat of the Egyptian sun made clothing unnecessary, and it was mostly for the sake of privacy that adults (both men and women) wore skirts.

10 THE RICH WORE WIGS
Egyptians with a lot of money wore wigs, while the poor wore their own hair long or in pigtails. Until the age of puberty, boys would have their heads shaved except for one plait. This was most likely to keep away lice and fleas.

9 NAPOLEON DIDN'T HARM THE SPHINX
There is a famous myth that Napoleon destroyed the nose of the Sphinx, but there are illustrations of the monument from before his time that clearly show the nose missing.

8 THE EARTH WAS FLAT

Unlike their Greek counterparts, the ancient Egyptians believed that the earth was flat and round like a pancake. They believed that the Nile, the life-giving force of Egypt, ran straight through its center.

7 SOLDIERS COLLECTED TAXES

Egyptians were famed for their valiant and numerous soldiers. When they weren't fighting battles for the Pharaoh, they were used as a national police force and to collect taxes. I suspect there wasn't a lot of tax evasion in those days!

6 NO SEPARATION OF CHURCH AND STATE

The pharaoh was the highest priest in ancient Egypt and it was his duty to perform all of the sacred duties in all the temples. As this was impossible since he was just one man, the chief priest of the temple would usually act on his behalf.

5 STEP PYRAMID OF DJOSER'S WALL

The famous Step Pyramid of Djoser (the first one built) originally had a 34-foot-high wall surrounding it. The wall had 15 doors, but only one was functional.

4 WOMEN HAD MONEY

Ancient Egyptian women had equal legal and financial powers to men. Despite this, they did not share equal social status.

3 ARTISANS BUILT THE PYRAMIDS

While we have all heard the tales of slaves building the pyramids for the Egyptians, skeletons of pyramid workers show that they were most likely Egyptian men who were in the full-time employ of the Pharaoh. There is even graffiti on some of the stones that suggests the men were members of building teams who took pride in their work.

2 THE HEART HELD THE SOUL

Egyptians believed that the heart was the container of the soul. For this reason, when all of the other organs were removed in the process of mummification, the heart was left in place.

1 RAMSES REALLY *WAS* GREAT

When Ramses the Great died in 1212 BC, he left behind a legacy of nearly 100 concubines and eight official wives! It's no wonder he was called "Ramses the Great."

10 CURIOUS FACTS ABOUT PORNOGRAPHY

10 INVENTED BY THE VICTORIANS

While nude images of humans have existed for as long as civilization, it was not until the Victorian era that pornography, in the sense that we know it, existed. Prior to the 19th century, there were a few laws regarding sexual behavior, but none regarding images of sexuality. The Victorians were a prudish bunch, and they outlawed the depiction of nudity for all but the upper class, who they felt had the moral strength to cope with the images. When Pompeii was discovered, all of its nude statues were quickly moved off to the Secret Museum in Naples. Despite this, pornography was very popular in the Victorian world, but people were discreet with their use of it.

9 EXTREME AUSTRALIAN LAW

Although Australia is an open democracy, it is illegal to sell any X-rated materials (or to rent them) in all but two of the states there. The two states that do allow it are the Australian Capital Territory (ACT) and the Northern Territory. Because of a discrepancy in Australian law, it is not illegal to own or transfer X-rated material across state lines, so ACT and the Northern Territory are home to almost all of Australia's mail-order porn companies. In 2007, the Australian government took possession of some X-rated material illegal for certain aboriginal communities.

8 ENTERTAINMENT FORMATS

The porn industry is a very powerful one, so much so that it has had major parts to play in the "format-wars" over the years. Not only did it play an important role in the HD DVD vs. Blue-ray battle, but it helped secure the victory of VHS over Betamax. With a market of well over 50 billion dollars a year, it is no surprise that porn producers hold much sway in entertainment. Porn revenue is larger than the combined revenues of all professional football, baseball, and basketball franchises.

7 PORN LEADS TO CRIME—OR DOES IT?

Contrary to what many people say, the countries with the easiest access to hardcore pornography also have the lowest sex-crime rates in the world. A good example of this is in Japan, where a study in 1995 found that "[s]ex crimes in every category, from rape to public indecency, sexual offenses from both ends of the criminal spectrum, significantly decreased in incidence. Most significantly, despite the wide increase in availability of pornography to children, not only was there a decrease in sex crimes with juveniles as victims but the number of juvenile offenders also decreased significantly."

6 PORNOGRAPHY ADDICTION

There are two main nongovernmental groups that oppose pornography: religious believers and feminists. Both these groups claim that pornography can become an addiction, characterized by an overuse or abuse of pornographic material. They believe that five steps in addiction exist and that they ultimately can lead to cheating on a partner or even sexual crime (contrary to the above evidence). Feminists also believe that pornography is demeaning to women. The Roman Catholic Church considers the viewing of pornography to be a "grave offense"—in other words, viewing pornography leads to damnation.

5 PAYDAY

The average male porn star makes anywhere between $50 and $1500 per scene (not per hour) and generally is not paid royalties. On the other hand, women can make up to quarter of a million dollars a year, and some female porn stars have become so wealthy that they have retired young and rich. The richest porn star is Jenna Jameson, who sold her $30 million business, Club Jenna, to Playboy for an undisclosed sum.

4 GETTING A START

If you are male and want to get into a career in pornography, your chances of being accepted for mainstream porn are tiny. If, however, you are willing to do gay porn, there is a huge hole in the market, and you will find that unless you are incredibly hideous, your opportunities are huge. But back to straight porn: if you want to get a job as a straight male porn star, you are most likely to have success by taking an attractive female with you who says that she is only willing to perform if you are involved. The high demand for attractive women will get you a foot in the door.

3 HOTEL SHENANIGANS

On average, 50 percent of hotel guests order pornography on their televisions. A survey of Hilton, Marriot, Hyatt, Sheraton, and Holiday Inn hotels  found that nearly 70 percent of their overall profits from room services come from the hire of porn movies. In some countries where it is illegal to broadcast or have pornography, hotels are exempt, in order to accommodate the "needs" of their foreign clients.

2 OVERALL INTERNET STATISTICS

The total number of pornographic websites is around 4.2 million at the time of writing. That totals up to around 370 million individual pages of porn. On a daily basis, there are about 68 million search requests for porn, and 2.5 billion spam porn e-mails. Twenty percent of men admit to viewing porn at work during the working week, while thirteen percent of women admit the same.

1 FLUFFER

In the early days of the porn film industry, people called "fluffers" were employed by studios to "arouse" the male participants prior to filming scenes, and they would perform sexual acts on the actor. They were also required to keep the actors "cleaned up" between scenes and were normally considered to be part of the makeup department. While fluffers are almost entirely a thing of the past, there are some studios that still employ them, particularly in "gang bang" type scenes. Digital cameras and drugs like Viagra have removed much of the need for fluffers.

10 FACTS ABOUT MAIL-ORDER BRIDES

10 THE SWEET ESCAPE

Most people think that Russian brides are desperate women who want nothing more than to marry a foreigner (preferably American), get the hell out of Russia and start a new life. But in fact, this is almost always incorrect. Russia has a man shortage: there are roughly eight men for every ten women in a culture that is very marriage-oriented. Consequently, many Russian women are compelled to look outside of Russia for a husband. As one mail-order bride company says, "[Russian brides] feel as if you were one of the guys who would approach her at a bar: where she can say, 'yes' if she likes you, and 'thanks, but no, thanks' if she doesn't."

9 DANGERS INVOLVED

Being a mail-order bride can be very dangerous. There are at least four recent cases of American men murdering (sometimes quite brutally) their mail-order bride. But it does go both ways: there is also a case of a mail-order bride murdering her American husband. Before involving yourself in the mail-order marriage industry, it pays to really consider the reasons behind using this method to find your future wife or husband. You might get lucky and meet someone leaving their home country for the reasons cited in item 10, but you might be one of the unlucky ones who ends up dead.

8 DIVORCE RATES

The United States Citizenship and Immigration Services (USCIS) reports that "marriages arranged through [mail-order bride] services would appear to have a lower divorce rate than the nation as a whole, fully 80 percent of these marriages having lasted over the years for which reports are available." The USCIS also reports that "mail-order bride and e-mail correspondence services result in 4000 to 6000 marriages between U.S. men and foreign brides each year."

7 AMERICAN FRONTIER

Believe it or not, mail-order brides were not uncommon in the mid-19th century on the American frontier. Many of the men who traveled West had a hard time finding a wife, and a cottage industry arose so that men could find wives from the East who would then travel to marry them.

6 HOW TO MEET
There are two ways to meet a mail-order bride. The first is to buy the contact information of the bride and organize a meeting in real life, and the second is to join a mail-order bride tour, in which men travel to a foreign country and attend special parties where the brides show off their wares.

5 STRANGE EDUCATION
Johns Hopkins University offers a course called "Mail-Order Brides: Understanding the Philippines in a Southeast Asian Context," which is supposedly a deep look into Filipino kinship and gender. Why a person would want to study this subject is beyond me, but there must be at least a small amount of demand out there.

4 UNFRIENDLY ATTITUDES
Australia is currently implementing schemes to put an end to what they deem "inappropriate immigration" after a public-affairs program showed the story of a Russian woman who arrived as a mail-order bride and was then confined as a sex slave by her husband in Sydney. While the original moves to clamp down on mail-order brides were mixed, the majority of people now support the changes.

3 MAIL-ORDER HUSBANDS
Because it is illegal to market mail-order marriages between Filipina women and foreign men, some clever people in the Philippines came up with a bright idea— mail-order husbands! These reverse publications allow men to advertise themselves to women. The end result is the same, but the method is different.

2 BIG PROFITS
The average cost of obtaining a mail-order bride is $10,000. Of that money, only $500 to $1000 will end up with the bride or her family. The rest goes to the marriage brokers. It is no surprise that such a lucrative market can attract some dishonest people...

1 DISHONEST MARKETING

In 2004, a jury in Maryland awarded a mail-order bride nearly half-a-million dollars in damages because she married a man who had a history of violence and abuse, which was concealed by the mail-order company. To make matters worse, the agency (prior to being found guilty) was advertising the bride as one of their greatest success stories.

10 COMMONLY BELIEVED MYTHS

10 FIVE SENSES

The Myth: We have five physical senses—sight, hearing, touch, smell, and taste.

Traditionally humans were considered to have five senses—sight, hearing, touch, smell, and taste. What most people don't know is that this number was never really considered to be the full count. Historically, we include the internal senses of imagination, memory, common sense (not to be confused with the sorely lacking common sense of many people), and the estimative power. In modern times, some scientists have gone so far as to say that we have over 21 senses!

9 THE RAINBOW LIE

The Myth: A rainbow has seven colors.

Unlike what most of us were probably taught at school, rainbows do not have seven colors. In fact, the rainbow is actually a continuous spectrum of color, and it is only an artifice of human color perception that makes us see seven bands. There are also special supernumerary rainbows, which have more than seven bands visible to the naked eye. Next time you see a rainbow, count the bands of color—you may be pleasantly surprised.

8 COLD COMFORT

The Myth: Drinking alcohol warms you up. This is entirely untrue, yet it is still commonly seen as an antidote to coldness in movies. It is probably at the root of another myth about Saint Bernard dogs carrying casks of liquor around their necks. Neither myth is true. In fact alcohol consumption causes your body temperature to drop. The feeling of warmth that one has after drinking is caused by the increased flow of blood to the surface of the skin; this gives the false perception of heat, when it is, in fact, wicking heat away. This myth was first debunked in 1866, so there really is no excuse for it to still be around.

7 QUAKE WITH FEAR

The Myth: Small earthquakes can reduce the chance of a big one. Statistically, for every huge quake there are a fairly consistent number of smaller quakes. This seems to disprove the notion that small quakes prevent big ones. Historically, the big ones keep coming regardless of how many small quakes occur.

6 DON'T SWIM

The Myth: You must wait 30 minutes after eating before swimming. While swimming after eating might make you feel uncomfortable, it will absolutely not cause you to get cramps. The myth comes from the mistaken idea that after eating the blood will divert to the gut, leaving the muscles with too little and thereby causing a cramp.

5 HOLY CELIBACY

The Myth: Catholic priests can't be married. It is only in the Western rites of the Catholic Church (such as the Roman Rite) that married men are not allowed to become priests. In the Eastern Rites, married priests are not uncommon. And while the Roman Rite has stuck with the idea of celibacy since it was first recommended by Saint Paul in the Bible, it does occasionally make exceptions for Anglican clergy converting to Catholicism or other married men who are called to the priesthood. It should also be noted, however, that once an unmarried man becomes a priest, he cannot get married in any rite of the Catholic Church.

4 CELL PHONE PLANE CRASH
The Myth: Using a cell phone on a plane can cause interference and, consequently, a crash.

We can tell right off that this is a myth by the mere fact that many airlines are now beginning to allow the use of cell phones during flights. After 25 years of testing by the Federal Aviation Administration (FAA), no evidence at all has surfaced to show that there is a danger when using cell phones on board.

3 GRUMPY OLD MEN
The Myth: When you get older, you become bad tempered.

Once you turn 30, you should expect little or no change in your personality for the rest of your life. It is a myth that age makes you bad tempered. If you see an elderly person who seems to be especially grumpy, they have either been like that their whole life, or they are suffering from a health condition such as a stroke or dementia.

2 RAW FISH
The Myth: Sushi is raw fish.

"Sushi" neither means "raw" nor does it always include raw fish. Sashimi, on the other hand, is raw fish. Sushi actually refers to the way that the rice is prepared (with a vinegar dressing). When you see those tasty little rolls of seaweed, fish, and rice, it is *makizushi*.

1 ARE YOU A COP?
The Myth: In the United States, a policeman must answer truthfully when asked if he is a cop.

Entrapment law in the United States does not forbid police officers from denying that they are police. It is more concerned with enticing people to commit crimes they would not, in the normal course of events, have considered. This is an error that is frequently seen in movies, or perhaps it is just that films are realistically depicting people who believe the myth, though I doubt it.

10 FASCINATING "FACTS" THAT ARE WRONG

10 THE NEW DEAL

The Myth: Franklin Roosevelt's "New Deal" was built upon the ideas of John Maynard Keynes.

Marriner Eccles was a prominent banker who saved his family bank from ruin when the Great Depression hit. It was he who told the Senate in 1933 that the key to stopping the Depression was spending. Eccles was later rewarded by President Roosevelt with the chairmanship of the Federal Reserve, a post he held for 14 years, and he wrote the Banking Act of 1935. In honor of his work, the headquarters of the Federal Reserve is housed in the Eccles Building.

Although Keynes' papers had been around in some form for the three years before the New Deal, the evidence indicates it was not a major influence on national economies until 1936. Keynes' work during the Depression consisted primarily with unemployment as a function of savings and investments (1930) and public spending (1933). His book *The General Theory of Employment, Interest and Money* did not come out until three years after Eccles' testimony and the beginning of the New Deal.

9 KING CHARLES III ... OR NOT

The Myth: Prince Charles will become Charles III when he assumes England's throne.

Although it has been officially denied (imagine talking about what name you'll have when your mom dies), based on reports from Prince Charles' friends, it is believed by many that he will take George VII as his regnal name when he assumes the throne. There are many theories as to why, with the two most popular being that Charles is an unlucky name for English monarchs (Charles I was deposed and Charles II very nearly so), and that George is to honor his grandfather, George VI.

8 PROHIBITION

The Myth: The 18th Amendment to the Constitution (Prohibition) outlawed drinking.

Drinking alcohol was never outlawed, only making, transporting, and selling it were. Liquor could legally be consumed provided that it was purchased before Prohibition. The 21st Amendment would later repeal the 18th but still make it illegal to transport alcohol in areas where it was banned (so-called dry counties).

From time to time, the 18th and 21st Amendments are still the basis for lawsuits between a state and the federal government. For example, in *South Dakota v. Dole* (1987), South Dakota claimed that the federal government's national minimum drinking age of 21 was a violation of the 21st Amendment, but the federal government's position was upheld seven to two under the Tax and Spend clause.

7 PAUL REVERE

The Myth: Paul Revere rode all the way to Concord, Massachusetts, on April 16, 1775, to warn American Minutemen that the English army was invading.

Dr. Joseph Warren sent Paul Revere and Charles Dawes to Concord to warn John Hancock and Samuel Adams of the English invasion, and they soon met Dr. Samuel Prescott returning home from an evening out. All three were captured by the British, but Dawes and Prescott (not Revere) quickly escaped. Some say that Dawes was then thrown from his horse and had to walk back to Lexington but others claim that after the escape he was lost and had to ride back to Lexington. Of the three, only Prescott finished the ride all of the way to Concord.

6 HONEST ABE

The Myth: Abraham Lincoln was a Republican when he won the 1864 election.

By changing the name of his party to "National Union Party," Lincoln was able to court Copperhead (War Democrat) voters who would never vote Republican. Further, he selected the only southern Democratic senator not to resign his seat, Andrew Johnson, to run as vice president. Despite a convention to raise support for midterm elections, the

Republicans in the party joined the ranks of the radicals. By March of 1867, Johnson was the only Unionist in office that had not defected, and it became a splinter group of the Democratic Party. Ironically, the Republicans kept the name of National Union Republicans for a while and consider it part of their lineage.

5 BOSTON TEA PARTY

The Myth: American colonists protested the Tea Tax with the Boston Tea Party because it raised the price of tea.

The American colonists preferred Dutch tea to English tea. The English Parliament placed an embargo on Dutch tea in the colonies, so a huge smuggling industry developed. To combat this, the English government *lowered* the tax on tea so that the English tea would be price-competitive with Dutch teas. The colonists (actually, some colonists led by the chief smugglers) protested by dumping the tea into Boston Harbor.

4 THE *CLERMONT*

The Myth: Robert Fulton's famous steamship was named the *Clermont.*

All of the official records list the boat as *North River Steam Boat*, and even Fulton called it the *North River*. A later biographer accidentally called it the *Clermont*, which was the city it was berthed at. There were other steamboats before the *North River*, but like many inventors, Fulton is given credit because he made the first practical one. His boat ferried passengers on the New York City/Albany run and usually took all day, including an overnight stop. Two side notes: the engine for the *North River* was built by another famous inventor who took an existing idea and made it practical—James Watt; also, Fulton built a working submarine and called it the *Nautilus.*

3 FRANKLIN ROOSEVELT'S DEPRESSION

The Myth: The U.S. President who dealt with the Great Depression by asking employers to reduce profits and not lower wages, promoting public works programs, and creating the Reconstruction Finance Corporation was Franklin D. Roosevelt.

Although Roosevelt gets the credit, President Herbert Hoover was actually the one who sowed the seeds of recovery after the stock market crashed. Despite the fact that he started federal programs that were the precursors of the New Deal, Hoover never really felt that the Depression would last as long as it did. Many people felt that Hoover was uncaring of the plight of the poor; however,

Hoover was independently wealthy before entering politics and gave all of his government checks to charity. He believed in charity, as his work in Europe during and after World War I shows, and when he became Secretary of Commerce in the United States, he worked to foster ties between business and government to improve service throughout the nation. Herein lies the fundamental problem that Hoover had in dealing with the Depression: when the Great Depression hit, he counted on the generosity of all Americans to help the country, and unfortunately, he was sadly mistaken.

It's interesting to note that in President Barack Obama's handling of the current recession, he is more like Hoover than Roosevelt, including his counting on banks to increase loans (which they were hesitant to do for both Hoover and Obama) and running deficit spending (it was campaigning against deficit spending that helped Roosevelt win the presidency in 1932).

2 LA PUCELLE

The Myth: Joan of Arc was convicted of heresy.

Joan of Arc denied all of the heresy charges against her and she was never convicted of that crime, despite the many traps the prosecution laid for her. During the trial, a prosecutor made an off-hand remark and asked if it was true that she dressed like a man during battles. Seeing no harm in telling the truth, she replied yes, and this was enough to seal her doom. This transvestism violated Deuteronomy 22:5 and was enough for the court to convict her of violating God's law. Since that particular law carries a death penalty, she was burned at the stake. Great care was made to give the appearance of a trial in accordance with canon law, but many aspects, including the official record, were fraudulent. Pope Callixtus III reopened the trial and Joan was exonerated and Bishop Pierre Cauchon was castigated for using a religious law to settle a secular dispute.

1 PRINCE OF DARKNESS

The Myth: In the Old Testament of the Bible, "Lucifer" refers to the fallen angel.

"Lucifer" (light-bearer) is a generic title referring to the morning star (Venus). As such, it has been used throughout history to refer to Satan, Christ, and others. With this in mind, Isaiah 14:12 starts out "How art thou fallen from heaven, O Lucifer, son of the morning!" Taken as an independent verse, this appears to refer to the battle of angels; however, the passage starts at Isaiah 12:4 with "Thou shalt take up this proverb against the king of Babylon," and toward the end is

Isaiah 14:22: "For I will rise up against them saith the Lord of hosts, and cut off from Babylon the name, and remnant, and son, and nephew, Saith the Lord." Thus in the Old Testament, Lucifer refers to some unnamed Babylonian king.

10 FASCINATING INTERNATIONAL "FACTS" THAT ARE WRONG

10 RUSSIA

The Myth: The former Soviet Union celebrated the October Revolution in October.

Although the Bolsheviks took control of Russia on October 25–26, 1917, this date was under the Old Style (Julian) calendar. One of the first things the Communists did was to modernize their calendar to the Gregorian calendar, thereby pushing the day ahead 13 days (into November). This became a major holiday in the Soviet Union, mostly because the official ban on religion made the biggest holidays civil ones, such as May Day and the October Revolution.

9 GERMANY AND BRITAIN

The Myth: The British King George I of Hanover used English or German when speaking with his cabinet.

Those who know history and realize George I was a German prince who spoke no English may then think that "it's obvious" he and his advisors spoke German. The reality is that since George I's cabinet did not speak German, the lingua franca in the meetings was French.

8 BRITAIN AND FRANCE

The Myth: The *Titanic* was the first ship known to use the distress code "SOS."

Although British ships preferred the traditional distress call CQD, most of the other European countries used the International Conference on Wireless

Communication at Sea standard set in 1908 of SOS. The French ship *Niagara* is known to have used SOS well before the *Titanic* did. Incidentally, in CQD, the CQ was a general call on a telegraph line, and the D stood for Distress. In James Cameron's film *Titanic*, he did get it right that the radio operator tried both CQD and SOS after the new distress call was suggested to him.

7 LEBANON

The Myth: President John F. Kennedy was the first to say "Ask not what your country can do for you, but what you can do for your country."

Yes, the misconception is American, but the backstory is international. This quote thought by many Americans to be pure Kennedy was actually from Lebanese writer Khalil Gibran in an article advocating his Lebanese brethren to rebel against the occupying Ottoman Turks. American politicians are renowned for plagiarizing their best lines from foreign sources. For example, Abraham Lincoln took the phrase "a government of the people, by the people, and for the people" from the preface of John Wycliff's 1384 edition of the Bible, and Vice President Joe Biden cribbed a few speeches while in the Senate from British Labour Party MP Neil Kinnock.

6 AUSTRALIA AND SCOTLAND

The Myth: Alexander Fleming invented the antibiotic penicillin.

Many will disagree with this since it is more a question of semantics than a misconception. Although Alexander Fleming, from Australia, discovered that the mold *Penicillium notatum* has antibacterial properties, he was not a chemist, and growing and culturing the mold was difficult for him. Scot Howard Florey, with the assistance of Ernst Chain, was able to purify the penicillin and put it in a form for use in humans, thereby inventing penicillin as a true antibiotic.

5 SWITZERLAND AND BRITAIN

The Myth: Watson and Crick discovered DNA (deoxyribonucleic acid).

Again, people might say "everyone knows that," but many people learn the simplified version of the story that James Watson and Francis Crick discovered DNA, probably because they won the Nobel Prize for their discovery of DNA's double-helix structure. The true discoverer of DNA was Swiss biologist Friedrich Miescher, who was analyzing pus cell nuclei in 1868 when he discovered nuclein. He was able to analyze this further and discovered an acid component to the nuclein, which he called deoxyribonucleic acid. Scientists Avery, MacLeod, and

McCarty were the first to show a link between DNA and heredity in 1943, and Rosalind Franklin did the first x-ray diffraction pattern study of DNA in 1952. What Watson and Crick did was to develop a model of DNA that accounted for all of the previous research discoveries.

4 FRANCE

The Myth: Château Mouton Rothschild is a top-grade Chateau claret. The five growths (classes) of red Bordeaux were determined in 1855. Four were considered first class: Lafite-Rothschild, Latour, Margaux, and Haut-Brion. Mouton-Rothschild did not like being placed in second class, so their motto is *"Premier ne puis. Second ne daigne. Mouton suis."* ("First I cannot be. Second I do not deign to be. Mouton I am.") All I know is I certainly would not turn down a glass of it.

3 SCOTLAND AND ITALY

The Myth: The fax machine was invented after the telephone.
Scottish inventor Alexander Bain had invented the electric clock back in 1841. In 1843, he used his work on the electric clock to patent a device that could be synchronized with a twin over telegraph lines, which according to some stories he did so he could transmit a picture of a newborn calf (if true, it would need to be a daguerreotype, which seems very unlikely for just a cow). Frederick Bakewell patented a better fax machine in 1848, two years before Bain updated his, and in 1861, an Italian, Giovanni Caselli, invented the first high-quality fax. All of this was done before both Alexander Bell and Elisha Gray filed for the telephone patent on February 14, 1876.

2 GERMANY

The Myth: Albert Einstein was a poor student.
The myth that Einstein was a poor student started when an American researcher mistranslated some of Einstein's report cards by not taking into account the grading system at the time. While Einstein was in school, students were given grades 1 to 6, 1 being the best. This was reversed (1 was worst) the year after Einstein graduated. Further research has uncovered a letter from Albert's mother to his aunt complimenting his grades, but I guess the image of Einstein going from failing school to being a top physicist is too good to be changed because of the truth.

1 CHINA

The Myth: Pandas eat only bamboo.

The reason that pandas eat so much bamboo is that it doesn't run away. They are omnivores that have adapted to a primarily bamboo diet, but they will eat anything they can catch, like small animals and carrion. The problem is that they are so slow from the fact that bamboo doesn't provide a lot of energy, so it is hard to catch anything else—it's a vicious cycle.

15 FACTS YOU PROBABLY DON'T KNOW

15 ARMADILLO BABIES

Some armadillos give birth to genetically identical quadruplets (in other words, they share exactly the same DNA). This is the only known case of more than two embryos developing in a single egg in nonhuman mammals.

14 MICROBES

Three pounds of the weight of every human is nonhuman microbial life, the likes of parasites and bacteria. Despite sounding incredibly disgusting, many of these are essential to the functioning of the human body.

13 POOP GERMS

The germs in feces can pass through up to ten layers of toilet paper. Don't forget to wash your hands!

12 EARWIGS

Earwigs, those odd-looking creatures with little pincers on their butts, have wings and can fly. Like some species of birds that are all but flightless, they are not particularly good at it, but it can come in handy if a quick escape is needed.

11 CUTTLEFISH EYES

Not all creatures have round eyes. For example, goats have rectangular eyes, and cuttlefish have perhaps the most bizarre of all—w-shaped pupils. Cuttlefish are also unable to see color, but they can see polarization of light, which helps them to see better due to contrast.

10 PYRAMIDS

While the ancient pyramids appear dusty and rough to us, this is how they always looked. When they were first built, they were usually coated with a highly polished white limestone, causing them to glitter from afar. The pyramid of Khafre still has some of this coating visible at the top point.

9 KOALA

Female koalas (which are actually marsupials, not bears) have two vaginas. Fortunately for them, male koalas have forked penises.

8 BLIND SPOT

Human eyes have a blind spot. The reason we don't notice it is that our brain is smart enough to fill the spot with information from the other eye and surrounding details.

7 AVOCADOS

The avocado is a ghost from evolution. It is only thanks to man that they remain today because of cultivation from our early history. Originally, the avocado was eaten by huge creatures such as woolly mammoths. If it had not been for humans liking the taste, avocados would now be extinct.

6 TRAFFIC LIGHTS

Have you ever noticed that people at traffic lights push the button repeatedly in the hopes that it will change the light faster? In fact, most traffic-light buttons are simply placebo buttons—they do nothing at all. Traffic lights generally run on timers, so whether you push it or don't push it, the lights will change anyway. This is also true for many elevator close-door buttons.

5 RAT LAUGHTER

When tickled, rats appear to laugh. While humans are the only creatures that have true risibility (the ability to laugh from rationality, as opposed to laughing due to sensation), rats do an extremely good job of mimicking it.

4 MERCURY

If you were to stand at the right point on Mercury's surface, you would be able to see the sun rise about halfway, then reverse and set before rising again, all within the same Mercurian day. Having said that, one day on Mercury is 176 earth days, so you would be waiting a long time to see it.

3 HITLER'S LOVERS

All four women who had a romantic relationship with Adolf Hitler attempted to commit suicide at least once. Of those four, two succeeded, one being Eva Braun, who committed suicide at Hitler's side.

2 SAND SHARKS

When a sand shark is pregnant, she develops two embryos. Of the two, the strongest will eat the other and any eggs that remain in the mother at the time. The technical name for this is "intrauterine cannibalism."

1 RAINBOW

When you look at a rainbow, the center is the shadow from your head. A primary rainbow is always on an arc 42 degrees around your head's shadow. This is called the antisolar point.

10 ASTONISHING FACTS ABOUT DREAMS

10 YOUR BRAIN IS ACTIVE WHEN YOU DREAM

Studies have provided evidence suggesting tremendous variation in brain activity during sleep. This has been demonstrated using EEG technology. Scientists have identified five distinct stages of sleep, characterized by differences in brain activity: stages 1, 2, 3, 4, and a final stage labeled rapid eye movement (REM) sleep. When awakened during REM sleep, subjects report dreaming. With the development of new brain-imaging technology in the early 1990s, we learned even more about brain activity during REM sleep. Researchers found that certain areas of the brain are extremely active during the REM sleep state, even more active than when we're awake. Studies have shown that certain visual areas of the human cortex, which decode complex visual scenes, are significantly more active during REM sleep. Intense activity is also observed in the limbic system, which is a set of structures heavily involved in human emotion.

9 ANIMALS AND DREAMS

We can't be 100% sure that animals dream in a similar way to humans, but they do enter into a state of REM sleep. REM sleep occurs in all mammals, although it excludes the egg-laying monotremes of Australia. The sentinel hypothesis of REM sleep, which was put forward by Frederic Snyder in 1966, proposes that many mammals wake up immediately after entering into REM sleep, leading him to

infer that the process was being used as a defense mechanism. Many birds also show signs of REM sleep, but reptiles and other cold-blooded animals do not. The echidna does enter into REM sleep, but only if its environment is around 25°C. Dogs and cats also experience this stage of sleep.

8 MARIJUANA AND DREAMS

Many people who smoke marijuana report having no dreams, yet after they quit, the same people report extremely vivid and intense dreams. Most vivid dreams take place during REM sleep, so the logical scientific question is "Does marijuana (THC) affect REM sleep?" A study conducted in 1975 compared the sleep patterns of experienced marijuana users with those of nonsmokers. The results showed reduced eye-movement activity and less REM sleep in the THC condition. They also reported an REM rebound effect, which is more REM activity upon withdrawal from THC. Scientific evidence exists that correlates marijuana use with a loss of REM sleep and dreams, so the next time you smoke marijuana and don't remember your dreams, you will know why.

7 EPIC DREAMS

Epic dreams are extremely vivid and can be life changing. These dreams are so compelling that they often generate a greater awareness of your natural surroundings and give you a fresh, new perspective on an aspect of life. When you wake up from an epic dream, you feel as if you have discovered something profound or amazing. The epic dream will remain with you for years. People who experience these types of dreams often report a continuous story line that constitutes an entirely different and ongoing life.

6 GENDER DIFFERENCES IN DREAMS

Many studies have been conducted to examine differences in the dreams of men and women. It has been shown that women dream of both genders equally, yet 67 percent of the time, the characters in men's dreams are predominantly male. Women's dreams tend to last longer and include more emotional content, whereas men's dreams are reported to include more violence, cars, and roads. On average, 8 percent of people's dreams include sexual activity. The primary gender difference in sexual dreams is that men tend to dream about unknown or public places and their dreams often feature strangers, while the opposite is true for the majority of women. Women more often dream of enclosed bodies of water, such as pools, lakes, and ponds. Of course, this data is based on general percentages and is not true for everyone.

5 SLEEP PARALYSIS

Sleep paralysis is a condition that affects many people in the world. It is directly related to the REM sleep stage and dreaming. Sleep paralysis corresponds with REM atonia, which is the state of paralysis that occurs during REM sleep. A person experiences sleep paralysis when the brain awakes from the REM sleep cycle, but the paralysis state remains. The person is conscious, but unable to move. They continue to dream and in many cases can visually experience their dreams in their room. A person experiencing sleep paralysis is not fully conscious, but well aware of what is happening. The experience has been described as distorted tunnel vision. The paralysis state may be accompanied by extreme hallucinations and a sense of danger. Many historical claims of alien abduction have been explained by extreme cases of sleep paralysis.

4 NIGHTMARES VERSUS NIGHT TERRORS

Ernest Hartmann has published many books and papers on the topic of nightmares. His work has indicated that the most common theme of a nightmare is being chased. Adults are commonly chased by a male figure, while children face animals or fantasy creatures. Nightmares are less common in adults than in children, who experience them most often between the ages of three or four and seven or eight. About 5 to 10 percent of people have nightmares once a month or more frequently. Hartmann's work suggests that nightmares directly correlate with daily activities and are an indicator of fear or anxiety that needs to be confronted. Some common triggers can be drug abuse, traumatic events, or the loss of a loved one.

Night terrors are quite different from nightmares. They occur during the first hour or two of sleep and during the non-REM cycle. Loud screaming and thrashing is common. The sleeper is hard to awake and usually remembers no more than an overwhelming feeling or a single scene. Night terrors are much less common than nightmares. Children from the ages of two to six are most prone to night terrors, and they affect about 15 percent of all children.

3 FAMOUS DREAMS

Dreams have often been credited with influencing world-changing events. Mary Shelley wrote Frankenstein after having a dream about the monster, saying that she "saw the hideous phantasm of a man stretched out, and then, on the working of some powerful engine, show signs of life, and stir with an uneasy, half-vital motion." Elias Howe was a sewing machine pioneer who greatly influenced the product in the middle of the 19th century. He is recorded as saying that he had a vivid dream about a group of cannibals that were preparing to cook him. They were dancing around a fire, waving their spears up and down. Howe noticed that in the head of each spear there was a small hole, which ultimately gave him the idea of passing the thread through the sewing needle close to the point, not at the other end. It was a major innovation in making mechanical sewing possible. The scientist Friedrich August Kekulé discovered the seemingly impossible chemical structure of benzene (C_6H_6) after having a dream about a group of snakes swallowing their tails. In 1953, James Watson and Francis Crick discovered the structure of DNA. Watson later reported that the idea came to him after dreaming of a series of spiral staircases. A few days prior to his death, Abraham Lincoln discussed a dream with his wife in which he previewed a dead body wrapped in funeral vestments surrounded by hundreds of mourners. He claims to have been told by a soldier that the president had been assassinated.

2 CHRONIC SNORING CAN LEAD TO A SLEEP DISORDER

Snoring is a major problem for millions of people. Many individuals who experience chronic snoring are suffering from an REM sleep disorder. During REM sleep, individuals will experience irregular breathing, a rise in blood pressure, vivid dreams, and paralysis. People who snore regularly do dream, but will not remember the dreams as often as normally sleeping individuals. They often will develop an REM sleep disorder. This disorder is a condition in which the individual does not experience any kind of paralysis when they sleep. The absence of this paralysis causes many people to physically act out their dreams. Such physical behaviors often include talking, yelling, punching, kicking, jumping out of bed, arm flailing, and even grabbing. The person will remain sleeping while acting out their dreams and will not remember the activity or dream the following day.

1 VIVID DREAMS HELP YOU LEARN

REM sleep begins when signals are broadcasted from the base of the brain, an area called the pons. The pons distributes signals to the thalamus, which directs them toward the cerebral cortex. The cerebral cortex is the area of the brain responsible for learning, thinking, and organizing information. The pons also sends signals that shut off the neurons in the spinal cord, causing temporary paralysis during REM sleep. REM sleep activates the area of the brain that we use for learning. This may be an extremely important factor in normal brain development during infancy. It may explain why small children spend much more time in REM sleep than adults do. In addition, REM sleep is associated with increased protein in the brain. Studies have been conducted that correlate REM sleep and learning mental skills. Separate groups of people were taught the same skill, and a larger percentage of individuals who fell into REM sleep during the night were able to recall the skill the next day. This theory is called the Ontogenetic Hypothesis of REM sleep.

15 FASCINATING FACTS ABOUT TOILETS

15 PSYCHO

The horror movie *Psycho*, directed by Alfred Hitchcock, was the first film to show a toilet being flushed. A large number of complaints were received by the studio because of it. Obviously no one minded the fact that there was a woman being slashed to bits in the shower!

14 AIR FRESHENER

The first air fresheners for toilets come from medieval times. They were made of pomegranate fruits, which were studded with aromatic cloves and hung in the vicinity of the toilet.

13 FANCY PAPER

Hermann Goering, a leading member in the Nazi party, had such a delicate bottom that he refused to use regulation toilet paper, instead preferring to use soft white handkerchiefs.

12 FRONT OR BACK?

First prize in stupidity goes to the $100,000 U.S. study to determine whether most people put their toilet paper on the holder with flap in front or behind. The answer was that three in four prefer the flap in front.

11 LANGUISHING ON THE LAVATORY

On October 25th, 1760, King George II of Great Britain died. His death was caused by his falling off the toilet.

10 THREE YEARS

The average person spends three whole years of their life sitting on the toilet.

9 STALL

The first toilet stall in a row is the least used (and, unsurprisingly, the cleanest).

8 LACK OF LOOS

An estimated 2.6 billion people worldwide do not have access to toilet facilities, particularly in rural areas of China and India.

7 ROMANS

The Roman army didn't have toilet paper, so they used a water-soaked sponge on the end of a stick instead!

6 FLUSHING FUN

The toilet is flushed more times during the Super Bowl halftime than at any other time during the year. It should be pointed out that there have been no studies done to confirm or deny this fact.

5 PHARMACEUTICALS
Nearly 90 percent of all drugs taken by humans end up going down the toilet—in urine. Studies by the EPA have found fish in the sewers with trace amounts of antidepressants, pain relievers, and antibiotics. I bet those fish don't get sick!

4 TOILET DEATHS
Each year around the world, 1.8 million people die due to a lack of proper sanitation. Many of those dead are children.

3 GERMS GALORE
On every square inch of a public restroom toilet handle, up to 40,000 germs are waiting for the next hand to come along and open the door.

2 THOMAS CRAPPER
While he didn't invent the toilet, Thomas Crapper perfected the siphon flush system we use today. He was born in the village of Thorne, which is an anagram of throne, which is what some British people call the toilet.

1 WORST TOILETS
In a 1992 survey, British public toilets were voted the worst in the world. Following quickly behind were those in Thailand, Greece, and France.

10 FACTS YOU DIDN'T KNOW ABOUT CHE GUEVARA

10 NOT SO GLAMOROUS NAME
The name Che Guevara either incites love or hate. The name is synonymous with freedom-fighting to some and butchery to others. What most

people don't know is that Che's real name was not quite so romantic; he was born Ernesto Lynch. That's right—Che Guevara was actually plain old Mr. Lynch. It doesn't have quite the same ring to it, does it? His surname comes from the fact that his family was half Irish.

9 STINKY CHE

Che Guevara as a youth was nicknamed "Chancho" (pig) because of his bathing habits (or lack thereof) and the fact that he proudly wore a "weekly shirt"—i.e., a shirt he changed once a week. All through his life people commented on his smelliness (though obviously not to his face once he had the power to execute people on a whim).

8 ERNESTO THE GEEK

Contrary to the image we all have of Guevara, in his youth he was quite the geek. He loved playing chess and even entered local tournaments. In between hanging out with his chess buddies, Ernesto read poetry, which he loved with a passion. His favorite subjects at school were mathematics and engineering. I think we could safely say that if he were a teenager today, he would be emo.

7 CUBAN OR NOT?

While Guevara is best remembered for his actions in Cuba, he was actually born in Argentina to wealthy parents, and he never became a Cuban citizen. When he was born, his father said, "The first thing to note is that in my son's veins flowed the blood of the Irish rebels."

6 DOCTOR OF MEDICINE

There seems to be some dispute about this fact around the Internet, but in June 1953, Guevara completed his medical studies and graduated as Doctor Ernesto Guevara. While studying, he was particularly (and oddly) interested in the disease leprosy.

5 AMERICAN TRIP

In 1964, Guevara traveled to the United States to give a speech to the United Nations in New York. While there, he condemned the U.S. for their racial segregation policies: "Those who kill their own children and discriminate daily against them because of the color of their skin; those who let the murderers of blacks remain free, protecting them; and furthermore, punishing the black population because they demand their legitimate rights as free men—how can those who do this consider themselves guardians of freedom?" Isn't it ironic?

4 FIVE CHILDREN
We tend not to see Guevara as a family man, but in fact he had one child with his first wife, Hilda Gadea, a daughter who was born in Mexico City on February 15, 1956, and he had four children with his second wife, the revolutionary Aleida March.

3 NO HANDS
After he was executed, Che's hands were chopped off by a military doctor. They were preserved for fingerprint identification and then later sent to Cuba as proof of his demise.

2 IRONIC ICON
The famous monochrome image of Guevara's face has become one of the most well-known icons in modern history. Ironically, it helps to fuel the consumerist culture that Che most despised.

1 SAINT ERNESTO
In Cuba, many consider Guevara to be a national hero, and some even worship him as a saint. In school, children pledge to "be like Che." Needless to say, Guevara has never been declared a saint and the adulation of him is opposed by the church.

15 FASCINATING FACTLETS

15 CHECKMATE
"Checkmate," the term used in chess to announce victory, comes from the Persian phrase "*shah mat*" which means "the king is dead."

14 BATMANIA
The great city of Melbourne, Australia, had an unusual first name due to the first man who settled there—John Batman. The city was originally called Batmania.

13 CANNULATED COWS
To make scientific study of cows easier, a round window is fitted to some of the animals. This allows easy visual access to the digestive system of the creature. Cows that have this window installed are called cannulated cows.

12 RABBIT TEST
In the 1920s, a woman's urine was injected into a female rabbit in order to test whether the woman was pregnant or not, because the hormone secreted by pregnant women causes a reaction in rabbits. Modern pregnancy tests use the same effect without the use of the rabbit.

11 DUCK GENITALS
Male ducks often have penises of up to 14 inches in length! They use these rather nasty spears to rape females who have a built-in system to help defend themselves: their vagina leads to three different canals, two of which are false. When raped, the female can close the real canal, forcing the male duck's sperm into a dead end.

10 FLATULIST
A flatulist is a performer who receives payment for farting in an amusing or musical manner. In *The City of God* (14.24), Saint Augustine mentions some performers who had "such command of their bowels, that they can break wind continuously at will, so as to produce the effect of singing."

9 SIX-HOUR CLOCK
In Thailand, a six-hour clock is used alongside the standard twenty-four hour clock. It counts the same number of hours in a day but divides the day into four quarters of six hours.

8 ORGAN2/ASLSP
Organ2/ASLSP (As SLow aS Possible) is a piece of music by avant-garde composer John Cage. As its title suggests, it should be played as slow as possible. A performance of this work began in 2001 and is scheduled to end in 2640.

7 PYROPHONE
A pyrophone is an instrument that is designed like a pipe organ, but instead of producing sound through air movement, it uses explosions to create music. The effect is rather frightening and definitely weird.

6 MONDEGREENS
We have all at some point or another sung along with a song only to find that we're singing the wrong lyrics because we misheard the original. This is called a mondegreen. For example, the Jimi Hendrix song "Purple Haze" has the lyrics "'Scuse me while I kiss the sky," which might be wrongly heard as "'Scuse me while I kiss this guy," a mistake that could lead to some embarrassment at karaoke parties.

5 FERRET LEGGING
The Official Dictionary of Unofficial English defines "ferret legging" as "an endurance test or stunt in which ferrets are trapped in pants worn by a participant." The world record for ferret legging is presently held by a retired miner in Britain who kept the ferret in his leg for five hours and 26 minutes.

4 STREETS OF JAPAN
Most Japanese streets don't have names. They are instead given numbers: one for the district, one for the block, and finally one for the house.

3 GLASS DELUSION
This is a bizarre psychiatric disorder from the middle ages in which sufferers believed themselves to be made of glass and prone to shattering. Even the famous were not immune to the disorder, as King Charles VI of France is said to have suffered from it.

2 MIRACLE FRUIT
This is a great fruit for party tricks. When eaten, the miracle berry plant (*Synsepalum dulcificum*) tricks the taste buds into thinking that sour is sweet.

This makes it possible (and this where the party tricks come in) to eat large quantities of lemons, and to even drink vinegar without flinching. This is not recommended, however.

1 FORER EFFECT

Next time you read your horoscope, think of the Forer effect. This is when a person sees vague information designed to apply to a large number of people and believes it to be specifically tailored for them. This is what makes fortune telling appear to be so accurate when it is actually fabricated.

10 MYTHS ABOUT NINJAS

10 NINJAS ARE MYTHICAL

The Myth: There are no real ninjas.

In fact, ninjas and the arts that they learned date back to over 800 years ago. The ninja families developed their skills in order to protect themselves against the likes of Samurai warriors. It is this humble beginning that gives *ninjutsu* its unique philosophy: escape if you can, and if you can't, kill. There was nothing unethical about this to the ninja—he would throw sand in the enemy's eyes, stab them when they were down, or do anything to protect life and limb. Over time, the ninjas were used as spies, bodyguards, and assassins for hire.

9 NINJAS AND SWORDS

The Myth: As a matter of course, ninjas caught swords with their bare hands. In fact, a true ninja knows that there is only one good way to deal with a sword blow: move out of its path. While movies may show ninjas catching swords barehanded, this really is just a Hollywood myth to sell more B-grade films. On the other hand, if getting out of the way of a sword really is not possible, a ninja may be carrying a hand claw that he could use to prevent the sword from doing any damage.

8 NINJAS WORE MASKS

The Myth: Ninjas wear masks and black clothes when fighting; it is their uniform.

This is entirely false. These days, most ninjas who are working as bodyguards wear suits or similar modern clothing. So when might a ninja have worn a mask? Maybe eight hundred years ago if they had to hide in the trees, but even then it was not part of a "uniform." A ninja wearing a mask is no different from a soldier wearing camouflage paint. It depends entirely on the environment and the need for concealment. Of course, this is also true of black clothing.

7 NINJAS VANISHED

The Myth: Ninjas were able to vanish.

This myth has come about because of the first ninja rule: get away. If a ninja can avoid fighting, he will. In order to achieve this goal, he might need to create a diversion of some kind, such as throwing *shuriken* (throwing stars), setting off smoke bombs, or throwing sand in the opponent's eyes. By the time the opponent recovered from the distraction, the ninja would be gone. There is no magic involved here—just common sense.

6 NINJAS AND PRESSURE POINTS

The Myth: Ninjas can't kill with just a touch.

I bet you weren't expecting that! In fact, there are a series of "touches" (this word is used lightly, as a decent amount of pressure is needed) that can render a person dead. This is quite logical when you consider that a firm-enough blow to the temple can kill a person. These deadly methods are normally only taught to the most advanced ninja students who, by that time, would never need to use them. Fundamental nonlethal pressure-point techniques, however, are taught from the very beginning of ninja training, and even the most basic student can take a person to the floor with one finger pressed firmly in the right part of the throat or in the eyeballs, for example. Pressure points cause a lot of pain when pressed in the right way, and they are indispensable tools for the ninja. Furthermore, simple techniques, like nipple squeezing, can also render an offender defenseless in seconds.

5 NINJUTSU

The Myth: Ninjutsu refers to fighting methods.

In fact, *ninjutsu* means the art of stealth and perseverance—it is about the strategy and tactics of fighting. The actual moves come from a variety of different martial arts disciplines. In the most common and most authentic version of *ninjutsu, Bujinkan Budō Taijutsu*, 18 disciplines form the main basis of training:

1. *Seishin-teki kyōkō* (spiritual refinement)
2. *Taijutsu* (unarmed combat, using one's body as the only weapon)
3. *Kenjutsu* (sword fighting)
4. *Bōjutsu* (stick and staff fighting)
5. *Shurikenjutsu* (*shuriken* throwing)
6. *Sōjutsu* (spear fighting)
7. *Naginatajutsu* (*naginata* fighting)
8. *Kusarigamajutsu* (*kusarigama* fighting)
9. *Kayakujutsu* (pyrotechnics and explosives)
10. *Hensōjutsu* (disguise and impersonation)
11. *Shinobi-iri* (stealth and entering methods)
12. *Bajutsu* (horsemanship)
13. *Sui-ren* (water training)
14. *Bōryaku* (tactics)
15. *Chōhō* (espionage)
16. *Intonjutsu* (escaping and concealment)
17. *Tenmon* (meteorology)
18. *Chi-mon* (geography)

4 SHURIKEN: KILLER STARS

The Myth: Shuriken (throwing stars) are used to kill from a distance.

In fact, *shuriken* are used as secondary weapons either to slash or stab. Normally they are thrown to cause a distraction. *Shuriken* come in two varieties: *hira-shuriken* (the famous ninja stars), which were originally household items such as washers and coins that were used to distract and were not usually sharp; and *bo-shuriken*, which are straight spikes up to 21 centimeters (about 8½ inches) in length that, like most ninja weapons, were also originally household items such as chopsticks or hairpins. Their origins certainly make it clear that *shuriken* were not intended to be killing weapons.

3 NINJA WEAPONS
The Myth: Ninjas only use ancient Japanese weapons.

Ninjas do use ancient Japanese weapons, but not exclusively. Ninjas are often trained in modern weaponry as well, and many of the so-called ancient weapons are not ancient at all—they are modern interpretations of ancient concepts, such as the *shuriken* whose origins lie in coins as mentioned in number 4, above. Ninjas have also long used gunpowder to their advantage, either to create smoke screens or even bombs, in the discipline *kayakujutsu*, the art of gunpowder.

2 NINJA STRENGTH
The Myth: Ninjas need to be strong and fast.

The whole point of *ninjutsu* is to use the body effectively, whether a ninja is fat or thin, short or tall. The ninja doesn't need speed, and in fact speed can work against him. What he needs is the ability to predict his opponent's move and outthink him. By making calm and steady movements, he gains control of the enemy and ultimately the fight. Much of *ninjutsu* is about foot movement and natural positioning, which allows the ninja to retain his balance in all manner of unusual situations.

1 PIRATES VERSUS NINJAS
The Myth: Pirates are better than ninjas.

This long-raging Internet debate is just silly. There is no doubt at all that ninjas are far better and that pirates just utterly suck in comparison. There has never been a recorded case of a pirate beating a ninja. A pirate may have a cutlass and a hook hand but he has little else to fight with—plus lots of lace and fancy clothes—whereas a ninja has a whole slew of weapons and light-weight clothes that give him an advantage before a fight even begins. Furthermore, if the pirate looks like he might be winning a battle at sea, the ninja can just jump off the ship and run on water to the nearest island.

10 MYTHS ABOUT
THE COMMON COLD

10 SWEAT IT OUT

We've all done it or at least seen others do it: covering up with extra blankets, sticking your head over a bowl of hot water, all in the hope that we will sweat the cold out. Unfortunately, this does not work and is completely ineffective. The only benefit this may have is to make you feel a little better because it addresses the cold's symptoms.

9 FLU SHOT DANGERS

Many people believe that you can catch a flu from the flu vaccine. This myth comes about from the misconception that the flu vaccine contains a weakened form of the flu virus. The vaccine actually includes only components of the virus, and not a complete version of it. Therefore, you won't catch the flu from a flu shot.

8 WEAK IMMUNE SYSTEM

A weakened immune system does not heighten the risk of catching a cold. Studies have shown that healthy and unhealthy people exhibit the same amount of susceptibility to colds. Interestingly, the same study found that 95 percent of people who had the cold virus directly applied to their nasal membranes became infected, but only 75 percent of them exhibited any symptoms of the cold. This is called an asymptomatic infection.

7 VITAMIN C

It is a myth that loads of vitamin C and zinc help to stave off or cure a cold. While it is often a good idea to take vitamin and mineral supplements, they have no effect on the cold virus. Once the cold hits, you are better off taking painkillers and waiting it out.

6 WINTER COLDS

Many people believe that most colds are caught during the winter, but in fact, most colds are caught in the spring and fall. The virus becomes much more active in those seasons and seems to become largely dormant in the winter.

5 DON'T DRINK MILK

A lot of people think that drinking milk while you have a cold is a bad idea because it causes more mucus to build up. Actually, milk does not cause a buildup of mucus at all—you can drink as much of it as you like and it will have no effect on your cold.

4 COLD KISSING

There is a popular myth that kissing a person with a cold will cause you to catch it. The reality is that the quantity of virus on the lips and mouth are miniscule, and a much larger dose would be required for you to become infected. It's the nasal mucus you have to worry about (so no nose-kissing).

3 COLD CAUSES A COLD

I bet most people here have been told, at one time or another, not to go out with wet or damp hair, or to wrap up warm so you don't catch cold. In fact, body temperature (or ambient temperature) makes no difference at all. You catch a cold when you come into contact with the cold virus; once the virus gets into your system you will get sick. It doesn't matter if you are hot, cold, warm, or dry.

2 DON'T TREAT COLD SYMPTOMS

Many people believe that the symptoms of a cold, like coughing and a running nose, are designed to help us get over the sickness quickly, therefore they don't believe that we should treat the symptoms with medicines. But the truth is that the symptoms not only make no difference to the duration of the cold, they can help spread the bug to other people. You should take comfort in knowing that painkillers and other cold medicines will not only make the illness more tolerable, they will help to keep it contained.

1 STARVE A FEVER

I am sure that everyone has heard the phrase "starve a fever, feed a cold." The fact is it is completely untrue. Eating has no negative impact on the body when you are sick; in fact, the opposite is true. Food provides the body with fuel to cope with illness, so when you're sick, it's a good idea to eat healthy and well. I recommend a good bowl of chicken soup for a start!

10 MISCONCEPTIONS ABOUT NEANDERTHALS

10 LACK OF SPEECH
The Myth: Neanderthals couldn't speak; they grunted.

It has been long believed that Neanderthals, having only a basic capacity for sound in their throats, couldn't speak like humans. But in 1983 at a cave in Israel, scientists found a Neanderthal hyoid bone (part of the vocal mechanism) that was identical to that of modern humans. This means that their capacity for speech (at least physically) is the same as our own. There is no reason to believe that they did not have at least a basic system of vocal communication.

9 OUR ANCESTORS
The Myth: Man is descended from Neanderthals.

In fact, Neanderthals and modern men existed side by side as two separate groups. Recent DNA studies have found that the Neanderthals were a distinct evolutionary line, a line which ultimately died out around 30,000 years ago. The extinction of Neanderthals was most likely caused by slightly lower birthrates and higher mortality rates than humans, combined with an increasingly unstable climate.

8 EXCESS HAIR
The Myth: Neanderthals were hairy.

There is absolutely no reason to believe that Neanderthals were any hairier than modern man. Computer models have shown that excess hair on Neanderthals would have caused overproduction of sweat, which would have frozen on the Neanderthals, potentially leading to death.

7 CLUBBING

The Myth: Neanderthals exclusively used clubs as weapons.

Actually, the Neanderthals had many highly developed tools and weapons, such as spears, for killing mammoths, and stone tools. They are thought to have used tools of the Mousterian class, which were often produced using materials like bones, antlers, and wood rather than stone. Many of these tools were very sharp. There is also good evidence that they used a lot of wood, although wooden objects are unlikely to have been preserved until today.

6 BENT OVER

The Myth: Neanderthals had bent knees and walked like chimps.

This is one of those very unfortunate cases of a discovery leading to much confusion. A Neanderthal skeleton discovered at the start of the 20th century had bent knees, giving rise to the popular belief that all Neanderthals did. In fact, it turns out the skeleton was of a Neanderthal that suffered from arthritis. Neanderthals walked upright in the same manner as modern humans; they were generally only five to six inches shorter than modern humans, contrary to a common view of them as "very short" or "just over five feet."

5 SAVAGES

The Myth: Neanderthals were savage.

There is actually much evidence to show that Neanderthals cared for the sick and old in their communities. There has been fossil evidence that shows potentially life-threatening injuries that were completely healed, indicating that the Neanderthal who suffered the injury was nursed back to health by another member of his group. There is also evidence (via fossilized musical instruments) that Neanderthals enjoyed and played music.

4 ETHNICITY

The Myth: Neanderthals were ethnically equal.

Because we use one term to describe all Neanderthals, we tend to think of them as a single group of people sharing identical traits and features, but it is most likely that there were different ethnicities in Neanderthals, just as there are in humans. A recent study has determined that there were probably three racial groups within the Neanderthal family, finding that, "The conclusions of this study are consistent with existing paleoanthropological research and show that

Neanderthals can be divided into at least three groups: one in western Europe, a second in the Southern area and a third in western Asia."

3 CAVEMEN
The Myth: Neanderthals lived in caves.

Okay, this is partially true—some Neanderthals did live in caves (hence "cavemen"), but many of them lived in tepee-style huts made from animal bones and covered with branches and skins. Around the huts were piled stones to keep the whole thing in place.

2 APE FACE
The Myth: Neanderthals had faces like apes.

This misconception came about through poor reconstructions from largely arthritic skeletons. In 1983, Jay Matternes, a forensic artist who did much work in fleshing out skulls for homicide investigations, performed a reconstruction on a much better Neanderthal specimen than had been seen before. The result clearly shows that the Neanderthals looked virtually same as us.

1 UNANSWERED QUESTIONS
The Myth: There are certain questions about the physical attributes of Neanderthals that we will never know.

As of 2009, the complete Neanderthal genome has been mapped. The most important implication of this is that it now becomes technically possible to clone a Neanderthal—to raise them back from the dead, so to speak. The current estimated cost of doing this is $30 million, and no one is putting up the cash. There are ethical questions that are always going to be raised regarding cloning, and this is also a hindrance. But there is absolutely no reason not to believe that we will, one day, be able to give birth to and raise a Neanderthal (or at least the closest thing possible to one).

25 FASCINATING FACTS ABOUT CIGARETTE SMOKING

25 $400 BILLION INDUSTRY

Cigarettes are the single most traded item on the planet, with approximately one trillion being sold from country to country each year. At a global take of more than $400 billion, it's one of the world's largest industries. These numbers are even more impressive when you take into account the World Health Organization's report that approximately 25 percent of cigarettes sold around the world are smuggled.

24 NICOTINE RISING

The nicotine content in several major brands of cigarettes is reportedly on the rise. Harvard University and the Massachusetts Health Department revealed that between 1997 and 2005, the amount of nicotine in Camel, Newport, and Doral cigarettes may have increased by as much as 11 percent.

23 BANNED FROM THE AIRWAVES

In 1970, President Nixon signed the law that placed warning labels on cigarettes and banned television advertisements for them. The last date that cigarette ads were permitted on TV was extended by a day, from December 31, 1970, to January 1, 1971, to allow the television networks one last cash windfall from cigarette advertising during the New Year's Day football games.

22 GLOBAL MARKET

U.S. cigarette manufacturers now make more money selling cigarettes to countries around the globe than they do selling to Americans. In fact, the American cigarette brands Marlboro, Kool, Camel, and Kent own roughly 70 percent of the global cigarette market.

21 CIGARETTE SMOKING MAY BE HAZARDOUS TO YOUR HEALTH

Cigarettes can contain more than 4000 ingredients, which, when burned, can also produce over 200 "compound" chemicals. Many of these "compounds" have been linked to lung damage. They also contain arsenic, formaldehyde, lead, hydrogen cyanide, nitrogen oxide, carbon monoxide, ammonia, and 43 known carcinogens. In the early 1950s, the Kent brand of cigarettes used crocidolite asbestos as part of the filter, a known active carcinogen.

20 TASTES LIKE URINE

Urea, a chemical compound that is a major component in urine, is used to add "flavor" to cigarettes.

19 FILTER FILLERS

The "cork tip" filter was originally invented in 1925 by Hungarian inventor Boris Aivaz, who patented the process of making the cigarette filter from crepe paper. All kinds of filters were tested, although cork is unlikely to have been one of them.

18 AGE RESTRICTION TO *BUY* CIGARETTES

In most countries around the world, the legal age for the purchase of tobacco products is now 18, raised from 16, while in Japan the age minimum is 20 years old.

17 NO AGE RESTRICTION TO *SMOKE* CIGARETTES

Contrary to popular social belief, it is not illegal to smoke tobacco products at any age. Parents are within the law to allow minors to smoke, and minors are within the law to smoke tobacco products freely. However, the *sale* of tobacco products is highly regulated with legal legislation.

16 NO SMOKING IN PUBLIC

Smoking bans in many parts of the world have been employed as a means to stop smokers from smoking in public. As a result, many social businesses have claimed a significant drop in the number of people who go out to pubs, bars, and restaurants.

15 TAKES YEARS OFF YOUR LIFE

Scientists claim the average smoker will lose 14 years of their life due to smoking. This, however, does not necessarily mean that a smoker will die young; they may still live out a "normal" lifespan.

14 SOME STATES SMOKE MORE

The U.S. states with the highest percentages of smokers are Kentucky (28.7%), Indiana (27.3%), and Tennessee (26.8%), while the states with the fewest are Utah (11.5%), California (15.2%), and Connecticut (16.5%).

13 AMERICAN WOMEN LIKE TO SMOKE

The United States is the only major cigarette market in the world in which the percentage of women smoking cigarettes (22%) comes close to the number of men who smoke (35%). Europe has a slightly larger gap (46% of men smoke, 26% of women smoke), while most other regions have few women smokers. The stats: Africa (29% of men smoke, 4% of women smoke); Southeast Asia (44% of men, 4% of women); Western Pacific (60% of men, 8% of women).

12 NICOTINE GETS INTO EVERY CORNER OF YOUR BODY

Nicotine reaches the brain within 10 seconds after smoke is inhaled. It has been found in every part of the body and in breast milk.

11 SUGAR HIGH

Sugar approximates to roughly 20 percent of a cigarette, and many diabetics are unaware of this secret sugar intake. Also, the health effects of burning sugar are unknown.

10 LITES AREN'T REALLY LIGHT

"Lite" cigarettes are produced by infusing tobacco with carbon dioxide and superheating it until the tobacco "puffs up" like expanding foam. The expanded tobacco then fills the same paper tube as "regular" tobacco. However, smokers draw on "lite" and menthol cigarettes harder (on average) than regular cigarettes, causing the same overall levels of tar and nicotine to be consumed.

9 HOLEY FILTERS

"Lite" cigarettes are manufactured with air holes around the filter to aerate the smoke as it is drawn in. Many smokers have learned to cover these holes with their fingers or their lips to get a stronger hit.

8 DEPLETES THE IMMUNE SYSTEM

The immune systems of smokers have to work harder every day than those of nonsmokers. As a result, a smoker's blood will contain fewer antioxidants, although a smoker's immune system may be quicker to respond to virus attacks due to its more active nature.

7 SMOKING MAY CAUSE HEARTBURN

Smokers often smoke after meals to "allow food to digest easier." In fact, the exact opposite is true. Blood is diverted from digestion because the body's priority moves away from the digestion of food in favor of protecting the blood cells and flushing toxins from the brain.

6 SMOKING FETISH

Some people (mostly males) can be aroused by the sight of a smoker smoking (usually females). This is called the Smoking Fetish, and it affects a small number of the population. As with most fetishes, the reason for this arousal can usually be traced back to incidents in childhood. However, cigarettes—particularly menthols—force blood away from the penis if smoked while aroused.

5 TEEN SMOKERS

Most smokers take up the habit in their mid teens, well before the legal age for purchasing cigarettes, and it is seen as a rite of passage toward adulthood. Other perceived rites of passage include: using aftershave, wearing stilettos, drinking alcohol, using drugs, and engaging in sexual intercourse; a number of these are sometimes cited as the main causes of teenage pregnancy.

4 NUMBER-ONE GATEWAY DRUG

Smoking tobacco is the ultimate gateway drug in that it is legally available and involves mastering a unique method of intake. Smokers looking to get high will very rarely do so from cigarettes after the initial stages of taking up the habit. Alcohol, on the other hand, is less likely to lead to the use of other substances because of the significant effect that users need look no further for stimulation.

3 SIDE EFFECTS MAY VARY

Smokers generally report a variety of after-effects such as calmness, relaxation, alertness, stimulation, concentration, and many others. In fact, smoking will produce a different effect in each individual depending on "what they expect to get," turning the cigarette into the world's most popular placebo (satisfying the brain's hunger for nicotine being the only "relaxation" factor). The smoker will then use these expectations as a reason for continuing the habit.

2 POTENT POTABLES

Several active ingredients and special methods of production are involved in making sure the nicotine in a cigarette is many times more potent than that of a tobacco plant.

1 TO TOP IT ALL OFF...

"Toppings" are added to the blended tobacco mix in cigarettes to add flavor and a taste unique to the manufacturer. Some of these toppings have included clove, licorice, orange oil, apricot stone, lime oil, lavender oil, dill seed oil, cocoa, carrot oil, mace oil, myrrh, beet juice, bay leaf, oak, rum, vanilla, and vinegar.

15 AMAZING FACTS ABOUT THE HUMAN BODY

15 STOMACH

The stomach's digestive acids are strong enough to dissolve zinc. Fortunately for us, the cells in the stomach lining renew so quickly that the acids don't have time to dissolve it.

14 LUNGS

The lungs contain over 300,000 million capillaries (tiny blood vessels). If they were laid end to end, they would stretch 1500 miles.

13 TESTICLES
A man's testicles manufacture 10 million new sperm cells each day—enough that he could repopulate the entire planet in only six months!

12 BONES
Human bone is as strong as granite in supporting weight. A block of bone the size of a matchbox can support nearly ten tons—that's four times as much as concrete can support.

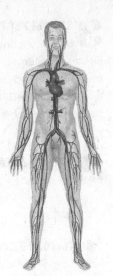

11 FINGERNAILS
Each finger- and toenail takes six months to grow from base to tip.

10 SKIN
The largest organ in the body is the skin. In an adult man it covers about 20 square feet. The skin constantly flakes away—in a lifetime, each person sheds around 40 pounds of skin.

9 HEIGHT
When you sleep, you grow by about 8 mm (0.3 inches). The next day you shrink back to your former height. The reason is that your cartilage discs are squeezed like sponges by the force of gravity when you stand or sit.

8 FOOD & DRINK
The average person in the western world eats 55 tons of food and drinks 11,000 gallons of liquid during his life.

7 KIDNEYS
Each kidney contains 1 million individual filters. They filter an average of around 1.3 liters (2.2 pints) of blood per minute and expel up to 1.4 liters (2.5 pints) of urine a day.

6 EYES
The focusing muscles of the eyes move around 100,000 times a day. To give your leg muscles the same workout, you would need to walk 50 miles every day.

5 TEMPERATURE
In 30 minutes, the average body gives off enough heat to bring a half gallon of water to boil.

4 BLOOD CELLS
A single human blood cell takes only 60 seconds to make a complete circuit of the body.

3 FORESKIN
The foreskin from a circumcised baby takes only 21 days to grow from a piece of skin the size of a postage stamp to skin that can cover three basketball courts. Amazing isn't it? Thanks to science, the laboratory-grown skin is used in treating burn patients.

2 VISUAL RECEPTION
The eyes receive approximately 90 percent of all the information we get, making us basically visual creatures.

1 OVARIES
The female ovaries contain nearly half-a-million egg cells, yet only 400 or so will ever get the opportunity to create a new life.

10 MYTHS ABOUT DINOSAURS

10 HUMANS AND DINOSAURS
The Myth: Humans lived alongside dinosaurs.
Dinosaurs and people coexist only in books, movies, and cartoons. The last dinosaurs—other than birds—died out dramatically about 65 million years ago, while the fossils of our earliest human ancestors are only about 6 million years old.

9 MAMMALS AND DINOSAURS

The Myth: Mammals only evolved after dinosaurs died out.

Tiny mammals lived in the shadow of the dinosaurs for more than 150 million years, occupying ecological niches as small, nocturnal animals weighing as little as two grams. The ancestors of mammals, animals called synapsids, actually appeared before dinosaurs.

Mammals remained relatively small until 65 million years ago, when the demise of the dinosaurs left a mass of niches for larger mammals to fill. Most of the types of mammals we know today evolved after this time.

8 EGGS FOR BREAKFAST

The Myth: Dinosaurs died out because mammals ate their eggs.

Dinosaurs coexisted with mammals for 150 million years. Although dinosaur nests were undoubtedly vulnerable, the most dangerous predators were probably smaller dinosaurs. Most mammals of the time were probably too small to eat the eggs of large dinosaurs.

7 ASTEROID CATASTROPHE

The Myth: An asteroid impact alone killed the dinosaurs.

A layer of iridium-rich rock marks the point of impact where a ten-kilometer asteroid hit the earth 65 million years ago in shallow water covering what is now Mexico's Yucatán Peninsula. That impact formed the 180-kilometer-wide Chicxulub crater. There is no convincing evidence that any nonavian dinosaurs

survived the aftermath of the impact, yet we are still not totally sure how the dinosaurs died. The impact itself could only have killed the dinosaurs in the immediate vicinity of the crater. But it also produced devastating after-effects, including giant tsunamis, rain that may have been as acidic as battery acid, and clouds of dust that darkened and cooled the globe for months or even decades. Another theory suggests that before the impact, the number of dinosaurs was already dwindling as falling sea levels and volcanic eruptions took their toll. A combination of those effects probably wiped out the dinosaurs.

6 EVOLUTION

The Myth: Dinosaurs died out because they were unsuccessful in evolutionary terms.

Dinosaurs survived for more than 150 million years, so they cannot be considered unsuccessful. Hominids have lived for only 6 million years, and *Homo sapiens* date back no more than 200,000 years. Dinosaurs out-competed other animals of their era, but they lost the battle to survive the effects of the asteroid impact.

5 EXTINCTION

The Myth: All dinosaurs died out 65 million years ago.

Birds evolved about 150 million years ago. Most experts believe they evolved from small predatory dinosaurs, which would classify them as dinosaurs according to modern methods of grouping animals. These avian dinosaurs probably suffered some losses after the asteroid impact, but they soon rebounded.

4 SLOW AND SLUGGISH

The Myth: Dinosaurs were slow and sluggish animals.

Early paleontologists thought dinosaurs must have been slow and sluggish to have lost the "evolutionary race" to birds and mammals. But modern studies find no sign that they were laggards, lazily dragging their tails behind them. Most dinosaurs were probably as mobile as large, modern mammals. Like lions, meat-eating dinosaurs were active predators that probably lay down and rested after eating their fill.

One study in 2000 of an exceptionally well-preserved hadrosaur fossil, found in a South Dakota riverbed, suggested that dinosaurs had powerful hearts more like those of birds or mammals than like modern reptiles. Researchers argue that the fossilized, four-chambered heart points to an active, birdlike metabolism.

3 LAND REPTILES

The Myth: All large land reptiles from prehistoric times were dinosaurs.

Terrestrial reptiles reached five meters in length before the first dinosaurs evolved 230 million years ago. Some—such as sail-backed dimetrodon, which flourished in North America during the Permian period (290 to 240 million years ago)—were related to dinosaurs, but were not true dinosaurs.

2 MARINE DINOS
The Myth: Marine reptiles, like the plesiosaurs and ichthyosaurs, were dinosaurs.

Several types of marine reptiles evolved during the dinosaur age, but all true dinosaurs were terrestrial animals. Marine crocodiles, like other crocodiles, were closely related to the dinosaurs and so were large, extinct marine reptiles called plesiosaurs, pliosaurs, mosasaurs, and ichthyosaurs.

1 FLYING DINOS
The Myth: Flying reptiles were dinosaurs.

Flying reptiles called pterosaurs first appeared just after the dinosaurs and then died out at the same time as the dinosaurs. The largest grew to the size of a small airplane. However, while they were close relatives, flying reptiles were not true dinosaurs.

10 BIZARRE FACTS ABOUT KIM JONG IL

Note: Facts 10 to 6 are propaganda spread by North Korean newspapers, while facts 5 to 1 are actual facts.

10 SUPERNATURAL
The "Fact": He had a supernatural birth.

According to North Korean historical literature, Kim Jong Il was born in a log cabin inside a secret base on Korea's most sacred mountain, Mt. Paektu. At the moment of his birth, a bright star lit up the sky, the seasons spontaneously changed from winter to spring, and rainbows appeared. This contradicts way less interesting Western accounts of his birth, which state the dictator was born in a guerilla camp in Russia while his father was on the run from the Japanese.

9 FASHION FORWARD
The "Fact": He is a fashion trendsetter.

According to North Korea's newspaper *Rodong Sinmun*, Kim Jong Il's iconic style has become a global phenomenon. The inspired look of his zipped-up khaki tunics with matching pants has been spreading across the world, an obvious testament to his outstanding image and influence. The paper didn't mention the popularity of the four-inch platform shoes Kim wears, but his oversized shades definitely seem to be a big hit with the women of Hollywood.

8 LOVED THE WORLD OVER
The "Fact": The world loves him.

According to state-run media, Kim Jong Il is the most prominent statesman in the present world, and people in countries the whole planet over celebrate his birthday with films and festivals. In reality, most nations are confused by his erratic foreign policy decisions on important issues such as North Korea's nuclear program.

7 HAMBURGERS
The "Fact": He invented the hamburger.

Since any American influences have long since been banned in his tiny communist country, Kim Jong Il had no choice but to create some new non-Western food by himself. The North Korean newspaper *Minju Joson* reported that Kim Jong Il invented a new sandwich called "double bread with meat" in an attempt to provide "quality" food to university students. He then built a plant capable of mass hamburger production to feed his students and teachers, despite the fact that the majority of his citizens battle famine on a daily basis.

6 GOLFING GLORY
The "Fact": He is the best natural golfer in history.

In 1994, it was reported by Pyongyang media outlets that Kim Jong Il shot 38 under par on a regulation 18-hole golf course—including five holes in one! That score is 25 shots better than the best round in history and is made even more amazing by the fact that it was his first time playing the sport. It's said that Kim Jong Il would routinely sink three or four holes in one per round of golf, and—lucky for the PGA—he has since given it up.

5 ADDICTION
The Fact: If he gets addicted to a drug, everyone else does too.

According to a book written by one of Kim Jong II's ex–staff members, he was once injured by falling off his horse when it slipped on loose rocks. He was afraid of becoming addicted to the painkillers that his doctors prescribed him, so he had members of his administrative staff injected daily with the same dosages he had to take. He did this so he wouldn't be the only one hooked on the drug.

4 IN THE MOVIES
The Fact: He once kidnapped a prominent director to film a *Godzilla* rip off for him.

Shin Sang-ok, a South Korean filmmaker, was kidnapped by Kim Jong II, sent to prison, and eventually forced to make a film called *Pulgasari* that was basically a communist propaganda version of *Godzilla*. After Shin and his wife managed to escape North Korea while location scouting in Austria, Kim Jong II shelved *Pulgasari* and all of Shin's other work. Kim Jong II has since given specific instruction to his Ministry of Culture and his communist filmmakers to "make more cartoons."

3 HITLER MUCH?
The Fact: He had disabled and short people deported from his capital.

In preparation for the World Festival of Youth and Students in 1989, Kim Jong II had disabled residents removed from Pyongyang. The government also distributed pamphlets advertising a wonder drug that would increase the height of short people. Those who responded to the pamphlets were sent away to different uninhabited islands along with the disabled in an attempt to rid the next generation of their supposedly substandard genes.

2 GREAT BOOZE
The Fact: At one time he was the world's biggest buyer of Hennessy.

For a few years in the early 1990s, it was confirmed by Hennessy that Kim Jong II was its best customer, spending about $600,000 to $850,000 annually on the liquor. He is partial to the Paradis cognac, which can sell for over $700 per bottle. In comparison, the average North Korean makes about $1000 per year.

1 CITY OF DREAMS

The Fact: He maintains a city that was built just to be looked at.

Kijong-Dong is a propaganda city that was originally built in the 1950s by Kim Jong Il's father right on the South Korea border to display the North's superiority

to the South and also to encourage people to defect. It has no actual residents, but an extensive effort has been put forth to simulate a functioning city, including lights on set timers and street sweepers to create an illusion of activity. The use of modern telescopes has revealed that the units lack window glass, and some buildings are just concrete shells that don't even have interior rooms. The city also houses the world's largest flagpole, complete with a 300-pound North Korean flag.

CHAPTER SEVEN
Heaven and Hell

10 POSSIBLE RESTING PLACES FOR THE HOLY GRAIL

10 ACCOKEEK, MARYLAND

The locals of the Accokeek area claim that a Jesuit priest stowed away on board Captain John Smith's ship as he sailed up the Potomac River sometime around 1606 or 1607, and that this priest had ties all the way back to the Knights Templar.

The legend states that the priest had the Grail for years in England and Europe, possibly taken from Glastonbury Tor (number 7 on this list) when treasure seekers started looking for King Arthur's grave. Somehow the Grail passed down to this nameless priest, who fled for environs where few people would care about it.

Its location in the Accokeek area is not known.

9 OAK ISLAND, NOVA SCOTIA

"The Money Pit" was discovered by three teenage boys playing on Oak Island in 1795, or so the story goes. Since then, six people have died attempting to excavate the mysterious treasure everyone is sure is there.

The more time passes, the wilder imaginations run: the Pit is no longer thought to hold merely chests of gold doubloons, but the Holy Grail itself, hidden there by the Knights Templar in the early to mid-1300s.

This is no idle assumption, since there is, in fact, an arrangement of boulders on the island that forms a perfect cross 250 meters long by 100 meters wide, oriented so that the head points due east. It's on the north side of the island in a clearing only 50 square meters larger than the cross. The Pit is due south through a woodlot.

The most compelling evidence for the Holy Grail's presence here seems to be the ingenious design of the Pit, which was fitted with a water channel booby trap leading up and out to the open water.

Whatever is down there lies at exactly 100 feet and has been described as "metal in pieces." They say the mystery will not be resolved until one more person dies in the Pit.

8 ROSSLYN CHAPEL, ROSLIN, SCOTLAND

One of the legends used by Dan Brown in *The Da Vinci Code*, this list item centers on secret stone chambers and channels under the Collegiate Chapel of St. Matthew, on Roslin Hill, and there are lots of extremely strange carvings in and around the chapel that add ominous weight to the story.

The chapel was built starting in 1456 at the behest of its founder, William Sinclair, a nobleman and knight. He is rumored to have been a descendant of the Knights Templar.

There are carvings of what appear to be Indian corn (maize) around the windows. Maize was unheard of in Europe at the time of the chapel's construction. There are also carvings of "green men," which seem to symbolize pre-Christian Celtic traditions regarding spring and summer.

The Apprentice Pillar is the real standout. No one knows why it was carved as it was, and there are no other pillars like it in the chapel or anywhere in Europe. The chapel's carvings took 40 years to complete, so they must have been significant to Sinclair, who died just before they were finished. The legend states that the Holy Grail resides inside the Apprentice Pillar.

Or perhaps it's in the family crypt under the basement. This crypt is sealed shut, and sealed very well. The Sinclairs still own the chapel and refuse to let anyone go digging up their ancestors (who can blame them?), as this would necessitate tearing down the whole chapel.

7 GLASTONBURY TOR, GLASTONBURY, ENGLAND

Tor is Celtic for "conical hill," and that is what Glastonbury Tor is. It's said to be the legendary Avalon, King Arthur's resting place while he heals from wounds suffered at the hands of his evil son, Mordred, whom he killed in a duel.

It's been called *Ynys yr Afalon*, Old English for "the Isle of Avalon," since at least AD 1100, and tradition states that in 1191, Arthur and Guinevere's coffins were uncovered at the top of the hill, although no evidence exists to support this.

The Arthurian and Templar legends are inseparable, and the story goes that the Knights Templar returned from the First Crusade with all the famous Biblical relics and hid them throughout the British Isles. The Holy Grail was buried somewhere on Glastonbury Tor, perhaps between Arthur and Guinevere's coffins, the most poetic place.

6 THE DOME OF THE ROCK, JERUSALEM, ISRAEL

Legend states that since the Holy Grail *was not* the Holy Chalice, it was buried with Jesus somewhere near his crucifixion site. This site is believed by some to have been a fissure between two rocks, one of which has since eroded away, the other of which is still there to be visited, at the top of the hill on which the Dome of the Rock now sits.

It's sacred to all three monotheistic religions: Judaism holds that Abraham almost slew Isaac on this rock; Christianity believes that Jesus' cross was planted between this rock and another; Islam holds that Muhammad sprang to heaven on a horse from the rock.

The Holy Grail is, properly, the cup, bowl, or plate that happened to be near the cross and catch the blood of Jesus as he died. It was then buried with him, by one of his disciples, his mother, or Joseph of Arimathea in his tomb. The location of the tomb is not known, but is described in the Bible as being nearby, which likely means somewhere on or around the hill.

5 CATTEDRALE DI SAN LORENZO, GENOA, ITALY

The Grail may not be lost, but found, and on display to the public for free in Genoa at the Cathedral of St. Lawrence. This relic is a bowl made of green glass, which was thought to be emerald until it was broken in the early 19th century. No one knows where it came from, but William of Tyre, in 1170, wrote that it first turned up in a mosque in Caesarea, Israel, in 1101. It has not been carbon dated.

4 CATEDRAL DE SANTA MARIA DE VALENCIA, SPAIN

Another contender is on display at the Cathedral of St. Mary in Valencia, and this is considered the most likely spot for the Holy Grail. Skeptics claim that *if* the Grail even exists, the Valencia Chalice is the best bet. It was carbon dated in 1960 to somewhere between the 300s BC and the AD 100s and manufactured in the Middle East, so it is possible. Even if it isn't the Grail, its age makes it extremely valuable.

The chalice is made of dark red agate and set in a gold stem, with another upside-down bowl of chalcedony as the base. It is the official Chalice of the Roman Catholic Church.

3 SANTA MARIA DE MONTSERRAT, CATALONIA, SPAIN

This legend ties in with the German Holy Grail legend of Munsalvaesche, which is another name for Corbenic, the castle where the Fisher King lived and where Sir Galahad was born.

Munsalvaesche is German for the Latin phrase *mons salvationis*, or "the mount of salvation." *Montserrat*, however, is Catalan for "jagged mountain." The monastery and abbey are nestled in the mountain, and the Grail is said to be hidden somewhere under the church grounds or elsewhere on the mountain. If so, it may well never be found, as the terrain is extraordinarily rugged and the mountain is gigantic. The peak, at 4055 feet, is called Sant Jeroni, "Saint Jerome," who features prominently in several Grail legends. He may have traveled to the area in the late AD 300s and hidden the Grail there.

2 SOMEWHERE IN THE JERUSALEM SEWERS

This legend states that the Knights Templar of the First Crusade found neither the Holy Grail nor the Ark of the Covenant because the sewer system provided the finest hiding place on earth at the time. Jerusalem has been attacked many times, and the Jews living at the time of the Ark's disappearance are sure to have lowered it into the sewers to protect it from Nebuchadnezzar in 586 BC.

The disciples may have known the location of the Ark and hidden the Grail with it, deep in the sewers, since the Ark had escaped notice for almost 600 years by then. Digging, which may undermine the buildings above, is expressly forbidden except for those professional archaeologists intent on uncovering sites of antiquity.

1 THE U.S. BULLION DEPOSITORY, FORT KNOX, KENTUCKY

Yes, you read that right. This legend is based on the premise that the Bullion Depository, commonly called Fort Knox, is probably the single most secure place on the planet. Some of its security measures are a mystery, but it is known that no one, not even the president, is allowed on the property, except the U.S. Mint police stationed inside.

The closest anyone can get to it is Highway 31, about 400 yards from the building. The security consists of multiple fences, the innermost electrified, alarms, cameras, armed guards, and the nearby Fort Knox units: 30,000 active troops who train every day with Apache helicopter gunships, M-1 Abrams tanks, armored personnel carriers, and heavy demolition.

This doesn't account for the unknown security measures, which probably include motion-activated minigun turrets, landmines, pressure sensors, and snipers, and that's before you even get inside.

Awful lot of security for some gold bricks, wouldn't you say? Unless there are other things inside. The combination to the vault is not known by any one person, but is composed of 10 combinations, each known by only one official working in the building. There are pistol ranges inside, a gym, and a dojo, and the vault is lined with solid granite. The gold resides in separate, small rooms, each fitted with a solid-steel door.

The main vault door is 22 tons of steel and can withstand a direct hit from a two-kiloton nuclear warhead. The Depository has housed a copy of the Magna Carta, the Hungarian crown jewels, the Crown of St. Stephen, the U.S. Constitution, the Declaration of Independence, and various other historical documents from all over the world.

The legend states that there's a special room somewhere in the vault that does not house gold or artifacts such as those cited above, but instead is home to the Holy Grail, the Ark of the Covenant (with a "Do Not Touch" sign), satellite pictures proving that the Ararat Anomaly is Noah's Ark, and the True Cross, complete with dried blood that has been analyzed as consisting of several strains of DNA, one of them encoded not on a double helix, but a triple helix.

10 POPES WHO DIED BRUTAL DEATHS

10 POPE ST. PETER, OCTOBER 13, 64

As one of the original apostles of Jesus and one of the greatest purveyors of Christianity at the time, the apostle Simon Peter became the ire of Emperor Nero of Rome, who despised Christians, going so far as to blame them for the Great Fire of Rome earlier in the year AD 64. Nero sent out an order for Peter's arrest, but he escaped. During his escape, Peter witnessed a vision of Jesus that inspired him to return to Rome and accept his martyrdom. It's said that he asked to be crucified as Jesus was, but to be turned on his head so as not to imitate Jesus' crucifixion. In this position, he wouldn't easily be able to suffocate to death as he would in an upright position, prolonging his death.

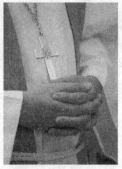

9 POPE ST. CLEMENT I, 99

According to legend, after being banished from Rome and sent to work in a stone quarry, Clement found that his fellow prisoners were suffering from dehydration. After kneeling to pray, he saw a lamb on a hill. He took a pickaxe and struck the ground where the lamb stood, and a stream of water came gushing out. As the story goes, upon seeing this, many locals and fellow prisoners were converted to Christianity on the spot. As punishment by the guards, an anchor was tied around Clement's neck and he was thrown into the Black Sea.

8 POPE ST. STEPHEN I, AUGUST 2, 257

Stephen was only pope for a scant three years but was burdened by controversy both within the church and from outside forces. Within the church, the debate roared on over the subject of rebaptism of lapsed Catholics. Outside the church, though, Emperor Valerian—who had once been an ally of Christians but later turned away from them—issued two edicts of persecution against the church. Stephen was sitting on his throne, celebrating Mass, when the emperor's men stormed the room and beheaded Stephen where he sat. The blood-stained throne was allegedly preserved by the church until the 18th century.

7 POPE ST. SIXTUS II, AUGUST 6, 258

Not too long after Pope Stephen I was killed, Sixtus II was elected the new pope. During this time, Emperor Valerian had made it law that all Christians were required to participate in ceremonies honoring the Roman gods, largely to avoid conflict with the government. As pope, though, Sixtus was able to avoid this. Unfortunately, not long after the first decree, Valerian sent out a second that condemned Christian priests, bishops, and deacons to death. While giving a sermon, Sixtus II was captured by the emperor's men and put to death by beheading—the first victim of the infamous 258 Persecutions.

6 POPE JOHN VII, OCTOBER 18, 707

Being the grandson of a senator and the son of a state official made John VII the first pope to be born from a distinguished family line. He was also pope during the time of the "Byzantine Papacy," when all popes had to be approved by the Byzantine emperor to ensure that all decisions made would suit the state; however, as with other popes during that time, things didn't always go so smoothly. But it wasn't the state that would see to John VII's end, but rather the enraged husband of a woman he was sleeping with who caught them in the act and beat the pope to death.

5 POPE JOHN VIII, DECEMBER 16, 882

Some consider him one of the greatest popes of his times, while others argue otherwise; but no one would disagree that John VIII's time was marred by political intrigue. It was only a matter of time before he would become the victim of this. There is some speculation as to whether it was a coordinated assassination, or simply done out of jealousy of the church's treasures, but one evening, a relative of John VIII visited the pope and poisoned his drink. Finding that the poison did not work quickly enough, the relative bashed in John's head with a hammer.

4 POPE STEPHEN VII, AUGUST 897

This one is actually a two-fer of sorts. The thing Pope Stephen VII is most famous for is not any particular decree or act of benevolence, but rather for putting a corpse on trial. Specifically, his predecessor, Pope Formosus, was put to trial in what would become known as the Cadaver Synod. Upon finding the dead Pope Formosus guilty of all charges, Stephen VII had him stripped of his papal vestments, three fingers removed from his right hand, his body thrown into the Tiber River, and all the former pope's laws and ordinations annulled. Sadly for Stephen VII, the trial caused a frenzy, and he was imprisoned and later put to death by strangling.

3 POPE JOHN XII, MAY 14, 964

When people think of the pope, the more devout picture a benevolent and compassionate leader, or failing that, at least a guy who's pretty nice most of the time. Not so with John XII. Shortly after being elected pope at the age of 18, John XII decided the whole celibacy thing wasn't for him and went around humping whatever he could. Gambling, theft, assassination, and incest are only a few things he was reported to have partaken in regularly. It's even alleged that he toasted Satan and Roman gods and demons during sermons and other celebrations. He was briefly deposed by Pope Leo VII after John XII handed the papal lands over to the German king, Otto I, but he was later reinstated. So after all that, it only seems a fitting end that John XII was beaten to death by a jealous husband who came home to find the pope having sex with his wife.

2 POPE BENEDICT VI, JUNE 974

It seems Benedict VI never did a whole lot himself, and yet he was destined to suffer for the transgressions of his predecessor, Pope John XIII, who during his time as pope made several enemies among the nobility in Europe. John at one point was captured and exiled, yet managed to return and have several of his enemies hung for their roles in his exile. John went on to die a natural death, but Benedict wasn't as fortunate. Only a year and a half after Benedict VI was elected pope, a priest named Crescentius I—brother of the late Pope John XIII—was ordered to capture and later strangle him to death.

1 POPE JOHN XXI, AUGUST 18, 1277

Along with being pope for only a very short eight months, John XXI was also a practicing physician and a prolific writer on subjects such as logic, philosophy, and medicine. It seems a fitting tribute, then, that John XXI would be immortalized in Dante's classic epic poem, *The Divine Comedy* (La Divina Commedia). He is actually the only pope shown as living in Paradise. But to get to paradise, John XXI met with an unfortunate accident. Shortly after a new wing was added to his palace in Viterbo, Italy, a section of the poorly constructed roof collapsed on him while he was asleep in his bed. He died of his injuries eight days later.

10 BIZARRE AND RIDICULOUS FATWAS

10 SUN AND EARTH

The Fatwa: Grand Mufti Sheikh Ibn Baaz—The Sun Revolves Around the Earth

In a 2000 fatwa titled "The Transmitted and Sensory Proofs of the Rotation of the Sun and Stillness of the Earth," Saudi Arabian Grand Mufti Sheikh Ibn Baaz asserted that the earth was flat and disklike and that the sun revolved around it. He had insisted that satellite images to the contrary were nothing but a Western conspiracy against the Islamic world.

9 SATANIC VERSES

The Fatwa: Ayatollah Khomeini—Kill for a Book None of Us Should Read!

In 1988, publication of Salman Rushdie's novel *The Satanic Verses* led Iranian revolutionary leader Ayatollah Khomeini to issue a fatwa against Rushdie, with a huge bounty for his death. This triggered several attacks on the novel's translators, publishers, and booksellers, including the murder of Japanese translator Hitoshi Igarashi. Millions of Muslims around the world who had never read a single line of the book wanted Rushdie dead. Interesting fact: 24 percent of Iranians at the time couldn't even read.

8 TOMBOYS

The Fatwa: Malaysian National Fatwa Council—Tomboy Fatwa

A University of Massachusetts study reported that girls who play sports have higher self-esteem and are less likely to enter (or remain in) abusive relationships than girls who don't play sports. Could this fact have threatened the he-men at the Malaysia National Fatwa Council? Maybe. Perhaps that's why Kuala Lumpur had a near riot on their hands when the Sisters in Islam marched against a Malaysian fatwa banning tomboys; the fatwa branded any girls who acted unladylike as violating Islamic tenets. Fortunately, the as-yet-undefined punishment for Malaysian girls in T-shirts and jeans hasn't been incorporated into Sharia law yet.

7 MICKEY MOUSE

The Fatwa: Muhammad Al-Munajid: Bring Me the Head of Mickey Mouse

That's right, somebody put a hit on Mickey Mouse. Calling Mickey "one of Satan's soldiers," Sheikh Muhammad Al-Munajid decreed that household mice and their cartoon cousins must be "killed in all cases," according to the UK's *Daily Telegraph*. And get this—the guy's not your average nut job, either: Munajid used to be a former diplomat at the Saudi embassy in Washington, D.C. He made the remarks on the Arab television network al-Majd TV after he was asked to give Islam's teaching on mice.

But don't worry, Mickey won't be alone. Munajid also put a hit on Jerry, of *Tom and Jerry*. Maybe they could rent an apartment with Salman Rushdie.

6 EMOTICONS

The Fatwa: Multaqa Ahl al Hadeeth—Emoticon Fatwa

I can almost get behind this one. Sure, emoticons are annoying, but evil? Really? Well, to a Muslim forum looking to make a name for itself, yes.

According to Muslim Internet forum *Multaqa Ahl al Hadeeth*:

> *Emoticons are forbidden because of its imitation to Allah's creatures whether it is original or mixture or even deformed one and since the picture is the face and the face is what makes the real picture then emoticons which represent faces that express emotions then all that add up to make them Haram.*

Additionally:

> *A woman should not use these images when speaking to a man who is not her mahram, because these faces are used to express how she is feeling, so it is as if she is smiling, laughing, acting shy, and so on, and a woman should not do that with a non-mahram man. It is only permissible for a woman to speak to men in cases of necessity, so long as that is in a public chat room and not in private correspondence.*

5 SOCCER

The Fatwa: Soccer Fatwa

No, not even the beautiful game is safe from stupid fatwas. As part of a government drive to eliminate frivolous fatwas, the Saudi newspaper *Al-Watan* lampooned one very real edict setting out new rules for soccer. Ridiculous demands included "do not play with 11 people like the heretics, Jews, and

Christians," and "play in your pyjamas or regular clothes [because] colored shorts and numbered T-shirts are not Muslim clothing." Especially ridiculous is the decree to "remove the crossbar in order not to imitate the heretics and in order to be entirely distinct from the soccer system's despotic international rules."

4 VACCINE
The Fatwa: Infidel Vaccine

Cases of polio are actually increasing in India, Nigeria, Afghanistan, and Pakistan. Why? Because an anti-polio fatwa by anti-Western clerics forbid Pakistani children from immunizations because the clerics say the vaccine is a conspiracy to make Muslims sterile. Ironically, it's the clerics' plans that would produce this result, since dead and paralytic kids don't breed all that much.

3 NUDITY AND SEX
The Fatwa: Rashad Hassan Khalil—No Nudity for Sex

In 2007, the former dean of Islamic law at Al-Azhar University in Cairo issued a fatwa that nudity during sexual intercourse invalidates a marriage between husband and wife. Debate was immediate. Suad Saleh, head of the women's department of Al-Azhar's Islamic Studies, pleaded for "anything that can bring spouses closer to each other"; Islamic scholar Abdel Muti concurred, saying, "Nothing is prohibited during marital sex, except of course sodomy."

For his part, Al-Azhar's fatwa committee chairman, Abdullah Megawar, backpedaled and said that married couples could see each other naked but should really cover up with a blanket during sex.

2 URINE
The Fatwa: Sheikh Ali Gomaa—Urine Fatwa

According to Egypt's Grand Mufti, Sheikh Ali Gomaa, drinking the urine of Muhammad is deemed a great blessing. What, do they have a lot of this stuff lying around, going to waste or something? Remember, Muhammad never claimed that he himself was divine—so why does his urine have magic properties? Failing to pass the laugh test with Muslim scholars, Mufti later recanted, saying it was only his "personal opinion."

1 BREAST-FEEDING

The Fatwa: Ezzat Attiya—Adult Breast-feeding in the Workplace

In May 2007, Ezzat Attiya wondered how unrelated men and women could work together in the same office when Islam forbids men and women who aren't married or related to be alone together. His answer: let her suckle him *five times.* Yes, that's right, an adult female breast-feeding an adult male coworker will defuse all sexual tension in the office. See, the woman will now be the man's foster mother, and they can be alone together anytime. Attiya's ruling was intergalactically mocked and quickly condemned on the home front as well. He was later suspended from his job and ridiculed in Arab newspapers; he issued a hasty retraction, saying it was a "bad interpretation of a particular case."

5 BIZARRE MYTHS ABOUT THE PAPACY

5 THE POPE IS THE GREAT BEAST

The Myth: The pope is the beast spoken of in Revelation 13. Verse 1 says he wears crowns and has "blasphemous names" written on his head. Verse 18 says the numerical value of his name adds up to 666. The pope's official title in Latin is *Vicarius Filii Dei* (Vicar of the Son of God). If you add that up using Roman numerals, you get 666. The pope's tiara is emblazoned with this title, formed by diamonds and other jewels.

This belief is especially popular with Seventh-Day Adventists, but it's also widely repeated in some Protestant circles. The letters in *Vicarivs Filii Dei* do add up to 666. Isolate the numbers and this is what you get: 5 (V) + 1 (I) + 100 (C) + 1 (I) + 5 (V) + 1 (I) + 50 (L) + 1 (I) + 1 (I) + 500 (D) + 1 (I) = 666.

But there are problems with this. The first is that *Vicarius Filii Dei* is not now, nor has it ever been, a title of the bishop of Rome. The second problem is that virtually no one, including many unsuspecting Catholics, knows that this papal "title" is a fabrication. To an untrained ear, it sounds enough like one of the pope's real titles, *Vicarius Christi* (Vicar of Christ), to pass the test. Unfortunately for those who traffic in this particular piece of pope fiction, *Vicarius Christi* adds up to only a measly 214, not the infernal 666.

Ironically, using the same math exercise above, the name of the woman who started the Seventh-Day Adventist Church, Ellen Gould White, also adds up to 666 in Latin (L + L + V + L + D + V + V + I = 666).

4 THE PAPACY IS A MEDIEVAL INVENTION

The Myth: The papacy is a medieval Roman invention. The early church knew nothing of a "supreme pontiff." Other bishops didn't regard the bishop of Rome (the pope) as having special authority to operate the way modern popes do.

The earliest account we have of a bishop of Rome exercising authority in another diocese comes from Pope St. Clement's Epistle to the Corinthians. It was written by Clement, bishop of Rome, around the year AD 80. In it he responds to the Corinthians' plea for his intervention. In the letter, he says, "But if any disobey the words spoken by Him [Christ] through us [Clement], let them know that they will involve themselves in sin and no small danger"; this clearly shows that he believed he had a special authority and demanded obedience.

Pope Victor I, who reigned from 189 to 199, worked to settle a dispute, known as the Quartodeciman controversy, among the bishops of the east and west over when to celebrate Easter. The other bishops recognized his unique authority when they followed his directive to convene local and regional synods to deliberate on the issue. Most of the bishops decided to adopt his proposal that the whole church celebrate Easter on the first Sunday after Passover. He threatened those who didn't with excommunication. The fact that no bishop in the world—not a single one—disputed his authority as bishop of Rome to carry out such an excommunication is a powerful piece of evidence that the early church recognized the unique authority of the bishop of Rome.

St. Irenaeus in the 1st century wrote of the church in Rome: "For with this church, because of its superior origin, all the churches must agree; that is, all the faithful in the whole world, for in her the apostolic tradition has always been preserved for the benefit of the faithful everywhere."

3 THE POPE CANNOT MAKE MISTAKES

The Myth: According to papal infallibility, the pope cannot make any mistakes—but they have! The popes once believed that the earth was the center of the universe and we know that is wrong.

This myth has arisen from a misunderstanding of papal infallibility, the actual definition of which is:

1. The pope must be making a decree on matters of faith or morals.
2. The declaration must be binding on the whole church.
3. The pope must be speaking with the full authority of the papacy and not in a personal capacity.

This means that when the pope speaks on matters of science, he can make errors. However, when he is teaching a matter of religion in an official capacity, Catholics consider that the decree is equal to the word of God. It cannot contradict any previous declarations and it must be believed by all Catholics. Catholics believe that if a person denies any of these solemn decrees, they are committing a mortal sin, the type of sin that sends a person to hell.

Here is an example of an infallible decree from the Council of Trent (under Pope Pius V):

> *If anyone denies that in the sacrament of the most Holy Eucharist are contained truly, really, and substantially the body and blood together with the soul and divinity of our Lord Jesus Christ, and consequently the whole Christ, but says that He is in it only as in a sign, or figure, or force, let him be anathema.*

The last section of the final sentence, "let him be anathema," is a standard phrase that normally appears at the end of an infallible statement. It means "let him be cursed." Catholics believe that the pope can err in nonreligious matters, and that popes have done so on many occasions throughout history.

2 POPE JOAN

The Myth: In the middle ages, there was a "Pope Joan," a woman who hid her gender and rose through the ranks of the church, became a cardinal, and was elected pope. No one knew she was a woman until, during a papal procession through the streets of Rome, she went into labor and gave birth to a child. She and the baby were killed on the spot by the mob, enraged at her imposture.

But the facts of history show otherwise. The primary proofs that this is all just a fable are these: first, the earliest point that we can trace the legend to is the mid-13th century, but it didn't really gain wide currency until the late 14th century. No evidence of any kind exists from the 9th century (when Pope Joan was alleged to have reigned), nor do we see any in the 10th through 12th centuries. None of the annals or acts of the popes that were written between the 9th and 13th centuries (nor any after that) mention her.

It's important to remember that even if there had been a female impostor pope, this would just mean that an invalid election had taken place, nothing more. Other invalidly elected claimants to the papal office have come and gone over the centuries. She would not have been pope; no one invalidly elected would be.

This is probably also a good time to point out that in order to be validly elected as pope, you must be over the age of reason (generally considered to be seven years old), male, and baptized.

1 SEDES STERCORARIA

The Myth: All popes when elected must sit on the Sedes Stercoraria, a chair with a hole in the center of the seat, without underwear on, in order to have their genitals touched, to prove that they are a man. This supposedly started after Pope Joan ruled to make sure that the same mistake would not occur again.

In the item number 2 above, we discussed the Pope Joan myth, which is the first step in disproving the myth of the Sedes Stercoraria. If Joan never existed, the need to prove the elected pope male also does not exist.

However, two chairs with holes in them do exist in the Vatican, but they're actually antiques from the ancient Romans and have no significance other than to symbolize the Church's view that it superseded the Roman Empire. The chairs' original Roman use is unknown, but it's speculated that they were either birthing stools or toilets.

Humanist Jacopo d'Angelo de Scarparia, who attended the 1406 coronation of Gregory XII during which the pope sat on two "pierced chairs," said, "The vulgar tell the insane fable that he is touched to verify that he is indeed a man."

10 APPALLING RELIGIOUS SCANDALS

10 WITCH HUNTS—PROTESTANTISM

When the Puritans settled in Massachusetts in the 1600s, they created a religious police state where doctrinal deviation could lead to flogging, pillorying, hanging, cutting off ears, or boring through the tongue with a hot iron. Preaching Quaker beliefs was a capital offense. Four stubborn Quakers defied this law and were hanged. In the 1690s, fear of witches seized the colony. Twenty alleged witches were killed and 150 others imprisoned.

9 ON THE JEWS AND THEIR LIES—LUTHERANISM

Unfortunately, the founder of Protestantism, Martin Luther, was also a religious bigot. In his most famous book about Judaism (written in 1543) we find the following gem: "base, whoring people, that is, no people of God, and their boast of lineage, circumcision, and law must be accounted as filth. They are

full of the devil's feces … which they wallow in like swine, and the synagogue is an incorrigible whore and an evil slut…"

Two other books by Luther, *Against the Papacy at Rome Founded by the Devil*, and *Against Hanswurst*, are described as "rivaling his anti-Jewish treatises for vulgarity and violence of expression," and "[are] so inexpressibly vile that a common impulse of decency demanded their summary suppression by his friends."

8 THE BOOK OF ABRAHAM—MORMONISM

The Book of Abraham is believed by Mormons to be the handwritten account of the prophet Abraham. In 1835, Joseph Smith, founder of the Mormon Church, was able to use his "Angel-given" tools to translate some Egyptian scrolls that he was given access to (at that time no one could read hieroglyphics). Upon inspection, Smith declared that they contained the Book of Abraham. He promptly translated the lot and it was accepted as scripture by the church (it's included as part of the Pearl of Great Price). The scrolls vanished and everyone thought the story would end there. But it didn't—in 1966, the original scrolls were found in the New York Metropolitan Museum of Art. The scrolls turned out to be a standard Egyptian text that was often buried with the dead. This fraud caused a number of Mormons to leave the church and is still a hotly debated topic among Mormons and their critics.

7 THE END OF THE WORLD—JEHOVAH'S WITNESSES

The Jehovah's Witnesses computed from a prophecy in the Book of Daniel, Chapter 4, that 1914 would be the start of the war of Armageddon. The writings referred to "seven times" and the Jehovah's Witnesses interpreted each "time" as equal to 360 days, giving a total of 2520 days. This was further interpreted as representing 2520 years, measured from the starting date of 607 BC. This gave 1914 as the target date for Armageddon.

Since late in the 19th century, Jehovah's Witnesses had taught that the "battle of the Great Day of God Almighty" (Armageddon) would happen in 1914. It didn't. When 1914 passed, they changed their prediction to say that 1914 was the year that Jesus invisibly began his rule. The next major estimate was 1925. *Watchtower* magazine predicted, "The year 1925 is a date definitely and clearly marked in the Scriptures, even more clearly than that of 1914; but it would be presumptuous on the part of any faithful follower of the Lord to assume just what the Lord is going to do during that year."

The Watchtower Society selected 1975 as its next main Armageddon prediction. This was based on the estimate "according to reliable Bible chronology Adam was created in the year 4026 BC, likely in the autumn of the year, at the end of the sixth day of creation." They believed that the year 1975 was a promising date for the end of the world, as it was the 6000th anniversary of Adam's creation. Exactly 1000 years was to pass for each day of the creation week. This prophecy also failed.

Realizing how stupid they were looking every time they made a new failed prediction, they announced that the end of the world would occur 6000 years after the creation of Eve, a date that cannot be calculated.

6 LISA MCPHERSON—SCIENTOLOGY

Lisa McPherson (February 10, 1959–December 5, 1995) was a Scientologist who died of a pulmonary embolism while under the care of the Flag Service Organization (FSO), a branch of the Church of Scientology. Following her death, the Church of Scientology was indicted on two felony charges, "abuse and/or neglect of a disabled adult and practicing medicine without a license," putting under trial the nature of Scientology's beliefs and practices. The charges against the Church of Scientology were dropped after the state's medical examiner changed the cause of death from "undetermined" to an "accident" on June 13, 2000.

A civil suit brought by her family against the church was settled on May 28, 2004.

5 BURMA—BUDDHISM

Human sacrifices were still occurring in Buddhist Burma in the 1850s. When the capital was moved to Mandalay, 56 "spotless" men were buried beneath the new city walls to sanctify and protect the city. When two of the burial spots were later found empty, royal astrologers decreed that 500 men, women, boys, and girls must be killed and buried at once, or the capital must be abandoned. About 100 were actually buried before British governors stopped the ceremonies.

4 AISHA—ISLAM

Aisha was the six-year-old girl who was betrothed to Muhammad. At the age of nine, she married him, becoming one of his 11 (or 13, depending on the source) wives. While most Muslims do not object to the marriage, it's a source of great scandal to many non-Islamic people. In Islamic tradition, Aisha is attributed as the source of many stories about the life of Muhammad. It is believed that she was his favorite wife.

3 METZITZAH—JUDAISM

Metzitzah b'peh is a controversial method of circumcision performed by some Haredi and Hassidic Jews in which, after removing the foreskin, the *mohel* (circumciser) sucks out the blood from the wound to clean it, then he spits the blood into a provided receptacle. Afterward, the circumcised penis is bandaged and the act is considered complete. *Metzitzah b'peh* was implicated in the transfer of herpes from *mohels* to eight Israeli infants, one of whom suffered brain damage. When three New York City infants contracted herpes after *metzizah b'peh* by one *mohel* and one of them died, New York authorities took out a restraining order against the *mohel*. In three studies done in Israel, Canada, and the U.S., oral suction following circumcision has been implicated in 11 cases of neonatal herpes.

2 THUGGEE MURDERS—HINDUISM

Members of India's Thuggee sect strangled people as sacrifices to appease the bloodthirsty goddess Kali, a practice beginning in the 1500s. The number of victims has been estimated to be as high as 2 million. Thugs were claiming about 20,000 lives a year in the 1800s until British rulers stamped them out. At a trial in 1840, one Thug was accused of killing 931 people. Today, some Hindu priests still sacrifice goats to Kali.

1 HUMAN SACRIFICE—ATZEC PAGANISM

The Aztecs began their elaborate theocracy in the 1300s and brought human sacrifice to a golden era. About 20,000 people were killed yearly to appease gods, especially the sun god, who needed daily "nourishment" of blood. Hearts of sacrifice victims were cut out, and some bodies were eaten ceremoniously. Other victims were drowned, beheaded, burned, or dropped from heights. In a rite to the rain god, shrieking children were killed at several sites so that their tears might induce rain. In a rite to the maize goddess, a virgin danced for 24 hours, then was killed and skinned; her skin was worn by a priest in further dancing. One account says that at King Ahuitzotl's coronation, 80,000 prisoners were butchered to please the gods.

10 WEIRD RELIGIOUS PRACTICES

10 MORMON TEMPLE GARMENTS

In some denominations of the Church of Jesus Christ of Latter-day Saints, the temple garment (or the Garment of the Holy Priesthood, or informally, the garment or garments) is a set of sacred underclothing worn by adult adherents who have taken part in a ritual ceremony known as the washing and anointing ordinance, usually in a temple as part of the endowment ceremony. Adherents consider them to be sacred and may be offended by public discussion of the garments. Anti-Mormon activists have publicly displayed or defaced temple garments to show their opposition to the LDS Church.

According to generally accepted Mormon doctrine, the marks in the garments are sacred symbols. One proposed element of the symbolism, according to early Mormon leaders, was a link to the "Compass and the Square," the symbols of freemasonry to which Joseph Smith, the creator of Mormonism, had been initiated about seven weeks prior to his introduction of the endowment ceremony.

9 SCIENTOLOGY E-METER

An E-meter is an electronic device manufactured by the Church of Scientology at their Gold Base production facility. It's used as an aid by Dianetics and Scientology counselors and counselors-in-training in some forms of auditing, the application of the techniques of Dianetics and Scientology to another or to oneself for the express purpose of addressing spiritual issues.

E-meter sessions are conducted by church employees known as auditors. Scientology materials traditionally refer to the subject as the "preclear," although auditors continue to use the meter well beyond the clear level. The preclear holds a pair of cylindrical electrodes ("cans") connected to the meter while the auditor asks the preclear a series of questions and notes both the verbal response and the activity of the meter. Auditors are trained to recognize many types of needle movements, each with their own special significance.

A 1971 ruling of the United States District Court, District of Columbia (333 F. Supp. 357), specifically stated, "The E-meter has no proven usefulness in the diagnosis, treatment, or prevention of any disease, nor is it medically or scientifically capable of improving any bodily function."

8 EXORCISM

Exorcism is the practice of evicting demons or other evil spiritual entities from a person or place which they are believed to have possessed. The practice is quite ancient and still part of the belief system of many religions, though it is seen mostly in the Roman Catholic and Eastern Orthodox churches.

Solemn exorcisms, according to the canon law of the church, can only be exercised by an ordained priest (or higher prelate), with the express permission of the local bishop, and only after a careful medical examination to exclude the possibility of mental illness. The *Catholic Encyclopaedia* (1908) enjoined: "Superstition ought not to be confounded with religion, however much their history may be interwoven, nor magic, however white it may be, with a legitimate religious rite."

7 JEWISH KAPAROT

Performed around the time of the High Holidays, Kaparot is a traditional Jewish religious ritual. Classically, it's performed by holding a live chicken by the shoulder blades and moving around your head three times, symbolically transferring your sins to the chicken. The chicken is then killed and given to the poor, to be eaten at the pre–Yom Kippur feast. In modern times, the ritual is performed in the traditional form mostly in Haredi communities.

In 2005 on the night before Yom Kippur, more than 200 caged chickens were abandoned in rainy weather as part of a Kaparot ritual in Brooklyn, New York; the chickens were starving and dehydrated, and some were rescued by the American Society for the Prevention of Cruelty to Animals. Jacob Kalish, an Orthodox Jew, was charged with animal cruelty for the drowning deaths of 35 of the chickens. In response, animal rights organizations have begun to picket public observances of Kaparot, especially in Israel.

6 SHAMANISM

Shamanism refers to a range of traditional beliefs and practices concerned with communication with the spirit world. There are many variations in shamanism

throughout the world, though there are some beliefs that are shared by all forms of shamanism. Its practitioners claim the ability to diagnose and cure human suffering and, in some societies, the ability to cause suffering. This is believed to be accomplished by traversing the axis mundi and forming a special relationship with, or gaining control over, spirits.

Shamans have been credited with the ability to control the weather, divination, the interpretation of dreams, astral projection, and traveling to upper and lower worlds. Shamans were used in Tibetan Buddhism as a form of divination by which the Dalai Lama was given prophesies of the future and advice.

5 DOWRY

This is a cultural practice rather than a religious one, and despite laws against it, it continues to exist across India. The girl child's dowry and wedding expenses often send her family into huge debt. As consumerism and wealth increase in India, dowry demands are growing. In rural areas, families sell their land holdings, while the urban poor sell their houses.

To stop the practice of dowry, the government of India made several laws detailing severe punishment to anyone demanding dowry, and a law in Indian Penal Code (Section 498A) has been introduced. While the law helps women and their families, it also puts men and their families at a great disadvantage. In urban India, many incidents of misuse of the law and extortion of men by brides and their families (called "sowry") have come to light.

4 MORMON BAPTISM OF THE DEAD

Since 1840, baptism of the dead, also known as vicarious baptism or proxy baptism, has been practiced in the Mormon Church. It's the practice of baptizing a living person on behalf of someone who is dead; the living person acts as the deceased person's proxy.

In the practice, a living person is baptized by immersion on behalf of a person of the same gender who is dead. The person performing the baptism calls the living proxy by name, and then says, "Having been commissioned of Jesus Christ, I baptize you for and in behalf of [full name of deceased person], who is dead, in the name of the Father, and of the Son, and of the Holy Ghost. Amen." The proxy is then briefly immersed in the water. Baptism of the dead is based on the belief that baptism is a required for entry into the Kingdom of God.

The Mormon Church vicariously baptizes people regardless of race, sex, or religion. This includes both victims and perpetrators of genocide. Some Jewish survivors of the Holocaust and their supporters have objected to the practice, and Pope Benedict XVI has banned all Catholic Churches from giving the names of the deceased to Mormons.

3 JAINIST DIGAMBARAS

Digambar, also spelled Digambara, is one of the two main sects of Jainism. Senior Digambar monks wear no clothes, following the practice of Lord Mahavira. They do not consider themselves to be nude—they are wearing the environment. Digambaras believe that this practice represents a refusal to give in to the body's demands for comfort and private property.—only Digambara ascetics are required to forsake clothing. They have only two possessions: a peacock feather broom and a water gourd.

2 ISLAMIC NIQAB

A *niqab* is a veil that covers the face, and it's worn by some Muslim women as a part of the sartorial *hijab*. It's popular in the Arab countries of the Persian Gulf, but it can also be found in North Africa, Southeast Asia, and the Indian subcontinent.

The *niqab* is regarded differently by the various schools of Islamic jurisprudence known as *madhahab*. Some see it as obligatory, or *fard*, while others see it as recommended, or *mustahab*, and a few see it as forbidden. The majority of scholars believe the *hijab* is required, but only a few see the *niqab* as required, although this is not the common perception among the general population.

1 JEHOVAH'S WITNESSES REFUSAL OF BLOOD TRANSFUSIONS

A fundamental doctrine of the Jehovah's Witnesses teaches that the Bible prohibits consumption, storage, and transfusion of blood, including in cases of emergency. This doctrine was introduced in 1945 and has been elaborated upon since then. Although it's accepted by a majority of Jehovah's Witnesses, evidence indicates that a minority does not wholly endorse this doctrine. Facets of the doctrine have drawn praise and criticism from both members of the medical community and Jehovah's Witnesses alike.

In 1964, Jehovah's Witnesses were prohibited from obtaining transfusions for pets, from using fertilizer containing blood, and were even encouraged to write to dog food manufacturers to verify that their products were blood free. Later that year, Jehovah's Witnesses who were doctors and nurses were instructed to withhold blood transfusions from fellow Jehovah's Witnesses. As for administering transfusions to non-members, *Watchtower* magazine stated that such a decision is "left to the Christian doctor's own conscience."

10 BIZARRE POST-MODERN RELIGIONS

10 DISCORDIANISM

Also known as: Paratheo-Anametamystikhood of Eris Esoteric

Symbol: The Sacred Chao, symbol of the hodge and podge

Founded by Malaclypse the Younger (aka Greg Hill) with Omar Khayyam Ravenhurst (aka Kerry Thornley) in 1958 or 1959

Main doctrine: "The Discordian Society has no definition."

It's still up in the air as to whether Discordia is a mock religion or not. Discordia is mostly about nothing; they teach that discord and anarchy are paramount. Discordians do not worship, but are very interested in Eris, the goddess of discord. They also believe that everything is true, even lies.

9 KIBOLOGY

Founded by James "Kibo" Parry in 1989

While Wikipedia lists Kibology as a religion satirizing Scientology, I can't seem to find any strong correlation to that fact. Kibologists, sometimes referred to as "kibozos," follow the humorous teachings of Kibo, who was a strong presence on the Internet in the 1990s. Most of the religious texts involve humorous anecdotes, facts, short stories, and decrees made by Kibo and his followers.

Kibo has run for the office of president of the United States. He also wrote a fact page very similar to many Chuck Norris jokes years before the Internet meme was created.

8 CHURCH OF GOOGLE

Also known as: Googlism

Founded by Matt MacPherson

Google.com, the world-renowned search engine, has a following. These people believe that Google, being omniscient and omnipresent, is the closest mankind will come to knowing and facing a god. Google can solve all their problems through knowledge, and knowledge is power. They even have nine proofs of Google's godliness.

7 LAST THURSDAYISM
Founded by Michael Keene in 1996

The omphalos hypothesis claims that there is no proof that history wasn't created and implanted by God as a test for us. Creationists use this in arguments about dinosaur bones being planted on Earth to test humans' faith. Last Thursdayism takes this to another level by claiming that there is no proof that everything wasn't created last Thursday. In fact, they believe that you are God, and you've created a copy of yourself, created the world, and are testing yourself. Any memories prior to Thursday have been implanted, as has your belief system. Oh, and everyone knows about it and is in on it, so you best behave well or else you will have to punish yourself on the day of reckoning (next Thursday).

6 CHURCH OF THE SUBGENIUS
Founded in the 1950s by J. R. "Bob" Dobbs, the world's greatest salesman (or Douglass St. Clair Smith and Philo Drummond in 1979)

The Church of the Subgenius parodies all. Science, New Ageism, Christianity, conspiracy theories, pop culture, and the government are not safe from the tauntings of this group. The fundaments of the church are based on achievement of "slack," which is freedom, humor, money, and luxury.

Of the postmodern religions I'm writing about, this is the one with the most richness to its background. The Church of the Subgenius has many holidays, including Hate for the Sake of Hating Day and the Feast of Weird Al Yankovic. They have a deity, "Bob," and his wife, Connie, the antivirgin. They also have a complex religious order, which you can be a part of for a one-time fee of $30.

5 CAMPUS CRUSADE FOR CTHULHU
Also known as: The CCC

Main doctrine: Why settle for a lesser evil?

The Dark, Tentacled Lord is coming and the CCC wants you to be part of it! If you join Cthulhu's minions, the group promises years of friendship, bonding, and fear-of-dying-at-the-hands-of-Cthulhu-free existence.

The religion's sole (soul?) purpose is to please the god Cthulhu, a deity created by debatably science-fiction author H. P. Lovecraft. Right now Cthulhu is sleeping, but when the day comes for his awakening, boy, are you going to be sorry (unless you're part of the CCC, whose souls he won't devour).

4 CHURCH OF EMACS

The editor wars began some time ago, pitting unix-based, emacs-using editors versus vi-using editors. I've done extensive research (read: too boring to actually learn, so I glanced at it) into the whole mess, and it seems silly. Reminds me a lot of the Lilliputians in *Gulliver's Travels*. Anyhow, the Church of Emacs upholds the teaching that emacs is good and vi is evil. The Church of Vi is the opposite.

3 IGLESIA MARADONIANA

Founded on October 30, 1998, by many rabid fans

This is, of course, a bizarre religion founded on the Argentine soccer player Diego Maradona. It has a surprisingly large following worldwide and is the subject of both ridicule and controversy.

2 THEE TEMPLE OV PSYCHICK YOUTH

Also known as: TOPY

Founded by musical groups Psychic TV, Coil, and Current 93 in the 1980s

TOPY was created to break through restraints many of the founding members were feeling, that society puts too much stigma on things being "right" or "wrong." They're are heavily involved in occult and "magickal" practices, as well as the arts.

1 PASTAFARIANISM

Also known as: The Church of the Flying Spaghetti Monster

Founded by Bobby Henderson in 2005

Oh, you thought I was going to forget Him, didn't you? His Noodlyness wouldn't be pleased.

In an open letter to the Kansas School Board, Bobby Henderson challenged the state to either include his version of intelligent design or eliminate it from the curriculum altogether. He gives a very convincing argument for the belief system of his Noodly Savior. Bobby claims that he has written documentation that the world was created by a flying spaghetti monster. He demands that if the school board is allowing schools to teach about the Christian God, then flying spaghetti monster lessons should be included as well.

10 MISCONCEPTIONS ABOUT THE CATHOLIC CHURCH

10 DISCOURAGE BIBLE READING

Misconception: The Church discourages Bible reading.

The very first Christian Bible was produced by the Catholic Church. It was compiled by Catholic scholars of the 2nd and 3rd centuries and approved for general Christian use by the Catholic Councils of Hippo in 393 and Carthage in 397. The very first printed Bible was produced under the auspices of the Catholic Church and was printed by the Catholic inventor of the printing press, Johannes Gutenberg. The Catholic Church also produced the very first Bible with chapters and numbered verses; it was the work of Stephen Langton, Cardinal Archbishop of Canterbury.

At every Mass in the world every day, the Bible is read aloud by the priest. In the traditional Mass, there is one reading from the general body of the Bible (excluding the Gospels), and two from the Gospels. In the modern Catholic Mass, there are two readings from the general body of the Bible and one from the Gospels. All Catholic homes have a Bible, and the Bible is taught in Catholic schools, as is its perennial tradition.

This myth has come about because Bibles were often locked away in Churches in the past, but that wasn't to prevent people having access—it was to prevent them from being stolen. These were handwritten Bibles that were incredibly valuable, due to scarcity. Furthermore, people think the Church forbade people from reading the Bible by putting it on the Index of Forbidden Books, but the Bibles placed on the Index were Protestant versions (which lacks seven books) or poorly translated versions, the most famous of which is the King James Bible, which Catholics are not allowed to use.

9 IDOLATRY

Misconception: Catholics worship Mary and are, therefore, committing idolatry.

In Catholic theology there are three types of worship, one of which is condemned in the Bible:

1. *Latria*—This is adoration that's given to God alone. Giving this type of worship to anyone else is considered to be a mortal sin, and it is the idolatry that's condemned in the Bible.

2. *Hyperdulia*—This is a special type of worship given to Mary, the mother of Jesus. It is only given to her and it is not considered to be idolatry, as it is not adoration, merely reverence.

3. *Dulia*—This is the special type of worship given only to the saints and angels. Like *hyperdulia*, it isn't idolatrous because it, too, is a form of reverence.

The distinctions were made by the Second Council of Nicaea in AD 787. The council was called to condemn the people who claimed that it was idolatrous to have statues and images of saints.

8 NON-CHRISTIANS

Misconception: Catholics aren't Christians.

In fact, Catholics were the first Christians. When reading over early Christian writings, you can see clearly that their doctrines and teachings are the same as the Catholic Church today. These texts include bishops, virgins living in community (nuns), priests, confession, baptism of infants, the bishop of Rome as head of the Christian religion, and reverence for the saints. Here are some comments by the early Church fathers who were, in many cases, the apostles of the Biblical apostles:

Bishops: For it will be no light sin for us if we thrust out those who have offered the gifts of the bishop's office unblamably and holily. —Pope St. Clement, Letter to the Corinthians 1, AD 96.

The Papacy: "[From] Ignatius . . . to the church also which holds the presidency, in the location of the country of the Romans, worthy of God, worthy of honor, worthy of blessing, worthy of praise, worthy of success, worthy of sanctification, and, because you hold the presidency in love, named after Christ and named after the Father."—St. Ignatius, Letter to the Romans 1:1, AD 110.

Holy Communion: "This food we call the Eucharist, of which no one is allowed to partake except one who believes that the things we teach are true, and has received the washing for forgiveness of sins and for rebirth, and who lives as Christ handed down to us. For we do not receive these things as common bread or common drink; but as Jesus Christ our Savior being incarnate by God's Word took flesh and blood for our salvation, so also we have been taught that the food consecrated by the Word of prayer which comes from him, from which our flesh and blood are nourished by transformation, is the flesh and blood of that incarnate Jesus."—St. Justin Martyr, "First Apology," AD 148–155.

Infant Baptism: "Baptize first the children, and if they can speak for themselves let them do so. Otherwise, let their parents or other relatives speak for them."—St. Hippolytus, The Apostolic Tradition 21:16, AD 215.

Confession: "[A filial method of forgiveness], albeit hard and laborious [is] the remission of sins through penance, when the sinner . . . does not shrink from declaring his sin to a priest of the Lord and from seeking medicine, after the manner of him who say, 'I said, to the Lord, I will accuse myself of my iniquity.'"—Origen, Homilies in Leviticus 2:4, AD 248.

From these quotes, it's obvious that the practices of the modern Catholic Church are very close to the practices of the apostles and early Christians. It should also be said that the majority of historians accept that the Catholic Church was the first Christian Church, as it is verifiable from ancient texts.

7 TOTALLY INFALLIBLE
Misconception: The pope is infallible in all things.
According to Roman Catholic belief, the pope is only infallible under certain circumstances. If he is speaking in a personal capacity, without the full authority of the papacy and not on matters of faith or morals, he can make errors. See number 3 in "5 Bizarre Myths About the Papacy" (page 320) for more information.

6 ANTI-SCIENCE
Misconception: The Catholic Church is opposed to science and rejects the idea of evolution.
In fact, may great scientific advances have come about through Catholic scholarship and education. The most recent and interesting case is that of Monsignor Georges Lemaître, a Belgian priest who proposed the big bang theory. When he put forth his idea, Einstein rejected it, causing Monsignor

Lemaître to write to him, "Your math is correct, but your physics is abominable." Eventually, Einstein came to accept the theory.

Also, unlike many of the American Protestant or evangelical religions, the Catholic Church does not reject the theory of evolution. Right from the early days of the theory, the Church remained mostly silent on the issue. The first public statements specifically regarding evolution came from Pope Pius XII, who said, "The Church does not forbid that…research and discussions, on the part of men experienced in both fields, take place with regard to the doctrine of evolution, in as far as it inquires into the origin of the human body as coming from pre-existent and living matter."

In 2004, a theological commission overseen by Cardinal Ratzinger (now Pope Benedict XVI) issued this statement:

> According to the widely accepted scientific account, the universe erupted 15 billion years ago in an explosion called the "Big Bang" and has been expanding and cooling ever since. [...] Converging evidence from many studies in the physical and biological sciences furnishes mounting support for some theory of evolution to account for the development and diversification of life on earth, while controversy continues over the pace and mechanisms of evolution.

Catholic schools all around the world (including the U.S.) teach scientific evolution as part of their science curriculum.

5 INDULGENCES

Misconception: Indulgences let you pay to have your sins forgiven.
First of all, we need to understand what an indulgence is. The Catholic Church teaches that when a person sins, they get two punishments: eternal (hell) and temporal (punishment on earth while alive, or in purgatory after death). To remove the eternal punishment, a person must confess their sins and be forgiven. But the temporal punishment remains. To remove the temporal punishment a person can receive an indulgence. This is a special "blessing" in which the temporal punishment is removed if a person performs a special act, such as doing good deeds or reading certain prayers.

In the Middle Ages, forgers who worked for disobedient bishops would write fake indulgences, which they claimed could remove eternal punishment for sin instead of merely removing temporal punishment, in exchange for money, which was often used for church building. Popes had been long trying to end the abuse, but it took at least three centuries for the sale of indulgences to finally end. True indulgences existed from the beginning of Christianity, and the Church continues to grant special indulgences today.

4 EMPEROR CONSTANTINE

Misconception: Emperor Constantine invented the Catholic Church in AD 325.

In AD 313, Emperor Constantine announced toleration of Christianity in the Edict of Milan, which removed penalties for professing Christianity. At the age of 40, he converted to Christianity, and in 325 he convened the first ecumenical Council of Nicaea. Because of the importance of this council, many people believe that Constantine created the Church, but in fact, there had been many councils (though not as large) prior to Nicaea, and the structure of the Church already existed. Constantine was at the council merely as an observer, and the Bishops and representatives of the pope made all the decisions. Before the Council of Nicaea, priestly celibacy was already the norm, baptism of infants was practiced, as were all seven sacraments, and the structure of priests and bishops was already 300 years old.

3 PRIESTLY CELIBACY

Misconception: Catholic priests can't get married.

In order to clear this one up, we need to first understand the nature of the Catholic Church. Within the universal church there are sections. The most common section is, of course, the Roman (or Latin) Catholic Church. Then there is the Eastern Catholic Church (not to be confused with the Eastern Orthodox Church, which is a different religion). Both of these churches fall under the jurisdiction of the pope and both believe the same doctrines. There are a lot of differences between the two groups, but these are all in matters of style of worship and certain rules. In the Eastern Church, priests are allowed to be married, but a married priest can't become a bishop.

It also happens that occasionally in the Roman Church, pastors who convert from other religions such as the Church of England are allowed to become priests even if they are married. This means that married priests can be found in all parts of the Roman Catholic Church.

2 MODIFIED BIBLE

Misconception: The Church added books to the Bible.

The Catholic version of the Old Testament differs from the Protestant version in that Catholic Bibles contain seven more books than Protestant Bibles do. These "extra" books are the reason many people consider the Church to have added to the Bible, but in fact, the books were considered the official canon by all Christians until the Protestant Reformation, during which Martin Luther removed them. Interestingly, some of the seven books contain affirmations of Catholic doctrines that Luther rejected. The reason the Catholic Church uses the original Greek edition of the Bible is that the Apostles used it exclusively in their preaching.

Luther decided to use the Jewish Masoretic canon (ca. AD 700–1000) instead of the apostolic canon. The seven books he removed were Tobit, Judith, 1 Maccabees, 2 Maccabees, Wisdom, Ecclesiasticus, and Baruch. While he initially wanted to remove at least one book from the New Testament (the Epistle of James, because it contradicted Luther's teaching that faith alone is needed for salvation [James 2]), Luther ultimately decided to keep the Catholic New Testament in full.

Interestingly, Hanukah is mentioned only in 1 and 2 Maccabees, which are not included in either the Jewish or Protestant versions of the Old Testament.

1 MEDIEVAL PAPACY

Misconception: The papacy is a medieval invention.

The pope is the bishop of Rome, and from the beginning of Christianity, he was considered the head of the Church. This fact is alluded to in many of the early Church documents and even in the Bible itself: "And I say to thee: That thou art Peter [Greek for "rock"]; and upon this rock I will build my church" (Matthew 16:18). Peter was the first bishop of Rome and he led the Church until his death in AD 64, at which point St. Linus became the second pope. St. Irenaeus mentions him here in Against the Heresies (AD 180):

> The blessed apostles, then, having founded and built up the Church, committed into the hands of Linus the office of the episcopate [office of bishop of Rome]. Of this Linus, Paul makes mention in the Epistles to Timothy [2 Timothy 4:21]. To him succeeded Anacletus [the third pope]; and after him, in the third place from the apostles, Clement [the fourth pope] was allotted the bishopric.

St. Irenaeus goes on to mention another six popes and the various tasks they undertook during their reigns, such as the imposition by Pope Linus of the rule that women cover their heads in church (a rule which, though often ignored, still exists today).

10 PSYCHOACTIVE SUBSTANCES USED IN RELIGIOUS CEREMONIES

10 "HEAVENLY BLUE" MORNING GLORY (*IPOMOEA TRICOLOR*)
Active Constituents: Ergoline alkaloids

This is a species of morning glory native to the New World tropics that's widely cultivated and naturalized elsewhere. The seeds have been used for centuries by many Mexican Native American cultures as a hallucinogen; they were known to the Aztecs as *tlitliltzin*, the Nahuatl word for "black." Their traditional use was first discovered in 1941, brought to light in a report documenting the seeds' use going back to the Aztecs. It was reported in 1960 that the seeds of *Ipomoea tricolor* were used as sacraments by certain Zapotecs, sometimes in conjunction with the seeds of *Rivea corymbosa*, another species that has a similar chemical composition. Hallucinations are the predominant effect after ingesting morning glory seeds. Vivid visual and tactile hallucinations, as well as increased awareness of colors, have been described.

9 FLY AGARIC MUSHROOMS (*AMANITA MUSCARIA*)
Active Constituents: Ibotenic acid

This fungus, with its red cap and white spots, brings up the quintessential image of a hallucinogenic "mushroom." It's native to birch, pine, spruce, fir, and cedar woodlands throughout the temperate and boreal regions of the Northern

Hemisphere. These mushrooms were widely used as a hallucinogenic drug by many of the indigenous peoples of Siberia. In western Siberia, the use of *Amanita muscaria* was restricted to shamans, who used it as an alternate method of achieving a trance state. In the East, the mushrooms were used by both shamans and common people alike, recreationally as well as religiously. Unlike the hallucinogenic Psilocybe mushrooms, *Amanita muscaria* are rarely consumed recreationally in modern times. Depending on habitat and the amount ingested per body weight, effects can range from nausea and twitching to drowsiness, auditory and visual distortions, mood changes, euphoria, relaxation, and loss of equilibrium. Amnesia frequently results following recovery.

8 JIMSONWEED, OR HELL'S BELLS *(DATURA STRAMONIUM)*
Active Constituents: Atropine, hyoscyamine, and scopolamine
Native to either India or Central America, jimsonweed was used as a mystical sacrament in both possible places of origin. Native Americans have used this plant in sacred ceremonies, and the *sadhus* of Hinduism also used it as a spiritual tool, smoked with cannabis in traditional pipes.

In the United States, it's called jimsonweed, hell's bells (based on the flowers' shape) or Jamestown weed. It got this name from the town of Jamestown, Virginia, where British soldiers were secretly (or accidentally) drugged with it while attempting to suppress Bacon's rebellion. They spent several days generally appearing to have gone insane, and failed at their mission. The effects of jimsonweed have been described as a living dream: users fall in and out of consciousness and converse with people who don't exist or are miles away. The effects can last for days.

7 WORMWOOD *(ARTEMISIA ABSINTHIUM)*
Active Constituents: Thujone
Native to temperate regions of Europe, Asia, and northern Africa, the religious association with wormwood began with its strong association with the ancient Greek moon goddess Artemis. In Hellenistic culture, Artemis was a goddess of the hunt and protector of the forest and children. Wormwood is perhaps more famously known as the key ingredient in absinthe, the favorite drink of 19th-century bohemian artists. The most commonly reported absinthe experience is a "clear-headed" feeling of inebriation, a form of "lucid drunkenness."

6 KAVA *(PIPER METHYSTICUM)*
Active Constituents: Kavalactones

The word "kava" is used to refer both to the plant and the beverage produced from it. An ancient crop of the western Pacific, it's used for medicinal, religious, political, cultural, and social purposes throughout the region. The cultures there have a great respect for the plant and place a high importance on it. The drink is used to this day at social gatherings to relax after work, although it has great religious significance and is used to obtain inspiration. The calming effects of the drink (it's also occasionally chewed), in order of appearance, are slight numbing of the tongue and lips, mildly talkative and sociable behavior, clear thinking, muscle relaxation, and a very euphoric sense of well-being.

5 SALVIA, OR DIVINER'S SAGE *(SALVIA DIVINORUM)*
Active Constituents: Diterpenoid, known as Salvinorin A

Salvia divinorum is native to certain areas in the Sierra Mazateca of Oaxaca, Mexico, where it is still used by the Mazatec Indians, primarily to facilitate shamanic visions in the context of curing or divination. Shamans crush the leaves to extract leaf juices; they usually mix these juices with water to create an infusion or "tea," which they drink to induce visions in ritual healing ceremonies.

Salvia can be chewed, smoked, or taken as a tincture to produce experiences ranging from uncontrollable laughter to much more intense and profoundly altered states. When salvia is smoked, the duration of the effects is much shorter than some other more well-known psychedelics; salvia typically lasts only a few minutes. The most commonly reported after-effects include an increased feeling of insight and improved mood, and a sense of calmness and increased sense of connection with nature.

4 MAGIC MUSHROOMS
Active Constituents: Psilocybin and psilocin

Magic (psilocybin) mushrooms have been part of human culture as far back as the earliest recorded history. Ancient paintings of "mushroomed" humanoids dating to 5000 BC have been found in caves in Northern Algeria. Central and South American cultures built temples to mushroom gods and carved "mushroom stones," which date to as early as 1000 to 500 BC. *Psilocybian* mushrooms were used in rituals and ceremonies among the Aztecs; the fungi were served with honey or chocolate at some of the holiest Aztec events. The experience of ingestion is typically inwardly oriented, with strong visual and auditory components. Visions and revelations may be experienced, and the effect can range from exhilarating to distressing.

3 PEYOTE *(LOPHOPHORA WILLIAMSII)*

Active Constituents: Phenethylamine alkaloids, principally mescaline

From early records (specimens from Texas have dated from 3780 to 3660 BC), peyote has long been used by indigenous peoples, such as the Huichol of

northern Mexico, and by various Native American tribal groups, like those native to or relocated to Oklahoma and Texas. Peyote and its religious association, however, are fairly recent in terms of usage and practice among tribes in the Southwestern United States; their acquisition of the peyote religion and use of peyote can be firmly dated to the early 20th century. Typically consumed as a tea, the effects last about 10 to 12 hours. When combined with an appropriate setting, peyote is reported to trigger states of deep introspection and insight, described as being of a metaphysical or spiritual nature. At times, these states can be accompanied by rich visual or auditory effects.

2 AYAHUASCA, OR YAGE

Active Constituents: Beta-carboline harmala alkaloids, MAOIs, and DMT (dimethyltryptamine)

This psychoactive substance includes both ayahuasca bine (*Banisteriopsis caapi*) and chacruna shrub (*Psychotria viridis*). The word "ayahuasca," meaning "vine of the souls," refers to a medicinal and spiritual drink incorporating the above plants. When brewed together and consumed in a ceremonial setting, these plants are capable of producing profound mental, physical, and spiritual effects. Ayahuasca is mentioned in the writings of some of the earliest missionaries to South America. It may be considered as a particular shamanic medicinal brew or even as an entire medicinal tradition specific to the Amazons. The effects of the drink vary greatly based on the potency of the batch and the setting of the ritual. They generally include hallucinogenic visions, the exact nature of which seem unique to each user. Vomiting can be an immediate side effect and is said to aid in "purification."

1 CANNABIS

Active Constituents: THC (tetrahydrocannabinol)

The cannabis plant has an ancient history of ritual usage as a trance-inducing drug and is found in pharmacological cults around the world. In India, it has been engaged by itinerant *sadhus* (ascetics) for centuries, and in modern times the Rastafari movement has embraced it. Some historians and etymologists have claimed that cannabis was used as a religious sacrament by ancient Jews, early Christians, and Muslims of the Sufi order. Elders of the modern religious movement known as the Ethiopian Zion Coptic Church consider cannabis to be the eucharist, claiming it as an oral tradition from Ethiopia dating back to the time of Christ. Cannabis plants produce a group of chemicals called cannabinoids, which produce mental and physical effects when consumed. As a drug, cannabis usually comes in the form of dried buds or flowers (marijuana), resin (hashish), or various extracts collectively known as hashish oil. The psychoactive effects of cannabis are subjective and can vary based on the individual. Some effects may include a general change in consciousness (altered perception), mild euphoria, feelings of well-being, relaxation or stress reduction, lethargy, joviality, enhanced recollection of episodic memory, increased sensuality, increased awareness of sensation, and occasionally paranoia, agitation, or anxiety.

5 MOST BADASS NUNS OF ALL TIME

5 SISTER CATERINA DE ERAZU—HIT MAN IN A HABIT

Caterina de Erazu was a runaway Spanish nun turned hit woman in the early 1600s. She ended her career as an almost-respectable Mexican mule-train driver after being personally pardoned by the pope. Clerics and religious figures were tried by clerical courts, and no one could figure out what to do with a badass nun, so they just kept moving the case to a higher court. The pope just found the whole thing fascinating and pardoned her.

Being a hit man in a habit is sufficiently badass to put Sister Caterina on this list, but wait, there's more: Sister Caterina died following a duel with the husband of a woman she was hot for! It appears that Sister Caterina was America's first lesbian independent teamster. Apparently her life story was written in 1641; unfortunately, I can't find the name of the book or its author.

4 ANI PACHEN—WARRIOR NUN

Ani Pachen was born in 1933 in Tibet. When she was 17, her parents decided to marry her off, but she had other plans. She ran away and moved into a Buddhist monastery (a three weeks' journey away) and became a Buddhist nun. In 1958, when her father died, she became the leader of her family clan. She took up arms and became a warrior nun, fighting to keep the communists from China out of her homeland. She led her people in guerilla warfare for a year. The Chinese caught her and threw her in jail because she refused to renounce the Dalai Lama. She was beaten and hung by her wrists for a week, spent a year in leg irons, and spent nine months in solitary confinement in an unlit jail cell. She spent the last 11 years of her sentence in the infamous Drapchi prison in the Tibetan capital, Lhasa.

As soon as she was released from a total of 21 years in prison, she went right back to her warrior ways, leading protests and demonstrations. She found out she was going to be put in jail again, so she ran away to the border of Tibet. She walked for 25 days in the deep snow to escape to Nepal. She died in 2002.

3 SAINT HILDEGARD OF BINGEN—GENIUS

Saint Hildegard of Bingen was born in 1098 to a wealthy family and dedicated herself to the church as a nun. When she was eight, she was sent to study with a famous abbess called Jutta (who was, herself, a badass: she lived in a tiny room with no doors and had to be fed through the window); she became the abbess of the nunnery when Jutta died. Hildegard turned out to be a genius; she wrote music (the first opera, in fact) and letters to popes, giving them advice (when popes were pretty much the bosses of the whole world), and she was the first woman to write about female sexuality:

> When a woman is making love with a man, a sense of heat in her brain, which brings with it sensual delight, communicates the taste of that delight during the act and summons forth the emission of the man's seed. And when the seed has fallen into its place, that vehement heat descending from her brain draws the seed to itself and holds it, and soon

*the woman's sexual organs contract, and all the parts that are ready to
open up during the time of menstruation now close, in the same way as
a strong man can hold something enclosed in his fist.*

She also invented her own version of Latin and a new alphabet, and she had
visions throughout her whole life, which she wrote about in her journals. She is
considered a saint, and her feast day is on September 17.

2 SISTER LUC GABRIEL—BETTER THAN ELVIS

Sister Luc Gabriel (née Jeanine Deckers) was best known as the Singing
Nun. She was so badass that her song "Dominque" became such a hit that it
knocked Elvis Presley off the charts! Overnight, she
was an international celebrity with the stage name
of "Soeur Sourire" (Sister Smile). She gave concerts
and appeared on the *Ed Sullivan Show* in 1964. Her
fame went to her head, and she eventually left the
convent to spend more time on her musical career.

At the same time, she shacked up with her
lesbian lover and released a song called "Glory Be
to God for the Golden Pill," singing the praises of the contraceptive pill. After her
first album, none of her music was very successful. In 1982, she and her girlfriend
committed suicide together by taking sleeping tablets with alcohol.

1 CHRISTINA THE ASTONISHING

Christina the Astonishing was born in 1150 in Belgium. When she was 21,
she had a massive seizure and died. Halfway through her funeral, she jumped
out of her coffin and flew to the ceiling! This caused everyone to run from the
church screaming. When the priest ordered her down, she said that she had seen
heaven, hell, and purgatory. She also said she could smell the sin on people.
Because the smell of sin made her sick, she would often fly (yes, really—fly) away
from people and sit on the top branches of tall trees. She also hid herself in ovens
and on roofs. Her lifestyle was considered to be poverty, even in the 13th century:
sleeping on rocks, wearing rags, begging, and eating what came to hand. She
would roll in fire or handle it without harm, stand in freezing water in the winter
for hours, spend long periods in tombs, or allow herself to be dragged under
water by a mill wheel, though she never sustained injury. Despite this incredibly
odd (and yet badass) behavior, she was highly regarded in her time and many
people asked her for advice.

10 ASTONISHING (AND SOMETIMES WEIRD) BIBLICAL MIRACLES

10 JESUS EXORCISES LEGION

Remember *The Exorcist*? Scary, right? Priests have to go through a whole litany of just the right stuff to say in order to irritate the demon until it leaves. It can take months, but not if you have faith, of which Jesus had quite a lot.

Legion's demon possession can be explained as possible mental illness, probably schizophrenia, since he calls himself, "Legion, for we are many." Never mind that, for he/they are immediately terrified of Jesus, who simply tells the demons to leave the man. They beg to enter a nearby herd of pigs, and Jesus permit this. The herd goes insane and swarm off a hillside into the sea; all the demons drown.

The most awesome part is that Legion is described as running wild in the hills, screaming madly, breaking the chains with which people tried to bind him, and cutting himself with stones. His confrontation with Jesus would definitely be a must-see.

9 TEN PLAGUES OF EGYPT

This one has been subjected to scientific analyses. The interesting part is that the first plague is blood. The Nile runs red, and all the fish die. This could have been red toxic algae (red tide), or a volcanic eruption depositing red-colored earth and silt into the water.

Once the fish die, the frogs, leaving the dirty water, would die on the land. Then the flies would swarm terribly to feed on the frog carcasses. Then the livestock would die from fly bites (which cause diseases like anthrax and malaria). Anthrax transmits from cattle to humans in the form of boils and sores. Then comes fiery hail, perhaps from the volcano eruption. Then locusts descend to feast on whatever crops are left after the hailstorm destroys them. Then darkness falls, perhaps via eclipse or the locusts themselves.

Or it could have been completely supernatural. Either way, it would have been a great show.

8 JESUS WALKS ON WATER

It's one of his most famous miracles, and yet it doesn't seem to serve a great purpose, like number 5 on this list. Jesus seems to be showing off. Yet, he does it to show his disciples that they can do anything, if only they will believe in themselves.

Imagine seeing a man walk nonchalantly three miles across the northern tip of the Sea of Galilee at night and arrive at his disciples' boat just before they reach the other shore.

What does it feel like to step on water and not go through the meniscus? Did his feet get wet?

7 BALAAM AND HIS TALKING DONKEY

I will never be able to read this passage, from Numbers 22:21, without hearing Eddie Murphy's voice as Donkey in *Shrek*. Balaam may be the biggest goof in the Bible. He tries to curse the Israelites three times, and three times God changes his curses to blessings.

But this is after he has a vision of an angel standing in the road. Actually, his donkey sees it first, and refuses to go near it. Donkeys are quite smart, and this story is written quite accurately to that end. Three times the donkey refuses and three times Balaam beats her:

> Then the LORD opened the donkey's mouth, and she said to Balaam, "What have I done to you to make you beat me these three times?"
>
> Balaam answered the donkey, "You have made a fool of me! If I had a sword in my hand, I would kill you right now."
>
> The donkey said to Balaam, "Am I not your own donkey, which you have always ridden, to this day? Have I been in the habit of doing this to you?"
>
> "No," he said.

Then the LORD opened Balaam's eyes, and he saw the angel of the LORD standing in the road with his sword drawn. So he bowed low and fell facedown.

The angel of the LORD asked him, "Why have you beaten your donkey these three times? I have come here to oppose you because your path is a reckless one before me. The donkey saw me and turned away from me these three times. If she had not turned away, I would certainly have killed you by now, but I would have spared her."

Imagine sitting on the roadside and seeing this all happen. Only the donkey, and then Balaam, can see the angel. But the donkey plainly opens her mouth and speaks Hebrew (with proper grammar!).

Priceless.

6 PARTING OF THE RED SEA

This is perhaps the most famous miracle in the Bible. Cecil B. DeMille instilled it in the household imagination with *The Ten Commandments*, his 1956 epic starring Charlton Heston. But this depiction is not quite right. In the film, the sea parts immediately, but in the Bible, the Egyptian and Israelite armies oppose each other all day and night, separated by a pillar of fire and smoke.

All that night, a strong east wind blows back the water and creates a narrow path; by dawn, the seafloor is dry ground, and the water stands up like walls on both sides.

It would definitely have been an awesome spectacle. The Egyptians were just a tad foolish for following the Israelites down between the walls of water.

5 JESUS FEEDS THE FIVE THOUSAND

It's in all four Gospels, so the writers must have considered this miracle important. In Matthew 14:13–21, Jesus feeds 5000 men, not counting women and children, which might have placed the number at 10000, maybe more. He has only five loaves and two fish, after which his Disciples collect 12 baskets full of uneaten leftovers. The number seven is interpreted to mean perfection. Twelve is the number of the Tribes of Israel.

Jesus performs the miracle again in Matthew and Mark, feeding 4000 men, plus women and children, with seven loaves, a few fish, and collecting seven baskets of leftovers.

It certainly would have boggled the mind of anyone watching closely. How did he continue to reproduce the food? There was no description of manna and quail from heaven. Jesus simply blessed it, broke it, and had his disciples distribute it.

4 JESUS RAISES LAZARUS FROM THE DEAD

Imagine if you were standing in Bethany, just east of Jerusalem, among the crowd of mourners. Jesus is walking in, and another crowd is following him. But Lazarus has been dead for four days. Jesus is too late to heal him.

Yet, he breaks down and weeps. This is traditionally interpreted not as love for Lazarus, since Jesus already knows what he's going to do. He is weeping over the lack of the crowd's faith in him.

The best part of this story is when Lazarus' sister, Mary, tells Jesus, "My Lord, he has been dead for four days. There will be a bad smell." Yes, the smell of rot. Jesus isn't perturbed, but tells her to have the tomb opened.

He commands Lazarus to come out, and he does so, wearing his burial linens. Aside from how unbelievably shocking this must have been for the onlookers, it leads you to wonder, "Where was Lazarus for those four days?"

Lazarus was a good person, so he didn't deserve hell. And you can be sure the question on everyone's mind was, "What's Heaven like?"

3 JOSHUA STOPS THE SUN

Joshua does battle with the Amorites in Gibeon, somewhere north of Jerusalem. Not only do Joshua and his army rout the enemy army, but as they flee the field, God himself rains down hailstones on them, which kill more people than the Israelites do. Ah, the Old Testament. Good, old-fashioned wrath-of-God stories.

The fight apparently seems to Joshua as if it will take too long, given the huge numbers of men, so Joshua asks the Lord to stop the sun and moon so the day lasts long enough for the Israelites to do their thing. Most importantly, Joshua arranges his army to attack with the sun at its back (classic field tactic).

Imagine 12 hours of midday sun, no shadows, and then it doesn't go away! Twelve more hours of midday sun! And then the next day begins anyway, so it's 12 more hours of sun! If this is true, it means Joshua asked the Lord, and the Lord agreed, to stop the rotation of earth.

2 THE RESURRECTION

You don't need to believe it to understand the awesomeness of what the resurrection means. There are, according to the Bible, only two people who do not suffer the bitterness of death: Enoch and Elijah. The first simply walks with God and is no more. The second is taken to Heaven in a fiery chariot and whirlwind.

Jesus actually does die. But he's the only person in the Bible who revives himself. For three days he's dead to the world. So where is he during that time? One tradition says that he goes to hell to preach to everyone who had died before him, thus without salvation. This sounds fishy, since no one in his right mind is going to sit in a lake of fire, and then say, "No! I refuse to change!"

But wherever he goes, it remains in the Bible that three days later, Jesus' spirit returns to his body and he gets right back up. Job done. A little tidying up and he goes home. He defeats death itself with his own supernatural power.

1 "LET THERE BE LIGHT"

It seems easy to interpret God's command as the big bang, since that's thought of as being an instant occurrence from which the four forces of the universe diverged from a single, infinitely small point. So what did things look like before? The Bible's beginning is the most famous depiction, by far, of what we think of now as the big bang. It has been depicted many times in films, educational programs, and other media as a massive burst of light in all colors, quickly forming into galaxies, stars, and, later, planets and other astral bodies.

But it wouldn't have made any noise, since before the big bang, there was no medium through which the sound could travel. And yet, sound can't travel through space as it is. So it may be that the creation of light never made a sound.

10 PEOPLE WHO GIVE CHRISTIANITY A BAD NAME

10 SUN MYUNG MOON

Sun Myung Moon is the founder of the Unification Church, which has spread worldwide since its origin in 1954. Moon was born in 1920 and has set himself up as the reincarnation of Jesus Christ. A lot of people go around saying, "I'm Jesus," but they're usually dismissed as insane or attention-seeking.

Moon has convinced anywhere from several hundred thousand to one million people to join his church and consider him "Jesus reincarnated." He is vehemently opposed to homosexuality. He is also extremely anti-Semitic, championing the Holocaust as divine vengeance against the Jews because they didn't support Jesus, which Moon claims brought about his murder by the Roman government.

And Moon leads an extraordinarily lavish lifestyle. Modern church founders typically make a lot of money, but Jesus didn't make one cent. Moon has been known to spend $2000 a day and give his children as much as $50,000 monthly allowances. His "True Family's" home is a huge mansion on 18 acres in Irvington, New York, with 12 bedrooms, a dining room complete with pond and waterfall, seven bathrooms, and a bowling alley. He also has mansions in Korea, England, Scotland, and Germany, and his kids have Thoroughbred horses, private tutors, Ferraris, motorcycles, and blank checks to take on their vacations (on which they travel first-class, of course).

Blessed are the meek, for they shall inherit the earth.

The funniest part is that he was convicted of tax fraud and served 18 months in prison. Remember the fish Jesus told Peter to catch? It had two coins in its mouth, one for each of them, to pay the tax. "Render therefore unto Caesar what is Caesar's, and unto God what is God's." Even Jesus paid taxes.

9 DAVID KORESH

David Koresh (born Vernon Wayne Howell) was a handsome, charismatic Texan, considered so poor a student in elementary and middle school that he was enrolled in special-ed classes. He memorized the New Testament by age 11, and impregnated a 15 year old when he was 19. He must have forgotten a few verses.

By 1983, after being kicked out of a Seventh-Day Adventist Church for fooling around with the pastor's daughter, he began calling himself a prophet. He was able to recruit followers because of his good looks and magnetic personality, eventually proclaiming himself Jesus Christ, "the Son of God, the Lamb who could open the seven seals." He taught that monogamy was the only proper relationship, but that polygamy was perfectly fine for him, and him alone. After his first wife died, he quickly had sex with Karen Doyle, called her his second wife, and proceeded to have sex with as many as 140 different women.

Karen Doyle did not get pregnant, probably because she was 14 years old, so he slept with Michele Jones, who was 12 years old. By proclaiming this to be God's will, he was able to have sex with any woman or girl whenever he liked. He tried to gun down George Roden, who was also a high-ranking member of Koresh's sect, and escaped conviction by mistrial.

By the time of the Waco Siege, he had, by his own admission, fathered at least 12 children, some by girls as young as 12. And the followers just kept coming. In my opinion, the FBI seriously botched the siege and used unnecessary force, but Koresh was the primary culprit of his followers' deaths, 82 of them, by fire. Which side started the fire is hotly disputed and will never be known, but Koresh told his followers, "Don't move until you see God."

They didn't see God before they burned alive, Koresh with them.

8 PAT ROBERTSON

Robertson is worse than the previous two men on this list because he doesn't even know how to lie convincingly. He swears that "the spirit of God comes mightily upon [him]" and enables him to leg press 2000 pounds even though he's 79 years old. This claim has been thoroughly debunked by weightlifting experts, and yet he persists in claiming it without proving it.

He has claimed to be able to deflect hurricanes by praying to God, and stated that Hurricane Katrina was God's punishment for abortion throughout America, thus showing that he did not pray for Katrina's deflection. He believes that the 9/11 attacks and Hurricane Katrina might be divinely connected.

He denounced Haiti after the January 12, 2010, earthquake, stating that Haiti deserved what it was getting because it swore a pact with the devil back in 1791 in order to drive out the French. Whether that pact was sworn or not, his comments were obviously intended to inflame and hurt, and they did so. How Christian of him. He was roundly denounced by most Christian denominations and still refuses to retract what he said.

He predicted doomsday in 1982. He predicted a tsunami in the Pacific Northwest in 2006, then a terrorist attack on American soil sometime in 2007. He defended this last failure by saying, "All I can think is that somehow the people of God prayed and God, in his mercy, spared us." He has made many other predictions, none of which has come true.

He has many times called for the destruction of Islam and all its followers and calls Islam "satanic." He calls Hinduism "demonic." He even claims that some Protestant Christian denominations harbor the spirit of the antichrist.

He has made quite a few anti-Semitic remarks, notably about Ariel Sharon, the former prime minister of Israel, whose stroke and subsequent vegetative state Robertson calls "an act of God."

7 MATTHEW HALE

Hale is currently serving 40 years in prison for attempting to solicit the murder of Judge Joan Lefkow. Not a very model preacher. But actually, he calls himself the Pontifex Maximus of the Creativity Movement, which is just another offshoot from the Ku Klux Klan. The church is for whites only, and it has its own bible, in which one finds passages such as, "You have no alibi, no other way out, white man! Fight or die!"

His church calls for a worldwide racial holy war to exterminate the Jews and all black people in order to establish "a white world." His reasoning: God is white; God created Jews and black people to test the faith and resolve of white people; thus, killing a Jew or black person is not a sin. After one of his followers, Benjamin N. Smith, committed a deadly shooting spree, targeting only minorities, Hale "defended" his actions on TV by saying, "We do urge hatred. If you love something, you must hate that which threatens it." He is recorded on audiotape laughing about the shootings and imitating the sounds of gunfire.

6 MICHAEL BRAY

Bray is not an ordained or college-educated minister, but he does preach a lot about abortion. He served 46 months of a ten-year sentence for conspiring to bomb ten abortion clinics in Maryland, Virginia, and Washington, D.C. He and his wife stand firmly on the Bible as the inerrant Word of God, and they say that because it preaches so firmly against homosexuality and adultery, anyone convicted of either in a court of law should be put to death, even though American courts have no problem with either. They might be sins, but they aren't felonies.

Bray didn't exactly help the Christian cause of conversion by allowing Richard Dawkins, the most famous atheist in the world, to interview him for a show called *The Root of All Evil.* Bray was thoroughly outmatched, of course, and made Christianity look like…well, the root of all evil.

He is now out of prison and living in Wilmington, Ohio; he is officially labeled as a terrorist.

5 PAUL JENNINGS HILL

Hill was a trained and ordained Presbyterian minister, but the church excommunicated him in 1993 for taking such a militant stand against abortion and for becoming a member of the Army of God, a Christian terrorist, antiabortion organization.

This ordained minister finally let his anger get the best of him when he traveled to Pensacola, Florida, on July 29, 1994, to an abortion clinic, and murdered one of the doctors and his bodyguard point-blank with shotgun blasts. He also wounded the bodyguard's wife. Then he calmly put down the shotgun in the grass and sat and waited for the police.

He was executed. The law does not permit vigilante justice, and come to think of it, "Love thine enemies" seems a fair argument against it also.

4 MARSHALL HERFF APPLEWHITE, JR.

And if you thought the last several entries on this list were weirdoes, Applewhite has gone down in history as a true psychopath. Born May 17, 1931, he proclaimed himself a prophet in 1972, and then, as they all seem to do, called himself Jesus Christ reincarnated. He was not as handsome as number 9 on this list, but he wasn't exactly ugly, either; he was married and seemed for all the world to be "blameless and upright before God."

Followers flocked to his forceful charisma when he told them that UFOs were coming to take them away to heaven. When the UFOs didn't show, the followers left, but he kept preaching to friends and their acquaintances, and by 1975 acquired a following of 93 men, women, and children.

He eventually recruited people from all 50 states and settled in Rancho Santa Fe, California. His wife died of cancer in 1985, and sometime between then and 1997, he had a nurse surgically castrate him, for purification. He called his church "Heaven's Gate." His congregation worshiped him fervently.

On March 19, 1997, as the comet Hale-Bopp was passing Earth, Applewhite recorded himself preaching to his congregation that suicide "was the only way to evacuate this earth." His congregation did not believe in suicide, but was so enamored with him, that 39 members took his word for it, and on March 24, 25, and 26, they killed themselves with mixtures of phenobarbitol and applesauce, followed by vodka. They also put plastic bags over their heads to be sure of asphyxiation, in case the poison didn't work.

Applewhite's idea was to die so his spirit would ascend to the UFO that was following Hale-Bopp, which would then take him and his followers to another plane, both physical and spiritual.

3 JIM JONES

But the number of people who died with Applewhite is nothing compared to the 909 people, 276 of them children, who became enamored with the handsome, charismatic founder of the Peoples Temple. James Warren Jones started out Methodist and seemed to have fine intentions, endeavoring to bring about civil right for blacks and integrate American society. Somewhere along the line, however, he went patently insane. He was an aggressive narcissist, just as entries 1, 4, 7, 8, 9, and 10 on this list. He never claimed to be the reincarnation of Jesus Christ, and the only reason he founded the Peoples Temple was for the money he could make via his congregation.

The strangest part is that his followers were not hopeless runaways or uneducated and uninformed. They were predominantly members of other Christian denominations. They were taken in by Jones' good looks and charm and his ability to lead and convince.

In 1974, the Temple went to Guyana with only 50 members. But Jones promised others back in the U.S. a tropical paradise, and they flocked by the hundreds to "Jonestown." Because he had always been an outspoken Communist sympathizer, and intended Jonestown to be a socialist safe haven, he drew the attention of the U.S. Government.

On November 17, 1978, investigating claims of abuse within the Peoples Temple, California congressman Leo Ryan went to Jonestown, and about 15 members wanted to leave with him. They attempted to depart via a nearby airstrip, and were fired upon by Temple security guards. Ryan was killed, along with four others, one a Temple member.

When the shooters returned to Jonestown, Jones and accomplices were preparing a mass suicide by poisoning: Flavor Aid loaded with cyanide, phenergan, Valium, and chloral hydrate.

There are graphic pictures of the dead lying en masse outside the pavilion, 909 of them. The children were probably not told that the drink was poisoned.

Jones shot himself in the head.

2 CHARLES COUGHLIN

Father Charles Edward Coughlin was a priest who used the radio to acquire a large audience for his political and religious propaganda. He was born in 1891 and was one of the first to use modern technology to mass communicate for such a purpose.

He started out innocently enough, using radio to decry the KKK for burning crosses on his church grounds, but ten years later, in 1936, he started praising and defending both Adolf Hitler and Benito Mussolini for their politics and spewing some of the most despicable virulence against Jews that the world had seen to that point.

He blamed the Great Depression on "an international conspiracy of Jewish bankers," then blamed Communism, the Russian 1917 Revolution, and Marxist atheism on "global Jewry, in its attempt to lead people astray from the perfection of Lord Jesus."

Coughlin plagiarized a speech by Goebbels, then delivered it himself in a rally in the Bronx on September 13, 1935, giving the "Hitler salute." And this is what he said: "When we get through with the Jews in America, they'll think the treatment they received in Germany was nothing."

He acquired thousands of followers who chanted things like, "Wait until Hitler gets over here!" Coughlin was linked with a group that attempted to overthrow the U.S. Government, after which he was abandoned by most of them. He still refused to change his politics, and fought a series of radio duels with Unitarian Walton Cole, who wanted the Catholic Church to put an end to Coughlin's vitriol.

Franklin Roosevelt himself was the man who shut Coughlin up for good, when the latter started railing against the New Deal. The courts ruled that the First Amendment did not apply to radio, and Coughlin's license was revoked. This forced him to pay for his own airtime, which he couldn't do for long.

On May 1, 1942, the Archbishop of Detroit, Most Rev. Edward Mooney, ordered Coughlin to stop his political activities and confine himself to his duties as a parish priest, warning that he would be defrocked if he refused. Coughlin complied and remained the pastor of the Shrine of the Little Flower until retiring in 1966. He died in 1979, at 88 years old, still publishing inflammatory articles against Judaism and Communism.

1 FRED PHELPS, SR.

Phelps has 13 children, four of whom have disowned him and their other siblings. Those four children, two men and two women, have denounced Phelps as "a vitriolic, megalomaniacal sadistic psychopath." I can't phrase it better than that, and yet, it still doesn't fully capture this man's personality. Ordinarily, the lister should remain objective about the list, but in this case, except for his congregation, which officially numbers 71, 60 of whom are Phelps' relatives, it's highly doubtful that anyone else on the planet agrees with, or even slightly supports, Phelps' savage, barbaric perversion of Christianity and its founder. So I don't feel quite so bad about being biased.

His "ministry" at the Westboro Baptist Church, which he founded, in Topeka, Kansas, is based almost entirely on antihomosexuality, which is one of the easiest, if not the easiest, sin to denounce by means of quoting the Bible. God condemns homosexuality at least twice in Leviticus, and from this principle, Phelps feels he can condemn the entire world, but especially the U.S., which he has described as a liberal hellhole that supports homosexuality. (That's a very, *very* cleaned-up paraphrase of his graphic, disgustingly profane words.)

While there are plenty of Bible verses to quote against hatred, as quoted above, Phelps and his worshipers petulantly ignore these parts of the Bible and enjoy themselves by hating others. For them it's a physical and emotional release, a pleasure just as sensual as that garnered by loving others.

Phelps may never have begun a sentence with "God loves…" For him, sermons ought to begin with "God hates…" Most of the time that blank is filled in with homosexual slurs. He extrapolates God's hatred for gay people to ridiculous lengths, denouncing the entire world as imminently doomed to hell, except for…you guessed it: him and his precious few followers.

His two estranged sons have described him as "a malignant narcissist, with the same short, viciously intemperate disposition as a serial killer toward his victims." The only reason he hasn't killed anyone isn't because he views it as a sin, but because it would give the rest of the world more universal ground on which to stand against him. He prefers to set himself up as God on earth, perfect and blameless.

His oldest daughter, Shirley Phelps-Roper, has defended the group's actions as righteous with every word, according to the Bible, forcing "the sinful American nation to open its mouth and condemn itself."

Phelps and his congregation picket at least six churches and political establishments around their hometown every day with signs that read "God Hates Fags," "Thank God for Dead American Soldiers," and "America is Going to Hell." They do this for the sole purpose of offending and causing emotional distress. They picket the funerals of dead soldiers, screaming at the families while they grieve at the gravesides that the soldier has gone to hell and so will they. Then they laugh. They have been sued at least once, but they successfully appealed the suit and paid nothing.

Phelps is the man responsible for sending these brainwashed fools, who revel in their own malice, across the country. He has condemned every single president, from the time he was old enough to care, as the antichrist. He has even used racial slurs to talk about President Obama on several occasions.

10 BIZARRE THINGS YOU DIDN'T KNOW ABOUT CHRISTMAS

10 INCEST, CORPSES, AND JESUS

What do incest, an embalmed corpse, and the baby Jesus have in common? Most people know that, according to the Bible, the magi brought myrrh, along with gold and frankincense, as a gift to the baby Jesus. Some people also know that myrrh (dried tree sap) was used as an embalming ointment or as incense for funerals and cremations to mask the smells. However, few people know that, according to Ovid's *Metamorphoses*, myrrh trees originated as a result of Myrrha's lust for her father, Cinyras. With the help of her nursemaid, Myrrha repeatedly had sex with her unsuspecting father. When her father realized Myrrha's identity and that he had been boinking his daughter, he attempted to kill her, but she escaped. The gods took pity on her, and to release her from her shame, they turned her into a myrrh tree. Presumably the magi did not think to include a gift receipt so that Jesus could return the myrrh, which then became the first unwanted Christmas present.

9 HOLY CRAP!

Everyone has seen a nativity set; the simplest consist of the baby Jesus, Mary, and Joseph and perhaps a few shepherds or animals, while the most extensive contain not just the Holy Family but entire cities with hundreds or thousands of inhabitants. In parts of Spain, Portugal, and Italy, one of these figures will often be the *caganer*. While traditionally the figure of a Catalan peasant, now it can be any person, even Santa Claus or the devil, so long as they are posed in the act of defecating. The *caganer* is usually placed in a discreet location not in close proximity to the manger. Presumably this is so as not to contaminate the animals' drinking water, one guesses.

8 DEAD KIDS

Rub-a-dub-dub, three dead kids in a tub! Jolly old Saint Nicholas is not only the patron saint of children, but, according to legend, he brought back to life three children after they were murdered and pickled in brine. Supposedly the three children spent the night at the house of an innkeeper or a butcher, who then killed, gutted, dismembered, and pickled the youngsters and was planning to pass off their remains as pork. Saint Nicholas happened along and miraculously resuscitated, reassembled, and reanimated the youths. In artistic portrayals of Saint Nicholas, you'll sometimes see children standing in vats or tubs; that would be why! This legend is also referred to in the French song "*La Légende de Saint Nicolas.*" No word is available on whether the kids were dill or garlic flavored.

7 BAN IT!

Let's celebrate Christmas like our forefathers did—by banning it! In the United States, every year there's a traditional argument over whether or not left-wing liberals, the ACLU, Communist agitators, Jews, the government, big business, or any combination thereof are involved in a nefarious plot to "destroy" Christmas. Most proponents of this theory endorse a return to Christmases such as those in the olden days, apparently unaware that, from 1659 to 1681, Christmas was actually banned in Massachusetts. There were several reasons for this. The Puritans did not consider December 25 to be a religious day (if God had wanted us to celebrate it, then He would have specified that date in the

Bible). Christmas was celebrated by Catholics and hence was anathema to the Puritans, and, perhaps most importantly, Christmas was not being celebrated by quietly spending the day at home with family or at church, but rather by spending the day "consumed in Compotations, in Interludes, in playing at Cards, in Revellings, in excess of Wine, in mad Mirth ..." according to the Rev. Increase Mather. I suspect that if most Americans were offered the choice of spending Christmas shopping or, as in the days of our forefathers, getting drunk, we'd return to a "traditional" Christmas in less time than it takes Santa to get back up the chimney.

6 MEOW

Krampus, aka Schmutzli, aka Knecht Ruprecht, is the companion of Saint Nicholas who punishes the bad children by stuffing them into his sack and taking them to the Black Forest to eat them, to hell, or to the river to drown them. While obviously this prospect would be a bit intimidating, at least children can save themselves from an unpleasant fate by good behavior, unlike the unlucky Icelandic children. According to an old Icelandic tradition, everyone has to get one new piece of clothing for Christmas. Anyone who didn't was in danger of being eaten by the Christmas Cat, a large vicious black feline who belonged to a family that was descended from trolls. (Children who didn't behave were eaten by the ogress troll-mother herself.) Rumor has it that WalMart is considering suggesting that the Christmas Cat had kitties who emigrated around the world in an attempt to increase next year's Christmas clothing sales.

5 UNCLE POOP

One of the more unusual bearers of Christmas presents, with a unique delivery method, is the *Caga Tió* (pooping uncle or, in this case, pooping tree trunk). Found in the Catalonia region, it consists of a hollow log. Beginning at the Feast of the Immaculate Conception, the family "feeds" the *Tió* and covers him with a warm blanket each night. Then, at Christmas, the family gathers together, sings songs, puts the *Tió* partly into the fire and beats it with sticks until it excretes presents of candy, nuts, or figs. When the *Tió* is finished pooping, it signals this by dropping salted herring, a head of garlic, an onion, or by "urinating," whereupon the entire log is burned. This is where the expression "If you don't give me a present I'll beat the crap out of you" originated.

4 WASSAILING

Wassailing sounds like such an innocuous, wholesome tradition: knocking on doors, singing a few songs, and perhaps being offered a warm drink or cookies. The original wassailers, however, were more aggressive and would invade a home, demanding food, drink, or money from the homeowners, and refusing to leave until they received their "recompense." If forcibly ejected, they would curse, threaten, and sometimes vandalize the property of their "hosts." Think of some of the later verses from "We Wish You a Merry Christmas": "Now bring us some figgy pudding...we won't go until we get some." If you are ever the victim of a home invasion, you could probably lighten the mood by pointing out the similarity between your attackers and people who sing "Don we now our gay apparel, fa-la-la-la-la-la-la-la-la."

3 MARI LWYD

The old gray mare, she ain't what she used to be. The Mari Lwyd is a horse's skull, decorated with bells and ribbons, which is set on a stick and carried by an operator hidden under a white sheet. The eye sockets are often filled with green glass and the jaw may be spring loaded so that the Mari can "snap" at passersby. She is to be found in Southeast Wales around the Christmas season, particularly at New Year's. The Mari and her male companions attempt to enter households or pubs via a contest where they trade insults with the householders via song (apparently an early precursor to rap contests). If the Mari and her male friends win, they enter and obtain food and drink. The Mari particularly enjoys this because, as the men get drunker and drunker, the Mari begins to appear prettier, younger, thinner, and less dead to them.

2 CASTRATIONS AND A CROSS

Leo V became Byzantine emperor in 813 after forcing the abdication of Michael I, whereupon Leo had Michael's sons castrated. On Christmas Day in 820, Leo was praying alone in front of the altar of Hagia Sophia. A group of conspirators disguised as priests and monks and led by Michael the Amorian (no relation to Michael I) entered and drew their daggers to assassinate Leo. Unarmed and alone, Leo tried to defend himself with an incense burner in one hand and a large wooden cross in the other. After an hour, he succumbed to his injuries. Michael was immediately declared emperor, and Leo's four sons were castrated. This was not the origin of Christmas tree balls, fortunately.

1 CHRISTMAS QUESTION

Q. What do you get a dead baby for Christmas? A. A dead puppy.

"The Coventry Carol" is an old song dating back to the 15th century. It was performed in Coventry, England, as part of a Christmas play known as *The Pageant of the Shearmen and Tailors*, and that particular song refers to

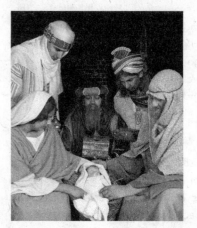

the Slaughter of the Innocents. This, according to the Gospel of Matthew, is when King Herod, fearing the competition from the newborn King of the Jews, sent his soldiers to slaughter all male children in and around Bethlehem who were age two or younger. In the pageant, the song was sung by the women of Bethlehem to their children to soothe them, right before the soldiers killed them. It seems to be an odd topic to have survived for so long, but I suspect that department store Santas may be its biggest fans.

CHAPTER EIGHT
Science and Nature

10 BIZARRE CASES OF MIND CONTROL

10 MELOE FRANCISCANUS

The blister beetle has an amazing way of perpetuating its existence. As a larva, it joins with other larvae to form a clump that resembles a female bee. The larvae then produce a chemical that fools male bees into believing the writhing clump is a potential mate. When the male arrives, the larvae latch on and wait for him to mate with a real bee. These horrifying little creatures then hop onto the female, who deposits them along with her eggs into the ground. The larvae eat the pollen she has provided and parasitize the baby bee. And so the cycle begins again.

9 ACACIA TREES

When we talk about mind control, the last thing we think of is plants, but here is one such case! The acacia tree produces certain chemicals that cause ants to go into a defensive frenzy. While in this state, the ants keep other plants and animals away. Once the tree is sufficiently safe and needs to produce fresh pollen, it sends out another chemical to get rid of the ants.

8 PHENGARIS ALCON

The alcon blue butterfly has very weird nannies for her young—ants. While still in its larval stage, the butterfly secretes a chemical that mimics that of ant larvae. Any ants that come upon the young butterfly carry it back to the nest and raise it as if it were their own child. Sometimes the ants take better care of the intruders than they do their own offspring. Alcon blue butterflies have been known to spend up to two years hibernating this way. Unfortunately for the ants, when the larva reaches the caterpillar stage, it often eats all the ants in the nest.

7 ICHNEUMON EUMERUS

Just when you were feeling sorry for the poor ants in the previous item, along comes *Ichneumon eumerus*, a wasp that parasitizes alcon blue butterflies! When it detects a butterfly in an ant nest, it sprays a chemical which forces all of the ants out. In the confusion, the wasp heads in and deposits an egg inside the alcon blue caterpillar. The wasp leaves, the ants return, and life continues as before, with the ants raising the caterpillar. But once the alcon has formed its chrysalis, what emerges is not a butterfly but a wasp.

6 MYRMECONEMA NEOTROPICUM

Myrmeconema neotropicum is a parasite of the cephalotes ant, found in South American rainforests. When infected by the parasite, the cephalotes ant, which is normally black, turns partly red and mimics the appearance of berries. This causes birds to eat them, killing the ants, but spreading the parasite in the bird droppings. These droppings are then eaten by healthy ants and the cycle continues.

5 PHORID FLIES

Ah, the poor ants—they just don't get any breaks. Phorid flies reproduce by laying their eggs in the thorax of an ant. The larvae then migrate to the ant's head and develop by consuming the muscle and nervous tissue there. In time, it consumes the entire brain of the ant, which then amazingly continues to walk aimlessly for about two weeks—until its head drops off. The phorid fly then pupates in the detached head.

4 TOXOPLASMA GONDII

Toxoplasma gondii is an ant parasite…just kidding. It's actually a very common parasite that can be found in all mammals, including humans, but it especially loves cats. If a rat or mouse becomes infected by the parasite, it modifies the rodent's behavior so that instead of being afraid of cats, it becomes attracted to them. The cat then eats the rat or mouse and the parasite begins to sexually reproduce inside the cat.

3 EUHAPLORCHIS CALIFORNIENSIS

This is a parasite that lives in shorebirds. It produces eggs, which are pooped out by the birds into marshes and ponds. The eggs are then eaten by snails. Once fully grown, the larvae leave the snails and find water, where they can parasitize killifish. In order to spread to other birds, the parasite makes the killifish swim around in circles at the top of the water so it will be eaten.

2 JEWEL WASP (AMPULEX COMPRESSA)

This one is not for the faint of heart. The jewel wasp stings a cockroach to paralyze it while it inserts a second sting directly into its brain. This causes the roach to lose its escape reflex. Astonishingly, the wasp then grabs one of the roach's antennae and leads it, like a dog, to its nest, where she lays an egg on its stomach and seals it up. Once the larva hatches, it consumes the living roach which lies there contentedly until it is dead.

1 HAIRWORM

The hairworm larva develops inside grasshoppers, crickets, and other similar bugs. As it grows, the hairworm eats the bug's internal organs until nothing is left but the head, legs, and outer shell. When it has expanded to three times the size of its host, it manipulates the host to seek out and enter a body of water, at which point the worm emerges and swims away, leaving the host to die.

10 BIZARRE SLEEP DISORDERS

10 RAPID EYE MOVEMENT BEHAVIOR DISORDER

When a human is in the rapid eye movement (REM) stage of sleep, the body is paralyzed so it does not act out actions while dreaming. When someone suffers from REM behavior disorder, this paralysis does not take place. The patient can then freely act out his dreams, which can be extremely violent. There are numerous cases of this disorder causing serious injury to the sufferer or his partner in bed.

9 NIGHT TERRORS

We have all suffered at one time or another from night terrors—the feeling of extreme terror coupled with an inability to wake up. When waking finally does come, the sufferer of night terrors is usually gasping, moaning, or even screaming. Most of the time, it is difficult or impossible to remember the dream that prompted the terrors. Perhaps the worst aspect of this sleep disorder is that if the sufferer is awakened, they can continue to suffer the terrors for up to 20 minutes in an apparently alert state.

8 BRUXISM

Bruxism is the rather fancy name for grinding your teeth during sleep. It is an extremely common problem, with up to 40 million Americans doing it on a regular basis. It can damage the teeth so severely that dentists often provide a special mouth guard, and in extreme cases, Botox injections are needed. There is no known cure.

7 RESTLESS LEGS SYNDROME

Restless legs syndrome is a disorder in which the sufferer feels uncomfortable unless they keep their legs (and sometimes arms or torso) constantly moving. The discomfort is often described as feeling like electrical charges or itching, and it can be experienced when the sufferer is asleep or awake. Medication used for restless legs syndrome often involves anticonvulsants and opiates, which is extremely controversial.

6 NON-24-HOUR SLEEP-WAKE SYNDROME

Most humans have a natural clock that keeps them tuned in to the 24-hour cycle of the earth. When this internal clock is dysfunctional, it results in non-24-hour sleep-wake syndrome. The sufferer can have a different sleep cycle every day and it can return to normal for short periods. Generally it takes one week for a person to complete a cycle that would normally take one day. Interestingly, this disorder mostly affects blind people, but there are also sighted people who experience it.

5 SLEEP APNEA

Sleep apnea is when breathing becomes erratic or even stops completely during sleep. It usually occurs repeatedly through the night and can be extremely dangerous. Most people who suffer from it are unaware of it, and it is only when someone sees them sleeping that it is brought to their attention. The most common treatment used for this disorder is a device that keeps a constant flow of pressurized air moving into the patient's mouth during the night.

4 KLEINE-LEVIN SYNDROME

Kleine-Levin syndrome is a disorder that forces the sufferer to need up to 20 hours of sleep per day (much like a cat). Oddly, it is usually accompanied by a super sex drive and excessive eating. There is no treatment for it, so the symptoms are alleviated with amphetamine-based drugs. Next time you fall asleep in a meeting, you might want to use this as an excuse so you don't lose your job.

3 SOMNILOQUY (SLEEP TALKING)

Sufferers of somniloquy will either murmur in their sleep from time to time or, in more extreme cases, may give entire speeches. Generally the talk is nonsensical, but this is not always the case. The only form of treatment for somniloquy is to wear a gag or, as doctors prefer to call it, a mouth guard.

2 NARCOLEPSY

Narcolepsy is a disorder that causes the sufferer to fall asleep at random times. This is the disease that led to many premature burials in the past (a far less regular occurrence these days, thankfully). Some narcoleptics suffer hallucinations during their sleep and others become paralyzed. The cause of narcolepsy is unknown.

1 SEXSOMNIA (SLEEP SEX)

Sexsomniacs make love in their sleep. It is a rare form of sleepwalking, and most people who have it know they have it but don't seek help because they are afraid people will think they are making excuses for willful behavior. Some people have sexsomnia and don't report it, as it bothers neither them nor their partner.

10 WEIRD AND WONDERFUL ODDITIES OF NATURE

10 MIRACLE MICE

Weird Fact: A mouse can fit through a hole the size of a ballpoint pen.
During the summer months, mice generally live outside and remain content there. But as soon as the weather begins to cool, they seek the warmth of our homes. Because of their soft skulls and gnawing ability, a hole the size of a ballpoint pen (about 1/4 inch) is large enough for them to enter en masse. Once inside, they constantly gnaw at virtually anything, including concrete, lead, and plastic. This is to keep their evergrowing teeth at a convenient length. Contrary to popular belief, mice don't generally like cheese, but will eat it on occasion. Mice can jump up to 18 inches, swim, and travel vertically or upside down. To mouseproof your house, check all small openings with a ballpoint pen—if it fits the hole, it will let mice in.

9 SQUARE EYES

Weird Fact: Unlike most creatures, goats have rectangular pupils.
We all imagine pupils to be round—since they are the type we see most often—but goats (and most other animals with hooves) have horizontal slits, which are nearly rectangular when dilated. This gives goats vision covering 320 to 340 degrees; this means they can see virtually all around them without having to move (for comparison, humans have vision covering 160 to 210 degrees). Consequently, goats can see better at night than humans can because they have larger pupils that can be closed more tightly during the day to restrict light. Interestingly, octopuses also have rectangular pupils.

8 BLIND HORSES

Weird Fact: Horses can't see directly in front of themselves.
Horses have considerably wide vision (and the largest eyes of any land mammal), being able to see a total field of up to 350 degrees. Horses have two blind spots: the first is directly in front of them and the other is directly behind their heads.

As far as seeing details, horses are red colorblind and have vision of 20/33 (compared to perfect human vision of 20/20).

7 SICK RATS

Weird Fact: Rats can't vomit.

Rats can't vomit or burp because of a limiting wall between their two stomachs and their inability to control the diaphragm muscles needed for the action. Neither rabbits nor guinea pigs can vomit, either. This makes rats particularly susceptible to poisoning (hence poison's popularity in controlling rat infestations). Because of this inability, rats will nibble at food to see if it makes them feel sick (they can't vomit, but they sure can feel like they want to!). If they don't feel nausea, they will scarf down the whole thing.

6 GORILLA GORILLA GORILLA

Weird Fact: The scientific name for a gorilla is *Gorilla gorilla gorilla.*

First off, let's just be clear: this is the scientific name for a particular type of gorilla—the Western Lowland Gorilla (this is the type you are most likely to see in a zoo, and the most common). For some reason, the poor gorillas got stuck with the weird names. If you aren't a *Gorilla gorilla gorilla*, you're a *Gorilla gorilla diehli*, *Gorilla beringei beringei*, or *Gorilla beringei graueri*. All clear? I didn't think so.

5 KILLER SWANS

Weird Fact: A swan can break a man's arm.

Next time you are feeding the beautiful swans and want to give one a nice pat on the back, don't do it! Swans are very protective of their young and will use their

incredibly powerful wings to fend off dogs (and sometimes humans). They have a wing span of around nine feet. In 2001, a young man in Ireland had his leg broken by a swan when he was trying to provoke it. The following year another person had their arm broken.

4 FRAGILE SPIDER

Weird Fact: If you drop a tarantula it will shatter.

First of all, unless you are allergic to tarantula venom, they are harmless to humans (though they pack a painful bite). Some tarantulas can also shoot the "hairs" off their legs, which can pierce human skin and cause great discomfort. Now, back to the weird fact. Tarantulas have an exoskeleton—meaning their skeletons are on the outside—like crayfish and crabs. They shed their exoskeleton regularly, normally by lying on their back. (When they are shedding their skeleton, it is a good idea to keep away from them as they will attack due to their vulnerable state.) Because the exoskeleton is very fragile, if a tarantula is dropped from a low height, it will shatter and die.

3 SCARY SPICE
Weird Fact: Nutmeg is poisonous.

Nutmeg is a hallucinogenic drug that is regularly used to flavor such lovely things as tarts and fruit cakes. It is also a poison that will kill you while you suffer a variety of extremely revolting (and one or two not-so-revolting) side effects on the way. Ingesting two grams of nutmeg will give you similar feelings to having taken amphetamines (the not-so-revolting side effect), but will also cause nausea, fever, and headaches. Ingesting 7.5 grams will cause convulsions, and eating 10 grams will cause hallucinations. Eating a whole nutmeg can lead to "nutmeg psychosis," which includes feelings of impending doom, confusion, and agitation. There have been two recorded cases of death by nutmeg (one in 1908 and one in 2001).

2 SHAKING LEAVES
Weird Fact: The telegraph plant is capable of rapid movement—even in the absence of wind.

The telegraph plant is a tropical plant usually found in Asia, but also in the South Pacific. The plant has the amazing ability to shake its leaves (which rotate on their axis and jerk up and down). There are a few other plants with rapid-movement abilities (such as the Venus flytrap), but this is the most bizarre and least known. It should be noted that when we refer to "rapid" in relation to plants, it is not super fast, but it is definitely visible with the naked eye.

1 BURNING ISSUE
Weird Fact: The bombardier beetle shoots boiling liquid as a defense mechanism.

The incredibly complex bombardier beetle has an amazing and unique ability: when threatened, it rapidly shoots boiling hot chemicals from its abdomen up to 70 times. The liquid is a combination of hydrogen peroxide and hydroquinones, which join together inside the beetle, causing a chemical reaction. The liquid is fatal to small insects and creatures and can be very painful to humans.

10 UNABASHED QUACKS IN MEDICAL HISTORY

10 PAUL CHAMBERLEN (1635–1717)

The purported inventor of the "Anodyne Necklace," Chamberlen claimed that the necklace would help "children's teethe as well as woman's labour." It is no shock that children during the 18th century often died as infants, and since babies teeth so frequently during infancy, it may have seemed natural that the teething itself was the source of illness and death. The Anodyne Necklace was invented to simply place around a baby's neck to prevent infant death during teething. Chamberlen deserves the last place on this list for preying and capitalizing on the grief and terror of parents who were more often than not resigned to the fact that their children would be more likely to die in infancy than to make it to adulthood. Unbelievably, such necklaces are still being sold today, despite an utter lack of evidence of their efficacy.

9 ALBERT ABRAMS (1863–1924)

Abrams invented the Dynamizer, which he claimed could diagnose any ailment simply by feeding into the machine a slip of paper upon which had been blotted a drop of the patient's blood. If a drop of blood was unavailable or the patient didn't want to give it, a handwriting sample would suffice! One made the Dynamizer work by connecting it with an electrode to the forehead of an assistant, who was stripped bare to the waist. Then the assistant was turned to face west under dim light, and his abdomen was struck repeatedly with a mallet. The vibrations coming off the assistant's abdomen would indicate to the doctor the nature of the disease. The medical community, ever the distrustful skeptics, sent Abrams a drop of rooster blood to be analyzed with the Dynamizer. The "patient" was diagnosed with malaria, syphilis, diabetes, and cancer.

8 BERNARD JENSEN (1908–2001)

Jensen was a famous American chiropractor and iridologist who asserted that all of the body's underlying dysfunctions and toxins can be identified through the iris (colored part) of the eye, despite the fact that the iris does not undergo major changes during a person's life. Nevertheless, Jensen insisted that darker areas of the iris, or areas that changed from lighter to darker, would be read as indications that there were problems or diseases in the corresponding part of the body. Different areas of the iris would represent different limbs and organs, and the left and right eye would be read differently. For instance, if the bottom of your right eye's iris had a dark fleck, your right kidney would be in grave danger.

7 DINSHAH GHADIALI (1873–1966)

Ghadiali invented the Spectro-Chrome, which he claimed could cure ailments by changing the color of the light to which the patient was exposed. His theory was that different colors corresponded to different elements (blue = oxygen, red = hydrogen, etc.), and the lack of those elements in the body was what caused disease. Hence, if the body was exposed to that color for a prolonged period, the deficiency would be remedied, and the disease cured. Any disease except broken bones could be cured in this manner; furthermore, the patient did not necessarily have to be exposed directly to the colored lights: he or she could also drink liquids out of an appropriately colored bottle in order to achieve the same effects.

6 D. D. PALMER (1845–1913)

The father of modern chiropractics, Palmer had a theory that misalignment of the spine is the most common cause of all illness in the human body. His scientific method boiled down to two incidents: 1) he whacked a deaf janitor with a book during some witty banter, and a few days later the man claimed he could hear better; and 2) he manipulated an undisclosed patient's spine and "cured" her vague "heart trouble." On these two incidents alone, Palmer postulated that there was a fluid called "Innate Intelligence" flowing through the body that could heal any ailment and that could be made to flow more easily by unblocking pathways through the manipulation of the spine. As chiropractics is a very common practice today, this will most likely be the most controversial of the entries on this list.

5 WILLIAM J. A. BAILEY (1884–1949)

President of "Radium Company" of New York and a self-proclaimed doctor who never received his medical degree, Bailey prescribed to his patients "Radithor," essentially a solution of radium in regular water, which he asserted would help invigorate tired patients. His most notable patient was Eben Byers, a wealthy industrialist, who drank 1400 bottles of Radithor before having his jaw fall off and subsequently dying from radiation poisoning. Upon Byers' death, it was discovered that the radium had eaten massive holes in his brain and skull. Bailey also marketed a radioactive belt clip (for portable "energy") and a radioactive paperweight (presumably to perk up lethargic businessmen).

4 JOHN HARVEY KELLOGG (1852–1943)

Immortalized in T. Coraghessan Boyle's book *The Road to Wellville* (which was later made into a movie starring Anthony Hopkins), and the brother of cereal magnate Will Kellogg, J. H. Kellogg is one of the few licensed medical doctors on this list. Well-known as an eccentric and monomaniacal leader of the "health movement," Kellogg ran a sanitarium in Battle Creek, Michigan, that drew large numbers of "patients" who apparently volunteered for such masochistic treatments as: complete abstinence from any sexual activity, since it was the source of most illness; yogurt enemas to cleanse the body; marching while eating meals to help digestion; carbolic acid applications to the clitoris to prevent female masturbation; and immersion in freezing water laced with radium. Apparently, he, not his brother Will, was the original Frosted Flake.

3 JOHN R. BRINKLEY (1885–1942)

The "goat gland" doctor, Brinkley performed hundreds of surgeries on men who feared that their most virile days were behind them by opening up their scrotal sacs and nestling goat testicles alongside the men's. There was no arterial conjoining, no grafting, no fusion—the goat gland and human testicle merely occupied the same sac, but Brinkley claimed that the extra flow of testosterone would revitalize a male patient's sex life.

Legend has it that Brinkley first tested his while he was working for a meatpacking company. He was astounded by the sexual voracity of the goats at the plant, thus prompting him to half-jokingly suggest to his undersexed patient that he should try goat glands; to this suggestion his desperate patient responded, "So, doc, put 'em in. Transplant 'em!" Brinkley went on to perform over 16,000 goat-gland transplants. He also arguably established the first radio advice talk show in order to advertise himself and his services to as many potential patients as possible. The book *Charlatan: America's Most Dangerous Huckster, the Man Who Pursued Him, and the Age of Flimflam* by Pope Brock is an excellent starting point to learn more about this irrepressible lunatic.

2 WALTER FREEMAN (1895–1972)

A prominent neurologist and psychiatrist, Freeman popularized the lobotomy by making it easy and convenient: he "perfected" the transorbital lobotomy, in which a sharp implement (the first was an ice pick from his own kitchen) was inserted through the inside corner of the eye, tapped with a small hammer until it broke through the skull bone, and entered into the frontal lobe of the patient's brain, then wiggled around like a stir stick to cut neural connections. These "surgeries" were performed outside of the operating room, without anesthetic, and after the patient was incapacitated by electroshock therapy. Freeman eventually developed his own instrument for performing the lobotomies called the "leucotome." He decided to refine his instrument further when one broke off inside a patient's orbital socket. Even after his medical license was revoked for killing a patient with his technique, he traveled the country in his "Lobotomobile" to service the needy and the isolated. He performed 3439 lobotomies during his career, though the psychological and physical damage caused by his practice of psychiatry is unquantifiable. For an amazing and heartbreaking first-person account of an 11-year-old victim's lobotomy by Freeman, *My Lobotomy* by Howard Dully and Charles Flemming is a must-read.

1 JOSEF MENGELE (1911–1979)

No list about quacks would be complete without mentioning this undisputed king of cruel and inhuman "research experiments." The "Angel of Death" at Auschwitz, Mengele's crimes against humanity during World War II at the concentration camp are well documented and well known. Some of the more notable and horrendous "experiments" he carried out were: injecting dyes into children's eyes to see if eye color could be changed; attempting to measure how much force would be needed to break a human being's skull (while living, of course); putting Jewish prisoners in a gigantic oven and testing how long it would take for human flesh to sustain first-, second-, and third-degree burns;

sewing twins together to see if he could create conjoined twins; and rubbing ground glass into injuries to see what the effect would be. The damage Mengele did to an entire race of people, to the human spirit, and to our perception of the depravity the human mind can invent is still unsurpassed.

10 TRULY BIZARRE SCIENTIFIC STUDIES

10 ELEPHANT RECOGNITION

The Study: Elephant Self-Recognition

Conducted by: New York's Wildlife Conservation Society

Three Asian elephants named Happy, Maxine, and Patty were observed by researchers after a large mirror was placed in the elephants' yard. Happy was marked with a white X painted above one eye, and a similar mark was made over her other eye in invisible paint of an identical smell and texture. When Happy saw her image in the mirror, she repeatedly brought her trunk to her own head to touch the white mark. This is the ultimate test of self-recognition. The elephants also made repetitive movements in front of the mirror and apparently used it to inspect their body parts. Maxine even put the tip of her trunk into her mouth and looked as though she were trying to study her mouth's interior.

Interesting Fact: Elephants have now joined apes and dolphins in being part of a small group of animals that are able to recognize themselves in the mirror.

9 SHEEP RECOGNITION

The Study: Sheep Recognizing Faces

Conducted by: The Babraham Institute

The Babraham Institute investigated sheep's ability to distinguish and remember faces of both other sheep and humans. Twenty sheep were presented with pictures of 25 pairs of sheep faces. The researchers had trained the sheep to associate one of each pair with a food reward. They determined that the sheep could recognize the individuals associated with a reward, even when they saw the faces in profile. The team further discovered that sheep can remember as many as 50 sheep faces, in addition to a familiar human face, for up to two years.

Interesting Fact: Scientists concluded that because sheep have such sophisticated facial recognition skills, they must have much greater social requirements than previously thought

8 LOOK-ALIKES

The Study: Do Married Couples Start to Look Alike?

Conducted by: Psychologist Robert Zajonc at the University of Michigan For this study, 110 participants were presented with random photographs of faces and were instructed to match the men with the women who most closely resembled each other. Two dozen of the photographs were of couples when they were first married, and another two dozen were of the same couples 25 years later. The judges were able to match husbands and wives far more often when the couples were older than when they were younger.

Interesting Fact: The results could not be explained, but there were some possible explanations. The first was diet, with the thinking that if both partners eat a high-fat diet, for example, their faces will both tend to look chubby. Another explanation was that couples are exposed to the same environment, which would affect the skin in similar ways. A third explanation was predisposition, the idea that people are more likely to choose partners who will grow to look like them. The most popular explanation was empathy. People grow to look similar because they are empathizing with each other, so the couple would copy each other's facial expressions. Then over time, because of all the empathizing, their faces come to look more similar.

7 SMART HIPS

The Study: Curvy Hips Intelligence

Conducted by: The University of Pittsburgh and the University of California, Santa Barbara

Researchers looked at data from a study of more than 16,000 women and girls that detailed their body measurements, as well as their education levels and scores on various cognitive tests. The women were measured by their waist-to-hip ratio, or WHR. The report indicated that women with waists that were about 70 percent of the diameter of their hips scored slightly better on intelligence tests and tended to have a slightly higher level of education than women with a higher waist-to-hip ratio. Also, women with lower WHRs and their children had significantly higher cognitive test scores. One theory is that the amount of omega-3 fatty acids in a woman's hips and thighs are a key indicator of her heart health. It's also important for the health of her brain and the brain of any child she may bear.

Interesting Fact: Scientists call the study intriguing but say the differences in cognitive ability that the researchers found were somewhat small. Because of this, they think it would be a mistake to overinterpret the findings that just because a woman has a curvy figure, she's smarter.

6 WOMEN IN RED

The Study: Are Women More Attractive in Red?

Conducted by: The University of Rochester

This study wanted to test whether men have different attitudes toward women based on the color the women are wearing. In one experiment, psychologists asked, "Imagine that you are going on a date with this woman and have $100 in your wallet. How much would you be willing to spend on your date?" Pictures of the exact same women wearing or framed by different colors were shown to men. The woman wearing red was more likely to be treated to a more expensive date. In all the experiments, women shown framed by or wearing red were rated significantly more attractive and sexually desirable by men than women in other colors.

Interesting Fact: One of the theories to explain the outcome of the study was that it could be due to deep biological roots because nonhuman male primates, such as baboons and chimpanzees, are known to be attracted to females displaying red.

5 HERRING GAS

The Study: Do Herring Communicate by Passing Gas?

Conducted by: Canada and Britain

Two teams carried out this research project. One studied Pacific herring in Bamfield, British Columbia, while the other focused on Atlantic herring in Oban, Scotland. It was discovered that the Atlantic and Pacific herring create a mysterious underwater noise. The noise was always accompanied by a fine stream of bubbles, and it turns out that the high-frequency sound was created by releasing air from their anuses. Researchers suspect herring hear the bubbles as they're expelled, helping the fish form protective shoals at night.

Interesting Fact: Researchers named the phenomenon Fast Repetitive Tick, which makes for a rather interesting acronym, FRT. Scientists say unlike the human version, these FRTs are thought to bring the fish closer together.

4 BOUNCING BOSOM

The Study: Bra Support for Bouncing Breasts

Conducted by: University of Portsmouth, England

Seventy women, including students at the University of Portsmouth, with bra sizes ranging from A cups to extra-large sizes (DD, E, FF, G, H, HH, J, and JJ), were recruited for the study. Each woman walked, jogged, and ran while wearing different bra types. During the exercise, biomechanical measurements were taken of breast movement in three directions: up and down, side to side, and in and out. During walking exercise, the women's breasts moved relatively the same amount in all directions. But when participants sped up to a jog or run, their breasts moved proportionally more in some directions than others: The overall pattern of the movement resembled a figure-eight. The study showed that for A-cup women, wearing sports bras reduced overall breast movement by 53 percent, compared with a 55-percent reduction for G-cup women wearing sports bras. It was concluded that whether women are flat chested or big busted, ordinary bras fall short when it comes to supporting bouncing breasts.

Interesting Fact: The momentum created by intense bouncing can stretch the breast's connective tissues, causing sagging and pain for many women. An estimated 50 percent of women experience breast pain during exercise.

3 FERTILITY SEXINESS

The Study: Do Women Walk Sexier When Fertile?

Conducted by: Meghan Provosat, Queens University, Canada

The idea behind this study was to determine whether women give subtle signals to men to advertise they are experiencing different levels of sex hormones. The lead researcher, Meghan Provost, had expected a sexy hip-swinging walk to be one of those signals. She analyzed the gait of female volunteers and the levels of sex hormones in their saliva. She then showed video clips of them to 40 men, asking them to rate the attractiveness of the way the women walked, and then she matched the results to the hormone tests. The results were so surprising that Provost repeated the experiment again with another group of male viewers. The researchers found those with alluring walks were the furthest away from ovulation and the women who were most fertile walked with fewer hip movements and with their knees closer together.

Interesting Fact: It was suggested that during the highest hormonal time, it is in a woman's best interests to form a closer attachment to one man to help raise children, rather than to advertise her fertile time and be approached by a larger number of competing males. Also, a sexy walk would be too obvious, so women are thought to use changes in smell and facial expressions that can be experienced only at close range.

2 SEXY SHOUTING

The Study: Why Female Monkeys Shout During Sex

Conducted by: The German Primate Center in Göttingen

To investigate the purpose behind the female monkey's shouting calls, behavioral scientists and primatologists focused on Barbary macaques (Old World monkey species) for two years in a nature reserve in Gibraltar. The researchers found that

females yelled during 86 percent of all sexual encounters. When females shouted, males ejaculated 59 percent of the time. However, when females did not holler, males ejaculated less than 2 percent of the time. To see if yelling resulted from how vigorous the sex was, the scientists counted the number of pelvic thrusts males gave and timed when they happened. They found that when shouting occurred, thrusting increased and led to more vigorous sex. It was concluded that female monkeys may shout during sex to help their male partners climax. Scientists found that without these yells, male Barbary macaques almost never ejaculated. The information in the study did not reveal how they were able to detect whether an ejaculation occurred, but I guess it's best to leave some things to the imagination.

Interesting Fact: Male and female Barbary macaques are promiscuous, often having sex with many partners. The females shout when they are most fertile so males can make the most use of their sperm.

1 BIG HANDS, BIG FEET, BIG...

The Study: Foot Size and Penile Length

Conducted by: University College London

In this study, the researchers measured 104 men's feet and their penises. Because there is no perfect way to measure a man's penis, they did what many other studies do that measure penis length: The researchers stretched the penis with a defined amount of force to determine how long it could get. This gives a pretty good indication of how long the penis would be when fully erect. The result of this study (to the relief of all size-seven-shoe-wearing males) was that there is no scientific support for the relationship between a man's shoe size and the length of his penis.

Interesting Fact: In another study, a group of Greek researchers measured height, weight, waist-to-hip ratio, finger length, and penis length of 52 men, aged 19 to 38. They found that age and body characteristics were not associated with penis size except for the "index finger length, which correlated significantly with the dimensions of the flaccid, maximally stretched penis." A similar study of 1500 men also found that length of index the finger was significantly correlated with penis dimensions.

10 MAMMALS WITH BIZARRE DEFENSES

10 OPOSSUM

Everyone knows that "playing possum" means playing dead. The American opossum (*Didelphis virginianus*), found from Canada to Costa Rica, usually reacts to danger as many other mammals do: by hissing, growling, and baring its teeth. It can also bite viciously if pushed too far. However, if this all fails and the situation becomes too dangerous, plan B is to feign death; the opossum collapses to the ground, drools as if it were very ill, and then remains motionless, with its mouth open and its teeth bared. It even produces a putrid, corpselike smell from its anal glands—move over, beaver-ass juice.

Many predators prefer to kill their own prey, and most will soon lose interest in an apparently dead animal, leaving the opossum alone. The most amazing thing about the opossum's defensive method is that it is not a conscious act; rather, it is a physiological response to a highly stressful situation, and the animal does fall into a comatose state that can last for hours. Usually, the opossum regains consciousness only after the enemy has left. Exactly how its body knows when to awaken is still a mystery.

9 POTTO

Found in the jungles of Africa, pottos may look like some kind of small, arboreal bear relative, but they are actually primates. They are nocturnal and feed on tree sap, fruit, and small animals. Due to their slow movements, pottos are vulnerable to a number of predators and have a very unusual defensive method: they have enlarged neural spines on their vertebrae, which protrude from the neck and shoulders. These spines have pointy tips and seem to be used as some kind of unlikely weapon, with the primate "neck-butting" its enemies and, perhaps, just making itself difficult to swallow. The spines may also function as some kind of shield, protecting the potto's neck from the killing bite delivered by some predators that is often aimed at the neck or back of the head.

8 PANGOLIN

Pangolins are very weird mammals whose bodies are almost completely covered in large scales, giving them an appearance somewhat reminiscent of a giant, living pine cone. They feed mostly on insects and are found in Africa and Asia. Although they have large, powerful claws on their forelimbs, they rarely use them as weapons; instead, when threatened, they coil into a ball so tight that's almost impossible to unroll. The sharp edges of their scales make them practically invulnerable to most predators. They can also lash out with their powerful, heavy tails, causing serious injury with the sharp scales.

And that's not all. A Sumatran pangolin was seen curling into a ball and then actually rolling down a slope at high speed to escape unwanted attention! The pangolin's last defensive resource is to spray a foul-smelling, gooey substance from its anus. Needless to say, this animal doesn't have many enemies to worry about.

7 THREE-BANDED ARMADILLO

Although we tend to think of armadillos as heavily armored creatures, protected by an almost-turtlelike shell, in most species, the shell offers no real protection against large predators, and the armadillos bury themselves into the ground to escape danger.

However, the South American three-banded armadillo is the only one that can roll into a perfect ball; this is accomplished thanks to its loosely jointed armor, which allows for a greater range of movement, and to its armored head and tail, which interlock when the animal rolls into a ball, thus making it completely invulnerable to most enemies.

This animal has also been known to shut closed at the last moment during an attack, making a snapping sound to startle its enemies as a clever additional defensive trick. Since it's so well protected, the three-banded armadillo doesn't need to be a good digger and will use the burrows of other animals instead of digging its own.

6 CRESTED PORCUPINE

Found in Africa and southern Europe (mainly in Italy), the crested porcupine is among the largest rodents in the world and also among the best-protected mammals. Its quills, which have black-and-white banding so that predators can spot them from a distance, are actually modified hairs covered with layers of hard keratin. These quills are longer in the front part of the porcupine's body, forming an erectile crest that gives the animal its name. However, the most dangerous quills are the short ones in the back of the body. When threatened by a predator, the porcupine usually shakes its tail quills, which are hollow and sound like a rattle; if this doesn't scare the enemy away, the porcupine charges backward, trying to stab the predator with its back quills.

These quills break off easily, and once they enter the predator's body, tiny barbs in the tip actually pull them deeper into the wound; many inexperienced predators die as the result of porcupine-quill injuries, either due to infection or because the quills work so deep into the flesh that they damage blood vessels or even internal organs! There are porcupines in North America, too, but these are usually smaller than their African relatives and spend much of their time in trees; interestingly, they have very powerful natural antibiotics in their blood. This is because they sometimes fall from the trees while foraging and are stabbed by their own quills. If it weren't for the antibiotics, many porcupines would die of infection after a fall.

5 PYGMY SPERM WHALE

Unlike its better-known relative the gigantic sperm whale, which can grow up to 65.5 feet (20 meters) long, the rarely seen pygmy sperm whale is only 3 feet 9 inches (1.2 meters) long. This makes it vulnerable to predators such as large sharks and orcas. To protect itself, the pygmy sperm whale employs a very unusual defensive method: it expels a jet of reddish, syruplike substance through its anus, and then uses its tail to stir it up, forming a large, dark cloud in the water. This momentarily conceals the whale from the predator's sight and allows it to quickly swim to safety.

There is a closely related species of cetacean, the dwarf sperm whale, which is known to use the same technique to escape predators; however, this is a very unusual defense for a mammal. In fact, the most similar defensive mechanism is found in cephalopods (squid and octopus), which are, ironically, the pygmy sperm whale's favorite meal!

4 DORMOUSE

These small, edible rodents are found in Europe, with some species scattered across Africa and Asia. They usually escape predators by fleeing, but they have an interesting defensive trick they use as a last resource. The skin in the dormouse's tail is very loose, and if a predator grabs the rodent by the tail, the skin comes off, allowing the dormouse to escape. This is a form of autotomy, losing a body part as a defensive mechanism. Autotomy is common among reptiles (lizards losing their tails is the best-known example) and invertebrates, but is very rare in mammals.

However, the dormouse can do this only once; after shedding the skin of its tail and escaping, the exposed tail bones usually fall off, or are gnawed off by the dormouse itself, since the skin does not grow back and the tail cannot be regenerated as it can in lizards. Some species of dormice have tufted tails that act as a decoy, driving the predator's attention away from the dormouse's head.

3 SKUNK

Everyone knows about skunks and their defensive method, but they deserved a place in this list anyway because their chemical weaponry is incredibly powerful. The skunk's defensive fluid is produced by a pair of glands in the anal region; although many other small carnivores have these glands (particularly those in the Mustelidae, or weasel, family), the skunk's glands are more developed and they have powerful muscles allowing them to spray the fluid as far as nine and a half feet (three meters)!

Skunks also have incredible aim (most impressive if we consider that they attack with their rear end facing the enemy) and usually spray directly at the predator's face; if an animal (humans included) is hit in the eyes by the skunk's liquid, it can go blind, so it is always better to leave these animals alone. Due to this and to the fluid's offensive smell, skunks have few enemies, the most important being the great horned owl, which practically lacks a sense of smell and can attack silently from above, therefore avoiding the nasty spray.

However, as usual in this list, the skunk's chemical attack is used only as a last resource since its fluid supply is limited, and it takes up to ten days for the glands to fully "recharge."

2 PLATYPUS

The bizarre platypus, once thought to be a hoax and now famous as one of the few mammals that lays eggs, is also unusual when it comes to defensive methods. In each hind limb, the male platypus has a sharp, retractable spur that is connected to a venom gland. When grabbed by a predator (or by a curious or ill-informed human), the platypus kicks with these spurs, injecting the venom, which is usually enough for the enemy to let it go. Although the venom can kill animals

 up to dog size, it is not lethal to humans. However, people who have been "stung" by these animals claim that it is among the most excruciatingly painful things that can be experienced, and the

effects of the envenomation can last for days and temporarily impair the victim. Some claim that the pain is strong enough to cause the victim to faint.

Interestingly, only the male platypus has a functional venom spur; the female poses no threat to other animals (except for the small invertebrates that make up its food, of course). This suggests that the venom spur is primarily an intraspecific weapon, used by male platypuses against each other during mating-season duels.

1 SLOW LORIS

This small, nocturnal primate is found in the rainforests of Southeast Asia. It measures around 13 inches (35 centimeters) long and feeds on whatever small animal it can capture (and sometimes it feasts on tree sap as well). Being small and slow would make the slow loris vulnerable to many predators if it weren't for its extremely unusual defensive mechanism. The slow loris has poison glands on its elbows (that's right, we're talking about a poisonous primate). But that's not all. It makes itself an unappetizing entrée by licking the poison and spreading it all over its fur. Female lorises also lick their poison onto their babies before leaving them to hunt.

And the best part: since it licks and sucks the poison into its mouth, the slow loris ends up having a venomous bite as well and, if pushed too far, it bites the venom into its enemy, causing intense pain and swelling. Some people have died as the result of anaphylactic shock after being bitten by slow lorises, even though the venom itself is usually not lethal to human-sized animals. Being a poisonous primate that gives a venomous bite is weird enough to grant the slow loris its number 1 status in this list. But in case you missed it, the coolest thing about this guy is that it can actually lick its elbows!

10 BIZARRE SPIDERS

10 BIRD DUNG CRAB SPIDER

This spider has one of the most effective camouflages of all animals: its body is covered with blobs and warts that give it the appearance of a fresh piece of bird excrement; it often produces a small thread of white silk and sits on it so that it looks like the white stains caused by bird droppings falling onto leaves. And as if this were not amazing enough, it also smells like poop. This camouflage has a double function: it makes the spider a rather unappetizing prey for most animals (especially birds themselves), and it serves as a lure for the small, excrement-loving insects, which are the spider's favorite prey. These spiders are found in Asia, from Indonesia to Japan.

9 ARGYRODES COLUBRINUS

This creature is usually known as the whip spider, although this name is also used for another arachnid and could lead to confusion. Found in Australia, this spider has a long, thin abdomen similar to a snake's body, hence its species name *colubrinus*, which means "snakelike." Its unusual appearance is, again, an example of camouflage. By looking like a small twig caught in spider silk, it escapes notice by most predators and is less easily spotted by its prey. The whip spider belongs to the same family as the dangerous black widow. It is not known how potent the whip spider's venom really is, but it is usually regarded as harmless due to its docile nature and short chelicerae (fangs).

8 SCORPION-TAILED SPIDER

This spider is so named because of the female's weird abdomen, which ends in a "tail" similar to that of a scorpion. When threatened, the scorpion-tailed spider arches this tail as a scorpion would. Only the female has a tail; the male looks more like an ordinary spider and is much smaller. These creatures are, again, found in Australia, and they seem to be completely harmless. They spin circular webs and are often found in colonies, although each female spider has its own web and doesn't venture into those of other females.

7 BAGHEERA KIPLINGI

This spider was named Bagheera kiplingi after Bagheera, the black panther character in *The Jungle Book*, and the book's author, Rudyard Kipling. It was seemingly named because of its pantherlike agility, which is common to all jumping spiders. However, while all the other known jumping spiders are predators, Bagheeras are almost completely vegetarian, feeding almost exclusively on acacia buds and nectar. They use their agility to escape the aggressive ants that usually protect acacia trees from other animals. Occasionally, the Bagheera spider feeds on ant larvae, and even, if very hungry, on other Bagheeras (it's still a spider, after all!). Funnily enough, there is a chapter in *The Jungle Book* in which, during a period of food scarcity, Bagheera the panther claims that he hopes he could be a vegetarian!

6 ASSASSIN SPIDER

Found in Madagascar and parts of Africa and Australia, these bizarre predators have long necks designed to support the weight of their enormous jaws, and they feed almost exclusively on other spiders, hence their name. Despite their fearsome appearance and name, they are completely harmless to humans. An interesting note is that these spiders are survivors from the age of dinosaurs! Perhaps that's why they look so alien nowadays.

5 WATER SPIDER

Also known as the diving bell spider, the *Argyroneta aquatica* is the only completely aquatic spider in the world. It is found in Europe and Asia, from the

UK to Siberia, and lives in ponds, slow-moving streams, and shallow lakes. Since it cannot take oxygen directly from water, the water spider builds an underwater retreat with silk and fills it with air it carries from the surface (by trapping air bubbles in the hairs that cover its body and legs). Once filled with air, the silk retreat becomes bell shaped and has a silvery shine, hence the spider's name (*Argyroneta* means "silvery net"). The spider spends most of its time inside the bell, and only has to replenish the air once in a while. It feeds on whatever aquatic invertebrate it can capture, including backswimmers, water striders, and diverse larvae; it also occasionally hunts tadpoles and small fish.

4 SPINY ORB WEAVER

Rather than being a single species, horned spiders, also known as spiny orb weavers, are a genus that includes as many as 70 known species, with many more yet to be discovered. They are found all around the world and are completely harmless, despite their frightening appearance; their horns and spines are supposed to be deterrents to birds. These spiders are also noted for adding small silk "flags" to the edges of their webs. These flags make the webs more visible to small birds, which can then steer away before becoming entangled in the web. Horned spiders are found all around the world, often in gardens and near houses.

3 PEACOCK SPIDER

Yet another Australian species, the *Maratus volans* is commonly known as the peacock spider due to the brightly colored, circular flap in the male's abdomen. Just like an actual peacock, the male of this diminutive species raises this flap like a colorful fan and uses it to catch the female's attention (they have extremely acute eyesight, as do most jumping spiders). It also vibrates its hind legs and abdomen for a more dramatic effect. Another common trait of the peacock and the peacock spider is that the male will sometimes court several females at the same time. Until recently, it was thought that the male peacock spider was capable of gliding through the air; according to some, it would extend the flap when leaping and therefore increase its jumping distance, hence its name (*volans* means "flying"). Today we know that the flap is for display purposes only. But that doesn't make it any less awesome.

2 MYRMARACHNE PLATALEOIDES

This spider is an incredible example of Batesian mimicry, when one animal deters potential predators by "disguising" itself as an unpalatable or dangerous animal of another species. In this case, it is a jumping spider that looks like a weaver ant. Weaver ants are noted for their painful bite and also because they produce two different chemicals that increase the pain in the bite wounds. They are very aggressive ants, and the effects of their bite can last for several days. Many birds, reptiles, and amphibians avoid these ants.

On the other hand, the *Myrmarachne* spider is harmless and shy; however, it pretends to be just as tough by looking and walking almost exactly like a weaver ant; its cephalothorax (the front section of a spider's body) is modified so that it looks like the distinct head and thorax of an ant, and it has two black spots that mimic the ant's eyes. Its forelegs mimic the ant's antennae, so the spider looks as if it has only six legs, like an actual ant. *Myrmarachne plataleoides* is only found in India, China, and Southeast Asia, but is not the only ant-mimicking spider; many other species are found around the world's tropics and they imitate many different kinds of aggressive ants.

1 HAPPY FACE SPIDER

No kidding. This is a real animal that is closely related to the black widow spider and found in the rainforests of Hawaii, where it is known as *nananana*

makaki'i. It is not known to be dangerous to humans in any way. The strange patterns on the spider's yellow abdomen often take the form of a smiling face, although in some individuals the markings are less obvious or even absent. Some happy face spiders can actually have markings reminiscent of a frowning or screaming face!

Although this is not the only spider with facelike markings, it is certainly the most notorious one. Unfortunately, it is the only spider in this list considered to be endangered, due to its limited range and the reduction of its natural habitat.

10 BIZARRE CAT TALES

10 THE LITTER KWITTER

Cleaning kitty litter is no walk in the park. According to statistics, it represents half of the expenses of keeping a cat. An interesting solution would be to train your cat to use the toilet. But how do you train your cat to do this? Enter the Litter Kwitter, a cat-friendly training system that teaches cats how to use a human toilet. The system consists of a special universal toilet seat (meaning it fits all toilets) and three toilet rings. The training is done in three stages. The first is the red stage, where your cat is trained to associate the toilet with the litter box, using a red ring fitted above the toilet that is filled with kitty litter. The amber stage follows, in which your cat is trained to balance itself on the toilet seat while using it, this time using an amber ring with a small hole that is surrounded with a little kitty litter. The final stage is the green stage, where your cat learns to use the toilet by balancing itself on the green ring, which has a larger hole this time. *Voilà!* A potty-trained cat!

9 RADIO STATION FOR FELINES

Nohl Rosen of Scottsdale, Arizona, is the proud owner of Cat Galaxy, an Internet radio and TV station catering specially to cats (and their owners, too).

Running for a strong nine years, the station has radio shows like *Morning Meows*, *Meow Mixing Monday*, and *Friday Night Feline Frenzy*. Most of the music from this station is "feline-approved" and ranges from jazz to R 'n' B. Plus, the station features interviews with various veterinarians and pet owners, as well. Oh, and the station's manager is none other than Rosen's own pet cat, Isis. Even the assistant manager and the program director are cats.

8 BRUMAS, THE PINK CAT

Brumas, a nine-year-old cat from Devon, England, was taking his usual stroll on September 3, 2005, and when he returned, his owners were surprised to see their pet's usual snow-white coat had turned a bright pink. "He was pink—Barbie pink. His head, ears, and right down his body, although not underneath, had gone a quite brilliant pink," said Joan Worth, the cat's owner. Worried, Joan and her husband Philip immediately went to the vet to examine Brumas. The vet said that Brumas was in good health, but they couldn't find an explanation for the cat's strange color. "They couldn't find any reason for it, although they decided it wasn't toxic, which was what I was worried about," said Mrs. Worth. Mr. Worth added, "We have thought about everything as to how this happened, from him being covered in some form of cow treatment to children's poster paints. We have no clue where he was that could have caused this to happen." However, paint is not believed to be the reason because Brumas' fur was not matted. As for Brumas, he seemed to be unaffected by the color change.

7 THE MEOW MIX HOUSE

Meow Mix, a popular cat food brand, launched the Meow Mix House, a reality TV series that followed a *Survivor* format. Ten cats chosen from various animal shelters across the country were pitted against each other in a battle of wits, brawn, and brain in a luxurious mansion on Madison Avenue in New York City. What's the first prize? A job as the feline Vice President of Research and Development in the Meow Mix Company. The reality series was shown on Animal Planet for ten straight weeks beginning June 16, 2006. Aside from the top prize, a second position in the company was awarded to the cat voted most popular by the viewers. The losers, however, got a year's supply of cat food, plus a new home and family, just like the two top winners. The top prize was given to Cisco from Miami, while Ellis from Portland won the popular vote.

6 PROJECT ACOUSTIC KITTY

Acoustic Kitty was a CIA project initiated by the Directorate of Science & Technology in the 1960s. It attempted to use cats in spy missions, particularly to bug secret conversations. It involved inserting a microphone and transmitter with battery to the body of the cat and wiring an antenna to its tail. The expenses used for the surgery and training were said to amount to 20 million dollars. However, when the project went on a trial run (a trial mission in which the cat was assigned to listen on two men in a park in Washington, D.C.), the project came to a halt when the test cat was run over by a taxi and killed. Due to the incident, not mentioning the various cons of the project, Acoustic Kitty was declared a failure.

5 GLOW-IN-THE-DARK CATS

In 2007, scientists at Gyeongsang National University in South Korea successfully created cloned cats that glow in the dark. The three white Turkish

Angora cats, weighing around 7 pounds each, were capable of glowing red under UV light. Here is a quotation from a report written by Alan Boyle, the science editor at msnbc.com, explaining the procedure: "They took skin cells from Turkish Angora female cats and used a virus to insert the genetic instructions for making red fluorescent protein. Then they put the gene-altered nuclei into eggs for cloning. The cloned embryos were implanted back into the donor cats, which effectively became the surrogate mothers for their own clones. Four kittens were born by cesarean section, but one of them died during the procedure, according to the *Korea Times*. The fact that the kittens' skin cells glowed under ultraviolet light served as evidence that they were really gene-altered clones."

4 FELINE CUTANEOUS ASTHENIA

Feline cutaneous asthenia (FCA) is a rare hereditary disease found in cats. The disorder, which is like a feline equivalent of the human disease Ehlers-Danlos syndrome, affects the way an afflicted cat's body produces collagen, an important component in skin tissue and tendons. The disorder has two forms, one caused by a dominant gene and one caused by a recessive gene. Both produce a similar symptom: abnormally soft and velvety skin that can easily tear. One common result of this is the formation of winglike folds or flaps on a cat's shoulders or back. FCA is said to be the cause of "winged" cats, like the cat owned by Granny Feng of Xianyang City, China, that has four-inch-long winglike appendages sprouting in its back.

3 THE MOSCOW CATS THEATER

Yuri Kuklachev, a former member of the Moscow State Circus, is the founder of the Moscow Cats Theater, a performing troupe that has 120 feline members. The idea for the troupe came to Kuklachev in 1971, when he saw a stray cat begging for food by standing on its hind legs. Realizing the cat's potential, he adopted it and soon incorporated it into his act at the state circus. Seventeen years later, Kuklachev left the state circus; two years after that he started the Moscow Cats Theater. The various acts that the troupe performs include tightrope walking, ball balancing, and riding a rocking horse. Maruska, one of the troupe's stars, can even do a handstand on Kuklachev's palm.

2 THE CAT WITH ETIQUETTE

When Faye Murrell's children left home, dining time became a lonely affair. So to have company at the table, she began giving her cat, Tessa, some table manners. The cat, a very quick learner, learned how to use a fork in no time flat. Not only that, but when noodles are served, Tessa can eat them with chopsticks, and when ice cream's on the table, she uses a spoon.

1 PIANO-PLAYING CAT

Nora, a gray tabby who was adopted from an animal shelter by music teacher Betsy Alexander, became a media sensation after a video of her playing the piano went on YouTube. Named after painter Leonora Carrington, she learned how to play by watching her owner's students practice while she sat under the piano. One night, she went up on the bench herself and started pawing the keys. With the encouragement of the owner, Nora's playing became a daily routine, and her performances were soon posted on YouTube. The videos found their way to the media, where they caught the attention of animal behaviorists, who find Nora an incredible case of animal intelligence. Her popularity made her an instant sensation, and she now has her own CD, DVD, and website.

10 BIZARRE SCIENTIFIC BELIEFS OF THE PAST

10 RAIN FOLLOWS THE PLOW

"Rain follows the plow" is the name given to a climatology concept that's now completely debunked. The theory said that human settlement caused a permanent increase in rainfall, thus enabling man to move to areas previously considered arid. It's this 19th-century theory that brought about the settlement of the Great Plains (previously known as the Great American Desert) and parts of South Australia. The theory was eventually refuted by climatologists, and in those arid areas of South Australia, drought brought an end to the attempted settlements.

9 WORLD ICE THEORY

This strange theory has a relatively normal name, but, rest assured, the concept is far from it. Hans Hörbiger, an Austrian engineer and inventor, received a vision in 1894 telling him that ice was the substance of all basic substances and had created the ice moons, ice planets, and a "global ether." He said, "I knew that Newton had been wrong and that the sun's gravitational pull ceases to exist at three times the distance of Neptune." Unbelievably, this theory got a great deal of support. One of the strongest supporters of the concept was Houston Stewart Chamberlain (British-born posthumous son-in-law of composer Richard Wagner), who went on to become one of the leading theorists behind the development of the Nazi Party in Germany.

8 ALCHEMY

Alchemy has its roots in ancient Egypt, where it combined with metallurgy in a form of early science. The Egyptian alchemists discovered the formulas for making mortar, glass, and cosmetics. From Egypt, the practice eventually spread to the rest of the ancient world and led to modern alchemy, in which men tried to turn metals into gold, to conjure up genies, and to perform all manner of bizarre, not-so-scientific activities. While alchemy has contributed in some ways to modern science, the discipline of true science caused the death of alchemy, which could not stand up to the rigorous testing of its pseudoscience.

7 CALIFORNIA ISLAND

From the 16th century, European experts in geography were convinced that California was an island separate from the North American mainland. Maps of the time show a large island on the left of the continent, and California continued to appear this way even into the 18th century. There was also a rumor that California was an earthly paradise like the Garden of Eden, or Atlantis. A romance novel from 1510 describes it thus:

> Know, that on the right hand of the Indies there is an island called California very close to the side of the Terrestrial Paradise; and it is peopled by black women, without any man among them, for they live in the manner of Amazons.—Las Sergas de Esplandián by Garci Rodríguez de Montalvo

The matter was finally put to rest indisputably on the 1774–76 expeditions of Juan Bautista de Anza. Interestingly, it's likely that within 25 million years, Baja

California and part of Southern California really will separate from North America due to tectonic plate movement.

6 GEOCENTRICITY

Geocentricity is the concept that the earth is the center of the universe and that all other objects move around it. The view was universally embraced in ancient Greece, and very similar ideas were held in ancient China. The idea was supported by the fact that the sun, stars, and planets appear to revolve around earth, and the physical perception that the earth is stable and not moving. This was combined with the belief that the earth was a sphere; belief in a flat earth was well gone by the 3rd century BC. The geocentric model was eventually displaced with the works of Copernicus, Galileo, and Kepler in the 16th century.

5 THE FOUR HUMORS

From classical antiquity right up to modern times, it was believed that the body contained four humors: blood, yellow bile, black bile, and phlegm. It was said that the right balance of these four humors made a person healthy, but an excess or decrease in any one would cause illness. Because of this belief, treatments of sickness included bloodletting, purges, and emetics. Occasionally, a mixture of herbs was used to restore balance. The concept of humors was not replaced until 1858, when Rudolf Virchow published theories of cellular pathology.

4 VITALISM

Vitalism states that the functions of living things are controlled by a "vital force" and not biophysical means. Vitalism has a long history in medical philosophies, and it has ties to the four humors (number 5 on this list). It's sometimes referred to as a "life spark," and even as the soul. In Eastern traditions, vitalism is essentially the same thing as *qi* or *chi*, which is heavily tied in to Eastern medicinal methods. The concept is (as can be expected) completely rejected by most mainstream scientists. In 1967, Francis Crick, the co-discoverer of the structure of DNA, stated, "And so to those of you who may be vitalists I would make this prophecy: what everyone believed yesterday, and you believe today, only cranks will believe tomorrow."

3 MATERNAL IMPRESSION

This is an old belief that a mother's thoughts while she's pregnant can impart special characteristics on the child in her womb. For many years, this idea was used to account for congenital disorders and birth defects. Maternal

impression was used to explain the disorder suffered by the Elephant Man: it was suggested that his mother was frightened by an elephant while she was pregnant with him, thereby imprinting the memory of an elephant on her child. Depression was also explained in this manner. If a mother had moments of strong sadness during pregnancy, it was believed that her child would ultimately suffer from depression in later life. Genetic theory caused the almost complete eradication of this belief in the 20th century.

2 PHLOGISTON

The theory of phlogiston dates to 1667 when German physicist Johann Joachim Bechera suggested that there was a fifth element (phlogiston) to go with the four classical elements (earth, water, air, and fire) which was contained within objects that could burn. It was believed that when an object burned, it released its phlogiston, an element without taste, mass, odor, or color, and left behind a powdery substance called "calx," which we now know to be oxide. Objects that burned in air were considered to be rich in phlogiston, and the fact that a fire burned out when oxygen was removed was seen as proof that oxygen could only absorb a limited amount of the substance. This theory also led to the idea that the human need to breathe had a sole function: to remove phlogiston from the body. The entire concept was superseded by Antoine-Laurent Lavoisier's discovery that combustion could only occur with the help of a gas such as oxygen.

1 SPONTANEOUS GENERATION

Before microscopes and theories of cells and germs, humans had other ideas about the creation of living things. They bizarrely believed that life arose from inanimate matter, such as maggots that come spontaneously from rotting meat. Proponents of this view (virtually everyone) used the Bible as a source of evidence, due to the fact that God made man from dust. However, the idea did exist before Christianity, and Aristotle said, in no uncertain terms, that some animals grow spontaneously and not from other animals of their kind. Earlier believers had to come up with some pretty strange ideas to make their theory work: Anaximander (a Greek philosopher who taught Pythagoras) believed that at some point in history, humans had been born from the soil spontaneously in adult form, otherwise they could never have survived. Before we laugh too hard at the ancients, we should note that many scientists right up to the 19th century believed this, and some even wrote recipe books for making animals. One such recipe calls for basil, placed between two bricks and left in sunlight, to make a scorpion. The theory was not finally put to rest until 1859, when Louis Pasteur proved it wrong once and for all.

10 ODD DISEASES WITH NO KNOWN CAUSE

10 GULF WAR SYNDROME

Gulf War syndrome is a relatively new disease that sprang up in the aftermath of the 1991 Persian Gulf war. Symptoms include birth defects in offspring of soldiers in the war and immune system faults. Some theories as to the cause of this disorder are that it is caused by the anthrax vaccine given to soldiers, or the use of depleted uranium for weaponry.

9 TWENTIETH-CENTURY DISEASE

If you have seen the very strange film *Safe* starring Julianne Moore, you'll be familiar with this controversial disease. Twentieth-century disease (also known as multiple-chemical sensitivity) is a chronic disorder in which a person seems to be allergic to virtually everything synthetic in the environment. Interestingly, when exposed to the chemicals in blind trials, the sufferers do not exhibit symptoms, but when told they are being exposed, they do.

8 STIFF PERSON SYNDROME

This is a horrifying disorder in which the sufferer has incredibly strong and painful spasms that cause their body to go rigid. The spasms can be caused by slight noises, such as the sound of a car horn. It can even be brought on by light touch and emotional distress. Many people with stiff person syndrome refuse to leave their homes due to the fear of a spasm.

7 MORGELLONS DISEASE

Morgellons disease is another controversial illness that some consider to not exist at all. The symptoms include crawling and tingling sensations around the body and finding fibers on or coming out of the skin. Despite the skepticism, when affected skin is studied under a microscope, it contains thousands of tiny hairs that do not appear to be human, plant, or synthetic.

6 CYCLIC VOMITING SYNDROME

Cyclic vomiting syndrome is when a person has repeated intense attacks of nausea, vomiting, and often headaches. It usually begins to appear in childhood and can last well into adulthood. Some sufferers have been known to vomit up to 12 times an hour. The cause is unknown, and there are no diagnostic tests to verify its presence.

5 ELECTROMAGNETIC HYPERSENSITIVITY

Electromagnetic hypersensitivity sounds like it comes straight out of Ripley's Believe It or Not. Those who suffer from the disorder are affected by electromagnetic fields such as those found near power stations. Sufferers are unable to distinguish between real and pretend exposure, which might suggest that it may be caused by hypochondria. The World Health Organization denies that there is any scientific basis for a person to be affected by electromagnetic fields.

4 NODDING DISEASE

The symptom of this serious disease, which leads to mental retardation in children, is pathological nodding. Perhaps the strangest aspect is that when the sufferer begins to eat or feels cold, the nodding begins, but the nodding ceases as soon as eating stops or the person becomes warm again.

3 PERUVIAN METEORITE ILLNESS

The Peruvian meteorite illness occurred in Peru when a meteorite fell to the earth in 2007. The impact created a large crater that began to leak water and steam. Shortly after, the local villagers began to suffer a variety of symptoms such as vomiting and confusion. As quickly as the disease came, it left, and there is no scientific consensus on what really happened that day.

2 SWEATING SICKNESS

Sweating sickness was a disease in medieval Europe. It swept across the continent multiple times until 1551, when it happened for the last time. The disease would strike suddenly, and death occurred within hours. Interestingly, the disease seemed to affect the rich more than the poor, and it took with it many members of royal households.

1 EXPLODING HEAD SYNDROME

This is a bizarre condition in which the sufferer experiences the sudden explosion of a very loud noise, which seems to originate in their own head. It's often described as the sound of loud voices, ringing, or waves crashing against rocks. The cause is unknown, but some doctors believe it may be caused by extreme fatigue and stress. Women are more likely to suffer it than men, and it can begin at any time in life.

10 BIZARRE HOME MENAGERIES

10 199TH STREET, NEW YORK

In September 2009, police raided a small home in Queens, New York, expecting to find the owners in possession of illegal substances. What they found was quite a bizarre surprise. The garage was littered with cages housing a monitor lizard, a baby python, and two iguanas. Also found at the home were: a baby caiman, four geckos, two marmosets, three tarantulas, seven adult pit bulls, one pit bull puppy, and a bulldog. The Center for Animal Care and Control was dispatched, and while the home itself was in a state of disrepair, reports were that the animals were fairly well taken care of.

9 A MODERN-DAY NOAH'S ARK

Former cab driver turned New York real estate billionaire Tamir Sapir, 61, had his luxury yacht boarded by the U.S. Customs and Border Protection in late

2007. Officers seized approximately $85,000 worth of specimens, including: bar stools upholstered with python and anaconda skin, seven carved elephant tusks, hides of jaguars, tigers, and zebras, a cigarette holder made from python skin, a cigar box wrapped in elephant hide, a zebra-skin-lined children's bed, and a fully stuffed and mounted lion. Sapir was charged with 29 counts of attempting to import items in violation of the Endangered Species Act and slapped with a $150,000 fine. A statement from his attorney explained that Sapir was not trying to smuggle the goods into America, but they were simply part of the decor of his "home away from home."

8 POLISH–UKRAINIAN BORDER

On a passenger bus traveling from Poland to Ukraine, border officials were conducting a routine inspection for prohibited items. All seemed fine until they reached the cargo hold, where, packed into various-sized luggage, they discovered: two miniature kangaroos, five miniature ponies (each about 20 inches in height), and 11 pheasants. One of the ponies appeared to be pregnant. The bus driver denied knowledge of any illegal activity and claimed the luggage was delivered to him with instructions to transport them to an unknown person in Lviv, Ukraine.

7 JANESVILLE, WISCONSIN

Local residents phoned police and the Rock County Humane Society when they became disturbed by the presence of a dog tied to the second-story balcony of a house. Upon entering the home, they discovered: six chickens, 13 rabbits, two ball pythons, one cat, a snapping turtle, several cages full of mice and rats, and, according to the source, "one native snake of unknown origin." Officials released the turtle and snake into the wild, while the remaining animals went to the care of the Humane Society. It's believed that the owners were planning to sell the animals, except for the rats and mice, which were used as food for the pythons.

6 GERMANTOWN, WISCONSIN

Police received several reports of a foul stench coming from a suburban Wisconsin home belonging to a woman named Jamie Verburgt. State Conservation Warden William Mitchell was asked to inspect the property, where he found nearly 200 animals, including: alligators, scorpions, 70 ducks, snakes, rats, turtles, toads, and carnivorous beetles. In an adjacent garage, Mitchell discovered the decaying corpses of "roadkill," which the owner had used to feed the animals. On top of this, carcasses of raccoons, rabbits, opossums, and squirrels were found in the owner's freezer. In a very closely related case, four years earlier, Verburgt's boyfriend, John Walters, was prosecuted for mistreatment of exotic animals. At the time, his home was raided by police, who seized a female cougar, a female leopard, a silver-tailed fox, a monitor lizard, two caracals, a coatimundi, a chinchilla, and a reticulated python.

5 APACHE JUNCTION, ARIZONA

Approximately 185 animals were found living in deplorable condition at a home in Apache Junction, Arizona. Neighbors suspected mistreatment of animals and made several pleading phone calls to police before any action was taken. Included were 47 dogs, 96 rabbits, 18 chickens, 13 goats, six horses, two cats, a pot-bellied pig, an African parrot, and a cockatiel. In a muddy area on the other side of the property, police found a horse, undernourished and poorly cared for; it was euthanized shortly after.

4 BARI, ITALY

A man was pulled over for a routine traffic check, and police were astonished when he opened his hatchback to reveal over 1000 animals cramped into the small space. There were 1000 terrapins, 216 budgies, 300 white mice, 150 hamsters, 30 Japanese squirrels, and six chameleons. The driver, Francesco Lombardo, admitted to smuggling the animals across Europe with the intention of selling them.

3 MICHAEL JACKSON'S NEVERLAND

How could we talk menageries without mention of Michael Jackson's collection of strange and wonderful animals? Since Jackson's death in June 2009, all the animals have been sent to new homes. Among the more memorable were Bubbles, the chimpanzee (sent to the Center for Great Apes, Wauchulu, Florida), Bengal tigers Thriller and Sabu (sent to Shambala, California), Rikki the African parrot (with Freddie Hancock at the Voices of the Wild Foundation), pythons, giraffes, anacondas, and two black caimans.

2 NOAH'S ARK, CHINA

This may be one for a Marine Mysteries list. In 2007, a deserted cargo ship was discovered off the coast of Qingzhou Island, China, after having lost engine power. On board were up to 5000 of some of the world's rarest species of animals. Packed into cramped wooden crates were 31 pangolins, 2720 monitor lizards, 44 leatherback turtles, 1130 Brazilian turtles, 21 bear paws wrapped in newspaper, and what was suspected to be an Asian giant turtle. The animals were transported to the nearby Guangdong Wild Animal Protection Centre.

1 HACIENDA NAPOLES

This famous 7.7-square-mile estate owned by drug lord Pablo Escobar is one of the largest privately owned menageries ever found. At the height of Escobar's success in the 1980s, he imported rare and expensive animals from all over the world. The zoo included giraffes, ostriches, elephants, ponies, rare antelopes, hippopotamuses, zebras, buffalos, camels, lions, an ocelot, and several species of exotic birds. After Escobar's death in 1993, many of the animals became property of the Colombian government, except for two hippopotamuses that escaped and were later shot dead by authorities. Today, Hacienda Napoles is an official zoo and considered a major tourist attraction.

15 TRULY BIZARRE CREATURES

15 KING VULTURE

Vultures are usually seen as dull, ugly, black birds. The king vulture, however, is a colorful creature. Its body is white on the top and black on the bottom, while its head is covered with colors ranging from red, orange, and yellow to blue and purple. It also has a wattle on its head. It doesn't have a voice box, but can still make low noises. According to Mayan mythology, these birds were the messengers of the gods, and when you look at one, you can see why.

14 JAPANESE SPIDER CRAB

The largest living arthropod, this huge crab has legs that can reach up to 13 feet in length and 45 pounds in weight! They are also said to live up to 100 years. Enjoy your nightmares!

13 SEA SPIDERS

These spiderlike creatures live in various depths of marine bodies. Their most notable characteristic, other than their habitat, is their huge legs (at least compared to the size of their bodies). They have no respiratory system; instead, they use diffusion to survive. The largest of these belong to the *Colossendeis colossea* species.

12 WHIP SCORPIONS

These frightening arachnids have large pedipalps (pincers) and "whips" at the end of their abdomen. More notably, they can spray various chemicals from their abdomen, including formic acid, chlorine, and a mixture of acetic acid and octanoic acid, depending on the species. The last spray has a vinegarlike smell, hence the whip scorpions' alternate name, vinegarroons. Similar creatures include whip spiders (also known as tailless whip scorpions) and micro whip scorpions.

11 UPSIDE-DOWN CATFISH

As their name states, these African fish are often found swimming upside down. It's thought they do this so they can reach food on the water's surface, such as insect eggs. Their coloration is also reversed: unlike most fish, their belly is darker than their back. This is to give them camouflage from predators who hunt them from above. They're popular aquarium fish and might be available at your local pet shop.

10 WATER BEARS

These tiny, caterpillarlike creatures are some of the most amazing in existence. They can live practically anywhere, from hot springs to arctic regions. More amazingly, they can enter a cryonic state that makes them almost impervious to environmental hazards. They can briefly survive temperatures of over 300°F, as well as near–absolute zero temperatures. They can withstand massive pressure, radiation, and even the deadly vacuum of space. In the cryonic state, their metabolisms grind to a near halt. They are most frequently found on mosses, lichens, and other damp places.

9 VAMPIRE MOTH
Not all butterflies and moths drink nectar: the vampire moth literally drinks blood! It uses its proboscis to pierce the skin of its target and drink the creature's blood. And yes, they occasionally bite humans. Fortunately, they do not cause any known diseases, but only the males bite.

8 MEGALOPYGE OPERCULARIS
These moths are very furry, especially as caterpillars. Known by several names, such as the pussy moth, puss caterpillar, southern flannel moth, and asp caterpillar, this moth is said to look like a Persian cat as a caterpillar. It may look "pet-able," but do *not* touch it! Like many caterpillars, these insects have a defense mechanism: those hairs are actually venomous spines. Touching one won't kill you, but it will *hurt* and cause a rash. First-aid is recommended if you accidentally make contact with one of these caterpillars. It uses its fur as its cocoon.

7 GIRAFFE WEEVIL
As you might expect, these weevils (although only the males) have long, slender necks to help in building nests. They are also quite colorful, and are mostly black with a red body.

6 DWARF SPERM WHALE
The sperm whale is a mighty creature. It's the largest of the tooth whales, dives to incredible depths, and is known to eat massive squids. However, this dwarf species is the smallest known whale. It's not much bigger than a human adult in length. Like a similar species, the pygmy sperm whale, it can expel a reddish substance to ward off predators.

5 CNEMIDOPHORUS UNIPARENS
These lizards might look normal on the outside, but on closer investigation, a surprising fact is revealed: some species, such as the New Mexico whiptail, consist entirely of females. They undergo parthenogenesis, which is embryo fertilization without a male, to produce new offspring. Despite this, however, these lizards still "mate" to increase fertility.

4 ANDEAN COCK-OF-THE-ROCK

The females of this species of bird are normal enough, but the males have an odd crest that looks like a large, red-orange bulge. Their feathers consist of reds and oranges in the front, black near the bottom, and a bit of gray. They are the national bird of Peru.

3 COCONUT CRAB

The largest living arthropod to dwell on land (weighing up to 9 pounds), this hermit crab is known to climb trees and eat coconuts. Unlike other hermit crabs, only the juveniles wear shells. The older crabs often wear coconut shells. They come in a variety of colors, such as orange and blue, and are rumored to steal shiny objects.

2 HAIRY FROG

This African frog gets its name from the hairlike structures found on the sides of the males. These hairs are used to increase the rate that the frog absorbs oxygen, since the males spend long periods of time guarding their eggs. Another impressive fact about these frogs is that they have retractable claws made of bone (as opposed to keratin). However, to get these claws out, the frog must break a bone nodule first. Ouch!

1 BARRELEYE FISH

Although this fish's existence has been known for quite some time, it was only in 2010 that scientists fully understood how bizarre it is. It has a mostly black body with a transparent head, which made it difficult to study since the head always shattered while the fish was being brought up to the surface of the water. Although it has two indentions in the front of its head, those are *not* its eyes, which are the green spheres in its transparent head. These eyes can be used to look above for food or look forward when stalking prey.

10 BIZARRE AND DREADFUL MENTAL DISORDERS

10 ZOOSADISM

Zoosadism, as its name implies, is when a person takes pleasure—often sexual—from causing animals to suffer. It is one of the three behaviors considered to be a precursor to sociopathic behavior and is, consequently, seen very frequently in the childhoods of serial killers. Studies have shown that at least 36 percent of sexual murderers have confessed to having abused animals in childhood; nearly one quarter of them expressed interest in zoosexual acts.

9 AUTASSASSINOPHILIA

There isn't a lot of information about this disorder, but I can assure you—it's weird! A person who suffers from autassassinophilia needs to put himself into a position of danger in order to become sexually aroused. The unfortunate upshot to this disorder is that it's not entirely uncommon for the sufferer to die in the process.

8 FOLIE À DEUX

Folie à deux means "madness shared by two." This is a truly bizarre disorder in which two people living in close proximity to one another share a mental disorder; in other words, the psychosis seems to spread from one person to another. Even stranger is the fact that there are reported cases of this occurring not just between two people but among entire families who all end up suffering from the same delusion. In those cases, the disorder is called *folie en famille*.

7 HYBRISTOPHILIA

We've all heard of people who fall madly in love with murderers on death row. These people are most likely suffering from hybristophilia, which is a sexual attraction to people who have committed an outrageous or gruesome crime. It's also sometimes referred to as "Bonnie and Clyde syndrome" and explains the large amounts of fan mail that killers often receive in jail.

6 VAGINISMUS

Vaginismus is a strange (and fortunately rare) disorder in which a woman is unable to engage in vaginal penetration (including the insertion of tampons) due to clamping of the pubococcygeus muscle. The cause is unknown but is considered to most likely be due to fear of painful sex, or the belief that sex is wrong and shameful.

5 TELEPHONICOPHILIA

We've all made crank calls in our youth (and if you say you haven't, you're lying!), but did you know there's a name for it, and it's even considered to be a disorder? Telephonicophilia is when a person gets sexual pleasure from making obscene phone calls. Most likely these are the heavy-breathing type, but who knows. Next time you get an obscene call, you might have a better idea of what's going on down on the other end of the line.

4 SYNESTHESIA

Synesthesia, while weird, can actually be a very useful disorder. The synesthete (one suffering from the disorder) exhibits all kinds of unusual characteristics relating to the senses. For example, some will see letters in color, making it easier to remember how to spell words, while others can smell or hear color or words. In a more bizarre twist, sufferers might mix sound and taste so that different noises have different tastes. It may be wise for synesthetes to avoid the brown note (if you don't know what that is, you don't want to).

3 PIBLOKTO

Piblokto (or Arctic hysteria) is a disorder exclusive to Eskimo groups in the Arctic Circle. It occurs mostly in winter, and the symptoms include hysteria (screaming and wild behavior), coprophagia (poop eating), insensitivity to the cold (leading to naked midnight runs in the snow), and more. It's mostly found in women and could be linked to a lack of vitamin A.

2 JUMPING FRENCHMEN OF MAINE

Jumping Frenchmen of Maine, a bizarre disorder with an equally bizarre name, is a rare mental disorder in which the slightest sound can cause the sufferer to become excessively startled, which makes them flail and jump around. Even odder, when a person with this disorder is given a loud direct order, they immediately obey with no control. For example, a sufferer will obey instantly if told to punch someone in the face.

1 WENDIGO PSYCHOSIS

Wendigo psychosis is a horrifying disease that makes a person crave human flesh and believe they're becoming a cannibal. It's mostly found in remote communities of aboriginal peoples. Strangely, witch doctors seem to have a considerably good success rate of curing this disorder. It's believed by some that wendigo psychosis may be behind some vampire and werewolf legends.

15 UNUSUAL PREHISTORIC CREATURES

15 DEINOTHERIUM

This genus of elephantlike creatures was not only huge, but it also had a pair of chin tusks. These odd tusks might have been used to dig up the soil to gain access to roots and vegetables. They also had relatively short trunks compared to other Proboscideans. They ranged from 12 to 15 feet high, making them one of the largest mammals to ever walk the earth.

14 THERIZINOSAURIDAES

This family of strange, mysterious theropods was notable for its long necks and large claws. However, unlike most other theropods, they were primarily herbivores. Some of them may have had feathers. The genus that the family is named after, *Therizinosaurus*, is actually only known from a few fossils, but their claws were quite large, likely reaching a meter in length.

13 EPIDEXIPTERYX

This birdlike dinosaur reveals an interesting part about the evolutionary history of birds. This member of the Scansoriopterygidae ("climbing wings") family had no flight feathers, but it did have four long tail feathers that were likely used in displays. Due to the dinosaur's age (it lived in China around 152 to 168 million years ago), it provides evidence that feathers, not surprisingly, evolved several million years before flight did. It was also one of the smallest dinosaurs, reaching just ten inches in height (not counting its feathers); that's about the size of a pigeon.

12 EPIDENDROSAURUS
Another birdlike dinosaur, this one belonged in the same family as Epidexipteryx. It's currently the earliest dinosaur known to have adapted for life in the trees, an important moment in the evolution of birds. More bizarrely, this dinosaur had an oddly long third finger, twice the length of its other ones. They may have been used to dig for insects.

11 MICRORAPTOR
Yet another birdlike dinosaur, this animal had four wings (and a feathered tail), although it could not fly. Instead, it likely glided from place to place, kind of like a flying squirrel. It's likely that this creature is one of the most recent common ancestors between birds and dinosaurs, its gliding ability eventually evolving into flight. Unfortunately for the genus, one fossil was used in a forgery, along with a fossil of a primitive bird, Yanornis, to create a fake fossil that was said to be the ultimate missing link between birds and dinosaurs: an archeoraptor. Although it could have been caught before the public noticed, it was published in *National Geographic* before it could be peer reviewed. When the fraud was exposed, it was quite embarrassing to the scientific community.

10 LONGISQUAMA
Living during the Triassic period, longisquama was a small, lizardlike creature that appears to have had a series of long feathers on its back. This implies that birds might have not evolved from theropods, but lizardlike reptiles instead. Of course, things are not always what they seem. Some scientists think the longisquama's "feathers" are just specially modified scales. Others think that the fossil's form is an optical illusion and that the feathers are just fern fronds. Due to the large number of feathered dinosaur fossils, it seems that these two possibilities are more likely.

9 TANYSTROPHEUS

When I describe a long-necked reptile, most people think of sauropods or even plesiosaurs. This Triassic reptile was neither of these. The tanystropheus was 20 feet long, but it had a 10-foot-long neck! Evidence indicates that this was a fish-eating reptile, since fossils of it have been found in mainly partially aquatic fossil sites, and fish scales and cephalopod tentacles have been found in their stomachs. They might have stayed on the beach, using their long necks to help them devour fish from the sea. It is also thought to have been at least semiaquatic.

8 SHAROVIPTERYX

Another gliding reptile, this Triassic critter glided similarly to the microraptor. However, the sharovipteryx had two "wings" on its hind legs and two small "wings" on its front legs. It might have used its wings while jumping from place to place on the ground. Some scientists think it was related to pterosaurs, but because it had wings on its legs instead of its arms, this link is questionable.

7 NYCTOSAURUS

This genus of pterosaurs is the only one that did not have claws on its wings. Otherwise, most species looked similar to the famous pterodon, until a new, as-yet-unnamed species was discovered in 2003. The species had a huge, antlerlike crest, larger than any other pterosaur's crest. Some speculate that there was a flap of tissue in between these antlers, like some other pterosaurs, which could have been used like a sail to enhance its flight. However, research shows that a crest that large would actually impair its flight, so it likely just had an odd set of antlers.

6 PTERODAUSTRO

This pterosaur had an unusual set of teeth, similar to the baleen of some whales. It almost certainly used these teeth to eat small, aquatic organisms, similar to the way a flamingo eats brine shrimp. Since flamingos get their pinkish hue from their diet, Pterodaustro might have been pinkish, too.

5 DUNKLEOSTEUS

One of the scariest creatures ever to live in the ocean, this devonian fish could grow up to 33 feet long, had an armored face, and likely had one of the strongest bites in history! It used a beaklike mouth instead of teeth to devour its prey. It was one of the largest of the Placoderms, a group of armored fish that are now extinct.

4 STETHACANTHUS

Sharks have lasted for over 400 million years. Although they have remained relatively unchanged throughout the fossil record, there have definitely been some oddballs. This particular shark had an anvil-shaped dorsal fin with small spikes on it, and also had a very bizarre growth on its head. The fin could have been used for courting mates or for defense.

3 HELICOPRION

This bizarre fossil was originally thought to be an ammonite, as the fossil looked like a spiraling, circular shell. However, after some examination, it was revealed that it wasn't a shell, but a spiraling set of shark teeth, a "tooth whirl." Unfortunately, cartilage doesn't fossilize as well as bone, so there wasn't much body to examine, and a guessing game began. The tooth whirl was thought to be on the shark's dorsal fin, tail, or even its snout. Thankfully, a skull of a related shark, ornithoprion, was found to have a tooth whirl on its lower jaw. The tooth whirl likely contained all of the shark's teeth that it would use in its life: its older teeth would be moved away to make room for its newer, better teeth. This didn't solve the problem, however. The tooth whirl was then placed on the tip of the lower jaw, but it turns out that would actually slow down the shark. Perhaps the most accurate representation is one in which the tooth whirl existed deep in the animal's mouth instead.

2 DEINOCHEIRUS

The only fossil of this dinosaur is a pair of arms, which look like they belonged to an ornithomimid, but they were eight feet long. This means that either the deinocheirus towered over the rest of the ornithomimids and most theropods, or it simply had very long arms for its body. The use of its arms is debated: some say it used them to tear apart large dinosaurs; others say that the claws were too blunt, so they were used as defensive weapons. Some have even said that the deinocheirus used its huge arms to climb trees, although this hypothesis is widely disregarded. Once again, the lack of a body in the fossil leaves many questions unanswered.

1 AMPHICOELIAS FRAGILLIMUS

This elusive fossil was discovered by the famed paleontologist Edward Drinker Cope, the same man who competed with Othniel Charles Marsh in the infamous "bone wars." Cope discovered many prehistoric fossils, but this one is by far the oddest. The only fossil that exists of it was a single vertebra fragment. It was 5 feet high, and estimated to be 8.8 feet high if the entire fossil were intact. (Compare that to *your* vertebrae!) Estimates vary, but they range from 131 to 196 feet in length, making it, by far, the longest creature ever, competing with the blue whale for being the heaviest creature ever (along with another, very elusive sauropod, bruhathkayosaurus). But, as luck would have it, the fossil just disappeared. It vanished without a trace. Was it a hoax? A misconception? Or was it really the largest animal to ever walk the earth? Sadly, we will probably never know.

10 BIZARRE MEDICAL TREATMENTS

10 SWEAT THERAPY

Sweat therapy is when excessive sweating is induced in order to make a person healthier. The practice has existed for thousands of years, like in Native American sweat lodges, for example. Despite its prevalence, there is very little scientific information on the practice and its supposed benefits.

9 MUD

We are all familiar with the use of clay in health resorts where people bathe in it to improve skin conditions, but what many people don't know is that clay (or mud) is also used in internal medicine. It's sometimes used as a coating on pills and is also consumed in larger doses for the treatment of bowel disorders. Even NASA uses clay treatments to deal with bone depletion in astronauts.

8 ELECTROCUTION

Electroconvulsive therapy is well-known from stories such as *One Flew Over the Cuckoo's Nest*, but despite the horrifying attitude that most of us have toward it, it's still commonly used in the treatment of severe depression, catatonia, and bipolar disorder. It was first used in the 1930s, and today it's estimated that up to 1 million people receive the treatment annually.

7 DOUSING

Dousing is an odd therapy in which water (usually cold) is poured or thrown over a person in order to create a shock reaction. Many people believe that this odd treatment kills harmful bacteria and leaves the good, stronger bacteria. There is no scientific evidence to support this at all.

6 URINE THERAPY

Urine therapy is when a person consumes urine or uses it for cosmetic reasons. A practitioner of urine therapy is sometimes called a psychopath. Just kidding—they're actually called uropaths. While some evidence exists to support the benefits of urine drinking, there are also obvious risks involved.

5 BLOODLETTING

Bloodletting is the practice of removing blood from a patient by various methods. It was originally thought to balance the humors (a medieval medical concept) and was almost always harmful to the patient. But bloodletting is still one of the most effective treatments of excess iron in the bloodstream, and it's also used for treatment of excess red blood cells, which can occur in diseases such as porphyria. In the old method, the patient was cut and a suction cup was placed over the wound to draw out blood. In modern medicine, syringes are used.

4 LEECH THERAPY

Leeches were not only popular in early history, they are extremely popular now. They're particularly helpful for clearing away debris and infection after

 surgery. In order to avoid some of the side effects that can occur through using leeches, scientists have invented "mechanical leeches," which do much the same job with far less risk of secondary infection.

3 HELMINTHIC THERAPY

Helminthic therapy is the intentional consumption of parasitic worms. People who use this treatment often consider it a cure-all and will use it for hay fever, asthma, and autoimmune diseases. The worms are taken orally, and after a number of weeks, worming tablets are taken to expel them. Efficacious or not, this is a treatment I never want to undergo.

2 FECAL BACTERIOTHERAPY

If you're eating, stop before you continue reading. Fecal bacteriotherapy is when a patient is given enemas containing poop from a healthy donor. It's bad enough thinking of an enema of your own poop, but this is an enema of a total stranger's. This therapy is used for the treatment of inflammatory bowel disorders such as ulcerative colitis. Oh, and just when you thought it couldn't get worse, sometimes the poop isn't delivered by enema, but instead through a tube inserted in the nose.

1 SMOKING

Smoking was long prescribed for a variety of illnesses, and even today some doctors still recommend it when the danger levels associated with other drug treatments are higher. Interestingly, there's evidence that smokers have a 50-percent-less chance of developing Alzheimer's and Parkinson's diseases. But I'm not a doctor, so I don't recommend it.

10 BIZARRE AND FASCINATING MEDICAL TALES

10 MAN WITH VULCAN BLOOD

Remember Mr. Spock and his green Vulcan blood in *Star Trek*? Apparently, it can happen. In October 2005, at St. Paul's Hospital in Vancouver, doctors were inserting an arterial line into a 42-year-old patient to relieve pressure in his legs after he fell asleep in a kneeling position when they were startled to see dark green blood trickle out of the patient instead of the usual bright red. The doctors' initial diagnosis was methemoglobin, a dangerous condition in which the hemoglobin in blood can't bind to oxygen. Analysis of the samples taken from the patient revealed another condition called sulfhemoglobinemia, a rare condition in which hydrogen sulfide combines with ferric ions in blood to form sulfhemoglobin, which causes the blood to turn dark green. According to the doctors, the disorder can be triggered by excessive doses of medications containing sulfonamides (in this case, sumatriptan, a migraine medication, although the true cause of the green blood is still unclear). The disorder usually goes away with red blood cell turnover, although blood transfusions may be needed in extreme cases.

9. WOMAN WITH TWO SETS OF DNA

When Karen Keegan, a 52-year-old Boston teacher, needed a kidney transplant, her three sons were tested to see if they were acceptable donors. Soon the tests revealed that two of Keegan's sons didn't match her genetic profile. Further tests showed that Keegan has chimerism, a condition in which two fraternal twins grow in the womb, but the first twin "absorbs" the other twin; the resulting embryo then contains two different sets of DNA, often in different parts of the body. To prove that Keegan is indeed the boys' mother, doctors began tracking the second DNA set in her body and found it in her thyroid gland.

8 MYSTERIOUS CASE OF NATALIE ADLER

Natalie Adler, a young woman from Melbourne, Australia, is the victim of an extremely rare disorder that left her practically blind three days out of every six. Her eyes will suddenly close involuntarily, and she cannot open them until three days later, when they will open again. It first started one Sunday morning when she was 11 years old. She had just contracted a sinus infection and a staph infection and woke up with swollen eyes. After that, the condition started. At first the clamping of the eyes occurred randomly, but after a while, it began following a cycle. Hundreds of eye specialists have run tests on Adler, but haven't found a direct cause or a cure for the disorder. For two years, however, doctors treated Adler using Botox injections on her face, making her see five days out of six, but the treatment no longer works.

7 PENCIL IN HER HEAD

After suffering numerous headaches and nosebleeds for 55 years, Margaret Wegner finally underwent surgery in August 2007. What was the surgery for? To remove a three-inch pencil that was lodged in her head after a childhood accident when she was four years old. Due to lack of technology and fear of irreversibly damaging Wegner's head, doctors delayed the removal of the pencil for more than five decades until the doctors found the exact location of the pencil in her head and safely took most of it out. "This was something unique because the trauma was so old," said Dr. Hans Behrbohm, an ear, nose, and throat specialist at Berlin's Park-Klinik Weissensee, who pinpointed the location of the pencil. "She shouldn't suffer any longer," he said.

6 GIRL WHO LAUGHED NONSTOP

Xu Pinghui, a 12-year-old girl from Chongqing, China, started laughing nonstop after developing a fever when she was just eight months old. Because of the mysterious condition, the girl lost the ability to speak at two years old and can only communicate through giggling. The cause of the disease is still a mystery, although doctors say that it might have been caused by damage to the frontal lobe due to the fever, and specialists are currently testing the theory.

5 IMPALED WITH A FAUCET

Yi Zhao, a 57-year-old man from Chongqing, China, was rushed into the emergency room after accidentally impaling his eye socket with a bathroom faucet after firefighters cut off the pipes. At the hospital, the faucet made it impossible to perform a CT scan, so a plumber was called to remove a foot of pipe jutting out of his eye. When it didn't work, an impatient Zhao decided to remove the faucet himself, with the doctor's guidance. Miraculously, there was little damage to the eye and no damage to the brain, but only fractures to the facial bones.

4 MAN "DIED" 100 TIMES

Jim McClatchey, 54 years old, of Atlanta, Georgia, was rushed to the hospital by his wife after she found him on the floor of their house unconscious. Doctors who were trying to revive him ended up shocking his heart 100 times as the patient kept having repeated cardiac arrests due to an unknown virus. In the first hour alone, McClatchey's heart stopped an incredible 50 times! He had to be defibrillated so frequently that he suffered second-degree burns to his chest. Bad pun alert: shockingly, he survived the ordeal and was back at work in no time flat.

3 HEART RECIPIENT
William Sheridan of New York was just recovering from a heart transplant when he inexplicably developed a passion for art and started making beautiful sketches. The 63-year-old found out later that his organ donor was an artist. This odd phenomenon, called cellular memory, is the theory that the brain is not the only part of the body that contains memory and human traits, and that other organs such as the heart and hands can contain them, too. Several studies have focused on this phenomenon, a notable one being Dr. Paul Peasall's study entitled "Changes in Heart Transplant Recipients That Parallel the Personalities of Their Donor," which was published in *Near-Death Studies* magazine in 2002.

2 EIGHT-LIMBED GIRL
Lakshmi Tatma, a girl born in 2005 in Bihar, India, was born a conjoined twin, with her parasitic twin's headless body joined to her at her pelvis, giving her the appearance of having four arms and four legs. Lakshmi (named after the many-armed Hindu goddess of wealth) has a rare condition called isciopagus, where her twin stopped developing in the womb and her remaining fetus absorbed the underdeveloped twin's body. Aside from the eight limbs, Lakshmi has two spines, four kidneys, two stomachs, and two chest cavities. That is, she did until she underwent a successful 27-hour surgery at a hospital in Bangalore to remove the extra parts.

1 THE MIRACLE WALKER
Mark Chenoweth gets the top spot on this list for his amazing story. Chenoweth, who has spent the past ten years in a wheelchair, was born with spina bifida, a crippling disease that left him unable to walk. In 1998, he consulted his doctor about taking scuba diving lessons, which the doctor immediately forbade. Against his doctor's orders, he took a vacation to Minorca and managed to persuade a diving center to give him scuba lessons. Diving to a depth of 55 feet, after he surfaced, he found out that he could walk again. Three days later, his legs lost sensation once more, so he immediately went back to scuba diving. After a while, he noticed that the deeper he got, the longer the time he could walk after. Now Chenoweth now uses his wheelchair only twice a year. It's not exactly known why this happened, but one theory suggests that the rich mix of

oxygen in the aqualungs divers use affected the nerve cells afflicted by the spina bifida, making them work temporarily.

10 EXTREMELY STRANGE PHOBIAS

10 AGYROPHOBIA—FEAR OF CROSSING THE STREET

Agyrophobics have a fear of crossing streets, highways, and other thoroughfares, or a fear of thoroughfares themselves. This, of course, makes it very difficult to live comfortably in a city. The word comes from the Greek *gyrus*, which means "turning" or "whirling," and agyrophobics avoid the whirl of traffic. The phobia covers several categories, wherein sufferers may specifically fear wide roads or suburban single-lane streets, and can also include a fear of jaywalking or crossing anywhere on a street, even a designated intersection. This phobia is considered independent from the fear of cars.

9 MAGEIROCOPHOBIA—FEAR OF COOKING

The name of this bizarre fear comes from the Greek word *mageirokos*, which means "a person who is skilled in cooking." This disorder can be debilitating and potentially lead to unhealthy eating if the sufferer lives alone. Mageirocophobics can feel extremely intimidated by people with cooking skills, and this intimidation and feeling of inadequacy is probably the root cause of the disorder for many.

8 PEDIOPHOBIA—FEAR OF DOLLS

Pediophobia is the irrational fear of dolls. Not just scary dolls—*all* dolls. Strictly speaking, the fear is a horror of a "false representation of sentient beings," so it also usually includes robots and mannequins, which can make it decidedly difficult to go shopping. This phobia should not be confused with pedophobia, also called pediaphobia, which is the fear of children. Sigmund Freud believed pediophobia may spring from a fear of the doll coming to life, and roboticist

Masahiro Mori expanded on that theory by stating that the more humanlike something becomes, the more repellent its nonhuman aspects appear.

7 DEIPNOPHOBIA—FEAR OF DINNER CONVERSATION

Admittedly, some dinner conversations can be very awkward, but some people are so terrified of the idea of speaking to another person over dinner that they avoid dining-out situations. In olden times, there were strict rules of etiquette that helped a person to deal with these situations, but they are (sadly) mostly forgotten now.

6 EISOPTROPHOBIA—FEAR OF MIRRORS

Eisoptrophobia is a fear of mirrors in the broad sense, or more specifically the fear of being put into contact with the spiritual world through a mirror. Sufferers experience undue anxiety even though they realize their fear is irrational. Because the fear often is grounded in superstitions, eisoptrophobics may worry that breaking a mirror will bring bad luck or that looking into a mirror will put them in contact with a supernatural world inside the glass. After writing this list, I realized that I suffer from a minor form of this disorder in that I don't like to look into a mirror in the evening when I am alone for fear of seeing someone (or something) behind me.

5 DEMONOPHOBIA—FEAR OF DEMONS

Demonophobia is an abnormal and persistent fear of evil supernatural beings in people who believe such beings exist and roam freely to cause harm. Those who suffer from this phobia realize their fear is excessive or irrational. Nevertheless, they become unduly anxious when discussing demons, when venturing alone into woods or dark houses, or when watching films about demonic possession and exorcism. Sufferers are most likely to be recognized by the strings of garlic around their neck or by carrying crucifixes, wooden stakes, and guns loaded with silver bullets. (Okay, I made that last part up.)

4 PENTHERAPHOBIA—FEAR OF A MOTHER-IN-LAW

Of all the phobias on this list, pentheraphobia is probably the most common. I'm sure that most married people have, at one time or another, suffered from this terrible fear. It's so common in Western society that it frequently appears in movies and other forms of entertainment. Of the many available therapies for this illness of the mind, divorce seems to be the most popular. A related phobia is novercaphobia, which is a fear of your stepmother, the most famous sufferer of which is Cinderella.

3 ARACHIBUTYROPHOBIA—FEAR OF PEANUT BUTTER STICKING TO THE ROOF OF YOUR MOUTH

I must say that finding information on this disorder is extremely difficult, which does make me wonder if it's perhaps the figment of an overactive imagination, but it's definitely bizarre and fairly well known, so it seems to deserve a place here. This disorder seems to be a fear that is quite easily worked around: don't buy peanut butter. However, for a child who is forced to eat peanut butter and jelly sandwiches every day, one can see how it might cause severe trauma in later life. Here is the testimony of one alleged sufferer: "Whenever I'm around peanut butter, I start to sweat excessively and my body starts convulsing. The roof of my mouth becomes coarse and itchy. I can't live with this fear anymore. My thirst for peanut butter must be quenched without me going into a full-blown panic attack."

2 CATHISOPHOBIA—FEAR OF SITTING

Cathisophobia (sometimes spelled with a "k") is a fear of sitting down. This disorder can be sparked by a particularly nasty case of hemorrhoids, but in some serious cases it can be due to physical abuse related to sitting on sharp or painful objects. Sometimes the sitting fear comes from punishment in the sufferer's school days, or it may be an indication of some other phobia, like sitting in front of elite and influential people. Cathisophobia is characterized by sweating, heavy or short breath, and anxiety.

1 AUTOMATONOPHOBIA—FEAR OF A VENTRILOQUIST'S DUMMY

I think we can all see the merit in this disorder; the very act of ventriloquism seems particularly nasty to me. It involves a man with his hand up a doll's butt, and then he proceeds to talk to the dummy. Sufferers of automatonophobia need not seek treatment—it's a perfectly valid reaction to a perfectly revolting concept. I think that is enough said on this topic.

11 UNBELIEVABLE MINIATURES

11 SEASHELLS IN THE SAND

Not to be confused with microscopic plankton and diatoms, these are, indeed, fully formed seashells on a minuscule scale. A great many gem and mineral societies worldwide have divisions devoted to the study and worship of these tiny homes that can be found in sand samples from around the world. And remember that impossibly tiny as these shells are, the original inhabitants were even smaller, as they had to fit inside. So far there's no evidence of any species of hermit crab that may have used these microshells as borrowed homes.

10 NANOMOTORS

Nanotechnology, nanorobotics, nanomachines. An everexpanding field of science and technology is expected to revolutionize the world as we know it. The simplest (though it's really hardly simple) of nanomachines are being constructed for biological study to better understand the mechanics of the cell and all its natural capabilities. The hope is that humans may be able to replicate some of these functions to better the health of mankind in the future. Scientists envision great strides in the fields of molecular biology, medicine, chemistry, physics, and nanocomputers through the development of these microscopic motors. Many of the machines are as small as half the width of a human hair, and others are so small that several hundred would fit in the space of the period at the end of this sentence.

9 SMALLEST BIBLE

In 2007, nanotechnology was pushed to another extreme when Technion, the Israel Institute of Technology, inscribed the entire Hebrew text of the Jewish Bible onto a space less half the size of a grain of sugar. The team etched the 300,000 words of the Bible onto a tiny silicone surface less than .5 millimeters square by blasting the silicone with gallium ions.

The previous smallest-known copy of the Bible measured 1.1 by 1.3 by 0.4 inches, weighed 0.4 ounces, and contained 1514 pages, according to Guinness World Records spokeswoman Amarilis Espinoza. The tiny text, obtained by an Indian professor in November 2001, is believed to have originated in Australia.

8 INSECT-POWERED AIRCRAFT

There are ancient stone tablets from the city of Ur that observe the natural flying power of the common housefly. The ancient Egyptians mused about how the housefly's powers may provide insight to the Pharaoh's journey into the afterlife. Even the great Nikola Tesla was curious about insect power:

> His 16-bug-power motor was, likewise, not an unqualified success. This was a light contrivance made of splinters forming a windmill, with a spindle and pulley attached to live June bugs. When the glued insects beat their wings, as they did desperately, the bug-power engine prepared to take off. This line of research was forever abandoned, however, when a young friend dropped by who fancied the taste of June bugs. Noticing a jarful standing near, he began cramming them into his mouth. The youthful inventor threw up.—from Tesla: Man Out of Time by Margaret Cheney, 1981.

Dr. Richard Brewer is given credit with manufacturing the first prototype fly-powered airplane in 1949, constructed of balsa wood and the cellophane from a pack of Lucky Strike cigarettes. Reportedly, Dr. Brewer's prototype plane was delivered to the Smithsonian Institute's National Air and Space Museum during the 1960s. Insect-powered aircraft have become quite a well-followed hobby, with many websites devoted to blueprints and instructions to construct miniature planes that utilize houseflies or flying beetles as their motors.

7 MINI-BEES

Called quasihesma, these minutely small bees come from Cape York in Queensland, Australia. Known as the smallest species of bee, these little guys are only two millimeters long. That's approximately the size of the head of a pin. They come from the family Colletidae and are often referred to collectively as plasterer bees, due to the way they smooth the walls of their nest cells with secretions applied with their mouthparts; these secretions dry into a cellophanelike lining. Another distinction of this group of bees is that they're solitary. Although they have been known to build nests in groups, they don't manufacture hives.

6 MATCHSTICKS

One of the many "humble" art mediums, matchsticks have been used to create a cavalcade of various structures and masterpieces. Commonly considered to be folk art, matchstick miniatures have also been classed as another form of "prison art," although the creators of the sculptures hardly need to have served time behind bars. The amount of artwork developed in this medium is immense and includes stick carvings, match-head sculptures, and homages to the engineering feats of mankind from every culture and civilization, created from minute lumber, one stick at a time.

Interesting Fact: The origin of matchsticks can well be dated back to 3500 BC. The Egyptians developed a small pinewood stick with a coating of a combustible sulfur mixture.

5 THAT'S THE PITS

For centuries, those pesky pits from peaches, plums, cherries, and olives have been thrown away with the garbage. But for quite a few folks with the ache to create and an extremely steady hand, those very pits are the "core" of their calling. The inspiration for this list, Mott's Miniatures Museum and Doll House Shop had quite a "large" collection of pit carvings. The American artist Bob Shamey has been featured by Ripley's Believe It or Not twice for his carvings. At the National Palace Museum in Taiwan, there's an olive pit carving of a tiny boat, with working shutters and facial expressions on all eight passengers.

4 CHECKMATE!

The Guinness World Record for the smallest handmade chess set was awarded in 2006 and went to M. Manikandan of Srivilliputtur, Tamil Nadu, India. His incredible creation was a chess board only 24 millimeters square. As for the playing pieces themselves, the largest piece was 10 millimeters high, and the smallest was half that, at 5 millimeters. A further search for mini chess sets revealed a beautiful solid gold set for sale on eBay that also measured 24 millimeters square. The owner of this set used slightly over six grams of 22-carat gold, for which he sought 100,000 rupees. Though that may sound like a king's ransom, converted into U.S. dollars, the amount comes down to a less-staggering $2175, or €1560.

3 RICE

Long considered a symbol of wealth and prosperity throughout the Asian world, rice has always held a position of high esteem and respect, not to mention being a daily staple food source around the world. It's only natural that respect for this most humble of grains would evolve into its own field of art. Rice writing originated in ancient Turkey and India, and one of the oldest known examples of this art is housed to this day in the Topkapi Palace in Istanbul. To have a grain of rice with your name written on it is still thought to be quite a lucky charm, so many companies have made a small fortune by providing such services. Most of these tiny art pieces are suspended in small glass vials filled with mineral oil to help magnify the writing on the minuscule grain.

2 THROUGH THE EYE OF A NEEDLE

The pinnacle of handmade miniatures would have to be sculptures that are smaller than the eye of a needle. The hands-down master of the art currently is Willard Wigan. An artist who started his career at only five years old, when he decided to start building homes for ants, he has continued to impress the world with his microcreations. He is often referred to as the "Eighth Wonder of the World." Wigan works primarily at the night, as even traffic noise from outside can destroy a piece he is working on. Using

microtools on a microscopic work field, he must control not only his pulse rate, but his breathing, as he has inhaled a few of his masterpieces due to a poorly timed breath.

1 THE WORLD'S SMALLEST SNAKE

The Barbados thread snake was discovered in 2008. Recognized as the world's smallest snake, the tiny reptiles will only reach a maximum size of ten centimeters long, or about 4 inches, and are reported to be "as thin as spaghetti." Due to their extreme tininess, females only lay one egg, which hatches out at half the size of the adult. A larger clutch of eggs would produce such small offspring that it would be near impossible for the baby thread snakes to find sustenance.

10 WRONGLY ATTRIBUTED INVENTIONS

10 COMPUTER DESKTOP AND GUI
Alleged Inventor: Microsoft
Actual Inventor: Xerox PARC

The GUI is a graphical user interface, the main system most people use to control their computer. It uses menu systems, a mouse to control a cursor, and windowlike boxes on the screen. Most people wrongly believe that Microsoft invented the user interface and the personal computer, but in fact it was invented by Xerox. Apple was shown the system by Xerox and loved it so much they emulated it and released it on their first graphical computer, the Macintosh. Microsoft saw the Macintosh, emulated Apple's efforts and released it under the name Windows.

9 AUTOMOBILE
Alleged Inventor: Henry Ford
Actual Inventor: Karl Benz

Most people when asked will say that the automobile was invented by Henry Ford. But this isn't the case at all. The inventor of the modern automobile is generally accepted as having been Karl Benz (of Mercedes Benz fame). In 1885, he was granted a patent for his design and was producing and selling his vehicles by 1888. It was not until eight years later that Ford created his first self-propelled automobile.

8 X-RAY PHOTOGRAPHY
Alleged Inventor: Thomas Edison
Actual Inventor: Wilhelm Röntgen

Thomas Edison is the man most people think invented x-ray photography—and Edison takes claim for many other people's inventions, as well—but it was actually Wilhelm Röntgen who took the very first x-ray photograph (of his wife's hand). His contributions to the science of x-ray photography were so great that they were originally called Röntgen rays.

7 MOVING PICTURES

Alleged Inventor: Thomas Edison (in fact his own moving-pictures concept was created by one of his staff, William Dickson)

Actual Inventor: Louis Le Prince

Edison, again, is usually given the honor of having invented moving pictures, but the very first moving picture ever created was filmed by Louis Le Prince in 1888. Two years later (coincidentally the same time as Edison "invented" his moving-picture system), Le Prince vanished on a train traveling between Dijon and Paris, and another two years later his son Alphonse was found shot dead in New York after testifying at a patent trial against Thomas Edison.

6 TELESCOPE

Alleged Inventor: Galileo

Actual Inventor: Hans Lippershey

Galileo is most famous for his invention of the telescope and the trial against him for heresy (for saying the Bible contained errors). But while he *was* tried for heresy, he was not the inventor of the telescope. That honor goes to Hans Lippershey, who created the first telescope in 1608, a mere year before Galileo used the design in his own telescope. By 1655, telescopes had become extremely powerful.

5 RECORDED AUDIO

Alleged Inventor: Thomas Edison

Actual Inventor: Édouard-Léon Scott de Martinville

Yet again, Edison is given undue honor for the invention of recorded audio. The true inventor of recorded audio was Édouard-Léon Scott de Martinville 17 years before Edison invented his phonograph. Most amazingly, Martinville was able to record sound on paper as waves, but had no mechanism to play it back, until some smart people in 2008 were able to use computer technology to bring the recording to life. At the time of the recording, France was ruled by Emperor Napoleon III, and James Buchanan was the president of the United States.

4 LIGHT BULB

Alleged Inventor: Thomas Edison

Actual Inventor: Sir Humphry Davy

With our fourth false-attribution to Edison, you start to wonder how many of his other inventions really were his! In 1879, Edison released his first commercial practical incandescent lamp. Believe it or not, 77 years earlier, the first incandescent lamp was invented in Great Britain by Sir Humphry Davy, to whom a great disservice is done by naming Edison as the real inventor.

3 RADIO
Alleged Inventor: Guglielmo Marconi
Actual Inventor: Nikola Tesla

Marconi introduced the radio in London in 1895, claiming it as his own invention. But some years earlier, Tesla had been working on the very same device (which is no surprise, since he is regarded as the father of wireless telegraphy). Here's what Tesla had to say about the issue: "The popular impression is that my wireless work was begun in 1893, but as a matter of fact, I spent the two preceding years in investigations, employing forms of apparatus, some of which were almost like those of today."

2 POWERED FLIGHT
Alleged Inventor: The Wright Brothers
Actual Inventor: Richard Pearse

Nine months before the Wright brothers' famous "first" flight at Kitty Hawk, Richard Pearse, a New Zealander, performed the same feat in Timaru, New Zealand. Pearse's machine much more closely resembled modern aircraft than that of the Wright brothers. Sadly, his ventures in flight are little known outside of New Zealand.

1 THE INTERNET
Alleged Inventor: Al Gore
Actual Inventor: Vinton Cerf

The Internet is a vast conglomeration of various technologies, the fathers of whom were Vinton Cerf, Lawrence Roberts, Leonard Kleinrock, and Robert Kahn. The Internet existed in a nonpublic form for many years before it was opened up to the world. The reason that Al Gore claimed to have invented it was because he provided funding for its growth; but the honor of inventing the Internet and the title "Father of the Internet" generally goes to Vinton Cerf.

10 SCI-FI INVENTIONS THAT SHOULD NOT BE INVENTED

10 FLYING CARS

Imagine being stuck in traffic. It sucks, right? Now imagine that you could flip a switch, and suddenly your car would begin to rise into the air. Gloating, you would fly over all those suckers stuck in traffic. Now that you're flying, imagine running into a tree. Next, imagine getting into a fender bender with another flying car and plummeting to your death in a flaming heap of twisted metal.

Flying cars would undoubtedly solve a number of problems. The only thing is they would create a whole new world of problems. To keep from running into every single power line and radio tower, we would need to create laws dictating where you could drive. It's kind of like creating flying roads. Of course, as soon as you get enough flying cars, you get a traffic jam on the skyways, thus negating the purpose of having a flying car.

9 CRYOGENIC FREEZING

Cryogenic freezing actually exists today. Every year, dozens of people elect to be frozen in the hope that medical advances will progress to the point where they can be thawed and cured of their diseases. Despite obvious risks and expenses, this process has been around for decades.

Now, let's assume that medical science advances to the point where it's possible to thaw the frozen bodies and heal any diseases they might have. The question is then, what happens to the population when people who would have otherwise died are brought to life in the future? Talk about overpopulation.

8 ARTIFICIAL INTELLIGENCE

Movies and literature are chock-full of robots. It's quite possibly one of the most cliché objects in sci-fi media. Despite this, robots are very real today and artificial intelligence is not far off. Wouldn't it be great, though, to have a servant who would do anything you asked? Or perhaps a lover who never ages? What about a machine that completely supplants all menial laborers?

The answer is no, it would not be great. A.I. is a common theme in sci-fi, and usually it causes more problems than solutions. If you don't believe me, think about the facts. The current trend is that every two years, computer processors double in speed, halve in size, and halve in price. Assuming this trend continues, in 20 years you'll be able to purchase a computer the size of a postage stamp that's smarter than the human brain for about $1. Now who's the superior species?

7 PREDICTING THE FUTURE

Wouldn't it be great to stop murders before they happened? How about wars? What about knowing next week's lotto numbers? Worthwhile goals, all of them. And they're entirely within reach with a time-viewing machine. Imagine how many problems would be solved. No more war, famine, or pestilence. The complete utopian society, right?

Wrong. So let's say, hypothetically speaking, that the U.S. has a time-viewing machine and this machine predicts that China is going to attack Los Angeles. To prevent this from happening, the U.S. issues a preemptive strike, thus starting a war in which China launches a missile headed straight for California, and thus the prediction becomes a self-fulfilling prophecy. This could be true of any major manmade catastrophe.

6 TELEPORTATION DEVICE

Imagine a world where you can travel to New Zealand on Saturday, then stop in Denmark for quick visit on Sunday, before you have to be at work at home on Monday. No longer do we have to use precious fossil fuel to travel. Terrorism in travel is a thing of the past—until a terrorist teleports a bomb into the White House.

First, let's assume that there is some sort of safety protocol in place to prevent things like that from happening. Technically, a teleporter breaks down all of the atoms in your body and sends them to the destination, where they are then reconstructed. The only problem with this is the actual transmission of the atoms. That's where the information age comes in. It makes far more sense to just transmit the blueprints of your atomic structure to a reconstruction device. Essentially, a teleporter is just a fax machine. The problem arises in the early use of such devices. Have you ever made a copy of a copy of a copy? Even using the highest-quality copy machine, the quality of the copy degenerates rapidly. At first, it might not be noticeable. What are a few atoms from a hair? Or a fingernail? Or your heart? We're not sure what even the smallest change in your atomic structure would do.

5 NANOBOTS

Cancer has been cured! The human lifespan numbers in the centuries. All degenerative diseases have ceased to exist. Major injuries heal within seconds. Recreational drug use no longer has any negative effects. Hangovers are a thing of the past. Nanobots have cured the world. These self-replicating robots are now injected into everyone as a natural immunization.

To describe the horrors these machine could cause, here's a passage from K. Eric Drexler's book *Engines of Creation*:

> Imagine such a replicator floating in a bottle of chemicals, making copies of itself....the first replicator assembles a copy in one thousand seconds, the two replicators then build two more in the next thousand seconds, the four build another four, and the eight build another eight. At the end of ten hours, there are not 36 new replicators, but over 68 billion. In less than a day, they would weigh a ton; in less than two days, they would outweigh the Earth; in another four hours, they would exceed the mass of the Sun and all the planets combined—if the bottle of chemicals hadn't run dry long before.

Part of the appeal of nanobots is that only a few need be injected and they can replicate in the human body. This also describes the danger. To put it succinctly: we are the Borg. Lower your shields. Your biological and technological distinctiveness will be added to our own. Resistance if futile!

4 WEATHER CONTROL

Welcome to the future. World hunger has been solved. The global community lives in utopian tranquility without hurricanes, tornadoes, or floods. The human race can now turn its gaze to more worthwhile things like space travel and beer.

The problem with weather control arises when we unleash specific weather on delicate ecosystems that cannot exist except under certain conditions. If this hurdle is overcome, there is no reason we shouldn't have a weather-control device. Until it breaks. Then a world lulled into complacency by good weather is suddenly thrown into a natural disaster. Or, in a worst-case scenario, a hostile foreign power takes over our weather-control devices and unleashes storms of unimaginable power and magnitude against us.

3 GENETIC ENGINEERING

Perfect humans. Engineered from before birth to be the best of the best. What could be better than having the perfect child with no possible risk of inherited flaws? And it would be all without the use of those messy nanobots. I think the movie *Gattaca* says it best:

> We want to give your child the best possible start. Believe me, we have enough imperfection built in already. Your child doesn't need any more additional burdens. Keep in mind, this child is still you. Simply, the best, of you. You could conceive naturally a thousand times and never get such a result.

The danger arises not from any physical aspect of genetic engineering, but rather the social aspects. When you begin to breed perfect humans, you create an entirely new social class. Bringing discrimination to new levels, the class you belong to will not be determined by social status, income, or skin color, but rather, genetic makeup.

2 HOLODECKS

After a stressful day at work, what could be more relaxing than coming home and relaxing in a nice peaceful meadow? Perhaps going for a relaxing drive in your flying car? With a holodeck, you can go anywhere, be anyone, or do anything. With the way videogames are heading, holodecks are not too far off. Imagine that you can have anything you want. Any fantasy is possible. And there is the danger.

It's the perfect drug. Why would anyone bother going dealing with their crappy life when they have the perfect life on the holodeck? Why would anyone bother dealing with reality? You want to be emperor of Rome? Sure! You want to be Blackbeard the Pirate? Why not? You want to have sex with Marilyn Monroe? Whatever you want is possible with the holodeck. It's been jokingly put forth that the holodeck would be the world's last invention. The thing is it would be. Why bother inventing anything else when you've already invented the perfect world?

1 REPLICATORS

Replicators are the solution to nearly every problem the world has. Imagine no more world hunger, no more energy crisis. Never again will there be a shortage of medical supplies. The perfect world where you can have anything you want.

Until the complete and utter collapse of society. You see, the replicator would make work obsolete. There would be no need for money. As a matter of fact, you would only need one large replicator and you could replicate another one. You could make anything from fresh pizza to a molecule-for-molecule exact reproduction of the Hope Diamond. The last day of the world will come when anyone can make anything.

10 MYSTERIES OF OUTER SPACE

10 SIMULACRUM IN EAGLE NEBULA

One of the strangest photos ever taken of space is that of the eagle nebula. The photo itself is supposed to show the birth of a star from gaseous clouds. However, when the photo was shown on CNN, hundreds of calls came in from people reporting they could see a face in the cloud. When the color of the photo was adjusted, a large human form seemed to appear within the cloud. Scientists haven't been able to explain this phenomenon.

9 WHERE DID GALAXIES COME FROM?

Scientists have only recently been able to explain where the stars and planets came from. Now, they've turned their attention to a much bigger mystery: where did galaxies come from? What's known is that galaxies are not scattered randomly throughout space; rather, they are found in clusters, known

as "superclusters." Scientists have two main theories to attempt to explain galaxy formation. First, the gas left over from the big bang clustered together to form galaxies, in which stars and planets were born. Second, the gas from the big bang created stars and planets all over the universe, and they migrated by gravity into galaxies. Neither theory has been universally accepted yet.

8 OTHER EARTHS

Our star, the sun, is just one of trillions in the universe. When you look at the fact that our star has eight planets, and do the math, it tells you that it's possible for there to be eight times as many planets in the universe than stars—an astounding figure. Is it not possible that just one of those planets might have life on it? It is a fact that, since the year 2000, hundreds of extrasolar planets have been discovered orbiting distant stars. Some of these were found to be earthlike, such as the planet Gliese 581d, a planet believed to have liquid water on its surface. Could it possibly contain life? Hopefully with advances in technology, we will soon know the answer. Until then, it remains one of space's greatest mysteries.

7 ARE THERE OTHER UNIVERSES?

This is one of the more controversial arguments out there. The theory is that there are an infinite number of universes, each of which is governed by its own set of laws and physics. Many scientists dismiss this argument as nothing more than speculation, as there is no evidence or mathematical law that allows for the existence of other universes. However, believers in this theory have argued that there are none that disprove it, either. This is one mystery that could only be solved if we were able to travel there; however, with the expansion of the universe, it is unlikely humanity will ever find the answer.

6 DARK MATTER

Albert Einstein's equation $E = MC^2$ is perhaps the best-known equation of the 20th century. However, when it's applied to space, an anomaly occurs. When we use it to determine how much matter the universe should have, we realize that we've only found four percent of the matter in the universe! Where is the rest of it? Many believe it's in the form of dark matter. Where is this dark matter? It's everywhere, wherever there is no visible matter. Scientists have yet to show any conclusive proof that dark matter does in fact exist. The fact that you can't see it, touch it, and light and radio waves pass right through it undeterred make it extremely hard to detect.

5 MARS–EARTH CONNECTION

When talking about life on other planets, some say we need go no further than our own solar system. Conspiracy theorists have always thought Mars may harbor life and that NASA is covering it up. Many photos have also called into question civilization on Mars, such as the face, pyramids, and photo of what appears to be an apelike figure sitting on a rock on Mars. While scientists have come out to debunk these photos, they've also admitted that they believe liquid oceans once covered the surface of Mars before its magnetic field disappeared. Is it possible that life did indeed once exist there? Current Mars exploration hopes to answer this question.

4 UFO SIGHTINGS BY NASA ASTRONAUTS

NASA astronauts are some of the most highly trained and specialized people in the world. Often they are expert scientists who can explain almost anything. So when they see something they can't explain, you can bet it's going to raise eyebrows. One of the most famous incidents occurred during a live broadcast on NBC in 1963. Major Gordon Cooper was at the end of his 22nd solo journey around the earth when he said that out of one of his windows he could see a glowing green object fast approaching. The object then made a sharp turn and shot away. He was sure he wasn't seeing things, as the radar in his spacecraft picked up the object as well. Upon his return to earth, interviewers wanted to ask him about the object; however, NASA officials didn't allow it.

3 WHITE HOLES

One of Albert Einstein's greatest accomplishments was proving, through mathematics, the existence of black holes. Through advances in technology, we have now been able to find several black holes and believe one to be at the center of our very own Milky Way galaxy. What's astonishing, however, is what Einstein also proved through his equations: white holes also exist. The exact opposite of black holes, white holes are believed to "spit out" an incredible amount of matter from seemingly nothing. Such an object should be easy to find, yet none have been. If one were found, it may help us explain other unknown mysteries, such as where the material that made the galaxies came from.

2 RUINS ON THE MOON

In this list we've discussed the possibility of life on distant planets and near planets. But could it possibly at one time have been as close as the moon? This conspiracy theory states that there are indeed ancient ruins and buildings on the moon, but the government has been censoring them from the public. This theory had no backing until two recent breakthroughs. A man who claims to have worked for the government censoring moon photos came forward with several, explaining how the censorship was done and that, indeed, there were structures on the moon. More recently, scientists announced they believe they've discovered water, possibly in ice or liquid form, under the surface of the moon. For conspiracy theorists, this was all the proof they needed, while critics dismiss it as "ridiculous speculation."

1 DARK ENERGY

Dark energy is the greatest mystery in the universe today because of the fact that it's believed to be all around us, and it explains why there seem to be anomalies within the law of gravity. According to the law of gravity, large objects, like galaxy clusters, should attract each other, and their gravitational pull should pull in other objects. This, however, is not the case, and the fact is most galaxy clusters are moving farther apart. This is due to the fact that the universe is expanding at an incredible rate. To answer the question of why this is, scientists developed the theory of dark energy, which has the opposite effect as gravity, pushing things apart. Mathematical calculations have shown that if it exists, it makes up 74 percent of our universe, outweighing gravity, and this is why the universe is expanding. However, we still have no conclusive proof, so it remains a mystery to us.

10 EXTINCT CREATURES THAT AREN'T EXTINCT

10 NEW HOLLAND MOUSE

The New Holland mouse was first described in 1843. It vanished from view after that and was presumed extinct until it was rediscovered in 1967. It's found only in Australia. The mouse is currently listed as endangered, and a number of the populations are now considered extinct, some due to the Ash Wednesday Wildfires in 1983.

9 TERROR SKINK

The terror skink (*Phoboscincus bocourti*) was long thought extinct until a specimen was discovered in 2003 in New Caledonia. The skink measures around 20 inches and has long, sharp curved teeth, which is unusual for a skink since they are normally omnivores. The only other known example of the skink was also discovered in New Caledonia in 1876.

8 GIANT PALOUSE EARTHWORM

The giant Palouse earthworm, from North America, was considered to be extinct in the 1980s, but recently it has resurfaced. Little is known about the worm, except that it's very strange. It can grow up to three feet in length and when handled it gives off a smell like lilies. The creature is believed to be able to spit in self-defense. It's albino in color.

7 TAKAHE

The Takahe is a flightless bird native to the South Island of New Zealand. It was thought to be extinct after the last four specimens were taken in 1898. After an extensive search for the bird, it was rediscovered near Lake Te Anau in 1948. The bird is currently endangered. Takahes have an unusual eating habit in which they pluck grass with their beak, grasp it in one claw, and eat only the softest parts at the bottom of the leaf. They then throw away the rest.

6 MOUNTAIN PYGMY POSSUM

The mountain pygmy possum was first described as a Pleistocene fossil in 1896. It was rediscovered alive in 1966 in a ski hut on Mount Hotham, Australia. The possum is mouse sized and is found in dense alpine rocks and boulders. The female possums live at the top of the mountain, while the males live lower down. In order to mate, the males travel up to the females. Because they needed to cross a road, their survival was in danger, so the Australian government built them a "tunnel of love" beneath the road.

5 GRACILIDRIS

Gracilidris is a genus of nocturnal ants that was only known through the fossil record. In fact, the only known fossil existing of this ant is a specimen preserved in amber. The ants were discovered alive and were described in 2006, but to this day very little is known about them. The ants live in small colonies and nest in soil.

4 BERMUDA PETREL

The Bermuda petrel, a nocturnal, ground-nesting sea bird, was thought extinct for 330 years. It's the national bird of Bermuda and was rediscovered in 1951 when 18 pairs were found. It was believed to have been made extinct after the English settled Bermuda and introduced cats, rats, and dogs. The bird has an eerie call that caused Spanish sailors to believe the isles were haunted by devils. For that reason, they never settled there.

3 LAOTIAN ROCK RAT

The Laotian rock rat (also known as the rat squirrel) was first described in 2005 by a scientist who classified it in its own family of creatures, Laonastidae. One year later, the classification was disputed by others who believe that the rock rat is actually a member of the extinct family Diatomyidae, which vanished in the late Miocene period. The animals are like large dark rats with squirrel-like tails. Surprisingly, the first specimens were found on sale as meat at a market in Laos.

2 LA PALMA GIANT LIZARD

The La Palma giant lizard was thought extinct from 1500. It lived in La Palma in the Canary Islands, and it's believed that the introduction of cats caused its final downfall. In 2007, it was rediscovered in its original location, despite the belief that the only lizards left in the Canary Islands were on Gran Canaria. An interesting side note is that the islands are named after dogs, not canaries—the name comes from the Latin *Insula Canaria* which means "Island of the Dogs," Canary birds are actually named after the islands.

1 COELACANTH

This entry is number one because it's the coolest—the coelacanth was thought to be extinct since the end of the Cretaceous period. In 1938, it was rediscovered in various African nations, making it a Lazarus taxon, one of a group of organisms that disappears from the fossil record only to come back to life later. Coelacanths first appear in the fossil record 410 million years ago. They normally live near the bottom of the ocean floor but have, on some occasions, been caught closer to the surface. They've been known to grow to be over 15 feet long, but there isn't a single attack on a human because the fish live so deep.

10 SURREAL CREATURES

10 OLM (*PROTEUS ANGUINUS*)

This amphibian, native to the deepest, darkest caves of Europe (most famously in Slovenia) and mistakenly identified in ancient times as a "baby dragon," has to be one of the most bizarre animals in the world. Completely blind and almost completely lacking body pigmentation, the olm lives in a very alien sensory universe. Despite being blind, it can pick up both chemical and electrical signals via receptors on its entire body, which come in handy to find the small invertebrates it feeds upon. Completely aquatic, the olm has a soft, pale skin that somewhat resembles that of a very pale human being, hence its local nickname of "human fish." There's a second subspecies of olm, the black olm, which is just as interesting but a tad less bizarre, since it has eyes and lacks the pale complexion of its cousin.

9 BLANKET OCTOPUS (*TREMOCTOPUS VIOLACEUS*)

There's no such thing as a "normal octopus." These extraordinary animals look like they came from another planet, took a dip in our oceans, and liked it enough to stay. The many strange traits of octopuses include their three hearts, venomous saliva, hidden parrotlike beaks, the ability to change the color and texture of their skin with incredible ease and speed (they are much better at it than, say, chameleons), and "intelligent arms" that don't seem to need instructions from the brain to perform certain actions.

That said, there are some octopuses that are more bizarre than others. The blanket octopus is one of them; for a start, the female is 40,000 times heavier than the male! The male is only one inch and leads an almost planktonic lifestyle, while the female is big, spectacular, and over two meters long. When she feels threatened, the female can also extend a capelike membrane between her arms that makes her look bigger and badder than she really is. Finally, an interesting fact is that the blanket octopus is immune to the deadly Portuguese man-of-war "jellyfish"; as self-defense, the clever octopus often tears off some man-of-war tentacles and uses them as weapons.

8 GLASS FROG (CENTROLENIDAE)

What makes these little tropical American frogs so surreal is that they have translucent skin, which basically makes them a living anatomy lesson without even having to cut open the frog! Indeed, some of their internal organs, such as the heart, intestines, and liver, are perfectly visible when you look at the frog's underside. Glass frogs are closely related and behave similarly to the better-known tree frogs.

7 BLOBFISH (*PSYCHROLUTES MARCIDUS*)

This gelatinous deep-water fish has a face that only its mother could love (although those who truly admire nature's boundless and sometimes macabre creativity will certainly appreciate it, too). Found in the oceans surrounding Australia and Tasmania, the blobfish leads a rather passive life, feeding on whatever piece of detritus floats within its reach. It lacks the muscular power of other fish and practically doesn't spend any energy while swimming thanks to its body, which is less dense than water. Rarely seen alive, the blobfish is occasionally captured as bycatch by fisherman's nets. However, I strongly doubt it's edible.

6 ASSASSIN SPIDER (ARCHAEIDAE)

The assassin spider is only two millimeters long, and, despite its name and creepy appearance, is completely harmless to humans. Its long "neck" has evolved specifically to support the weight of its immense jaws, which are armed with venomous fangs and act as deadly traps for the other smaller spiders that are its main food.

5 HATCHETFISH (STERNOPTYCHIDAE)

Viewed from the front, the hatchetfish looks otherworldly, and in a way it does live in a different world from ours. This deep-water fish is found in all the oceans except for the coldest regions, and, like the olm and blobfish, spends its entire life in almost complete darkness. The only life it sees is produced by living creatures, including itself, via special "photophores" or light-producing organs on its sides, which allow it to lure prey and to escape predators. As scary as it may look, the hatchetfish is only a few centimeters long and poses no threat to humans.

4 HAIRY CRAB (*KIWA HIRSUTE*)

Also known as the Yeti crab, this crustacean is covered in what at first glance appears to be fur, but is actually a dense covering of setae, like those found in the legs of some shrimp. These setae seem to function as a filter, detoxifying the water in which the creature lives. This is very useful when your habitat is a deadly hydrothermal vent that's constantly throwing poisonous minerals into the water. The hairy crab is blind and colorless and lives its entire life in darkness, just like the olm, blobfish, and hatchetfish. It seems that nature sends many of its most bizarre creations to the places where humans are most unlikely to see or reach them. Maybe because they'll last longer that way?

3 LEAFY SEA DRAGON (*PHYCODURUS EQUES*)

This fish, closely related to the sea horse, survives by pretending to be a floating bunch of sea weed. It swims very slowly, which adds to the effect, and its dorsal and pectoral fins (which do all the swimming) are transparent and practically invisible. I strongly suspect most predators don't even know the leafy sea dragon exists at all! These amazing little creatures have weird reproductive habits: the female lays the eggs into the male's body via a long tube, and the male carries the brood until the baby sea dragons hatch. This fish is found on the southern and western coasts of Australia.

2 SATANIC LEAF-TAILED GECKO (*UROPLATUS PHANTASTICUS*)

Evolution made this lizard look so much like a decaying, dry leaf that it's seldom seen, let alone eaten, by any predators. It's found only in Madagascar, where it shares the forests with other fantastic reptiles. It's an insect eater, and despite its infernal name, scary eyes, and defensive threat display (which it uses only when camouflage doesn't work, which is very rarely), it's completely harmless to humans. Unfortunately, this incredible species is endangered due to overcollecting for the pet trade and the devastation of its natural habitat—

Madagascar's forests have been reduced by 90 percent, and most of its iconic species are either gone or on the verge of extinction.

1 HEMEROPLANES CATERPILLAR

Yes, a humble caterpillar is number one on this list, and I think it really deserves it. This is, in my opinion, a living masterpiece of nature, and although all animals are amazing, this has to be one of the most awe-inspiring. Incredibly rare to see and found only in the rain forests of Mexico and Central America, this little creature is usually normal looking and has rather drab colors, but if threatened by a potential predator, it undergoes an incredible transformation: it hangs from a branch with its hind legs and inflates the front part of its body, until it looks just like a small pit viper ready to inject its deadly venom.

Not only does it mimic the snake's triangular "head," fierce eyes, and shiny scales perfectly, but it also pretends to "strike" at enemies (it's just a bluff, since it's not venomous or dangerous in any way). Surely many of its potential enemies—including some humans!—fall for this incredibly accurate imitation and leave the caterpillar alone. As an adult, the hemeroplanes is a rather nondescript moth that has absolutely nothing viper-ish about it. The hemeroplanes caterpillar is little known and sadly endangered due to deforestation.

10 CREATURES THAT CRAWLED OUT OF YOUR NIGHTMARES

10 GIANT ISOPOD

We'll start with perhaps the least harmless on this list. These bottom-feeding deep-sea crustaceans bear some resemblance to common woodlice, but they can reach up to around a foot in length. Close your eyes and imagine sitting in the yard, playing with potato bugs, when this thing gets jealous and comes hurtling out of the bushes for its turn. An impossible scenario, considering the isopods are deep-sea kinda guys, but you can see why a hypersized version of the only bug cute enough to handle is nightmare material.

9 BOMBARDIER BEETLE

This looks like a little weevil! Why is it on the list? Chemical warfare. This bug is about as cute as a beetle can be, and the largest ones are tiny at best. Nightmare material? Hardly. But it isn't called the bombardier beetle for nothing. When it's threatened, the beetle aims its convenient butt-nozzle at its attacker and instantly makes them regret their choice of dinner. At the end of the beetle's abdomen, two separate chambers store hydroquinone and hydrogen peroxide. When it's threatened, the beetle contracts the chambers, combining the two materials, which violently react and produce a spray roughly the same temperature as boiling water.

8 GIANT PACIFIC OCTOPUS

It would have been too easy to include any number of squid on this list, but I think it's about time for the giant octopus to get some recognition. Normally shy by nature, the octopus can be deadly when it wants to be, but the main source of nightmare material here is its size. While 33 pounds doesn't sound too bad, a 14-foot wingspan just sounds terrible. I won't even mention its venomous beak.

7 GIANT ANACONDA

Naturally, at least one enormous snake had to make the list. It isn't the longest snake, but at 20 feet and 550 pounds, the giant anaconda is the biggest. The wetlands-dwelling serpents regularly make lunch out of jaguars and caimans. Humans tend to be a bit too big for breakfast, lunch, or dinner, but attacks on people aren't unheard of. Keep the children close in South America.

6 CAMEL SPIDER

While the first spider on our list isn't actually technically a spider, you cringed anyway. So did I. Camel spiders belong to a distinct, separate scientific order from other spiders, like scorpions do. While many different species actually inhabit territories all over the world, the most well-known remain the desert dwellers (they can also be found in grasslands or forest habitats). Many urban legends exist that vastly exaggerate all qualities of these monsters, such as that they're over three inches long (although their leg spans can reach up to five inches). Other myths are that they numb humans and eat part of them while they sleep, that they disembowel camels, and that they scream or squeal and leap through the air. All false. However, the creatures have been known to hit up to ten miles per hour in speed.

5 STONEFISH

You're walking along a beautiful beach, shin-deep in the foamy, churning waves. You can feel the algae-covered stones beneath your feet. You step around the larger ones onto the smaller ones, feeling them with your bare toes. All of a sudden, you feel a sting on the bottom of your foot. You yelp in pain, run out of the water, and look at the small puncture wound on the bottom of your foot. The neurotoxin from the world's most venomous fish seeps into your body, and the countdown commences. You must seek help immediately, or else you will face death. The stonefish, disguised convincingly like a rock, goes about its business, flustered at most by the intrusion. You run to get help, trying not to step on the wound caused by the fish's poisonous spur on its backbone.

4 LION'S MANE JELLYFISH

This fairly common jellyfish isn't really too bad overall. It varies in size and its sting is very painful but rarely fatal (although it may leave a nasty burn), but that's just about it. Generally speaking, it's not the best contender on a list of nightmarish creatures, but the lion's mane jellyfish has been known to reach enormous sizes. The bell of the jellyfish can reach up to 8 feet in diameter, and the tentacles may trail up to 100 feet! Now visualize yourself diving in the vast open ocean with one of these suckers for company.

3 BLACK MAMBA

The black mamba enjoys sunning himself, eating rodents and birds, and fighting off elephants. This serpent can exceed eight feet in length. As far as venomous snakes go, black mambas are beaten only by the 16 feet achieved by the king cobra. But why is the black mamba on here and not the cobra? Well, every snake will run when it can, and attack when it's cornered, except the black mamba. It usually runs, but when it's startled, its knee-jerk reaction is to bite first, then run, even if it has plenty of time to slither away. Also, it has been known, when pursued, to just get sick of running and turn around to face its attacker. These snakes can also slither at speeds of up to 12 miles per hour, and a single bite is enough to kill 20 to 25 grown men.

2 HONEY BADGER

Those who have heard of the honey badger know very well why it's on the list. For those who don't know, allow me to tell you. First of all, I know. "Honey badger"? On this list? Doesn't sound all that bad. Truthfully, it kind of sounds like an animal I wouldn't mind having as a pet. I think I could probably feed it potato chips through the hole in my screen door. Well, don't. Not if you value your fingers. Honey badgers are the most aggressive animals alive. They will consume venomous snakes, stand up against elephants, and eat honey straight out of the hive while being swarmed by bees. They will quickly identify their enemies' weakest points (e.g., the gonads of a human male) and relentlessly attack.

1 SYDNEY FUNNEL WEB SPIDER

Oh, Australia, what beautiful, majestic creatures you have. And by "beautiful majestic creatures," I mean marsupials, venomous snakes, and the God-awful Sydney funnel web spider. Incredibly aggressive, dark colored, and glossy, with huge killer fangs and nature's worst attitude, getting bitten by one of these things should be on your "Things to Never Do Ever" list. The spiders dig tunnels or take up residence in trees, creating tunnels with trapdoors complete with trip lines so they know when to open them.

The male spiders wander and are attracted to water. They can survive being stuck in the pool for up to 24 hours! Approaching one or, God forbid, attempting to handle one is a very excellent way to get bitten. They bite multiple times, nearly always delivering a full dose of venom, and don't let go. They must be grabbed and removed, as trying to shake them off usually isn't enough to loosen the grip of their gigantic fangs. They have what is called atraxotoxin, which is highly toxic to primates, such as humans. I'm thoroughly convinced that if there is a hell, one of its gates (or at least a fire exit) opens in Sydney, Australia.

CHAPTER NINE

Entertainment

10 BIZARRE KUNG FU MOVIES

10 SWORDSMAN WITH AN UMBRELLA

A frequent addition to $5.99 kung fu movie box sets, *Swordsman with an Umbrella* gives you exactly that: a swordsman out for revenge who totes around a Japanese-style umbrella. While this isn't too strange in itself, the weirdness factor gets turned up when he uses the umbrella to fly, Mary Poppins–style, or throws it like a Frisbee at his enemies, accompanied by goofy cartoon sound effects. Keep in mind this movie is not a comedy—or at least it's not meant to be one.

9 DEADFUL MELODY

Starring popular Jackie Chan collaborator Biao Yuen and *The Bride with White Hair* star Brigitte Lin, *Deadful Melody* tells the story of a haunted lyre (a musical instrument similar to a harp) that can kill when the right notes are played. In a memorable final battle, Brigitte Lin's character uses the lyre to fight off an entire army, reducing them all to empty clothing with bizarre "magic bullets" fired from the lyre, all with pretty music being played over the screams of the dying.

8 THEY CALL ME PHAT DRAGON

This flick, also known as *The Invincible Kung Fu Master*, features Sammo Hung, star of TV's *Martial Law*, in his breakout role as a fat master of martial arts who hones his students' skill with "food-based" training. A memorable scene involves the famished hero trying to cross a slippery tile floor to get to his lunch before his master can finish eating it. Effective training indeed. Check out the Wu-Tang Clan's remastered DVD release, complete with trailers and an original music video.

7 DUEL TO THE DEATH

While it's an all-out classic martial arts film, *Duel to the Death* is also one of the weirdest. In the film, a Japanese master of the sword and a Chinese master of the sword seek to see who's better, while a group of ninjas tries to stop the duel by using some seriously bizarre tricks, such as merging together, Voltronstyle, into a giant ninja, or transforming into a naked woman to distract a chaste monk. The film takes gore to unintentionally hilarious levels when the villain is beheaded and the head flies after the hero, gets impaled on a stick, says a line ("YOU WILL DIIIIIIEEEEE," if I recall correctly), and explodes!

6 FILTHY GUY

Also known as *Return of the Secret Rivals* and *Emperor of the Filthy Guy*, this is another Sammo Hung vehicle that chronicles the rise of one of the first emperors of the Chin Dynasty, who, God knows why, was known for having serious scalp problems. If that's not weird enough, throughout the film the hero uses his slimy, infected scalp as a weapon, forcing enemies to smell it or using it to block sword blades and even break walls (for some reason his scalp disease makes his head seemingly invincible). One memorable scene involves the hero waking up an entire monastery as he rings the two-ton temple bell with his head to scratch an itch.

5 GOD OF COOKERY

Before Stephen Chow made two of the most watched Hong Kong films of all time, *Shaolin Soccer* and *Kung Fu Hustle*, he made this little gem. In the film, Chow plays a hack celebrity chef who enters an epic cooking competition with his rival. Kitchen utensils act as weapons, people turn into bulldogs, and it's revealed that Chow's character was exiled from heaven for giving out God's culinary secrets to earth. Keep an eye out for Stephen Chow's flaming dumpling attack!

4 NINJA HUNTER

This diamond in the rough was unearthed in the clearance bin at a Family Dollar Store in Orrville, Ohio, and I consider it well worth the 99 cents. The film has so much action it's hard to even keep up with the complex story, but every fight scene is a goofy work of art in itself. Suffice it to say, in this movie, you'll see ninjas douse themselves in acid to attack the good guys, a ninja that fights with steak knives, and one who transforms into what appears to be a flying picnic blanket to attack his enemy. You'll also see a man who gets his power by absorbing women while they're making love, and a ninja who's a dead ringer for Adolf Hitler wearing cat ears.

3 FIVE VENOMS VERSUS WU TANG

A great pick for a Halloween, this Chinese zombie film features "hopping" zombies from Chinese folklore, and the magicians whose job it is to put them back in the ground. The opening sequence sets the stage for what's to come: an amateur magician uses hand-written spells to take control of a group of zombies and makes them do a calypso dance number. Later in the movie, a group of children fights to protect a "baby zombie" and return it to his zombie parents, and then there's a duel between two magicians who constantly sic the zombie hordes on each other and throw magical frogs and butterflies from the tips of their swords.

2 LEGEND OF RED DRAGON

Also known as *The New Legends of Shaolin*, this Jet Li vehicle is a loose remake of the Japanese series *Lone Wolf and Cub*, with Jet Li fighting bad guys with his son in tow. The film is one of the best of Jet Li's early career, and it's chock-full of weird. You'll see two dart-throwing masters begin fighting with loogies, Jet Li's magical spear that uses super moves like the "Wonder Screw," and a group of five-year-old martial arts masters taking on a sword-wielding eunuch. Not weird enough for you yet? Keep in mind that the guy Jet Li burns to death in the beginning comes back to life as a charred zombie, who (and I'm not kidding) transforms into a car. Dragon Dynasty has a great version of this film, but if you want things even more crazy, get the older release with all the poorly translated subtitles, like "I'm gonna eat that chicken's ass!"

1 FANTASY MISSION FORCE

With Jackie Chan, Brigitte Lin, TV star Adam Cheng, and *One Armed Swordsman* star Jimmy Wang Yu, this movie, also known as *Dragon Attack*, packs some serious star power, but I'm sure most of the actors would rather forget it ever happened. Watching a film this weird makes you wonder what the producers were thinking. It seems to be an attempt at remaking *The Dirty Dozen*, where a general hires a group of misfits that includes a hobo, an escape artist, and a biker chick with a bazooka to rescue the military commanders of several different countries (including the "African" general, an obviously Chinese man with brown shoe polish on his face who uses phrases like "soul brother") who were taken prisoner by Nazis. The final scene shows that these "Nazis" are actually hundreds of bandage-gear-clad road-warrior types who ride on the back of Dodge Chargers with swastikas painted on the side. This description is entirely inadequate at capturing the sheer weirdness of this movie—it has to be seen to be believed. You'll find yourself so overcome with the absurdity of this movie that you'll laugh out loud.

10 BIZARRE TV SHOWS FOR KIDS

10 MAX AND RUBY (CANADA)

This animated show is fairly innocent. It's about two bunnies, Max and his big sister Ruby. What makes the show slightly bizarre is that their parents are never there. Ruby takes care of Max as if she were his mother, despite the fact that she's supposed to be seven years old. Surely social services would have something to say about this.

9 LAZYTOWN (ICELAND)

On this show, the main character, Stephanie, is human, and she arrives in LazyTown to live with her uncle, who's a puppet. She then urges all her new friends, who are all puppets, to play outside. Robbie Rotten, a human, tries to make them eat junk food instead. The mix of humans and puppets is pretty weird to me. And the whole show is just so keyed-up that it makes my head ache.

8 TELETUBBIES (UK)

Maybe I'm just too old, but I'm still puzzled by *Teletubbies*. I mean, what are they supposed to be? Why do they have screens on their stomachs? Who is the voice? Why is there a baby in the sun? Also, *Teletubbies* has been rumored to be gay propaganda because of Tinky Winky's color, the triangle on his head, and the fact that he carries a handbag. At one point, the Polish Ombudsman for Children planned to investigate this, but she dropped it.

7 OOBI (U.S.)

OK, so apparently children love this show, but it's hands with eyeballs! The creators could at least have used hand *puppets*. Also, the hands don't speak in proper sentences but just utter a few words. After watching this, I am now sure to get nightmares about talking hands.

6 VEGGIETALES (U.S. AND SOUTH KOREA)
So, what's more bizarre than anthropomorphic vegetables playing instruments (even though they have no arms)? Anthropomorphic vegetables playing instruments and teaching Biblical values!

5 SHIMA SHIMA TORA NO SHIMAJIROU (JAPAN)
I must admit that I've only watched one episode of this, but that was bizarre enough. The boy Shimajirou is taught how to use the toilet. His parents sing about what he's doing on the toilet, the toilet itself invites him to sit on it, and the "wee wee" says "Yahoo!" as it goes down the drain.

4 LUDWIG (UK)
This is a crystal playing the violin. There's really little else that can be said about this extremely strange television program from the United Kingdom.

3 BOOBAH (UK AND U.S.)
This show is best described as five splotches of color who dance while they're seemingly high on speed. They have names like Zing Zing Zingbah and Jingbah. They live in the Boohball, a big white ball that appears out of thin air. They don't talk, they squeak. To sum it up: bizarre!

2 THE JUNIOR CHRISTIAN SCIENCE BIBLE LESSON (U.S.)
This show includes aspects such as the very scary puppet Chip the Black Boy, a man who can neither play the guitar nor sing but does it anyway; and Teddy Eddie, a singing panda who constantly tells the kids "not to do drugs." Frankly, I've never wanted to do drugs as much as after watching this.

1 TOMORROW'S PIONEERS (PALESTINE)
With episode titles such as "Farfour and the AK-47," this show definitely goes a bit further than teaching children about the alphabet. Antisemitism, anti-Americanism, and Islamism are common themes on the show. Three of the characters have been Farfour, a Mickey Mouse look-alike, Nahoul, a bumble bee, and Assoud, a rabbit. In the show, they're all killed in the war against the Israelis, making them into martyrs.

10 MYSTERIOUS FICTITIOUS ISLANDS

10 THE ISLAND
First appeared in: *Lost* (2004)

"The Island" is the major setting of this six-season-long television show, as well as a video game, that features time travel, slave ships, supernatural monsters, large deadly non-native-to-the-island animals, hidden treasures, scary scientists, potential to sink into the ocean, supervillains, references to antiquity, and more—i.e., just about as much of a combination of the various aspects of the other islands on this list rolled into one.

9 SHANG TSUNG'S ISLAND
First appeared in: *Mortal Kombat* (1992)

Shang Tsung's Island appears as the tournament setting in a video-game version of the secret martial arts tournament, a premise seen in such earlier films as *Enter the Dragon*. It adds much more in the way of the supernatural, and, in 1995, resurfaced in the theatrically released film version. Shang Tsung is a powerful and deadly wizard; he's the primary antagonist in the series and is a shapeshifter who absorbs the souls of those he slays in order to maintain his youth and power.

8 ISLA NUBLAR
First appeared in: *Jurassic Park* (1990)

For *Jurassic Park*, Steven Spielberg used the island of Kauai as a stand-in for Isla Nublar (intended to mean "Cloud Island" in Spanish). Aside from serving as the primary location of this blockbuster film and novel, Isla Nublar is perhaps the only island people can actually visit, in a manner of speaking, due to its replication as one of the Islands of Adventure at Universal Studios Orlando.

7 ARKHAM ISLAND
First appeared in: *Batman* #258 (1974)

Over the years, the Batman franchise added many special bat caves to the story line. It's the Arkham bat cave that's associated with Arkham Island and the asylum there (which undoubtedly adds to the island's mysterious nature). With appearances in major comic books, films, and video games, the island serves as a setting for bizarre and creepy villains and harrowing violence. Video-game players can experience the Island in the 3D "Game of the Year" release of *Batman: Arkham Asylum* for the PlayStation 3.

6 HAN'S ISLAND
First appeared in: *Enter the Dragon* (1973)

This island's name served as one of the alternate titles for the film and as the main location for a mysterious martial arts competition, setting the stage for such later, similarly plotted (albeit more fantastical) films as *Mortal Kombat* (1995). Interestingly, a similarly named island (Hans Island) is a tiny island in the Nares Strait over which both Canada and Denmark claim ownership. This disputed claim led to a Google war when each nation spammed Google search results in support of their ownership.

5 SKULL ISLAND
First appeared in: *King Kong* (1933)

Skull Island is the home of King Kong and several other species of creatures, mostly prehistoric (in some cases species that should have been extinct long before the rise of mammalian creatures such as gorillas), along with a primitive society of humans. It's the main setting of three major films and a tie-in video game, as well as a pseudodocumentary and companion book about expeditions to and the animal life on the island.

4 THE ISLAND OF DOCTOR MOREAU
First appeared in: *The Island of Doctor Moreau* (1896)

This island is home to Dr. Moreau, who spends his time creating animal-human hybrids that terrorize the book's protagonist. Multiple film adaptations of this story, and the whole notion of animal experimentation by a mad scientist, serve as a definite precursor to *Jurassic Park*, if not a few of the story lines in *Lost*. The British Union for the Abolition of Vivisection was formed two years after the publication of this novel.

3 TREASURE ISLAND
First appeared in: *Treasure Island* (1883)

Treasure Island is a tale of "pirates and buried gold" by Robert Louis Stevenson. In addition to the numerous film and television adaptations of the novel, the characters, setting, and events of this novel have greatly influenced modern imagery of pirates, including treasure maps marked with an "x," schooners, the Black Spot, tropical islands, and one-legged seamen with parrots on their shoulders.

2 LINCOLN ISLAND
First appeared in: *The Mysterious Island* (1874)

The original "mysterious island" that first appeared in a novel has since served as the main plot location in at least a half-dozen films. *Mysterious Island* (the book) was a sequel to Jules Verne's famous *Twenty Thousand Leagues Under the Sea* and *In Search of the Castaways*, although, thematically, it's vastly different from those books. While on the island, the main characters find a message in a bottle that serves as part of the mystery.

1 ATLANTIS
First appeared in: *Timaeus* (360 BC)

Arguably the inspiration for many of the other islands listed above, Atlantis, which first appeared in Plato's writings, makes incredibly diverse appearances on television and in video games, from being the main setting for TV's *Stargate: Atlantis* to being playable levels in *Arctic Thunder* and *Guitar Hero: Smash Hits*. Of course, while I'm reasonably confident that no actual island has housed Dr. Moreau's experiments, smoke monsters, or Batman's arch-nemesis, Atlantis may have actually existed. Sure, the search for it has attracted the attention of fictional heroes such as Indiana Jones, but many real-life archaeologists and explorers have devoted much time and effort in to the quest as well.

10 MOST EVIL DISNEY VILLAINS

10 STROMBOLI *(PINOCCHIO)*
"Large," "loud," and "evil" are the words that come to mind when Stromboli is mentioned. He's a heartless showman who burns his marionettes for firewood when they grow too old to perform. This puppeteer's sole passion is money, and when he discovers Pinocchio's potential as a stringless puppet who can sing and dance, he kidnaps him and forces him to work.

9 CRUELLA DE VIL *(101 DALMATIANS)*
This fur-loving woman is a danger to all animals. She'll do whatever it takes to get her hands on the dalmatians. Anyone who kills cute little puppies to make coats is evil in my books. With a quote like this, how could she not be on the list: "Poison them, drown them, bash them on the head!"

8 GOVERNOR RATCLIFFE *(POCAHONTAS)*
This money-hungry governor is as greedy as they come. He does not trust the "savages" and sends his men to attack them because he believes they're hiding gold he most desperately wants. Even when it's discovered that the Native Americans don't possess the riches, he still declares that he must "sound the drums of war."

7 JAFAR *(ALADDIN)*
This evil sorcerer is seen in his advisor attire for the majority of the movie. However, he also goes through quite a few transformations. These include: an old cripple, a sultan, a cobra, and a frightening genie. He pretends to be a faithful advisor to the sultan in an attempt to steal his throne and rule Agrabah.

6 LADY TREMAINE *(CINDERELLA)*
This self-centered wicked stepmother psychologically abuses Cinderella. She ruthlessly toys with the poor girl's hopes and dreams, treating Cinderella as a slave rather than a child. In an attempt to prevent Cinderella from attending the grand ball, she locks her away with no chance of meeting the prince. Lady

Tremaine successfully manages to inflict extreme suffering on Cinderella without laying a finger on her.

5 SHAN-YU *(MULAN)*

This ruthless leader of the Huns is determined to conquer China. He and his army climb over the Great Wall and invade the land to prove Shan-Yu's superiority to the emperor. Shan-Yu feels no hesitation when it comes to taking a life. Sometimes, for his own amusement, he kills without remorse, which he demonstrates when he asks "How many men does it take to deliver a message?" to which one of his henchmen replies "one" as he aims his arrow at one of two Chinese spies.

4 URSULA *(THE LITTLE MERMAID)*

This manipulative, lip-pouting octopus has a mean hobby of collecting souls so that they can suffer in misery for the rest of their existence. She manipulates Ariel with empty promises in order to collect her soul and lure King Triton into her clutches in the process.

3 SCAR *(THE LION KING)*

The evil brother of Mufasa will do anything to become king of the pride lands, even if it means killing his brother and his nephew, Simba. Although he only succeeds in murdering Mufasa, he convinces his nephew that it was his fault, leaving Simba to live with the guilt of his father's death. Scar tells the cub to "run far away, Simba, and never come back."

2 THE QUEEN *(SNOW WHITE AND THE SEVEN DWARFS)*

When "the fairest of them all" reaches an age at which her radiance is fading, she plots to have her stepdaughter, Snow White, killed and demands that she have her heart to feed on. She even uses witchcraft to transform into an old lady, which allows her to give a poisoned apple to a naive Snow White.

1 MALEFICENT *(SLEEPING BEAUTY)*

Maleficent's evil knows no bounds, and all of her insidious plans are devised out of spite. The malicious enchantress casts a spell on Princess Aurora to ensure that "before the sun sets on her 16th birthday, she shall prick her finger on the spindle of a spinning wheel and die." With her devil-like horns, she is easily seen as the most evil villain of all. If you don't agree, look up "maleficent" in the dictionary: the definition is "doing evil or harm."

10 BANNED CONTROVERSIAL ALBUM COVERS

10 *THE ORIGIN OF THE FECES*, TYPE O NEGATIVE (1992)

What better way to kick off this list than with goth-metal band Type O Negative's album, the title of which plays on Darwin's *On the Origin of Species*. Upon first release, the album featured quite a "cheeky" cover photo of a derriere allegedly belonging to the band's lead vocalist, Peter Steele. Apparently their label, Roadrunner Records, had second thoughts soon after release (what a surprise), and later issues of the album were given the more tame "green skeleton" cover, rendering the original an immediate collectable.

9 *FAR BEYOND DRIVEN*, PANTERA (1994)

As long as we're delving into the anal theme here (no pun intended), the original cover of this album artistically depicts a large drill bit, that's, um… far beyond driven into a place where the sun don't shine. I can hear the record company execs now: "Well, gee, apparently that crossed some sort of line, so let's just replace that picture with an image of the drill bit impaling a skull instead, shall we? Problem solved."

8 *AMORICA*, THE BLACK CROWES (1994)

I guess the horror of exposing a few strands of pubic hair was enough to cause an uproar about the Black Crowes' original cover photo that was used on their album *Amorica*. Urban legend at the time had it that this was actually a photo of a male model with some strategic "tucking" involved, but in reality the image was first used on the cover of a 1976 issue of *Hustler* magazine, which makes that seem unlikely to be true. Right? Please say it ain't so. The photo was later replaced in some markets (namely, the U.S.; ironic given the album's title and stars-and-stripes theme) by a blacked-out version that just showed the flag triangle (sans pubic hair) against a black background, as if to say, "Move along people, nothing to see here."

7 APPETITE FOR DESTRUCTION, GUNS N' ROSES (1987)

"Appetite for Destruction" is the title of a painting by popular "lowbrow" artist Robert Williams and was the basis for the cover of Guns N' Roses' debut album of the same name. Unfortunately, the geniuses in Geffen Records' marketing department didn't consider that a graphic depiction of rape might cause some problems with conservative retailers in the U.S., who refused to stock the album until a change was made to the now-more-widely-recognized cross and skulls cover. Williams' artwork was retained, but it was relegated to an interior sleeve insert. Prices for sealed first pressings of this record with the original artwork on the cover can run you upward of $100.

6 HOLY WOOD (IN THE SHADOW OF THE VALLEY OF DEATH), MARILYN MANSON (2000)

This album was Manson's first release following the April 1999 Columbine High School shootings, for which he had been crucified in the press for being an inspiration to the killers (this claim was later determined to be totally unsubstantiated). Consequently, this album explores such themes as parental roles and America's hypocrisy of conservative values and culture juxtaposed with its mainstream acceptance of violence and the fame attained by people whose publicly displayed deaths have been romanticized. Various major retail chains in the U.S. refused to stock the record at all, and some only would with an alternative cover. Manson's response was:

> The irony is that my point of the photo on the album was to show people that the crucifixion of Christ is, indeed, a violent image. In fact, the picture itself is composed of a statue of Jesus taken from a place of worship. My jaw is missing as a symbol of this very kind of censorship. This doesn't piss me off as much as it pleases me, because those offended by my album cover have successfully proven my point.

5 LOVE IT TO DEATH, ALICE COOPER (1971)

Original versions of this album cover are affectionately known as the "thumb cover" among fans and collectors because that wacky Vincent Fernier (aka Alice Cooper) surreptitiously poked his thumb through an opening in the front of his cape during the photo shoot in such a way that it appears to be his penis on display. Released under the Straight label (owned by Frank Zappa), this clever gag was allowed to slide. But when Warner Brothers acquired the label, the cover on later re-issues of the album had a version of the photo with the offending digit airbrushed out.

4 BLIND FAITH, BLIND FAITH (1969)

This legendary supergroup's only album, the self-titled *Blind Faith*, featured a topless 11-year-old girl provocatively holding an aircraft-type object that some interpreted as a phallic symbol. Nice, eh? Apparently not. Well-known San Francisco rock-and-roll photographer Bob Seidemann, who was a personal friend of band member Eric Clapton, produced this artwork, which according to him was supposed to depict human creative achievement in technology (represented by the aircraft), borne though innocence (represented by the young child). Whatever. In the U.S., the record was issued with an alternate cover. But I'm telling you, if this blatant use of what pretty much amounts to child pornography to sell records wasn't bizarre enough, you ain't seen nothin' yet:

3 VIRGIN KILLER, THE SCORPIONS (1976)

How anyone in their right mind thought this cover photo was a good idea is beyond me. The Scorpions have several controversial covers in their discography, but this one of an erotically posed 10-year-old girl takes the cake (the shattered glass pattern obscuring her genitals is an intentional part of the image). The inspiration came solely from label RCA Records' marketing personnel; the band members had nothing to do with it, but early on they did stand behind it and tried to defend its use as being an artistically symbolic representation of the title track's lyrical theme: that time is the killer of virgin innocence. Not surprisingly, the image was soon replaced by a more acceptable alternative cover depicting the band (in a rather ridiculous pose). More

recently, some band members, in particular former lead guitarist Uli Roth, have expressed regret over the cover and their original support of it.

In May 2008, U.S. conservative media group WorldNetDaily reported Wikipedia's hosting of this image to the FBI, which led to an investigation but no resultant actions. However, on December 5, 2008, the URL for Wikipedia's image page of this photo was added to the UK-based Internet Watch Foundation's blacklist, which resulted in the content being blocked by most of the UK's major Internet service providers. This unfortunately caused some undesirable problems, as subscribers temporarily could not edit or contribute to any Wikipedia pages. The blacklisting was rescinded four days later through the reasoning, in part, that the photo was already widely available in the public domain.

2 *DIAMOND DOGS*, DAVID BOWIE (1974)

The sleeve of this album features a stylish painting by Belgian artist Guy Peellaert. This striking piece is a somewhat freakish representation of Bowie as a half-man/half-dog creature. An anatomically correct creature by the way, to which RCA Records immediately took exception by withdrawing the albums and ordering the artwork to be reproduced with the canine genitalia airbrushed out (which is amusing in comparison to the previous entry—just two years later, RCA deemed the cover of *Virgin Killer* acceptable). Inexplicably, a few unaltered versions survived and are quite valuable today, reportedly approaching close to $10,000 in value. But buyers beware: 1990 Rykodisc re-issues with the restored original image are somewhat easy to come by, and although they can be worth a couple hundred dollars in their own right, they aren't the real deal.

1 *YESTERDAY AND TODAY*, THE BEATLES (1966)

The Beatles' infamous "butcher-baby" cover is perhaps the most well-known banned cover of all time and is likely the most valuable as well. The cover featured the Beatles sitting with chunks of raw meat and bones scattered over them along with dismembered baby dolls. The original version of this album wasn't actually released for sale to the general public, but advance copies and promo material were sent to radio stations and a few retailers, and the immediately ensuing outcry caused Capitol Records to quickly withdraw all inventory that was ready for distribution (about 750,000 copies). Rather than destroy all the sleeves, Capitol instead chose to slap a much more conservative photo of the band posed around a steamer trunk over the original art and then re-issue the records to retailers. It didn't take long for fans to figure out how to peel the trunk photo off to reveal the butcher photo underneath, which eventually led to a cottage industry of professional peelers. A collectors' jargon evolved to distinguish "first state" (original uncovered version), "second state" (paste-over version), and "third state" (peeled) copies.

Over the years, so many paste-overs have been peeled (or damaged or lost) that these days, second-state butcher-baby versions are becoming scarcer and are increasing in value. If in good condition, they can easily fetch a couple thousand dollars, and thus are more desirable than even professionally peeled third-state copies. Not surprisingly, first-state originals are the most valuable; factory-sealed copies, in particular, are extremely rare and worth in the tens of thousands of dollars or more depending on condition. By the mid '80s, there were only two stereo and fewer than ten mono sealed first-state butcher copies known to exist. In 1987, a case of 24 sealed original butcher-babies (five stereo and nineteen mono) turned up at a Beatles convention in the hands of Peter Livingston, whose father, Alan, was president of Capitol Records at the time of the recall. These are known as the "Livingston copies" and are the most valuable of all, given their pedigree.

To determine if your copy of *Yesterday and Today* is a paste-over, look for a faint v-shaped bleed-through of Ringo's black shirt in the white background area of the trunk photo midway down the right edge. If you're lucky enough to discover a previously unbeknownst one in your collection, my advice to you is don't even think about trying to peel it! In all my years of record collecting, my second-state butcher-baby version in very good condition is the most prized item.

10 ROCK ACTS THAT SABOTAGED THEIR CAREERS

10 BILLY SQUIER
Sabotaged by: Music Video

Boston rocker Billy Squier was the lone hard rocker still hitting the charts when synthesizers and drum machines crowded everything else out of '80s radio. With the excellent *Don't Say No* and *Emotions in Motion* already under his belt, record executives were salivating over the chance to market his 1984 album, *Signs of*

Life. For the music video of the first single, "Rock Me Tonight," they convinced him to dance on a bed wearing a pink tank top. The album sold gangbusters, but the video lost Squier his fan base (his dancing was compared to a French pastry chef whose soufflé had fallen). The shame of it was that in concert, Billy just strapped on a Telecaster and rocked. Subsequent albums predictably fizzled.

9 CHEAP TRICK
Sabotaged by: Japan

After three critically acclaimed but poor-selling albums, Cheap Trick was ready to launch their best record with *Dream Police*. But then their quickie live set in Tokyo went uber-platinum. Put on hold for a year, *Dream Police* sold well when it finally saw the light of day, but critics complained the band had abandoned their Budakon sound (even though the concerts were recorded after *Dream Police* was already completed). Desperate for another hit, record executives paired the band with producer after producer, even though nobody knew why the live album sold when the studio versions didn't. Only after their record contract expired did Trick get their edge back on *Cheap Trick '97* and *Rockford*, both produced on independent labels.

8 QUIET RIOT
Sabotaged by: Trash Talk

Quiet Riot has the dubious honor to be the very first heavy metal band to score a top-ten hit with a cover of Slade's "Cum On Feel the Noize." But they'd shot their wad creatively, and they had to release another Slade cover as a follow-up. The band probably could have weathered this, but when lead singer Kevin DuBrow insulted Mötley Crüe, he angered fans on all sides. Heavy metal found its first pariah in a movement supposedly populated by outcasts. Oh, the angst!

7 OZZY OSBOURNE
Sabotaged by: Reality Television

Oh, he's all warm and fuzzy now, but back in the day, Ozzy was a bat-biting, ant-eating, dove-killing badass backed by guitar whiz Randy Rhoads on "Crazy Train," "Over the Mountain," and "Flying High Again." But by letting MTV into his L.A. mansion (instead of the creepy dungeon we all pictured him in) to film *The Osbournes*, Ozzy cashed in the last of his credibility for a permanent Trivial Pursuit mention and loads of cash.

6 METALLICA
Sabotaged by: Napster

As file sharing made anonymous, consequence-free theft absurdly easy, Metallica drummer Lars Ulrich stood up for musicians by refusing to sell Metallica content digitally. Musicians applauded the stand, but the fan base saw Metallica as out of date and hypocritical, since mix-tape trading was largely responsible for Metallica's getting noticed by the major labels. It took five years and group therapy before the band recovered most of its reputation.

5 ROD STEWART
Sabotaged by: Urban Legend

You know the one, don't you? Sure, you do. About how Rod Stewart had to have his stomach pumped because he had a gallon of human semen in it? Regardless of which way Rod swings, he claims his career was unaffected. For the record, Rod later married model Rachel Hunter. Incidentally, the same urban legend has also been applied to Elton John, David Bowie, Mick Jagger, Jon Bon Jovi, Alanis Morissette, Britney Spears, and Lil' Kim.

4 THE BEATLES
Sabotaged by: Jesus

In a press interview, John Lennon made a cynical, off-the-cuff remark that Beatlemania had made his band "more popular than Jesus now." The backlash was instantaneous and resulted in mass protests and record burnings. Management quickly scheduled a press conference, and Lennon recanted, according to a script we're all too familiar with these days. Me? I think Jesus let him off with a warning.

3 THE BEATLES (AGAIN!)
Sabotaged by: Yoko Ono—NOT

Bands have always had to tolerate the singer's girlfriend, but damn, this was The Beatles. Post-Yoko, the rift between John and Paul grew unfixable, leading to the group's demise before they could get old and start sucking. Wait…

2 JERRY LEE LEWIS
Sabotaged by: Marriage

Just as his star was burning brightest ("Whole Lotta Shakin Goin' On" and "Great Balls of Fire" were established hits), Jerry Lee Lewis had the brainstorm that marrying his 13-year-old cousin was a really good idea. As you can imagine, it was career suicide, but it's hard to appreciate how much of an outrage it must have been in the 1950s. Let's try: today, Marilyn Manson can vivisect a leopard seal in an elementary school crosswalk and no one bats an eye. But we all still abhor Jerry Lee Lewis. Yeah. It's that bad.

1 MICHAEL JACKSON
Sabotaged by: Plastic Surgery

How bad must you be to beat Jerry Lee Lewis in a creep-out contest? Try cosmetic surgeries numbered in scientific notation, resulting in a bleached, noseless rictus that makes the old guy from *Poltergeist II* look huggable. And if that doesn't seal the deal, throw in cash settlements for pedophilia charges and dangle a blindfolded baby out a window. At his obese and addicted worst, Elvis looks angelic next to this abomination of too much fame, money, and wasted talent.

10 CLOWNS YOU DON'T WANT TO MESS WITH

10 KRUSTY

Krusty the Clown should be well-known; he is, of course, one of the characters from the popular television program *The Simpsons*. Krusty is famous for being loved by all the kids for his humorous antics on screen while being rather different off screen. Krusty is a hard-living entertainment veteran, sometimes depicted as a jaded, burned-out has-been who's been down-and-out several times and remains addicted to gambling, cigarettes, alcohol, Percodan, Pepto-Bismol, and Xanax. He instantly becomes depressed as soon as the cameras stop rolling. Krusty wastes money almost as fast as he earns it: lighting his cigarettes with hundred-dollar bills; eating condor-egg omelets; spending huge sums on pornographic magazines; and losing a fortune gambling on everything from horse races to operas to betting against the Harlem Globetrotters. So why is Krusty on this list? For the simple reason that a person who takes copious amounts of drugs and booze and sells products that kill (like cereal with a jagged metal Krusty-O in each box) can never be trusted!

9 PULCINELLA

Pulcinella (often called Punch or Punchinello in English) is a classical character that originated in the *commedia dell'arte* of the 17th century, a form of professional masked theater. His main characteristic, from which he acquired his name, is his extremely long nose, which resembles a beak. His traditional temperament is to be mean, vicious, and crafty; his main method of defense is to pretend to be too stupid to know what's going on, and his secondary tactic is to physically beat people. Pulcinella has appeared in a round-about way in modern fiction as well. Konrad Beezo and his son, Punchinello, are the antagonists in the novel *Life Expectancy* by Dean Koontz. While by no means the most evil of clowns on this list, Pulcinella can be said to be a progenitor of the evil-clown genre and definitely deserves an entry here.

8 RONALD MCDONALD

This is no joke. Ronald McDonald, the famous mascot for the fast food joint, is a clown you don't want to mess with! The reason, however, is slightly different from some of the other entries here. Most countries with McDonald's restaurants have a Ronald McDonald actor who is often hired for children's parties. Because he is so famous and drives kids wild, he travels with an entourage of bodyguards, other McDonald's staff who are trained in the job. Now this is where the danger comes in. If you're a kid and you get too close to Ronald, the bodyguards are trained to keep you back—with violence. The methods they're taught included pinching children and stamping on their feet. So remember, next time you see Ronald, keep your distance. Otherwise, you might end up injured.

7 DOINK

In the early 1990s, an evil clown character was featured in the World Wrestling Federation (WWF). Doink the Clown was portrayed as a villain early on in his career. He would do cruel things such as pop children's balloons with a cigar, splash water on the audience, and use a fake prosthetic arm to attack opponents. Once he even attacked an opponent with a car battery. His entrance theme music was a typical happy circus tune that would quickly segue into dark and menacing music, complete with evil cackling sound effects.

6 KILLER KLOWNS FROM OUTER SPACE

A list like this would not be complete without the title characters in the movie of the same name. An army of sadistic extraterrestrial lifeforms that resemble clowns lands their circus-tent ship in the sleepy American town of Crescent Cove. The Klown Army advances into Crescent Cove, inflicting genocide during their occupation. They harvest the unsuspecting population, blasting random victims with a ray gun that cocoons them with lethal cotton candy. The Klown Army uses a variety of seemingly innocent methods to ensnare their victims, such as killer shadow puppets, bloodhoundlike balloon animals, and a ray gun that looks like a child's toy. Since the methods themselves appear whimsical, the townspeople don't know they're in danger until it's too late. It isn't quality, it isn't serious, but it sure is ridiculously funny.

5 UBU ROI

Ubu Roi (King Ubu), a play by Alfred Jarry, premiered in 1896. It is one of the precursors to the Theatre of the Absurd and the greater surrealist art movement of the early 20th century. The main character, Ubu (who is certainly a clownlike figure), lives in a world of greedy self-gratification. He is an antihero— fat, ugly, vulgar, gluttonous, grandiose, dishonest, stupid, jejune, voracious, cruel, cowardly, and evil. With the urging of his wife, Ubu murders the king who helped him, usurps his throne, and is in turn defeated and killed by his son. In its first performance, after only the first word (*merde*, the French word for "shit") a riot broke out and the play was banned from the stage, so it moved to a puppet theater. It has since had a very popular revival.

4 POLTERGEIST CLOWN

Those of you who have seen the excellent horror series *Poltergeist* will remember the clown scene in which the young boy is assaulted by his toy clown. The scene has been parodied by both *Family Guy* and *Scary Movie 2*, in which the clown sexually assaults his victim. The famous clown scene is not the best in the film, but it is certainly one that makes it worth seeing.

3 THE JOKER

The Joker is the famous wicked character from the *Batman* stories. Probably the most sinister portrayal is by the late Heath Ledger, who managed to bring a believable evil to the screen in *The Dark Knight*. Throughout his original comic book appearances, the Joker was portrayed as a master criminal whose characterization varied from that of a violent psychopath to a goofy trickster-thief. His appearance is not typical of most clowns, but he shares sufficient traits with them that he should certainly be included in the genre. The origin of his looks varies from source to source, but the most common is that he fell into a vat of chemical waste that bleached his skin, turned his hair green, and made his lips bright red.

2 PENNYWISE

Pennywise is the clown form of the shapeshifting eponymous character from the Stephen King novel *It*. In the overall scheme of King's writing, It comes from part of the greater universe that also encompasses some of his other works. While It appears mainly as Pennywise the clown (particularly when stalking children), It also appears as a giant spider. Humans never truly see its full form as it "naturally" exists beyond the physical realm in a place called the "deadlights." Every 30 years, It comes back to life to terrorize and destroy. At the end of the novel, It is revealed to be female and it lays eggs.

1 POGO

Pogo had to be number one on this list for one very good reason: if you messed with him, you really would end up dead. Pogo was the name of the clown character used by John Wayne Gacy to make connections with young men so he could rape, torture, and murder them. Gacy taught himself how to apply clown makeup and made all his own costumes. He intentionally painted his mouth with sharp corners instead of the normal round corners that are generally preferred so as to not frighten children. Gacy performed countless times at local children's parties and hospitals. There is no doubt he epitomizes the concept of the "evil clown." Pogo's death toll was between 25 and 30.

10 BIZARRE AND TRAGIC HOLLYWOOD SUICIDES

10 RUSLANA KORSHUNOVA (JULY 2, 1987–JUNE 28, 2008)

Ruslana Korshunova was a Kazakh supermodel of Russian heritage. She posed in *Vogue* and represented designers such as Vera Wang and Nina Ricci. She was discovered in 2003 and was immediately distinguished by her knee-length chestnut-colored hair. Part of what made her suicide so bizarre was the method she chose. June 28, 2008, somewhere around 2:30 p.m., Ruslana "fell" out of her ninth-floor balcony in Manhattan after having watched the movie *Ghost* with a former boyfriend. Friends have said that she was usually a cheerful person and had never shown any signs of distress or feelings of failure, although there were things written on some social networking sites that seemed to suggest otherwise. She at one time stated, "Death is a celebration of life... there is hope," and, "I'm so lost. Will I ever find myself?" Ruslana Korshunova's death was ruled a suicide because the police could find no other witnesses. However, something odd that was noticed at the time of her death was that her trademark hair was considerably shorter and looked as if it had been cut in haste.

9 MARY KAY BERGMAN (JUNE 5, 1961–NOVEMBER 11, 1999)

I'm sure everyone is familiar with the popular show *South Park*, but maybe not so familiar with this leading lady who contributed to making the show so beloved. Mary Kay Bergman was born in Los Angeles, California, to Jewish parents and was a self-proclaimed nerd. Science fiction and fantasy were two main passions of hers, but she had always been an avid fan of Disney. She not only voiced the parts of Ms. Cartman and Wendy on *South Park*, but she also was the voice of Timmy Turner in *The Fairly OddParents* and was the official voice of Snow White for Disney. Bergman had been married for nine years and seemed happy. Until her death, no one had known that she suffered from chronic and acute depression for many years, despite having reached many of her goals and achieving a dream profession. Sadly, though, on a Thursday night, Mary Kay Bergman shot herself in the head. She was found an hour and 20 minutes later by her husband and friend, and she left two suicide notes that have not yet been released.

8 RYAN JENKINS (FEBRUARY 8, 1977–AUGUST 23, 2009)

I'm sure that some may argue over this person's status as a celebrity because they only starred on reality television. Although his status isn't nearly the same as some others on this list, I am absolutely addicted to reality television, so it's enough for me. Although the reasons behind the suicide are difficult to hear, it was certainly bizarre and shocking enough to bear noting. Ryan Jenkins was a Canadian, born in British Columbia, who was also a self-made millionaire. He appeared on the VH1 show *Megan Wants a Millionaire* and went on to star on *I Love Money*. On that show, he won the first-place prize, along with $250,000 dollars. Only a few episodes of *Megan Wants a Millionaire* aired, and *I Love Money* never aired, following the discovery on August 15, 2009, of the body of Jasmine Fiore. She was a former model who met Ryan in a Las Vegas casino, married him two days later, and was brutally killed shortly thereafter. Fiore was found in a suitcase with no teeth and her fingers had been cut off. She had been strangled, and her body had been crushed, mutilated, and beaten. Had she not had breast implants, her identity might never have been discovered. Five days later, after an intense search for Fiore's killer had begun, Jenkins hanged himself with a belt in a motel room in Canada.

7 PAULA GOODSPEED (1979–NOVEMBER 11, 2008)

Anyone who watches *American Idol* will likely be familiar with Paula Goodspeed. Paula was a devoted fan of *American Idol* and especially of Paula Abdul. She had auditioned to be on the show to meet her idol and in the hopes of becoming infamous. She achieved infamy, but sadly for the wrong reasons. It was said that she was rejected from the show because of her outlandish fashion and flat audition, and that she was ridiculed for having braces. Five months later, Goodspeed wrote on a social-networking website that auditioning may have been a mistake and that reading fans' comments about her were hurtful. As a consequence of her very serious crush on Paula Abdul (Goodspeed identified as being gay), an audition gone wrong, and cruel remarks from her peers, Paula Goodspeed's body was found outside Paula Abdul's home, having killed herself with an overdose of prescription pills.

6 BRYNN HARTMAN (APRIL 11, 1958–MAY 28, 1998)

Brynn Hartman was the third wife of well-known actor and comedian Phil Hartman, and the third time, in this case, was anything but a charm. Most people remember Phil Hartman from his work on *Saturday Night Live*. Brynn was a former model who had a history of drug and alcohol abuse throughout their marriage, as well as behavioral problems. No one knows if it was their two children or Phil's undying love for Brynn, but he was determined to make this marriage work. It ended up costing him his life. On the evening of May 28, Brynn and Phil had one of many arguments about her drug use. Phil then went to sleep and was later shot three times by a high and intoxicated Brynn. Phil is believed to have died instantly. Brynn then confessed the murder to two people before she shot herself in the head, taking her own life. There was speculation that actor Andy Dick had provided Brynn Hartman with the cocaine she took that night, which caused her psychotic behavior, but he denies those claims to this day.

5 ELLIOTT SMITH (AUGUST 6, 1969–OCTOBER 21, 2003)

Elliott Smith was born in Omaha, Nebraska, and lived for a long time in Portland, Oregon. He had a gift for creating music that took you to another place, and his voice was totally unique. He was best known for playing a large role in creating the soundtrack for *Good Will Hunting* and for an Academy Award nomination for his song "Miss Misery." Elliott had existing suicidal tendencies, having tried to jump off a cliff while drunk, only to have a tree break his fall. While he lived in Portland, he began to dabble in drugs. Following an argument with his girlfriend in late October 2003, Smith was found in the kitchen with a knife in his chest after his girlfriend heard him scream. Elliott Smith died at 1:36 p.m.

4 JONATHAN BRANDIS (APRIL 13, 1976–NOVEMBER 12, 2003)

Jonathan Brandis was born in Danbury, Connecticut, and began his film career at age five. He starred in films such as *The Neverending Story II: The Next Chapter* and *Ladybugs*, with Rodney Dangerfield. His most well-known role was on the Steven Spielberg TV series *SeaQuest*, which turned him into a teen idol. Friends of the actor said he seemed to be depressed about his lack of a career as an adult, despite the fact that he was working on a film in his directorial debut and had projects in the works. Jonathan Brandis hanged himself on the evening of November 11 and died in the hospital the next day.

3 ANDREW KOENIG (AUGUST 17, 1968–FEBRUARY 14, 2010)

Andrew Koenig was best known as the character Boner on the sitcom hit *Growing Pains*. He also played The Joker in a short film based on the *Batman* series, but otherwise didn't have too extensive a resume. Koenig was said to have mostly enjoyed working behind the scenes, and he was deeply involved in human rights. In February 2010, Koenig went to Canada to see the Olympics and never returned. He was later found hanged in Vancouver.

2 DANA PLATO (NOVEMBER 7, 1964–MAY 8, 1999)

Dana Plato was born in Moore, Oklahoma, and was best known for her role as Kimberly on *Diff'rent Strokes*. She was fired from the show because of an unplanned pregnancy. Unable to reach the status she wanted, she became involved in darker pastimes and was arrested for armed robbery in 1991. She got breast implants and appeared in *Playboy* in the hopes of regaining stardom. She later worked on films of an erotic nature. She appeared on *The Howard Stern Show* the day before her death and claimed she had been sober for ten years. Callers called to defend her and commend her on turning her life around, but Dana went on to overdose on pills the following day in a vehicle outside of her fiancé's mother's house. Sadly, in May 2010, Dana's son also committed suicide.

1 PEG ENTWISTLE (FEBRUARY 5, 1908–SEPTEMBER 16, 1932)

Peg Entwistle may be the oldest on the list, but her story certainly isn't the least interesting. Born in Port Talbot, Wales, her dream, like so many others', was to become an actress. She started out on Broadway and went on to be known as a comedienne. Her only film was called *Thirteen Women* and, apparently, received very poor reviews. Upset by the comments of the critics, as well as her small amount of screen time, Peg walked up the hill featuring the famous Hollywood sign, climbed atop the "H," and jumped off. Strangely enough, the following day, a letter came in the mail for Entwistle offering her a role in a play about a woman who commits suicide.

10 MOST EVIL VILLAINS IN ANIME

10 **GRIMMJOW JEAGERJAQUES** *(BLEACH)*
Despite being one of the weaker of the ten espada (the highest-ranked men in Sosuke Aizen's army), Grimmjow made a mark on the *Bleach* series for being cruel, belligerent, and ruthless. He has an undying desire to kill his opponents in battle, no matter what it costs him. Among the espada, he represents destruction.

9 **PALADIN ALEXANDER ANDERSON** *(HELLSING)*
Gleefully destructive and completely unwilling to use his brain or listen to reason, Alexander lives to kill, and he wants to kill the hero, Alucard. His prejudices against the Hellsings and the Protestant English blind him and prevent him from being in any way a good guy, even though he does ostensibly kill monsters most of the time.

8 **OROCHIMARU** *(NARUTO)*
Classic evil. Orochimaru's childhood might give you a moment of pity for him, but his life will suck any more mercy right out of you. Even as a young man, he demonstrated malice, power-lust, and a darkness that even friends and a good master couldn't heal. He's determined to become immortal, and he doesn't care what he has to do to get there. Evil experiments on people, betrayal, slavery, mind control, necromancy, possession, murder—he stops at nothing.

7 **TETSUO** *(AKIRA)*
Yes, Tetsuo's also the hero of *Akira*. But he's a very tragic kind of hero who destroys an entire city and causes the death of countless citizens. Unfortunately, no one said you had to "mean it" to become a villain, or that the viewer can't empathize with the villain. After all, having depth of character and a good past is what makes him so interesting a character, and the story about him into a classic. He can't control his power and doesn't seek assistance doing so in time to contain it, causing him to become the prototypical accidental villain.

6 FRIEZA *(DRAGON BALL Z)*

Frieza makes this list for being notorious as the first true villain of the *Dragon Ball Z* series. When he is first introduced, he's feared by many, destroyed planets with his finger, and was all around scary. His forms (the various shapes he can take on) easily induce fear because each and every transformation does something to prove his evil. His first form impales Krillin and beats Gohan, his third nearly kills Piccolo, and his final form kills Dende, Krilln, Vegeta, almost kills Piccolo again, and destroys planet Namek. He is truly one evil bastard.

5 SOSUKE AIZEN *(BLEACH)*

Aizen is one cunning, confident, and mastermind villain in the *Bleach* series. He plans his own death, has been secretly working behind everyone's backs for possibly centuries, betraying many and plotting too often, and even the most cunning of ideas are mere whims to him, not to mention he has immense power that's on par with the leader of the 13 Captains himself, and that's without showing his *bankai*.

4 NARAKU *(INUYASHA)*

Naraku gets high points for being possibly the stingiest villain ever. Almost nothing can kill him, and he's one evil bastard, doing things like creating puppets of the dead or making demonic servants to do his bidding. He does so much it would take a while to count, but he makes a very big impact on the show for being a target for so many, yet living for so long.

3 PROFESSOR KAKUZAWA *(ELFEN LIED)*

Kakuzawa tortures children and thinks he's right to do it. He doesn't just excuse it because it's what he wants; he actually thinks he's noble and doing good. Kakuzawa is an example of the most frightening of evils—the evil we've seen in our own world and in our own time, the evil of thinking you're doing the right thing, or "doing evil to do good." On top of that, his idea of "good"—the most basic prejudice and racism—is itself evil.

2 VICIOUS *(COWBOY BEBOP)*

Very well-known for a reason, Vicious was once Spike's partner, and it's because of him that Spike's life is shattered. A would-be leader of their crime syndicate, Vicious is smarter and more directly violent than a lot of the villains in anime. He's old-fashioned destructive, plus a soupçon of malice par excellence.

1 GRIFFITH *(BERSERK)*

Griffith is the proud leader of the group of elite mercenaries known as the Band of the Hawk. He gets an offer from a group of demons to become an immortal apostle, as long as he gets rid of everything that he ever loved. As a result, he kills most of his trusted and loyal soldiers, takes out his closest friend's eye and his arm, and rapes another friend (his best friend's lover), thus deforming the unborn child. That's pretty evil.

10 WEIRD AND CONFUSING FILMS

10 *FIGHT CLUB*

I had to put *Fight Club* on the list, not because it's the most confusing movie ever, but because I fear backlash. Objectively, this movie is confusing. The basic premise is that two men join together to form an underground, bare-fisted boxing club, and while the plot gets a lot more complicated, the most confusing aspects are the subliminal messages created by splicing the film together. Is there any meaning behind them? That's one question that I have trouble answering, because this film has been interpreted in many different ways, which is part of being a confusing movie. Confusing movies, at least the good ones, will leave a need to solve the problems that the film creates. *Fight Club* is relatively straight-forward compared to the rest of the movies on this list, and so ultimately it can't really be put up any higher.

9 *DONNIE DARKO*

Probably the only good movie Jake Gyllenhaal will ever do, this film is quite a confusing one. There have been analysts who think that this is the deepest film ever, and those who think it's crap. In fact, all ten of the movies on this list could be argued the same way, because I've heard many arguments about all of them being stupid and "poorly written." But it's the significant lack of information that a film like this gives that creates a need for a deep meaning.

That's the wonder of confusing films though. They can compel audiences to interpret their meanings just with significant images and dialogue, but in reality, all ten could be shallow schemes to make the writers and directors seem genius (and that alone is pretty genius). In *Donnie Darko*, a young man has visions of a demonic-looking rabbit that control his life. The film's strangest elements occur near the end of the film when we see distortions in time, and the sequence of events becomes confused.

8 ERASERHEAD

There are two filmmakers who can create movies that stand out above all others as very confusing: David Lynch and Stanley Kubrick. Kubrick respected Lynch a lot and thought of *Eraserhead* as one of his favorites, even screening the movie for the cast of *The Shining* to get them in the right mood; but I'll return to Kubrick later. Other fans of *Eraserhead* include Mel Brooks (who hired Lynch for *The Elephant Man*) and George Lucas (who tried to hire Lynch for *The Return of the Jedi*—imagine *that*). As for the film itself, it's a cult classic, and, like all cult classics, it's bizarre. The basic conflict is that a man has to survive a hostile environment and a mutant child. That odd premise is then augmented by the significant lack of dialogue, which makes the whole thing confusing. The somewhere-between-odd-and-disturbing imagery is layered with potential meaning, leaving the whole thing open to interpretation. Many people have tried to figure *Eraserhead* out, but no one has ever really found the right answer (although Kubrick probably came pretty close).

7 MEMENTO

This film is quite interesting. The set up is great because it's a concept that seems to have never really been done before: the main character suffers from short-term memory loss, so he needs to write down his memories so he can investigate a murder. The confusion of it all is in the fact that it's told out of chronological order because of the memory loss. Many films have told stories out of chronology, such as *Pulp Fiction*, but *Memento* is a puzzle because the lack of a straight-forward timeline makes each scene hard to put into context. The confusion is necessary to fuel the plot because it's a psychological thriller.

6 BIG MAN JAPAN

This movie is mostly so straight-forward that the confusing aspect of this film caused it to be completely forgotten. A 40-year-old man occasionally turns into a giant, and you don't question anything that happens before the ending, but you question what the ending itself means. I expect that anyone who sees this film will come out in an awkward state between confusion and entertainment. This is a good film, a gem that not many people know about, but it leaves you wanting resolution. You can assume all you want about the story, but you won't get a satisfying answer. What's even weirder is that this film is a comedy *and* a mockumentary, making the ending so out of place with anything that came before it that you won't know what to think.

5 THE SHINING

In case you've missed this one, a husband and wife and their son move to a mountain hotel during the off season to act as caretakers, only to discover the hotel is haunted. People don't give *The Shining* enough credit for being confusing, but all you need to do is watch the bear-fellatio scene and suddenly it'll all come back to you. This movie is bizarre, but people still respect it because bizarre works in a horror movie. What's really bizarre is that nobody notices any details. There are theories that the entire room 237 sequence is a dream, with Danny symbolically represented by Jack, and with Jack symbolically represented by the naked lady in the tub. Of course, people just enjoy it for what it is, a bizarre, scary story, but if you ever try to figure out what's actually going on, prepare for one of the most confusing rides of your life.

4 MULHOLLAND DR.

Confusing is the first word that comes to mind when David Lynch is involved. David Lynch has made some straight-forward movies, but then there are films like this. It gets a lot of credit for being really confusing, and I can't blame people. In the tangled story, a woman loses her memory and tries to rediscover her identity. Characters are played by multiple actresses, there are an insane number of identity issues, and some theories suggest that the first three-quarters of the film are all just a dream sequence. *Twin Peaks* was Lynch's TV show, and even though this was going to be *Twin Peaks'* successor, instead it came out as a movie.

3 PRIMER

An underrated science fiction film that was made for $7000 dollars with a cast you could count on one hand, *Primer* was Shane Carruth's attempt at a re-envisioning of the tried-and-true plot of time travel. *Primer* is an anomaly for confusing movies, because there is not one person in the universe who can fully comprehend it. Carruth didn't know what he was doing while he was writing it; it just sort of came. The plot—four friends invent a time-travel device—doesn't really make complete sense because the film's dreamlike qualities leave you thinking "I don't know what it is, but it's good." Furthermore, Carruth plays the lead role, which contributes to the confusion. The two main characters don't know what's going on, and so the *characters* are confused. On top of that, they speak in engineer talk, so the viewer feels like an eavesdropper. You don't really learn anything more than the characters do. *Primer* is confusing for the writers, the actors, the characters, and the audience. It's a creation that far exceeds the knowledge of those surrounding it.

2 THE MATRIX TRILOGY

This whole series is based on the premise that a man discovers that the world as he knows it is just a dream that exists inside human beings, whose bodies are being used by machines as batteries. There's compelling evidence as to how confusing not just one of these movies is, but *all* of them are. So let's look at the first one. *The Matrix* raised nothing but questions, the most important being "Is what I perceive to be real actually real?" Then instead of answering that question, *The Matrix Reloaded* made you question the movie itself. The questions went from your reality to the movie's reality. The shocking ending scene with the sentinels actually made some people theorize that the entire series is one giant matrix and the scenes outside the matrix are *still* inside the matrix, and even speculate as to how that is possible. Then, the third movie, the one that would answer all the questions came out. Can you guess what it did? Raise more questions! People were enraged, but it's ultimately a good series. First the filmmakers made you question what reality meant, then they made you question what the movie's reality meant, and then they made you question why you even bothered with the series at all. The third movie cancelled out the two that came before; instead of resolution, you get a complete head scratcher. Most people perceived it as garbage and gave up, but either way, not one person could come out of any Matrix movie with any real answers.

1 2001: A SPACE ODYSSEY

This is the most confusing movie you'll ever see. Kubrick is the master of obscuring the motives and themes behind a movie, and this is the pinnacle of his work. The films before this one were not really confusing at all; in fact, they were very straight-forward. After *2001*, he followed up with *A Clockwork Orange*, which is also often referred to as his best work (as is *Dr. Strangelove*). As Kubrick's movies progressed, they became less subtle, and even though his later films were all very deep, not one of them was as confusing as this one. *2001* presents a journey through time and space during which man discovers his true origins. Rather than being fast-paced, like Kubrick's *Full Metal Jacket*, it just festers, with striking images and  slow pacing, and then suddenly, you just enter another dimension completely separate from the rest of the movie. The ending itself raises five million questions, and even though it helps to make the rest of the film seem straight-forward in comparison, it just isn't the case. From the very first to the very last shots of this film, all you get is more questions, and the purpose isn't for Kubrick to answer them, it's for you to answer them for yourself, which ultimately makes it even more confusing.

10 MOST RIDICULOUS COMEDIES

10 BEAVIS AND BUTT-HEAD DO AMERICA

Beavis and Butt-Head was known as a show that could be considered "intelligent." The whole premise was both realistic and yet ridiculous. When the movie came out, many people were skeptical of how the TV show would translate to a movie. Fortunately it didn't let people down. The movie has a very ridiculous premise to begin with. Beavis and Butt-Head wake up to find their TV stolen and go around looking for it. They wind up all over America and eventually at the White House. The movie gets really ridiculous when Beavis eats a cactus that makes him hallucinate, as well as when Beavis becomes his alter ego, "Cornholio."

9 HOT SHOTS! PART DEUX

I remember this movie for one thing: being very ridiculous. It's a spoof of the over-the-top action genre where movies like *Commando* and *Rambo* fit in. It's full of odd moments, such as when Charlie Sheen's character dips his hands in caramel and Skittles to toughen them up for a fight, or when Saddam Hussein has a fight against the president of the United States. Definitely a ridiculous movie, and a must-see for fans of the style.

8 ACE VENTURA: WHEN NATURE CALLS

I've been formulating a theory that the more sequels a series gets, the more ridiculous the series gets. Ace Ventura confirms the theory. *Ace Ventura: Pet Detective* is already a ridiculous movie about a pet detective who takes his job—but nothing else—seriously, and the sequel brings things up a notch. With Jim Carrey in the lead role, the movie is bound to be absurd. Throw in silly moments such as him escaping the butt of a rhino robot or when he battles against the Wachootoo tribe's greatest fighter, and you have a ridiculous movie like no other. Although not as praised as the first one in the series, this follow-up definitely is more absurd.

7 AUSTIN POWERS IN GOLDMEMBER

The Austin Powers series has always been ridiculous, and this one is definitely the craziest. Centering around Austin Powers' spy missions against Dr. Evil, this spoof of the James Bond series is the funniest I've seen. It's full of hilarious moments, from the fountain scene to the scene with Mini Me and Austin behind the curtain. The first two movies are also quite ridiculous, and this spoof series is another that deserves to be viewed. All three movies are good, but the third is the craziest.

6 MONTY PYTHON AND THE HOLY GRAIL

It would be hard not to put this on the list, because this movie is a classic. It's a movie that seems to have been slapped together in ten minutes. It's about the knights of Camelot, and God sends them on a quest to find the Holy Grail. It's near impossible to name the most ridiculous moments in the movie because from the very first to the very last seconds of the film, every moment is incredibly absurd. My favorite moments are the tale of Sir Lancelot, the Bridge of Death, and the Black Knight. This is a must for anybody who has a sense of humor.

5 BLAZING SADDLES

Another movie that is up there on the list of best comedies with *Monty Python and the Holy Grail*, *Blazing Saddles* is Mel Brooks' most well-received movie. It spoofs Westerns and, like every Mel Brooks comedy, is extremely ridiculous. The movie's premise is that in order to drive people out of a town for convenience of the railroad, State Attorney General Hedley Lamarr appoints a black man as sheriff. The story becomes even more hilarious when the townspeople start to enjoy his company. The most ridiculous part, however, is when the movie breaks the fourth wall and a climactic battle scene ends up migrating onto another movie set and turns into a pie fight. Besides the end, one of the most ridiculous parts is when the Waco Kid shoots the guns out of six men's hands in just a couple seconds without even visibly moving. Another staple for comedy lovers and a very influential film.

4 SPACEBALLS

The next movie on the list is another Mel Brooks film, but it's not as critically acclaimed as *Blazing Saddles*. This film parodies science fiction, primarily the Star Wars films. The premise is that the idiot race of Spaceballs have used up their air and plan to steal the air from Druidia. The movie is much more ridiculous than *Blazing Saddles* because it's in a more allowing universe. There are moments such as when they go to ludicrous speeds that are too over-the-top to watch with a straight face, and there's a great scene that parodies the movie *Alien*. *Spaceballs* is the best Star Wars spoof around, the most ridiculous Mel Brooks movie, and definitely worth watching.

3 AIRPLANE!

This is another movie that is often thought of as one of the funniest movies ever. This movie makes all modern spoofs look terrible. The movie spoofs airplane disaster movies in a sort of tongue-in-cheek manner. Every character is completely straight faced, and that is what makes it so funny. It was Leslie Nielsen's breakthrough comedy performance, and the whole thing is definitely hilarious. Everybody in the movie just accepts very weird things. It all seems so absurd and in a world of its own that you could honestly watch ten minutes and get the same impact as if you watched the whole thing. Of course, it's definitely smarter to see the whole thing, and this isn't one to miss on your list of comedy classics.

2 IDIOCRACY

To stray away from popular movies for a while, *Idiocracy* is definitely a very ridiculous movie and deserves more attention than it got when it came out. The premise is that an average man in the Army and a prostitute are put in time capsules for a year. Unfortunately, the project is canceled and they're left inside. Over the course of 500 years, the world slowly becomes stupider to the point that when the soldier and the prostitute get out of their capsules, they're the smartest people on the planet. The premise is hilarious on its own. Of course, this film was made by Mike Judge, who created *Beavis and Butt-Head*, and *Idiocracy* is way more over the top. The funniest moments are too many to count, because in a world of idiots, there's never a dull moment.

1 DEAD ALIVE

I can't think of a better movie to put at the top spot. This movie is the most ridiculous I will ever see because it's a black comedy that could easily win the title of "goriest movie ever." It's full of zombie gore moments that make you both cringe and laugh, but it's not scary. It's a slapstick form of zombie comedy that pioneered its own genre, "Splatstick." It's directed by Peter Jackson, who is much more well-known for the Lord of the Rings movie series. Not too many people know about his earlier work, which was much more humorous, at the same time very gory. The most ridiculous scene in movie history is the lawnmower scene in this movie, and the second most ridiculous being the graveyard scene. Some honorable mentions are when the protagonist's mom's ear falls into someone's soup and they eat it, as well as when he beats up a zombie baby in public. If you want to see the most hilarious movie ever made, this is it—but if you have a weak stomach, you might want to skip it.

10 SUPERHUMAN FEATS IN CHESS HISTORY

10 THE GRAND OLD MAN OF CHESS

In 1935, in Moscow, Dr. Emanuel Lasker, at 66 years old, took third place behind Mikhail Botvinnik and Salo Flohr who tied for first at only half a point ahead of him. Lasker lost no games and beat the much younger José Raúl Capablanca, as well as Kan, Goglize, Pirc, Cechover, and Menchik. He drew the rest, and proved that age means comparatively little next to fighting spirit, which he had in greater, more intimately understood abundance than any player in history.

9 RUBINSTEIN'S IMMORTAL GAME

In 1907, in Lodz, Poland, Akiba Rubinstein destroyed Georg Rotlewi with what has been called by several grand masters "the most magnificent combination of all time." This is all the more amazing given that it came from the mind of a player known for a quiet, positional style, as opposed to an aggressive, sacrificial one.

Rotlewi was a local master, but not world-class, and handled the opening 12 moves or so sloppily, allowing Rubinstein to take the initiative firmly. He developed all his pieces into fine coordination in the center, connected his bishops, and proceeded to sacrifice his knight, then his bishop, then his rook and queen at the same time, then his other rook, all in successive moves, until Rotlewi was faced with unavoidable checkmate.

Games have seen more sacrifices than this, but none has ever been as beautiful.

Rubinstein was a Polish Jew, and survived the Holocaust because he went insane, retiring from chess in 1932 because he suffered from anthropophobia (literally, "fear of people") and schizophrenia, and entered an asylum in Krakow. In 1942, an SS unit cleared out the asylum's patients for the death camps, but the SS lieutenant was an avid chess player; when he read Rubinstein's clipboard, he recognized him and couldn't bring himself to send such a pitifully insane chess legend to his death. The last the lieutenant saw of him, he wrote in a letter, Rubinstein was looking out a barred window, singing a song of unknown origin in Polish about being a grasshopper hiding in the dust of a butterfly's wings. He died in 1961.

8 THE IMMORTAL VICTOR

Victor Korchnoi was born March 23, 1931. He challenged Anatoly Karpov for the world title in 1978, at the age of 47, and lost by only one point. Since then, his play has steadily declined, but at an extraordinarily slow rate; he won the World Senior Championship in 2006 without one loss.

He has played world-class chess for a record 55 years. Not even Lasker (numbers 10 and 6 on this list) can make such a claim. Korchnoi is the oldest active grand master on the current tournament circuit. In 2003, at 72 years old, he beat grand master Helgi Gretarsson in 23 moves, after sacrificing his knight, rook, and bishop.

7 FISCHER'S PERFECT TOURNAMENT

Bobby Fischer vied for the U.S. Championship eight times and won eight times—a record. He was the youngest ever, at 14, and in 1963 and '64, he did the unthinkable, winning 11 out of 11 games, with no losses and no draws.

It's happened more rarely than baseball pitchers have pitched perfect games. Lasker, Capa, and Alekhine did it once each, among other players. But Fischer managed it against extremely strong competition, including Larry Evans, Robert Byrne, and Pal Benko. He also took the First Brilliancy Prize with his win against Byrne.

The tournament director congratulated Larry Evans, in second place, "for winning the tournament," and Fischer "for winning the exhibition."

6 LASKER TAKES A BITE OUT OF THE BIG APPLE

The 1924 New York tournament was the strongest in history up to that time, and Capablanca, the reigning champion and "Chess Machine," was expected to win with ease. He did very well, scoring 14.5 points out of 20 games. But Lasker, at the ripe old age of 55, took the number-one spot with 16 points and only one loss, to Capablanca.

He breezed right through the competition, beating everyone but Capablanca at least once, including Alekhine, the future world champion. He beat the following world-class masters two for two: Reti, Maroczy, Bolgoljubow, and Janowski.

5 THE DOUGHBOY BLINDFOLDED

Harry Nelson Pillsbury had one of those rare personalities: a chess player who entertained the masses. Chess is not a spectator sport, but Pillsbury was a barnstormer.

He is estimated to have had an IQ of 190, which he used to telling effect in 1901 in Chicago, by playing ten games of chess, ten games of checkers, and a game of whist (a card game) simultaneously, and not looking at the boards. The whist game was against three other men, and he meanwhile called out his moves for the chess and checkers games as soon as his opponents had called out theirs.

Just to ice the cake, he agreed to memorize a list of very long words, some made up on the spot, given to him by two psychologists. He glanced at the list for two seconds, gave it back, and proceeded to recite the words perfectly. Then he recited them backward.

He won every game of chess, every game of checkers, the game of whist (when the other players quit or ran out of money), and met the psychologists the next day, and recited the words for them again, forward and backward.

4 KARPOV UNLEASHED

The Linares Tournament will forever be linked to the name Garry Kasparov, who won it a record nine times. But the victory every chess player will remember most from Linares is Anatoly Karpov's 1994 devastation of the strongest field in history up to that time, a category-18 tournament with an average rating of 2685.

Karpov won with a score of 11 points out of 13 games. He won nine games and lost none, drawing only four. It remains the most stunning tournament victory of all time, to date, especially given that several of his wins were beautiful displays of sacrificial and positional artistry.

The most notable of these is his victory over Veselin Topalov, who later became world champion and, as of this writing, is the second-highest-rated player in the world. In their game, Karpov sacrificed both rooks, one of them twice, and ripped Topalov's king protection to pieces. When the smoke cleared, Karpov had a queen and bishop, Topalov a queen and rook. But Topalov had no pawns left. Karpov had five, and they could not be stopped.

3 CAPABLANCA'S TEN YEARS OF PERFECTION

José Raúl Capablanca played the most crystal-clear, pristine positional chess in history, as attested by almost every grand master today. He rose to prominence in 1909 when, as an unknown player, he defeated Frank Marshall, the most vicious attacker in the world, by eight to one in a match.

For an entire decade—from 1914 to 1924—Capablanca made no mistakes. He just kept getting better. He hit his prime in 1914, and his absolute best years lasted from 1919 to 1922, during which time he beat Lasker for the championship, four to zero, no losses. That was unheard of—Lasker was thought invincible. And from 1914 (when he lost two games, to Lasker and Tarrasch) to 1924 (when he lost one to Reti), Capablanca played 99 tournaments and match games versus the greatest players in the world, over and over, and lost none. The only reason he didn't win some of the tournaments in which he played is because he played a cool-headed, positional style and drew many games because of it, while aggressive players bowled over inferior opponents and won more points.

But it was this perfect decade that earned him the nickname "Chess Machine," playing what remain some of the most precisely correct games in all of chess. Boris Kostich had a score of nothing but draws against him in tournaments, and so a ten-game match was organized in 1919 in Havana. Capablanca beat him five times in a row, and Kostich resigned the match without continuing.

Another highlight of this decade of perfection was Capablanca's victory over Frank Marshall in New York in 1918, when Marshall unleashed his "Marshall Attack" variation of the Ruy Lopez for the first time. It remains one of the most fearsome, dreaded attacking variations in the opening repertoire. Capablanca met it cold, having no idea what was in store for him, and still won, seeing his way through the bewildering complications and savage assaults against his king, without ever playing a bad move.

"I don't understand it," Marshall told a newspaper later. "I could have beaten Lasker with that opening. No one can lead Capa astray. He just never gets scared, because he always knows how the game will end: in his favor."

2 GARRY KASPAROV JUST WILL NOT QUIT

No one would have believed, in the last months of 1984, that Anatoly Karpov was being watched, coldly and keenly, by an intelligence that was as great as his own and yet as fearless as a wolverine's, which slowly and surely drew its plans against him. (Bonus points to anyone who recognizes the book spoofed in this paragraph.)

That intelligence was Garry Kasparov, who, at 21 years old, was the young lion intent on taking Karpov's crown. But at 33 years old, Karpov was still firmly in his chess prime. Chess players do not begin their decline until about 35 years old, or often 40.

The match between them began on September 10, 1984, and Karpov got off to the start everyone expected: four wins and no losses in nine games. The rules demanded six wins in order to win the match. Kasparov's immediate future looked bleak, but he sank his teeth in like a British bulldog and battled Karpov heroically to 17 draws in a row. It was Rocky versus Ivan Drago.

Then Kasparov lost another. Karpov was winning five to zero. One more win was all he needed. He could afford five losses in a row if he wanted, playing recklessly aggressive chess. But he was getting tired. Kasparov was also, but he was younger, and had nothing to lose. The match became the first and only world championship to be abandoned without a winner.

1 THE METEORIC YEAR OF BOBBY FISCHER

Actually, this list item is something of a misnomer, since meteors go down, not up. But in the spirit of the phrase, Bobby Fischer's skill at the game became unrivaled in about 1970. The only two players on the planet, or so it was thought, who could cause him serious problems were Boris Spassky and Tigran Petrosian.

But in 1971, on the road to the World Championship versus Spassky, Fischer had to make it through Interzonal tournaments, then Candidates' matches, three of them, to become the number-one contender. This is how FIDE, the World Chess Federation, handled the championship back then (and they should return to it).

First Fischer met Mark Taimanov, the ninth-highest-rated player in the world. The match rules were "first to six wins, draws not counting," and Fischer proceeded to beat Taimanov six times in a row, no draws, no losses, no sweat.

No one in the chess world could believe what they had seen because Taimanov didn't make more than two or three blunders throughout the match. Then came the truly astounding feat: Fischer met Bent Larsen, the third-highest-rated in the world, and beat him six times in a row, no draws, no losses.

Then, his final test before facing Spassky: a six-win match versus Petrosian. Fischer won 4.5 to 2.5, trouncing one of the absolute finest defensive players in the history of the game.

Then he beat Spassky without even trying hard, by a four-point margin, 12.5 to 8.5. He had single-handedly bowled over the entire Soviet chess machine.

Players were required to use seconds, one or two players who worked over the games after adjournments or focused on methods for defeating a particular opponent's style. Spassky had three official seconds: Iivo Nei, Nikolai Krogius, and Efim Geller, who was one of the top ten in the world at the time. Fischer had just one, William Lombardy.

But Spassky really had the entire Soviet Union, a virtual "Who's Who" of the top-100-rated players in the world backing him up—which is cheating. They labored like scholars over Fischer's style, his games, and adjourned positions.

Lombardy, Fischer's second, has said many times that the only thing Fischer had him do was bring up room service: plate after plate of cheese sandwiches. Fischer did the rest himself.

12 MOST CONTROVERSIAL VIDEO GAMES

12 MANHUNT

Manhunt is a third-person stealth horror game released in 2003. A sequel, *Manhunt 2*, was released four years later. Since 2003, the games have stirred incredible amounts of controversy but have also garnered great success for the creators, Rockstar Games. The games center around your character being forced to kill numerous different people (called "hunters") over several different levels (or "scenes"); the gruesomeness of your kills affect your "rating" at the end of the scene. Each kill is shown during a short cut scene, in which your character murders the victim with the weapon you've selected. These weapons include hammers, knives, carrier bags, crowbars, chainsaws, guns, and cheese wire, among others. The kills can vary in their grittiness, which is up to the player to choose as he approaches the victim.

The game's apparent glamorization of violence gives it the feel of a snuff film, with the glorification of vigilantism and voyeurism. The game was linked to the 2004 murder, in Britain, of Stefan Pakeerah, who was killed by his best friend with a claw hammer in a method similar to those used in *Manhunt*. The killer, Warren LeBlanc, was found to be an obsessive player of the game, which his mother admitted in court after he had pleaded guilty. After this case, *Manhunt* was taken off the shelves in UK stores and was banned in several countries. Despite its controversies, it's still a successful franchise.

11 LEFT BEHIND: ETERNAL FORCES

Left Behind: Eternal Forces is a real-time strategy game, released in 2006 for Windows. It is based on the Left Behind series of Christian novels and features the "Tribulation Force"—a Christian group whom the player fights for in New York as they combat global warming and a world government run by an antichrist. The game can be likened to other strategy games such as *Age of Empires*, or *Command and Conquer*. However, in *Left Behind*, the Christian mass fights various enemies using their faith as you try to convert everyone in order to be saved. Conversion is encouraged first; however, lethal force is authorized when necessary. This provided the basis for the game's negative reception—it was accused of inciting a "convert or kill" message. It was branded as a "violent Christian video game" that promoted "religious bigotry, intolerance, and warfare." The Anti-Defamation League, a Jewish organization, defended the makers of the game, stating, "Conversion to Christianity in the game is not depicted as forcible in nature, and violence is not rewarded."

10 BEAT 'EM & EAT 'EM

This game was released in 1982 for the Atari 2600 by a company called Mystique, the same company who also released number 9 on this list in the same year. The company later went out of business during the video game crash of 1983. The idea of *Beat 'Em & Eat 'Em* is to control two nude women who move back and forth across the bottom of a building, catching semen from a man who is constantly masturbating on top of the building. Catching semen gives you points, and you gain an extra life for every 69 points you get. A gender-reversed version of the game, called *Philly Flasher*, was released later. In this game, you play two nude men who move across a building catching breast milk from a witch (you read that right). Upon catching all the milk, the men masturbate and ejaculate. Although it was unbelievably risqué and rated as one of the worst games of all time, it became infamous.

9 CUSTER'S REVENGE

Among the three sex games that Mystique released for the Atari 2600, *Custer's Revenge* is perhaps the most notorious. It was at the center of an $11 million dollar lawsuit, as well as numerous protests from Native American groups, women's rights activists, and critics of the video game industry in general. It's widely regarded as one of the worst games of all time, in both appearance (with characters that looked like Lego blocks) and game play. The idea of the game is to control General Custer as he moves across the screen with a large erection, avoiding arrows, in order to make it to a nude Native American woman tied to a post and rape her.

8 BATTLE RAPER

The game *Battle Raper* (as well as number 6 on this list) was made by a Japanese game company called Illusion. Illusion is famous for developing 3D "eroge" games, a genre whose name is a portmanteau of "erotic game." These games feature anime-style eroticism and are usually either visual novels or romance simulators. Some eroge games are harmless, such as girlfriend simulators, while others include voyeurism, rape, and molestation. *Battle Raper* is, as the name suggests, a fight game, with moves involving molestation and humiliation affecting your opponent's health, along with the usual punches and kicks. The winner of a match can then rape the loser however they want, with rape cut scenes that are unlocked at the end of the game.

7 JFK: RELOADED

This game was released for download in 2004 by Scottish company Traffic Games; the release date coincided with the 41st anniversary of the assassination of John F. Kennedy in 1963. The game puts you in the position of Kennedy's assassin, Lee Harvey Oswald, as he attempts to assassinate the president. The playability of the game comes from a points system, where you must try and accurately re-create the actual bullet path of the assassination and the events described in the Warren Commission report. It's been argued that *JFK: Reloaded* isn't so much a game as a historical simulation. Either way, the company ran a competition in 2005 to see who could get the highest score and get closest to a 100-percent accurate simulation of JFK's death. A man from France won $10,000 with a score of 782 out of 1000. A spokesman for Edward Kennedy, John Kennedy's brother, called the game "despicable." He is quoted as saying,

"Why would someone make this game? This should have never been allowed on the market."

6 RAPELAY

RapeLay is another Japanese 3D "eroge" video game, released for PC in 2006. It follows the story of a man who stalks and rapes a mother and two daughters, with the player, of course, helping him do this. The game is a sexual simulator, with mouse clicks and scrolls allowing clothing to be removed and molestation to occur. Many different game modes are available, ranging from stalking the girls and watching wind blow up their skirts, to having full sexual intercourse with all three females at once. The game even features an "internal ejaculation" counter that can result in pregnancy or "game over." Obviously, the game received a negative reaction from every critic that reviewed it; some claimed to be "horrified" at the game content and said that games like *RapeLay* are the reason tighter laws must be applied to control game content. On the other hand, some people defending the game have argued that rape is considered a less-serious crime than murder, and that the majority of games out now feature the murder of numerous people in order to finish the game.

5 SUPER COLUMBINE MASSACRE RPG!

The idea behind this game was, in part, to parody video games and their supposed role in the 1999 Columbine shootings, as well as present a critique on how the media sensationalized the shootings. Opinions of the game vary greatly. Some believe it to be a sordid trivialization of an unjust crime and the impact it had on numerous victims. Others find the game's cartoon graphics and side plot into the shooter's perdition in hell to be  original and worthy of praise. Either way, the game puts the player in control of Eric Harris and Dylan Klebold in a re-created high school. The majority of the game is played with an overhead view of your character as you move around, collecting weapons and experiencing flashbacks of the shooter's lives, including things that may have inspired them to carry out the shooting. "Battles" are fought with various people around the school, with digital photos of the actual Columbine high school and sound clips in the background. In these battles, weapons can be chosen and used to take the "enemies'" health.

The game was created by Danny Ledonne in 2005, and it was downloaded 10,000 times in its first year. It didn't gain much media attention until 2006, after which downloads increased dramatically, with 30,000 in the first half of May 2006. By March 2007, the game had been downloaded over 400,000 times. Most of the media coverage, as expected, was negative. *SCMRPG!* was seen as a game that "glamorized murder" and was an "example of a game that worships terrorism." The small amount of positive feedback the game got was from people who accepted Ledonne's message of critique and parody. A survivor of the shootings even said, "It probably sounds a bit odd for someone like me to say, but I appreciate the fact, at least to some degree, that something like this was made."

4 BABY SHAKER

Baby Shaker was an iPhone application that had to be seen to be believed. As with most apps, the phone can be shaken and moved to control the action on screen. In this primitive "game," however, you were presented with a cartoon picture of a baby and had to shake the iPhone to stop it from crying. When you had shaken it enough, red crosses appeared over its eyes, signifying that it had died. The game caused huge upset with the public, and two parents, whose babies were victims of being shaken, protested outside an Apple store; the application was taken off the Apple store.

3 MUSLIM MASSACRE: THE GAME OF MODERN RELIGIOUS GENOCIDE

This shoot-'em-up game was made by a forum member under the name of "Sigvatr" in 2008. The protagonist was an American hero who parachuted into the Middle East with the aim of killing as many Muslims as possible. There were numerous weapons, including pistols, a shotgun, a machine gun, grenades, and rocket launchers. Some enemies were civilians (whom you must also kill) and some were suicide bombers that could do damage to you. Each stage lasted around a minute. The bosses of each level were Osama Bin Laden, Muhammad, and Allah. Game companies tried to ignore the game's controversial nature and branded it "boring and tedious," while many Muslim groups called it "unacceptable, tasteless, and deeply offensive," claiming it encouraged young people to kill Muslims. Two days after a September 11th anniversary, the game was taken off the Internet, and an apology was issued due to large amounts of negative comments. However, the apology was found to be fake, and the game is still in circulation. An article in the *LA Times* printed an anonymous comment that said, "If it were a game showing Muslims killing Israelis, the whole world would have sought revenge."

2 ETHNIC CLEANSING

The premise of this game is to control either a skin-headed white supremacist or a member of the Ku Klux Klan and to move through the ghetto, shooting and killing any black and Latino people you find. You then descend into the subway and kill Jewish people, before finding a Jewish Control Center and killing the former prime minister of Israel, Ariel Sharon. The game was released in 2002 by an underground record label specializing in neo-Nazi and white supremacist music called Resistance Records. The game has been protested, and the game engine that was used to create it, Genesis3D, has even been encouraged to change their licensing to prohibit the creation of racist games. The game's description is as follows: "The Race War has begun. Your skin is your uniform in this battle for the survival of your kind. The White Race depends on you to secure its existence. Your people's enemies surround you in a sea of decay and filth that they have brought to your once clean and White nation. Not one of their numbers shall be spared...."

1 KZ MANAGER

Numerous versions of *KZ Manager* have been made since 1990, when it was first released for the Commodore 64, Amiga, MS-DOS, and Windows systems. The game is a text-based resource-management game that simulates the construction and running of a Nazi concentration camp. Many other management simulation games, such as the Sim City series, are hugely successful, but instead of managing resources like water, electricity, and food, *KZ Manager* has the player manage the prisoners (Jews, Gypsies, or Turks—your choice), poison gas, and money, as well as monitoring public opinion and camp productivity. Money can be made by forcing the prisoners to work; public opinion can be raised with regular killing of the prisoners. More prisoners can be bought, and the corpses of those you have killed are put on a garbage pile. Most versions of *KZ Manager* are in German, which is strange, considering the modern German regulations against the uses of Nazi symbols and practices. *KZ Manager* is freeware, and the latest Windows version, called *KZ Manager Millennium*, is available through the Internet.

10 ODDEST VILLAINS FROM SCOOBY-DOO

10 THE TAR MONSTER
First appeared in "The Tar Monster," 1978

The Tar Monster appears several times throughout the *Scooby Doo* series, and he's a monster made out of tar! The villain behind him in the original series is Mr. Stoner, who tries to scare away the archaeologists from the Sanctum of Byzantium so that he can steal the temple's ancient treasure.

9 THE PTERODACTYL GHOST
First appeared in "Hang in There Scooby-Doo," 1977

This is another one of those monsters that makes you think, "Wow, those Hanna-Barbera guys really ran out of ideas." The monster is actually Jonathan Jacobo, who terrorizes a local hang-gliding contest so he can win with no competition. The Pterodactyl Ghost also appears in *Scooby-Doo 2: Monsters Unleashed*.

8 THE GHOST ANIMALS OF AFRICA
First appeared in "Safari, So Goodi!," 2002

This is a fairly strange scheme: the Hunsecker couple tries to kidnap various African animals to sell as exotic pets back home. They do this by painting the wildlife with fluorescent paint and then emitting a supersonic pitch from their boat, which makes the animals go crazy, so everyone thinks they're demons.

7 THE WAX PHANTOM
First appeared in "Don't Fool with a Phantom," 1970

This monster just looks so awesome. The Wax Phantom is the owner of a radio station who wants to get away with embezzling a lot of money from his station by blaming his crime on the crazy butler. However, the gang manages to catch up to him and captures him with a wax shower. They also get Scooby and Shaggy caught in the wax shower, which in real life would kill them instantly.

6 IT
First appeared in "Spooky Space Kook," 1969

Here's another monster that just looks crazy. "It" is the creation of a farmer who wants the military to move off his land. The artsy flair the cartoonists add to "It" and his spaceship make this villain way cool. It's also interesting because the show started to probe into a dangerous area for TV at that time: the military being not so nice.

5 GHOST CLOWN
First appeared in "Bedlam in the Big Top," 1969

Here's one that I picked just because it's so creepy. Personally, I'm very afraid of both clowns and hypnotists, so a hypnotist clown ghost is incredibly frightening, and the villain in this episode is the recently fired circus hypnotist.

4 THE GHOST OF ZEN-TUO
First appeared in "Mystery Mask Mix-up," 1970

This one wows with the incredible racism in its episode. No Chinese voice-actors were used for this episode, so the American actors had to improvise the ghost's with garish fake accents. There are racial slurs throughout the episode, and the villains act very, very stupid. On top of how bad that is, there are a lot of animation goofs.

3 THE MYSTERY MACHINE
First appeared in "It's Mean, It's Green, It's the Mystery Machine," 2002

This monster is odd in a few ways. For one, the monster is actually the gang's van, Mystery Machine. For another, we get to hear a lot about the backstory of the Mystery Machine and Freddy. The villain here is a crazed soccer mom bent on getting her kid's band back together.

2 THE TITANIC TWIST
First appeared in "Wrestle Maniacs," 2005

Almost breaking the limits of violence and creepiness for *Scooby-Doo*, the Titanic Twist is a wrestling ghost who goes around beating people for no apparent reason. There's actually blood in this episode, and the portrayal of wrestling culture is more than a little creepy.

1 **THE GOLD MONSTER**
First appeared in "Gold Paw," 2005

Okay, a monster made out of gold? How cool is that? And he can also melt through walls and turn other things into gold. He's a pretty epic monster, made even more awesome when it turns out he's actually a robot made out of cookie dough engineered by an old lady to break into Fort Knox.

10 MOST CONTROVERSIAL STAR TREK EPISODES

10 **"THE CITY ON THE EDGE OF FOREVER"—*STAR TREK*, 1967**
With its classic time-travel story, this episode is widely considered one of the best in Trek history. However, behind the scenes, it caused a firestorm between the producers and the episode's writer. Harlan Ellison, a noted sci-fi author who penned the episode, was upset with the changes producers Gene Roddenberry and D. C. Fontana made to his story. These included taking out drug-addicted *Enterprise* crewman and a hostile Kirk-Spock relationship. Ellison wanted his name removed from the final episode, but Roddenberry wouldn't do it. There was bad blood between the two for years. In 2009, Ellison sued Paramount for failing to compensate him for all the decades of merchandising the studio did for the episodes. An Los Angeles federal court ruled in Ellison's favor.

9 **"SPOCK'S BRAIN"—*STAR TREK*, 1968**
This was the first episode of the third season, and the first to air after the series was renewed. Too bad it would end up being considered one of the worst *Star Trek* episodes of all time. As the title suggests, it concerns Spock's brain—it's gone missing, and the crew must find it. Leonard Nimoy says

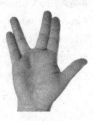

he felt embarrassed throughout the episode, though it's possible to watch it and think it's so bad that it's good.

8 "PLATO'S STEPCHILDREN"—*STAR TREK*, 1968

Under the control of aliens, Kirk and Uhura kiss, and it just so happens that Kirk is white and Uhura is black. Although it's often called the first interracial kiss on TV, it wasn't. However, NBC was frightened at the possibility that Southern TV stations would be angered by the kiss, and they did two takes: one with the kiss and one without. But Nichelle Nichols, who played Uhura, deliberately flubbed the latter take, so the kiss remained. There isn't any evidence this episode caused any real controversy when it aired, save for a single irate letter from a Southerner.

7 "CONSPIRACY"—*STAR TREK: THE NEXT GENERATION*, 1988

Parasites infect the Federation, threatening to take it over. The controversy comes from a particularly violent scene at the end of the episode. Picard and Riker confront Remmick, a Starfleet officer infected by the parasites. They shoot him with phasers, causing his body to explode, and revealing the mother bug inside. This scene was so violent that the BBC removed it when airing the episode, and the Canadian sci-fi channel still runs it with a warning.

6 "SHADES OF GRAY"—*STAR TREK: THE NEXT GENERATION*, 1989

This episode is *Star Trek*'s only clip show. Riker falls into a coma, and the only way to save him is have him relive painful memories. Paramount told the producers they wanted to do a clip show because other episodes had big budgets. Even one of the episode's co-writers thought it was pretty bad, calling it a "piece of shit."

5 "THE HIGH GROUND"—*STAR TREK: THE NEXT GENERATION*, 1990

This episode concerns terrorism and a planet that wants the Federation to join their fight for freedom. The Brits are to blame for the controversy on this one. Data has a line in which he says Ireland was eventually unified by terrorism in 2024. Sensitive about such a mention when the troubles in Northern Ireland were still ongoing, the BBC cut the line when the episode first aired. "The High Ground" has never been shown on Ireland's RTE channel, and sometimes when the episode is aired in the UK, the line is still cut.

4 "REJOINED"—*DEEP SPACE NINE*, 1995

Star Trek is infamous for avoiding overt references to homosexuality, something fans have complained about for decades. This is one of the few episodes to make even an oblique reference to it by showing a female kiss. Jadzia Dax and Lenara Kahn are Trills, an alien species that lives on in symbionts implanted in host bodies. Two of their previous hosts had a romantic relationship that was never resolved, hence the same-sex kiss. One TV station in the South removed the scene, and the producers received a large number of negative calls in response.

3 "TO THE DEATH"—*DEEP SPACE NINE*, 1996

Notable because most of the controversy happened before the episode was aired, "To the Death" was the first *Star Trek* episode ever cut for violence. When the *DS9* crew travel to a planet with an Iconian Gateway—a portal to practically anywhere—they encounter hoards of the vicious Jem'Hadar. Hand-to-hand combat ensues. Originally, 52 Jem'Hadar were shown getting killed, but this is trimmed to just 20 victims, losing 45 seconds of the episode. The BBC censored it even further. Fans complained the result felt choppy and disjointed.

2 "TSUNKATSE"—*VOYAGER*, 2000

Seven of Nine is forced to compete in an alien gladiator sport. Among her combatants is an alien champion played by…The Rock. To many fans, "Tsunkatse" was simply an attempt to cash in on the popularity of another UPN show, *WWF Smackdown!* The Rock even used his signature moves and eyebrow raising, to the delight of his alien audience. Despite negative fan reaction, the episode was the highest rated of the season, and you can be sure that's what the producers wanted.

1 "HARBINGER"—*ENTERPRISE*, 2004

Romantic tension between the Vulcan T'Pol and Commander Trip Tucker culminates in a "love scene" in which T'Pol lets down her garment and displays her bare backside, including her naked rear end. Ten days before the episode aired, Janet Jackson had accidentally displayed her bare breast at the Super Bowl, which surely factored into the network's decision to crop the scene and hide the bare bottom. The scene was shown without cuts in Canada and exists intact on the episode's DVD.

10 HIDDEN IMAGES FOUND IN CARTOONS

10 GUEST APPEARANCES

During the sequence in *The Hunchback of Notre Dame* in which Quasimodo sings "Out There" (one of the best songs on the soundtrack) as we pan over a view of Paris from the bell tower, characters from other Disney movies can be seen in the background. Most prominent is Belle (*Beauty and the Beast*) strolling along in her blue dress and reading a book. More sharp-eyed viewers may also spot Pumbaa from *The Lion King* being carried by two men; a street merchant shaking out the flying carpet from *Aladdin*; and, incongruously, even a satellite dish on one of the rooftops.

9 POCAHONTAS

If you go through the movie *Pocahontas* and look at each scene carefully, you'll find it is full of references to sex. Some are pretty obscure, but others are very, very clear—clear enough to be fairly convincing evidence of their intentional inclusion in the movie.

8 THE PHALLIC PALACE

This is a more popular one. The rumor was that during the making of *The Little Mermaid*, a disgruntled artist who was going to lose his job drew the phallic object in the castle in annoyance over his impending redundancy. However, the artist himself says that he was not about to be fired, but was forced to hurry in drawing the design so that he could meet his deadline and did not realize at the time the exact shape of what he had drawn. Well, at least he didn't until he was contacted by a disgusted member of his church youth group who had heard about the controversy. Obviously, later versions of the video had the infamous spire removed.

7 HARD-UP MINISTER

In keeping with *The Little Mermaid* theme, another popular accusation for the Disney producers came when someone noticed the rather odd shape protruding from the minister's pelvic region during the scene in which Ursula (disguised as "Vanessa") attempts to marry Eric using Ariel's voice. However, later shots in the film show that the minister had rather bandy legs that blended in with his tunic, and the "erection" was actually his knees.

6 SIMBA AND THE SEXY CLOUD

This is another popular one. Long has been the controversy over a dust cloud in *The Lion King*. In the scene just before Simba meets Rafiki, he tiredly flops down on the edge of a cliff, and a cloud of dust rises that allegedly, for a few frames, spells the word S-E-X. The debate is that the special-effects team put the cloud in, intending it to read S-F-X to leave their little mark on the film. I say judge for yourself, but it looks like "sex" to me.

5 RACIST DONALD DUCK

Disney characters and Warner Bros. characters interacted for the first time in the 1988 film *Who Framed Roger Rabbit* and cartoon fans cheered. However, during an evening at the Ink & Paint Club, Donald Duck and Daffy Duck duet on the piano together and the relationship turns nasty when Donald allegedly calls Daffy a "nigger." Anybody who has seen a Donald Duck cartoon should know that it can sometimes be quite difficult to understand what Donald says, but thinking you hear him scowling "God damn stupid nigger" takes the cake. Closed captioning in the film says that the line is "Goddurn stubborn nitwit"; others claim it is "You doggone little..." But this is not the first time Donald has been busted for his language. In 1995, WalMart pulled a Disney video of Mickey Mouse cartoons from its shelves after complaints that Donald shouted "Fuck you!" in the episode called "Clock Cleaners."

4 TAKE OFF YOUR CLOTHES

The scene in *Aladdin* on Jasmine's balcony, in which the hero is trying to brush off the growling tiger Rajah, he can apparently be heard whispering "Good teenagers take off your clothes." The script says that the line is "Good kitty, take off and go." The clip sounds like someone other than Aladdin has whispered the line, but no matter which is true, the allegation got Disney in hot water with the

American Life League, who used it to try and get Disney films banned, claiming they had been sneaking sexual messages to children for years.

3 JESSICA RABBIT'S LADY GARDEN

A cartoon temptress, *Who Framed Roger Rabbit*'s Jessica Rabbit has helped to turn a lot of young boys into men over the years. Wishes came true with the claim that cheeky animators sneaked in a few frames of her without underwear during the scene in which Jessica and Bob Hoskins' character are riding in a taxi that runs into a lamp post. As she is thrown from the car, Jessica lands, causing her red dress to hitch up, revealing her apparently unclothed nether regions. In some cases, it has been tradition for animators to slip racy shots into films for a split second, but it seems that their fun can be spoiled by young men pausing at this scene in which Jessica Rabbit spreads her legs. Now why they would do that, I have no idea…

2 THE RUDE RESCUERS

In 1999, Disney studios announced that they would be recalling the home-video version of the 1977 movie *The Rescuers* because a few shots contained an "objectionable background image." During the scene in which the mousy heroes, Bernard and Bianca, fly through the city in a sardine tin (about 38 minutes into the movie), a photographic image of a topless woman can be seen in the windows they pass. While some of the items on this list are questionable and some have been proven wrong, this one is pretty clear, and Disney studios had to hang their heads in shame. It was confirmed by a Disney spokesperson, who simply said that the tampering "was done more than 20 years ago," and the company recalled 3.4 million copies of the video that had been sold.

1 SEXY BEAST

In the movie *Beauty and the Beast*, we see many references to sex, but we also see some satanic references. In the scene in which the prince stabs the beast, there are some very blatant symbols of evil such as a skull and the sign of the horns. You need to look carefully to see them, but they're definitely there.

10 VILEST VILLAINS OF FICTIONAL LITERATURE

10 THE WICKED WITCH OF THE WEST (*THE WONDERFUL WIZARD OF OZ* BY L. FRANK BAUM)

The Wizard himself believes that the witch's magic is more powerful than his own and could kill him in an instant if he goes near her. He offers Dorothy a trip back to Kansas if she kills the witch. That's how loathsome she is to the embodiment of all that is good in Oz. The witch actively tries to kill Dorothy and company several times, with wolves, bees, the winged monkeys, and crows. She captures the Cowardly Lion and tries to starve him to death, she tries to burn the Scarecrow to death, and it's all to force Dorothy to give up the slippers. She steals one of Dorothy's slippers by tripping her over an invisible bar. Dorothy finally has enough and throws a bucket of water on the witch. Why does it kill her? Because water is pure, and the witch is thoroughly corrupt in all respects and is thus the embodiment of impurity.

9 PAP FINN (*THE ADVENTURES OF HUCKLEBERRY FINN* BY MARK TWAIN)

No wonder Huck Finn doesn't really care for religion. Why should he honor his father if his father is a drunken child beater? When he first appears, Pap Finn is pasty white, sweaty, filthy, stinky, and repeatedly threatens to beat Huck to death. He is probably the only character in the story that Huck really hates, but Huck is also scared to death of him and reluctantly obeys him as much as he has to. Pap kidnaps Huck and forces him to live with him, tries to sue the local judge for the money Huck finds at the end of *The Adventures of Tom Sawyer* on the pretense that Huck is Pap's property because Pap made him, and thus the money belongs to Pap and was never Huck's to give away. Huck finally escapes from him out of terror and loathing. Jim finds Pap dead later and doesn't tell Huck until the end of the story. No one sheds a tear.

8 COUNT DRACULA (*DRACULA* BY BRAM STOKER)

Forget all that sexual stuff you see in the vampire movies. Dracula *vants* one thing: blood. He requires the blood of humans to survive, and has no qualms at all about killing everyone in the whole *vorld*, *vone* neck bite at a time, to keep his thirst quenched.

The interesting thing about Dracula is that he kills one person at a time and yet manages to wipe out the entire crew of a Russian cargo ship bound for England. He does this in the form of a wolf, because as a wolf, he is supremely savage, ripping people to pieces and lapping their blood off the ground.

His motive for traveling to England is simply that he currently lives in a remote area of Transylvania, and there aren't a lot of people to suck dry. England has "teeming millions," as he puts it. The main characters of the book start to get in his way, and he immediately starts wiping them out, one by one, turning Lucy Westenra into a vampiress, scaring her mother to death. Van Helsing starts plotting against him, and he retaliates by going after Mina Harker, the most dear to every one of his rivals. Dracula is *vicked*, cruel, and heartless right to the end, *ven* they cut his head off and stab him through the heart.

7 SAURON (THE LORD OF THE RINGS TRILOGY BY J. R. R. TOLKIEN)

All Sauron wants is the whole world of Middle Earth brought under his control. Power, power, power—that's his motive. He also has a generous capacity for revenge against the Valar and the elves for defeating him at the end of the Second Age, before the story begins.

He has no one to answer to as the most powerful entity in Middle Earth, and as a result he rampantly commits atrocities across the whole land. He sends his armies into Gondor, Rohan, and the Shire without provocation, for the sole purpose of finding his Ring of Power and killing everyone in the way.

He is finally undone, destroyed into permanent spirit form, by one of the smallest creatures of Middle Earth, but according to the lore of the story, he isn't dead. He has merely been dealt so severe a blow that he will never rise again (we hope).

6 AARON THE MOOR (*TITUS ANDRONICUS* BY WILLIAM SHAKESPEARE)

Aaron's final words are, "If one good deed in all my life I did, / I do repent it from my very Soule." That's the vilest "screw you" in literary history. He's the main instigator of the carnage throughout the play, and yet his only motive is that he enjoys what he's doing. He loves to hurt people and he wants people to hate him. It's ecstasy to him. He proclaims in his big speech, while standing with his head in a noose, that his only regret is that he wasn't 10,000 times worse before he was caught.

He convinces Demetrius and Chiron, the sons of the Queen, Tamora, to kill Lavinia's betrothed, Bassianus, in front of her, just to make her grieve. They do this, then rape her and cut her tongue out and hands off so she can't tell. It's all delicious fun for Aaron.

Then he frames Titus' sons for Bassianus' murder and lies to Titus that if one of his family will cut off his hand and send it to the emperor, the emperor will spare his two sons. Titus complies, cutting off his hand, which is returned from the emperor, along with Titus' sons' heads anyway. Aaron knew it would happen and loves every minute of it. He's finally caught and forced to die by starvation and dehydration. He refuses to show remorse.

5 BILL SIKES (*OLIVER TWIST* BY CHARLES DICKENS)

Early in the novel, Dickens describes Bill Sikes thus:

> ... a stoutly-built fellow of about five-and-thirty, in a black velveteen coat, very soiled drab breeches, lace-up half boots, and grey cotton stockings which inclosed a bulky pair of legs, with large swelling calves;—the kind of legs, which in such costume, always look in an unfinished and incomplete state without a set of fetters to garnish them. He had a brown hat on his head, and a dirty belcher handkerchief round his neck: with the long frayed ends of which he smeared the beer from his face as he spoke. He disclosed, when he had done so, a broad heavy countenance with a beard of three weeks' growth, and two scowling eyes; one of which displayed various parti-colored symptoms of having been recently damaged by a blow.

Bill Sikes is Fagin's finest protégé from years back, and now he is well trained to steal and burglarize, but he is depicted as being just as likely to kill a man when no one is looking rather than try to pick his pocket without being noticed. He has absolutely no moral scruples of any kind and is only out to make a buck for himself. Nancy, the poor whore he sleeps with, thinks he loves her, and because she used to be a pickpocket also, trained by Fagin, she feels unstable. Sikes seems to offer her stability, until he beats her to death for trying to stop him from beating Oliver to death.

He regularly beats his dog, Bull's Eye, until the poor dog needs stitches. The dog is so patently terrified of him that it follows him around, afraid to run. Sikes is finally undone by the London mob, which hounds him through the streets until he accidentally hangs himself.

4 SATAN (*PARADISE LOST* BY MILTON)

Satan's motive for attempting to overthrow God is that he believes himself to be more beautiful, more powerful, and thus rightfully deserving of the Throne of Heaven. So he and his minions, whom he has corrupted from God, wage war against God and his minions. Not smart. They lose, although they make a better fight than expected, because they can't be killed if they're already in heaven.

Then they're thrown into hell, where Satan immediately decides on revenge. But he doesn't want open war. That failed once, so there's no sense in trying again. If he can't beat God, he'll ruin all of God's work. It's all Satan has left as a weapon. It makes him repugnantly underhanded—he's no longer willing to stand and fight like a man.

He stabs God in the back, as it were, by corrupting his greatest creation, humans, and introducing sin into the mortal universe. It will require the death of God's own Son as recompense. Satan's story is easily the most vengeful ever told.

3 POLICE INSPECTOR JAVERT (*LES MISERABLES* BY VICTOR HUGO)

Jean Valjean is released from prison after 19 years, all for stealing a loaf of bread for his starving family. Once he gets out, he finds it difficult to function as a citizen and steals out of habit. But a bishop pities him and covers for him so he doesn't go back to prison. Valjean then turns over a new leaf and, six years later, has become mayor of Montreuil-sur-Mer.

Enter Javert. He is Montreuil's chief police inspector and used to work at the prison where Valjean was incarcerated. He suspects the mayor to be Valjean when Valjean lifts a horse cart off a helpless man. Only Valjean could be so strong, Javert remembers.

What follows is almost a thousand pages of abject misery for Jean Valjean as Javert hounds him all over France. His motive? The law must be upheld. Valjean had stolen a child's silver coin out of habit as soon as he was released. He then tried to give it back but couldn't find the child.

Over and over, although Javert witnesses the magnanimous good deeds Valjean commits, he refuses to give up the chase. Valjean finally gets the drop on him but refuses to kill him even though Javert's pursuit is the primary reason for several of Valjean's family members' deaths.

Jean Valjean releases Javert, who cannot reconcile this mercy with his conscience, and drowns himself in the Seine, rather than live in a world where there is good.

2 GRENDEL (*BEOWULF*)

Grendel is the most classic monster in all of literature. Except for his lineage, directly back to Cain of the Bible, he has no motive for killing and devouring as many of the innocent townsfolk of the meadhall, Heorot, as he can. It isn't explicitly stated, but he's sure to enjoy the meal of 30 people at once. Beowulf arrives and rips his arm off, and Grendel flees rather than staying to fight like a man. Beowulf finds him in his mother's cave, like a spoiled bully finally beaten. He is cowering in a corner, and Beowulf beheads him. Good riddance.

1 IAGO (*OTHELLO* BY WILLIAM SHAKESPEARE)

He is petty, underhanded, and the embodiment of the prime blemish of mankind: envy. Iago has been said to have no motive for destroying the life of every major character in the play, other than revenge, at first, for Othello's passing over him for the post of lieutenant. Othello chooses Cassio for lieutenant, while Iago believes he's better for the promotion from ensign. He then sets about ruining both Othello and Cassio's lives with a web of lies. He cannot fight Cassio or Othello face to face because he is afraid they will kill him.

So he corrupts Roderigo, a local moron, who's in love with Desdemona, Othello's wife. Thus, Roderigo does all of Iago's dirty work for him, causing Othello to go mad with jealousy over his wife's apparent affair with Cassio. By the time it's over, Roderigo gets in a fight with Cassio and they wound each other. Then in the confusion, Iago stabs Roderigo in the back to silence him. Othello kills Desdemona, whose best friend, Emilia, rats on her own husband, Iago, who immediately kills her to save himself.

How do you kill a fiend so vile? It's left somewhat ambiguous at the end, with Lodovico promising to torture Iago. Whether he will be killed is not stated.

10 BIZARRE TOYS FOR KIDS

10 PEE WEE HERMAN DOLL

Given the strange circumstances under which Paul Reubens, who played Pee Wee Herman, was arrested, one wonders why any company would agree to produce a child's doll of him. That aside, the doll itself is horrifying—it looks like a monstrous grinning clown without its red nose. The ill-fitting suit and strangely long fingers make this a doll that no parent would want for their child.

9 LOOK-ALIKE DOLL

If you're worried that your child isn't narcissistic enough, this is the toy for them! The Look-alike Doll is a small action figure made to look exactly like its owner. Just send in a photo and wait for your doll to arrive in the mail.

8 REBORN BABY

Reborn Baby is the brainchild of Deborah King from Scotland. While there's no denying her artistic talent, the dolls she produces are macabre, to say the least. She attempts to make her dolls as lifelike as possible—complete with an optional beating heart. The unfortunate thing is that she makes it look so real that the lack of movement and the frozen pose make it look like an embalmed infant corpse. Any child that jumps for joy at receiving one of these for Christmas needs to get to a therapist, pronto!

7 ADOLF HITLER DOLL

Unless you're a member of your local Ku Klux Klan or any other racist bigoted organization, you're not at all going to want this hideous (and very lifelike) doll for your child. It even comes with a removable Nazi uniform in case you want to see Hitler's missing testicle.

6 EPIDERMITIS

This hideous toy has a covering that feels like human skin, and hair that feels like human hair. It's headless (the hair comes out of its neck) and has a tail made of a metal rod. Whatever benefit a young child (and that is the age group the Epidermitis is marketed at) would get from his grotesque bundle of fake human flesh is beyond me. Here's what the company says about it: "They require minimal maintenance, can be stored in state of forced hibernation in standard refrigerators, and are customizable with different body, skin, and hair selections and through tanning, tattooing, and piercing."

5 PEE AND POO PLUSH TOYS

Pee and Poo plush toys are designed to make your children comfortable with pee and poo. Why you want to make them comfortable with the idea of playing with pee and poo is unclear. While these are undoubtedly designed to help with toilet training, it seems that teaching children that handling poo is okay is not a good idea.

4 GOD ALMIGHTY

God Almighty is an action figure sold by the "Jesus Christ Superstore." It features a God-like figure with a long white beard wearing a flowing white coat. The figure also comes with a Kalashnikov AK-47 (yeah right, because God really needs one of those), and the unfortunate logo on the box reads, "his [sic] is the kingdom, the power and the glory." Tacky.

3 CHOPPED-UP LADY

Only in Japan would a toy like this be developed. This toy is a bag filled with an anatomically correct woman who has been chopped into pieces. She comes complete with blood oozing out of her wounds and blood splatters on her face. Perfect for the parent who wants to distract their future serial-killer child from maiming animals.

2 STRIPPER POLE

Believe it or not, a British company produced a stripper pole toy for young girls to practice their pole dancing. Fortunately, some officials decided to yank it from the shelves, but sadly not before dozens of parents bought them for their daughters. The marketing campaign for this product is quite unbelievable: "Unleash the sex kitten inside...simply extend the Peekaboo pole inside the tube, slip on the sexy tunes, and away you go!" Remember—this was made for preteen girls.

1 BREAST-FEEDING DOLL

Yes, it's another doll, but I'm certain you will understand why it is number 1 on this list. Let's start with the product tagline: "Because you shouldn't have to wait until you have breasts before you start breast-feeding your baby." I beg to differ. This doll comes with a special top for pre-pubescent girls to wear that has little flowers in the place of nipples. When the doll is placed on the flower it begins to suckle. This doll is seriously, seriously wrong. It is made by the Spanish company Berjuan.

CHAPTER TEN

Around the World

10 BIZARRE TOURIST ATTRACTIONS

10 NOODLE BATH (JAPAN)

The Japanese do everything that other people do, but sometimes in very different ways. One day because he thought it was mundane to take a bath with water and soap, a man decided to bathe in noodles, and soon enough other people wanted to do the same. Apparently, pepper collagen, an ingredient used in pork broth, improves metabolism and clears your skin. Acne is also said to vanish after one session. This same bathhouse previously filled their spas with chocolate and Beaujolais wine.

9 VALE DE LA PREHISTORIA (CUBA)

Even Michael Crichton, the creator of *Jurassic Park*, would feel a little bizarre in the milieu of life-size dinosaurs built by inmates from a nearby prison. Spread over an area of 11 hectares, the 200 life-size prehistoric creatures in the Santiago de Cuba province range from the brontosaurus to cave men, creating a kind of Communist theme park with shades of the Flintstones thrown in.

8 KARNI MATA TEMPLE (INDIA)

Rajasthan, India, is the land of maharajas, palaces, deserts, camels, and the Karni Mata temple, which not only serves as a refuge for rodents but a place where they're worshipped as well. Built in the early 20th century by Maharaja Ganga Singh of Bikaner in reverence to Karni Mata, a female Hindu sage, the temple's ostentation serves as no indication of the experience a visitor is going to get. So high is the status of rats in this citadel of devotion that an accidental death of one of the inhabitants requires a replacement with a solid-gold replica.

7 INTERNATIONAL FRIENDSHIP EXHIBITION HALL (NORTH KOREA)

In the city of Pyongyang, which one journalist described as being a "Stalinist theme park," lies the International Friendship Exhibition Hall. The structure houses 90,000 or more gifts accumulated over the years by the great leader Kim Il Sung. The list of Kim Il Sung's admirers includes former Soviet prime ministers Gregory Malenkov and Nikolai Bulganin, Palestinian leader Yasser Arafat, Cuba's Fidel Castro, and Zimbabwe's Robert Mugabe. The gifts themselves are even more interesting—silver chopsticks from Mongolia, a gold cigarette case presented by Marshall Tito of Yugoslavia, chess boards from Colonel Gaddafi of Libya, and a grinning alligator offering drinks from a wooden tray sent all the way from Nicaragua. Surely, friendship has its rewards.

6 ISLA DE LAS MUNECAS (MEXICO)

Julián Santana Barrera collected dolls that had been discarded and brought them to this island. Legend had it that he did it to appease the spirit of a girl who drowned in the river there. When you navigate through the canals of Isla de las Munecas, the dolls stare at you from where they hang in the trees. To make the story more interesting, Barrera drowned, succumbing to the same fate as that little girl for whom he labored so hard.

5 COCKROACH HALL OF FAME (UNITED STATES)

Ross Peroach, David Letteroach, and Marlin Monroach are some of the characters you'll become acquainted with when you visit Michael Bohdan's Cockroach Hall of Fame in Plano, Texas. A pioneering pest-control specialist, Bohdan took it upon himself to impersonate famous characters in the most bizarre way possible: by re-creating their likenesses with deceased cockroaches. However, if you aren't into dead ones, he has Madagascar hissing roaches as well—and they're alive and kicking.

4 BANG KWANG PRISON (THAILAND)

Most travelers aren't bored in Bangkok, but if malaise sets in, there's always the Bangkok prison to visit. Why? Because for a fee you can interact with the inmates, some of them Western travelers whose holidays went horribly wrong. Brought into the spotlight by the 1999 movie *Brokedown Palace*, this highly fortified bastion derives its allure from the possibility of actually showcasing 7000 specimens imprisoned for crimes ranging from drug smuggling to murder. Moreover, you quickly learn not to commit such offenses when you are in Thailand.

3 NEUTRALITY ARCH (TURKMENISTAN)

If you ever hazard to travel the silk route like the pioneering traders centuries ago, the city of Ashgabat in the former Soviet republic of Turkmenistan will introduce you to one of its own great denizens: Saparmurat Niyazov. Niyazov, Turkmenistan's leader after independence, etched his name onto everything in the country, but most

famously he built for himself the Neutrality Arch. To secure his place in history as a megalomaniac, he ordered his statue to be placed at the top of the structure, revolving continuously so that he always faces the sun. And to top it all off, he called it the "Neutrality Arch," which you can hardly use to describe a man who ruled with an iron fist.

2 SEKIGAHARA WAR WORLD (JAPAN)

In Japan's Gifu prefecture is an oddball theme park that re-creates the great battle of Sekigahara. As if a solemn monument were not enough, an enterprising businessman re-created the scene with life-size concrete structures of beheading, ritual suicides, and hand-to-hand combat. If you aren't satisfied with the gore, the song titled "Ah, the Decisive Battle of Sekigahara" played on an endless loop will soothe your ears.

1 KARNER BONE HOUSE (AUSTRIA)

Perhaps the unlikeliest of places to host an ossuary, the Karner Bone House in the bucolic Austrian town of Hallstrat would far more easily be associated with the *Sound of Music*. However, it's more noted now for playing host to skulls painted with decorations such as flowers, leaves, and serpents. Why? Because of the acute lack of space and the urgent need to recycle graves.

10 SPOOKY TRAVEL DESTINATIONS

10 HILL OF CROSSES (LITHUANIA)

Walking up to the Hill of Crosses can be an extremely disturbing experience. You're greeted by the site of hundreds of thousands of crosses of varying sizes all placed in seemingly random order. The origin of the first crosses here is unknown, but despite the Communist government's many attempts to destroy them and suppress the devotion there, the crosses kept coming back. The Hill of Crosses is in Kryzių Kalnas, 12 kilometers north of the city of Siauliai.

9 ST. LOUIS CEMETERY NO. 1 (U.S.)

It would be wrong to write a list like this without the inclusion of at least one cemetery. The Saint Louis Cemetery is actually three Roman Catholic cemeteries in New Orleans. They frequently feature in movies because most of the graves are above-ground vaults, which make the perfect setting for thrillers and horror movies. Tourists are advised not to enter the cemeteries alone due to the high risk of crime. This graveyard is a "Who's Who" of famous celebrities and criminals, from a voodoo witch to Bathelemy Lafon, the architect who became one of Jean Lafitte's pirates. Also rumored to be buried here is the murderous New Orleans socialite Delphine LaLaurie.

8 MARY KING'S CLOSE (SCOTLAND)

Mary King's Close is a subterranean town in the old part of Edinburgh, Scotland. It has been perpetually shrouded in myths and mysteries. History recounts tales of walled-up plague victims and ghosts, and other horrible stories. It's believed that when the plague hit the area, the local council contained it by walling up the Close with all the living and the dead left inside, which led to its nickname, the Street of Sorrows.

7 LEAP CASTLE OUBLIETTE (IRELAND)

Leap Castle is four miles north of Roscrea in Ireland. Originally built in 1250 and renovated in 1659, the castle history is full of tales of executions, hauntings, and the famous oubliette—a dungeon where people were chained and left to die alone. When excavation work was done in the oubliette, three cartloads of human remains were removed from it. The most horrifying specter seen in the castle is that of a hunched creature that carries with it the stench of rotting flesh.

6 CHÂTEAU DE MACHECOUL (FRANCE)

Château de Machecoul is not as well known as it should be. It was home to one of medieval history's most vile serial killers, Gilles de Rais (1404–1440). Gilles was a knight and even a companion-in-arms to Saint Joan of Arc. After his warring days ended, he retired, dabbled in devilry, and spent his wealth. To regain his riches, he turned to satanic practices that involved the slaughter of hundreds of children. Here is an excerpt of the transcript from the trial of Gilles de Rais:

> When the said children were dead, he kissed them and those who had the most handsome limbs and heads he held up to admire them, and had their bodies cruelly cut open and took delight at the sight of their inner organs; and very often when the children were dying he sat on their stomachs and took pleasure in seeing them die and laughed...

He was hanged at Nantes on October 26, 1440. Gilles de Rais was the inspiration behind the tale of Bluebeard. All of his crimes took place in the Château of Machecoul, which remains to this day, although it's in ruins. His victims' bodies were stuffed in the walls, dropped down chimneys, and buried around the site.

5 POENARI CASTLE (ROMANIA)

Vlad the Impaler (Vlad Tepes) was a name to strike fear into the hearts of one and all. He was the inspiration behind Bram Stoker's character Dracula, and Poenari Castle was his home. It was built in the 13th century, and by the 15th century it was the primary stronghold of this bloodthirsty ruler. After Vlad's death, the castle went to ruins, but it's still possible to visit (as long as you don't mind climbing 1500 steps to get to it). It's considered one of the most haunted places on the planet.

4 CAPUCHIN CATACOMBS OF PALERMO (ITALY)

The Capuchin Catacombs of Palermo are burial catacombs in Sicily. The monks of the monastery would lay their dead brethren to rest in the catacombs, and because of the nature of the soil in the region, the monks were preserved extremely well. The walls are lined with row upon row of monks and nobles in full dress (providing an extremely rich history of clothing to historians). In 1880 the catacombs were officially closed, but tourists continued to visit and a few more burials took place, the most notable being the last: in the 1920s, Rosalia Lombardo, a two-year-old girl, was the last body laid to rest there. To this day she looks as if she has just fallen asleep.

3 POVEGLIA (ITALY)

Poveglia is a small island in Venice that's forbidden to visitors. It was home to Venice's plague victims during the three major outbreaks in the Middle Ages. After it was a plague pit, it became a leper colony and then later housed an insane asylum. It's about as good as it gets when you're looking for a horrifying spot. It's believed that the core of the island may be filled with the remains of the dead, and local fishermen avoid the place for fear of uncovering a corpse and unleashing the plague.

2 AOKIGAHARA (JAPAN)

Aokigahara, the sea of trees, is a forest at the foot of Mount Fuji in Japan. It's believed to be home to countless paranormal phenomena, and it's the second most popular suicide location in the world (second only to the Golden Gate Bridge). The highest number of suicide victims found in the forest in one year is 78, in 2002. Every year there's a "body hunt" undertaken by local volunteers to clear out all the human remains.

1 EUROPEAN OSSUARIES

Unlike the Capuchin Catacombs, the ossuaries across Europe are home to bones and not preserved corpses. Ossuaries are usually built to house skeletal remains when cemetery space becomes limited. In the most famous ossuary—Santa Maria della Concezione dei Cappuccini, a church in Rome, Italy—the remains of over 4000 friars can be seen laid out in elaborate patterns and ornamental designs. This is truly a scary place to visit.

10 BIZARRE MICRONATIONS

10 THE GRAND DUCHY OF WESTARCTICA

When the Antarctic Treaty was signed, it split up the territory in Antarctica among several different countries; but there's an area in Western Antarctica called Marie Byrd Land, between the claims of Chile and New Zealand, that had no territorial claim attached to it. In 2001, Travis McHenry saw the area was unclaimed and declared it an independent nation with himself as the ruler. He sent declarations of his claim to all the nations that signed the Antarctic Treaty; the letters were of course universally ignored, as there are no year-round residents of the area and no one who claims to part of the nation's government has even been to the location thus far. Very little is known about the intentions of the founder, or the "nobility" of the nation. The most that's come out of the country has been a few coins and stamps, and a free e-mail service for "citizens."

9 PITCAIRN ISLAND

Of all these micronations, this one by far has the most interesting history. We're all at least somewhat familiar with the story of the mutiny on the *Bounty*, when the evil Captain Bligh was overpowered by mutineers who wished to return to Tahiti instead of going back to England. What most don't know is that many of the mutineers actually did eventually relocate to Tahiti, though some settled in a tiny island called Pitcairn in the South Pacific, where a few of their descendants still live today. Officially, the island is not considered a nation but an unincorporated territory. It's legally a democracy, with the town's mayor considered the ruler, but isn't considered a country. With a population of roughly 50 as of 2003, this island is officially the smallest democracy in the world.

8 MOLOSSIA

Started by Kevin Baugh in 1977 as a school project, the Republic of Molossia is a mock dictatorship in northern Nevada described as a "hobby" by its de facto ruler. Kevin Baugh calls Molossia an "enclave nation" because it's surrounded by the United States, and while the country has a constitution and a national assembly, Baugh claims martial law due to the "everpresent foreign threat" of the U.S. The micronation also has territorial claims in Pennsylvania and Northern California, and has recently laid claim to the Neptune Deep (the floor of the deepest trench in the Pacific Ocean) and the province of "Vesperia," located on the planet Venus. Baugh has also decreed national bans on firearms, incandescent light bulbs, and smoking, along with more outlandish bans against onions, catfish, walruses, and anything from Texas. The property is mainly considered a tourist trap; visitors get a 45-minute guided tour of the country by Kevin Baugh himself, who expects them to present their passports at the gate.

7 FREETOWN CHRISTIANIA

While not a traditional micronation (if there is such a thing), Freetown Christiania certainly qualifies for this list as a self-governing area with a small resident population. Freetown was established in 1971 in an abandoned military base in Copenhagen, Denmark, by freethinkers and hippies with ambitions of building a free society. Depending on who you talk to, Freetown Christiania is either "the world's first fully functioning anarchistic society" or an area overrun with squatters and drug dealers. It's also either a "safe, quiet town where one is free to be oneself" or a crime-ridden slum, where people are often raped, mugged, or murdered.

Since the area is, indeed, in a state of anarchy, no official numbers exist on crime rates, so it's hard to tell if the lofty vision of the founders actually lines up with reality. The "town" consists of an area

less than a kilometer square, and citizens still pay taxes and city utilities to Copenhagen, but the residents claim Freetown has its own set of laws and public services. The local laws forbid firearms, cameras, "hardcore" drugs, and cars, though it's unclear how these laws are enforced since the town also boasts it has no police. The main attraction for visitors is "Pusher Street," where people can buy marijuana and related paraphernalia in an open-air market, despite the fact it's illegal in the rest of Denmark. While it has something of a bad reputation, Freetown is still known for being the origin of many famous Danish writers, artists, and theater groups. It's considered by some to be a shining example of how anarchy is a plausible system of government.

6 THE NATION OF CELESTIAL SPACE

If I were rating these nations by territory claimed, this would be the hands-down winner. The so-called Nation of Celestial Space was established on January 1, 1949, by James Thomas Mangan when he wrote to his local board of deeds and titles to lay stake to some previously unclaimed territory. What was this territory? The entire universe, minus the earth. While this bizarre claim was ignored by most, it didn't stop Mangan from printing coins, bills, and postage stamps for his "nation." When the U.S. and Russia began flying high-altitude aircraft, he wrote letters of complaint to their respective state departments claiming that these flights were infringing on his territorial claim without his permission. Strangely, Mangan wasn't the only person to establish an extraterrestrial micronation before the Outer Space Treaty was signed in

1967, forbidding territorial claims in outer space. Other contenders included the Other World Nation, which claimed the other planets of the solar system, and the Celestial Solar Kingdom, which claimed the surface of the sun.

5 ROSE ISLAND

In 1968, Italian architect and real estate investor Giorgio Rosa constructed a 400-square-meter platform in the Adriatic Sea seven miles from the Italian town of Rimini. The platform was meant to be a tourist spot, sporting its own souvenir shop, fishing pier, and radio station. Soon after it was opened, Rosa declared sovereignty and renamed the platform the Republic of Rose Island and started claiming he was going to begin printing his own currency. Worried that this was a ploy to avoid taxes, the Italian government evicted Rosa and his employees soon after, and the Italian navy destroyed the platform with explosives. In a snarky retort, Rosa began printing postage stamps with an image of the platform's destruction and issued them from his "Government in Exile."

4 CONCH REPUBLIC

An example of a micronation founded in the name of both protest and comedy, the Conch Republic was established on April 23, 1982, to protest the building of a U.S. border checkpoint between the Florida Keys and the mainland. The checkpoint was meant to curb an influx of illegal immigration and smuggling from Cuba and other Caribbean islands, but inadvertently caused gridlock on the only highway bridge that led to the Keys, inhibiting tourism and shipping. Mayor of Key West Denis Wardlow declared himself prime minister of the republic and during the secession ceremony declared war on the United States by breaking a stale loaf of Cuban bread over a nearby naval officer. He then quickly surrendered and applied for one billion dollars in foreign aid from the United States.

While the secession was never serious, the Keys are still jokingly referred to as the Conch Republic, and the protest did succeed in persuading the Border Patrol to remove the checkpoint. The people of the Conch Republic also banded together in 1994 to reopen a national park that the federal government had closed. During the closure, the prime minister declared, "The U.S. government is closed, but the Conch Republic can still issue passports." Indeed, passports and other souvenirs are available on the country's website. Their national motto is "We Seceded Where Others Failed."

3 REPUBLIC OF MINERVA

Wishing to create a libertarian utopia with no taxes, subsidies, or welfare, real estate millionaire Michael Oliver started a project to create an island and declare it an independent nation. In 1971, he succeeded. In the Minerva reef, between Tonga and New Zealand, tons of sand was poured into the shallow reefs to bring it above sea level and create a small island. The citizens of this tiny island had high hopes, thinking they could attract tourists, fisherman, and even industry after adding more sand to the island, which at the time was barely stable enough to hoist a flag on. The group elected a president, Morris C. Davis, and wrote up a declaration of independence and sent it to nearby nations. Suspicious of the group's intentions, nearby Tonga issued a proclamation that the island was inside their territorial waters and used soldiers to forcibly evict the residents and lower the flag. This action was supported by the South Pacific Forum, so there wasn't much Oliver could do but fire the "president" of his nation and cut his losses. Years later, former president Davis returned with an expedition of American settlers, intending to reoccupy the reef, but was again kicked out by Tongan troops. A more recent expedition has found that the artificial island has been "more or less reclaimed by the sea."

2 PRINCIPALITY OF SEALAND

Sealand started its life as an offshore anti-aircraft platform called "HM Fort Roughs" placed in a British shipping lane during World War II to fend off German mine-laying aircraft. During the war, the platform housed 107 UK sailors on its 550-square-meter deck and observation towers. In 1967, Pirate Radio broadcaster Paddy Roy Bates occupied the platform and set it up as a base for his pirate station, *Radio Essex*. A year later, Bates' son fired a rifle at a work crew that was repairing an automated buoy near the platform, and was arrested for firearms violations since Bates and his family were still considered British citizens. Bates was acquitted because the platform was three miles outside of the UK's oceanic claim and in international waters. Seeing an opportunity, Bates declared the platform the Principality of Sealand, giving his tiny nation the motto *E Mare Libertas* (From the Sea, Freedom), wrote a national anthem, and started issuing stamps and currency. He stated that the British court ruling gave him the right to declare the open-sea platform as a sovereign nation.

Since Sealand exists in international waters, there was little the British government could do about the pirate broadcasts (and the Bates family's habit of shooting at passing boats while "defending their waters"), but to this day, no one has officially recognized the sovereignty of the platform.

1 PRINCIPALITY OF HUTT RIVER

Likely the most well-known micronation on this list, the Principality of Hutt River was founded by Leonard George Casley in 1970. It consists of about 75 square kilometers (about 30 square miles) of farmland near the town of Northampton in Western Australia. It came into being due to a wheat quota law Casley called "Draconian." The government imposed quotas that only allowed him to sell 99 acres of wheat when he had grown 9900 acres. He initially fought the unfair quotas in court, even appealing to the British royal family. When all else failed, Casley resorted to an obscure tort law that allowed British colonies to secede in similar circumstances. Leonard George Casley dubbed himself "His Royal Highness Prince Leonard" and declared his independence.

Despite nearly 40 years of calling itself a sovereign state, the Principality of Hutt River hasn't been recognized by the Commonwealth of Australia, nor any international entity. However, the principality has issued stamps, passports, and coins (one bearing the profile of former American President Bill Clinton) and claims approximately 18,000 citizens "living abroad," as you can apply for citizenship for a small fee on the country's website. It has a standing military (mostly consisting of Casley's children and grandchildren), and even though it's landlocked, it claims to have a navy. The Australian government, while not honoring Hutt River as a real country, regards it as simply an eccentric old man selling souvenirs to tourists. Many Australian wildernesses tours include a stop at Hutt River, billing it as "the second biggest nation on the continent."

10 PLACES YOU CAN'T GO

10 MEZHGORYE

Mezhgorye is a closed town in Russia that's believed to be the home of people working at a highly secret military base in the mountains towering above it. U.S. satellite imagery has shown large excavation projects taking place there, and when the Russian government has been questioned about it, they've given contradictory replies. Some believe it may be a secret nuclear bunker for the nation's leaders.

9 VATICAN SECRET ARCHIVES

Actually, the archives here aren't secret, despite their name. You can view any document you wish. But you can't enter the archive. You must submit your request for a document and it will be supplied to you. Despite what Dan Brown's novel *Angels and Demons* will have you believe, the documents are all available and there are no copies of suppressed scientific theories or great works that were banned. The only documents you can't access are those which are not yet 75 years old (in order to protect diplomatic and governmental information). Indexes are available for people who want to see if a document exists in the archives. The Vatican Secret Archives have been estimated to contain 52 miles of shelving, and there are 35,000 volumes in the selective catalogue alone.

8 CLUB 33

Contrary to popular belief, Disneyland has a full liquor license that is used when the place closes down to the general public to accommodate private parties. But there is one place in Disneyland that's always open to sell booze: Club 33. Club 33 has a full liquor license and it is available to members only. Membership fees range from 10 to 30 thousand dollars. There is currently a waiting list of over 14 years.

7 MOSCOW METRO-2

Metro-2 is a secret underground rail system in Moscow that runs parallel to the public metro. It was built by Stalin for the purposes of easy and swift transportation of the KGB during his reign of terror. The government continues to this day to deny its existence.

6 WHITE'S GENTLEMEN'S CLUB

White's is an exclusive English club for men only. But even if you're a man, you can only join by invitation. Unless you belong to a royal family or are a powerful politician, you're unlikely to be invited to become a member.

5 AREA 51

This entry is almost certainly the one most would expect to see here. Area 51 is the name of the U.S. military base in Nevada that's off-limits to all but a few special people. It's rumored to be the home to captured alien technology from the Roswell event. Signs around the perimeter warn people that they will be shot on sight if they enter the area.

4 ROOM 39

Room 39 is the most secret area in one of the most secret nations in the world: North Korea. It's home to the men who seek ways to secretly obtain foreign currency for the current despotic ruler, Kim Jong Il. It's the hub of the "court" economy, the financial world of the Kim family. There are also persistent rumors that Room 39 is involved in international drug smuggling and illegal weapon sales.

3 ISE GRAND SHRINE

The Ise Grand Shrine is the most sacred spot in Japan. It has been in existence since the 5th century BC, and it's home to the most sacred item in Japanese imperial history: the sacred mirror. Tradition states that if the mirror is destroyed, the Japanese empire will fall. The only people who can enter the shrine are members of the royal family, or the priest or priestess.

2 MOUNT WEATHER EMERGENCY OPERATIONS CENTER

This is a place that's not only closed to the public, but that the public hopes to never have to enter! In most "end of the world" films, there's a highly classified area where U.S. government officials and a chosen few get to go in the hopes that they can escape the impending doom. The Mount Weather Emergency Operations Center is the real thing. It was set up in the 1950s because of the Cold War, but continues to operate today. It's a "last hope" area.

1 MECCA

Mecca is a city in Saudi Arabia and is believed by Muslims to be the place in which Muhammad first spoke of his new religion. Mecca is off-limits to all non-Muslims. The approach to the city includes special roads to divert non-Muslims away from it. Some descriptions of Mecca by non-Muslims exist, but they are all from people who have pretended to be Muslim in order to satisfy their curiosity about the place. The city is a fairly typical Saudi city, and a non-Muslim would be unlikely to see anything especially unusual except for the large number of Muslim pilgrims who visit there more than anywhere else in the world.

10 PLACES YOU DON'T WANT TO VISIT

10 GREAT PACIFIC GARBAGE PATCH (PACIFIC OCEAN)

The Great Pacific Garbage Patch, sometimes called the Pacific Trash Vortex, is a gyre of litter in the central North Pacific Ocean, located between about 135° to 155°W and 35° to 42°N. Most current estimates state that it's larger than the state of Texas, and some claim that it's larger than the continental United States; however, the exact size is not known for sure. The patch is characterized by exceptionally high concentrations of pelagic plastics, chemical sludge, and other debris that have been trapped by the currents of the North Pacific Gyre. The patch is not easily visible because it consists of very small pieces, almost invisible to the naked eye, and most of its contents are suspended beneath the surface of the ocean. This is not a place the average Joe would want to visit.

9 IZU ISLANDS (JAPAN)

The Izu Islands are a group of volcanic islands stretching south and east from the Izu Peninsula of Honshū, Japan. Administratively, they form two towns and six villages that are all part of Tokyo. The largest is Izu Ōshima, usually called simply Ōshima. Because of their volcanic nature, the islands are constantly filled with the stench of sulfur (extremely similar to the smell of thousands of farts, or rotten eggs). Residents were evacuated from the islands in 1953 and 2000 due to volcanic activity and dangerously high levels of gas. The people returned in 2005 but are now required to carry gas masks with them at all times in case gas levels rise unexpectedly.

8 THE DOOR TO HELL (TURKMENISTAN)

While drilling in Darvasa in Turkmenistan in 1971, geologists accidentally found an underground cavern filled with natural gas. The ground beneath their drilling rig collapsed, leaving a large hole with a diameter of about 50 to 100 meters (about 165 to 330 feet). To avoid poisonous gas discharge, scientists decided to set fire to the hole. Geologists had hoped the fire would go out in a few days, but it has been burning ever since. Locals have named the cavern the Door to Hell.

7 ALNWICK POISON GARDEN (ENGLAND)

Inspired by the Botanical Gardens in Padua, Italy (the first botanical garden, which was created to grow medicinal and poisonous plants in the 1500s), the Alnwick Garden in Alnwick, England, is devoted entirely to plants that can kill. It features many plants grown unwittingly in backyards and those that grow in the British countryside, as well as many more unusual varieties. Flame-shaped beds contain belladonna, tobacco, and mandrake. The Alnwick Garden has a home-office license to grow some very special plants, namely cannabis and coca, which are found behind bars in giant cages—for obvious reasons.

6 ASBESTOS MINE (CANADA)

Asbestos is a set of six naturally occurring silicate minerals highly prized for their fire-resistance and sound-absorption abilities. On the downside, exposure to this stuff causes cancer and a variety of other diseases. It's so dangerous that the European Union has banned all mining and use of asbestos in Europe. But, for those curious enough to want to get close to the stuff, all is not lost. In Canada at the Thetford Mines, in Quebec, you can visit an enormous open-pit asbestos mine that's still fully operational. The workers in the mines aren't required to wear any sort of respiratory protection, and in some sections of the nearby town, residential areas are butted up against piles of asbestos waste. The mine offers bus tours of the deadly environment during the summer months. Tickets are free (would you expect it to be any other way?). If you decide to visit, don't forget your full-body biohazard suit.

5 RAMREE ISLAND (BURMA)

Ramree Island in Burma is a huge swamp home to thousands of enormous saltwater crocodiles, the deadliest in the world. It's also home to malaria-carrying mosquitoes and venomous scorpions. During World War II, the island was the site of a six-week battle in the Burma campaign. Here's a description of one of those horrifying nights:

> That night [February 19, 1945] was the most horrible that any member of the M. L. [motor launch] crews ever experienced. The scattered rifle shots in the pitch-black swamp punctured by the screams of wounded men crushed in the jaws of huge reptiles, and the blurred worrying sound of spinning crocodiles made a cacophony of hell that has rarely been duplicated on earth. At dawn the vultures arrived to clean up what the crocodiles had left…Of about 1,000 Japanese soldiers that entered the swamps of Ramree, only about 20 were found alive.

4 YUNGAS ROAD (BOLIVIA)

The North Yungas Road leads from La Paz to Coroico, 35 miles northeast of La Paz in the Yungas region of Bolivia. It's legendary for its extreme danger, with estimates stating that 200 to 300 travelers are killed yearly along it. The road includes crosses marking many of the spots where vehicles have fallen off. It was built in the 1930s during the Chaco War by Paraguayan prisoners, and it's one of the few routes that connects the Amazon rainforest region of northern Bolivia to its capital city. Because of the extreme drop-offs of at least 2000 feet, its narrow width—most of the road is no wider than 10 feet—and its lack of guardrails, the road is extremely dangerous. Further, rain, fog, and dust can make visibility precarious. In many places, the surface is muddy and can loosen rocks from the road.

3 MUD VOLCANOES OF AZERBAIJAN (AZERBAIJAN)

In the spring of 2001, volcanic activity under the Caspian Sea off the Azeri coast created a whole new island. In October 2001, there was an impressive volcanic eruption in Azerbaijan at Lokbatan, but there were no casualties or evacuation warnings. But Azerbaijan does not have a single active volcano, at least not in the usual sense of the word. What Azerbaijan does have are mud volcanoes—hundreds of them. Mud volcanoes are the little-known relatives of the more common magmatic variety. They do erupt occasionally with spectacular results, but are generally not considered to be dangerous—unless you happen to be there at the wrong time. Every 20 years or so, a mud volcano explodes with great force, shooting flames hundreds of feet into the sky, and depositing tons of mud on the surrounding area. In one eruption, the flames could easily be seen from nine miles away on the day of the explosion, and were still burning, although at a lower level, three days later.

2 THE ZONE OF ALIENATION (EASTERN EUROPE)

The Zone of Alienation is the 19-mile exclusion zone around the site of the Chernobyl nuclear reactor disaster and is run by a special administration under the Ukrainian Ministry of Extraordinary Situations. Thousands of residents refused to be evacuated from the zone, or they illegally returned there later. Over the decades, this primarily elderly population has dwindled, falling below

400 in 2009. Approximately half of these resettlers live in the town of Chernobyl; others are spread in villages across the zone. After recurrent attempts at expulsion, the authorities became reconciled to their presence and even allowed limited support services for them. Because of looting, there is a strong police presence, so be warned—if you visit, you may either be shot or get radiation poisoning, and we all know how awful that can be.

1 ILHA DE QUEIMADA GRANDE (BRAZIL)

Off the shore of Brazil, almost due south of the heart of São Paolo, is Ilha de Queimada Grande (Snake Island). The island is untouched by human developers, and for very good reason. Researchers estimate that on the island live between one and five snakes per square meter. That figure might not be so terrible if the snakes were, say, two inches long and nonvenomous. The snakes on Queimada Grande, however, are a unique species of pit viper, the golden lancehead. The lancehead genus of snakes is responsible for 90 percent of Brazilian snakebite-related fatalities. The golden lanceheads that occupy Snake Island grow to well over a half-meter long, and they possess a powerful, fast-acting venom that melts the flesh around their bites. This place is so dangerous that a permit is required to visit.

10 SCARIEST
FILIPINO MONSTERS

10 ASWANG

The *aswang* are probably the most common of Filipino monsters since there are so many different kinds. In general, they are shapeshifters who are humans by day, and dogs, pigs, bats, cats, or snakes by night; the type of animal depends on regional lore. *Aswang* break into funeral homes and steal recently deceased corpses. They're also known to enter homes to drink human blood and can turn humans into *aswang* by tricking people to bite them in return. The *aswang* are especially hungry for human fetuses, so some of the more superstitious stories include neighborhood patrols set up in front of the home of a pregnant woman to protect her from wandering stray animals in case they're the *aswang* in disguise.

9 MATRUCULAN

The *matruculan* is one of many Filipino creatures that attack pregnant women. This particular monster first impregnates a virgin before coming back later to kill the woman and eat the fetus (although some stories say that both mom and baby are eaten). Some stories claim that the woman is not a virgin, but rather married and already pregnant. To protect the mother and child, the husband must swing a *balisong*, or butterfly knife, above the woman's belly while she is in labor. This leads one to wonder which is scarier: an invisible mythological creature, or the father of your unborn child brandishing a knife above your abdomen?

8 KAPRE

These are hairy giants with glowing eyes and a cigar that never burns out. They can usually be found sitting atop trees, waiting for darkness to scare naughty children who are outside of their homes late at night. The *kapre* are unique Filipino monsters because they don't steal fetuses, eat people, or cut them up. They simply enjoy scaring children. Some stories claim that *kapre* are actually very friendly beings who can grant wishes if you find their magical white stone. You can assume a *kapre* is nearby when trees sway while there is no breeze or you see faint smoke from high above, probably from the *kapre*'s cigar.

7 DUWENDE

These are tiny, humanlike creatures that live underground. There are two main types of *duwende*: the *duwende puti*, who are supposedly kind creatures who bring about good luck, or the *duwende itim*, who are mean folk that like to play pranks on humans. They generally keep to themselves and only interact with humans when their homes are disturbed. For example, a kindly farmer who takes care of his land may be rewarded by the *duwende puti* with a greater abundance of crops than usual. However, someone who kicks an anthill on or near the home of a *duwende itim* will be punished with a myriad of ailments, from a twisted mouth to swollen testicles. The best way to avoid *duwende* of any kind is to say *tabi-tabi po* aloud before entering what might be their space.

6 TIYANAK

The *tiyanak* is similar to the Greek mythological siren in that it lures prey with its voice. A person hears a baby cry from deep in the woods and then follows the sound to rescue the baby. Some stories say the person wanders aimlessly in search of the baby and becomes hopelessly lost. Others claim that the person eventually finds a baby in the middle of the woods. When it's picked up, the baby then shapeshifts into a monster with large, sharp teeth. It eats the person and transforms back into a baby to await its next victim. With either version, the story ends with "… and he was never found again."

5 SIGBIN

Depending on the region and storyteller, the *sigbin* resembles either a hornless goat, a reptilian crow, or something vaguely along the lines of the *chupacabra*. What is most common with all accounts is that the *sigbin's* head hangs between its forelegs, which are much shorter than its hind legs. Whether because of physiology or because it makes the *sigbin* seem scarier, it's also known to crabwalk backward. The *sigbin* also has a long, whiplike tail that emits a foul stench and two grasshopperlike legs on its neck that enable it to jump far distances. *Sigbins* wander around at night in search of children to devour, but they keep the hearts to make amulets. Most stories and sightings originate from the Cebu region, but in 2005, scientists in Borneo, although it's some distance away, discovered a "cat-fox-like carnivore" with hind legs longer than forelegs, giving it an awkward gait and physical appearance that somewhat fits many of the descriptions of the *sigbin*. No conclusive evidence has been found yet to link the two together.

4 TIKBALANG

The *tikbalang* is described as having the head of a horse, the body of a man, and the hooves of a horse where human feet would be. In northern regions of the Philippines, the *tikbalang* is considered a nuisance but generally harmless. They enjoy disorienting weary travelers and making them imagine things that don't exist. Travelers can easily stop the pranks by turning their own shirt inside out and asking the *tikbalang* to stop bothering them. The stories of *tikbalang* from southern regions paint the creature as a much more sinister monster. He has glowing red eyes, a large cigar, and smells of the stench of burning hair. When angered—and he angers easily—the *tikbalang* will stamp you to death. To tame the beast, the person must pluck the one of three unusually long hairs found in its mane. After that, the *tikbalang* is your slave. Folklore states that when the sun shines through the clouds while it's raining, two *tikbalang* are getting married.

3 KUMAKATOK

In the middle of the night, a knock will sound at the door, and outside will be three hooded figures, one a pretty, young woman and two elderly men. There are no stories of how the group was formed or where it originated, but tales about the three figures have popped up all over the Philippines, and with more frequency around the time of disease outbreaks. Legend has it that a visit from the *kumakatok* is an omen that someone in the family will soon die. There are no paintings or hangings that can keep them at bay. Leaving the door unanswered doesn't help, either. They simply knock and leave, and someone still dies shortly thereafter.

2 THE WHITE LADY (*KAPEROSA*)

The White Lady is a specific kind of *multo*, or ghost. Most *multo* tend to be family members who come back to certain relatives to take care of unfinished business, but the White Lady is unique in that she doesn't appear to only her relatives or even to specific people she knew when alive. Many sightings have reported her in empty buildings, near forests, and on cliffs. However, she is most commonly seen along Balete Drive in Quezon City. She was a young lady who was raped and killed by two Japanese soldiers during World War II. While there haven't been stories of the White Lady being a purposefully malicious being, she has been reported to be the cause of more than a few car accidents by drivers who looked in their rearview mirror and saw a young lady in the backseat wearing a white dress. Sure, some strange, unknown lady sitting in your backseat is bad enough, but the White Lady is also said to have no face, or a face covered in blood.

1 MANANANGGAL

The *manananggal* are sometimes considered to be a special breed of the *aswang* (number 10 on this list). They are sometimes referred to as *tik-tik* because of the sound they makes while in flight; to confuse a victim, the *tik-tik* sound becomes fainter as the *manananggal* nears. The *manananggal* generally takes on the form of a beautiful woman with large, leathery bat wings. The lower half of her body roots to the ground while the upper part detaches as she flies in search of food. The *manananggal* has a taste for human blood and a particular craving for the hearts of human fetuses, which it retrieves with its long, proboscislike tongue. Like the Western culture's vampire, the *manananggal* hate garlic and salt, so hanging garlic or placing a bowl of salt near the window is the best way to keep them away. To kill a *manananggal*, you must find the lower body and spread salt or ashes on the open wound. That prevents the two halves from joining and transforming back to human form when daylight breaks.

10 BIZARRE CREATURES FROM JAPANESE FOLKLORE

10 KAPPA

At first glance, there's nothing too "outlandish" about a *kappa*. It's a little goblinlike creature frequently referred to as a water monkey. A *kappa* has a dent in its head that's full of water from its native spring, and if the water spills out of its head, it loses its magical powers. *Kappas* generally drink blood but can be either good or evil, and are known for being polite and always keeping promises. They love to eat cucumbers, and a family wishing to gain the favor of a *kappa*, or at least avoid a bad *kappa*'s wrath, writes their names on a cucumber and throws it into the *kappa*'s pond. The strangest thing about them is that there are over a dozen different, weirdly specific categories of *kappa*. There are different names for one-eyed *kappas*, hairy *kappas*, cowardly *kappas*, mountain-climbing *kappas*, and even party animal *kappas*.

9 HEIKEGANI

The *heikegani* are on this list for one very cool reason: they actually exist. *Heikegani* crabs are a species of arthropod native to Japan. Originally, Japanese myth said that these crabs bore the faces of *heike* samurai that died in the battle of Dan-no-ura, and indeed, their bodies do in fact resemble human faces. Carl Sagan proposed that, in the past, Japanese people only ate *heikegani* crabs that didn't resemble samurai faces, therefore ensuring that those with markings resembling a human face would survive and have offspring. These days, most crabs have bodies resembling human faces; however, at a mere one or two inches in diameter, they're not eaten very often.

8 KASA-OBAKE

The *kasa-obake* is a type of *tsukumogami*—an object that spontaneously comes to life after existing for 100 years. The idea of inanimate objects spontaneously developing spirits after a certain amount of time seems reasonable enough when you consider how strange legends and folklore usually are to begin with. The bizarre thing about the *kasa-obake* is that, apparently, umbrellas were animating so often that someone eventually decided that they required their own name, just to separate them from other *tsukumogami*. That's right, *kasa-obake* is the name of an animated parasol.

7 NUPPEPPO

There's not nearly enough information about the *nuppeppo* to satisfy my curiosity. *Nuppeppos* are animated lumps of human flesh. They walk around on their hands and are most often spotted in graveyards or deserted temple areas at midnight. Where do they come from? Why are they alive? Do they smell bad? Why do most images of them seem to be downright cute? We don't have nearly enough information about this horror-film fodder.

6 MAKURA-GAESHI

Here we have another case of Japanese folklore being bizarre if for no other reason than its specificity. The *makura-gaeshi* is a trickster spirit notorious for moving pillows while people sleep. Some sources say they also sprinkle sand in eyes and steal souls, but, really, what they're known for is moving pillows. Stories don't specify how far the pillows are moved; some sources claim that they move pillows all the way to the foot of the bed while the victim is peacefully asleep.

5 MOKUMOKUREN

The *mokumokuren* is another example of a bizarrely specific creature. In ancient Japan, sliding walls made of paper were fairly common. Paper, however, can collect holes and become torn. A *mokumokuren* is a spirit that inhabits a sliding paper wall with a hole in it. If the owner of the wall is careless, the wall may collect more holes, and the more holes there are in the wall, the more likely somebody is to notice the eyes of the *mokumokuren* peeking out. This probably becomes a bit unnerving over time, and the only way to get rid of a *mokumokuren* is to repair the holes in the wall.

4 KONAK JIJI

The *konak jiji* is simply a malicious little creature. It takes the form of an infant and lurks in remote mountain areas, waiting for an innocent traveler to pass by. When a victim is in sight, the *konak jiji* begins to cry. It's human nature to want to stop a baby from crying, and so most kindhearted travelers seek out the wailing infant and, of course, make the fatal mistake of picking it up to comfort it. Once the *konak jiji* is picked up, it grows unbearably heavy. Some sources say that they can grow to weigh over 750 pounds, enough to do serious damage to anyone holding them. It's not all bad, though—if you manage to survive the crushing weight of the *konak jiji*, it may give you magical gifts.

3 AKANAME

The *akaname* is on this list because it's both bizarrely specific and just plain bizarre in its own right. *Akaname* can be translated to "filth licker," and that's no misnomer. The *akaname* is a hideous type of Japanese bogeyman that quite literally licks dirty bathrooms clean with its tongue and the aid of poisonous saliva. It's believed that the monster may have originated as a way for parents to motivate their children to keep the bathroom clean.

2 ITTAN MOMEN

The *ittan momen* looks harmless enough; after all, it's only a strip of white cloth that's, oh, 33 feet long or so. It has a habit of flying around at night, which is a bit weird, but not too frightening. It's not frightening, that is, until the *ittan momen* becomes scared or if it's just plain evil. Then it may wrap around your head and crush your skull or smother you to death. It's not all bad, though—*ittan momen* enjoy being worn by people who have gained their trust. Although how, exactly, one gains the trust of a giant strip of cloth seems to be a mystery.

1 SHIRIME

Time for something a little crass: *shirime* was the name given to an apparition of a man with an eyeball where his anus should have been. Now, we're not given much, if any, information on why such an apparition should exist at all. In fact, there's only one recorded story of the *shirime*, but the idea was apparently so well liked by the Japanese poet and artist Yosa Buson that he included it in several of his paintings of supernatural creatures. The story of the *shirime* simply states that a lone samurai was walking down a road at night when somebody called to him. He turned to see a mysterious man undressing and pointing at his derriere when a large, glittering eye opened from the indicated area. The samurai was, understandably, so horrified that he ran away screaming, and the *shirime* was never seen again.

15 TRULY ODD GEOGRAPHICAL FACTS

15 TAUMATAWHAKATANGIHANGAK OAUAUOTAMATEATURIPUKAKA PIKIMAUNGAHORONUKUPOKAIWHE NUA KITANATAHU

The second-longest accepted geographical name in the world is Taumata-whakatangihangak oauauotamateaturipukaka pikimaungahoronukupokaiwhe nua kitanatahu (85 letters), which is a hill in New Zealand. It's a Maori phrase that translates to "place where Tamatea, the man with the big knees, who slid, climbed, and swallowed mountains, known as land-eater, played his flute to his loved one." Although the *Guinness Book of Records* still regards it as the longest, it has been supplanted by Krung thep maha nakorn amorn ratana kosin mahintar ayutthay amaha dilok phop noppa ratrajathani burirom udom rajaniwes mahasat harn amorn phimarn avatarn sathit sakkattiya visanukamprasit (163 letters) in Thailand.

14 LESOTHO, VATICAN CITY, AND SAN MARINO
Lesotho, Vatican City, and San Marino are the only countries completely surrounded by one other country. Lesotho is enclosed by South Africa, while Vatican City and San Marino are both surrounded by Italy.

13 LLANFAIRPWLLGWYNGYLLGOGERYCHWYRNDROBWYLL-LLANTYSILIOGOGOGOCH
Llanfairpwllgwyngyllgogerychwyrndrobwyll-llantysiliogogogoch is the longest village name in the world (and third-longest geographical name). It's located in Wales, and, yes, there are four "l"s in a row!

12 Å
The shortest place name is Å, and it's located in both Sweden and Norway. In Scandinavian languages, Å means "river." The road signs for the area are frequently stolen for their novelty value.

11 VATICAN CITY
Vatican City is the smallest country in the world at only .2 square mile. That's smaller than the average city! The largest country is (surprise, surprise) Russia.

10 HULUNBUIR, INNER MONGOLIA
The largest city in the world, based on surface area, is Hulunbuir, Inner Mongolia, which is 101,913 square miles.

9 EL AZIZIA, LIBYA, AND VOSTOK, ANTARCTICA
The hottest temperature recorded on Earth was in El Azizia, Libya, at 136°F; the coldest was -134°F in Vostok, Antarctica. The hottest average temperature is in Western Australia, where it's around 96°F year-round.

8 SAN MARINO

San Marino claims to be the world's oldest constitutional republic. It was founded in 301 by a Christian stonemason fleeing persecution under Emperor Diocletian. Its constitution of 1600 is the oldest written constitution in the world.

7 ECUADOR'S MOUNT CHIMBORAZO

Though Mount Everest is the highest altitude on the planet in terms of sea level, Ecuador's Mount Chimborazo is the closest to the moon. The Mariana Trench, in the Pacific Ocean, is the lowest place on earth.

6 ALASKA

Alaska is the most northern, eastern, *and* western state in the U.S. It's the only state that enters the Eastern Hemisphere, making it also the most eastern-lying and western-lying state.

5 MID-ATLANTIC RIDGE

Located along the middle of the Atlantic Ocean, the Mid-Atlantic Ridge is the longest mountain chain on earth, at about 25,000 miles. Iceland is the only part of this chain that's above water. The Andes form the longest exposed mountain range, at about 4300 miles.

4 ITALY'S MOUNT CIRCEO

Mount Circeo on Cape Circaeum on the western coast of Italy was once called Aeaea (five vowels in a row with no consonants). It was believed in mythology to be the home of the witch Circe. Two other vowel-only geographic locations are the town of Aiea, Hawaii, and Eiao, one of the Marquise Islands.

3 GLACIERS

Glaciers store between 70 and 80 percent of all the freshwater on the planet; 99 percent of those glaciers are in the Arctic and Antarctic regions.

2 19TH-CENTURY EARTHQUAKES

In 1811 and 1812, three earthquakes measuring around 8.0 on the Richter scale caused the Mississippi River to flow backward. These earthquakes also created Reelfoot Lake in Tennessee.

1 KOLA SUPERDEEP BOREHOLE

The deepest hole ever drilled by man is the Kola Superdeep Borehole in Russia. It reached a depth of 40,226 feet, or 7.62 miles. It was drilled for scientific research and produced some unexpected discoveries, one of which was a huge deposit of hydrogen so massive that the mud coming from the hole was "boiling" with it.

10 COMMON MISCONCEPTIONS ABOUT BRITAIN

10 BRITISH NATION

Misconception: Britain is a country.

While "Britain" and "Great Britain" do refer to the general area, neither refers to a country. "Britain" is a general term for Wales, Scotland, and England collectively, while "the British Isles" also includes Ireland (both Northern Ireland and the Republic of Ireland). England is most often incorrectly named in this way, and English people are often referred to as "British." Northern Ireland is part of the "United Kingdom of Great Britain and Northern Ireland," which differentiates between the part of Ireland that's governed by England and the Republic of Ireland, which is a self-governing nation.

While calling an English person British is technically correct, it's very unspecific in the same way that calling a Canadian person "North American" would be, except that Britain isn't a continent.

9 WARM BEER

Misconception: British people drink beer warm or at room temperature.

It's unclear where this idea comes from. Walking into a British bar and ordering a beer any way but cold would raise eyebrows just like it would everywhere else. In fact, the most popular lager beers in Britain tend to be of the "extra cold" variety,

and this applies to most bitter beers and ales, too! Nobody likes a warm beer, the British included.

Having said that, most Americans like their beer super cold, so an English beer may appear to be warm by comparison, but it's still cold. Chilling beer too much can damage its flavor.

8 THE BOOK OF BRITISH SMILES

Misconception: British people have bad teeth.

This one is commonly referred to in comedy shows poking fun at Britain, but it's believed by many to be hard fact. While a percentage of the British population, just like in any other country, suffers from dental problems, the standard of oral hygiene is generally very high. In fact, the shortage of available dentists is a constant issue in England. Just like anywhere else in the world, in Britain, a person with bad teeth is considered the slightly gross exception, not the rule.

7 GOD SAVE THE QUEEN

Misconception: "God Save the Queen" is the national anthem of England.

That's right, I said England, not Britain. "God Save the Queen" is the national anthem of Britain, but not England itself. Despite this, even English people will insist that the song is their country's anthem, which isn't the case. Wales has its own national anthem, as do Scotland and Northern Ireland. What sets England apart is that, in fact, it doesn't even have an official national anthem at all!

So what happens when (for example) England plays against Scotland in a game of soccer? Both countries can't use "God Save the Queen." This isn't a problem for Scotland, who can bring out their own anthem, but England's choice varies. Common stand-ins for when "God Save the Queen" can't be used for whatever reason are "Land of Hope and Glory," "I Vow to Thee My Country," or "Jerusalem," all of which are popular contenders for becoming the official national anthem, although sadly, none of them is.

6 ABSOLUTE POWER

Misconception: The Queen is the ruler of Britain.

Did I hear you say, "But she *is* the ruler of England!"? Sorry, you're still wrong. The monarchy has not had political power in Britain for a long time. Each British country has its own parliament and are ruled politically by its own prime minister.

While the monarchy does technically rule Britain, it doesn't have any power outside of ceremony. The Queen doesn't have power in Britain any more than she does in Canada and other commonwealth countries. All of these countries are technically "ruled" by the Queen, but she doesn't have power in any of them. The British monarchy exists today mainly for ceremonial and tourist reasons.

5 HOW NOW BROWN COW
Misconception: British people speak the "Queen's English."

Or, to use the more common term, British people talk "posh." Watch and listen to any representation of Britain from a foreign country, and you'll hear British people speaking in a manner that's considered just as ridiculous to most of Britain as it is to foreigners. We all know what that kind of English sounds like; if not, take a look at Fry's Holophonor tutor in *Futurama*. Know what I mean? Then read on.

This may come from the way in which English is generally written in Britain. It's always taught that you should write "properly" and use correct language in formal writing so that it's easier to understand when read. Despite this, British people rarely speak the way they write. In reality, Britain has a wide variety of accents, some even bordering on dialects, the majority of which do not sound remotely like how British speech is presented in foreign media. To see some examples of this, try watching some British television movies. (But *don't* watch the news! Newsreaders are told to use the Queen's English so they can be understood by all; it's even called "BBC English.") Good examples of everyday British language are *Trainspotting* (Scottish accent), *28 Days Later* (modern London and Manchester accents), and *Sweeny Todd* (old London accent).

4 FREE HEALTHCARE
Misconception: Britain has free universal healthcare.

Sadly, as is commonly unknown to people outside of Britain, the National Health Service (NHS) is not free, nor will it cover any illness or injury. The NHS is paid for through taxes and donations and will only provide certain approved services or treatments. While it's true that emergency treatment is almost always free of charge, treatment for long-term illness or injury is almost always charged. Certain drugs will be provided for certain illnesses, but if your illness or the drugs and treatment you require isn't on the "approved" list, you won't get it from the NHS. This is always a controversial issue in Britain.

The NHS is also not available to non-British citizens, except in the case of emergency. Even then, the emergency must have taken place within Britain.

3 SCOTTISH MONEY

Misconception: Scottish money is legal tender in the rest of Britain.

If you've ever attempted to use Scottish pounds sterling in England, Wales, or Northern Ireland, you will know that many places won't accept it.

Scottish pounds sterling are not legal tender in all of Britain, and shops outside of Scotland are not legally obliged to accept it. Banks outside of Scotland will accept it, but legally it's up to the manager's discretion whether or not to accept it in any other location. What's the difference between Scottish pounds sterling and the pounds sterling used in the rest of Britain? Actually nothing, aside from how it looks.

So why do many places outside of Scotland refuse to accept it? The most common reasons are that either the Scottish pounds sterling aren't commonly seen and so aren't recognized, or that their design and the fact that most people outside of Scotland rarely see the pounds sterling make them easy to forge.

2 RAIN, RAIN EVERYWHERE

Misconception: It always rains in Britain.

When people think of Britain, we all tend to immediately think of bad weather. We see rain clouds, storms, bitter wind, and general misery. However, compared to many other parts of the world, Britain enjoys comparatively pleasant weather! During the winter, the average temperature can become bitterly cold (between 32 and 43°F), but the average summer temperature ranges between about 60 and 75 degrees, and often higher. Britain ranks a comfortable 46th in a chart of worldwide average rainfall, falling well behind such countries as New Zealand (29th) and even the U.S. (25th).

Why does Britain have a reputation for bad weather? Most likely because winters tend to be longer than summers in Britain, most artwork of Britain depicts the weather based on expectation, and we all like to dwell on a period of bad weather, even if the weather is generally good.

1 BRITISH TEA

Misconception: British people drink excessive amounts of tea.

There are many ways of looking at which regions drink the most tea, but whichever way you look at it, Britain is not the biggest tea-drinking region by a long shot. Taking population into account, Britain ranks somewhere around third worldwide, falling well behind Turkey and India. Depending on your source, China still sits above Britain in the tea-drinking league tables, even when considering population.

So where does this misconception come from? Well, it's true that Britain does drink a lot of tea, but it is far from the top consumer. Britain actually drinks almost as much coffee as it does tea. The misconception may actually stem from a linguistic difference between Britain and other English-speaking regions. In most places, the evening meal is referred to as "dinner" or "supper." This is correct terminology in Britain, too, but an evening meal is very often referred to as "tea." So when a British person invites you over for tea, they're inviting you for a meal, not to just sit and drink tea, which is how some people imagine the situation. This is also true of the commonwealth nations, where "come for tea" usually means "come for the main evening meal." A British person will almost never invite you over solely to drink tea, although if you stop by it will commonly be offered. Tea is most often drunk after a meal at dessert, or after strenuous activity as an alternative to coffee.

10 ODDITIES OF THE BRITISH PARLIAMENT

10 NO CONSTITUTION

Or to be more accurate, there is no single document setting out how the country should be governed. The UK is one of only a handful of nations without a written constitution (the others being Israel, New Zealand, and San Marino). It instead relies on a huge number of separate laws and traditions, which evolved over hundreds of years.

A surprising number of features central to the British political system are nothing more than convention. There is no constitutional requirement for there to be a prime minister, for example; it is simply a role that has developed over time.

The lack of a concrete constitution is likely to become a serious political debate in the near future, as the Liberal Democrat party has begun campaigning for constitutional reform.

9 ROYAL ASSENT

Before a bill can become law, the Queen must give her approval, or "royal assent." She still has the power to grant (accept), withhold (refuse), or reserve (postpone) the royal assent of any bill from Parliament.

In reality, no monarch has refused a bill passed by Parliament since 1708, so it is assumed that the Queen will grant assent to any Parliamentary bill presented to her.

8 VOTING SYSTEM

The number of votes a political party gets and the number of seats they win in Parliament rarely show any relationship. Voters pick a candidate for their local area, and the person with the most votes wins the seat. If a candidate wins with 60 percent of the vote, the other 40 percent of votes are discounted.

It's a simple system, but in a nation with three major parties, it can create some anomalies, which has led some of the public to question how representative the voting system is. Those discounted votes soon mount up and can lead to results such as the 2005 election, in which the Labour Party got only 37 percent of the vote but 55 percent of the seats, and the Liberal Democrats got 22 percent of the vote but only 9 percent of the seats.

The voting system does, however, tend to produce a clear overall winner, which leads us on to…

7 CHOOSING THE PRIME MINISTER

British citizens have no say in who becomes PM—the best they can do is vote for their party's Member of Parliament (MP) and hope. As you might expect from a system built on ancient conventions, the process of deciding who becomes PM is far from straight-forward. After the results of the general election have been announced, the leader of the party with the overall majority (i.e., with more MPs than all of the other parties put together) goes to Buckingham Palace and asks the Queen for permission to form a government. Luckily for them, this is another convention: the Queen will never say no to the leader of the biggest party.

The system is not very democratic; in fact, in most elections, less than 40 percent of the people have voted for the largest party.

6 HUNG PARLIAMENT
The voting system usually makes sure the winning party has a strong overall majority, but occasionally the votes don't produce a clear winner. These "hung parliaments" force the parties with a sizable share of the seats to make deals, and sometimes two of them agree to work together until the next election.

If none of the parties can work together to form an overall majority, the convention is that the previous prime minister stays in office. This means, for example, that if the PM belonged to the Labour Party, there is the possibility that the Labour Party could come third in an election, but Britain would still have a Labour Prime Minister!

5 CALLING AN ELECTION
There is no fixed amount of time between elections. The law states that a government must have an election at least every five years, but an election can be called at any point within that time. The Queen has ultimate power over the dissolution of Parliament, but convention allows the prime minister to choose when this should be.

When the PM decides the time is right to have an election, they ask the Queen to dissolve Parliament. This often proves advantageous to the government, who usually wait until they are ahead in popularity before putting the vote to the public.

4 HOUSE OF LORDS

The Members of Parliament sitting in the House of Commons are not the only politicians in Parliament, although you could be forgiven for thinking so. Parliament also has an upper chamber, the House of the Lords, composed of the Lords Temporal, who are appointed by the Queen on recommendation of the government, and 26 prominent bishops of the Anglican Church.

All bills successfully passed through Parliament are debated and ratified by the House of Lords. The Lords can and do reject bills, but the ultimate power lies with the House of Commons, which can invoke the "Parliament Acts 1911 and 1949" to pass the bill regardless. This has only happened seven times since 1911, including a 2004 ban on hunting with dogs.

As the upper chamber is made up of unelected members and ultimately powerless against the House of Commons, there have been calls for change from some MPs who favor an elected second house similar to the U.S. Congress.

3 UNPARLIAMENTARY LANGUAGE

When in session, MPs are forbidden from using language that might "offend the dignity" of Parliament. This commonly includes swearing, personal insults, and, most seriously, accusing another MP of dishonesty. Many words have been deemed unparliamentary by House Speakers over time, including "coward," "guttersnipe," "hooligan," "liar," "traitor," and "git."

Many MPs have perfected the art of insult while avoiding reprimand from the House Speaker and enjoy mocking their rivals with phrases such as being "economical with the truth" (lying) or "unusually fatigued" (drunk).

2 THE CEREMONIAL MACE

The Mace of the House of Commons is an ornate golden staff that rests in the center of the chamber when Parliament is in session. The staff represents the authority of the Queen and must be present in the chamber for the meeting of the House to be legal.

The mace has seen its fair share of action over the decades; it has been thrown, snatched, and even wrestled from MPs protesting Parliament's decisions. In 2009, Labour MP John McDonnell was suspended for picking up the staff and disrupting a debate on the expansion of Heathrow Airport in London.

1 PARLIAMENTARY VOTING

The House of Commons makes use of an old and rather eccentric method of voting. After the vote has been announced by the Speaker of the House, the MPs present are given eight minutes to move into one of two rooms: the "aye" or the "no" room. When the time is up, the doors are locked and the MPs line up to be counted.

Secretaries of state and even the PM vote on important matters and can often be seen scrambling for the correct room among the MPs. Despite looking ridiculous, the voting system provides an excellent opportunity for MPs to meet and talk with the PM and the rest of the government.

10 PLACES WITH MORBID NAMES

10 THE SKELETON COAST, NAMIBIA

The rusted, dilapidated remnants of hulking ships, recent and ancient, litter this stretch of coast in this southwestern African nation, which the Namibian Bushmen called "The Land God Made in Anger." Many ships are covered by the sands of time, and only their bows can be seen jutting through sandbars, while others are completely unseen, buried in their beachy graves. Over time, punishing winds and currents, rocks, and fog have resulted in the demise of many ocean vessels as well as marine animals such as whales, whose bleached bones can be

found intermingled with decaying hulls, and for which the coast gets its name.

Countless shipwrecked sailors came face to face with death here. If they were "fortunate" enough to avoid drowning and make it to land, they were greeted with an arid, salty wasteland of massive sand dunes that extended for a hundred miles inland with no opportunity for finding sustenance. Eventually, they perished from thirst or exposure. Although the area is slightly more accessible today, it's still very remote and notorious, and ships go out of their way to stay far out to sea when passing by it.

9 TOMBSTONE, ARIZONA

In the Southwest American desert, the town of Tombstone is a reminder of the Old West's violent, lawless past. It received its name when a prospector looking for valuable rocks was told that all he would find out in the harsh area would be his own tombstone. However, the prospector stumbled upon silver, named his mine the Tombstone, and the town sprung up from there.

Although the inception of the town's name was a tongue-in-cheek joke, it lived up to its moniker; perhaps it was a self-fulfilling prophecy. A substantial part of the town consisted of saloons and whorehouses that attracted various unsavory characters, including many outlaws. One of these brothels, the Bird Cage Café, was reported by the *New York Times* as being "the wildest, wickedest night spot between Basin Street and the Barbary Coast." Violence and bloodshed became the norm in Tombstone, with the shootout at the OK Corral between Wyatt Earp and his brothers and a gang of outlaw "cowboys" being the most famous event. Not ironically, Tombstone is home to a number of cemeteries that are tourist attractions today.

8 DEAD SEA, ISRAEL AND JORDAN

This body of water in Israel and Jordan certainly doesn't have a shortage of bleak or depressing nicknames. Lake of Asphalt, Salt Sea, Sea of the Devil, and Stinking Lake are a few, even though it holds some biblical importance. Its high mineral content, which makes it ten times saltier than the world's oceans, allows nothing to live in its waters except some bacteria. It lies at the lowest point of dry earth on the planet, plunging 1300 feet below sea level. Being so low, water doesn't drain but can only evaporate, leaving a strong concentration of minerals. An estimated seven million tons of water evaporates daily.

The mineral deposits are actually sought after and are used for things such as medicines, fertilizers, and cosmetics. Health spas and resorts were also commonplace on the sea because it was, and still is, believed that the water has healing properties. However, scientists are warning that the Dead Sea is, in fact, dying itself. In recent years, it has been rapidly shrinking, with the southern end disappearing altogether. Over the past 50 years, the water level has dropped 80 feet, and the sea has lost a third of its volume. To make matters worse, the only thing that flows into the sea is raw sewage with virtually no fresh water replenishing it. While officials are devising ways to keep the Dead Sea as pristine as they possibly can, it's evident that it will never be the same again and its destiny is to continue to dwindle. Strict conservation efforts must be put into effect to at least slow the inevitable.

7 MURDER ISLAND, NOVA SCOTIA

The Tusket Islands lie off the coast of the Canadian province of Nova Scotia. Although they're picturesque and beautiful, they're also home to the mysterious and ominous Murder Island.

Stories surrounding the island are quite cryptic. One tale has the origin of the name going back to 1735, when the brig *Baltimore* was discovered on the shore with its interior splattered in blood and deserted except for one mysterious woman. She told confusing stories of a convict revolt and an Indian massacre that were never substantiated or fully explained. Before a concrete conclusion could be reached, the inscrutable woman disappeared along with the knowledge of what had really happened.

Another story tells about a smallpox epidemic that ran rampant through a French fleet stationed near the island sometime in the 1700s. Hundreds of corpses were unloaded onto the diminutive island and buried there. Reports of human bones popping up through the island's beaches continued through the 20th century. Whether or not these stories can be proven, it's probable that Murder Island holds some checkered secrets.

6 GALGBACKEN (GALLOWS' SLOPE), STOCKHOLM

Also known as Gibbets' Slope ("gibbets" is another name for gallows), Gallows' Slope was the largest and last place of execution in Sweden's capital city. The last execution took place in 1862, and the preferred method of execution was, obviously, hanging. However, beheadings were also quite popular. Criminals of all ilks, including murderers, rapists, embezzlers, and counterfeiters, were put to death here. A number of those sentenced to die were also prominent figures of the day. In the 1930s, construction workers found human skeletal remains while beginning construction on residential housing on the site. There's no doubt that bones of those unlucky enough to meet their death on the gallows still lie buried at Gallows' Slope.

5 HELL'S KITCHEN, NEW YORK CITY

A neighborhood in Midtown Manhattan, Hell's Kitchen was infamous for crime, sex, and violence. It's thought to have gotten its name from a rough, dangerous hostel long since gone. Irish and German immigrants first settled the neighborhood, with most of them working on the docks as longshoremen, or in slaughterhouses and factories. The immigrant influx led to a filthy shantytown and the rise of multiple street gangs. After the Civil War, the population swelled even more, and tenements rose above the streets, resulting in further squalid conditions. More gangs formed, violence grew exponentially, and the neighborhood became known as "the most dangerous area on the American continent."

When Prohibition banned the production and sale of alcohol in the 1920s, some of the gangs evolved into organized crime rackets dealing in bootlegging, gambling, prostitution, and extortion. In the 1950s, Puerto Rican immigrants populated Hell's Kitchen, which resulted in much racial tension and subsequent violence with the other ethnic groups there. This strife became the inspiration for the movie *West Side Story*. A bit later, the Westies, an extremely violent and powerful Irish-American gang, operated from their base in the neighborhood.

Today, Hell's Kitchen has undergone gentrification, and real estate agents prefer to call the neighborhood "Clinton." However, there are still hints of the neighborhood's tawdry past, as some pornography shops and strip clubs are still sprinkled throughout the area.

4 THE DEATH ZONE

This is not a specific location per se, but it describes an altitude on Earth exceeding 26,240 feet. Some mountaineers define it as an altitude over 25,000 feet. Almost all the peaks in the death zone are located in the Himalaya and Karakoram ranges (which is technically part of the Himalayas). At this particular height, oxygen is so scarce that life simply cannot be sustained. Climbers can't

acclimatize themselves to this altitude, can't digest food, and without oxygen tanks their bodily functions deteriorate at a rapid pace, resulting in unconsciousness, deliriousness, hallucinations, and eventually death.

Although there are no definitive numbers, hundreds of climbers have died climbing peaks in the death zone. On a macabre note, the bodies of all who have succumbed on these mountains simply remain there, since removing them would be such a painstaking and dangerous, if not impossible, task. Therefore, the death zone is essentially the world's highest graveyard.

3 GOLGOTHA (PLACE OF THE SKULL), JERUSALEM

A biblical entry, Golgotha was an ancient site located outside the walls of 1st-century Jerusalem. It's said that Jesus was crucified on this site, as were many who were convicted of crimes by the Roman Empire. There are a few theories about how the hill got its name. Some believe the name refers to the number of abandoned skulls and bones that were found there. Others say the craggy, rocky hill physically resembled a skull. Still others claim that Golgotha loomed over a cemetery, so it naturally would be bestowed with a gruesome name.

It was a Jewish religious requirement that all executions take place outside the city of Jerusalem, and the Romans were believed to have honored this tradition. Therefore, the site of Golgotha was established just outside of the walled city. Due to many parts of Jerusalem being destroyed and rebuilt throughout history, the exact site of the hill is disputed. However, many scholars agree that the site lies within the Church of the Holy Sepulcher, which was built by the emperor Constantine. According to tradition, this is also the site where Adam (the first man) was buried. Wherever the current-day location of Golgotha may be, it's a historically documented site where grisly executions actually took place.

2 DEVIL'S ISLAND, FRENCH GUIANA

Located off the coast of French Guiana, Devil's Island was a notorious penal colony. The main prisons were actually located on the mainland, but the whole complex collectively became known as Devil's Island. Originally a leper colony, it operated as a penal colony from 1884 to 1952. Conditions were probably worse than any modern-day prison in any country today. While wearing nothing but pairs of shoes and straw hats, and being barraged by malaria-carrying mosquitoes, prisoners would work waist deep in water while their skin baked in the unrelenting sun. If they didn't meet their daily quota of work, such as chopping enough wood, they would only be fed a paltry piece of dry bread for the day.

In Kourou, which was the deadliest camp on Devil's Island, 4000 prisoners died within a span of three years. All throughout the penal colony, thousands of men died from exhaustion, thirst, hunger, heatstroke, dysentery, malaria, and murder. The only hope many of the convicts had was escape.

Most escapees fled through the dense jungle, where they had to compete with hostile natives, piranhas, flesh-shredding brush, and the same mosquitoes and oppressive heat they faced in the colony. If they were lucky enough, they made it to Dutch Guiana, where they would find sanctuary. Some attempted to escape by sea on makeshift rafts; some were successful, others died a watery death. Those who were caught and brought back to Devil's Island were labeled as "incorrigible." They were put into solitary confinement, made to work like animals all day, then shackled in irons overnight until it was time for them to go to work again.

Prisoners stopped being sent to Devil's Island in 1938, and in 1952, the prison was closed. When accounts of the horrors were revealed to the general public, people were appalled that a civilized country such as France would propagate such atrocities. Today, Devil's Island is a museum and tourist attraction.

1 DEATH VALLEY, NEVADA AND CALIFORNIA

Lying in America's Mojave Desert, Death Valley is one of the hottest, driest, inhospitable places on earth. It's 3.3 million acres of barren wilderness consisting of towering mountains, canyons, rifts, salt flats, and sand. The lowest point in North America is here at the Badwater Basin, where the elevation sinks to 282 feet below sea level. Temperatures commonly reach over 100°F, with the highest temperature recorded at 134°F, two degrees short of the highest ever recorded on Earth.

The hardships early pioneers, as well as intrepid individuals following them, faced in the various regions of Death Valley gave rise to equally morbid names. Some of them include: the Funeral Mountains, Dante's View, Furnace Creek, Devil's Golf Course, Desolation Canyon, Devil's Cornfield, Black Mountains, Stovepipe Wells, Hell's Gate, and the aforementioned Badwater Basin. People first attempted to traverse the burning sands of the area during the California Gold Rush of 1849. They were known as the Death Valley 49ers, and many of them never got to lay their eyes on gold since they became victims of the hellish conditions. In 1933, Death Valley was established as a national park. Many people visit each year, but if you go off the established and official roads and trails, it's crucial that you are with an experienced guide; rescue operations are an all-too-common occurrence in this unforgiving landscape.

10 MOST DANGEROUS PLACES ON EARTH

10 UNITED STATES OF AMERICA

For the average traveler, the U.S. is fairly safe, but the numbers don't lie. There are more than 200 million guns in the U.S. and more than 50 murders a day, which is ten times the rate of Germany. Nearly 5000 people die a year in truck crashes, about 6000 pedestrians die on the streets, and 31,000 people end their own lives. The U.S. now leads all nations in violent crime, and incarcerations now stand at 2.3 million, the most of any country. American citizens also make up the greatest number of criminals serving time in overseas prisons. Militias, hate groups, and other right-wing radicals all spread their message of violence and are known to throw around the odd pipe bomb. The government is not much better, spending a whopping $600 billion a year on defense in order to contain the handful of nations hostile to it.

9 BRAZIL

For anyone traveling to Brazil, it's not a matter of whether you get mugged, it's a matter of when! Grinding poverty still lives alongside incredible wealth in a country that's riding a wave of economic growth. But with prosperity, rates of crime have also soared. Street crime is rampant in parts of Rio de Janeiro and São Paolo, and while many victims are left unharmed, having a broken bottle put to your throat for your jewelry is not pleasant. The incidence of "quicknappings" has risen in major cities. This involves being abducted and taken to an ATM to pay your ransom. If you can't pay, thanks to mobile technology, your family is only a call away. Along with street crime, organized-crime groups have waged wars against police and public institutions that were unable to be bribed. Prison riots are brutally suppressed, drugs and narco-terrorism claim civilian casualties, and if you survive all that—the piranhas are waiting.

8 SOUTH AFRICA

Any nation described as the "rape capital of the world" should be one to take extraspecial care in. Although rape there had shown a declining trend in 2004, it increased in 2005. Another damning statistic for South Africa is its appallingly high murder rate. The 2010 World Cup host is consistently in the top-five list of countries by homicide rate. Most crime is confined to poor areas but it hasn't stopped gated communities from springing up all over South Africa and wealthy tourist groups from traveling with armed guards. Farming in South Africa has become one of the most dangerous professions in the world—the murder rate for farmers there is about eight times the national average. And like anywhere, sex can be very dangerous in South Africa, where more than ten million people are infected with HIV.

7 BURUNDI

This small, densely populated, poor nation has giant problems. A civil war between Hutus and Tutsis tore the nation apart between 1993 and 2006. A ceasefire was declared; however, most of the agreement's provisions have not been implemented. Mass murder and mayhem compete with environmental problems as the biggest headaches for the people of Burundi. The list of assassinated leaders is extensive, and control of the nation has changed hands numerous times in the last 50 years. Crimes committed by roaming gangs and armed children are risks for visitors. Muggings, carjackings, and kidnappings await, so you are advised not to stop the car for souvenirs. Should you be injured or harmed while in Burundi, you may need to be well trained in first-aid, as local clinics have almost no resources to assist you.

6 ANTARCTICA

While murder, rape, and robbery may not be big problems in this part of the world, the hostile conditions are. Antarctica is home to some extreme weather conditions, with the mercury regularly dropping below -100°F and winds tearing in at more than 65 mph. If exposed to this weather for more than an hour, you will most certainly die. Antarctica has no hospitals, no food to forage, and, if you get lost, not a lot of hope. Stay with the tour groups. At least there is a McDonald's at Scott Base (if you manage to find it).

5 AFGHANISTAN

For hundreds of years, this nation has been one of the world's most strategically important and lusted-after territories. However, it also remains one of the poorest, undeveloped, and unstable. During the Soviet invasion, the Red Army planted more than 12 million landmines in Afghanistan. Hundreds of people are killed, shredded, and maimed each year due to these insidious devices. Following the Soviets were the Taliban, whose control meant women were banned from jobs and universities. In 2001, the United States overthrew the Taliban, but banditry, tribal rivalries, and drug-related violence have left the nation unstable. Suicide bombings are a constant threat, and no one in Afghanistan is safe. The most lethal suicide attack occurred in Baghlan Province in November 2007, killing more than 70 people. Did I mention Afghanistan is also the world's largest supplier of top-grade hashish and opium?

4 SOMALIA

Somalia is a failed state known for its anarchy, corruption, lack of government, and starvation. Travelers are warned against entering Somalia, the self-proclaimed "independent Republic of Somaliland," or even sailing near the Horn of Africa. Pirates patrol these waters armed with AK-47s and will seize craft and hold crews for ransom. Interclan fighting has claimed thousands of lives in the north of the country, while territorial control in the capital, Mogadishu, is carved up between many clans and warlords. Ethiopia attacked Islamic troops in Somalia in late 2006, resulting in hundreds of casualties and the internal displacement of thousands. Heck, if this place is too much for the Marines, what chance do you stand? Make sure your insurance is fully up to date.

3 SUDAN

Desperation, death, and destruction are synonymous with Sudan. Terrorism is a mainstay of this nation, which has been controlled by Islamic military regimes since its independence. Some of the world's most famous killers have earned their stripes in Sudan, finishing with degrees in car bombing, rocket launching, and genocide. Violence is rife in the Darfur region among government-backed militias, government troops, and local insurgent groups. Sudan has been in open warfare with Chad partly due to the Darfur conflict. Since 2003, 230,000 Sudanese refugees have fled to eastern Chad from Darfur. More than two million have died during the two civil wars during the last 50 years. Along with its bleak desert conditions, this all makes Sudan one of the worst places on the planet.

2 COLOMBIA

Kidnapping is the main worry in Colombia. There were 2338 kidnappings in Colombia in 1998. Of the victims, 138 were killed by their captors. Ranked fourth in the world for murders in 2006, the popular targets are mayors, and dozens of them are slain each year. And, of course, who can forget cocaine? Colombia provides 75 percent of the world's supply, and thanks to Pablo Escobar and the

Cali Cartel, paramilitary groups have waged war on the government in a bloody conflict with no end in sight. Even those working in the name of charity are not excluded from the frenzy. In 2005, five Catholic missionaries were murdered, down from nine in 1999. Colombia's beautiful coast and rugged mountains should make it a tourist paradise; instead, it's among the most feared destinations you can visit.

1 IRAQ

It doesn't matter whether you're George Bush, Pele, or Chuck Norris—you aren't safe in Iraq. Despite its rich history and oil reserves, it's a ruined nation that's wracked with violence, despair, and confusion. Since 2003, the United States has occupied Iraq, which has led to a civil war claiming the lives of more than 650,000 civilians. Al-Qaeda, Sunni insurgents, Shiite security forces, Kurdish rebels, American soldiers, Turkish troops, and criminals are involved in a cycle of violence that, unfortunately, will not abate any time soon. Improvised explosive devices (IEDs), explosively formed penetrators (EFPs), and mines are constant threats, as are suicide bombers, who have slain hundreds. Kidnappings and random killings are reported with almost mind-numbing frequency. Since 2003, 2 million Iraqis have fled to neighboring countries, and another 1.9 million in Iraq remain internally displaced. Depleted uranium used as armor-piercing ammunition will poison Iraqi civilians and U.S. servicemen for decades. Truly, a hell on earth.

10 INCREDIBLE REAL-LIFE CASTAWAY TALES

10 JOHN F. KENNEDY (1917–1963) AND CREW

Survived: 6 days on Plum Pudding and Olasana islands

In 1943, John F. Kennedy was the 26-year-old skipper of *PT-109*. As the *PT-109* was prowling the waters late at night, a Japanese destroyer suddenly emerged and in an instant cut Kennedy's craft in half. Two of his 12-member crew were killed instantly and two others were badly injured. The survivors clung to the drifting bow for hours. At daybreak, they embarked on a 3.5-mile swim to the tiny, deserted Plum Pudding Island. They placed their lantern and the non-swimmers in their group on one of the timbers that had been used as a gun mount and began kicking together to propel it. Braving the dangers from sharks and crocodiles, they reached their destination in five hours. After two days on the small island without food and water, Kennedy realized they needed to swim to a larger island, Olasana, if they were to survive. Kennedy and his men were found and rescued by scouts after surviving six days on coconuts.

Interesting Fact: The island where Kennedy's crew washed ashore has become a minor attraction and has been renamed Kennedy Island.

9 LEENDERT HASENBOSCH (CA. 1695–1725)
Survived: About 6 months on the Ascension Islands

Leendert Hasenbosch was a Dutch soldier who went aboard a VOC-ship as the bookkeeper. After the ship made a stop at Cape Town, South Africa, in 1725, Hasenbosch was sentenced for sodomy and set ashore on Ascension Island. He was given a tent and the amount of water to last about a month, some seeds, a Bible, clothing, and writing materials. Hasenbosch survived by eating sea turtles and seabirds, as well as drinking his own urine. It's believed he probably died in a terrible condition after about six months.

Interesting Fact: Leendert Hasenbosch wrote a diary that was found by British mariners in 1726 who brought the diary back to Britain. The diary was rewritten and published a number of times.

8 MARGUERITE DE LA ROCQUE (CA. 1523–?)
Survived: 2 years on the Isle of Demons

In 1542, French explorer Jacques Cartier led a voyage to Newfoundland, accompanied by 19-year-old Marguerite de La Rocque. During the journey, Marguerite became the lover of a young man. Displeased with her actions, Marguerite's uncle, Lieutenant General (and pirate) Jean-François Roberval marooned her on the "Isle of Demons" (now called Harrington Island) near the Saint-Paul River. Also marooned were Marguerite's lover and her maid servant. Marguerite gave birth to a child while on the island, but the baby died (probably due to insufficient milk), as did the young man and the maid servant. Marguerite survived by hunting wild animals and lived in a cave for two years until she was rescued by Basque fishermen.

Interesting Fact: Returning to France after her rescue, Marguerite achieved some celebrity when her story was recorded by the Queen of Navarre in 1558.

7 CAPTAIN CHARLES BARNARD (1781–1840) AND PARTY

Survived: 18 months on Eagle Island (part of the Falkland Islands)

In 1812, the British ship *Isabella* was shipwrecked off Eagle Island. Most of the crew was rescued by the American sealer *Nanina*, commanded by Captain Charles Barnard. However, realizing that they would require more provisions for the extra passengers, Barnard and four others went out to retrieve more food. During their absence, the *Nanina* was taken over by the British crew. Barnard and his men were left on Eagle Island by the very men they had saved. Barnard and his party were finally rescued in November 1814.

Interesting Fact: The evening Barnard's ship rescued the *Isabella*, Barnard dined with the *Isabella* survivors, and, finding that the British party was unaware of the War of 1812, informed them that technically he was at war with them. (Maybe he shouldn't have mentioned that). Barnard later wrote a narrative, *Marooned*, detailing his experience.

6 ADA BLACKJACK (1898–1983)

Survived: 2 years on Wrangel Island

In the fall of 1921, a team of five people were left on Wrangel Island north of Siberia. Arctic explorer Vilhjalmur Stefansson planned the expedition with the intention of claiming the island for Canada or Britain. A 23-year-old Eskimo woman, Ada Blackjack, was hired as a cook and seamstress and was paid 50 dollars a month. Ada needed the money for her son, who was suffering from tuberculosis. The plan was to stay one year on the island and bring six months' worth of supplies. This would be enough to sustain them for a year while they lived off the land itself. The men were unable to find enough food and began to starve, so in January 1923, three of the men made a desperate attempt to seek help. Ada was left to care for the fourth man, who was sick with scurvy. The three men were never heard from again, and the man she was caring for eventually died. Ada somehow learned how to survive until she was rescued in August 1923 by a former colleague of Stefansson's. Ada used the money she earned to take her son to Seattle to cure his tuberculosis.

Interesting Fact: Except for the salary that Ada made on the trip and a few hundred dollars she got for furs that she trapped while on Wrangel Island, Ada did not benefit from the subsequent publication of several very popular books and articles concerning her survival story.

5 ALEXANDER SELKIRK (1676–1721)
Survived: 4 years and 4 months on Más a Tierra Island

Alexander Selkirk was a Scottish sailor and a skillful navigator, which led to his appointment as a sailing master on the *Cinque Ports*. The captain of the ship was a tyrant, and after a few sea battles with the Spanish, Selkirk feared the ship would sink. So in an attempt to save his own life, he demanded to be put ashore on the next island they encountered. In September 1704, Selkirk was dropped off on the uninhabited island of Más a Tierra, over 400 miles off the West Coast of Chile. He took with him some clothing, a musket, some tools, a Bible, and tobacco. At first, Selkirk simply read his Bible and awaited rescue, but it soon became apparent that rescue wasn't imminent. He resigned himself to a long stay and began to make island life habitable with only rats, goats, and cats for company. Finally, in February 1709, two British privateers dropped anchor offshore and Alexander Selkirk was rescued. In 1713 Selkirk published an account of his adventures, which many believe were fictionalized six years later by Daniel Defoe in his now-famous novel *Robinson Crusoe*.

Interesting Fact: In 1966, Más a Tierra Island was officially renamed Robinson Crusoe Island. At the same time, the most western of the Juan Fernández Islands was renamed Alejandro Selkirk Island.

4 ERNEST SHACKLETON (1874–1922)
Survived: 105 days on Elephant Island

Ernest Shackleton was an Anglo-Irish explorer who launched the Imperial Trans-Antarctic Expedition in 1914. During the expedition, the ship *Endurance* became trapped in ice and for ten months drifted until the pressure of the ice crushed and sank the ship. Shackleton and his men were stranded on ice floes, where they camped for five months. The men sailed three small lifeboats to Elephant Island, which was uninhabited and provided no hope for rescue. Shackleton and five others set out to take the crew's rescue into their own hands. In a 22-foot lifeboat, they survived a 17-day, 800-mile journey through the world's worst seas to South Georgia Island, where a whaling station was located. The six men landed on an uninhabited part of the island, so their last hope was to cross 26 miles of mountains and glaciers (considered impassable) to reach the whaling station on the other side. Shackleton and two others made the trek and arrived safely in

August 1916 (21 months after the initial departure of the *Endurance*). With the help of the Chilean government and its navy, Shackleton returned to rescue the men on Elephant Island. Not one member of the 28-man crew was lost.

Interesting Fact: It would be more than 40 years before the first crossing of Antarctica was achieved by the Commonwealth Trans-Antarctic Expedition, 1955–1958.

3 JOHN ADAMS AND THE *BOUNTY* MUTINEERS (1768–1829)
Survived: On the Pitcairn Islands

After the famous mutiny on the *Bounty* in 1789 and several months of landing and sailing around the eastern islands of Fiji, the *Bounty* mutineers decided to settle on the uninhabited Pitcairn Islands to elude the Royal Navy. To prevent the ship's detection and anyone's possible escape, the ship was burned to the water. Nine crewmen along with six Tahitian men, and 11 women, including one with a baby, had found a home. The Tahitians were treated poorly, which led them to revolt and kill some of the mutineers. By 1794, crewmen Young, Adams, Quintal, and McCoy were left to care for a household of ten women and their children. McCoy, who had once worked in a distillery, discovered how to brew a potent spirit from the roots of the *ti* plant. By 1799, Quintal had been killed by Young and Adams in self-defense, and McCoy had drowned himself. Adams and Young used the ship's Bible as their guide for a new and peaceful society. As a result, Adams and Young converted to Christianity and taught the children to read and write using the Bible. Then in 1800, Young died of asthma, leaving John Adams as the sole male survivor of the party that had landed just ten years earlier.

Interesting Fact: Later, in 1808, the ship *Topaz* arrived at Pitcairn Island and found Adams ruling over a peaceful community of ten Tahitian women, including his wife, and several children. The Royal Navy granted him clemency in 1825, and he died four years later.

Also, the main settlement and capital of Pitcairn, Adamstown, is named for John Adams.

2 JAN PELGROM AND WOUTER LOOS (CA. 1611–?)
Survived: On mainland Australia

In 1629, a Dutch East India ship, the *Batavia*, with 316 people on board, was wrecked off the coast of Western Australia. Most of the people on board made it safely to the nearby Abrolhos islands. A fanatic named Jeronimus Cornelius led a mutiny, and with 36 men under his command began systematically murdering, raping, and torturing men, women, and children. Before help arrived, 125 people had been killed and their bodies dumped in mass graves. Cornelius and the other mutineers had their hands cut off after they signed a confession, and then they were hanged. Two of the youngest mutineers, Wouter Loos and Jan Pelgrom, avoided execution when they were sentenced to be marooned on the Australian mainland. They were given some provisions and put ashore near the mouth of the Murchison River and were told to explore the land and to try and make contact with Aborigines. They were instructed to keep watch for a vessel to take them off after two years. They were never seen again, and might be considered Australia's first-known European residents.

Interesting Fact: Later European exploration recorded Aborigines with blue eyes, suggesting at least one of the men survived. Also, the mass graves were later excavated and became a morbid tourist attraction. The story is frequently taught in schools and has even been made into an opera.

1 JUANA MARIA, THE LONE WOMAN OF SAN NICOLAS (?–1853)

Survived: 18 years on San Nicolas Island

In 1835, Russian sea otter hunters clashed with Indian people living on remote San Nicolas Island. The bloody conflict drastically reduced the native population. Missionaries requested that these Indians be moved to the mainland for their own safety. When a ship was sent to pick them up, high winds forced it to depart early, leaving Juana Maria behind. In 1853, a party headed by sea otter hunter George Nidever found the Indian woman alive and well. Clad in a dress of sewn-together cormorant skins, she lived in a shelter made from whale bones. She willingly went with her rescuers, bringing along only a few possessions. Nidever brought her home to live with him and his wife in Santa Barbara, California. No one, including the local Chumash Indians, could understand her language. The new living conditions altered her diet and affected the woman's health. She contracted dysentery and died after she had been on the mainland for only seven weeks. The Lone Woman was baptized conditionally with the Christian name Juana Maria (her Indian name is unknown). She is buried at Mission Santa Barbara, where a plaque remains in her memory.

Interesting Fact: Juana Maria's life story was turned into a book, *Island of the Blue Dolphins.*

10 UNIQUE AND AMAZING PLACES ON EARTH

10 THE DOOR TO HELL (TURKMENISTAN)

The Door to Hell, as local residents at the nearby town of Darvaza have dubbed it, is a 230-foot-wide crater in Turkmenistan that has been burning continuously for 35 years. In 1971, geologists drilling for gas deposits uncovered a huge underground cavern. The drilling caused the ground over the cavern to collapse, taking down all their equipment and their camp with it. Since the cavern was filled with poisonous gas, they dared not go down to retrieve their equipment. To prevent the gas from escaping they ignited it, hoping it would burn itself out in a couple of days. Unfortunately, there was a slight miscalculation as to the amount of gas that was trapped, and the crater continues to burn to this day.

9 MOUNT RORAIMA (VENEZUELA, BRAZIL, AND GUYANA)

Mount Roraima is a pretty remarkable place. It's a tabletop mountain with sheer quarter-mile-high cliffs on all sides. There's only one "easy" way up, on a natural staircaselike ramp on the Venezuelan side; to get up any other way takes an experienced rock climber. On the top of the mountain, it rains almost every day, washing away most of the nutrients for plants to grow and creating a unique landscape on the bare sandstone surface. This also makes for some of the highest waterfalls in the world that cascade over the sides of the cliff (Angel Falls, the tallest waterfall in the world, is located on a similar tabletop mountain some 130 miles away). Though there are only a few marshes on the mountain where vegetation can grow properly, they contain many species unique to the mountain, including a species of carnivorous pitcher plant.

8 METEOR CRATER (ARIZONA)

Meteor Crater is a meteorite impact crater located about 43 miles east of Flagstaff, near Winslow, in the northern Arizona desert of the United States. Because the U.S. Department of the Interior Division of Names commonly recognizes names of natural features derived from the nearest post office, the

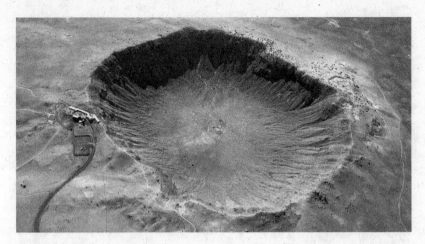

feature acquired the name of "Meteor Crater" from the nearby post office named Meteor. The crater was created about 50,000 years ago during the Pleistocene epoch when the local climate on the Colorado Plateau was much cooler and damper. At the time, the area was an open grassland dotted with woodlands inhabited by woolly mammoths, giant ground sloths, and camels. It was probably not inhabited by humans; the earliest confirmed record of human habitation in the Americas dates from long after this impact. The object that excavated the crater was a nickel-iron meteorite about 160 across that hit the plain at a speed of several miles per second.

7 THE GREAT DUNE OF PYLA (FRANCE)

Since Europe has no deserts, you'd think the title of "Europe's largest sand dune" would go to something that wasn't particularly impressive. But you'd be wrong. The Great Dune of Pyla is nearly two miles long, a third of a mile wide, and 100 meters high, and for some reason, it formed in a forest. The dune is very steep on the side facing the forest and is a famous paragliding site. At the top, it also provides spectacular views out to sea and over the forest (since the dune is far taller than any of the trees surrounding it).

6 SOCOTRA (REPUBLIC OF YEMEN)

Socotra has been described as one of the most alien-looking places on Earth, and it's not hard to see why. The island is part of an archipelago in the Arabian Sea. It's very isolated, with a harsh, dry climate, and as a result, a third of its plant life is found nowhere else, including the famous Dragon's Blood Tree, a very unnatural-looking umbrella-shaped tree that produces red sap. There are also a large number of birds, spiders, and other animals native to the island, and coral reefs around it that similarly have a large number of endemic (i.e., only found there) species. Socotra is considered the most biodiverse place in the Arabian Sea and is a World Heritage Site.

5 83-42 (GREENLAND)

This is really just a curiosity and isn't visually impressive, but 83-42 is believed to be the northernmost permanent point of land on Earth. It's tiny, only 115 feet long, 50 feet wide, and 13 feet high, but it's about 400 miles from the North Pole. It beat the previous record holder, ATOW1996, when it was discovered in 1998, and lichens were found growing on it, suggesting it was not just one of the temporary gravel bars that are found in that region, which are regularly pushed around by the rough seas.

4 ROTORUA (NEW ZEALAND)

Rotorua is a city on the southern shores of the lake of the same name, in the Bay of Plenty region of the North Island of New Zealand. The city is known for its geothermal activity, with a number of geysers, notably the Pohutu Geyser at Whakarewarewa and the boiling mud pools located in the city. This thermal activity owes itself to the Rotorua caldera on which the city lies. Rotorua is also a top adventure destination and is New Zealand's Maori cultural heartland. Rotorua city is renowned for its unique "rotten eggs" aroma, which is caused by the geothermal activity that releases sulfur compounds into the atmosphere. If you ever visit New Zealand, this is a city you must see. It was once home to the famed Pink and White Terraces, and you can visit thermal wonderlands as well as other sights that are truly astounding.

3 DON JUAN POND (ANTARCTICA)

With a salinity of over 40 percent, Don Juan Pond is the saltiest body of water in the world. It's named after the two pilots who first investigated the pond in 1961, Lieutenants Don Roe and John Hickey. It's a small lake, only 330 feet by about 1000 feet, and on average it's only about 4 inches deep, but it's so salty that even though the temperature at the pond regularly drops to as low as -22°F, it never freezes. Don Juan Pond is 18 times saltier than sea water; as a comparison, the Dead Sea is only 8 times saltier than sea water.

2 ICEBERG B-15 (ANTARCTICA)

Iceberg B-15 was the largest iceberg ever recorded. It had an area of 1200 square miles, making it larger than the island of Jamaica, and was created when part of the Ross Ice Shelf broke off in March 2000. In 2003, Iceberg B-15 broke apart, and one of the larger pieces (called B-15a) drifted north, eventually smashing into a glacier in 2005, breaking off a three-square-mile section and forcing many Antarctic maps to be rewritten. It drifted along the coast and eventually ran aground, breaking up once again. In 2006, a storm in Alaska (that's right, Alaska) caused an ocean swell that traveled 8400 miles over six days to Antarctica and broke up the largest remaining part even more. Almost a decade later, parts of the iceberg have still not melted, and the largest remaining part, still called B-15a, has an area of 665 square miles.

1 GUAÍRA FALLS (BRAZIL–PARAGUAY BORDER)

Located on the Parana River, Guaíra Falls was, in terms of total volume, the largest waterfall on Earth. Each second, 1,750,000 cubic feet of water toppled over this waterfall on average, compared to just 70,000 cubic feet per second for Niagra Falls. However, the falls were flooded in 1982 when a dam was created to take advantage of this massive flow rate. The Itaipu Dam is now the second most powerful hydroelectric dam in the world, after the Three Gorges Dam. The Itaipu Dam supplies 90 percent of the power consumed by Paraguay and 19 percent of the power consumed by Brazil, including Rio de Janeiro and São Paolo.

10 MOST TERRIFYING PLACES ON EARTH

10 RIDDLE HOUSE

The History: The Riddle House in Palm Beach County, Florida, was originally a funeral parlor. The Victorian house was dismantled and rebuilt in Yesteryear Village at the South Florida fairgrounds. In the 1920s, the house became privately owned by Karl Riddle.

The Terror: Joseph, one of Riddle's former employees, committed suicide by hanging himself in the attic of the house. Joseph, for whatever reason, hated men, and his ghost displays this hatred by attacking men who enter the attic, although men are no longer allowed in. Other places in the house are haunted as well, and furniture is frequently moved by unseen forces.

9 HELLTOWN

The History: The northern part of Summit County in Ohio is known by the eerily blunt moniker Helltown. In the 1970s, Boston Township was the site of a government buyout and subsequent mass eviction of citizens. The houses were intended to be torn down and the land used for a national park, but the plans never quite manifested. Legends spawned wildly, and who can blame the rumor mongers? Driving through the dark, wooded landscape was enough to give you chills even when it was populated, let alone when you now have to drive by boarded-up houses standing next to the burned-out hollows of others (the local fire department has used some of the Helltown buildings for practice).

The Terror: Whether based on a kernel of truth or cooked up in the heads of creative visitors, the persistent legends of Helltown add to the creep factor. The steep Stanford Road drop off, which is immediately followed by a dead end, is aptly named The End of the World. If you get stuck at this dead end for too long, according to ghost story enthusiasts, you may meet your demise at the hands of many members of the endless parade of freaks patrolling the woods. Satanists, Ku Klux Klan members, an escaped mental patient, an abnormally large snake, and mutants caused by an alleged chemical spill proudly march in this parade. And if you stray from the roads, you may find Boston Cemetery, home to a ghostly man, grave robbers, and, the quirkiest of all, a moving tree.

8 STULL CEMETERY

The History: Stull, Kansas, is a tiny, unincorporated town in Douglas County (aka the middle of nowhere). Ten miles west of Lawrence and thirteen miles east of Topeka puts it far from anything resembling a large population center. The population of Stull is approximately 20 people.

The Terror: Don't let the deceptively quaint village fool you: a darker side lurks behind the bushes and in the shadows. In the early 20th century, two tragedies rocked the tiny settlement (please observe, these are not legend or folklore, but fact). First, a father finished burning a farm field only to find the charred corpse of his young son in the aftermath. The second incident was that a man went missing and was later found hanged from a tree. As far as legends go, the infamous cemetery is where you can find your fill of supernatural lore. The book *Weird U.S.* by Mark Moran and Mark Sceurman has this to say on Stull Cemetery:

> There are graveyards across America that go beyond merely being haunted and enter into the realm of the diabolical. They are places so terrifying that they say the devil himself holds court with his worshippers there. The cemetery on Emmanuel Hill in Stull, Kansas, is one of these places.

Rumors exist that Stull Cemetery is one of the seven gateways to hell. While the old church is now demolished, many attempt to sneak in at night for a peek at the unsavory goings-on. But be warned, the police patrol heavily, especially on Halloween and the spring equinox. The place is supposed to be so unholy, in fact, that some claim Pope John Paul II refused to allow his plane to fly over eastern Kansas on his way to an appearance in Colorado. The validity of this last claim is up for debate, but none can deny that legends or not, Stull Cemetery is a terrifying place to be.

7 THE RIDGES

The History: Originally known as the Athens Lunatic Asylum, the Ridges was renamed after the state of Ohio acquired the property. The hospital saw hundreds of lobotomies, and often declared masturbation and epilepsy to be the causes of insanity in patients.

The Terror: Athens, Ohio, is listed as the 13th most haunted place in the world, per the British Society for Psychical Research. The nearby Ohio University (which currently owns most of the property on which the Ridges is located) is said to be heavily haunted. Billy Milligan, the notorious rapist with dissociative identity disorder, was housed at the facility for years. The most famous story, however, is that of a 54-year-old female patient who ran away and was missing for six weeks. She was found dead in an unused ward. She had taken off all of her clothes, neatly folded them, and lay down on the cold concrete, where she subsequently died. Through a combination of decomposition and sun exposure, her corpse left a permanent stain on the floor, which is still visible today. Her spirit now haunts the abandoned ward.

6 HUMBERSTONE AND LA NORIA

The History: In 1872, Humberstone was founded in northern Chile as a saltpeter mine and business boomed. However, after several heavy blows (including the Great Depression), the business declined and then collapsed in 1958, and the town of Humberstone and those that surrounded it, including La Noria, were abandoned by 1960. Treatment of workers in both towns bordered on slavery, and now the towns are left standing derelict.

The Terror: These towns are so terrifying that the residents of nearby Iquique refuse to enter them. The former residents never left: they can be seen walking around and children have been heard playing; ghostly images frequently show up in photographs taken in Humberstone. It's rumored that the dead of the La Noria cemetery rise at night and walk around town. Regardless of whether that's true, the cemetery contains opened graves where the bodies are fully exposed, leaving you to wonder: is it ghosts or grave robbers? (As if either prospect is very appealing.)

5 BYBERRY MENTAL ASYLUM

The History: In Pennsylvania, the Philadelphia State Hospital at Byberry, also known simply as Byberry, was the poster image for patient maltreatment. The hospital was founded in 1907 and known as the Byberry Mental Hospital. It exceeded its patient limit quickly, maxing out at over 7000 in 1960. It housed everything from the mentally challenged to the criminally insane. Due to its atrocious conditions and the subhuman treatment of its patients, the hospital was closed and abandoned in 1990. It then became a nuisance for the neighborhood, as it was a breeding ground for vandals, arsonists, satanists, and urban explorers. Byberry was demolished in 2006, in spite of the fear of spreading asbestos (which is what kept it standing for 16 years).

The Terror: The terrifying aspect of this location isn't so much its hauntings or the unsavory characters that lurked after dark (although you would have been wise to be wary of both while exploring the building). The terror comes from the facts of how the hospital was run. Human excrement lined the hallways, which were also where many patients slept. The staff was abusive and frequently exploited and harassed patients. One patient had a tooth pulled without anesthetic, while another female patient was killed and dismembered. Although the killer, Charles Gable, was never caught, the victim's body was strewn across the property, and another patient was found playing with her teeth. Even as the hospital was in the process of closing, two released patients were found dead in the Delaware River two days after their release.

4 LEAP CASTLE

The History: While this Irish castle is perhaps the most popular location featured on this list, it's worth recapping its long and often gruesome history. Although it was built by the O'Bannons in the late 15th century, the castle was taken over by the ruling O'Carrolls, to whom the O'Bannons were subject. After the death of Mulrooney O'Carroll, a fierce rivalry erupted, culminating in two brothers struggling for control. One of the brothers, a priest, was brutally murdered in his own chapel, in front of the family, by the other brother. The chapel is now known as the Bloody Chapel, for obvious reasons. Many people were held prisoner and even executed at the castle.

The Terror: Leap Castle is rumored to be haunted by a vast number of spirits, including a violent, hunched beast known only as the Elemental, which is most recognizable by its accompanying smell of rotting flesh and sulfur. While renovating the castle, workers discover an oubliette, which is a dungeon accessible only through a ceiling hatch, into which prisoners are thrown and then forgotten and left to die. This particular oubliette contained three cartloads of human remains and was filled with spikes to impale those thrown into its depths.

3 SHADES OF DEATH ROAD

The History: This New Jersey road winds through seven miles of countryside, and the stretch gives us no definitive clues as to the origin of its eerie name (Shades of Death is not a nickname given by locals, but is in fact the road's official moniker). While the explanation for this highly unusual name has been lost, many theories abound. Some say that murderous highwaymen would rob and kill those along the road. Others say the reason was violent retaliations by the locals against the very same highwaymen, resulting in their lynched corpses being hung up as a warning to others. Some attribute it to three murders that occurred in the 1920s and '30s: the first murder saw a robber beating his victim over the head with a tire iron; in the second, a woman decapitated her husband and buried the head and body on separate sides of the road; the third murder consisted of poor Bill Cummins being shot and buried in a mud pile. Some say the name comes from the massive amounts of fatal car crashes there, while others consider it the fault of vicious wildcats from nearby Bear Swamp. The most likely explanation, however, is that malaria-bearing mosquitoes terrorized the locals every year, and the remoteness of the area prevented them from receiving good medical attention. This is supported by the fact that, in 1884, most of the swamps in the area were drained.

The Terror: Gruesome history and spooky name aside, you have much to fear along this byway. South of the I-80 overpass lies an officially unnamed lake, which most will tell you is called Ghost Lake. This lake is frequently the home of specterlike vapors, and the sky is supposed to be unusually bright, no matter what time of night you're there. As per the name, ghosts of the highwaymen's victims roam the area, and they are most frequently noticed in the abandoned cabin across the lake. The dead-end road known as Lenape Lane is home to thick fogs and apparitions, and visitors may be chased off by a white light. I'll let Wikipedia detail the most disturbing aspect of Shades of Death Road:

> One day during the 1990s, some visitors found hundreds of Polaroid photographs scattered in woods just off the road. They took some and shared them with Weird NJ, which published a few as samples. Most of the disturbing images showed a television changing channels, others showed a woman or women, blurred and somewhat difficult to identify, lying on some sort of metal object, conscious but not smiling. Local police began an investigation after the magazine ran an item with the photos, but the remainder disappeared shortly afterwards.

2 TUOL SLENG MUSEUM OF GENOCIDE

The History: Welcome to Phnom Penh, Cambodia, home of the Tuol Sleng Museum of Genocide. This former high school was converted in 1975 to Security Prison 21 by the Khmer Rouge. The prison was used as a base to

torture and murder prisoners. Most of the prisoners were former soldiers and government officials from the Lon Nol regime. However, the Khmer Rouge leaders' paranoia soon caught up with them, and they began shipping people from their own ranks to the prison. Many prisoners were tortured and tricked into

naming their family and associates, who were then also arrested, tortured, and murdered. The museum is now located within the prison grounds.

The Terror: The ghosts of the estimated 17,000 victims of Tuol Sleng continue to roam the prison halls, and odd happenings around the place are often attributed to them—and it isn't hard to see why. Most were forced to confess to crimes they didn't actually commit. Although most victims were Cambodian, many foreigners fell victim to the death machine, including Americans, French, Australians, Arabs, Indians, Pakistanis, Vietnamese, a New Zealander and a Briton. Only 12 people are thought to have survived. To close the entry on this sad history, I'll leave you with the actual security regulations, the ten rules all prisoners had to abide by (all imperfect grammar is from the original poor translation):

1. You must answer accordingly to my question. Don't turn them away.
2. Don't try to hide the facts by making pretexts this and that, you are strictly prohibited to contest me.
3. Don't be a fool for you are a chap who dare to thwart the revolution.
4. You must immediately answer my questions without wasting time to reflect.
5. Don't tell me either about your immoralities or the essence of the revolution.
6. While getting lashes or electrification you must not cry at all.
7. Do nothing, sit still and wait for my orders. If there is no order, keep quiet. When I ask you to do something, you must do it right away without protesting.
8. Don't make pretext about Kampuchea Krom in order to hide your secret or traitor.
9. If you don't follow all the above rules, you shall get many many lashes of electric wire.
10. If you disobey any point of my regulations you shall get either ten lashes or five shocks of electric discharge.

1 THE MINES OF PARIS

The History: The seemingly infinite tunnels that run below the streets of Paris should not be confused with the Catacombs of Paris, the famous underground ossuary, although the mines are often mistakenly referred to as catacombs. Exploring the mines is illegal, and penalties include heavy fines. The mines were used to dig out minerals from Paris' varied sediment (Paris' location was submerged underwater for millions of years), and the tunnels are what was left behind.

The Terror: The mines are now unkempt, unpatrolled, and unsafe. Legends report that ancient cults and creatures patrol the depths. Spirits dwell in the infinite shadows, and if you wander deep enough and survive, you may even enter Hades itself. As far as reality goes, those legends can take a backseat. The tunnels stretch for close to 375 miles throughout the Parisian underground, and most of them are unmapped. Saying it's easy to get lost there is an understatement. It's nearly impossible *not* to get lost. Many parts of the catacombs are hundreds of feet below street level. Some hallways are flooded, or are so narrow you have to crawl through them. There are holes that drop hundreds of feet, and manholes that are unreachable, luring unwary urban explorers in with false promises of freedom. The infinite underground maze absorbs sound, making it unlikely you will hear someone yelling for help, even if they are not far away. Or, worse yet, making it unlikely someone will hear *you* yelling. Thousands of human bones litter the tunnels due to overcrowding in many of Paris' cemeteries. Weird paintings adorn the walls. Are they ancient? Are they new? Are they warnings? Or pleas for help? If you have claustrophobia, avoid the mines at all costs. If you don't have claustrophobia, you probably will after a trip here. Bring plenty of batteries, backup flashlights, clean water, a friend, and say a prayer before entering the mines of Paris. You will need them all.

10 AMAZING CITIES YOU'LL NEVER VISIT

10 DONGTAN, CHINA

The highly publicized planned city of Dongtan was supposed to be the first mega eco-city of its kind. However, after much anticipation, it was announced that it would not become a reality.

As people in China moved from the countryside to the cities, they created more environmental waste, which spurred a movement for more environmentally friendly projects. Dongtan was by far the most ambitious. Slated to be twice the size of Manhattan, the site was an island near Shanghai and was to change the way humans interacted with their environment.

The self-sustaining city would have produced its own energy from solar, wind, bio-fuel power, and recycled city waste. Public transportation would have been powered by clean technologies such as hydrogen fuel cells, and a vast network of foot and bicycle paths would have substantially cut down on vehicle emissions. In addition, organic farming methods were to be used inside the city limits.

It was to be a green model for the entire world, but, like most projects of this scale, resistance and problems arose. Many considered it a pipe dream that was never really plausible, while others claimed the environmental impact of China's rapidly developing cities would negate any benefits Dongtan presented. When Shanghai's mayor (the project's biggest supporter) was arrested for property-related fraud in 2006, the plan fell into further disarray, with permits lapsing and enthusiasm waning. Eventually, the global recession all but sank the undertaking, and the innovative ideas planned were put on hold.

9 TRITON CITY

Buckminster Fuller was a brilliant visionary, scientist, environmentalist, and philosopher who in the 1960s developed a bold design. It was dubbed Triton City and was intended to be a utopia for up to 5000 residents. The giant, floating city was designed to encourage people to share resources and conserve energy.

Fuller was initially commissioned by a wealthy Japanese patron to design a floating city for Tokyo Bay. The patron died in 1966, but astoundingly enough, the U.S. Department of Urban Development commissioned Fuller for further design and analysis. His designs called for the city to be resistant to tsunamis, provide the most outdoor living possible, desalinate the very water that it would float in, give privacy to each residence, and incorporate a tetrahedronal shape, which provides the most surface area with the least amount of volume. Everything from education to entertainment to recreation would be a part of the city. Fuller also claimed that the low operating costs would result in a high standard of living.

The city plans were sent to the U.S. Navy, where they were dissected and analyzed even further. The city of Baltimore, upon hearing of the project, became interested and petitioned to have Triton City moored off of its shores in Chesapeake Bay. However, as municipal and federal administrations changed, the project languished and was never brought to light. Today, there are derivatives of Triton City, such as the artificial island Kansai and its airport in Osaka, Japan, but they pale in comparison to the scope of Triton City.

8 BROADACRE CITY

Originally designed by one of the most famous and respected architects in history, Frank Lloyd Wright, in 1932, Broadacre was meant to be a "new town" utopia. It didn't fit into its own category because it had many characteristics of a conventional city of the time, and it incorporated the principles of an agricultural nation that Thomas Jefferson championed. In essence, Wright wanted to abandon the crowded, machine-age, industrial city, but avoid a rural community.

Just like Jefferson believed every citizen should have their own "vine and fig tree," Wright planned the city so that each denizen would grow their own food on their one acre plot of land. In what was a controversial characteristic, citizens of all social classes would intermingle much more than in any other city or town of the day. Wright also despised centralization, so it was essential that the city be sprawling and widespread, which severely differentiated itself from a typical town. In Broadacre, homes, factories, offices, and municipal buildings would all be separated by large expanses of parks planted with lawns and trees. Cleanliness was paramount, and there was to be only light industry and all utility wiring would be buried underground.

Opponents of Wright's city were vociferous, however. Because he believed that the automobile was "the advance agent of decentralization," he envisioned extremely little mass transportation, which many city planners vehemently disagreed with. Wright's vision was never realized, and the closest things we have today are the sprawling suburban communities that blanket much of the planet.

7 DISNEY RESORTS

These are not cities by definition, but anyone who has been to a Disney resort knows that they are basically self-sufficient cities in their own right. Considering the amount of real estate the conglomerate already owns and operates, it's amazing how many other things they planned that never came to fruition. It's also interesting to realize what we could have had from the world's largest entertainment company, since most of these would have been great places to visit:

- *Mythia:* A Greek and Roman myths and legends–inspired park planned to be built near Disneyland.
- *WestCOT:* A West Coast EPCOT Center planned for California.
- *Disneyland East:* A large park to be built on the site of the 1964 World's Fair in Queens, New York.

- *Port Disney:* An American version of Tokyo DisneySea planned for California.
- *Disney's Asian, Venetian, Persian, and Mediterranean resorts:* Resorts that were to be built near Disney World.
- *Disney America:* A patriotic theme park that was to be built in Virginia.
- *Discovery Bay:* A land inspired by Jules Verne's works, such as *Around the World in Eighty Days.* Some ideas were later incorporated into Disneyland Paris.
- *Beastly Kingdom:* A mythical-beings land planned near Animal Kingdom in Florida.
- *Dark Kingdom* (Shadowlands): A park near Disney Word that would have showcased all of Disney's villain characters and be the antithesis of the Magic Kingdom. Maleficent's Castle would have been in the center of the park.
- *Sci-Fi City:* Planned for Tokyo Disneyland, this would have been an immense park with an endless amount of science-fiction rides and attractions. If built, it would have been the most extensive and impressive "tomorrowland" ever created.
- *Disney's Snow Crown:* A Disney-themed ski resort situated at the Mineral King glacial valley in Northern California; construction was ultimately prevented by preservationists.

These are the biggest resorts and parks that were conceived by Disney but never built. There are hundreds more attractions, rides, and restaurants whose ideas were put to paper but never became reality.

6 SLUMLESS, SMOKELESS CITIES

Sir Ebenezer Howard was the father of the garden-city movement, which is a suburban town near a large, metropolitan city that's designed to not be reliant upon its bigger neighbor. Garden cities were intended to provide pleasant environments with open public land while at the same time containing industry and agriculture. Howard succeeded in spearheading the building of many garden cities, beginning in the United Kingdom, to mixed results. But his vision of the slumless, smokeless cities model has gone unbuilt.

Howard's design is very interesting, and if you peruse his self-drawn diagram, the aesthetics appear quite pleasing. A number of characteristics are notable. The entire design resembles a big wheel, with the Central City as the hub for six smaller, surrounding garden cities. Each city is surrounded by a circular canal, and one large circular canal, the Inter Municipal Canal, connects each of the six outer cities. Independent straight canals cut through all six outer cities and run directly into the Central City. Roads also ran along these straight waterways. Running through the outer towns was the Inter Municipal Railway. Inside the railway, Howard planned for such things as farms, an insane asylum, reservoirs, an agricultural college, industrial homes, cemeteries, and a "home for waifs."

The overall design was to relieve the huddled crowdedness and dirtiness of big cities but still have the feeling of connectivity. Since it would have been such a daunting project, and there wasn't quite enough support for Howard's plan, these connected cities never materialized.

5 CALIFORNIA CITY

While this actually *is* a city you can visit, you'll never see its original plan fulfilled. Nat Mendelsohn was a developer who had a dream of developing a city that would rival Los Angeles in terms of grandeur. He ambitiously began building on a 124-square-mile piece of land in the middle of California's Mojave Desert; the plans were complete with a huge park and artificial lake. If you were to look at a satellite picture of the city, it may seem like Mendelsohn had at least come close to realizing his dream. However, upon closer inspection, you would notice something conspicuously missing: houses.

Although hundreds of streets crisscross in one continuous, gigantic grid, the network is just one, prodigious ghost town. But at least ghost towns have structures; these streets are lined with absolutely nothing, not even a telephone pole. It kind of looks like an intricate crop circle, or like threadbare hiking paths run amok, twisting through the dirt and sand.

Mendelsohn had the same idea as many real estate developers of the time. He would buy a vast amount of land, divide it into thousands of home plots, then sell the plots to families who longed for a piece of property to call their own. The gamble didn't pay off for him, however, because 50 years later, decaying streets still lie there empty. One reason is that dust storms are a common occurrence in the area, but he mainly overestimated demand.

The city isn't empty, though. It has a population of roughly 14,000 people, comprising a small town. The entire town, however, only takes up a small corner on the outskirts of the boundless, barren grid. Although it has services, it will never be the large city like Los Angeles that Nat Mendelsohn conceptualized.

4 MINNESOTA EXPERIMENTAL CITY

The Minnesota Experimental City (MXC) was the brainchild of a private partnership between the University of Minnesota and the federal government in the 1960s, and would be intentionally open to observation and evaluation by urban studies experts. Like its name suggests, the city would be a combination of experimental ideas never before tried on such a large scale.

The city would accommodate about 250,000 people, and it would focus on open spaces such as parks, farms, and wilderness. Only one sixth of the area would be paved, and the city would be partially covered by a geodesic dome (designed by Buckminster Fuller, whose Triton City is number 9 on this list). This design is extraordinarily strong, hurricane and tornado proof, and widely used today. The city would be car free, with cars parked at the edge and people-movers whisking people into the center of the city. A futuristic and highly advanced automated highway system, in which magnetic, driverless cars were used, would connect people to the outside world.

Perhaps the most drastic and controversial departure from conventional cities was that there would be no schools. Instead, citizens would teach the practice of lifelong learning, which states that everyone is a teacher as well as a student and that education takes place through social interactions, observations, and joining groups and clubs, among other things.

Budgetary problems as well as logistics quashed the city's groundbreaking.

3 WELTHAUPTSTADT

Welthauptstadt Germania (World Capital Germania) was to be the jewel of the Third Reich. Adolph Hitler, unmatched in his hubris, was convinced that Germany would become the center of Europe, and perhaps the world, and even before World War II began, he had begun to plan his capital city, which was a rebuilt Berlin. His goal was to exceed the quality and splendor of other world capitals such as London, Paris, and Washington, D.C.

Plans for this grandiose city included a stadium that could house 400,000 spectators; a Chancellery with a lavish hall twice as long as the one at the Palace of Versailles; the Triumphal Arch, based on the Arc de Triomphe in Paris but much, much larger; and a giant open square to be surrounded by large government buildings. The centerpiece of the new city would be the Volkshalle, or People's Hall, which would include a humongous domed building designed by Hitler himself and chief architect Albert Speer. If this domed building were built, it would still today be the largest enclosed space in the world, 16 times larger than the dome at St. Peter's Basilica in Rome.

Even though the war began before construction could start, all the necessary land was acquired and engineering plans were developed. Hitler's plan was to win the war, finish construction on Welthauptstadt, hold an extravagant World's Fair there in 1950, then retire. Needless to say, the crushing of the Nazi regime and Third Reich at the hands of Allied forces put an end to the future of the great city.

One humorous aspect of the planning of Welthauptstadt is that the marshy ground of Berlin never could have supported the monstrous structures Hitler wanted as the showpieces of his city.

2 SEWARD'S SUCCESS

The name of this planned city, across the bay from Anchorage, Alaska, was a reversal on "Seward's Folly," which was the moniker bestowed on the transaction that Secretary of State William Seward made when he purchased Alaska from Russia. It was to be a city unlike any in the world.

First and foremost, it was to have a colossal glass dome covering it that made it completely climate controlled. The city would have amenities for 400,000 citizens, including a sports arena, mall, schools, and petroleum center. Transportation would be quite innovative and included moving sidewalks and an aerial cable-car line that would shuttle people around the city and to nearby Anchorage. Skylights and large windows would give people the sense of openness but would not compromise the climate-controlling properties of the dome. Cars would be nonexistent inside because it was a city "for people, not cars," and all energy used in the city would be provided mostly by natural gas. Later, plans called for a subway under the bay that would also lead to Anchorage.

Failure to make lease payments on the land, and the impracticality of it all, ensured that Seward's Success would, in the end, not live up to its name.

1 BOOZETOWN

No, this was not an insincere idea concocted by someone just to garner attention. Back in the 1950s, it was the dream of one man who doggedly fought to make it a reality. BoozeTown was to be a resort city completely centered around the culture of drinking, where alcohol would be embraced, loved, and revered.

Mel Johnson loved to drink. As a young man, he traveled the world to see the great drinking cities: Dublin, New York, Havana, Rio, Barcelona, New Orleans, and Paris. But the drinking culture of these cities just wasn't enough for him; he wanted something more. He was a very intelligent man who dropped out of Harvard University and served in the armed forces, but after World War II he had an epiphany and set out to create BoozeTown.

His city would be composed of dozens upon dozens of bars and nightclubs, all with different themes. He was meticulous in his planning and fleshed out every detail. Street names would allude to alcohol, such as Gin Lane, Bourbon Boulevard, and 21st Amendment Avenue; there would be a moving sidewalk and an electric trolley system that would help escort staggering drunks home (or to another bar); much of the alcohol would be brewed or distilled inside the town, which would produce revenue; every bar and liquor store would be open 24 hours a day, seven days a week; drinks would be allowed everywhere, even banks and places of worship; the city would have its own currency, BoozeBucks; there would be a police force, the Party Police, but instead of harassing drinkers they would be there to assist them; the *BoozeTown Bugle* would keep citizens abreast of the current news; and no children would be allowed inside. There would be a big daycare just outside city limits for visitors. Johnson figured that the permanent populace would consist of "retirees, artists, and goof-offs," people who wouldn't be responsible for children in the first place. He believed that famous artists, writers, and actors would in time flock to the city to live. In the middle of the city would be a towering building shaped like a martini glass in which Johnson would have his home and headquarters.

He scouted out areas for BoozeTown, such as somewhere in the Midwest, northern Nevada, or an island off of the western coast of Mexico. Johnson had money from the death of his wealthy father, but he needed much more capital and held numerous, lavish fundraisers in order to get it. He printed up a plethora of trinkets such as maps, postcards, and matchbooks with BoozeTown's logo on them to help persuade investors. At times, he believed he had enough money and set various opening dates for his city. However, very few people were actually serious about ponying up the money Johnson needed. This, added to the fact that he was acting increasingly more erratic and eccentric and that the press was vilifying him, basically ended Johnson's dream of BoozeTown. In 1960, he gave up on the dream and was later committed to a hospital and diagnosed with paranoid schizophrenia. He died just a few years later.

You can almost picture yourself driving down an open stretch of road in the middle of nowhere, then, suddenly, seeing a titanic martini glass pop up on the horizon beckoning you to come experience BoozeTown, "Where It's Always Happy Hour."

15 BOGEYMEN FROM AROUND THE WORLD

15 JAPAN

The *namahage* visits each house on New Year's to ask if any misbehaving children live there. If the parents are able to report that their children aren't lazy and don't cry, he moves on to the next house.

14 KOREA

The Korean bogeyman is called Kotgahm, which is the word for persimmon. The legend is that a mother told her crying child that she would feed him to a tiger if he didn't behave. A passing tiger, hearing the threat, waited outside the door for his meal. But the mother gave the child a persimmon, a *kotgahm*, and the crying stopped. The tiger thought the *kotgahm* must be a terrifically fierce creature to be more frightening than a tiger. Today, Kotgahm is most often pictured as an old man with a mesh sack who carries naughty children away.

13 SPAIN AND MEXICO

Duérmete, niño, duérmete ya. Que viene el coco y te comerá. (Go to sleep child, go to sleep now. The coconut man will come and eat you.)

If you think of a coconut as a head, with the three holes as the features of a face, you can see how El Coco might be transformed in the mind of a child to a hairy little man. During the 16th and 17th centuries in Spain, there were orphan collectors who took children away in sacks. The misbehavior? Refusing to go to bed and sleep.

12 FINLAND

One of the most unusual of the world's bogeys is Groke, a giant blue blob who is so lonely and sad that the ground beneath her feet freezes as she walks. She isn't malevolent, just lonely. But she frightens people, and they run from her.

11 ENGLAND
There are many theories about the origin of the word "bogeyman." One is that it devolved from "buggy man," the driver of the cart picking up corpses during the Black Plague that decimated Europe. As in the United States, the bogeyman may be nothing more clearly defined than a mist or fog scratching at windows, or he is sometimes thought of as a tall, gaunt, scarecrowlike man.

10 SCOTLAND
The boggart is a malicious fairy who causes personal calamities, small and large. It sometimes puts a cold hand on people's faces at night. You must not name it, or it will become unreasonable and follow your family wherever you go. A horseshoe over the doorway will protect you from boggarts.

9 BAHAMAS
The Small Man has a rolling cart and captures children who are out after sundown. If he gets you, you will become a Small Person yourself, and ride in his cart forever.

8 BULGARIA
The anti–Santa Claus, Torbalan lurks in the shadows in Bulgaria, waiting to snatch misbehaving children and carry them away in a sack.

7 CZECH REPUBLIC AND POLAND
Bubak is a scarecrowlike man who hides on riverbanks, making sounds like a lost baby to lure adults as well as children. He drives a cart pulled by cats and weaves clothing for the souls he steals.

6 NETHERLANDS
The *bolman* has claws and fangs. He hides under your bed or in your closet, waiting to grab you and put you in the basement if you don't sleep.

5 PHILIPPINES
Pugot Mamu is a gigantic, headless shapeshifter who lives in trees and deserted houses. Self-beheaded, he eats children through the hole in his neck.

4 QUEBEC
The Bonhomme Sept-Heures (the Seven O'clock Man) may have been taken from the English "bonesetter," an old name for a traveling medicine man. The Bonhomme Sept-Heures steals children, but can only get you if you're awake.

3 NORWAY
The *nokken*, a lake monster, will get you if you don't come in when called.

2 TRINIDAD AND TOBAGO
The *jumbies*, postdeath misbehavers, live here. They're shapeshifters, so children are taught not to play with random animals, lest they turn out to be *jumbies*. There are several ways to defeat *jumbies*, however: you can leave your shoes outside because *jumbies* have no feet and will spend the night trying to get the shoes on; you can leave a container of sand or rice outside the door so *jumbies* will have to count each grain; you can cross a river because *jumbies* won't cross water; or you can leave a rope with many knots so the *jumbies* will have to untie each one.

1 ITALY
Italy has l'uomo Nero, a tall man with an unseen face, a heavy coat, and a black hat. He hides under the table, and parents knock on the table to warn their children that l'uomo Nero is present and will take them away if they don't eat their dinner.

10 BIZARRE TRAVEL GUIDES

10 *THE SPACE TOURIST'S HANDBOOK*
Believe it or not, a travel book exists for those who wish to pay the millions of dollars it costs to travel to outer space. This book will teach you the ins and outs of space travel, like what to expect, how to prepare, and much

more. It's a definite must-have for all those billionaires who can afford to toss $20 million on a strange vacation.

9 UP SHIT CREEK
As the name implies, this book is a collection of tales about misadventures relating to toilets, poop, and river rafting. Written by a river-rafting guide, this is actually a pretty hilarious book, and while it's definitely up there in the bizarre stakes, it's an enjoyable read.

8 LAID TO REST IN CALIFORNIA
If you're planning to travel to California for a vacation, or you're already there and are sick of the sight of celebrity homes, why not check out some celebrity final resting places? This book takes you on a who's who tour of celebrities via the graveyard.

7 BIKING TO THE ARCTIC CIRCLE
Have you ever wanted to bike to the Arctic Circle? No? Me neither. Nevertheless, someone did, and he wrote this book all about his experiences. It's definitely an odd travel guide but not sufficiently odd to make it farther up on this list.

6 TRAVEL BY CARGO SHIP
So you want to travel on the cheap—this guidebook outlines 120 itineraries of all kinds of cargo vessels that you can book passage on. It gives you the fares and descriptions of the different vessels, their facilities, and the likelihood of being murdered by Somali pirates.

5 ROUND IRELAND WITH A FRIDGE
On a wager, the author of this book traveled around Ireland for a month with a refrigerator at his side. Perhaps more bizarre than the subject matter is the fact that this book is an international bestseller!

4 MINI-TRIPS FOR MAXI-FUN
Ah, McDonald's—who else would write a travel book with the intention of luring unsuspecting readers into all of these dreadful hamburger joints? This book was written in the 1970s by McDonald's staff and outline small trips you can make as a family, each involving a stop off at, you guessed it: McDonald's.

3 THE COMPLETE MEDICAL TOURIST

Need a tummy tuck? Fancy a face-lift? Desperate to change genders? Instead of paying out thousands to your local surgeon, this book shows you where you can travel through Asia and the rest of the world for plastic surgery on the cheap.

2 OTHER PEOPLE'S BUSINESS

Here are 192 pages describing over 100 free tours of factories in Ohio. Oh boy! Yes, please! Joking aside, this is such a dreadfully dull topic that it absolutely needs to be on a list of weird travel books.

1 FLATTENED FAUNA

Here is the ultimate guide to the dead animals that litter the highways and streets of North America. If you love checking out carcasses flattened like pancakes in the middle of the road, this guide is an essential for the glove compartment.

CHAPTER ELEVEN
Sports

10 ODD DISCONTINUED OLYMPIC SPORTS

10 SWIMMING OBSTACLE RACE

This was a highly unusual yet undeniably fun 200-meter race. Competitors first had to swim to a pole, climb up and down it, then swim a bit, clamber over two boats then swim under two more, and then swim to the finish. The race was held only once, during the 1900 Olympics, and was won by Frederick Lane of Australia.

9 DISTANCE PLUNGING

A silly sport that almost certainly attracted equally silly people, this event was held only once, in 1904. Competitors would dive into the pool and remain motionless for 60 seconds or until their heads bobbed out of the water, after which their distance plunged was measured. The winner was an American, William Dickey, who must have been very proud. Interestingly, all the entrants were American.

8 *JEU DE PAUME*

That's "game of palm" to us non-Francophiles. This game was a precursor to modern tennis, and was essentially tennis with your hands or a small paddle in lieu of rackets. Still played today, although it's rare, this sport started as an exhibition event in 1900, became part of the Olympic program in 1908, and was brought back as an exhibition in 1924.

7 ROQUE

An American variation on the French sport of croquet, this was played during the 1904 St. Louis Olympics. Understandably, as the sport was virtually unknown outside the U.S., all the competitors were American. The event was dropped after the St. Louis Games and is widely believed to have been included for the sole purpose of boosting the U.S. medal count.

6 TUG-OF-WAR

Tug-of-war actually has a real shot at coming back to the modern Olympic program, considering that it was held in the Ancient Olympics. It was an Olympic sport during the 1900, 1904, 1908, 1912, and 1920 Games, and the British won the most medals in the sport, including the 1908 Games, where the gold medal was won by the London police force.

5 STANDING TRIPLE JUMP

It may seem odd to take arguably the most dynamic field event and limit it to a pedestrian pace, but back in the early Olympic Games, all jumping events (long, triple, and high) were also played from a standing position. The event was in the Olympics between 1900 and 1912.

4 ROPE CLIMB

Another sport with a chance of returning, the rope climb was actually part of the gymnastics program and was held sporadically between 1896 and 1932. At the 1904 Games, the event was won sensationally by American George Eyser, who competed with one wooden leg. Eyser went on to win five more gymnastics medals, including two more golds.

3 DUELING PISTOLS

An aristocratic sport for men of bravery and honor, right? Well, not when your opponent is a mannequin, as it was in the dueling pistols event during the 1906 Games. Competitors took turns shooting at a mannequin dressed in fancy clothes from 20 and 30 meters away. The event returned to make a brief appearance at the 1912 Games before being banished forever (hopefully).

2 SOLO SYNCHRONIZED SWIMMING

Synchronized swimming already has a somewhat controversial reputation at the Games, and it's hard to understand the motive for introducing it into the Olympics, especially when it was preceded by solo synchronized swimming, an event held during the 1984, 1988, and 1992 Games. A single woman would get into the pool and try to synchronize with the music being played. Yes, it really is as bad as it sounds.

1 LIVE PIGEON SHOOTING

Held during the 1900 Games, this event was the only time when animals were killed for sport during a modern Olympics. Over 300 pigeons were killed during the Games, many of them from the gun of Belgian Leon de Lunden, who took gold with 21 kills. Understandably, the sport was dropped from the program after the 1900 Games and was eventually replaced with clay-pigeon shooting.

10 SPOOKY SPORTS CURSES

10 THE CURSE OF THE BAMBINO

In perhaps the most famous of sports curses, the Boston Red Sox decision to sell Babe Ruth to the Yankees in 1920 brought down an 83-year championship drought for the New York team. Before the trade, the Red Sox had won five World Series, and the Yankees had won none. From the trade in 1920 until 2003, the Yankees won 26 series, while the Sox won none. The curse's reputation was enhanced by the Red Sox repeatedly coming close to winning the title and falling short. The team made four World Series appearances (1946, 1967, 1975, and 1986) and each went the full seven games. In 1986, the Red Sox were one out away from winning the Series in six games when the tying run scored on a wild pitch and was followed by Mookie Wilson's ground ball rolling through Bill Buckner's legs to put the New York Mets ahead. In game seven, the Sox took an early 3–0 lead only to blow it and lose 8–5. But the Curse of the Bambino finally ended in 2004. First, the Red Sox beat the Yankees in the American League Championship Series despite losing the first three games. They then swept the St. Louis Cardinals in the World Series. The Sox added another Series win in 2007 with a sweep of the Colorado Rockies.

9 THE CURSE OF BILLY PENN

Philadelphia long had a policy of not allowing buildings higher than the statue of city founder William Penn that stands on top of City Hall. This ended in 1987 with the completion of One Liberty Place, which is nearly 400 feet taller than City Hall. Penn apparently responded to his demotion by cursing Philly's pro-sports teams. Over the next 20 years, the Flyers lost the Stanley Cup twice (1987, 1997), the Phillies lost the World Series (1993), the 76ers lost the NBA Finals

(2001), and the Eagles lost the Super Bowl (2004). In 2007, when the Comcast Center became Philadelphia's tallest building, workers tried to break the curse by attaching a figurine of Penn to the final beam. It worked, and the Phillies won the World Series the next year.

8 THE CURSE OF THE COLONEL

When the Hanshin Tigers won the 1985 Japan Championship Series, celebrating fans in Osaka grabbed a statue of Colonel Sanders from a Kentucky Fried Chicken and threw it off a bridge into a canal. Over the next 17 years, the Tigers finished last in their league ten times, inspiring a rumor that the team will never win another championship until the Colonel's statue is recovered. The Tigers won the League Championships in 2003 and 2005, only to lose the Japan Series both years. Before too much blame is given to the Colonel, it should be noted that the Tigers had previously gone 21 years between League Championships (1964 to 1985) without any known curse affecting them. The statue was discovered on March 10, 2009, by a construction crew building a new boardwalk.

7 THE CURSE OF COOGAN'S BLUFF

When the Giants left the Polo Grounds at Coogan's Bluff in New York City for San Francisco in 1957, betrayed fans reportedly hexed the team so it would never win a World Series away from New York. The Giants have not won the Series since 1954, despite earning the National League pennants in 1962, 1989, and 2002. Furthermore, in two of those Series they played in, games in San Francisco were delayed by nature's wrath: game six of the '62 Series was held up for three days by extremely heavy rains, and game three of the '89 Series was postponed ten days by a massive earthquake that damaged the Giants' home field, Candlestick Park.

6 THE CURSE OF MARTY MCSORLEY

During game two of the 1992 Stanley Cup, the Los Angeles Kings held a 2–1 lead over the Montreal Canadiens. As the game was winding down, Canadiens coach Jacques Demers became suspicious of the curvature of the stick of Kings defenseman Marty McSorley and asked that it be measured. Referees determined the blade was "too curved" and sent McSorley to the penalty box for two minutes for using illegal equipment. Montreal capitalized on the one-man advantage, and Canadien Eric Desjardins scored to tie the game.

During overtime, Desjardins scored again to win the game for the Canadiens and tie the series at one game each. Montreal won the next three games and the Stanley Cup. Since then, no other Canadian team has won the championship. Four teams got to the Stanley Cup Finals only to lose to an American rival: the Vancouver Canucks were defeated by the New York Rangers (1994), the Calgary Flames lost to the Tampa Bay Lightning (2004), the Edmonton Oilers fell to the Carolina Hurricanes (2006), and the Ottawa Senators lost to the Anaheim Mighty Ducks (2007). Granted, none of this explains why all of Canada would be punished instead of just Montreal, or why the team that didn't cheat is the victim of the curse, but no one said curses had to be either logical or fair. One Canadian team did manage to find a loophole in the curse: the Quebec Nordiques moved to Denver in 1995, became the Colorado Avalanche, and won Stanley Cups in 1996 and 2001.

5 THE MADDEN CURSE

Since 1999, the covers of the *Madden NFL* video games have featured top players, many of whom have suffered injury or setback. For example, Michael Vick appeared on the cover of *Madden NFL 2004* and suffered a leg injury that sidelined him for most of the 2003 season. When Donovan McNabb was chosen for the *Madden NFL 2006* cover, he declared, "I don't believe in the curse at all." He suffered a hernia in the first game of the 2005 season, played despite the pain for eight more games, and then was reinjured, opted for surgery, and missed the last seven games. In 2006, Shaun Alexander, the previous season's MVP, was featured on *Madden NFL 2007* and sustained a foot injury that caused him to miss six starts. When EA Sports announced that LaDainian Tomlinson would be on the 2008 cover, superstitious fans created the website SaveLTfromMadden.com to urge him to reconsider. Tomlinson eventually declined the offer, but said it was over his payment, not concerns about the curse.

4 THE CURSE OF BOBBY LAYNE

Quarterback Bobby Layne led the Detroit Lions to three NFL Championships (1952, 1953, and 1957). Despite this, the Lions, thinking he was past his prime, traded him to the Pittsburgh Steelers in 1958. When Layne left, he reportedly declared that Detroit wouldn't win for 50 years. Over those 50 years, the Lions have had the worst winning percentage of any NFL team and have had only a single post-season victory (1991). On the 50th anniversary of the trade, the curse went out with a bang when the Lions became the first NFL team to go 0–16.

3 THE SOCCEROOS' WITCH DOCTOR CURSE

According to the autobiography of soccer player Johnny Warren, during the 1970 World Cup qualifiers, Australia's Socceroos hired a witch doctor to curse their opponents. Australia proceeded to beat Rhodesia 3–1. However, when the players were unable to come up with the 1000-pound fee the witch doctor demanded, he reversed the curse onto the Socceroos, who then lost their next match to Israel, partly because three players fell ill during the match. In 2004, Australian comedian and filmmaker John Safran read Warren's book and traveled to Africa to reverse the curse. He found that the original witch doctor was dead, but hired a second one who performed a rite in which he killed a chicken and splattered the blood over Safran. The Socceroos not only qualified for the 2006 World Cup, but they advanced to the second round, the best result they ever had.

2 THE CURSE OF THE BILLY GOAT

William Sianis, owner of the Billy Goat Bar, brought his pet goat to Wrigley Field to watch game four of the 1945 World Series. During the seventh inning, Chicago Cubs owner Philip Wrigley personally had Sianis and the goat ejected because of complaints from other spectators about the smell. A furious Sianis reportedly declared, "Them Cubs, they aren't gonna win no more." The Cubs proceeded to drop the next three games and lose the Series to the Detroit Tigers, prompting Sianis to send Wrigley a telegram asking, "Who smells now?" The Cubs have not made it to a World Series since. Several attempts have been made to break the curse, ranging from Sianis' nephew Billy bringing a goat onto the field to fans hanging a butchered goat from the statue of Harry Caray in Chicago. According to Sam Sianis, William's nephew-in-law, the curse can only be lifted by the Cubs organization showing a genuine fondness for goats and allowing them into Wrigley Field because they truly want to and not simply for publicity.

1 THE *SPORTS ILLUSTRATED* COVER JINX

According to legend, the athletes appearing on the cover of *Sports Illustrated* go on to experience bad luck. *SI's* first cover subject, baseball player Eddie Mathews, was also the first victim of the jinx, suffering a hand injury one week later that forced him to miss seven games. Over the years, the jinx has produced losses (the 1987 baseball preview featured the Cleveland Indians with the declaration "Believe it! Cleveland is the best team in the American League," only for the team to lose 101 games and finish dead last); injuries (golfer Jim Venturi was named 1964's Sportsman of the Year and then spent the next season battling carpal tunnel syndrome); and even death (Pat O'Connor, pictured on the 1958 Indianapolis 500 preview issue, was killed in a 15-car pileup on the last lap of the race). On the other hand, Michael Jordan has appeared on the cover a record 49 times and made it through with life and limb intact. *Sports Illustrated* did their own analysis of the phenomenon for a 2002 issue and concluded that 37 percent of their cover subjects suffered demonstrable misfortune or decline in performance following their appearance.

10 BIZARRE SPORTS

10 CANINE FREESTYLE

Canine freestyle is an incredibly bizarre sport in which dogs perform freestyle dance—a mix of obedience, tricks, and dancing—with their owners in time to music. There are two types of canine freestyle: in the first, the dog and owner dance together; in the second, the dog must keep at the heel of the owner while the owner dances.

9 SWAMP SOCCER

As its name suggests, swamp soccer is a form of soccer played in bogs or swamps. It originated in the north of England as an endurance event for soldiers but has since been opened to everyone. There are currently 260 swamp soccer teams around the world.

8 TRACTOR PULLING

Truck and tractor pulling is a competition in which tractors or trucks are used to pull very heavy sleds along a track. The pulling vehicles produce enormous amounts of pollution and noise, which add to the sport's popularity. It's especially popular in rural areas where there's an abundance of trucks and tractors.

7 BUN CLIMBING

Bun climbing is a Hong Kong sport in which people scurry up a tall tower covered in steamed sweet buns. The winner of the so-called Bun Scramble is the person who is able to gather the most buns on his way up the pole.

6 MOUNTAIN UNICYCLE

When I think of unicycles, I think of clowns at the circus, not rugged men taking them to some of the most dangerous terrains on earth. Unicycles are some of the hardest things to ride, right next to pogo sticks, and in this sport, people ride them on rocky terrain. This is just a sport of pure insanity, but it has gotten national coverage on major news channels like FOX. It's not a graceful sport by any stretch of the imagination.

5 CHESS BOXING

Those are two words you never thought you'd see together. Chess boxing is a sport for nerds. It involves a two-minute boxing round and a four-minute chess competition. There is even a governing body, the World Chess Boxing Association, and their motto is. "Fighting is done in the ring, but war is waged on the board."

4 PUNKIN CHUNKIN

Punkin Chunkin is another sport involving the use of heavy machinery. In the competition, any large mechanical device can be used to toss a pumpkin as far as possible. People come from all around with their homemade catapults, slingshots, and air cannons to win the glorious title of Greatest Punkin Chunker.

3 OUTHOUSE RACING

Outhouse racing, as its name implies, is a sport in which someone sits on a toilet in a portable outhouse and gets pushed and dragged around by his friends. The inventor of the event calls it "the best case of the runs you'll ever have."

2 AIR SEX

Air sex is a Japanese sport in which (fully clothed) men pretend to have sex with invisible partners. Often the simulated sex acts are set in time to music and involve exaggerated sexual motions. The current holder of the world-champion title goes only by the mysterious name of Cobra.

1 MIND BALL

Mind ball is the most mind-numbingly boring sport invented. Two players sit opposite each other with electronic instruments attached to their heads. They then use the power of the mind to move a ball around a table. It takes considerable time to see the ball move. Next time you're invited to a mind ball championship, I recommend that you stay home and watch paint dry instead.

10 INCREDIBLY DANGEROUS SPORTS

10 STREET LUGING

Climb a big hill on a busy highway, lie supine on an elongated skateboard, and start rolling. Gather speed and try not to die. That's going to be difficult because you have no brakes, you're an inch from a road surface that's itching to see what bone marrow looks like, and you present a visual profile to passing vehicles that's only slightly easier to see than a puddle—which is what you'll be if you have anything close to a lapse in concentration or luck.

9 HELI-SKIING

There's a reason some things are so inaccessible—it's God's way of saying, "Don't be stupid." Still, people pay top dollar to be helicoptered (at $500 a pop) to untouched snowcaps, where they leap onto virgin slopes and ski far from crowds but very close to avalanches. Even the helicopter ride can be dangerous, and many would-be skiers have died en route to untouched powder, such as Frank Wells, former president of the Walt Disney Company, who died in a helicopter crash during a heli-skiing trip in 1994.

8 BIG-WAVE SURFING

Let's not get crazy here: no one's saying surfing isn't fun. But any sport with rules for when a shark enters the field of play is not for those with functioning frontal lobes. Big-wave surfing cranks the dial to 11 by towing surfers into monster 50-foot waves strong enough to crush villages. So if the brute force of the wave doesn't kill you or bury you so far underwater that you drown, you could still bash your head on submerged rocks or fail to avoid your own board (fickle thing!) hurtling past you like a fastball. And where would that leave you at Frankie and Annette's luau?

7 BULL RIDING

Rodeo started as the gymnastics of ranching: a series of highly specific competitions taken from key aspects of cattle ranching in the Old West. But there never was and never will be any damn reason to ride a bull—its only practical application is to make you appreciate your own job, even if you're unemployed. Straddling 1800 pounds of leaping pissed-off beef (an effect achieved by constricting bovine genitals with rope or *tasers*) routinely results in the rider being thrown ten feet into the air with a landing cushioned by a mere inch of dirt and feces. And if you don't break your jaw, ribs, or collarbone on reentry, you still have that bull to worry about (and he's still bitter).

6 BULL RUNNING

Bull running (*encierro*) is a "sport" that involves running in front of bulls that have been let loose on a course of a town's streets. There are actually several *encierros*, but the most famous is in Pamplona, Spain, and it was mentioned in Hemingway's *The Sun Also Rises* and *Death in the Afternoon*. The purpose is to entice or herd the bulls from offsite corrals to the bullring. Any fool over 18 with more bravado than brains can participate. Every year, between 200 and 300 people are injured, mostly with contusions due to falls. Since 1910, 14 people have been killed in Pamplona's Running of the Bulls.

5 CHEERLEADING

Forget the wimps wearing pads and helmets at football games—the real danger is on the sidelines, where estrogen and adrenaline combine in one of the newest recognized sports. It has been estimated that there are over 20,000 reported cheerleading injuries a year, making cheerleading the most injury-prone sport in the world for women. Many common injuries include broken legs and spinal damage. Think about it—it's like diving on land, with easily distracted co-eds serving as the water.

4 MOTORCYCLE RACING

Motorcycling is the most dangerous motorsport in the world. Just one example is the Isle of Man TT event, which has a rich 100-year history. However, during that time, there have been over 220 deaths. The drivers in the race are required to maintain their balance while driving through all types of obstacles such as rocks and trees, all while traveling at an extremely high speed.

3 HIGH-ALTITUDE CLIMBING

Today, about one death occurs for every six successful summits on Mount Everest, and each victim had to pass corpses on the way up. Real mountaineers face every threat you can imagine, including drowning. Gravity has to get in line for its chance to kill you, since hypoxia, hypothermia, frostbite, and pneumonia all have prior reservations. Even a relatively minor injury can be fatal, as rescue helicopters simply can't get to you, and your buddies may be too gassed to help. But if you do reach the summit (and you'll probably have to wait in line), keep those glasses on, or you'll burn up your corneas from excess UV radiation. Kinda defeats the purpose, huh? To date, 179 out of 1300 Everest climbers have died, but mortality rates have started to decline since 1990. Nope, I'll just buy the $945 North Face jacket and read *Into Thin Air*, thank you.

2 BASE JUMPING

You know, we used to call this behavior "attempted suicide." BASE jumpers willingly hurl themselves from Buildings, Antenna, Spans, or Earth with nothing but a hand-deployed parachute to prevent "deceleration trauma." In this game, there's no need to keep score: the winner is the one who *doesn't* die. Lucky losers get slammed back into the object they just jumped off, or they break everything they have that's made of, say,  bone. Between five and fifteen people die each year, according to Harry Parker of the International PRO BASE Circuit. This sport is illegal almost everywhere, and with good reason.

1 CAVE DIVING

The idea for this sport came about when someone was disposing of a dead body. Take all the regular hazards of diving—itself a dangerous activity—and uncharted territory, freezing temperatures, low-visibility conditions, and cramped quarters. And don't forget that ticking clock on your air supply—you can't just go "up" to breathe. On top of that, it's still a wilderness experience, and some of the caves actually have wild animals living in them. According to a recovery team based in San Marcos, there have been more than 500 deaths from this sport since the 1960s. The risks are so high that experience affords little protection; many victims have been diving instructors and technical divers. As a result, the National Speleological Society defines a "successful" cave dive as "one you return from." Perhaps they should follow that logic and define an "intelligent" cave dive as "one you don't take."

10 MARTIAL ARTS FROM OUTSIDE ASIA

10 HIGHLAND WRESTLING

The Scots have always been known as fierce fighters, but few would compare Jackie Chan and William Wallace, even though most Scotsmen have a good amount of martial arts training. Highland wrestling is the first kind of fighting taught to young Scots, and family techniques are often handed down from father to son. It's recorded that English knights were frequently caught off-guard by the skill of an unarmed Scotsman who could drag fully armored knights off their horses with ease. Highland wrestling is mainly used today by reenactment societies and "living historians" since many of the actual techniques are lost to history.

9 PANKRATION

The ancient Greek Olympics were brutal in general, but the most punishing of the events was the Pankration, which roughly translates to "anything goes."

This fierce combination of boxing and wrestling allowed almost any attack, from groin punches to eye gouges and even finger breaking. The intention of all the Olympic events was to keep every man in the city ready to serve in the military, and the art of the Pankration came in mighty handy when fending off the barbarian hordes. Today, the Greeks continue to practice Pankration as a sport, and the techniques developed thousands of years ago still make it into mixed martial arts events.

8 EUROPEAN FENCING

Swordsmanship in western Europe during the 14th and 15th centuries was an important skill for any young man to have, as most gentlemen of noble upbringing carried their rapiers around at

all times and were prone to calling for duels at the drop of a hat. European fencing is a surprisingly sophisticated and complex fighting art, producing literally thousands of manuals and guides printed all over Europe. Fencers were known for precision strikes, delicate footwork, and full-body control on par with any samurai. Each country and region in Europe had a distinctive style, as well as a different technique for a number of swords.

7 APACHE KNIFE FIGHTING

The Apaches mastered the use of many weapons for attacks against settlers or other Native American rivals, and while many of those weapons were terrible to face, the Apaches were deadliest with little more than a knife. Every Apache had at least one knife at all times because they were useful for any number of things in a hunter-gatherer society, but in battle, Apaches would carry as many as a dozen knives on their person. They could throw them with fearsome accuracy or cut down men with close, surgical strikes to the chest, throat, or Achilles tendon. Currently, the U.S. military employs several trainers of Apache ancestry to teach special-forces troops survival and knife fighting. It's no wonder Navy SEALs are considered the best knife fighters in the world.

6 SAMBO

Sambo is a relatively modern martial art, combat sport, and self-defense system developed in the Soviet Union. It was recognized as an official sport by the USSR All-Union Sports Committee in 1938, presented by Anatoly Kharlampiev. There are three generally accepted competitive-sport variations of *sambo*: sport *sambo*, which is stylistically similar to amateur wrestling or judo; combat *sambo*, which was used by and developed for the military and resembles modern mixed martial arts, including extensive forms of striking and grappling; and freestyle *sambo*, which uses a uniquely American set of competitive rules created by the American Sambo Association.

5 *NGUNI* STICK FIGHTING

The bedrock of the Zulus' legendary fighting skill is the art of stick fighting, in which two Zulus armed with fresh-cut saplings attack each other with only a small hide shield to defend themselves. While the sticks don't cause a lot of damage to the body aside from shallow cuts, being whacked with one is extremely painful, and in a fight you're guaranteed to get hit a number of times. Combat with the sticks helps the Zulus shrug off pain and fear, which is the reason they could charge straight into British gunfire without flinching. Famous South African leader Nelson Mandela says he participated in stick fighting as a child.

4 KRAV MAGA

This deadly fighting art from Israel had its origins on the streets; it was developed by Jewish vigilantes who defended their neighborhoods from anti-Jewish gangs. Krav Maga differs from most martial arts in that it's focused on ending a fight as quickly as possible by using "overwhelming force," making Krav Maga techniques some of the most downright lethal of any martial art. Today it is considered a martial art reserved for military and police use, and is utilized by U.S. Special Forces and the FBI.

3 *JEET KUNE DO*

Many falsely identify *jeet kune do* as an Eastern martial art, but in truth it was developed in America by Bruce Lee (an American citizen) because he admired the simplicity of Western fighting styles like boxing and wrestling. Tired of the overly complex methods of kung fu, Lee stripped combat down to its most basic elements when he developed *jeet kune do*, teaching that the most important move is the one that wins the fight. Many celebrity friends of Lee practiced the art, like Kareem Abdul-Jabbar, John Saxon, Jim Kelly, and Steve McQueen.

2 SAVATE

Developed in France during the 19th century, *savate* was developed by street fighters who used to put on their old heavy boots and try to kick each other in the head; in fact the word *savate* is an old slang term for an old shoe. *Savate* moved from the street into boxing schools and is still a popular form of unarmed competitive fighting in France, known for brutal kicks to the head and face meant to down a man in one blow. *Savate* schools have also started teaching weapon skills. Typical of a martial art that originated in street fighting, these weapons include walking canes, short knives, and, strangely enough, the wooden chair.

1 CAPOEIRA

A combination of combat and dance, *capoeira* is possibly one of the most beautiful fighting styles to watch. It started in Brazil with African and Native American slaves who taught themselves to fight with only their feet while their hands were shackled. After slavery was abolished,

the emperor of Brazil deemed *capoeira* techniques too dangerous for freed slaves and forbade its practice. The *capoeira* community then began to disguise training matches as "games" and set them to music to look like a dance. To this day, *capoeira* matches are always set to music and look like a highly acrobatic dance, but *capoeira* involves many impressive kicks, throws, and take-downs that can be quite useful in a real fight.

10 WORLD CUP CONTROVERSIES

10 WAGS DESCEND ON DEUTSCHLAND

We'll kick off this list with a sad, and pathetic, subculture that rears its ugly head whenever England plays a major international tournament. At World Cup 2006, the WAGs—wives and girlfriends—of the England players had a grand old time. The England team manager, Sven Goran Eriksson, had allowed the WAGs to travel to the tournament and spend time with the players in between training and matches. These WAGs were extremely wealthy, since some of their partners were earning upward of 100,000 pounds a week.

The WAGs turned England's World Cup experience into an absolute circus. The country was constantly bombarded by the tabloids, with images of Victoria Beckham and company dripping with jewelry and designer clothes, and dragging their entourage of paparazzi all over quaint little German towns. It was distracting for the players, distasteful for the fans, and detracted from the soccer showpiece that is the World Cup.

9 DISASTROUS FRENCH DEFENSE

This is probably only an unsavory event for the France fans out there. For the rest of us, it certainly qualifies as unexpected. Leading up to World Cup 2002, the French team was on top of the world. They were the current World Cup champions, having won in France in '98, and the current European champions, having won at Euro 2000. The team had two of the top strikers in the world, David Trezeguet and Thierry Henry, who were scoring goals for their clubs like it was going out of fashion. France had an eminently winnable group that included Uruguay, Denmark, and Senegal, which was playing its World Cup debut. Heavily installed as pre-tournament favorites, the only blemish on the French preparation was an injury to Zinedine "Zizou" Zidane that saw him unable to play in the team's first two matches.

Senegal shocked France with a 1–0 win in the first match—one of the biggest upsets in World Cup history. France was then held to a goalless draw by Uruguay in game two. Zidane, the heartbeat of the French side, was rushed back from injury to play in the third match against Denmark, but was not fully fit and was ultimately unable to prevent a 0–2 loss. France was eliminated in the group stages, losing all three matches and not even scoring a single goal, thus completing the worst defense of the World Cup in history.

A memorable incident was when Trezeguet, after a number of near misses by the French team, hit the crossbar with a shot in the third match. He put his hands on his hips, shook his head and stared at the heavens incredulously, ruing their incredibly bad luck. Later, when questioned about France's terrible performance, Thierry Henry blamed it on Zidane's injury, remarking, "It was because we didn't have Zizou."

8 JUNG-HWAN HUNG OUT TO DRY

One of the most incredible fairy tales of the World Cup is South Korea's unexpected charge to the semifinals at World Cup 2002. Along the way, they claimed some high-profile scalps, the first of which was Italy in the knock-out round of 16. The match was highly controversial in terms of refereeing decisions (the Italians were probably entitled to feel somewhat resentful).

South Korean Jung-Hwan Ahn scored the extra-time goal that sealed the Italians' fate. At the time, Jung-Hwan's club team was the Italian team from Perugia. After scoring the golden goal to knock Italy out of the World Cup, Perugia fired Jung-Hwan. The owner, Luciano Gaucci, said, "That gentleman will never set foot in Perugia again. He was a phenomenon only when he played against Italy. I am a nationalist and I regard such behavior not only as an affront to Italian pride but also an offense to a country which two years ago opened its doors to him. I have no intention of paying a salary to someone who has ruined Italian soccer."

7 DAVID BECKHAM

At World Cup 1998, England was pitted against arch-nemesis Argentina in the knock-out round of 16. Early in the second half, David Beckham was felled by Argentinean Diego Simeone in a certain yellow-card offense. However, as Beckham was lying on the ground, he kicked out at Simeone in retaliation, triggering an instant (and warranted) dismissal. England would have to play out the rest of the match with only ten men and, after a gallant effort, would eventually go out on penalties.

The unpleasantness of this incident came from the treatment of Beckham in the weeks and months that followed. The English press needed a scapegoat and were baying for his blood. A long period ensued when Beckham was mercilessly pilloried in the papers across the nation. He spent the remainder of the season in the United States, fearing for his personal safety. There were attacks on his home, vitriolic hate mail, and even burning effigies. Soccer can bring joy and happiness to all corners of the globe, but it's sad that it can also generate this level of hatred and revulsion.

6 RONALDO—WHAT A WINKER

World Cup 2006 saw England play Portugal in the quarter finals. It was something of a grudge match, as Portugal had beaten England on penalties at the last European Championships in 2004. England talisman Wayne Rooney has something of a fiery temperament, and this was especially obvious in his more tender years. In the game against Portugal, Rooney became visibly more frustrated by the minute. He was starved of service from the English midfield, which just didn't seem to be able to string passes together. He was also getting close physical attention from the Portuguese defender, and was leading the line by himself. Rooney was starting to boil, and every England fan knew it was only a matter of time before he lost his cool, which he duly did in the 62nd minute by stamping on Portuguese defender Ricardo Carvalho.

But it's not Rooney's foul that makes this list; it's the actions of his Manchester United teammate Cristiano Ronaldo, who was playing on the Portuguese team for the Cup. Playing in the Portuguese midfield, Ronaldo sprinted some 40 yards to remonstrate vigorously with the referee following Rooney's foul. Surrounded by three or four shouting Portuguese players, the referee duly red-carded Rooney and sent him off the field. Directly after the incident, Ronaldo winked toward his bench, sending the UK media into an uproar. The wink suggested "mission accomplished," that the Portuguese had been planning on goading the notoriously hot-tempered Rooney with close attention and underhand off-the-ball contact in a bid to get him sent off. To do this to a close club teammate made it particularly unpalatable on Ronaldo's part.

5 CARD COUNTING WITH GRAHAM POLL

At World Cup 2002, the last Group F match between Australia and Croatia was refereed by Englishman Graham Poll. He had a wealth of experience in the English Premier League and took control of many high-profile matches. As testament to his ability, Poll was selected as England's representative at two World Cup tournaments and one European Championship.

Poll had successfully refereed two matches at World Cup 2002, and the marks he received from the assessors indicated that he was likely to referee the final game, a fact he laments in his autobiography. It all went wrong for Graham in the Australia–Croatia group match, when he inadvertently issued three yellow cards to the same player before sending him off.

When Poll issued a second yellow card to Croatian Josip Simunic, who was player three for his team, he inadvertently noted down the name of the Australian number three, Craig Moore, failing to send Simunic off. Simunic continued to play for some time before committing another transgression and being issued a third yellow card (which Poll thought was his second) and finally being sent off the field. This is probably the highest-profile, and most blatant, refereeing blunder in World Cup history, and it's a shame that it had to happen to such an experienced, and otherwise excellent, referee in his final showing at an international tournament.

4 RONALDO'S MYSTERY AFFLICTION

At World Cup 1998 in France Ronaldo was the world's most recognizable soccer player. Prior to the World Cup, the Brazilian had signed a monumental sponsorship deal with sports giant Nike and became the first globally mass-marketed soccer player on the planet (yes, even predating the meteoric rise of brand Beckham). In part because of Ronaldo's fame, the events before the final in Paris would go down in World Cup folklore.

On the morning of the day of the final match—Brazil versus France—rumors began circulating in the press that Ronaldo had been violently sick the night before and would be unable to play. As the speculation worked up to a fever pitch, almost every manner of illness was reported, and even wild conspiracy theories were dreamed up involving French Secret Service agents dressed as bellhops slipping something into his food.

Sure enough, when the Brazilians released their team sheet less than two hours before the final, Ronaldo was excluded. Predictably, this sent the media into a frenzy that only relented some 30 minutes before the final when the team sheet was changed and Ronaldo was included. Brazil would lose the final 3–0, and Ronaldo was a shadow of the player that had scored four goals in the tournament thus far. He looked jaded, tired, and his play was just not normal.

After all the fury died down, the accepted explanation was that he suffered a convulsive fit, resulting in his exclusion from the lineup. Ronaldo says that his late inclusion was at his own request. A prevalent alternative explanation (or conspiracy theory, as the case may be) is that his late entry was at the behest of Nike, who—unable to bear the scenario of their most significant soccer investment not playing in the World Cup final—applied intense pressure to force his inclusion. Given how much money is in soccer, this is certainly not beyond the realm of possibility.

3 RIVALDO'S THEATRICS

At World Cup 2002 in the group match between Brazil and Turkey, Brazilian player Rivaldo indulged in some Oscar-worthy playacting. In the closing stages of the match, the ball went out of play and Brazil was awarded a corner. Rivaldo stepped up to take it and motioned for the ball. Instead of amicably rolling it over to him, Turkish defender Hakan Unsal spitefully booted it directly at him. The ball clearly struck Rivaldo on the thigh, but in a bid to mislead the referee, he sank to the ground clutching his face and moaning and writhing in pain. Unsal was sent off with his second yellow card.

Without condoning Unsal's childish petulance, Rivaldo's behavior is exactly what we don't need defacing the beautiful game of soccer. Diving, simulation, playacting—whatever you want to call it—is just plain cheating and is absolutely disgraceful. Rivaldo was fined by FIFA for his antics, but some people feel that incidents such as this should be much more harshly punished. A three-match suspension, for example, would make any player think twice about cheating.

2 KEANE ABANDONS IRELAND

Talismanic Ireland captain Roy Keane was a soccer "hard man"—an aggressive, passionately driven midfielder with an explosive temper. He could have one hell of a fight and would never back down.

Upon arrival at the Irish base camp for World Cup 2002, Keane was extremely unimpressed with the facilities and team management. Following a massive argument with manager Mick McCarthy, Keane withdrew from the squad and went home. Ireland went on, without their captain, to do exceptionally well at the World Cup. How much further could they have gone if Keane had stayed? Well, that was the speculation that was always going to hang over them; such is the respect afforded Keane as a player.

Keane's actions polarized opinions in his native country and across the globe. His supporters say that he was absolutely right to stand up for his principles and point out a deep-seated amateurism in the Irish Football Association. His detractors say he unforgivably turned his back on his country. Others, like Piers Morgan of the *Daily Mail*, contends Keane is a "humorless, nasty, violent, foul-mouthed, selfish, disloyal thug who resides on a *Citizen Kane*–style pedestal of egotistical, lonely, unjustified self-adoration."

1 ZIDANE'S MOMENT OF MADNESS

Zinedine "Zizou" Zidane was, arguably, the finest soccer player of his generation and will go down in history as one of the greatest to have ever played the game. The French team was struggling to qualify for World Cup 2006 in Germany when coach Raymond Domenech urged Zidane to come out of international retirement to help the team. With their captain reinstated, France went to the World Cup and performed brilliantly throughout the tournament. To cap off his extraordinary career with another World Cup winner's medal would have been a fairy-tale ending for Zidane. However, he would end up tainting his reputation after a moment of sheer madness in the last minutes of extra time in the final game against Italy.

Zidane was sent off the field for a violent head butt to the chest of Italian defender Marco Materazzi. Though the incident occurred off the ball, it was squarely captured on camera and replayed all over the world for weeks and months to come. There followed much speculation in the press as to what Materazzi must have said to prompt the assault. After months of silence from both parties, Zidane (and later, Materazzi) came out and clarified the situation. Frustrated at being marked so closely by Materazzi, Zidane made the sarcastic remark, "If you want my shirt so badly, I'll give it to you after the match." Materazzi replied, "I'd prefer your sister," and the rest is history.

15 WORST SPORTING MOMENTS OF ALL TIME

15 STEVE HOWE

Steve Howe was a relief pitcher for the Los Angeles Dodgers and the New York Yankees. During his seven-year career, he was suspended by Major League Baseball seven times for substance abuse. He spent years in rehab attempting to control both his cocaine addiction and alcoholism. In 1992, he was offered a new contract with the Yankees and seemed to be under control, until his continuing use of cocaine got him banned for life by the MLB. Fans seemed happy with this outcome, until Howe successfully appealed the ban and in 1994 played in 40 games, recording a 1.80 ERA (earned run average). After a few struggling seasons, How was released from his contract and retired from baseball in 1997. His 1989 autobiography stated that he had overcome his problems with a commitment to evangelical Christianity. In 2006, he was killed in a car accident, and the autopsy revealed a large amount of methamphetamine in his body. Howe became the standard story for athletes getting preferential treatment by the judicial system.

14 GREG LOUGANIS

As an Olympic diver, Greg Louganis hit his head on the board during a dive and fell into the water. He got out of the pool, was stitched up by trainers, and went back onto the board to win his gold medal. For years, people thought of it as a great comeback and a touching story for everyone in sports. In 1995, seven years after the incident, Louganis publicly announced that he had AIDS and had known about it since before the 1988 Olympics. The media, fans, and fellow divers were disgusted by the idea that Louganis would knowingly put all of them at risk and not tell anyone that he had tested positive for AIDS even after his blood had gotten into the pool when he hit his head. He didn't even think to tell the trainer who treated him on site. Instead, Louganis was too selfish to tell the truth and put everyone who entered that pool after him at risk.

13 JOE THEISMANN

In 1985, after two Super Bowl appearances and one win, an MVP award, and having set the most records for the quarterback position within the Washington Redskins' organization, Joe Theismann was playing a Monday-night game against the Redskins' division rival, the New York Giants. On an attempted flea-flicker play, the Giants defense blitzed and Lawrence Taylor sacked Theismann for a loss of yards. Taylor immediately jumped to his feet and signaled for the Redskins to send out medical personal. Theismann's leg was broken midway between the knee and ankle, breaking both the fibula and tibia. A reverse-angle replay showed the extent of the damage, as viewers saw Theismann's lower shin lying flat on the ground, and the upper half of his leg sticking up at a 45-degree angle.

12 DAVE DRAVECKY

To survive cancer is a miraculous event, and to return to your job on national television after surviving cancer is something else entirely. Dave Dravecky was an outstanding pitcher for the San Francisco Giants when doctors discovered a tumor on his arm. He had the tumor removed, and after recovery time he appeared to be healthy again. After some rehab, he seemed ready to return to the mound and did so on August 10, 1989. He pitched eight solid innings and got the win in what appeared to be a feel-good story for every baseball fan. In his second start a few days later, Dravecky went five innings until, in the sixth, his humerus bone snapped in half while he was throwing a pitch, leaving him in agonizing pain and rolling on the ground in anguish. His career was ended, and two years later his arm was amputated. The story was one that many were following, and no one had expected such a dramatic and painful end to a great career.

11 DAVID BUSST

The benchmark for horrific injuries is David Busst. Busst was a promising English soccer defender who had played in the Premiership and had been considered as a potential member of the national English squad. While playing for Coventry, Busst was defending a corner kick in the early minutes of a match against Manchester United. Busst collided with two other players and suffered extensive fractures to both his tibia and fibula. The game was stopped for 12 minutes while groundskeepers cleaned the blood off the field. Many players reported being physically ill after seeing the injury, and many even required counseling afterward. Busst's leg became infected and at one point was nearly amputated. After 26 operations, Busst officially retired from soccer and later became a coach.

10 ALBERT HAYNESWORTH

Albert Haynesworth had long been considered one of the most dominant defensive ends in the NFL. In 2006, he was playing for the Tennessee Titans. During a regular season game against the Dallas Cowboys, the Dallas running back Julius Jones scored a touchdown on a short run. Dallas' center, Andre Gurode, had fallen to the ground and lost his helmet. Haynesworth tried to stomp on Gurode's head but missed. In a second effort, Haynesworth's metal cleats cut open Gurode's head, narrowly missing his eye. Haynesworth received a 15-yard penalty, and then another 15 when he protested the call. Gurode on the other hand, was taken off the field, where it took medical staff 30 stitches to close the wound on his head. Gurode suffered headaches and blurred vision for over a month following the incident. The NFL commissioner suspended Haynesworth for five weeks, and many expected the Titans to also enforce a punishment, but they never did. Haynesworth served his suspension and returned to football in November of the same season. Many called for a harsher penalty after the commissioner, Roger Goodell, said that there was "absolutely no place in the game, or anywhere else" for Haynesworth's behavior.

9 CLINT MALARCHUK

In 1989, hockey player Clint Malarchuk was playing goalie for the Buffalo Sabers in a game against the St. Louis Blues. Two players skated into each other and they both collided with Malarchuk. Steve Tuttle's skate caught Malarchuk's throat and slit his jugular vein. Pools of blood collected on the ice while Malarchuk skated off to the locker room with the assistance of trainers and referees. He said later that he was thinking that he was going to die, but wanted to get off the ice because his mom was watching the game on TV and he didn't want her to see him bleed to death. He asked for a priest and someone to call his mom and say that he loved her. A quick-thinking trainer, Jim Pizzutelli, reached into Malarchuk's neck and pinched the vein shut. After doctors arrived, it took them 90 minutes and 300 stitches to repair his neck. There were reports of fans fainting at the sight of the injury, two of them suffering heart attacks. At least three players vomited on the ice after witnessing the incident.

8 MARK MCGWIRE

In 1998, Mark McGwire and Sammy Sosa put on one of the best shows in the history of baseball. They battled all season, piling on the home runs in a chase that would leave them in the record books. They combined for 136 home runs and broke the all-time record for home runs in a season. The two had "saved"

baseball, drawing in huge numbers of fans who had been alienated by the game. And then in 2005, Jose Canseco released a book full of accusations about steroids, including saying he had personally injected McGwire with the substances. McGwire denied the accusations publicly and eventually had his chance to set the record straight in front of Congress. Instead, he pleaded the Fifth Amendment, his right to silence. Fans took this as an admittance of guilt. The records were tainted. The steroids scandal is one of the worst in sports history and is still ongoing. McGwire breaking Roger Maris' record for most home runs in a season is considered by many the death of baseball's purity.

7 HAND OF GOD

In the World Cup 1986 quarter final, Argentina found themselves tied 0–0 with England. Only six minutes into the second half, Argentinean Diego Maradona and English goalie Peter Shilton went to play a ball in the penalty area. Maradona reached the ball first and with his left hand knocked the ball into the net. The match referee didn't see the infraction and the goal was allowed. Argentina went on to win the match after Maradona's second goal, known at the "goal of the century" and a late goal by England. Following the match, Maradona told reporters that the goal was scored with "the head of Maradona and a little with the hand of God." The name Hand of God stuck, and many English fans are still embittered by the obvious rule infraction.

6 THE UNDERARM CRICKET INCIDENT

In the final match of the 1981 Benson and Hedges World Series Cup, New Zealand was looking for a six to tie the match and force the cricket series into another match against Australia. Australia's captain, Greg Chappell, directed the bowler, his brother Trevor, to bowl underarm, thus denying Brian McKenchie an opportunity to tie the matchup. McKenchie threw his bat in disgust and was the only one censured for his act. Technically, at the time an underarm bowl was not against the rules, but it was seen as unsportsmanlike. Australia's own fans booed them off the field following the victory. Afterward, the prime ministers from both countries involved called the underarm bowl cowardly and disgraceful.

5 PISTONS–PACERS BRAWL

With only a minute left in a 2004 regular-season basketball game between the Detroit Pistons and the Indiana Pacers in Detroit, the Pacers were preparing to walk away with the game by 15 points. Ben Wallace of Detroit went in for a slam dunk when he was fouled hard from behind by Ron Artest. Wallace reacted immediately, shoving Artest. The incident should have ended there, with the rivals finishing the final 45 seconds of the game. Instead, Wallace kept going after Artest. Both teams tried to get in the way, but Wallace wouldn't quit. Artest, shielded by coaches and referees, lay down on top of the scorers' table and at one point even put on a headset to talk to the broadcasters. The teams were nearly separated when a Detroit fan tossed a beer from the stands onto Artest, who jumped up, went into the stands, and attacked the wrong fan. Other players followed him as the brawl continued. The referees disappeared, calling the game over, but the security guards were also conspicuously absent. Artest threw several more punches before team staff managed to escort him into the locker room. Both teams left the court while beers and even a folding chair were thrown at them. Nine fans were injured in the event after many had fled onto the court to escape the brawl. Nine players were suspended for at least one game, while Artest missed the rest of the season. The incident was called the worst in NBA history.

4 BEN JOHNSON

When thinking of world-class sprinters today, most people don't think about Canada. However, in the 1980s, one of the biggest names in running was Ben Johnson. In 1987 he set the world record for the 100 meters and became one of the most endorsed and beloved athletes in Canada. At the '88 Olympics, Johnson lowered his own world record to 9.79 seconds, took the gold medal, and became an international hero. He only held the medal for three days before his urine test came back positive for steroids. After an investigation he was stripped of all records and his gold medal. Johnson attempted a comeback in 1991, but once again tested positive for steroids.

3 ZINEDINE ZIDANE

What will you remember from the 2006 World Cup? How about from the career of Zinedine Zidane? It's probably just this one incident. In the 110th minute of play of the final game of the World Cup, France and Italy were tied 1–1. When Italian player Marco Materazzi made choice comments about Zidane's sister, Zidane turned around and rammed his head into Materazzi's chest. He received a red card and left the field of play, while Italy went on to win the game in penalties. Zidane retired from soccer, leaving himself with a disgraced legacy and his country without the World Cup title.

2 DALE EARNHARDT, SR.

The most controversial NASCAR driver of all time, Dale Earnhardt was a seven-time champion and known as "The Intimidator." He would fight for every race and is remembered as one of the greatest drivers ever. In 2001, he went into the final turn of the Daytona 500 in third place. He fended off Sterling Marlin momentarily, until his car was tapped and careened head-first into the outside wall at 150 mph. Earnhardt's neck snapped when his entire body was jolted and the blow of his head against the steering wheel killed him on impact. It was a sad day, and no one even considered celebrating Michael Waltrip's long-awaited victory. No fan will ever forget Kenny Schrader leaping out of his car, looking in Earnhardt's window, and immediately signaling for the paramedics.

1 DUK KOO KIM

On November 17, 1982, Duk Koo Kim entered a lightweight boxing match against Ray Mancini in Las Vegas. The match was supposed to go 15 rounds, which Kim had never done before. The two men traded punches pretty evenly at the beginning of the fight, but things quickly got vicious. Mancini's ear was torn open by one punch, while his hand quickly swelled to twice its normal size. The fight was being televised live, and many viewers turned off the TV to keep their children from watching a fight like this. At one point in the 13th round, Mancini landed 39 punches in a row. Despite the terrible turn the fight was taking, the referee decided to allow it to continue into the next round. When the 14th round began, Mancini landed two rights and knocked down Kim, who hit his head hard on the mat. Mancini was declared the winner on a technical knockout, while Kim was rushed to the hospital. Despite an emergency brain surgery, Kim slipped into a coma and died four days later. After the fight, Mancini struggled with blaming himself, while both Kim's mother and the bout's referee committed suicide. Many rules were changed in boxing to protect a fighter's health, and the fight was one of the last televised nationally.

10 DEATHS OF PRO WRESTLERS

10 BRUISER BRODY

Frank Donald Goodish, also known as Bruiser Brody, was a professional wrestler who worked for several major wrestling promotions worldwide.

On July 16, 1988, Brody was in the locker room before a match in Puerto Rico, when Jose Huertas Gonzalez came up and asked him to go into the shower to discuss business. At the time, Huertas was one of the men who made decisions at the Puerto Rico World Wrestling Council meetings, and it's rumored that Brody had upset him on numerous occasions by refusing to do jobs.

Huertas got into the shower area first, and when Brody bent his head to enter the shower area as well, Huertas allegedly grabbed his hair and stabbed Brody several times in the stomach and the chest. According to fellow wrestler Bret Hart, the other wrestlers in the locker room were "too scared to help Brody, so they sat there for over an hour while he died." Brody was taken by ambulance to the hospital, but he died hours later while undergoing a second surgery.

Huertas, who always maintained his innocence, was tried for murder and was acquitted by a jury of his peers, citing self-defense. A number of wrestlers refused to work in Puerto Rico in protest of the jury verdict, which temporarily crippled the Puerto Rican wrestling scene.

9 CRASH HOLLY

Michael John Lockwood, or Crash Holly, as he was known in the ring, was an American professional wrestler best known for his time with World Wrestling Federation (later World Wrestling Entertainment, or WWE). He wrestled as a crafty hardcore fighter who managed to work his way out of the trickiest situations, a skill that earned him the nickname "The Houdini of Hardcore."

Lockwood died on November 6, 2003, at the age of 32. In Florida, at the home of wrestler Steve Richards, Lockwood was found partially clothed, with a pool of vomit around his face and empty prescription medication bottles and a partly consumed bottle of alcohol nearby; he had recently received divorce papers from his wife. Although it was first believed that he died by choking on his own vomit, Lockwood's death was later officially ruled a suicide.

8 TEST

Canadian pro wrestler Andrew Martin, who fought under the ring name Test, wrestled for the WWF and the WWE from 1998 to 2004, and later from 2006 to 2007. He last worked under the ring name "The Punisher" for Total Nonstop Action Wrestling.

On March 13, 2009, at the age of 33, Martin was found dead in his home in Tampa, Florida. After seeing him appearing motionless through a window for several hours, a neighbor called the police. The cause of death was determined to be an accidental overdose of oxycodone. Forensic pathologist Dr. Bennet Omalu later found that Martin had severe chronic traumatic encephalopathy, an Alzheimer's-like form of brain damage (after his death in 2007, fellow pro-wrestler Chris Benoit, number 1 on this list, was found to have suffered from the same condition). It's caused by repeated concussions and subconcussive head injuries.

7 THE VON ERICH FAMILY

At one time, the Von Erichs were the biggest stars in wrestling, but things went bad for the family rather quickly. Out of five brothers that wrestled, only one lived to see age 35. David died in 1984 from gastroenteritis. Mike suffered an injury and during surgery contracted a virus that nearly killed him. He was never the same again and killed himself. Kerry was a former World Champion who lost his foot in a motorcycle accident. He wrestled for a few more years, but drug charges led him to kill himself. The youngest Von Erich brother, Chris, killed himself because he felt he could never be as good as his brothers were.

6 BRIAN PILLMAN

Brian Pillman was a football player and professional wrestler; he wrestled for the World Wrestling Federation, Extreme Championship Wrestling, and World Championship Wrestling. He was known as "The Loose Cannon," a wrestling gimmick that made him infamous for his unpredictable character.

On October 5, 1997, sometime during the night or early morning before the "In Your House: Badd Blood" pay-per-view fight in St. Louis, Pillman died in a Bloomington, Minnesota, motel room at the age of 35. An autopsy found that drugs, alcohol, and a previously undetected heart condition, arteriosclerotic heart disease, had led to his death; it was the same condition that had led to the death of his father.

5 MISS ELIZABETH

Elizabeth Ann Hulette, best known as Miss Elizabeth, was a professional wrestling manager. She was the manager to "Macho Man" Randy Savage, whom she married in real life in 1984 after several years of dating. However, the marriage ended in divorce in 1992. After the divorce, Hulette dated and even married again, but none of the relationships lasted. It was then that Hulette became involved with another professional wrestler, Lex Luger. Although they never married, they did live together.

In 2003, fans were shocked to find out that Miss Elizabeth had died from an overdose of a combination of pain pills and alcohol at the home she shared with Luger. It was found out that just two weeks earlier, Luger was arrested for allegedly striking her in a domestic dispute. After a police search of the premises, he was charged with multiple drug possession charges.

4 ANDRE THE GIANT

André René Roussimoff, better known to fans as Andre the Giant, was a French professional wrestler and actor. Andre was born with acromegaly, a medical condition that made him famous for his large size but was also partially responsible for his death. Eventually, his disease began to take its toll on his body. By the late 1980s, André was in constant, near-crippling pain, and his heart struggled to pump blood throughout his massive body. In 1993, Andre died in his sleep of a heart attack shortly after attending the funeral of his father. In honor of Andre, the WWE created a Hall of Fame and made him the first inductee.

3 EDDIE GUERRERO

Eddie Guerrero was a Mexican-American professional wrestler born into the Guerrero wrestling family. He had a well-documented battle with substance abuse that almost cost him his life, career, and family. However, Eddie appeared to overcome his addiction and even reached the top of the wrestling world, becoming World Champion. On the night of November 13, 2005, he was scheduled to wrestle for the championship. However, earlier that morning he was found unconscious in his hotel room by his nephew Chavo. Chavo attempted CPR, but Guerrero was pronounced dead when paramedics arrived on the scene. He was 38 years old, and in the prime of his career. An autopsy revealed that Guerrero died as a result of acute heart failure from arteriosclerotic cardiovascular disease (the same condition that killed Andrew "Test" Martin, number 8 on this list). Guerrero's wife Vickie Guerrero claimed that he had been unwell in the week preceding his death. Throughout his career, Guerrero won 23 titles including the WWE Championship, and was posthumously inducted into the WWE Hall of Fame in 2006.

2 OWEN HART

Canadian pro-wrestler Owen Hart was best known for working for the World Wrestling Federation. A member of the Hart wrestling family, Hart was the youngest child of WWE Hall-of-Famer Stu Hart and Helen Hart. Owen was cited by a number of peers as one of the WWF's most talented professional wrestlers.

On May 23, 1999, Hart fell to his death in Kansas City, Missouri, during the "Over the Edge" pay-per-view event. He was supposed to make a dramatic entrance and be lowered from the rafters to just above ring level, at which time he would act "entangled," then release himself from the safety harness and fall flat on his face for comedic effect. But something went wrong with the stunt harness and the release mechanism was apparently triggered early. Hart fell 78 feet into the ring and landed chest-first on the top rope, throwing him into the ring. Dazed, Hart managed to sit up in the ring, but then lost consciousness.

Fans watching the match at home didn't see the incident or its aftermath; the live broadcast showed only the audience, while medical personnel worked on Hart in the ring. The TV announcer kept saying that Hart was actually badly hurt and the injuries weren't a wrestling stunt. Hart was pronounced dead on arrival at the local hospital. His death was later declared to be from internal bleeding from a severed aorta.

1 CHRIS BENOIT

Chris Benoit was a Canadian professional wrestler. He held a total of 32 championships during his pro-wrestling career and is tied for the most world championship reigns in history.

On June 25, 2007, police officers entered Benoit's home and discovered the bodies of Benoit, his wife, Nancy, and their seven-year-old son, Daniel. It was determined that Benoit had committed the murders.

On June 23, Chavo Guerrero, another professional wrestler, exchanged phone calls and voice messages with Benoit, and was "concerned about Benoit's tone and demeanor."

On June 24, five text messages were sent from Chris and Nancy Benoit's cell phones. Four of them were the Benoits' address; the fifth said that the family's dogs were locked in the home's pool area and noted that a side door to the garage was open.

It was found that on June 22, Benoit killed Nancy in an upstairs room of their home. Her body was wrapped in a towel and her limbs were bound, and a Bible had been left beside her. Her injuries suggested that her murderer had pressed a knee into her back while pulling on a cord around her neck, strangling her. Blood found under her head indicated she may have tried to fight off her attacker.

Daniel Benoit had been suffocated in his bedroom. Like his mother, a Bible was left by his body. The boy had internal injuries to his throat area but showed no bruises. Reports indicate that Daniel had been sedated with Xanax and was likely unconscious when he was killed. A large knife was also found underneath Daniel's bed, but was unused in either of the murders.

After killing both his wife and child, Chris Benoit hanged himself with a noose made from the cord of a weight machine. When the weights were released—about 240 pounds—it strangled him.

10 EVENTS THAT HAVE KILLED BOXING

10 THE SAD SAGA OF JAMES BUTLER

Butler was a very promising young fighter from New York City known by the nickname "The Harlem Hammer." In November 2001, he fought Richard "The Alien" Grant for a charity event to benefit survivors of the 9/11 attacks. After losing by unanimous decision, Butler made his way to the middle of the ring to purportedly congratulate Grant. Grant reacted by stretching his hand out in a motion to embrace Butler, but instead, Butler (who had already removed his gloves) threw a vicious right hook to Grant's face. Grant suffered numerous facial injuries including a broken jaw, lacerated tongue, and several stitches. Butler, in turn, was arrested and convicted of assault and served prison time for the attack.

Unfortunately, the tale doesn't end there. Butler continued his career after serving his sentence but could never duplicate his earlier success. In October 2004, Butler was arrested and charged with murdering Sam Kellerman, brother of HBO boxing analyst Max Kellerman, with a hammer and setting his body on fire after a dispute. Butler pled guilty in 2006 and was sentenced to 29 years in prison.

9 THE RIOT AT MADISON SQUARE GARDEN

Polish-born Andrew Golota entered the ring on July 11, 1996. with an exceptional 27–0 record and on the cusp of superstardom. All he had to do was get past the 38–1 former undisputed heavyweight champ Riddick Bowe. Golota didn't just perform well—he performed brilliantly. He clobbered the ex-champ almost into submission. He was well ahead on points and seemingly close to scoring a knockout.

Golota then (for reasons only he knew) began repeatedly punching Bowe below the belt line. The Polish fighter was warned several times and even received point deductions, but his behavior continued. After several more blatant low blows, the referee was forced to disqualify him. Riddick Bowe's corner responded by rushing the ring and viciously attacking Golota and his team. This triggered a full-scale, racially charged riot that spilled into the stands. Dozens of fans, boxing officials, and police were injured in this disgraceful and bizarre incident.

8 ONLY IN AMERICA

Not everyone can own a professional football franchise. Not everyone can own a baseball franchise. But anyone can promote a fight, even a convicted killer and numbers operator from Cleveland. In 1974, Don King very

shrewdly promoted his first professional fight. It turned out to be the famed Ali versus Foreman "Rumble in the Jungle" in Zaire. This megaevent instantly transformed King into *the* major player in boxing for the next 30 years.

But, alas, Don King likes to play dirty, and his many exploits are infamous. He's perpetrated fraud after fraud on any and all promising fighters to join his stable. King has been implicated in incidents of murder, bribery, theft, bookmaking, breach of contract, and Mafia-assisted racketeering. Someone once said, "Don King wears his hair that way so he can hide his horns."

7 SONNY LISTON AND THE MOB

By all accounts, Sonny Liston had a woeful childhood. Extremely poor and physically abused, Liston left home at an early age and participated in numerous violent crimes. While incarcerated, his boxing skills were discovered and he soon began destroying a string of opponents on his way to the heavyweight title. Liston's prowess caught the attention of several Mafia associates, including Frankie Carbo and "Blinky" Palermo, two men who were linked to numerous counts of match fixing.

By the time Sonny Liston fought a young Cassius Clay on May 25, 1965, the general public already suspected that Liston was controlled by the mob. He nevertheless participated in one of the most obvious fixes in sports history. In the very first round, Liston took a dive and allowed himself to be counted out after Clay threw his famous "Phantom Punch." Coincidently, their first fight also ended controversially when Liston refused to come out of his corner for the seventh round. Sonny Liston would died years later under very suspicious circumstances.

6 THE CORRUPT RICHARD STEELE

A very rare event occurred on March 17, 1990. On this night, two undefeated champions, who were both in the same weight class and in their primes, met in the ring. Julio Cesar Chavez, who was 68–0 (and promoted by Don King) met Olympic gold medalist and welterweight champ Meldrick Taylor in a fight refereed by Richard Steele. Chavez was the favorite, but it was Taylor who dominated the fight from the opening bell.

As the match wore on, Taylor's trademark speed began to wane, but he still held a commanding lead on all scorecards going into the final round. Moments before the end of the match, Chavez scored a knockdown, but Taylor rose to his feet quickly; had the fight continued, Taylor would have still won by unanimous decision, but it was not meant to be. Richard Steele stopped the fight with a mere two seconds left and awarded the victory to Chavez. There were immediate protests from Taylor's camp, but the decision stood. Taylor's career and health were subsequently ruined, and Steele, who notoriously favored Don King's fighters, forever tarnished the sport.

5 INTERNATIONAL BOXING FEDERATION RANKING SCANDAL

The way boxing works is that each sanctioning body has a champion. Champions are only allowed to fight boxers ranked in the top 15. Ranking committees determine who gets ranked. Ranking committee chairmen have the final say and are notoriously corruptible.

In November 1999, International Boxing Federation (IBF) president Bob Lee, Sr., was indicted on 32 counts of racketeering. Lee was conspiring with his rankings chairman, C. Douglass Beavers, to rig the rankings system to favor boxers whose promoters and handlers paid cash bribes. The duo routinely took thousands of dollars from the likes of Don King and Cedric Kushner in return for artificially inflating the rankings of their fighters. Promoters who didn't pay didn't see title fights. The result was a completely corrupt system that was not in any way based on merit. Another black eye for boxing.

4 JIM NORRIS: BOXING'S NOT-SO-GOLDEN AGE

James D. Norris was a very wealthy and extremely powerful man in the mid-20th century. He owned many companies, including an NHL franchise, a major stake in Madison Square Garden, and champion-caliber racehorses. Jim Norris was also a very unsavory individual and was widely known to associate with criminals. As president of the International Boxing Club (IBC), Norris had a virtual monopoly on championship fights because of a lucrative contract the IBC had to broadcast fights on national television.

Jim Norris was personally responsible for fixing numerous bouts, including Harry Thomas versus Max Schmeling in 1937, and Jake Lamotta versus Billy Fox in 1946. His corruption knew no limits. Besides match fixing he was also manipulating the ranking system, unofficially managing many boxers (usually against their will), and persuading fighters to hire his associates as advisors. Norris' actions perpetuated a chain of farces that were passed off as competitive bouts to an unsuspecting public and helped erode boxing's integrity.

3 SEOUL, KOREA, 1988 OLYMPICS

Many people remember a young Roy Jones, Jr., being robbed of a gold medal by corrupt Olympic judges, but few remember an even uglier incident that preceded it. New Zealander Keith Walker was officiating a bantamweight bout between Byun Jong Il of South Korea and Alexander Hristov of Bulgaria. The fight was an ugly, foul-filled affair, and Walker had to repeatedly penalize Jong for head butting.

At the conclusion of the fight, Hristov was announced the winner, but this only incensed Jong's countrymen. Numerous South Korean boxing officials and coaches stormed the ring and viciously attacked referee Keith Walker with punches, kicks, bottles, and even chairs. The terrified Walker barely escaped serious injury and immediately headed to the airport and took the first plane back to New Zealand. Shamed and embarrassed, the Korean Boxing Federation president and the president of the Korean Olympic Committee both resigned after this deplorable incident.

2 THE ACTIONS OF PANAMA LEWIS

Carlos "Panama" Lewis was a world-class trainer; his character, on the other hand, was anything but classy. Already under a cloud of suspicion for gambling on fights he was involved in and giving his boxers water spiked with illegal stimulants, Lewis concocted a wicked plan for his fighter Luis Resto against undefeated rising star Billy Collins, Jr., on June 16, 1983.

Knowing Resto was overmatched, Panama and another trainer removed padding from his gloves and poured an illegal hardening agent on his hand wraps. Resto proceeded to brutalize his unsuspecting opponent for ten rounds. After being declared the winner, Resto approached Collins' corner. Collins' father touched Resto's hand and immediately notified ringside officials. Both

Panama Lewis and Luis Resto had their licenses revoked and were given prison sentences. Sadly, Billy Collins, Jr., would never fight again. His promising career was shattered by the injuries he received. He was dead less than one year later; suicide was suspected.

1 THE DEATH OF DUK KOO KIM

A superstar in South Korea, Kim had risen all the way to being the number-one lightweight contender and earned a shot at the world title against the great Ray "Boom Boom" Mancini on November 13, 1982. The bout was extremely brutal, especially for Kim, who began to wear down in the latter rounds after absorbing tremendous punishment from the champion Mancini. In the early part of the 14th round, Mancini hit Kim with a crushing blow that caused him to fly toward the ropes and hit his head on the canvas.

Kim managed to rise, but the referee stopped the fight. Minutes later, Kim collapsed into a coma and was carried out of the ring and taken directly to the hospital. The Korean star died four days later from severe brain trauma. Out of the hundreds of recorded ring fatalities, Kim's death was one of the saddest. His opponent, Ray Mancini, was never the same fighter again, and it was widely reported that he blamed himself for Kim's death. Duk Koo Kim's mother committed suicide just three months after her son's death by drinking a bottle of pesticide. The bout's referee, Richard Green, consumed by guilt, also committed suicide shortly after the fight.

10 STORIES BEHIND CRAZY SPORTS TRADITIONS

10 C OF RED

The best way to show support for your favorite team is to proudly wear the team colors. Greater solidarity comes from tens of thousands of your fellow sports fanatics all wearing it, too. This tradition's beginnings may have come from the NHL's Calgary Flames during the 1986 Stanley Cup Finals. The Edmonton Oilers' fans were in the midst of "Hat Trick Fever" as they tried to win their third consecutive championship. In response, Calgary promoted "C of Red" to encourage their fans to come dressed entirely in red. During the next year's first-round playoffs, Calgary's opponent responded with the "Winnipeg White Out." Now the practice is extremely popular at American universities, like Penn State's Code Blue and Virginia Tech's Orange-Maroon Effect.

9 SOUTH AFRICA'S VUVUZELA

This is a fairly recent fixture in the FIFA scene even though the vuvuzela has been popular in South African games since the 1990s. The vuvuzela is a simple blow horn originally made of tin but mass-produced in plastic for games. You blow into it as you would a trumpet, and the vuvuzela emits a loud monotone note similar to elephant calls. It's stirred up some controversy because there were many who tried to have vuvuzelas banned from the 2010 World Cup in South Africa. The complaints range from "too loud" to "not fit for a sports arena." The vuvuzela supporters say it doesn't detract from the game any more than anything else that fans have with them, and that it is a strong part of the South African culture.

8 THE HAT TRICK

This popular hockey tradition may have gotten its inspiration from the sport of cricket. In cricket, a hat trick happens when a bowler dismisses three batsmen with consecutive deliveries. The custom crossed over to hockey with Ontario's Biltmore Mad Hatters. When one of the players scored three goals in a game, the team owner, Mr. Biltmore, would present him with a new fedora. Many stories describe Mr. Biltmore throwing his top hat onto the ice to salute the player, and soon enough, the fans also tossed their own hats onto the floor. After they're collected, the hats are donated, thrown away, or saved for a gigantic display case that showcases the franchise's hat-trick history.

7 FOOD RACES

During intermissions in games, many fans race to the concession stand to grab some more food before play resumes. In certain stadiums, the food does the running! The most famous is the Klement's Sausage Race at Miller Park, home of the Milwaukee Brewers. The tradition began in the early '90s as a computer-animated race on the stadium scoreboard, but the sausages made their first live appearance in 1994. At the bottom of the sixth inning of every Milwaukee Brewers home game, employees of Miller Park and a select few highly honored guests don the seven-foot-three-inch foam sausage costumes and race from third base down to home plate and back up to first base. To date, there are five sausages: Brett Wurst the bratwurst, Stosh the Polish sausage, Guido the Italian sausage, Frankie Furter the hot dog, and Cinco the Chorizo. Bratwurst is currently the race leader, with 18 wins. The race gained fame outside of baseball in July 2003 when then–Pittsburgh Pirate Randall Simon used a bat to hit Guido (worn by employee Mandy Block) on the sausage's head. Given where he hit Guido, the bat never came near Mandy Block's head, but since the costume is so top-heavy, Guido easily fell and took Frankie Furter down as well. Simon was arrested, given a fine, and suspended by the MLB for three games. Despite reprimands by the authorities, some found the situation comical. Mandy Block asked for Simon's autograph on the infamous bat, and T-shirt companies made a tidy profit with shirts saying "Don't whack our weiner!"

6 THE TERRIBLE TOWEL

The Terrible Towel is as much a symbol of the NFL's Pittsburgh Steelers as their three-star logo. Its creation comes from the mid-1970s after the Steelers won their first-ever Super Bowl in 1974 and were strong contenders at the 1975 playoffs after winning 12 of 14 games during the regular season. Around that time, general manager Ted Atkins, sales manager Larry Gerrett, and broadcaster Myron Cope brainstormed ideas to market the team's success. The first idea was to sell a mask of head coach Chuck Noll, but it was dismissed due to price issues. The next idea was the more cost-effective "Terrible Towel" because it was cheap, durable, and easy to carry around. They had less than two weeks to promote the Terrible Towel, so Myron Cope went on TV and radio telling people to bring, buy, or dye a dish towel yellow, gold, or black. By the next game, somewhere between 30,000 and 50,000 fans were spinning towels over their heads, and the numbers have only grown since then. The following year, the Steelers' franchise printed the official Terrible Towel image onto bright yellow towels, and the tradition became official. All proceeds from Terrible Towel sales go to the Allegheny Valley School, which is "a residential and educational facility for children and adults with intellectual and developmental disabilities." To date, the Terrible Towel has made over $2.5 million for the school.

5 BLEACHER ROLL CALL

At the old Yankee baseball stadium, the fans in section 39 had a history of bad behavior. They heckled visiting teams and high school marching-band students, they ignored the warnings of stadium ushers, and they even badgered fellow Yankee fans who weren't part of their tight-knit group known as the Bleacher Creatures. As a result of their bad attitudes, section 39 lacked access to the rest of the stadium, and beer sales were banned in just that area. However, negotiations between the Yankee organization and the Bleacher Creatures ensured that the group would get to sit together in section 203 of the new Yankee Stadium in exchange for some changes to a few of their more belligerent Bleacher Creature traditions. Now seen more as "extremely loyal fans" rather than a group of nasty hecklers, Yankee home games aren't really complete until they deliver their Bleacher Roll Call. At the top of the first inning, "Bald Vinny" Milano shouts the name of a Yankee player and the entire section chants that particular baseball player's name until he recognizes the Bleacher Creatures with a wave or salute. They go down lineup until every Yankee player has been called.

4 THE PLAYOFF BEARD

This is a tradition that started with the NHL's New York Islanders. From 1980 to 1983, the team won the championship and lifted the Stanley Cup high above their whiskered faces. Since then, many teams and their fans have put away the razorblade for the duration of their playoff run. In addition to discussing team strategies and playoff series, fans also get into debates over which players can grow the best, worst, or the most nonexistent playoff beards. Many teams also sponsor Beard-A-Thons, in which players and fans grow a playoff beard to fundraise money for various charities. The playoff beard tradition is strongest within hockey, but it has found its way into other sports through players like the NFL's Jake Plummer and tennis pro Björn Borg.

3 THE UNOFFICIAL MASCOTS

Fans love to show their support by wearing their team colors. Some may take it to the next level with brightly colored face paint or tattoos (temporary or not), but there are a select few superfans who dress so bizarrely that everyone takes notice. The NFL's Washington Redskins have the Hogettes. When the group was formed, no one had even thought it would become an unofficial football mascot. As Hogettes founder Michael Torbert describes it, he attended a Halloween party at his grandmother's retirement home dressed in her tea party finest; he was so popular in the old woman's clothes that he and his friends thought they could take this act to local hospitals to cheer up sick children. As lifelong Redskins fans, they decided to go attend a game in their drag wear, including pig snout masks referencing the offensive linesmen, who were nicknamed the "Hogs." The Hogettes have become a fixture within the Redskins community, and through their fame, they have found greater exposure for their many charities. To date, the Hogettes have raised over $100 million for charities like the Ronald McDonald House and the March of Dimes.

2 #1 HECKLER

Heckling is one of the least favorable traditions in pro sports fandom, but jeers and taunts are as common at games as the cheers and applause. No one has a heckling career quite as prestigious as that of Robin Ficker, an ardent fan of the former Washington Bullets (now known as the NBA's Washington Wizards). For 12 years, Ficker held season tickets to Washington Bullets games, and his seats were directly behind the visiting team's bench. He would taunt players through his megaphone; he made fun of coaches' outfits. When the Chicago Bulls came to play, Ficker would read the sex passages of Bulls' coach Phil Jackson's 1975 autobiography, *Maverick*. Ficker's had some supporters over the years, including basketball player Charles Barkley, who had flown him to Phoenix when his team was in the finals against the Chicago Bulls. In 1997, the former Bullets moved to the MCI Center and Ficker decided not to renew his season tickets because the new seats were too far from the visitors' bench. He faded from the sports world to focus on his political career but has recently taken to attending and heckling at wrestling matches at the University of Maryland.

1 DETROIT'S LUCKY OCTOPUS

A practice that remains strong for the Detroit Redwings of the NHL but (hopefully) won't catch on with the other teams in the league is the tossing of octopuses onto the rink. The origins of this tentacled tradition began in 1952 when fewer NHL teams meant that the road to the Stanley Cup only took eight playoff wins. To mark this occasion, brothers Pete and Jerry Cusimano threw the eight-legged octopus onto the ice to represent the Redwing's eight games against the Toronto Maple Leafs and the Montreal Canadiens. Since then, hundreds of octopuses have rained down onto the Redwing rink, including one tossed by Bob Dubisky and Larry Shotwell that weighed 50 pounds. With every octopus purchased for the purpose of tossing, the Superior Fish Market gives out an "Octoquette" which is a pamphlet of recommended guidelines for octopus tossing, including boiling the octopus for half an hour (raw octopus tends to stick to the ice and leave a slimy residue when removed); launching them only after a Redwing goal, as any other time may result in a delay-of-game penalty; and toss the octopus in a direction away from any players, officials, and personnel.

10 STIRRING AND UNEXPECTED OLYMPIC MOMENTS

10 KOREA'S MARCH UNDER THE SAME FLAG

They were divided at the 38th parallel but reunified in Sydney. It was probably only symbolic—and perhaps even delusional—but when an event can bring two countries that are officially at war to march under the same flag, it gives the spectator an idea of the strength of the Olympic movement. At the 2000 Olympics in Sydney, Australia, a flag with the map of an undivided Korea in blue over a white background was carried by Park Jung Chon, a North Korean judo coach, and Chun Un Soon, a South Korean basketball player, while the band aptly played an emotional folk song. Same uniform, same flag, same song—it seemed that for one fleeting moment in history, the two nations forgot the past and embraced the future.

9 AN AFRICAN DELIGHT IN BARCELONA

The two were as different as they come: one, a white South African; the other, an Ethiopian. Derartu Tulu and Elena Meyer had just finished first and second in the 10,000-meter race. What followed was perhaps the most poignant victory lap in history. Hand in hand, the two Africans celebrated their victory together. For many, it heralded South Africa's re-entrance into the sporting arena after years of apartheid, but it was the beauty of two African athletes, to recognize each other's performance in their hour of glory, that seemed to provide the shining light for the African continent.

8 PYAMBU TUUL RUNS THE RACE

Pyambu Tuul represented Mongolia in the marathon at Barcelona in 1992. He came in last. When asked why he was so slow, he replied "No, my time was not slow, after all you could call my run a Mongolian Olympic marathon record." Not satisfied, another reporter asked him whether it was the greatest day of his life, to which came a reply that can throw anyone off their seat:

> And as for it being the greatest day of my life, no, it isn't. Up till six months ago, I had no sight at all. I was a totally blind person. When I trained, it was only with the aid of friends who ran with me. But a group of doctors came to my country last year to do humanitarian medical work. One doctor took a look at my eyes and asked me questions. I told him I had been unable to see since childhood. He said, "But I can fix your sight with a simple operation." So he did the operation on me and after 20 years I could see again. So today wasn't the greatest day of my life. The best day was when I got my sight back and I saw my wife and two daughters for the first time. And they are beautiful.

Simple, ain't it? It's the races we run within ourselves that are most important.

7 DAN JANSEN'S REDEMPTION

It seemed to be happening all over again. A sense of déjà vu had set in. Dan Jansen, the speed skater who had promised so much but had failed to deliver, was competing in the 1000-meter finals at Lillehammer in 1994. Surely, it was his last chance at redemption. Four years earlier at the Calgary Games, he had competed in the 500-meter speed skating event hours after hearing the news of his sister Jane's death. He had failed to make much of an impact in the race. The jinx continued in Albertville in 1992. Call it what you will—destiny, an act of divine providence, whatever—in Lillehammer, he skated like never before, set a world record, and took home the gold. And if there is anything called poignancy in sports, it's this: Dan Jansen, holding his little girl and looking up to the heavens, saying, "This is for you, Jane."

6 MIRACLE ON ICE

Lake Placid, New York, 1980. The Soviets had invaded Afghanistan. President Carter was not sending an American contingent to the Moscow Summer Olympics. It was in this cauldron of spite that the American team comprising mostly amateurs had just taken the lead against the mighty Soviets. Ten minutes of intense hockey followed, but the Soviets could not breach the American defense. With the clock winding down, ABC's Al Michaels' immortal words—"Eleven seconds, you've got ten seconds, the countdown's going on right now! Morrow, up to Silk. Five seconds left in the game. Do you believe in miracles? YES"—were accompanied by jubilation on the rink as well as the stands. Decades later, it's still the video you show your kids to teach them what it is to be American.

5 JOHN STEPHEN AKHWARI IN MEXICO

Momo Walde won the marathon gold in the high altitude of Mexico City in 1968. One hour later, a little-known Tanzanian runner, John Stephen Akhwari, entered the Olympic stadium—the last man to do so. Wounded after a fall and with a dislocated knee, he hobbled up to the track for one last surge to the finish. He then retired to a thunderous applause by a small crowd that was lucky enough to get a glimpse of this gallant champion. It was later written of his perseverance, "Today we have witnessed a young African runner who symbolizes the finest in the human spirit. A performance that gives true dignity to sport—a performance which lifts sports out of the category of grown men playing in games." But Akhwari was far more modest. When asked why he did not quit, he replied, "My country did not send me 5000 miles to start the race. They sent me 5000 miles to finish the race."

4 BLACK POWER AND A SYMPATHETIC AUSTRALIAN

It's an image that, even if you saw it a thousand times, spoke to your heart in so profound a manner that it embodied the spirit of the times. The image is that of Tommie Smith and John Carlos raising a hand covered in a black glove, with Peter Norman donning the Olympic Project for Human Rights badge. It will be remembered as the most iconic image of protest at the Olympic Games, but all three of them were ostracized after. It was only years later that their act was to be recognized as a demonstration of dignity. It's one of those moments when sports cease to be just games and assume the task of being a vehicle of change and progress.

3 DEREK REDMOND PERSONIFIES COURAGE

With a career plagued by injuries, Derek Redmond arrived at Barcelona with an eye on the gold medal. It wasn't to be. With 175 meters to go in his 400-meter semifinal, he pulled his hamstring. The dream had ended it seemed. Not to Redmond though. The events that followed are etched in the minds of millions. Crying, he stands up again, only to try to finish on one leg. His father, watching from the sidelines, joins him with words of comfort—"We'll finish together." "Strength is measured in pounds. Speed is measured in seconds. Courage? You can't measure courage," were the words used by the IOC to promote the Olympic movement with the act of perseverance. But for Derek Redmond, it was the only plausible thing to do.

2 LUZ LONG AND JESSE OWENS EMBRACE IN BERLIN

At the 1936 Games in Berlin, in full view of the Führer, a 19-year-old German athlete, Luz Long, gave American Jesse Owens some advice before they competed in the long jump: "Play it safe. Make your mark several inches before the takeoff board, and jump from there." Owens, the grandson of a slave and the son of a sharecropper took the advice, qualified for the finals and took his tally of gold medals to four. The first to congratulate him was Luz Long. "It took a lot of courage for him to befriend me in front of Hitler…You can melt down all the medals and cups I have, and they wouldn't be a plating on the 24-carat friendship that I felt for Luz Long at that moment," he said, recounting his rendezvous with the blue-eyed German. But for all his heroics, the African American Owens had to take the freight elevator in the Waldorf Astoria to attend his own reception.

1 ALI LIGHTS THE OLYMPIC FLAME

In Atlanta in 1996, at last he emerged from the background: a body weathered by Parkinson's, but a mind astute as ever. Shivering, he lit the flame. No other athlete in the history of sports had meant so much to so many as Muhammad Ali, for the dignity of the man was consummate; never relinquishing ideals for money or fame, Ali was the people's champion, the underdog in sports and life. "They didn't tell me who would light the flame, but when I saw it was you, I cried," said Bill Clinton. He wasn't the only one.

14 THINGS YOU DON'T KNOW ABOUT THE ANCIENT OLYMPICS

14 UNKNOWN ORIGINS

No one actually knows what the origins were of the very first Games. One myth suggests that Heracles, the divine son of the god Zeus, ran a race in Olympia and decreed that it be repeated every four years.

13 ORIGINALLY A RELIGIOUS CEREMONY

The Olympic Games were one of two central rituals in ancient Greece. (The other was the Eleusinian Mysteries, initiation ceremonies for people joining the cult of Demeter and Persephone.) In its heyday, the games lasted five days. The first three were for the sporting events, and the other two days were for rituals and celebration. On the final day, all participants attended a feast in which 100 oxen (killed on the first day as a sacrifice to Zeus) were eaten.

12 THE STATUE OF ZEUS

The Statue of Zeus, one of the Seven Wonders of the Ancient World, was housed in a temple at Olympia, the site of the ancient Olympics.

11 USED AS A MEASUREMENT OF TIME

An olympiad (a period of four years, which refers to the time between two Games) was used as a measure of years by the ancient Greeks in much the same way as we now use the terms "AD" and "BC." This idea was devised by the historian Ephorus. Previously, every Greek state used its own different method of time measurement, which led to a great deal of confusion.

10 ONLY ONE RACE

The only event at the first Olympics was the *stadion* race—a race of about 190 meters, measured after the feet of Zeus. The event was named after the building in which it took place, and it's the source of the English word "stadium."

9 TAKE YOUR MARK

Unlike the modern starting position for foot races, runners (20 of them) started in a fully erect standing position with their arms stretched in front of them. If there was a tie, the race would be rerun.

8 OLIVE BRANCH AWARDS

The winner of the first-recorded Olympic Games, the first gold medalist in a sense, was Coroebus of Elis, a baker from Eleia, the region in which Olympia was found. He won in 776 BC. Instead of winning a gold medal as is now the norm, he received an olive branch—more a symbol than a prize. The town of Eleia still exists today, with about 150 citizens.

7 NAKED GAMES

It's believed that the Greek tradition of athletic nudity started at the games in 720 BC, and it was most likely introduced by the Spartans or Megarian Orsippus. It's from this practice that we have our word "gymnasium," derived from the Greek word *gymnos*, meaning "naked." Competing naked was meant as a tribute to the gods and to encourage aesthetic appreciation of the male body.

6 SHOWING OFF THE GOODS

While the competitors were naked during the Games, it's possible that some wore a *kynodesme*: a thin leather strip tied tightly around the part of the foreskin that extended beyond the glans to prevent the glans from showing. The leather was then tied around the waist to expose the scrotum, or to the base of the penis, making it appear to curl upward. Not all athletes wore the *kynodesme*.

5 TEMPORARY TRUCE

During the Games, all of Greece was under a truce (*ekecheiria*): there could be no use of capital punishment, and no wars or battles. This was in order to ensure the safety of competitors and spectators on the way to Olympia. While the rule was generally adhered to, at least one account exists of a possible breach by the Spartan army. They were punished with a large fine and a ban from attending the Games that year.

4 THREE OTHER GAMES

The Olympic Games were part of four Games that were held so that there would be one set of Games each year. The other three were the Pythian, Nemean, and Isthmian Games, but the Olympic Games were the most important.

3 FOR GREEKS ONLY

Although the first Games were "international" in a sense, in that all Greek city-states were allowed to enter, only men who spoke Greek could compete. Eventually, members of the Greek colonies were also able to enter.

2 HOPLITODROMOS

The last foot race added to the ancient Games (after the addition of two longer-distance races) was the *hoplitodromos*, in which competitors would run 400 or 800 yards in full armor with shields and a helmet or greaves (leg armor). This was introduced in 520 BC. Runners would often trip over each other or stumble on shields dropped by other competitors.

1 2000-YEAR GAP

As part of the move toward making Christianity the official religion, the ancient Olympic Games were finally suppressed by either Theodosius I in AD 393 or his grandson Theodosius II in AD 435. The Games would not return until 1896. They were held in Athens, Greece.

CHAPTER TWELVE

Miscellaneous

10 URBAN LEGENDS THAT CAUSED A MORAL PANIC

10 RAINBOW PARTIES

A rainbow party is a sexual party said to be popular among adolescents. Girls wearing different shades of lipstick take turns performing oral sex on the boys attending the party, leaving an array of colors on their penises so they vaguely resemble rainbows. This urban legend was publicized on several talk shows and publications, leading parents to believe that rainbow parties were not only factual, but also rampant among teenagers. However, apart from questionable testimonials, little evidence exists that rainbow parties are real, and sex researchers, as well adolescent health care professionals, believe the practice to be nonexistent and nothing more than the cause of a moral panic.

9 VODKA-SOAKED TAMPONS

The rumor that both women and men are inserting vodka-soaked tampons into their vagina and anus, respectively, as a new way to get drunk quickly reached the status of an urban legend through the media coverage that it received, alarming parents that the dangerous practice was prevalent among teens. Getting drunk via a vodka-soaked tampon purports to have several benefits, such as helping fool Breathalyzer tests by eliminating alcohol breath, providing a quicker way to get drunk by speeding alcohol into the bloodstream, and preventing vomiting caused by intoxication. All these claims seem credible; however, all, except for getting people drunk faster by only a matter of minutes, have been proven to be false, leading to the question of why anyone would want to ingest alcohol in such a manner and dismissing the story as a false urban legend.

8 SNUFF FILMS

Said to portray the actual death or murder of those being filmed, snuff films continue to cause a tremendous stir by playing to people's emotions and by relying on their plausibility. While some people maintain that snuff films have been distributed commercially, police investigations by various law enforcement agencies, including the FBI, have revealed that no snuff films have been produced and that no market exists for them, undermining the claims that the films are made for financial gain. While some deaths and murders have been caught on camera, such as suicides and executions of death row inmates, none of them has been explicitly recorded for the purpose of entertainment or profit.

7 KIDNEY HEIST

The story goes that a well-organized, well-funded crime ring with very skilled personnel is drugging travelers and surgically removing one of their kidneys, leaving the victims to wake up submerged to their neck in a bathtub full of ice. This urban legend has been associated with numerous major U.S. cities, from Las Vegas to Houston to New Orleans, where it caused quite a commotion on the days prior to Mardi Gras, prompting the New Orleans Police Department to issue an official statement declaring the allegations of kidney theft as "completely without merit and without foundation." The National Kidney Foundation also took part in the fight to dispel the credibility of the legend by asking individuals who claim to have been victims of kidney theft to contact them; so far no one has.

6 JENKEM

Jenkem is supposedly a drug made by fermenting raw sewage that causes a euphoric high followed by strong hallucinations when its gases are inhaled. It took the world by storm, fooling several news outlets, including the *Washington Post*, which reported the drug as a new popular way to get high among American teenagers, and appealed to its gross factor by calling it "the human-waste drug" and "butthash." The media frenzy was sparked by an intelligence bulletin published by the Collier County Sheriff's Office, which cited Jenkem as "a popular drug in American schools." However, the information contained in the bulletin came from a source that later dismissed it as a hoax, and the belief that Jenkem was a new popular drug was based on nothing but gossip.

5 WALMART GANG INITIATIONS

By addressing the issue of gangs, rumors that gang initiates were required to kill children or women at a WalMart as part of the initiation process caused widespread panic and flooded police phone lines. The rumors portrayed those most vulnerable, children and women, as being at risk, and spread quickly through text messages and media coverage. Many people avoided shopping at WalMart on the days following the surge of the rumor, failing to notice that it bore some similarities to another false urban legend in which gang initiates would kill unsuspecting drivers who flashed their headlights at them. The WalMart gang initiations were said to take place in stores across the U.S. and even in the province of Alberta, Canada. Police departments in several states were quick to reassure concerned callers and issued statements declaring the rumors as "not credible," "hoaxes," and "urban legends."

4 PIN PRICK ATTACKS

These hypothetical attacks involved injecting blood tainted with AIDS into unsuspecting targets at movie theaters, raves, and night clubs. The unwary victim would feel a slight prick on their arm and later discover a note attached to their clothes carrying the message "Welcome to the world of AIDS." Variations of the urban legend quickly spread through e-mail, and some claimed to be a warning being circulated by the Dallas Police Department, which later declared the attacks as false. Although attacks have been carried out using syringes as weapons, in none of the attacks were the syringes contaminated with HIV or AIDS, except for two events. In New Zealand, a man intentionally infected his wife with a syringe of his blood. In Australia, an inmate at Sydney's Long Bay Jail managed to jab a guard with a syringe filled with HIV-positive blood. Prison guard, Gary Pearce contracted the disease and died, despite the 1 in 200 chance of infection. The motive behind this urban legend was to frighten people and to keep them from visiting leisure establishments by playing on the public fear of AIDS.

3 SEX BRACELETS

According to the legend, gel bracelets, also known as jelly bracelets, or "awareness bracelets," are being used by teenagers as a sexual code to indicate their willingness to participate in different acts, which range from hugging and kissing to oral sex and intercourse. The acts are determined by the bracelet's color, and if a boy snaps a girl's bracelet off her wrist, he is awarded a "sexual coupon" that can be exchanged for the act that corresponds to the color of the bracelet. Several schools banned the bracelets in response to the rumors of the bracelets' hidden meaning, which in turn led news outlets to believe that the rumors were in fact true, citing the banning of the bracelets as proof positive. Alarmed parents expressed shock and disbelief, ignoring the fact that gel bracelets served only as a fashion accessory, and that the idea of the bracelets being used as "sexual coupons" was nothing more than wishful thinking on part of the adolescents.

2 BLUE STAR TATTOOS

Playing on parents' fears and on society's instinct to protect those who are most vulnerable, the blue star tattoos legend takes the form of a warning, declaring that LSD-laced rub-on tattoos are being distributed to children to get them addicted at an early age. The "warning" has been attributed to several health institutions and police departments. Despite the fact that the information contained in the warning regarding the effects of LSD is inaccurate, and that LSD is not an addictive drug, the blue star tattoo legend continues to fool and alarm parents, journalists, and school administrators. The legend resurfaces from time to time, bringing with it a familiar wave of panic and concern, regardless of the fact that no documented cases of actual LSD distribution to children exist.

1 POISONED CANDY

This is by far the most popular urban legend on this list and the most widely believed to be true. Retold each year on the days leading up to Halloween, it manages to instill unease by casting doubt on the integrity of others. Rumors that unscrupulous people hand out poisoned candy to unsuspecting children on Halloween have become a staple of urban legend lore, due in part to the horrifying nature of the act and to the mass media coverage that false claims have received. No evidence and no documented cases exist that tampered candy has been randomly and knowingly distributed to trick-or-treating

children with the intent to harm or possibly kill. In one case of premeditated murder, however, a cyanide-laced Pixy Stix was given to a child by his father, who intended to kill him and collect the insurance money. Attempts at debunking this urban legend haven't been able to put it to rest, and as with all other urban legends on this list, it continues to be passed off as true, causing a moral panic despite its obvious falsity and blatant sensationalism.

10 BIZARRE COLLEGE COURSES

10 THE UNBEARABLE WHITENESS OF BARBIE

A mandatory course for some freshmen at Occidental College, "The Unbearable Whiteness of Barbie: Race and Popular Culture in the United States" tries to explore ways in which "scientific racism has been put to use in the making of Barbie." Elizabeth Chin, the course instructor, warns students that the course itself is no child's play. With assigned readings ranging from Sandra Cisneros to Karl Marx, the course incorporates some pretty hardcore academic content. Nevertheless, a class on race that describes the whiteness of Barbie as unbearable seems incredibly unscientific. Wonder if this course was offered when a certain gentlemen named Barack Obama was roaming the corridors of this West Coast institution...?

9 THE THEOLOGY OF EATING

Since such an important aspect of everyday living must have theological implications, Loyola College decided that the inextricable link between God and eating was to be explored. Students are taught the "complex religious aspects associated with eating," exploring the texts to expound the intricacies of etiquette in a canonical context. The evolution debate may not have been decided, but common sense predicts problems for those who do not eat a balanced diet. However, if free food is part of the deal, it may help all those poor souls dissect (food) theology.

8 STUPIDITY

Occidental College makes another appearance on the list, this time for the accommodation of stupidity. Of course, the word refers to the name of the course rather than a quality possessed by its students. The course itself uses works of Friedrich Nietzsche and Gilles Deleuze, among others, to clarify that "stupidity is neither ignorance nor organicity, but rather, a corollary of knowing and an element of normalcy, the double of intelligence rather than its opposite." Only those who indulge in it must know.

7 THE JOY OF GARBAGE

No matter how useless garbage sounds, Virginia Matzek of Santa Clara University will try to change your impression of it. A "science class for non-science majors," the Joy of Garbage is apparently a "serious class where students are required to do research and learn how to work with data." Among the questions asked are, "What is the difference between 'garbage,' 'discard,' and 'waste'?"

6 THE ART OF SIN AND THE SIN OF ART

The Rhode Island School of Design attracts aspiring artists and designers from around the country, but it's inconceivable to think that some of them might want to "lust with the saints and burn with the sinners." However, if any one of them accepts the invitation, they can spend the semester analyzing the moral dimensions of the works of classical as well as modern artists. Being the artsy school that RISD is, the course and the teacher should have a cult following. Well, different strokes for different folks.

5 PHILOSOPHY AND *STAR TREK*

Philosophy students at Georgetown University read works by Aristotle, Kant, and others. However, it's done under the pretext of understanding the philosophical depths of *Star Trek*. The course serves as an introduction to metaphysics and epistemology and tries to dissect the major philosophical questions that come up in the science-fiction entertainment drama. Another proof that the ingenuity of educators has conjured ways of teaching that were hitherto unknown.

4 ZOMBIES! THE LIVING DEAD IN LITERATURE, FILM, AND CULTURE

The American South is still the bastion of conservatism and evangelism, but that doesn't stop them from trying to expound zombies. The credit for this pioneering course must go to Sean Hoade, professor of English at the University of Alabama at Tuscaloosa, who draws parallels between American consumption patterns and zombies. His observation that "zombies act as a mirror for Americans, not only as we see ourselves but also as the rest of the world sees America in the time of George W. Bush: as a roaming, voracious killer turning its victims into soulless creatures like itself" may be a little far-fetched, but Hoade's students aren't complaining.

3 MAPLE SYRUP: THE REAL THING

Those who decide to attend Alfred University in a bucolic part of western New York state may find themselves in a classroom studying the subtleties concerned with the production of maple syrup. The only prerequisite for the course is the "willingness to work for long periods in snow, cold, and mud." The class dissects the production techniques invented by the Native Americans, and visits to local producers, restaurants, and festivals augment the process. It's the "real thing, so students can find jobs easily with this course on their resume!

2 THE ART OF WALKING

The art of walking might seem trivial to some, but not to Dr. Ken Keffer, Professor of Modern Languages at Centre College in Kentucky. He conducts a class dedicated to the understanding of "intelligible and sensual design in inner and outer nature," first expounded by Immanuel Kant. Apart from the customary walks he takes with his students to the nearby Perryville Battlefield and the surrounding areas, Dr. Keffer assigns freelance walking assignments for students to appreciate the subtleties of walking. Now, where is this college again?

1 THE PHALLUS

The people at Occidental College decided that in the course of human events it becomes necessary for students to delve into the "signification of the phallus" and the "relation of the phallus to masculinity, femininity, genital organs, and the fetish." Since it's self-evident that the phallus occupies a central theme in the psychoanalytic theories of gender and sexuality, the course occupies a pivotal role in the Intercultural and Queer program.

10 BIZARRE CASES OF MASS HYSTERIA

10 MUMBAI SWEET WATER

In 2006, the water at Mahim Creek in Mumbai—one of the most polluted waterways in India—miraculously turned sweet; or at least that's what the residents of the village claimed. Raw sewage and industrial waste spill into the creek by the thousands of tons every day. Within hours of the announcement of the sweet water, people in Gujarat claimed that the seawater at a nearby beach had turned sweet as well. Despite warnings not to the drink the water, many locals gathered it up in bottles, while trash and plastic floated by on the current. By 2 p.m. the next day, the sweet water devotees said the water had returned to normal.

9 TANGANYIKA LAUGHTER EPIDEMIC

In 1962, an outbreak of mass hysteria occurred in Tanganyika (now Tanzania). Apparently a pupil at a local school told a joke that caused some students to begin laughing. But the laughter began to spread, and it caused such an epidemic in the region that the school was shut down. The laughter moved to the surrounding areas, and thousands of people were affected. It took 18 months for this most bizarre case of mass hysteria to finally die out.

8 HINDU MILK MIRACLE

In 1995, Hindu statues across India began to drink milk that was offered on a spoon. While holding spoons to the mouths of the statues of Ganesha, the milk would appear to vanish as if he were slowly sipping it. The reports continued for a number of days, with scientists putting forward various explanations for it. Many Hindus continue to believe that it was a miraculous event.

7 JUNE BUG EPIDEMIC

In 1962, at a textile factory in the U.S., workers in the dress-making department began to develop flulike symptoms. Those affected claimed to have been bitten by an unseen bug, and a search was led to find the cause. Eventually, no evidence of a bug was found nor were any bite marks found on the sufferers. The U.S. Public Health Service concluded that it was a case of mass hysteria.

6 SOAP OPERA HYSTERIA

Morangos com Açúcar is a Portuguese soap opera aimed at children and teenagers. In 2006, the show aired an episode in which the characters suffered from a strange disease. All of a sudden all over Portugal, school children began to report the symptoms of the disease from the show, including rashes and dizziness. Schools were closed. Eventually the Portuguese National Institute for Medical Emergency stated that they found no evidence of a true illness and it was chocked up to mass hysteria.

5 THE TOXIC LADY

The Toxic Lady, Gloria Ramirez, was rushed to the hospital in 1994, suffering from severe effects of cervical cancer. All of the hospital staff who treated her or went near her began to get sick, and many collapsed. This strange epidemic seemed to affect women more than men, and all tested showed normal blood-test results. The health department issued a statement saying it was mass hysteria, but some believed that the medication Gloria was taking may have caused her body to exude a dangerous toxin.

4 THE WAR OF THE WORLDS

The War of the Worlds is now famous all over the world due to the mass hysteria it caused. In 1938, Orson Welles broadcast an adaptation of the book over the radio in such a way that it sounded like an authentic news recording declaring an alien invasion. All over the United States, panic ensued; police were involved in order to calm the crowds.

3 THE MONKEY MAN OF DELHI

In 2001, a strange, monkeylike creature was reportedly roaming the streets of New Delhi attacking people. Eyewitnesses said he was four feet tall and covered in black hair, with a metal helmet, red eyes, and claws. Many people reported being scratched by the creature, and 15 people suffered bites and bruises. Unfortunately, this case of mass hysteria led to death; three people died leaping from buildings to escape the alleged monkey man.

2 PENIS PANIC

Penis panic is a strange hysteria in which large numbers of men in a community believe that their penises are shrinking to the point they're going to disappear. It frightens some men so badly that they use devices such as needles and hooks to prevent their penises from vanishing entirely. In 1967, there was an outbreak of penis panic in Singapore, and it took a massive government campaign and media blackout to prevent its spread.

1 THE DANCING PLAGUE

The Dancing Plague occurred in 1518 in the Roman Empire. It started when Frau Troffea began to dance erratically and unstoppably in the middle of the street. Within days she had been joined by 34 more people, and within a month over 400 people were dancing themselves to death. And that's exactly what happened—most of those afflicted died of dancing.

10 BIZARRE BODY MODIFICATIONS

10 BRANDING

Human branding is the process in which a mark, usually a symbol or ornamental pattern, is burned into the skin of a living person with the intention that the resulting scar makes it permanent. This is performed using a hot or cold iron, using the techniques of livestock branding on humans.

9 SUBDERMAL IMPLANT

A subdermal implant refers to a kind of body jewelry that's placed underneath the skin, allowing the body to heal over the implant and creating a raised design. Many people who have these implants use them in conjunction with other types of body modification to create a desired dramatic effect.

8 EARLOBE STRETCHING

A person who is either obsessed with stretching their piercings, or with showing off their stretched piercings, is known as a "gauge queen." Some wear this term with pride, others use it derisively. Most

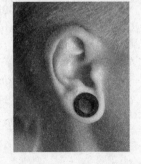

people can stretch their earlobes to at least one-quarter inch and still have the tissue return to normal when they remove the jewelry, but there really are no guarantees. Don't stretch your ears unless you're certain you'll want it forever. Once the elastic limit of the skin has been passed, or a large amount of additional tissue has built up, the hole won't close again completely.

7 TONGUE SPLITTING
Also known as tongue bifurcation, in this body modification, the end of the tongue is forked by cutting it down the middle from the tip toward the base. In most cases, the split is created with a scalpel or surgical laser. People who split their own tongues do it through a long, very painful process by inserting nylon bindings through an existing tongue piercing and gradually tightening them.

6 TOOTH FILING
Tooth filing is a form of body modification in which people file their natural teeth to create a desired look or shape.

5 TIGHTLACING
Tightlacers wear very tight corsets, which they call training corsets, to achieve extreme permanent body and posture modification that gives the appearance and feeling of wearing a corset.

4 PEARLING
To enhance the appearance of the genitals and heighten the sexual pleasure of partners during intercourse, pearling involves permanently inserting small metal beads under the skin of the labia, for women, or the shaft or foreskin of the penis, for men. The practice seems to have been fairly common across world cultures and is still done today.

3 CORNEAL TATTOOING
Eyeball tattooing has been around for a long time; in the 19th century it was commonly used to correct cosmetic defects in blind eyes. The procedure can be performed with a traditional tattoo needle or a syringe. The eye is simply held open while the pigment, which is the exact same type used in a regular tattoo, is injected into the eyeball.

2 ANAL STRETCHING

The process of anal stretching is a lot like earlobe stretching, except you don't wear the "jewelry" around the clock. Like stretching a piercing, it involves slow and increasingly larger gauges over an extended period of time.

1 EXTRAOCULAR IMPLANT

Apparently first done in the Netherlands, the practice of implanting jewelry in the outer layer of the eye has come to the U.S. According to Dr. Christopher Rapuano, a corneal surgeon at Philadelphia's Wills Eye Hospital, "You can think of it as crazy. I mean, this is invasive surgery where you are cutting the surface layer of the eye open to put a little piece of jewelry in. The first time I read about this I said, 'Oh, my God, who is doing this?'" The safety of the procedure will have to prove itself over time, since it hasn't been performed on many people, but the possibility for infection and complications is definitely there.

10 MOST CONTROVERSIAL FLAGS

10 THE RAINBOW FLAG

The rainbow flag, also known as the pride flag or the gay pride flag, of the lesbian, gay, bisexual, and transgender (LGBT) community is a symbol of LGBT pride and social movements, in use since the 1970s. The colors reflect the diversity of the LGBT community, and the flag is often used to stand for gay pride in LGBT rights marches. It originated in the United States but is now used worldwide. Designed by San Francisco artist Gilbert Baker in 1978, the design has undergone several revisions, but the most common variant consists of six stripes, with the colors red, orange, yellow, green, blue, and violet. The flag is commonly flown horizontally, with the red stripe on top, as the colors would appear in a natural rainbow.

9 THE ANGUS FLAG

In 2007 in Angus, Scotland, one of the country's 32 local government council areas, the Angus Council decided to scrap the Saltire (the flag of Scotland) and replace it with a new Angus flag. This move led to public outcry across Scotland, and more than 7000 people signed a petition opposing the council's move, leading to a compromise whereby the Angus flag would not replace the Saltire but be flown alongside it on council buildings. The new flag was criticized as a waste of time and money, as well as a politically motivated move. The design consists of four quarters containing a crowned lion passant, a cinquefoil, a checked strip crossed with a buckled belt, and a depiction of the heart of Robert the Bruce; the sections represent the four ancient earldoms of Angus.

8 THE SUN OF VERGINA FLAG

On August 11, 1992, the newly independent Republic of Macedonia adopted a new flag to replace the old Communist "red star" insignia. The flag depicted a stylized yellow sun centered on a red field with eight main and eight secondary rays emanating from it, tapering to a point. This ancient symbol was known as the Vergina Sun or Vergina Star, named after the town in Greece where it was discovered in archaeological excavations of the ancient Macedonian city of Aigai. The symbol had also been adopted by many in the then Socialist Republic of Macedonia to represent historical connections between that country and ancient Macedonia, and had been paraded in demonstrations by ethnic Macedonians at home and abroad.

The flag, the new Republic of Macedonia's constitution, and its name all became the focus of a bitter dispute between Greece and the Republic, during which Greece imposed an economic blockade on the Republic beginning in February 1994. In July 1995, Greece lodged a request with the World Intellectual Property Organization (WIPO) for exclusive copyright to the Vergina Sun. Greek objections also prevented the flag from being flown at the United Nations Headquarters building in New York. The blockade was lifted in October 1995 when an agreement was reached to change the flag, modify the constitution, and resolve the naming dispute through United Nations–sponsored negotiations.

7 THE PRE–ISLAMIC REVOLUTION IRANIAN FLAG

Like the country's current flag, the former Iranian flag contains horizontal bands of green, white, and red, but the emblem in the middle contained a lion, sun, and sword, rather than the four crescents and sword introduced by the

Islamic regime in 1980. Recently, the appearance of the pre–Islamic Revolution Iranian flag at U.S. rallies against the re-election of President Mahmoud Ahmadinejad has stirred tension between two generations of protesters. While they all came out to express solidarity with protesters in Iran, each group views the flag very differently. Supporters of Iran's deposed shah often bring out the flag at demonstrations, and some would be happy to see a constitutional monarchy restored in Iran or a secular democracy with no royal figurehead. Younger protesters don't want to give Iran's rulers any excuse to accuse them of links to a movement that seeks to overthrow the current regime, and often plead with older protesters to put away their flags.

6 JAPAN'S RISING SUN FLAG

The Rising Sun Flag is the military flag of Japan. It was used as the ensign of the Imperial Japanese Navy and the war flag of the Imperial Japanese Army until the end of World War II. It's also presently the ensign of the Japan Maritime Self-Defense Force and the war flag of the Japan Ground Self-Defense Force. It's also waved during the Japanese New Year and in sporting events. The design is similar to Japan's national flag in that it has a red circle close to the middle signifying the sun; the difference is the addition of extra sun rays (16 for the ensign) exemplifying the name of Japan as "The Land of the Rising Sun." The flag was used in overseas actions from the Meiji period to World War II. When Japan was defeated in August 1945, the flag was banned by Allied occupation authorities. However, with the re-establishment of a Self-Defense Force, the flag was re-adopted in 1954. The flag with 16 rays is today the ensign of the Maritime Self-Defense Force while the Ground Self-Defense Force uses an 8-ray version. This flag is often considered offensive in countries that were victims of Japanese aggression, particularly China and Korea, where it's considered as a symbol of Japanese imperialism.

5 THE PATRIOTE FLAG

The Patriote flag is a politically charged symbol often used by hard-line nationalists in Quebec, Canada. It was used by the Patriote movement in Lower Canada (present-day Quebec) between 1832 and 1838. It's highly similar to the civil flag of the German *Bundesland* of North Rhine–Westphalia. Some theories about its origins pretend that the color green was adopted to represent the Irish of Lower Canada, the color white for the French Canadians, and red the English of the territory. Some also say the tricolor style was inspired by the

French tricolor, the symbol of the French Revolution that inspired the Patriotes. It became the national flag of the Republic of Lower Canada at the Declaration of Independence of Lower Canada in 1838.

Nowadays, it's used by contemporary Quebec independence supporters as a symbol of their movement and ideal. As such, it serves a purpose similar to the Estelada flags, symbols of the Catalan independence movement. It's often seen in crowds at Quebec National Day concerts and gatherings and was featured at the voting day assembly of YES supporters of the 1995 Quebec referendum on independence.

4 THE FLAG OF EUROPE

The Flag of Europe is the flag and emblem of the European Union (EU) and Council of Europe (CoE). It consists of a circle of 12 golden stars on a blue background. The blue represents the West, the number of stars represents completeness, while their position in a circle represents unity. The stars don't vary according to the members of either organization, as they are intended to represent all the peoples of Europe, even those outside European integration.

In 1985, the EU, which was then the European Economic Community (EEC), adopted the flag of Europe as its own flag (having had no flag of its own

before) at the initiative of the European Parliament. The flag is not mentioned in the EU's treaties, its incorporation being dropped along with the European Constitution, but it is formally adopted in law. Despite it being the flag of two separate organizations, it is often more associated with the EU due to the EU's higher profile and heavy usage of the emblem. The flag has also been used to represent Europe in sporting events and as a pro-democracy banner outside the Union. Euroscepticism, a general term for opposition to the European Union or the process of European integration, however, makes its use controversial in some cases.

3 THE IRAQ FLAG

On January 21, 2008, a new flag was confirmed by the Iraqi parliament. In this current version, the three stars were removed, while the *Takbir* (the words *Allaahu Akbar*, or "God is Great") was left written in green Kufic script. The flag is controversial, as some Iraqis refuse to accept the legitimacy of a government while foreign troops remain active in Iraq. Some Sunni tribal leaders took offense at the purging of the stars, a symbol of the nation's former Sunni regime. However, as of April 2009, Anbar province raised the new Iraqi flag as is evident on the official site of Anbar province. *The New York Times* reports that the flag design recently imposed is intended to be temporary and mentions that Iraqis have "expressed varying opinions about the new flag."

2 THE CONFEDERATE FLAG

The Confederate battle flag, also called the Southern Cross, Stars and Bars, Dixie Flag, or the Rebel Flag, has been described variously as a proud emblem of Southern heritage and as a shameful reminder of slavery and segregation. In the past, several Southern states flew the Confederate battle flag along with the U.S. and state flags over their statehouses. Others incorporated the controversial symbol into the design of their state flags. The display of the Confederate flag remains a highly charged and emotional topic, generally because of disagreement over the nature of its symbolism. As a result of these varying perceptions, there have been a number of political controversies surrounding the use of the Confederate flag in Southern state flags, at sporting events, at Southern universities, and on public buildings.

According to Civil War historian and native Southerner Shelby Foote, the flag traditionally represented the South's resistance to Northern political dominance; it became racially charged during the Civil Rights Movement of the 1950s and '60s, when fighting against desegregation suddenly became the focal point of that resistance.

1 THE U.S. FLAG

Also called the Stars and Stripes, Old Glory, and the Star-Spangled Banner, the American flag features 50 stars, representing the 50 states, and 13 stripes, which represent the original 13 colonies that rebelled against the British crown and became the first states in the Union.

The American flag is to some a symbol of the freedom, liberty, and opportunity found in the U.S., while to others it stands for America's military presence around the world or economic dominance. While it's not uncommon to see news footage of the American flag being burned in protest in the Middle East, it's also sometimes burned in protest within the country. The United States Supreme Court has ruled that, due to the First Amendment to the United States

Constitution, it's unconstitutional for a government (whether federal, state, or municipal) to prohibit the desecration of the American flag, due to its status as "symbolic speech."

10 BIZARRE THEORIES AND THE FACTS SURROUNDING THEM

10 MAGIC

The Theory: By using certain objects, such as a candle or a dagger, you can bend the universe to your will, completely ignoring the laws of physics and the practical laws of the universe.

The Facts: Many people claim that they can use powers such as summoning demons or angels or having out-of-body experiences under laboratory conditions, but no one has been able to prove it so far. There are incidents that do defy logical explanations, such as some people's claims of successfully using Ouija boards, although since none of these events can be proven, it's very weak evidence.

9 REPTOIDS

The Theory: This has to be one of the most outlandish theories ever brought forth. It's claimed most famously by David Icke, but by several others as well. It states that the royal family of Britain, President Bush's family, and many other such clans are actually aliens here to secretly take over earth, feeding off humans to maintain their "human forms."

The Facts: Most of the theorists' proof consists of enhanced photos of people such as George Bush with reptile-looking eyes, although they have come forth with many other forms of evidence such as videos proving the presence of the reptoids here on earth. All the videos brought forth have been proven fakes or are so obviously fake no one has wasted time and resources to look into them.

8 2011 IS ACTUALLY 1714

The Theory: The early Middle Ages never existed and we have been counting the earth as almost 200 years older than it actually is.

The Facts: Well, there's no solid way to prove or disprove it, since the very theory says the carbon dating that has been done for this age is flawed. Those who believe we've miscounted history also claim that the written material from the "Middle Ages" is a forgery. However, no one has put forth a reason why the Middle Ages were made up, and there is no solid evidence to prove the theory since the basis of it stops anyone from being able to scientifically prove they are wrong. Since all this claim says is that the carbon dating is incorrect and the writings are forgeries—even though scientists and historians have an almost perfect timeline with the carbon dating they use—we can almost cast this one aside without proof.

7 NAZI ADVANCES

The Theory: The Nazis were much further ahead than technology would allow them to be at the time. This theory ranges wildly, but one of the most popular versions is that the Nazis landed on the moon as early as 1942 and established a base on the moon's dark side. They also had establishments with at least half a dozen alien civilizations, and the remaining Nazis remain on the moon to this day.

The Facts: There are so many holes in this theory: for example, most skeptics believe that we haven't had any contact at all with aliens as of yet, and the dark side of the moon is freezing, so Nazis would need amazing machinery to survive there. They would need a way to renew all their resources, which could be explained by growing plants to create food and air. But they would also need an energy source of some kind, although whatever they used would have to be something not yet discovered on Earth.

6 HOLLOW EARTH

The Theory: The earth is actually hollow and is not filled with magma. Claims range from there being several layered shells (usually four) on the inside of the planet, to the inside having ground and soil like ours with 800 miles of crust between us and the other world at the Earth's center; most believers usually say there is also an inner sun.

The Facts: Though this is not quite as insane or as impossible as some others on this list, it's still highly unlikely. We don't know for sure what's under our

Earth's crust, but this theory completely forgets to mention where the magma that erupts from volcanoes comes from if the Earth is hollow. Moreover, the inner sun would pose numerous problems, such as the inner inhabitants most likely being sucked into its gravity or caught in its solar flares. This theory is often supported by the fact that it's currently impossible to search the bottom of the Arctic to find the Earth's core. There's also a castle in Europe with defenses set to ward off an attack from the Earth's inside out. Since the hole to the inner Earth is under a chapel in the castle, that would involve taking down the castle to check this theory; the castle's owners won't allow this, and many often use it as proof. Note sometimes this and theory number 7 on this list have been mixed together, saying the remaining Nazis fled to the inner Earth.

5 TERRAFORMED MARS

The Theory: Mars is already being terraformed behind our backs by groups such as NASA and the ESA (European Space Agency). This is a fairly new claim and is supported only by speculation and a few pictures.

The Facts: First off, it seems almost no theorist takes price into account when they come up with these ideas. NASA is already having trouble as it is keeping itself funded. The cost of bringing something to Mars that could turn it into a habitable, Earthlike planet would cost billions, possibly even trillions of dollars. The computer technology required to make sure every little thing was right would cost even more. Not to mention the time it takes a spaceship to get to Mars from Earth, so something that big would take years to get there and might not even work when it did. Our best bet for terraforming Mars at the moment is to take prehistoric microbes that feed off carbon dioxide and other gases and let them change Mars in the same way scientists think they changed and formed Earth. Of course, this in itself would take millions of years, and at the present there seems no way to terraform Mars and no reason to.

4 HEALING THOUGHTS

The Theory: Using your mind to think positively and encourage yourself and others to feel better really helps and can replace medicine.

The Facts: Sadly, this is believed by many people, and it certainly can't hurt as "treatment" for the common cold, since rest and relaxation are the best things for that, after all. For more serious diseases, people who really believe in this idea may not go to a doctor, and as such they can damage their body or even kill themselves. This is no more effective than healing prayer, which when it does seem to work can be explained away as coincidence. Many people actually do believe in healing thoughts, and luckily for some of them, the placebo effect has often proven successful: since they think they're getting better, their bodies get stronger and they do sometimes pull through.

3 CHAKRAS

The Theory: We each have seven chakras going down from the top of our head to our feet. They can be used for a variety of things, and awakening one can usually help you with a specific thing.

The Facts: There is no way to prove these things exist, but people believe in them, some more than they believe that humans have souls. They're usually connected with paranormal cases, and as such usually don't have any specific stories all their own, although there have been some reports of people having slightly greater abilities when their charkas are awakened, or knowing that something will happen before it does. This is usually explained by a "sixth sense," often 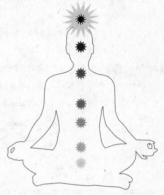 described as the brain's way to activate the subconscious mind, which helps us gather information and process it in such a way that we don't know how we acquired it. This can explain why people think they've been to places they never have, or other similar feelings, and it can also explain away almost all the chakra stories.

2 HOLOGRAPHIC REALITY

The Theory: Life doesn't exist. We're all in fact test programs in a giant virtual reality, or the players of that reality itself.

The Facts: Once again, there is no specific way to disprove this theory. Though it would mean in reality we would probably look much different or not exist at all. There is not much of a base for this to stand on, since it is another "can't prove can't disprove" paradox, it is back to our own judgment. Strange as it may seem, this theory could explain a lot of the problems with the world. If we all are just test subjects in a large-scale virtual-reality test, then all of the anomalies we find in the world and many of its mysteries could be explained as bugs and glitches in the program. There's no solid proof that it does exist, though, and the claim is most likely just generated by people's fears of technology we're stepping into and what it may do to us.

1 RELIGION

The Theory: Though the theory varies greatly from religion to religion, most believe that there is a being or beings greater than anything else in the universe that created the Earth. It's generally accepted in Western civilization that there is a god.

The Facts: We find ourselves at another paradox: there is no way to prove or disprove any religion. Many believers in a religion will often say God is testing us, as he has faked many of the things we see in history, such as dinosaur bones being millions of years old. However, skeptics usually point out other facts, such as that the second you accept one religion you are literally rejecting thousands of others. Skeptics will also point to the overwhelming evidence that all so-called effects of prayer can be explained through mere coincidence.

10 HUMAN SIDESHOW FREAKS

10 JOSEPH MERRICK—THE ELEPHANT MAN

Joseph Merrick (often wrongly named John Merrick), born in 1862, suffered from severe disfigurement and growths on one side of his body. Because of these growths, he was unable to work and ended up in a sideshow where, contrary to popular belief, he was treated extremely well and was well paid. After he was seen by a doctor, Merrick was taken to live in a hospital. At 27 years of age, he died of suffocation while he slept.

9 JUAN BAPTISTA DOS SANTOS—THE MAN WITH TWO PENISES

Juan Baptista dos Santos was the man with two penises (and a third leg). He was born in Portugal in 1843, and while he turned down a considerable amount of money to appear in a traveling circus as a freak, he did tour hospitals demonstrating his unusual deformity to medical congresses. In addition to his two penises and three legs, he had three scrotums and three pairs of testicles (though one pair retracted into his body in his youth).

8 MYRTLE CORBIN—THE FOUR-LEGGED LADY
Josephine Myrtle Corbin was born in Tennessee in 1868. She suffered from a disorder called dipygus, which means she had two pelvises side by side. Each pelvis had a pair of legs; the extra pair was believed to have been from a twin that didn't split correctly. The center legs were much smaller than the outer legs, and while they functioned they weren't strong enough for walking. Despite her disorder, Corbin had five children.

7 MADEMOISELLE GABRIELLE—THE HALF LADY
Gabrielle Fuller was a Swiss-born woman who joined the circus at the 1900 Paris Exhibition. She spent many years traveling with the Ringling Brothers and also made appearances at the Coney Island Dreamland show. She was born with a perfectly formed upper body, and nothing else.

6 MARY ANN BEVAN—THE UGLIEST WOMAN
Mary Ann Bevan (née Webster) had the unfortunate honor of being labeled the ugliest woman because she suffered from a form of gigantism. However, despite her unpleasant appearance, she managed to marry and have four children. She died in 1914.

5 MARTIN LAURELLO—THE HUMAN OWL
Martin Emmerling, whose stage name was Martin Laurello, was called the human owl because he could turn his head 180 degrees (meaning that he could literally look behind himself). He worked for many sideshows over the years, and appeared in the Ripley's shows right up until 1945.

4 MADAME CLOFULLIA—THE BEARDED LADY OF GENEVA
Madame Clofullia was a hairy woman who had a two-inch beard by the time she was eight years old. By 14, she was touring Europe as a sideshow attraction. For publicity reasons, she shaped her beard like that of Emperor Napoleon III, and he gave her a diamond out of admiration.

3 WANG—THE HUMAN UNICORN
Wang's fame comes entirely from a single snapshot taken of him by a Russian banker who was traveling in China in the 1930s. Wang was perfectly

normal except for an extraordinarily large horn growing from his head. Large cash rewards were offered in exchange for any information on him, as Robert Ripley wanted him to travel in his sideshow, but no one ever came forward.

2 LIONEL—THE LION-FACED BOY
Stephan Bibrowsky was born in 1890 in Poland. He had a rare disorder that caused his entire body to be covered with six-inch-long fur. He became famous throughout Europe because of his disorder. He enjoyed his fame and loved to demonstrate to people that he was a highly cultured young man who spoke five languages fluently.

1 ELLA HARPER—THE CAMEL GIRL
This is the text from Ella Harper's pitch card, which was an advertising flyer for attractions at a sideshow:

> I am called the camel girl because my knees turn backward. I can walk best on my hands and feet as you see me in the picture. I have traveled considerably in the show business for the past four years and now, this is 1886 and I intend to quit the show business and go to school and fit myself for another occupation.

10 BIZARRE GOVERNMENT PUBLICITY STUNTS

10 THE PRODUCTION OF *MONGOL*
Kazakhstan had slipped the world's attention before a certain Borat Sagdiyev gave the world an insider's scoop of his country. Needless to say, this infused a sense of patriotism in the Kazakhs, who used the same medium, albeit far more conventionally, to produce *Mongol*, an Oscar-nominated movie depicting the life of Genghis Khan. By adopting Khan as their own, Kazakhs

created a hero with whom they could counter the liabilities that Borat had heaped on their country. The only problem was that more people (a lot more) watched Sacha Baron Cohen's *Borat* than saw *Mongol*.

9 THE TAEPODONG ISSUE

Madeleine Albright was witness to a publicity stunt of gigantic proportions when she visited Kim Jong Il in Pyongyang, North Korea. Kim emerged with her at a stadium spectacle where tens of thousands of placard-flipping North Koreans converged to depict the testing of the Taepodong missile. Kim Jong Il rumored to have quipped to Albright, then secretary of state, that the performance was a goodwill gesture with the aim of assuring America that the 1998 missile test would be the last ever. For all the effort of those who made the event possible, that promise was never kept and the reclusive North Korean leader returned to his old ways.

8 BOIGANY'S CITY

Not satisfied with the existing capital of Abidjan, Felix Boigany shifted the seat of government of the Ivory Coast to Yamoussoukro. He built the Basilica of Our Lady of Peace at a whopping cost of $300 million in an effort to immortalize himself. To that end, Felix ordered a stained-glass window of his image to be placed beside a gallery of similar artwork depicting Jesus and the apostles. However, his people were hardly impressed, as the country's foreign debt doubled with this expenditure.

7 EVITA PERON'S REPÚBLICA DE LOS NIÑOS

When Evita Peron died of cancer at the tender age of 33, her legacy was assured in the annals of Argentinean folklore. Her titles included Vice President of Argentina, First Lady, Spiritual Leader of the Nation of Argentina, and the founder of the Children's Republic. Children's Republic? The República de los Niños was a miniature city where all the buildings were scaled down to the size of a ten-year-old child. It included a Parliament, Palace of Justice, Government House, and buildings for military forces all in children's sizes so that young citizens could witness a "real republic." It was a well-intentioned project, but it seems Peron forgot that ten-year-old kids are more inclined to show interest in games rather than the intricacies of political life.

6 BAHRAIN EMBRACES MICHAEL JACKSON

Having been acquitted of child molestation charges in 2005, Michael Jackson wanted a break. So, what did he do? He simply hopped on a plane and went to the Kingdom of Bahrain. Jackson was received by Abdullah Hamad Al Khalifa, the crown prince, who lavished him with thousands of dollars and boundless attention, even going so far as calling the pop star his "brother." However, two months later, Jackson—being Jackson—decided that his Middle East sojourn should come to an end. A couple of years later, the prince sued him for seven million dollars, and the "close, personal relationship" that he enjoyed with MJ was let out in the open.

5 BEIJING'S SPITTING CLAMPDOWN

In an effort to raise the "cultural and ethical standards" of Beijing before the 2008 Olympics, authorities went on a quest to root out spitting in public areas. The Beijing Capital Ethics Development Office declared spitting the city's number-one bad habit and proceeded to impose fines on those who disregarded the new law banning it. Hundreds of uniformed "mucus monitors" were installed to patrol the streets and hand out free spitting bags to those who could not control themselves. Chinese authorities left no stone unturned in promoting their idea of the perfect Olympics, assuring prospective foreign visitors a phlegm-free Games. It's amazing what Communist countries can achieve, isn't it?

4 ENVER HOXHA'S BUNKERS

If his close relationship with Joseph Stalin weren't bizarre enough, Enver Hoxha built 750,000 to 1 million bunkers to convince his fellow Albanians that the country could defend itself from foreign invasions. For a small country with a population of about one million people, these pillboxes, constructed at "strategic areas," served as a psychological bulwark against the nation's seemingly ubiquitous enemies. When Communism was toppled and the world got more access to this Eastern European nation, it became clear that Albania was not the developed country that its leader had claimed it to be. As for the bunkers, it was determined that it took the same amount of money to build two of them as it would take to construct a two-bedroom apartment.

3 CHESS CITY IN KALMYKIA

Kalmykia is a remote republic in the southwest of the Russian federation. It would have gone unnoticed were it not for its enterprising president, Kirsan Ilyumzhinov, whose love for chess and acute public relations expertise have transformed the republic into an eerie example of post-Soviet anachronism. Ilyumzhinov, being the president of the World Chess Federation, took up the task of promoting chess by building a city dedicated to the sport. With a California-style housing development rising from the parched brown steppes of the capital city of Elista and a large domelike monument where chess masters practice their trade, the president has more than fulfilled his duties to chess' governing body. However, there's one small problem: 300,000 Kalmykians live in poverty, and the source of funding for the construction of the chess city is… not divulged.

2 IDI AMIN ASSUMES HIS TITLES

Idi Amin Dada was a character beyond comparison. His size and manner made him a cartoonist's dream, and he went out of his way to provide enough material all throughout his reign. His long trail of actions, including the expulsion of Asians from Uganda and the nationalization of 85 British-owned companies, proved to be unacceptable to the former colonizers, who broke off diplomatic relationships with the eccentric general. Losing had never occurred to Amin, and he promptly conferred on himself the title of "His Excellency, President for Life, Field Marshall Al Hadji Doctor, Idi Amin Dada, VC, DSO, CBE, MC." He might have been the Conqueror the British Empire (CBE) in his own mind, but MC? Some thought it meant "Mental Case."

1 TINA TURNER TURNS WHITE

Courtesy of the South African government, Tina Turner became a white person for a brief period. Well, almost. When the apartheid government of South Africa realized the importance of black musicians playing for black audiences, they roped in a host of African American musicians, including Clarence Carter, Curtis Mayfield, Millie Jackson, and Tina Turner, to perform at open-air stadiums. They thought it would reiterate their position on racial segregation, and they proclaimed the artists to be "honorary whites," which gave them access to hotels, restaurants, and other facilities otherwise prohibited to ordinary blacks. Subsequent events proved that this publicity stunt was simply an attempt to appease South Africa's black community, but it will always be remembered for the lengths to which politicians will stoop to retain power.

10 BIZARRE MODERN PARANORMAL PHENOMENA

10 LITTLE CREATURES

Ever since the discovery that a Hobbit-like race actually once existed on Earth, science has been re-examining the possibility that other reported little people may not be entirely mythical. Putting science aside, there have always been those who insist that small humanoid creatures exist among us. Reports have been made of gnome- or elflike creatures sometimes spotted unawares in remote locations. They're often described as being no more than nine inches tall, though with the physical features of a humanoid. Some of them are said to be very hairy.

In Mexico and the Caribbean, *duendes* are small gnomelike creatures that sometimes invade the world of normal human beings, either to steal food or for more sinister reasons. Either because of their utter strangeness or some power they possess, *duendes* have been said to shock witnesses almost into paralysis until they make their escape.

In Iceland, belief that elves and other little creatures have real abodes beneath the Earth is very strong. People who construct malls and large buildings are sometimes physically impeded from disturbing areas where these little creatures are believed to live so as not to incur their wrath. Many Icelanders claim their beliefs are based on actual sightings of these beings. So can we dismiss the elves, gnomes, fairies, or whatever we like to call the little creatures we grew up reading about in fairy tales as mere myth? Or are they based on very tangible creatures that still exist and are sometimes inadvertently witnessed today?

9 GIANT RAPTORS

Raptors are birds of prey that hunt for food or feed on carrion. They are usually larger than average birds and have a specialized physiology, such as powerful beaks and talons, that helps them seize and tear apart their prey. Eagles, vultures, and falcons are all considered types of raptors. In recent times, however, sightings of giant raptorlike birds have been reported. Disturbed witnesses often describe a raucous cry emitted by the birds. Reports of wingspan averages have varied between 12 and 18 feet, with the birds' height being estimated at around 3 to 5 feet. Many reports describe the birds' prehistoric appearance, as well as the scaly, lizardlike skin on their legs. Giant raptors have been spotted in places such as Kansas and Oklahoma, usually in wooded areas or near canyons. Witnesses have reported the creatures having a stench of rotted meat, which would be understandable given their diet. Raptors have been seen by single witnesses as well as by fairly sizable groups of five or more persons. Like the elusive Big Foot, conclusive evidence of the raptors' existence in our modern world is yet to be obtained. Are they real remnants from an age past that have somehow survived in small numbers today? Are they all just "misinterpretations" of already known large birds? The questions, and the random sightings, continue.

8 DOPPELGANGERS

An enigmatic German-derived word, a doppelganger is basically a person's exact double. Apparently, they have been seen since early times, and are sometimes known as "fetches." In the modern era, paranormal message boards have several posts from persons claiming to have seen someone in one place, only to meet them later and realize the first sighting was impossible.

One woman looking through a large picture window clearly saw her husband being dropped off at home by a coworker. She went to the door to let him in, only to find no sign of either person or the car outside. Her husband arrived home hours later, and confirmed that at the time she thought she saw them, he and his colleague were still four hours away from home. One person was told that he was "heard" arriving home with a friend five minutes before he actually did so. When he and his partner actually did get home, his waiting friends said their arrival sounded exactly the same, and that made the same noises and even uttered the same words that were heard the first time. Weird, yet apparently not so uncommon.

A few people even claim to have undeniably seen themselves, even wearing the same clothing, stating that the double looked equally astonished at the sighting. In folklore, seeing one's doppelganger is a harbinger of one's death. Seeing someone else's "fetch" was also said to portend death. Such notable persons as Percy Shelley and Abraham Lincoln reported having doppelganger experiences. Can these events all be explained as tricks of the subconscious mind or the easily misled eye?

7 TIME SLIPS

Time slips and lost time are unnerving experiences. They have been surmised to be extraterrestrial encounters, dimensional shifts, or even brain strokes. The most disturbing reports are those corroborated by more than one person experiencing the same impossible time jump. Characteristically, time slips occur when someone sets out on a journey, long or short, along a familiar path that's clearly defined and should take a specific time to complete. The journey appears normal, except at the end the person realizes they have covered a number of miles in an impossibly short space of time. They are unsettled to find themselves at their destination sometimes hours earlier than is possible. There have even been cases of "time loss," when a person set out on a journey, traveled normally, yet arrived at their destination hours later than is explainable. Where did the missing time go? Usually it's only upon arrival that the time discrepancy is noticed. Are there dimensional "warps" we sometimes inadvertently pass through? Could physics someday confirm and explain the existence of these time slips? Enough people continue to have these experiences to justify scientific investigation into this phenomenon.

6 THE *CHUPACABRA*

The *chupacabra* has been variously described as a doglike creature with long canine teeth. It was first spotted in Puerto Rico in the 1990s and has since been sighted in the Americas and Mexico. Sometimes witnesses report that the animal has a kangaroolike gait. Its name is derived from the Spanish words for "goat sucker." This refers to its horrifying ability to creep into livestock farms at night and literally suck the blood of animals until they die. Obviously, the similarity to vampire lore and the possibility of the animal attacking humans lead to panic in communities. What is this weird creature? Is it really a new animal, or, as has been suggested, some kind of starved, mutated coyote? Alleged *chupacabra* carcasses have been found and examined, but no real conclusions were drawn. Reports of exsanguinated livestock corpses, however, appear to have increased in recent times. Many farmers have adopted armed nighttime watches, hoping to kill this weird predator before it eventually becomes bolder.

5 PANIC IN THE WOODS

The woods are a mysterious place, full of unseen life and fraught with danger for the unwary. Forests are places of menace in fairy and folk tales. But in our enlightened modern times, could nature inspire sheer, unreasoned panic? There are those whose experiences make them certain that nature has an intelligence—one that doesn't always welcome humans. PANic in the woods has been associated with the mythological Greek god Pan, protector of wild places, whose unseen presence inspires causeless terror. Victims experience a feeling that there is a powerful, sinister force nearby and sense imminent danger. This usually leads the person to flee the area, desperately seeking out civilization. One curiously common characteristic of PANic is that people often describe the woods becoming quiet and strange just before the fear starts, except for an unusual, escalating, buzzing sound. At least one article on the phenomenon called "Landscapes of Panic" has been written for *Fortean Times* magazine by Patrick Harpur. Many other alleged actual experiences of panic have been posted on paranormal forums. Is there really a spirit of the woods that shuns humanity? And if so, is PANic its way of warning us—and fighting back?

4 DOG-HEADED MEN

Encounters with men with the heads of dogs have been reported since ancient times. Cynocephali were supposed to be a race living in Africa that cannibalized humans. But seeing such beings in modern times would seem incredible, yet there have been increasing reports of these creatures. Most sightings occur at night, though some have happened during daylight hours. Bizarrely, some people have reported the men indifferently walking along main roads, attired normally, except they have the head of a dog. Most witnesses insist the head is too real in appearance and lifelike motion to be a mask. Some more sinister reports claim the creature has been caught unawares lurking around at night near woodlands or the darkness of a backyard. One nighttime jogger reported that a dog-headed man kept pace with him as he ran across a field, staying alongside until the petrified runner finally made it to his well-lit doorway. There was one report of a dog-headed man seen through a window from outside a house, lurking near the kitchen. Other cases describe dog-headed men that stand outside homes at night and look in through windows.

3 BLACK-STICK MEN

The black-stick man is another entity encountered in modern society. Not to be confused with shadow people (number 2 on this list), incredibly, he is even stranger. Stick men are supposed to look like completely black, thin, stick-figure drawings. They have been reported as between average height to impossibly tall. Their heads are just black circles with no discernable facial features. They are totally two dimensional without any depth. Usually they've been sighted walking along roads at night or at transitional times, such as twilight or just before dawn. Bizarrely, some people have reported them wearing what appears to be a top hat. Their walk is described as a weird "lolloping" gait. They're surprised when actually seen, and have followed unfortunate witnesses on occasion. Their pace remains leisurely as they approach. Obviously, to be pursued by such an otherworldly creature would be anything but pleasant, and those who have encountered them have been understandably terrified. So far, however, apart from being creepily frightening, they have done no physical harm and ultimately just disappear.

2 SHADOW PEOPLE

What are shadow people? No one seems to know for sure, even as sightings of these entities continue to be reported. Generally shadow people appear as dark, silhouetted figures, usually male, that suddenly walk across

hallways, through walls, appear in rooms only to disappear again, and sometimes stand looking at a sleeping person, only to eventually vanish once the sleeper awakens. They have no purpose and don't seem to be harbingers of anything. Are they from another dimension? The afterlife? Whatever they are, they've scared enough people to have drawn increased attention to their shadowy selves.

1 BLACK-EYED KIDS

It started in 1998 when journalist Brian Bethel gave an account of being approached by two boys as he entered his car. The boys allegedly asked him for a lift. He described experiencing a sudden feeling of fear and panic, while at the same time having an overwhelming urge to open the door for the boys.

He then noticed their eyes—they were entirely coal black, with no whites visible. Bethel drove away in fear even as the teens became more insistent. Since his story, several reports of encounters with black-eyed children have been recorded. In one case, a woman claimed they asked to be let into her home, and became agitated when she refused. Their main characteristics are their completely black eyes, their tendency to inspire sudden fear and panic, and their need to be invited into a person's space.

10 BIZARRE ENIGMAS THAT DEFY EXPLANATION

10 ICE WOMAN

Nature performs many astonishing feats, yet it's a different matter altogether when we human beings push past the boundaries of normal. It was a viciously cold morning in Lengby, Minnesota, when a man discovered his 19-year-old neighbor, Jean Hilliard, lying in the snow. Her whole body was frozen solid from the night before, when temperatures dropped 25 degrees below zero. Apparently, Jean was trying desperately to reach her neighbor for help when her car skidded off the road. When her body was discovered, she was immediately sent to the local hospital, where her condition stunned the doctors. One of the nurses said that Jean was "so cold, it was like reaching into a freezer" and that "her face was absolutely white, just this ashen, death look." Jean was also seriously frostbitten, and none of her limbs would bend or move.

The hospital staff did everything possible, yet the situation was dire. Even if Jean were to regain consciousness, she would more than likely have severe brain damage, and she was frostbitten to the degree that both her legs would have to be amputated. Her family gathered in prayer, hoping for a miracle. Two hours later, Jean went into violent convulsions and regained consciousness. She was perfectly fine, mentally and physically, although a bit confused. To the doctors' amazement, even the frostbite was slowly disappearing from her legs. She was released from the hospital 49 days later without even losing a single finger and sporting only minor scars.

9 IRON PILLAR OF DELHI

Iron, the king of metal, is used for just about everything, from the skeleton of your house to the chains on your bike. Unfortunately, iron can never escape its destiny to slowly transform into rust, with the exception of this phenomenal structure: meet the Iron Pillar of Delhi. Standing in at 23 feet tall and weighing more than six tons, this iron giant has managed to defeat corrosion for over 1600 years! But how can something that's 98 percent iron withstand decay for over a millennium? Scientists have found the answer to that question, but how ancient ironsmiths discovered the fact so long ago still amazes archaeologists today.

8 CARROLL A. DEERING

About 50 years after the mysterious disappearance of the crew of the *Mary Celeste*, which some call the greatest maritime mystery of all time, a similar event occurred when the schooner *Carroll A. Deering* was spotted around the coast of North Carolina on January 31, 1921. When rescue ships finally reached her, they discovered to their shock that the Deering's entire crew was missing. Though evidence in the galley suggested that food was being prepared for the following day, nothing else was found of the crew. Eerily enough, no personal effects, no ship logs, and no traces were left behind, much like the case of the *Mary Celeste*. Theories have pointed to paranormal activity because the *Carroll A. Deering* was in the region that is today known as the Bermuda Triangle. Others have concluded it was the work of pirates or of Russians attempting to steal the schooner's cargo.

7 HUTCHISON EFFECT

The Hutchison Effect refers to the number of eerie phenomena that occurred when inventor John Hutchison attempted to replicate a few of inventor Nikola Tesla's experiments. Some of the strange events witnessed include levitation, fusion of objects completely different in matter (such as wood and metal), and disappearances of some smaller objects. Even stranger is that after his experiment, Hutchison was unable to repeat the project with the same results. This experiment was so popular it even sparked the interest of NASA and the U.S. military, both whom have failed to reproduce the Hutchison Effect.

6 FACES OF BELMEZ
For over 20 years, the faces of Belmez are strange stains that the Pereira family keeps finding on the walls of their home. The faces can resemble males or females, and they also arrive with different expressions every time. Strangely, the faces only stop at the house for a quick visit before disappearing. Studies have been performed on the house to discover what was causing the faces to spontaneously pop up. One investigation exhumed and removed a human body from under the house, but that still didn't stop the faces from making appearances. Several hypotheses have been formed to help explain this strange recurring phenomenon, but overall, no conclusions have been reached.

5 DISAPPEARING LAKE
On May 2007, a lake in Patagonia, Chile, literally disappeared, leaving behind a 100-foot-deep pit, icebergs, and dry soil. However, this wasn't a small lake or pond—it was an astonishing five miles long! The last time geologists saw the lake in March 2007, they detected nothing strange about it. However, something happened during the two-month span that not only caused the lake to vanish, but also reduced a river that flowed from the lake to a tiny stream. Geologists were puzzled as to why a lake of that size would simply cease to exist. Perhaps, they suggested, an earthquake drained the lake, yet there were no reports of any quakes in that particular area during spring. Meanwhile, UFO enthusiasts concluded that a spaceship drained it. The mystery remains unsolved.

4 RAINING BLOBS
The townspeople of Oakville, Washington, were in for a surprise on August 7, 1994. Instead of their usual downpour of rain, the inhabitants of the small town witnessed countless gelatinous blobs falling from the sky. Once the globs fell, almost everyone in Oakville started to develop severe flulike symptoms that lasted anywhere from seven weeks to three months. Finally, after exposure to the goo caused his mother to fall ill, one resident sent a sample of the blobs for testing. What the technicians discovered was shocking—the globs contained human white blood cells. The substance was then brought to the Washington

State Department of Health for further analysis. In another startling reveal, they discovered that the blobs had two types of bacteria, one of which is found in the human digestive system. However, no one could successfully identify the blobs or how they were connected to the mysterious sickness that plagued the town.

3 THE BLACK HELICOPTER

In May 7, 1994, a black helicopter chased a teenage boy for 45 minutes in Harrahan, Louisiana. Unable to run any farther, the terrified boy explained that the helicopter's passengers descended from the vehicle and pointed weapons at him. To this day, the boy has no idea why he was targeted by the helicopter or why, mysteriously, they let him go. One week later, people traveling in a car near Washington had a similar experience when they, too, were pursued by the helicopter. Unable to escape, they witnessed men in black uniforms coming down from the aircraft on a rope ladder bearing weapons. However, the drivers were let off free, much to their confusion. Black helicopters feature much in UFO-lore and while there are simple explanations for some appearances, others (such as these two) remain unsolved.

2 ANIMALS IN STONE

There are several documented cases in which frogs, toads, and other small animals have been found concealed within solid stone—alive. There are other instances, too, of workers who cut down trees and found hoards of frogs inside. Weirder still, people have found creatures within not just natural formations such as rocks and trees, but manmade locations. In 1976, a Texas construction crew was breaking up concrete they had set over a year before. To their disbelief, they found a live green turtle within the concrete, in an air pocket that matched the shape of the small reptile. If, somehow, it got in when the concrete was poured a year earlier, how did it manage to survive during that time? After all, there were no signs of holes or cracks in the concrete through which the turtle could have entered.

1 DONNIE DECKER

Dubbed the Rain Boy in 1983, Donnie Decker was visiting his friend's house when he abruptly went into a trancelike state. Immediately after, the ceiling began to drip water and a mist filled the room. His friends called the landlord, who was alarmed by what he saw. Some time later, Donnie was at a restaurant with different companions when rain started pouring down on their heads. The restaurant owner immediately forced him out. Years later, due to a petty crime, Donnie was put in jail, where he caused chaos when rain started to pour down in his cell. After angry inmates complained, Donnie explained that he could make it rain when he wanted to, and he proved his point by dumping rain on the jailor. Eventually, he was released from prison and found a job as a cook at a local restaurant. His present whereabouts are unknown, as is the cause of the mysterious rain.

10 ROADS THAT WILL SCARE YOU STUPID

10 A229 FROM SUSSEX TO KENT, ENGLAND

"In November 1992 Ian Sharpe was heading up the A229 from Sussex into Kent. A girl in white with 'beautiful eyes' stepped in front of his car and she disappeared under the front wheels. In total despair Sharpe stopped the car believing he had killed her and was powerless to help. On leaving the car he found nothing there. No girl, no body, no white dress—or even any wildlife; a fox a badger or a rabbit. Not a sausage... I think you get the point." (*BBC Strange Stories: Britain's Most Haunted Road?*)

The local police are not strangers to calls of people plowing into pedestrians, or more specifically, a woman in white, only to lose track of the body. The ghost lady is generally thought to be Judith Langham, who was tragically killed in a collision of her wedding day, still in her dress.

9 PALI HIGHWAY, HONOLULU, HAWAII

According to legend, if you dare to travel this highway, don't bring pork unless you want angry, hungry spirits to break down your car. Or it could be Pele, but who's keeping track? And while you are in the area, look up Old Pali Road so you can say "aloha" to the ghost girl with half of her face missing. Ah, paradise!

8 REFORMATORY ROAD, MANSFIELD, OHIO

Phoebe Wise was an eccentric hermit. In the early 20th century, she lived alone, was unmarried, and was generally just odd. As the youngest of eight children, she inherited her family's house on Reformatory Road after her parents died, along with a few thousand dollars (a pretty good sum, if not filthy stinking rich for the time). She also sold some land for undisclosed amounts of money. Long story short, rumors spread of a hidden fortune. Some men broke in, tied her up, tortured her for her loot, and got very little to show for it (turns out, no treasure). They threatened to kill her if she left her house, and then they booked it. She had a hard time dragging herself out to telegraph the police, considering the burglars had scorched her feet with a torch. Phoebe survived and continued to live alone until 1933. Now she is said to walk the road, patrolling to keep an eye out for unwary burglars trying to ransack her home for lost treasure.

7 MARY ANGELA ROAD, MEMPHIS, TENNESSEE

Mary Angela Road is a lonely backwoods road that leads to the source of its legends: Voodoo Village. A small compound said to host many weird rituals and animal sacrifices, Voodoo Village is certainly an unsettling place to be. It's disputed how evil this place is, and many rumors probably come from local residents' ignorance, but between the weird, colorful paintings there and the numerous unexplainable statues, it isn't hard to see why people would think it's haunted! The local inhabitants despise the name Voodoo Village, and will definitely get angry if you take pictures there. Walsh Harris, founder of the community, used to belong to the Masonic Lodge, and much of the artwork there pertains to Masonic symbols and scripture. It's a weird place for sure. Don't expect to be greeted with a smile, and don't be too surprised if they block you in with a truck so you can't leave...

6 PACHECO PASS, CALIFORNIA

This road is notorious for numerous car accidents, as well as for its ghosts! Many a sleepy driver has met an untimely end on the road, but many of its ghost stories aren't even related to the accidents. A "time warp" of sorts is said to occur on Pacheco Pass, accounting for many reports of "lost time" and strange lights that illuminate the sky, and men in Old West garb and a stagecoach make the occasional appearance here. And if that weren't enough, the nearby San Luis Reservoir is said to host a mysterious light beneath the water. Side effects of driving on the road may include overwhelming feelings of dread or impending doom, unexplainable sadness, extreme apprehension, or diarrhea. (One of those is a joke—try to guess which.)

5 BALETE DRIVE, PHILIPPINES

According to legend, balete trees, which are numerous along this road, attract ghosts and other paranormal entities. You would be wise to keep your eyes up front while driving there. A glance in your rear-view mirror may make your stomach turn with a truly disturbing surprise. A lady in a white dress will have hitched a ride with you; she'll have long, flowing hair, and—no face. The last thing you want to do is check for cars behind you and be greeted with the silent likes of *that*. And if No-Face decides not to take a ride with you, you can still admire the road's three haunted mansions, whose previous owners were simply too attached to let them go.

4 SWEET HOLLOW ROAD, MELVILLE, NEW YORK

The woods surrounding this road, and the road itself, are rumored to be quite heavily haunted. A few pictures from local ghost hunters have turned up some very odd images. It isn't hard to see why! Three teenagers, who were apparently in some kind of bad way in their lives, decided to commit suicide by hanging themselves from the overpass. Some say you can still see their bodies swaying in the breeze on cool, dark nights. Mary, a nurse from the nearby hospital, wanders the road, perhaps to try and resuscitate the deceased teenagers. And if that isn't all bad enough, don't get pulled over there: the cop who routinely patrols the area isn't alive. The good news is that he won't write you a citation, he'll just silently stare at you with blood running down his shoulders. After he feels you've gotten the point, he'll turn around, exposing the gaping exit wound in the back of his head where the fatal bullet left his skull.

3 LAWLER FORD ROAD, ST. LOUIS, MISSOURI

This incredibly narrow road (nicknamed Zombie Road) carves a lonely path through two miles of woods, only to dead end at what used to be a rock quarry. The road soon became all but abandoned, and the road sign has been replaced by a chained gate. Among the resident freaks are a young boy who plummeted to his death from the nearby bluffs; a man struck and killed by a train; a crazy old lady who yells at you from her house at the end of the road; Native American spirits roaming the woods; and plenty of Satan worshippers. The name of the road, however, wasn't derived from these weirdoes. Credit for the spooky nickname goes to a mysterious killer known as The Zombie. He would wait in his old shack for lovers and partygoers to show up and attack them. Perhaps he isn't gone—reports of visitors disappearing aren't uncommon.

2 EL CAMINO DE LA MUERTA, BOLIVIA

This is the only road on this list where its ghosts take a backseat to the road itself! And yes, the name translates to "The Road of Death." Appropriate. The road is an incredibly dangerous winding highway that cuts through the mountains of Bolivia. Think 3000-foot drop-off with no guardrail, passing buses and trucks despite this, and the road being littered with debris and rock from the hillside. It has its fair share of ghosts, but if I were you, I'd be keeping my eyes on the road ahead, rather than scanning for spirits.

1 SHADES OF DEATH ROAD, NEW JERSEY

If this list were solely based on names, Shades of Death would surely still be number one. Shades of Death can't be too bad, but it runs right by...Ghost Lake? Seriously? Somebody was just demanding this place be haunted! And haunted it is, according to most. Between a murderer (or murderers?), a violent gang of criminals, and a mysterious plague, this road has been no stranger to death. Some say that at times, the population of malaria-carrying insects was so high that victims were laid out on the roadside in hopes of a traveling doctor happening by and curing them. Ghost Lake, home to mysterious columns of mist and a haunted cabin, is the most popular stop on the drive. If you're lucky (or unlucky) enough, you may just catch a faint glimpse of a murder victim out for a stroll in the fog. Yes, New Jersey wins it again, I know. But Bolivia wasn't in it to win it because it wasn't so much the scary ghosts on El Camino de la Muerta as much as the scary road planning! And let's be honest, between the stories, the lake, the name, and the history, Shades of Death was a worthy contender.

20 WEIRD SUPERSTITIONS

20 A BIRD IN THE HOUSE IS A SIGN OF A DEATH.

19 A LOAF OF BREAD SHOULD NEVER BE TURNED UPSIDE DOWN AFTER A SLICE HAS BEEN CUT FROM IT.

18 NEVER TAKE A BROOM ALONG WHEN YOU MOVE. THROW IT OUT AND BUY A NEW ONE.

17 IF THE FIRST BUTTERFLY YOU SEE IN THE YEAR IS WHITE, YOU'LL HAVE GOOD LUCK ALL YEAR.

16 IF A BLACK CAT WALKS TOWARD YOU, IT BRINGS GOOD FORTUNE, BUT IF IT WALKS AWAY, IT TAKES THE GOOD LUCK WITH IT.

15 AN ACORN AT THE WINDOW WILL KEEP LIGHTNING OUT.

14 A DOG HOWLING AT NIGHT WHEN SOMEONE IN THE HOUSE IS SICK IS A BAD OMEN.

13 IT'S BAD LUCK TO LEAVE A HOUSE THROUGH A DIFFERENT DOOR THAN THE ONE USED TO COME INTO IT.

12 A HORSESHOE HUNG IN THE BEDROOM WILL KEEP NIGHTMARES AWAY.

11 IF YOU CATCH A FALLING LEAF ON THE FIRST DAY OF AUTUMN, YOU WON'T CATCH A COLD ALL WINTER.

10 IF A MIRROR IN THE HOUSE FALLS AND BREAKS BY ITSELF, SOMEONE IN THE HOUSE WILL DIE SOON.

9 DROPPING AN UMBRELLA ON THE FLOOR MEANS THERE WILL BE A MURDER IN THE HOUSE.

8 ALL WINDOWS SHOULD BE OPENED AT THE MOMENT OF DEATH SO THE DECEASED SOUL CAN LEAVE.

7 IF THE GROOM DROPS THE WEDDING BAND DURING THE CEREMONY, THE MARRIAGE IS DOOMED.

6 TO DREAM OF A LIZARD IS A SIGN THAT YOU HAVE A SECRET ENEMY.

5 IF A FRIEND GIVES YOU A KNIFE, YOU SHOULD GIVE HIM A COIN, OR YOUR FRIENDSHIP WILL SOON BE BROKEN.

4 YOU SHOULD NEVER START A TRIP ON FRIDAY OR YOU WILL MEET MISFORTUNE.

3 DREAMING OF RUNNING IS A SIGN OF A BIG CHANGE IN YOUR LIFE.

2 IF A CLOCK THAT HASN'T BEEN WORKING SUDDENLY CHIMES, THERE WILL BE A DEATH IN THE FAMILY.

1 IT'S BAD LUCK TO LIGHT THREE CIGARETTES WITH THE SAME MATCH.

20 FANTASTICALLY NAMED PEOPLE

20 CANAAN BANANA

Canaan Banana served as the first president of Zimbabwe from April 18, 1980, until December 31, 1987. A Methodist minister, he held the largely ceremonial office of the presidency while his eventual successor, Robert Mugabe, served as prime minister. Banana was later convicted on charges of sodomy and imprisoned. He died 2003.

19 PRAISE-GOD BAREBONE

Praise-God Barebone was an English leather seller and radical preacher. He is best known for being elected to the Nominated Assembly of the English republic in 1653. The Assembly was known commonly as Barebone's Parliament due to its domination by religious and political eccentrics such as Praise-God, who was a Fifth Monarchist and believed in the imminent end of the world and return of Jesus. He died in 1679.

18 WALTER RUSSELL BRAIN

Walter Russell Brain was an eminent neurologist who authored the standard work on the subject, *Brain's Diseases of the Nervous System*, and was also the long-time editor of the neurological medical journal *Brain*. He was knighted in 1952 and made Baron Brain in 1962. He died in 1966.

17 MARC BREEDLOVE

Marc Breedlove is a professor of neuroscience at Michigan State University. He is known for his work on the study of sexual attraction and sexual behavior. His most influential work was in discovering that lesbians have a more masculine digit ratio than heterosexual women, a finding that has been replicated in his and many other labs and which indicates that lesbians, on average, are exposed to more prenatal testosterone than are straight women.

16 THURSDAY OCTOBER CHRISTIAN

Thursday October Christian was the first son of Fletcher Christian, leader of the mutiny on the *Bounty*, and his Tahitian wife, Maimiti. He was conceived on Tahiti and was the first child born on the Pitcairn Islands after the mutineers took refuge there. Born on Thursday, October 14, he was given his unusual name because Fletcher Christian wanted his son to have "no name that will remind me of England." He died in 1831.

15 THOMAS CRAPPER

Crapper was a noted English plumber who made significant contributions toward the improvement of the flushing toilet. He held many toilet-related patents, including the floating ballcock, and founded the plumbing company Crapper and Co. He died in 1910.

14 PRINCE OCTOPUS DZANIE
Dzanie is an amateur boxer from Ghana who competed in the 2008 Summer Olympics and the 2006 Commonwealth Games.

13 ARGELICO FUCKS
Fucks is a Brazilian professional soccer player. He won the Rio Grande do Sul State league, the Brazilian Cup, the Brazilian Champions Cup, the Conmebol Cup, plus the Portuguese league, cup, and supercup. He also represented Brazil internationally at the under-20 level, winning both the South American Championship and the Youth World Cup.

12 LEARNED HAND
Learned Hand was an influential United States judge and judicial philosopher. He served on the Southern District Court of New York and the United States Court of

Appeals for the Second Circuit. Hand has reportedly been quoted more often than any other lower-court judge by legal scholars and by the Supreme Court of the United States. He was a strong supporter of civil rights, civil liberties, and judicial restraint. He was an expert in statutory law in patents, torts, and antitrust. His writings remain admired in the history of legal literature. He died in 1961.

11 IMA HOGG
Ima Hogg, known as the First Lady of Texas, was an American philanthropist, patron, and collector of the arts, and one of the most respected women in Texas during the 20th century. She received an honorary doctorate in fine arts from Southwestern University and was a large contributor to Houston's Museum of Fine Arts. Very wealthy due to her family's oil business, Hogg founded the Houston Child Guidance Center, which provides counseling for disturbed children and their families. She also established the Hogg Foundation for Mental Health at the University of Texas at Austin in 1940. Hogg successfully ran for a seat on the Houston School Board in 1943, where she worked to remove gender and race as criteria for determining pay and established art education programs for black students. Hogg never married and died in 1975.

10 RUSTY KUNTZ

Kuntz is a former Major League Baseball player and the first-base coach for the Kansas City Royals. He was part of the Detroit Tigers team that defeated the San Diego Padres in the 1984 World Series.

9 CHUCK LONG

Chuck Long is the head football coach at San Diego State University. He played quarterback in college at the University of Iowa and professionally with the Detroit Lions and the Los Angeles Rams. He is an inductee of the College Football Hall of Fame.

8 ADOLF LU HITLER MARAK

Adolf Lu Hitler R. Marak is a politician in the state of Meghalaya, India. It may be noted that his name is not particularly curious within Meghalaya, where other local politicians are named Lenin R. Marak, Stalin L. Nangmin, Frankenstein W. Momin, or Tony Curtis Lyngdoh. Hitler Marak told the *Hindustan Times*, "Maybe my parents liked the name and hence christened me Hitler… I am happy with my name, although I don't have any dictatorial tendencies."

7 TEN MILLION

Ten Million was a minor league baseball player who played for various teams in the Northwestern League in the years prior to World War I. He's most famous for appearing on the first set of Obak baseball cards, where his name made him very popular. He died in 1964.

6 CHRIS MONEYMAKER

Chris Moneymaker is an American poker player who won the main event at the 2003 World Series of Poker. His victory is generally credited for being one of the main catalysts for the poker boom in the years following the win. He is one of the most successful touring poker players, with total live tournament winnings of over $2.8 million as of 2010.

5 REVILO OLIVER

Revilo Oliver was an American professor of Classical philology, Spanish, and Italian at the University of Illinois at Urbana-Champaign, who wrote extensively for White Nationalist causes. Oliver also briefly received national notoriety in the 1960s when he published an article following John F. Kennedy's assassination, suggesting that Lee Harvey Oswald was part of a Soviet conspiracy against the United States; in response, he was called to testify before the Warren Commission. As per his family's tradition, his name is a palindrome. He died in 1994.

4 RICHARD PLANTAGENET CAMPBELL TEMPLE-NUGENT-BRYDGES-CHANDOS-GRENVILLE

Richard Plantagenet Campbell Temple-Nugent-Brydges-Chandos-Grenville was a British statesman and close friend of Benjamin Disraeli. His name arose through successive generations of people with double surnames. He died in 1889.

3 PEERLESS PRICE

Peerless Price is a football wide receiver who was originally drafted by the Buffalo Bills in the second round of the 1999 NFL Draft, and has also played for the Atlanta Falcons and the Dallas Cowboys.

2 JAIME SIN

Jaime Sin was a Filipino bishop who later became archbishop of the Roman Catholic Church of the Philippines and was henceforth known as Cardinal Sin. He was only the third native Filipino Archbishop of Manila following centuries of Spanish, American, and Irish episcopacy. Cardinal Sin died in 2005.

1 WOLFGANG WOLF

Wolfgang Wolf is a German soccer coach who once managed Wolfsburg FC.

10 HUMAN CREATIONS ATTRIBUTED TO ALIENS

10 ANCIENT CAVE PAINTINGS

Discoveries of ancient artwork depicting mysterious figures have helped give rise to the "Ancient Astronaut Theory," which claims that alien beings visited prehistoric humans, possibly interacting and sharing knowledge with them. Advocates of this theory usually point to specific examples, such as a particular rock carving in the Val Camonica site in Italy, as well as the Wandjina Petroglyph sites in Australia. Using these examples as evidence reaches unsturdy ground when held up to scientific scrutiny. The popular image of two "alien" figures in Val Camonica was selected from over 200,000 drawings, a pretty clear sign of confirmation bias. Testing at the Wandjina site showed some drawings had been repainted numerous times over, with the images evolving over time at the artists' discretion, rendering the original artwork unknown.

9 EGYPTIAN CARVINGS

According to many UFO enthusiasts, the Temple of Osiris at Abydos in Egypt contains definitive proof of advanced ancient technology. The glyphs seem to include depictions of a helicopter, a jet plane, and some sort of flying saucer. Unfortunately for believers, the glyphs are a result of erosion and actual replacement and recarving of hieroglyphics. The original text is part of the titulary of Seti I, which had been changed to reference Ramses II. Modifying and defacing inscriptions was common in ancient Egypt's history, and in this case yielded some strange-looking results. Even stranger, UFO enthusiasts do not find it odd that there are no other examples like this in the thousands of hieroglyphs discovered elsewhere, nor is there any mention of flying machines anywhere in Egyptian literature.

8 NAZCA LINES

The Nazca Lines are a series of hundreds of ancient geoglyphs located in Peru. These include depictions of animals, birds, fish, and humans, along with simple lines and geometric shapes. Some of them are over 600 feet across and can only be viewed properly from the air. This has led to speculation by the Ancient Astronaut crowd that the ancient Peruvians were capable of advanced flight or were trying to communicate with beings that were. Scientists have claimed the lines were of spiritual significance, possibly pertaining to the availability of water. Also, historians have since re-created similar lines using primitive techniques without aerial assistance.

7 ANTIKYTHERA MECHANISM

The Mechanism is a clocklike instrument from around 85 BC that was discovered in 1900 near Antikythera, Greece. It was used aboard ships as a navigation tool because it could accurately predict locations of the sun, moon, and the five known planets at any given date. The device contained a complex system of gears, built with sophisticated technology that rivaled that of 14th-century clocks. Because of the precision involved in its construction, its almost-exact predictions of cosmic bodies, and the apparent 1300-year gap in technology, UFO enthusiasts have cited the Antikythera Mechanism as evidence of alien contact, as humans could have never figured its complex workings at that time. However, if aliens were to blame, they would have probably told the Greeks about more than just five planets, or at least given them a magnetic compass. Of course, ancient Greek literature mentions mechanisms like this one without mentioning otherworldly visitors.

6 SAQQARA BIRD

Found in a tomb excavation in 1898, the Saqqara Bird has been rumored by believers in the Ancient Astronaut Theory to be evidence of advanced flight in ancient Egypt. Theorists note that the vertical tail of the "bird" resembles a tail on an aircraft, as opposed to the horizontal tail feathers of a real bird. The lack of legs and the angle of the wings has lent to speculation about the design's capability of aerodynamic lift. Tests performed on re-creations of the artifact have shown it to have no aerodynamic properties conductive to flight. Modern scientific theories suggest it's either a religious artifact or even just a simple children's toy.

5 DOGU

Dogu are small humanoid figurines created in prehistoric Japan. Their unusual appearance has been claimed to resemble some sort of space suit, supposedly complete with goggles, armor, and hoses. Adding to the mystery, the *dogu*'s exact purpose remains unclear to historians. Ancient Astronaut proponents tend to ignore the fact that the "goggle-eyed" figures are only one of many types of *dogu*, and that archaeologists have pointed out the similarity of the figure's eyes to Inuit snow goggles. *Dogu* are seldom discovered intact, with limbs having been cut or broken off. This in conjunction with the *dogu*'s exaggerated hips, buttocks, and breasts suggests a possible usage in fertility rituals.

4 CROP CIRCLES

In 1966, a man claimed to have seen a saucer-shaped craft over a field near Tully, Australia. The saucer allegedly left a circular pattern of flattened reeds over the area it had taken off from. Years later, the story inspired two English pranksters to create their own patterns of flattened crops in local fields using simple tools. The fad quickly spread, and crop circles became increasingly complex and intricate. While some believe this is a result of alien technology or the increasingly complex nature of an extraterrestrial "message" to humans, the overwhelming majority of crop circles have been revealed as products of deception, artistic expression, and/or business or tourist interests.

3 NORWEGIAN SPIRAL

In December 2009, an enormous spiral appeared in the sky over northern Norway, leading to speculation of an extraterrestrial visit. The unusual visual phenomenon lasted for two to three minutes, and consisted of a blue light originating on the horizon, which gained altitude, culminating in a large white pinwheel effect before disappearing "into a wormhole." UFO enthusiasts cited this as evidence of extraterrestrial intelligence, while the official explanation from the Russian government wasn't quite as fantastic. Apparently, a Russian military missile test went haywire, and the spiral effect was either the result of a broken stabilizer engine, or the missile circling an airborne misfire beacon until it ran out of fuel and fell into the sea.

2 STONEHENGE

With its enormous stones dating past 2400 BC, the purpose and construction methods of Stonehenge have long been debated. Humans are generally accepted to have built the actual monument, as comparably large stones have been erected in modern times using primitive tools. However, Ancient Astronaut Theorists claim that the positions of the stones confirm an ancient ability to predict eclipses. This ability would mean the ancients had knowledge of lunar nodes, the two points in space where Earth's orbit intersects the moon's. This knowledge wouldn't be possible without extraterrestrial influence—or by generations of astute study that was continuously passed down and improved upon. Modern science obviously leans toward the latter, but it's possible that scientists have also attributed too much astronomical meaning to the placement of the stones.

1 PYRAMIDS OF GIZA

Similar to many other megalithic sites around the world, the Pyramids of Giza have been repeatedly attributed to extraterrestrials, mostly because of the sheer magnitude of their construction. According to believers, the technology needed to build the massive monuments was not available to the Egyptians during the time the pyramids were built. The cuts and placement of the stones are said to be so precise that we cannot re-create them even in modern times. The placement of the pyramids themselves and the measurements contained within are also said to support the Ancient Astronaut Theory, such as the height of the Great Pyramid being an accurate, scaled-down measurement of the distance between Earth and the sun, or the three Giza pyramids correlating with the constellation Orion. Modern measuring techniques have proven hopeful ideas like those to be false, yet the rumors persist. The Pyramids of Giza do display a remarkable knowledge of engineering and measuring for their time, but one would think that if creatures capable of interstellar travel were actually responsible for them, they would have done a better job.

10 BIZARRE AND OBSCURE CONSPIRACY THEORIES

10 THE MAJESTIC TWELVE

In 1947, President Harry Truman supposedly gave an order for a secret committee of world-renowned scientists, generals, and politicians—12 people—to investigate the Roswell Incident. The committee concluded that the incident truly was an extraterrestrial spacecraft that crash-landed, killing all occupants, typically numbered at 3 or 4.

The group, M-12, for short, suggested an executive order to create a military installation solely to contain and study the aliens and their spacecraft, thus creating Area 51. Plenty of images of government correspondence relating directly to this organization are circulating the Internet, including the famous 1947 letter from President Truman authorizing the CIA to create M-12. Skeptics argue that the letter is clearly forged.

This theory of M-12 and the purpose of Area 51 is based primarily on such documentation, all of which may be forged or nonexistent. One excerpt: "The official U.S. Government policy and results of Project Aquarius is [sic] still classified TOP SECRET with no dissemination outside channels and with access restricted to 'MJ TWELVE.'"

The most convincing evidence, however, believed even by many skeptics to be authentic, is a document currently housed in the National Archives in Washington, D.C., which is headed, "Memorandum for General Twining, from Robert Cutler, Special Assistant to the President, Subject: 'NSC/MJ-12 Special Studies Project.'" (NSC stands for National Security Council.)

9 THE CLINTON BODY COUNT

This conspiracy theory at least seems plausible, as it has nothing to do with science fiction. It states that Bill Clinton, while he was president and before, was quietly assassinating his associates (ostensibly anyone who got in the way of his career, such as Vince Foster). The Clinton Body Count is a list of about 50 to 60 of Clinton's associates who have died "under mysterious circumstance." The list began circulating over the Internet starting in the mid-1990s. The list grew out of a 1993 compilation of about 24 names prepared by the pro-gun lobby group American Justice Federation, which was led by Linda Thompson. The list was posted to the group's bulletin-board system.

The facts concerning Vince Foster's death are that he died an untimely death on July 20, 1993, of apparent suicide by gunshot in the mouth. His body was found in Fort Marcy Park, Virginia, and gunshot residue was found on the hand that had held the gun. Foster and Clinton were boyhood friends, both lawyers, and theorists believe that Foster got too close to uncovering some embarrassing truth about Clinton, probably of a sexual and/or dishonest nature; he had been on Clinton's White House staff less than a year.

The theorists argue that it's unlikely that a man with a wife, three children, and an extremely lucrative law practice, earning him $300,000 a year, would have manic depression, but Foster was diagnosed with it and prescribed antidepressants.

8 THE CHRIST MYTH THEORY

Yes, you read that right. According to this conspiracy theory, Christ himself never existed. His life story, his ministry, and his status as the divine Son of God are fabrications of the Roman Catholic Church. Those who have proposed one form or another of this theory have documented the similarities between stories of Jesus and those of Krishna, Adonis, Osiris, Mithra, and a pre-Christian cult of Jesus (Joshua) within Judaism. Some authors attribute the beginning of Christianity to a historical founder who predates the time Jesus is said to have lived.

The theory appears to have been originated by two French Enlightenment thinkers, Constantin-Francois Volney and Charles Francois Dupuis, in the 1790s. The idea has always been largely dismissed by academic circles and biblical historians, but the theorists have simply elaborated on the original claim. They say that not only did Jesus never exist, his presence in the New Testament is utter fiction, created by the Roman Catholic Church sometime in the late 2nd century or very early 3rd century AD as a means by which to control people. The authorities passed down the idea to their successors until Constantine considered it a very good means of control and called the Council of Nicaea to organize the Church into global domination.

Despite all the historical proof that Jesus did exist—and there is plenty of it—there are still many people who would like to think he didn't.

7 THE ANTICHRIST

Satan is alive on earth, and has created the Antichrist, Numerologists believe that the Antichrist is not yet old enough but will soon make his appearance at the age of 30, symbolically equal to Jesus beginning his ministry. He will do so in a very political manner, taking over some powerful organization, such as the United Nations. Every generation, since St. John the Divine wrote Apocalypse, has sworn that it would witness the Great Tribulation, Armageddon, and the second coming of Jesus. "The end is near," everyone said.

Now though, with the advent of global communications, especially the Internet, the theory has swelled exponentially. Christians who previously didn't think much of it have changed their minds. It can be argued that the worldwide availability of press coverage only serves to heighten fear of terrible things happening at any moment. 9/11 was the most well-covered tragedy in human history, and whenever an event like that occurs, people who believe in the Christian end-times scenarios flock to church to pray away their fears.

With the ability to control the entire world actually conceivable, the paranoia of the Antichrist showing up has become quite the pandemic. Most terrorists believe he will be male and come from Western Europe; and some swear he'll be French. Plenty are sure, however, that President Barack Obama is, in fact, the Antichrist.

Terrorism, the current U.S.-led war against a global hotbed of political unrest, and the fact that almost every Arab nation seems to be threatening an invasion of Israel at any second all serve to make this theory feel very real. Every day, CNN is loaded with horror stories about the Holy Land, and it just seems to keep getting worse. "The end is near."

6 THE ELECTRIC CAR

It's a verifiable fact that in 1899, an electric car set the human land-speed record at 65 mph. Steam and gasoline-powered automobiles didn't achieve this for another 20 to 25 years. Today, technology has progressed immensely, and yet we still have no readily available, affordable electric cars. The best-

production model accessible to the general public is the Toyota Prius, which gets 50 miles per gallon. This only intensifies the conspiracy theory that the U.S. oil companies currently possess the technology for purely electric cars that you can plug into an ordinary, American wall outlet at night and charge up for a cross-country trip by morning.

But, theorists claim, because this would bankrupt the oil companies, they refuse to release the technology. A 2006 documentary called *Who Killed the Electric Car?* fueled the fire that if the technology is documented to have existed as early as the 1830s, why did it appear to hit its peak at the turn of the 20th century, and then decline? Why are we still waiting for accessible electric cars? Edison patented one in 1913. All the electrical pioneers of that time tinkered with the idea, and plenty of reasonable examples were produced.

5 HAARP

The High Frequency Active Auroral Research Program does exist. It's a research project funded jointly by the U.S. Air Force, the U.S. Navy, the University of Alaska, and the Defense Advanced Research Projects Agency (DARPA). When you put that many government organizations into one sentence about new technology, conspiracy theorists come running. Did you see the 2003 movie

The Core? It concerns a stall in the Earth's magnetic field, which allows the sun's microwave radiation to cook the planet until a team goes into the Earth and jumpstarts it so it spins again and the magnetic field resumes.

The movie explains that the stall was accidentally caused by HAARP, which is researching the ability to create earthquakes for use as a weapon. The program's official description of itself is that it functions "to provide a research facility to conduct pioneering experiments in ionospheric phenomena… used to analyze basic ionospheric properties and to assess the potential for developing ionospheric enhancement technology for communications and surveillance purposes."

This sounds like the opposite of deep-earth experiments, but conspiracy theorists believe the program is a cover for a kind of particle-beam weapon first invented by Nikola Tesla, which has, in fact, been perfected, or brought close to perfection, by HAARP. The theory also claims that the ionospheric research is not a lie, but is being developed for use as a weapon to shoot down enemy spacecraft or ballistic missiles, the latter popular especially given that HAARP's facilities are all in Alaska, near Russia. Theorists even speculate that the weapon could become Tesla's most infamous invention: the Death Beam, which would be able to project a beam of extremely powerful electricity from the Alaskan facility to any point on the planet and create an explosion as devastating as a hydrogen bomb.

4 THE VRIL SOCIETY

It has been suggested that there's a secret form of energy, called Vril, that's used and controlled by a secret subterranean society of matriarchal socialist utopian superior beings. Yes, you read that correctly. The theory also claims that Nazi Germany discovered this underground race and its technology at Shambhala, Tibet, and used it to create flying saucers.

The whole claim is based on an 1871 sci-fi novel by Edward Bulwer-Lytton titled *Vril: The Power of the Coming Race*. It's generally considered an early example of science fiction, but because this genre was just getting off the ground at the time, it was seen by many as a nonfiction account of the subterranean race and their technology, a theory which persists today. The idea really took off in the 1960s.

3 THE SUPPRESSION OF FREE ENERGY

This conspiracy theory actually sounds plausible. Nikola Tesla claimed that free energy was indeed possible and worked for most of his career to achieve it. The claim is that he did, in fact, succeed just before his death in 1943 in discovering the mathematics and mechanics involved, but that the FBI immediately broke into his home and seized all his papers and work, and has never released any of it to the public.

The concept of free energy is, in very general terms, the ability to input x amount of energy into a machine, which will output x + 1 amount of energy. This seems to conflict with the law of conservation of energy, which states that energy can neither be created nor destroyed. Tesla believed the law to be incorrect. He invented the Tesla Coil as an attempt to create free energy.

If it's possible, free energy could be perfected and result in the entire planet being powered by a single power source, such as a nuclear power plant, and output all the energy anyone could ever need. An infinite supply of energy would be at our fingertips, all based on electric output.

You can see how this would irritate the oil companies. They are the cause of the suppression of free energy, the theory claims, as no one would have to depend on fossil fuels anymore. Electric input is just as viable as coal input or gasoline input. Thus, the electricity required to power a light bulb could be all we need to drive the whole world, invent spacecrafts capable of interstellar travel and utilize anti-gravity, to name a few potential gains from Tesla's discovery.

2 JESUS WAS A DIFFERENT SPECIES

This theory is a lot of fun. It has been alleged that the U.S. and Israeli governments led archaeological digs in the past that discovered the True Cross, on which Jesus was crucified (along with many others, as crosses were reused). The theories disagree on the location of the cross; most claim it was found in Jerusalem, but many believe it was at Rosslyn Chapel in Scotland, or various places in England.

Minute traces of blood were discovered on the cross and analyzed. The DNA was of several strains, and one was encoded not on a double helix, but on a triple helix! (Is this good stuff or what?) The DNA is unlike any other known and was labeled as a new species, Homo superioris. The theory continues that there are other people of this species currently living underground in various places around the world, including most major cities, and they have been around as long or longer than Homo sapiens. Jesus made the unprecedented decision to come up to the surface and live among us and try to teach us to be good, kind, and peaceful.

Jesus' supposed species possesses phenomenal supernatural abilities, including telekinesis, levitation (walking on water), telepathy (knowing people's thoughts), and healing. They're also very difficult to kill, and when no one was looking, presumably during the freak storm and earthquake described in the Bible, Jesus got down off the cross and disappeared, having done his job.

1 INELIGIBLE PRESIDENT

This theory apparently started as Republican/Conservative petulance once it appeared that Barack Obama might actually win the presidency, and it came across as a smear campaign trying to discredit him. But now that he is in the Oval Office for the duration, the claim still hasn't gone away, and even former skeptics and Independent Party members have joined the accusation that Obama is not a natural-born American citizen.

The U.S. Constitution is clear that no one may be elected president of the United States who was not born in one of those states. Obama's birth is officially credited as occurring at Kapi'olani Maternity and Gynecological Hospital in Honolulu, Hawaii. This qualifies him as a natural-born citizen, but the theory claims that his mother, Stanley Ann Dunham, a white woman from Wichita, Kansas, was actually born to a British father, who was not an American citizen, and that her birth occurred somewhere in eastern sub-Saharan Africa, probably Kenya, Tanzania, or South Africa. Dunham never applied for American citizenship, the theory continues, but grew up in Kansas, California, Texas, and other locations. She had a Ph.D. in anthropology and characteristically traveled the world studying various cultures, gave birth to Obama in either Kenya or Tanzania, and died in Honolulu in 1995. If these details of her birth and Obama's birth, are true, he is not a natural-born American citizen.

The most convincing evidence that there is at least something worth investigating on this subject is the absence of Obama's true official birth certificate. One copy of it should be on file in the Honolulu hospital, and another should be at Honolulu's City Hall. There should certainly be a third copy somewhere in Washington, D.C., but the conspiracy theory states that the only one that has turned up is currently in the Honolulu hospital and is a forgery. It's true that the other two hard copies, and any others that should be floating around, are nowhere to be found. It is easy to search the Internet for an image of the birth certificate, but the theory claims these images are all copies of the one in the Honolulu hospital.

10 WEIRD THINGS CARS HAVE BEEN COVERED WITH

10 NAIL POLISH

Yvonne Millner of Hopkins, South Carolina, decided to give her 1996 Mitsubishi Mirage a different look, so she decided to paint the car—with nail polish. She started by drawing a smiley face, but today she has designs, patterns, and slogans painted all over the vehicle. She would sometimes spend three to four hours a day on designing the car (which she nicknamed Smiley) and has used hundreds of bottles of nail polish in different shades, thus giving the car a unique, colorful appearance.

9 POSTAGE STAMPS

E. Hadley, of Casper, Wyoming, owns an automobile with a difference. Serving as a rolling stamp exhibit, his car is covered with approximately 10,000 postage stamps. To plaster the stamps to the car, five girls worked steadily for six weeks covering the vehicle with the stamps, which came from 60 different countries. The car was later varnished to protect the stamps from the elements.

8 COINS

Ken Burkitt of Ontario, Canada, has covered several vehicles, including a 1969 Austin Mini Cooper, with thousands of gold-plated English pennies. The coins used were covered with at least eight coats of polyurethane to prevent discoloration or rusting. To ensure that every inch of the car is covered, Burkitt uses a vice to bend coins into the shape of the surfaces they will cover.

7 CHOCOLATE

A Chinese car company covered a Volkswagen Beetle with 440 pounds of chocolate for Valentine's Day in 2007. Several workers first covered the Beetle with plastic wrap, then the melted chocolate was spread all over the car and candy was used to decorate it. The chocolate Beetle was then displayed outside a grocery store in Shandong province.

6 STICKY NOTES

Scott Ableman and a dozen of his colleagues from a company in Washington, D.C., decided to pull a fantastic prank on their coworker Walt. In less than two hours, the group covered Walt's Jaguar with 14,000 colorful sticky notes. Every inch of the car was covered except the hood ornament and the license plates. After finding out about his car, Walt went along with the prank and, after removing the notes from the windshield, drove it home to show to his family.

5 TOY CARS

James Ford, a young UK artist, after purchasing a 1981 Ford Capri on eBay, decided to turn the car into an art project. The result: General Carbunkle, an homage to General Lee (the car from *The Dukes of Hazzard*), which is covered with around 3500 to 4500 toy vehicles. The toy cars mostly came from donations from around the world, although Ford obtained 2000 of the toy cars used by posing as a toy-store owner and buying them at a trade fair.

4 GRASS

Brooklyn artist Gene Pool's medium is grass. He first puts adhesive on the surface of his soon-to-be artwork, spreads grass seeds all over it, waters the plants, then waits for the grass to germinate, and *voila*! Instant art. Pool has used the technique on various items like suits, hats, shoes, and briefcases,  but his crowning achievements are the two Buick LeSabres that he covered with Manhattan Perennial Rye #2, as well as a grass-covered St. Louis Cardinals bus.

3 MUSICAL INSTRUMENTS

Harrod Blank created "Pico de Gallo" ("spicy salsa" in Spanish), a Volkswagen Beetle covered with working musical instruments. The car also features a stage on the roof and a stereo system. It's currently displayed at the Art Car World Museum in Arizona.

2 CIGARETTES

The Stink Bug is a Volkswagen Beetle owned by Carolyn Stapleton of Orlando, Florida. The car serves as a moving antismoking advertisement because it's covered with thousands of used cigarettes. The words "kick butt" can be seen on the windshield, and a skull-and-crossbones adorns the hood.

1 CRYSTALS

Remember Ken Burkitt from number 8? He and his wife, Annie, get the top spot on this list for their amazing work on a 2004 Mini Cooper, which is covered with more than a million genuine Austrian Swarovski crystals depicting various U.S. landmarks and symbols, like the Statue of Liberty, the White House, and Mount Rushmore. The masterpiece, entitled "American Icon," took four artists six months to create because it was all done by hand. The crystals used were all of the same size and in 50 different colors to represent the 50 states of America. Burkitt said of the work, "We wanted to create something that would pay tribute to America in an eye-catching way. The car takes on a completely different look as the lighting changes throughout the day. The crystal design takes on a life of its own."

10 BIZARRE HUMAN MYSTERIES

10 ENTRANCING HEALERS

Shamanistic practices were once much more prevalent in the world and considered a profound foundation of the tribes that believed in them. In many cultures, these spiritually based rituals are still found today and revered as legitimate procedures. In the Philippines, an entrancing healer has the ability to materialize and dematerialize matter. The shaman enters a mild trance where they gain the supernatural ability to perform surgeries with little to no contact with the patient. They are then able to remove foreign objects within the body, such as glass and metal, and provide alleviation from similar pains.

Many of these shamans have been discovered as fraudulent, proving the use of slight-of-hand tricks and passing them off as legitimate procedures, but that isn't the case for all of shamans. Some entrancing healers can pull out molars with their bare hands, while others can remove and replace eyeballs. There is still no evidence dismissing what these shamans have been able to achieve for decades.

9 PSYCHIC SURGEONS

Much like entrancing healers, psychic surgeons can perform procedures that would normally require tools and what we consider conventional medical supplies, like anesthesia. But unlike the healers, psychic surgeons go deep into the patient's body and literally pull out tumors and organs from their patients.

These types of surgeons are mostly found in Brazil and the Philippines, where people strongly believe in spirits that aid every procedure and treatment. Patients are told to recognize that negative feelings and thoughts toward disease and illness only serve to aggravate the condition and can't be healed if the patient doesn't believe in the possibility of overcoming it. In other words, they must form a bond between the mind, body, and spirit to achieve the balance required for recovery; the body can't be healed if the mind and spirit aren't aligned. This is also the reason psychic surgeons argue that outsiders who come to them seeking help are more difficult to work on because they lack that faith.

8 SPONTANEOUS HUMAN COMBUSTION

Spontaneous human combustion (SHC) is burning from the inside out. It certainly sounds strange, but by now, many of us are familiar with this supposed phenomenon. Famous cases include Jack Angel's account of SHC that led to his hand needing amputation, to Mary Reeser, who was burned to a crisp and found with a shrunken skull. Even fiction has its examples of SHC, like in Charles Dicken's novel *Bleak House* (Dickens was fascinated by the topic and researched it thoroughly).

Already you can probably come up with a few facts off the top of your head that would debunk this mystery, but consider this: crematoriums preheat their furnaces to about 1837.4°F because the human body is relatively difficult to burn. It takes between one and two hours for tissue and major bones to become ashes. SHC victims are usually found in a liquid form, meaning their bodies had to burn at a temperature exceeding 2998°F. And in some cases, the entire body isn't burned; if the burning were from something like a house fire, there would likely be burn marks all over the body.

7 FIRE IMMUNITY AND FIRE STARTER

On the subject of fire, we come to the Leidenfrost effect. The effect actually creates an insulating, protective barrier of vapor that forms over a liquid exposed to extreme heat. This same effect protects you when you pinch out candles with wet fingers. It's a phenomenon we're all capable of doing given the right circumstances, like in firewalking, but that's only a fraction of what people with fire immunity experience.

Nathan Coker was a blacksmith in Maryland who could stand on white-hot metal, swill molten lead shot into his mouth until it solidified, and hold red-hot coals. His skin was so dexterous he never even showed signs of burn marks. Is it a practice of mind over matter, or did his skin, over years of handling fire, get tough enough to keep him from feeling the burn?

On the opposite end of the spectrum, pyrokinetics can attract or project fire. A. W. Underwood was able to cause a handkerchief to burn to flames by blowing on it. The idea of starting a fire with the mind or a wave of the hand is rejected much quicker than that of people with fire immunity, but the former remains the favorite in fiction.

6 DOWSING

Dowsing has existed as early as the 15th century. Using a divining rod, a dowser may find water, metals, and other substances in the ground without the use of scientific tools. The thought is that divining rods amplify invisible movements of the hand of the dowser, who has some ability to sense magnetic fields or may possess a form of ESP.

One way to explain the phenomenon is by exploring the environment. If a dowser can detect hints about their surroundings, then they make subconscious movements with their hands, forcing the rods to shake and dip, indicating they've found something of value. Most dowsers can't offer a plain explanation of how the process works, but the practice has been used to locate substances successfully throughout the centuries.

5 BIOELECTRICITY

You could probably search online for videos of people showing signs of bioelectricity. As early as the 19th century, there have been cases of people being electrically charged or magnetized, resulting in an odd electromagnetic effect on the objects around them. Some people even show allergic reactions to technology, finding it difficult to live around devices that emit too much magnetic and electrical charge.

There have been cases of people being so charged that they're able to illuminate light bulbs simply by holding them. Others cause fuses to blow out without any means of controlling the effect. It's even been recorded that people with this strong force can give a continuous static electricity shock that's powerful enough to actually hurt someone.

4 BIOLUMINESCENCE

Surprisingly, most cases of bioluminescence in humans come from ill patients. Anna Monaro had asthma, and for several weeks, a blue glow would emit from her chest while she slept. In his book *Death: Its Causes and Phenomena*, Hereward Carrington reported the body of a boy radiating a blue glow after his death from acute indigestion.

This glowworm effect still doesn't have enough cases to draw statistical significance, but Japanese researchers have discovered that the human body glimmers. The light we emit is about 1000 times lower than the naked eye can see. This light fluctuates during the day in cycles, leaving us brightest in the afternoon (the skin around your mouth lightens most around this time of day, too) and dimmest in the evening.

3 LEVITATION

D. D. Home was a famous medium who had many witnesses claim he could indeed levitate. Home's most incredible feat happened in 1868 when he floated out one window and into another during a séance. His abilities were never proven to be fraudulent, even by Harry Houdini, who attempted to duplicate many of Home's "tricks."

It was considered normal for levitation to occur during a séance not just by the people in attendance, but by the objects around them as well. Today, levitation is common during magical performances. If you ever want to experience levitation for yourself, try the Light as a Feather, Stiff as a Board game. It's been scaring kids for years now.

2 ESP

ESP is extrasensory perception, the ability to gain information through use of a sense unknown by science. Before getting into ESP, first you should realize you do in fact have more than five senses: you can also sense temperature, variations, proprioception (position of your muscles), and the force of gravity (you do this by knowing at what angle your head is in while your eyes are shut). ESP covers the other additional senses that are left.

There's plenty anecdotal evidence of ESP, but what about legitimate scientific proof? In the 1930s, the Ganzfeld experiments took place. People claiming to have ESP were told to lie down and then forced to listen to white noise to clear their minds. Someone observing from another room would then attempt to mentally send the clairvoyant an image. Afterward, that person would pick which image it was they saw in their mind from four choices. Critics predicted a 25-percent accuracy, but were surprised to learn that the subjects picked the correct image 35 percent of the time. That isn't statistically a lot more, but this experiment was used to show that perhaps there was something to ESP after all.

1 PROPHECY

The Delphic oracle did it. Nostradamus did it. Hell, you can call fortunetellers over the phone nowadays to hear about the future. History is riddled with people claiming to know the future. Some have visions that come and go, others have foretelling dreams. There are those who seek the future by means of ritual, and then there are people who are struck with precognition randomly. You might have experienced it yourself. Ever thought of a friend and they called you (or in this modern age, they e-mailed you) seconds later? Is that an example of precognition, or is it just coincidence?

Nostradamus had a number of prophecies that, when interpreted in a certain manner, predicted the Great Fire of London and the rise of Adolf Hitler. However, Nostradamus was purposefully vague and cryptic in each of his predictions, leaving them open for interpretation. To say that he unmistakably foresaw those events in history would be a bit of a stretch. Still, among all the items on this list, the ability to see the future is the most abundant bizarre trait people believe they possess.

10 TRULY RIDICULOUS CRIMINAL ACTS

10 NOT LION ABOUT ANY OF THESE

This one won a Darwin Award in 1989. Direct from Melbourne, Australia, a 24-year-old black belt in Chinese kung fu, on receiving his 1st-degree belt, was pumped up by his instructor with the brilliant knowledge that he could now overpower and kill a wild animal with his bare hands.

He immediately put the idea to the test by driving to the Melbourne Zoo, sneaking in after dark, and jumping into the lion exhibit. Not that the lions couldn't have taken him one on one, but they saw no need to fight fair. All the police and zookeepers found in the morning were his hands, clenched with red fur in them.

This qualifies as a crime, since it's illegal to trespass in a zoo after closing time, and besides this, the lions had to be retrained not to attack humans, as they now had a taste for human flesh.

9 READ THE SIGNS

On July 29, 2007, two burglars thought the prime target in North Richland Hills, Texas, would be a store that sells personal home-defense security systems and accessories. In their defense, the criminals managed to stuff over $10,000 worth of surveillance equipment, mostly security cameras and house alarms, into a couple of trash cans in only one minute and 15 seconds. Of course, this was all while being recorded by 17 security cameras of the same make and model as the ones they were stealing. There were no fewer than 12 warning signs across the front of the store advising to criminals that, among other things, "Someone besides Jesus is watching you, and neither that someone nor Jesus is going to be happy if you break the law."

There was at least one very good vantage point of their getaway car, including the license plate, which was not stolen, but registered in one of their names. When the police tracked them down, they still pled "not guilty."

8 BARNEY FIFE WAS A ROCKET SCIENTIST

On August, 17, 1981, Miss Terry Johnson of Chicago was woken at about 2:30 in the morning by two men wearing police uniforms, complete with badges, utility belts, handguns, cuffs, and hats. Their nameplates read Tyrone Pickens and Stephen Webster, and Miss Johnson stated later that she was more bewildered than scared. She thought that either these men had stolen the uniforms or they were policemen who thought she was a thief and were confiscating the stolen property before arresting her.

She waited for them to leave, then wrote down their badge numbers, names, and the number of their police car, and found out by the end of the day that the uniforms were real and belonged to the two men, who were, in fact, police officers. They had used police equipment to break into her home, robbed her with their uniforms on, while on duty, and not fled the city afterward.

7 DON'T TRUST THOSE YOU ROB

In February 2006, a New Zealand shoplifter named Amy Adams returned within a day to the butcher shop she had robbed because she saw her picture on a local TV news station stating that she had won the lottery and had to appear in person to claim her prize. She rapidly drove back to the shop, announced her name, pointed herself out in a still photo from a surveillance video, and was promptly handcuffed by undercover policemen. She still denied having broken any law all the way through her trial until the judge explained that she was guilty and had no hope of convincing anyone to the contrary. She then pled guilty, and still claimed she was innocent.

6 WRONG MOVE, WRONG TIME

In Raleigh, North Carolina, on December 11, 2007, someone was stabbed multiple times in an intersection, and ten police officers responded to the scene. While they were there, in the middle of the day, Anthony William, not the stabber, decided that the traffic jam at the intersection made for some ripe vehicles to steal. He waited for a woman to get out of her car, then walked right up, jumped into it, and tried to drive away. Every policeman in the area came down on top of him, one of them even banging on the car hood and shouting for him to get out. This officer had been less than 15 feet away from him and watching him the whole time while he committed the theft.

When William insisted on driving away, the police all memorized his license plate and let him go to avoid a dangerous pursuit. He was picked up in Virginia when he tried to sell the car to a used car dealer.

5 SILENCE! I KILL YOU!

In early 1994, an Islamic terrorist organization in Jordan ordered violent reprisals against all Jordanian stores that sold either videos or liquor. This meant bombing such stores. On February 1, Eid Saleh al-Jahaleen, 31 years old, accepted $50 in U.S. currency to plant a bomb in a Turkish movie theater in Zarqa. He entered and discovered that the theater was showing Turkish pornography. He had never seen anything of the sort, and was immediately fascinated.

He stowed his bomb under a seat in the center of the theater, as instructed, then sat down in the same seat and watched the show. Ten minutes later, the bomb blew off both his legs and his testicles. His penis was relatively unscathed, since it was safely inside his right hand. He bled to death in the aisle.

4 MY KINGDOM FOR A BLACKBEARD

On April 1, 2010, Somali pirates deliberately attacked the USS *Nicholas*. These Somali pirates are primarily armed with AKMs (AK-47 upgrades), RPGs, pistols, and grenades. The USS *Nicholas*, a guided-missile frigate, is armed with 40 harpoon antiship missiles, one Otobreda, a three-inch artillery rifle that fires 120 rounds per minute, two triple-tube torpedo launchers, four .50-caliber machine guns, and one 20-milimeter computer-automated Vulcan gatling cannon that fires 4500 rounds per minute.

Assuming the pirates simply failed to notice the *Nicholas'* massive armament, they might have considered the standard U.S. Navy steel-gray paint and the ships 453 foot length as somewhat different from the private yachts on which pirates prefer to prey. But, alas, it was not to be. The Somali pirates opened fire with their small arms. The sailors on board the *Nicholas* ran to general quarters, the Vulcan cannon shot down three of the four rocket-propelled grenades, and sailors manning one of the .50-caliber machine guns disabled the pirate skiff. The pirates' grenade that made it through the hail of cannonfire struck a bulkhead of the frigate's superstructure and dented it. The three pirates on board surrendered, and then the *Nicholas* sighted their mothership, an ex-shrimping schooner converted into an armed trawler of sorts. This ship simply turned and fled, but the *Nicholas* overtook it and two more pirates were captured.

The bulkhead dent was hammered out and repainted.

3 FILMING YOUR OWN CRIME

Not all idiotic criminal acts are funny. The Abu Ghraib Prisoner Abuse scandal of 2004 resulted in a nearly worldwide condemnation of the United

States (not that the United States was particularly popular before then) for "sinking to the terrorists' level," as it were. The primary guilty person was Specialist Charles Graner, the ringleader who incited numerous other guards to torture and humiliate prisoners, or at least look the other way while others did.

What makes these criminals' acts truly idiotic is that the perpetrators filmed themselves committing them with cell phone videos and photos. They collected the evidence that would have convicted them in any court of law on the planet. Others responsible for the torture were PFC Lynndie England, Staff Sergeant Ivan Frederick, Sergeant Javal Davis, and soldiers with ranks up to lieutenant colonel and colonel. Iraq was, at the time, utterly anarchic, and the guilty persons were under the impression that their crimes wouldn't be noticed and that no one would care.

2 BAD ITEM TO STEAL

On August 22, 1911, Vincenzo Peruggia hid in a janitor's closet in the Louvre, in Paris, France. He waited until well after the museum had closed and then walked out with the *Mona Lisa* hidden under his coat. His motive was multifold. He was Italian, and so is the painting and its painter, and he wanted it returned to an Italian museum. That might have been construed as selflessly patriotic, except that he didn't just give it to an Italian museum, he tried to sell it to one: the Uffizi Art Gallery in Florence. He also intended to make some money through a friend who would sell replicas of the painting, because with the real one out there somewhere, replica buyers would play the lottery, as it were, trying to buy the real one for cheap. The problem with all of this is that you can't exactly resell the real Mona Lisa.

The Uffizi curators somehow discovered that the painting must have come from the Louvre, since, after all, there's *only one Mona Lisa* and the Louvre is well-known for housing it, in which case the Louvre wasn't likely to have sold it to one of its part-time employees. Peruggia was arrested on the spot. Nevertheless, he was hailed as a hero throughout Italy, as he had hoped, and only served six months in prison.

1 WRONG PERSON TO MUG

If someone were to ask you who the last person anyone should ever dare to mug is, who would be your answer? I'm betting on 80 percent or better of respondents answering, "Chuck Norris."

Astoundingly, two idiots managed to try just that. Norris mentions the whole thing in his autobiography, *Against All Odds*. And, by his testimony, this is what happened:

In 1994, right at the beginning of his run as *Walker, Texas Ranger*, Norris was, and still is, living in Dallas, Texas, where the show was filmed. One day he was walking down the street by himself with no entourage, no fans following him, no bodyguards, not even his wife. He turned onto a commercial block in the city's downtown area and saw two men a little bigger than him coming straight for him from the other end of the block.

They were staring right at him, and he figured they wanted autographs, which he enjoys signing. So he walked up to them and stopped with a smile, whereupon they stood in front of him, whipped out a couple of large pocketknives, and one of them demanded, "Give me your wallet, Chuck! Give it here!"

Norris actually opened his mouth wide and then asked, "Are you insane!?"

"No! We know who you are! And we know you got a lot of money! Now give it up, or you're dead!"

Now before we go further, let's just go over a few of the particulars. All jokes aside, Chuck Norris truly does have the following black belts: 1st degree in Brazilian jiu-jitsu, 8th-degree grand master in taekwondo, 9th degree in *jeet kune do* under Bruce Lee and Lee's best student, Dan Inosanto; 10th degree in *shito ryu karate*; 10th degree in *tang soo do*; 11th degree in *chun kuk do*.

Granted, the last martial art is his own concoction, a hybrid of all the best moves he's learned over the years blended for both self-defense and competition, and you are only allowed a 10th degree or better in anything when you found your own *dojo*. But suffice it to say, the muggers didn't even use guns, they used knives from within arm's reach. What happened next was rather anticlimactic.

The police arrived about four minutes later, three officers in two cars, and they were greeted by the scene of two men with severely broken arms (the bones had gone through the skin) sitting on the curb, two bloody knives in the gutter, and Chuck Norris, the Almighty Himself, leaning against the wall, wearing his beard, jeans, cowboy boots, and a cowboy hat. He shrugged at them. The police started laughing so hard that they bent over, holding their sides, unable to put the handcuffs on the muggers. One of them managed to ask, "Did you not know who he was?!"

One of them said, "Yeah, we knew who he was! We figured all that crap on TV was fake!"

7 ESSENTIAL ZOMBIE SURVIVAL TIPS

7 PULL YOUR SHIT TOGETHER!
If it's a zombie infestation, the cops, firemen, and ambulance technicians will all be rather busy, or dead. When the first zombies are seen, the police will take them to hospitals. Do not lock yourself in your apartment and wait for the police to save you. Do not cooperate with the authorities. They know nothing about zombies, as they believe that zombies are a myth.

6 GET ARMED
You do not want to face zombies and be unarmed. Even if they're not so smart or quick or powerful, they'll be too dangerous to fight bare handed. Firearms are good, but you should also have some side weapons you can use if you run out of bullets or if the zombies get too close. Anything's good—knives, swords, axes, or even poleaxes—if you know how to use it properly. Blunt weapons are also good, but you must wear protective goggles and a mask, or something to protect your face from the splash of their rotting flesh.

5 GET ARMORED
You must try to protect your body as much as you can, especially your neck, arms, and legs. These are the most exposed parts for them to bite. You can find lots of body armor from army surplus stores, or even martial arts and hunting shops. Jeans also offer good protection from bites.

4 LEAVE TOWN
If the zombie infestation catches you in a big city, you must leave immediately. It's one thing to face 10 zombies, but another thing to face 10,000.

Best thing is to go to the country. Farms are quite easy to defend, and the open spaces won't let you get caught by surprise.

3 GATHER SUPPLIES

Gather as many supplies as you can, everything from bottled water to gas—you'll need it. And it won't be hard to do; if everyone else is dead, it won't be stealing! Best thing is to get a truck and start looting the largest stores in the area. Don't go into big towns, and don't start looting until you are 100 percent sure there won't be a zombie attack, let alone a big one! You don't want the authorities to stop the onslaught, nor do you want to end up in jail for looting.

2 BARRICADE

Some barbed wire and a whole bunch of gas-filled bottles can do wonders when defending your homestead from a zombie attack. Also, alarms are a very good idea. You can make them yourself (some cans and pots on a wire) or get a real one, with motion sensors and everything (see number 5 for looting tips; gas and generator required).

1 SEARCH FOR SURVIVORS

After you have enough supplies and your home and the surroundings are safe, you should start searching for survivors. Even if you are the only one of your group still alive, you'll end up going mad if you remain alone. Start with the small towns around you. It will be quite easy if you have a zombie-proof car. Just go to the city limits and honk. If zombies are there, they will head in your direction and you can just leave; alternatively, you'll recognize the survivors and can form a group. Safety in numbers!

Photo Credits

All photos are from shutterstock.com:

p. 2: © Susan Chiang
p. 12: © 58405423
p. 14: © Yellowj
p. 16: © Bocos Benedict
p. 19: © Tadeusz Ibrom
p. 24: © ribeiroantonio
p. 32: © Carolyn M Carpenter
p. 34: © Condor 36
p. 41: © 6493866629
p. 45: © CSLD
p. 49: © dwphotos
p. 53: © lafoto
p. 57: © Ryan M. Bolton
p. 61: © Daniel Alvarez
p. 71: © c.
p. 73: © Milan Vasicek
p. 74: © Sirk
p. 80: © Kevin H Knuth
p. 86: © Hugo Maes
p. 89: © Catalin Petolea
p. 91: © photofun
p. 94: © Susan Montgomery
p. 99: © Audrey Hsia
p. 101: © Pakhnyushcha
p. 102: © Perov Stanislav
p. 106: © Makarova Viktoria (Vikarus)
p. 110: © Patryk Kosmider
p. 112: © David P. Smith
p. 117: © Filip Fuxa
p. 118: © Jose AS Reyes
p. 121: © StudioSmart
p. 134: © Jerry Horbert
p. 140: © Lim Yong Hian
p. 142: © Monkey Business Images
p. 145: © Mindy w.m. Chung
p. 148: © Viktor1
p. 154: © Geoffrey Kuchera
p. 157: © wmiami
p. 159: © Ragnarock
p. 162: © Liz Van Steenburgh
p. 165: © erkanupan
p. 168: © K.L. Kohn
p. 177: © Richard J Ashcroft
p. 181: © Strakovskaya
p. 185: © piotrwzk
p. 189: © Pavel Mitrofanov
p. 191: © MISHELLA
p. 196: © mitzy
p. 204: © maryp
p. 211: © Lagui
p. 223: © Pallando

p. 228: © All32
p. 230: © Maridav
p. 236: © Mark Payne
p. 239: © vishstudio
p. 243: © domhnall dods
p. 247: © J.Schelkle
p. 250: © Arvind Balaraman
p. 256: © Dan Breckwoldt
p. 260: © Bobkeenan Photography
p. 262: © Vladislav Sabanov
p. 264: © Daria Filimonova
p. 267: © Vacclav
p. 273: © Khoroshunova Olga
p. 276: © otolibor
p. 281: © Elnur
p. 284: © Francis BossÈ
p. 287: © Ronen
p. 291: © Sean Prior
p. 297: © Sayanski
p. 300: © hkannn
p. 302: © Linda Bucklin
p. 305: © Sergey Peterman
p. 307: © CREATISTA
p. 314: © inginsh
p. 320: © Izabela Zaremba
p. 324: © Norbert Derec
p. 329: © ostill
p. 334: © Aleksandra Duda
p. 336: © Alessandro D'Esposito
p. 344: © hjschneider
p. 347: © CREATISTA
p. 349: © Denise Kappa
p. 364: © Anyka
p. 368: © orionmystery@flickr
p. 370: © rSnapshotPhotos
p. 372: © Ozerov Alexander
p. 375: © Beth Van Trees
p. 382: © Ronald van der Beek
p. 384: © mlorenz
p. 387: © Susan Flashman
p. 391: © Arnold John Labrentz
p. 392: © Andrejs Pidjass
p. 398: © Dean Mitchell
p. 407: © Wong Hock weng
p. 409: © Marcio Jose Bastos Silva
p. 415: © Ruslan Nabiyev
p. 422: © John Black
p. 426: © Jakub Krechowicz
p. 434: © Dmitriy Karelin
p. 438: © Hugh Lansdown

p. 442: © Oleksii Abramov
p. 446: © James van den Broek
p. 449: © djgis
p. 453: © Planetphoto.ch
p. 460: © alarich
p. 465: © Ronald Sumners
p. 479: © Bruce Rolff
p. 485: © Snezana Skundric
p. 491: © CREATISTA
p. 496: © Howard Sandler
p. 512: © Sergey Khachatryan
p. 514: © Caitlin Mirra
p. 518: © Thomas La Mela
p. 523: © Alexey Stiop
p. 527: © Boudikka
p. 536: © Alexander Chaikin
p. 538: © Luca Grandinetti
p. 543: © Rui Saraiva
p. 545: © kbremote
p. 548: © my-summit
p. 554: © Norman Chan
p. 561: © Walter G Arce
p. 568: © Sam DCruz
p. 581: © Alan Bassett
p. 585: © Vladimir Wrangel
p. 591: © TFoxFoto
p. 594: © Vasily Smirnov
p. 596: © olly
p. 598: © Fanfo
p. 607: © David Lee
p. 616: © Diego Cervo
p. 620: © Greg da Silva
p. 626: © lsantilli
p. 629: © Panos Karapanagiotis
p. 635: © Bochkarev Photography
p. 638: © Henk Jacobs
p. 641: © slon1971
p. 646: © Fotogroove
p. 651: © ivaskes_b&w.eps
p. 656: © tamir niv
p. 662: © Feng Yu
p. 664: © Ajay Bhaskar
p. 667: © Chee-Onn Leong
p. 671: © Sari ONeal
p. 674: © Rafa Irusta
p. 677: © Jarno Gonzalez Zarraonandia
p. 683: © marvellousworld
p. 688: © sprinter81
p. 690: © Juriah Mosin

Acknowledgments

My thanks go out to all the people involved in some way with this book and with Listverse. I'm especially thankful to the Listverse administration team and editors.

A big thank you is owed to all of the great writers (amateur and professional) who have contributed lists to the website, many of which have now ended up in this book.

Thanks also to the staff at Ulysses Press for their untiring efforts in getting this book to print. In particular, thanks to Claire Chun, production manager at Ulysses, who has coordinated and managed the process of putting it all together.

About the Editor

Jamie Frater was born in 1974 in Naenae, a suburb of Lower Hutt, New Zealand. He studied postgraduate music at the Royal College of Music in London, after which, due to an insatiable desire to share fascinating, obscure, and bizarre facts, he created Listverse.com where he presents a new top-ten list every day. He has been a guest speaker on numerous national radio and television stations in the United States and Great Britain. Jamie now writes full-time for his California-based website from his home, which he shares with his partner of seven years and his pet Bengal cat, Dexter.